Good Cookery!

Marshall Cavendish London & New York

Published by
Marshall Cavendish Books Limited
58 Old Compton Street
London W1V 5PA

© Marshall Cavendish Limited 1976, 1977,
1978, 1979

This volume first published 1979

This material was first published by
Marshall Cavendish Limited in the
partwork Good Cooking

Printed in Great Britain by
Redwood Burn Limited,
Trowbridge & Esher

ISBN 0 85685 705 X

CONTENTS

Tender treatment

The more economical cuts of meat, which would be tough if open roasted, can be turned into tender succulent dishes by pot roasting or braising. For both these related methods the meat is first browned on top of the stove, then cooked gently and slowly in the oven. Pot-roasted meat cooks in its own juices without any, or with little, additional liquid. Braised meat is often marinated first and cooked on a mirepoix, or bed, of diced vegetables, moistened by wine, stock or some other suitable liquid.

Pot roasting and braising are methods by which the meat is first browned in hot fat to seal in the meat juices and then cooked very slowly until it is so tender that it virtually falls off the bone or into pieces. These two methods differ in several respects from covered roasting (described in detail on pages 9–19) which, though another form of slow cooking, is an oven-only process where the meat is not browned to seal in the juices before cooking, but is cooked slowly from the beginning.

After the fast browning, pot-roasted meat is cooked slowly in the oven (or occasionally on top of the stove over reduced heat). If the casserole is flameproof the meat can be browned and oven-cooked in the same pan, otherwise it must be browned in a frying-pan and then transferred to a covered ovenproof casserole. In either case the lid must

1

fit tightly. A small quantity of liquid and vegetables can be added if liked. Basting is not usually necessary but a lean cut should be well larded.

For braising, meat can be marinated before browning to seal it. It is then placed on top of a mirepoix of chopped, mixed root and other firm vegetables. These may be sweated or gently fried first. They form a bed for the meat to rest on, and pork or bacon rind is also sometimes included. A small quantity of liquid is added, usually just enough to almost cover the vegetables. If more is used for a special recipe, this is reduced during cooking so that the eventual liquid is well flavoured and is barely more than a few spoonfuls per serving.

After fast browning at the beginning, the meat cooks slowly in the steam heat generated by the liquid. The liquid must be barely simmering and should on no account boil fiercely otherwise the meat will not be tender.

The gentle, slow cooking of both pot roasting and braising is suitable for most large and medium-sized cuts of meat. Braising, which involves the addition of some liquid, is also suitable for smaller cuts such as chops or braising steak.

Because both pot roasting and braising produce very tender results, they are particularly suited to tougher meat such as mutton and the coarser cuts of beef. They can acquire a delicious flavour and texture— particularly if first marinated—instead of the rather dry, tough result you would get if they were open roasted. But it is vital that the cooking temperature is not too high because the meat may become stringy and tough.

Chicken, especially the smaller birds with little flavour of their own, also benefit from the slow covered cooking particularly with additions such as herbs, stuffing or chopped, mixed vegetables.

Prime cuts of meat can also be pot roasted or braised, and these methods can lend distinction to high quality meat because, although the true roast flavour is missing, the lengthy cooking allows the flavours to blend and harmonize in a way that straight roasting cannot do. These make good dishes for a special occasion, but in general it is sensible to cook prime cuts of meat by the open-roasting method and ring the changes by pot roasting or braising the cheaper cuts.

EQUIPMENT AND ITS USE
In France, the traditional pot for braising, called a braisière, had a concave lid into which was put charcoal or boiling water. This ensured that although the meat was cooked over the fire, it in fact cooked evenly all round.

Nowadays the classic method for both pot roasting and braising involves starting the meat on top of the stove and completing the cooking in the oven, or sometimes on very low heat on top. This means that it is essential to use a flameproof casserole with a heavy level base and a well-fitting lid. If, however, you do not own a flameproof casserole, the initial browning can be done in a frying-pan on top of the stove and the meat and vegetables can then be transferred to a thick-based ovenproof casserole for the oven cooking.

Do not use too large a casserole, as the meat and vegetables should fit into it snugly. If you use a pot which is too big, more liquid has to be added, which means that the special flavours are diluted. When liquid is not being used, as for pot roasting, the fat disperses, tends to burn and the meat sticks to the pan.

Make sure the casserole lid fits really tightly. The braised meat is cooked in the damp heat and the steam from the simmering liquid must not be allowed to escape. If in doubt, put a layer of aluminium foil under the lid first to effect a better seal.

Some braised dishes can be cooked for considerably longer than their stated time without any harm coming to them, as long as the temperature is low enough. It is possible to use one of the low-temperature electric casseroles, also known as crockpots, for either braising or pot roasting. As these use roughly the same amount of electricity per hour as a light bulb they are a good investment if you do a lot of this kind of cooking. Follow manufacturers' instructions for cooking times.

SUITABLE CUTS
In general, the same cuts that are suitable for pot roasting are also suitable for braising. But, in addition, you can braise smaller cuts such as braising steak or chops. The addition of liquid stops them becoming dried out and sticking to the pan. Pot roasting and braising make the most of the less expensive scrag or middle neck cuts. The cooking time for smaller pieces of meat is proportionately longer than for a large roast.

Suitable cuts of beef include aitchbone, topside, top rump, top rib, brisket, silverside, thick flank, bladebone and chuck.

Suitable cuts of mutton and lamb are leg, shoulder, breast, best end, middle neck and scrag.

Suitable cuts of pork are spare ribs and hand and spring.

All chicken, except boiling fowl, can be used.

There is no reason why the better cuts of meat should not also be used, but they are of course more expensive.

As well as these, most cuts of veal, which can get very dry when open roasted, benefit from the steamy atmosphere of pot roasting or braising and this is discussed in a later course on cooking veal. Other meats such as bacon, oxtail, tongue and offal can also be braised. For offal and tongue see pages 123–145.

Choosing
A good butcher is always worth getting to know as fresh, quality meat is essential. Avoid any dried and/or discoloured looking meat.

Although good quality and freshness is always important, even with coarser cuts, sometimes the cuts from older animals may be used for pot roasting and braising. These methods give better results than the faster, open roasting methods as the slow cooking brings out the mature flavour.

Quantities
As for covered roasting, allow between 125-225 g [¼-½ lb] of boneless meat per person, depending on appetite, and about 175-275 g [6-10 oz] of meat with an average amount of bone.

COOKING TIMES AND TEMPERATURES
As a general rule allow 40 minutes per pound, plus an extra 40 minutes at 150°C [300°F] gas mark 2. The main thing to remember when pot roasting or braising any cut of meat is that it should cook very slowly in the oven. This means that it should be just simmering.

Because ovens can vary, check early on in the cooking that the meat really is simmering. If it is cooking too fast, turn the oven down slightly, and check again 30 minutes later. If it doesn't seem to be even simmering, then turn it up slightly. This is important, particularly with thick cuts of meat, which may otherwise not cook right through. Chicken must also be cooked through to the centre; if eaten slightly raw, it can give you salmonella poisoning.

If either the meat or vegetables have been reserved while the other is cooking and have therefore become cool, you can start off the cooking at a slightly higher temperature and then turn the oven down after 30 minutes.

At the end of the cooking time check that the meat is really tender. It should be almost falling into pieces and you should be able to cut it with a spoon. If in doubt, leave a little longer. Large, coarse cuts need slightly more cooking time than the better quality cuts of meat.

FATS AND LIQUIDS
The best fats for pot roasting or braising are good dripping or olive oil. You can also use vegetable oil. The amount required depends on whether the meat is on the fat or lean side, but as long as the pan is not much bigger than the meat and the lid fits tightly, you need probably less dripping or oil than you think—45-60 ml [3-4 tablespoons]—enough to stop the meat from sticking or the fat burning, but not so much that the meat is sitting in a sea of fat.

If there is a thick layer of fat around the meat, cut off the excess fat and render it down by melting it in a pan over a low heat.

After you have rendered the fat down, it can be used for the frying but remove the scraps of crisped fat before you brown the meat.

Liquid is not usually added to the pan for pot roasting, with occasional exceptions, such as a glassful of wine or cider to give a particular cut additional flavour.

Braised meat is often marinated first and the strained liquid from the marinade can be added to the braising pan together with stock or water. Alternatively you can use only stock or water, a mixture of the two, white or red wine, or cider. The wine can be inexpensive rough wine (dry rather than sweet) so should not really add greatly to the expense of the dish.

In braised dishes the meat sits on a bed of diced vegetables and as a general principle the liquid does not come up higher than about two-thirds of the vegetables. If, however, you are going to use a calf's foot or pig's trotter to make jelly, rather more liquid is used.

OTHER ADDITIONS
Vegetables, particularly root vegetables, are added to both pot roasts and braising dishes. For pot roasting, for instance, turnips, parsnips and onions can be added whole, either for all or part of the cooking time. For braising, vegetables such as onions, celery and carrots are cut into dice and gently cooked in fat and the meat is then placed on top of them. This is called a mirepoix.

Root or firm crisp vegetables are used because the long cooking process would disintegrate softer vegetables. Peeled, fresh or canned, tomatoes or tomato purée can also be added to a braised dish and the amount of other liquid reduced accordingly.

Garlic, herbs and spices all add flavour to the meat. These may either be used in a marinade or added separately to the cooking pot. Herbs that go well with meat include parsley, sage, basil, rosemary, marjoram, thyme, tarragon and bay leaves. Tarragon is also often used to flavour chicken.

Useful spices include cloves, mace, juniper berries, nutmeg, allspice and coriander.

A calf's foot or pig's trotter is used

in many classic braising dishes, particularly beef. The animal's foot gives the gravy a rich gelatinous quality. Ask the butcher to split the foot in half when you purchase it. Before use it should be thoroughly scrubbed in cold water and cut up. **Bacon and pork rind** can also be added to the pan. Because pot roasted or braised pork is cooked without the rind, the pork rind can be added to the pan separately in the same way as a calf's foot to enrich the gravy. Cut away the surplus fat (which can be rendered down separately) as otherwise you will end up with too much liquid fat in the cooking pot. The rind is removed before serving.

POT ROASTING

Wipe the meat with a damp cloth, then dry with kitchen paper. If it has been boned or stuffed it will need to be tied into a good shape for the pot. A cut of meat without much fat might dry out during cooking, so it should be larded with strips of bacon fat to prevent this.

Melt the dripping or oil in the flameproof casserole. When really hot put in the meat and brown it thoroughly on all sides over a high heat to seal in the juices. Take off the heat, surround with root vegetables such as carrots or turnips and season with salt and pepper and any herbs or spices. Cover and roast in a slow oven. Liquid is not usually added, but a small quantity of wine or cider is sometimes included to add flavour.

Some experts recommend that a pot roast should be looked at every hour or so and basted or turned over. This should not be necessary if the pot is the right size, the lid fits tightly and the temperature is sufficiently low, because the meat is cooking in a combination of dry, and sometimes steam, heat which should keep it sufficiently moist to prevent it sticking to the pan.

BRAISING

Meat to be braised is browned in the same way as for pot roasting. It is then placed on a bed of mixed diced vegetables, called a mirepoix, and liquid is added to the pan. This should generally come up no higher than two-thirds of the vegetable bed because the meat itself should cook gently in the steam rising from the bottom of the pan.

Marinating

Braised meat is very often marinated first to increase tenderness and flavour. (For step-by-step marinating see details on page 12). When the meat is taken out of the marinade it is important to dry it thoroughly with kitchen paper before it is put into the hot fat to seal in the juices. If wet, it would not brown and thus frying would not be effective.

Very lean meat should be larded, as for pot roasting.

Mirepoix

The classic mirepoix is made from onions, carrots and celery cut into fairly large diced pieces, with the addition of a few parsley stalks, a bay leaf and some thyme. To make a 'bed' for a 1.4-2 kg [3-4½ lb] cut of meat you need about four medium onions, six carrots and a half head of celery. There is no reason why other vegetables such as turnip, red cabbage, chicory, celeriac or swede should not be used.

When the meat is browned, it is removed from the pan and kept warm, and the diced vegetables are sweated, or browned gently, in the pan. The meat is then replaced on top of the mirepoix and the liquid added.

DISHING AND SERVING

Fat should be skimmed from both pot roasted and braised dishes before using the liquid for gravy or sauce. You can make a thin gravy by adding stock or vegetable water to the juices in the pan and checking the seasoning. Or you can thicken the gravy by mixing a spoonful of cornflour with cold stock, or water. Remove vegetables then add some of the hot juice to the cornflour and stir it into the casserole off the heat, return to the heat and let it boil for a minute or two to thicken.

The meat should be sliced thickly and arranged on a hot serving dish with the gravy poured over it or this may be served separately. The vegetables can also be served on the same dish, either surrounding or surrounded by the meat.

Alternatively a piquant sauce, made from new ingredients, with or without the addition of the pan juices, can be served, but this depends on what meat is being cooked.

1.4 kg [3 lb] meat
45 ml [3 tablespoons] fat or oil

For the marinade:
1 onion
1 carrot
1 garlic clove
150 ml [¼ pt] wine
bouquet garni
6 peppercorns

For the mirepoix:
4 onions
6 carrots
½ head celery

For the gravy:
250 ml [½ pt] stock
30 ml [2 tablespoons] cornflour

4 Heat fat in flameproof casserole. Brown meat on all sides over high heat. Remove and keep warm.

8 Remove meat from casserole and keep warm. Skim fat from the top of the juices in the pan.

Step-by-step to braising meat

1 Chop onion and carrot. Crush garlic clove. Put in dish with wine, herbs and peppercorns.

2 Lard meat, or remove excess fat. Marinate for several hours in a cool place, turning occasionally.

3 Heat oven to 150°C [300°F] gas mark 2. Remove meat from marinade. Dry with kitchen paper.

5 Peel and dice onions and carrots. Clean and dice celery. Brown vegetables gently in casserole.

6 Place meat on top, add strained marinade and stock to two-thirds mirepoix depth. Season.

7 Cover pot tightly. Braise in centre of oven. Check during cooking that liquid is just simmering.

9 For a thin gravy, add some stock if needed to the pan. Season. Strain stock to remove vegetables.

OR for thick gravy, mix cornflour to paste with cold stock. Add some hot pan juices and cook.

10 Slice meat thickly on to hot dish. Surround with vegetables. Pour gravy over, or serve separately.

Pastitsatha is a Greek dish of brisket served with spaghetti. An apricot stuffing is used to turn a rolled breast of lamb into a tasty treat.

PASTITSATHA

This is a Greek pot roast, served with boiled spaghetti and sprinkled with grated Parmesan cheese—allow 50 g [2 oz] of cheese.

SERVES 6–8
rolled brisket weighing 1.4 kg [3 lb]
45 ml [3 tablespoons] oil
3 medium-sized onions
4 garlic cloves
salt
freshly ground black pepper
15 ml [1 tablespoon] sugar
5 ml [1 teaspoon] ground cinnamon
1 bay leaf
3 cloves
150 ml [¼ pt] stock
45 ml [3 tablespoons] tomato purée

1 Check the meat is a good shape for the pot and tie if necessary. Wipe clean with a damp cloth and dry with kitchen paper.

2 Heat the oil in a flameproof casserole.

3 When hot, brown the meat on all sides in the oil over a high heat. Remove the meat from the cas-serole and keep it warm.

4 Peel and chop the onions finely. Peel and crush the garlic.

5 Brown the onions in the pan. Add garlic, salt, pepper, sugar, cin-namon, bay leaf and cloves.

6 Heat the stock in a small sauce-pan.

7 Add tomato purée and hot stock to the casserole. Stir.

8 Place the meat on top of the onion and tomato mixture. Cover tightly and cook in centre of oven at 150°C [300°F] gas mark 2 for 2½ hours until tender.

6

9 Remove the meat from the casserole and keep warm.

10 Skim any surplus fat off the top of the juices in the pan. Add more stock to dilute the juices if necessary and check the seasoning.

11 Cut meat into thick slices on to a serving dish. Pour the juices over the meat and serve with boiled spaghetti and grated Parmesan cheese.

APRICOT-STUFFED BREAST OF LAMB

Apricots go particularly well with lamb and this pot roast recipe turns an inexpensive cut into an out of the ordinary dish. Buy several small breasts rather than fewer large ones. The oil and lemon marinade adds flavour to the meat. Serve with the pot roasted vegetables plus steamed new potatoes if you wish.

SERVES 6–8
4 breasts of lamb, boned
45 ml [3 tablespoons] oil

For the marinade:
30 ml [2 tablespoons] oil
1 lemon

For the stuffing:
50 g [2 oz] dried apricots
15 ml [1 tablespoon] oil
4 rashers streaky bacon
1 large onion
100 g [¼ lb] cooked long-grain rice
25 g [1 oz] sultanas
2 sprigs rosemary, crushed
salt and black pepper
1 egg

For the garnish:
12–16 baby onions
12–16 baby carrots
4–6 celery sticks
150–250 ml [¼–½ pt] stock or vegetable water

1 Mix 30 ml [2 tablespoons] oil and the juice from one lemon. Pour this mixture over the boned lambs' breasts and leave overnight, in a cool place.

2 Put the dried apricots into a bowl, pour boiling water over them to just cover, and leave them to stand while preparing the other ingredients (about 20 minutes).

3 Heat the oven to 150°C [300°F] gas mark 2.

4 Remove the rinds from the bacon, chop up small and fry in 15 ml [1 tablespoon] oil until the fat runs. Remove bacon from pan to a bowl.

5 Peel and chop the onion finely; fry gently in the pan until soft but not coloured. Add to the bacon.

6 Add the cooked rice, sultanas, crushed rosemary and seasoning to the bacon and onion.

7 Drain the apricots. Chop up small and add to the mixture. Mix well.

8 Break the egg into a small bowl and beat it with a fork. Add to the stuffing mixture and stir in well.

9 Remove the lamb from the marinade and dry well with kitchen paper.

10 Place a portion of the stuffing on each breast, roll it up and tie it securely with string (do not use nylon string).

11 Heat 45 ml [3 tablespoons] oil in a flameproof casserole. When hot, add the rolled breasts of lamb and brown on all sides over a high heat.

12 Cover the casserole tightly and pot roast in oven for about 2 hours or until the meat is really tender.

13 In the meantime, peel the onions, scrape the carrots and wash the celery. Cut the celery into large pieces, and add all the vegetables to the meat about 1 hour before cooking is completed. Check there is enough fat in the pan so that the vegetables do not stick.

14 When cooked, remove the meat and vegetables to a hot dish and keep warm.

15 Skim the fat from the pan juices. Add enough stock to make a gravy. Check seasoning, bring to the boil and strain into a sauce-boat.

16 Cut the meat into neat thick slices with the stuffing in the middle. Arrange on a hot serving dish, surrounded by the vegetables, and serve the gravy separately.

POT ROASTED CHICKEN

This method of cooking chicken has much in common with the French method of roasting chicken in that the bird is turned several times to brown it evenly on all sides. The bird may be cooked in the oven after browning, but is cooked on the stove top in this recipe. Oil is the best fat to use because the chicken is less likely to stick than with butter. The stuffing also helps to keep the bird moist as well as adding to the flavour. Serve with new potatoes, tossed in butter and parsley, and a fresh green salad, made with a crisp lettuce, sliced cucumber and chopped spring onions.

SERVES 4
1 oven-ready chicken weighing about 1.2 kg [2½ lb] including giblets
bacon and celery stuffing
salt
freshly ground black pepper
1 small onion
60 ml [4 tablespoons] olive oil
60 ml [4 tablespoons] thick cream

1 Make the stuffing.

2 Rinse the giblets in cold water and blot dry. Cut up the chicken liver and add to the stuffing.

3 Wash, drain and dry the chicken. Sprinkle the body cavity with salt and pepper. Rub salt over the skin.

4 Peel the onion and insert in the body cavity.

5 Stuff the chicken at the neck end with the bacon and celery stuffing. Retruss the chicken if necessary.

6 Put the oil in a heavy-based flameproof casserole. When hot, put in the bird and lightly brown on all sides. Add the giblets.

7 Lay it back on one breast, cover tightly and cook over a low heat, tightly covered, for 25 minutes.

8 Turn the bird on to its other breast, basting with oil from the pan. Take care not to break the skin. Cover again and cook for another 25 minutes.

9 Turn the chicken upright on to its back, baste again, and cook for a further 25 minutes.

10 Test that the chicken is cooked by piercing with a skewer. The meat should be very tender and the juices which run out should be clear.

11 Remove the chicken from the pan, tilting it so that the juices run from the body cavity into the casserole. Put the chicken on to a warm serving dish, and keep warm until the sauce is ready.

12 Remove the giblets and skim the fat off the surface of the pan juices. Add the cream and bring very gently to the boil. Season and pour into a sauce-boat.

PORK WITH ORANGE SAUCE

This is a delicious way of braising pork on the bone—a hand and spring is a suitable cut. The meat is marinated with a dry marinade at least 4 hours before cooking, so allow time for this. To add richness to the sauce you can add the pork rind to the pan, but cut off all fat first. The orange segments should be prepared while the meat is cooking so they will be ready to poach when the meat has been cooked. Serve with sautéed parsnips.

SERVES 6–8
**piece of pork on bone,
    weighing about 2 kg [4½ lb]
125 ml [4 fl oz] white stock
275 ml [½ pt] dry white wine
3 oranges**

**For the marinade:
3 garlic cloves
salt
45 ml [3 tablespoons] oil
15 ml [1 tablespoon]
    freshly chopped parsley**

**5 ml [1 teaspoon] marjoram
2 sprigs rosemary, crushed
freshly ground black pepper**

1 Remove rind and as much fat as possible from the pork (the fat can be rendered down for separate use).

2 Peel and crush the garlic with the salt. Mix with the oil and add parsley, marjoram, crushed rosemary and pepper.

3 Rub the marinade mixture all over the pork. Leave the pork in a dish for at least 4 hours or overnight, in the refrigerator or a cold larder, to absorb the flavours.

4 Heat the oven to 150°C [300°F] gas mark 2.

5 Scrape the herbs off the meat with a knife. Brown the meat over a high heat in a flameproof casserole. It will be oily from the marinade but add a little extra oil if necessary.

6 Add the stock, wine and the juice

Pork with orange sauce is braised without the rind after marinating four hours in an oil and herb marinade.

of one orange to the pan and bring to the boil. Cover tightly.

7 Transfer to the oven and cook for about 3½–4 hours or until really tender.

8 Remove the meat from the pan and keep warm.

9 Skim the fat from the pan juices.

10 Peel and segment the remaining two oranges. Poach the segments in the pan juices for just long enough to warm them through.

11 Slice the meat and arrange on a hot serving dish. Surround with orange segments.

12 Strain pan juices into sauce-boat and serve with meat.

Put a lid on it

Covered roasting has, in many ways, more in common with steam or casserole cooking than with the more traditional open-roasting methods of cooking meat. Nonetheless, because no liquid is added to the meat, it is a roasting technique and has some advantages over open roasting. It is a more economical method of cooking because the meat shrinks less as there is no loss of juices. The slow, steamy cooking helps to tenderize the less expensive, coarser cuts which are not generally considered 'roast' meats.

Everyone loves a roast, but the high cost of prime roasting cuts makes it impossible to serve this treat to the family as often as they would like. This is a pity because roasted meat goes a long way and usually provides enough in the way of leftovers to make another meal.

There are cheaper, coarser cuts of beef, lamb, pork and veal sold for roasting but if you have ever tried roasting these by conventional means, you will know just how stringy and tough the results are. The best method for these cuts is to roast them covered. This will enable you to serve roast meat more often. This long, slow method breaks down coarse cuts and makes them as tender and tasty as prime roasts.

Now that there are so many aids to covered roasting, such as foil, roast-

Roasting in a transparent bag enables you to check progress without uncovering meat.

ing bags, covered roasting tins, electric casseroles and plug-in multi-cookers (if you have one of the latter you do not need an oven), covered roasting is increasing in popularity. More and more cooks are discovering that when meat is roasted under cover, shrinkage and loss of juice are reduced to a minimum, flavour is preserved and, as a bonus for the busy cook, there are no nasty splashes to clean off the oven.

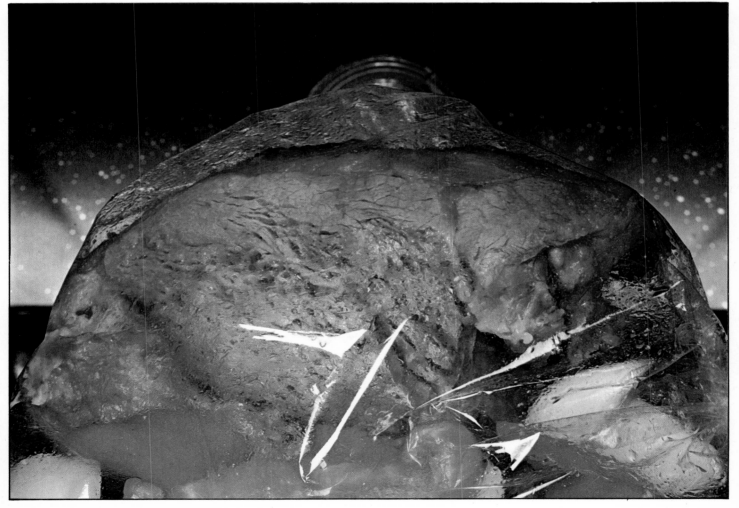

SUITABLE CUTS OF MEAT FOR COVERED ROASTING

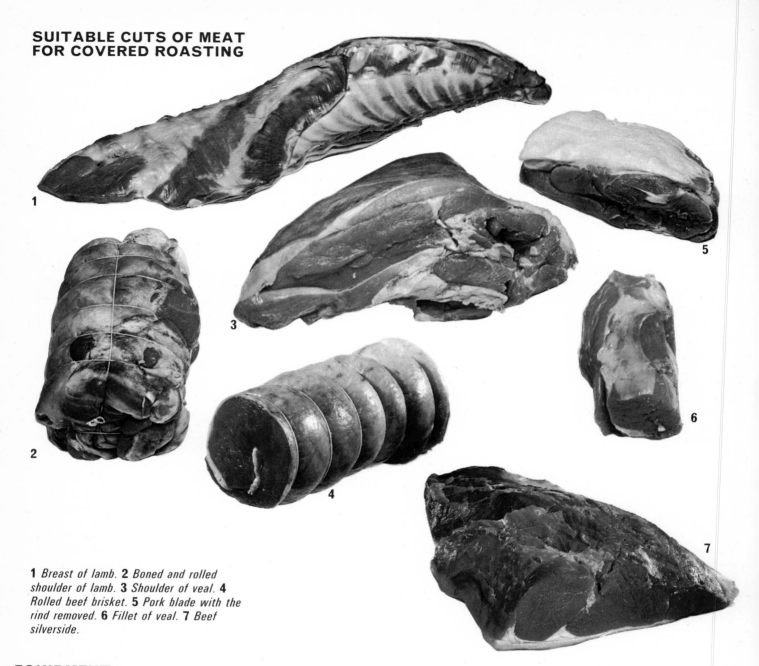

1 *Breast of lamb.* 2 *Boned and rolled shoulder of lamb.* 3 *Shoulder of veal.* 4 *Rolled beef brisket.* 5 *Pork blade with the rind removed.* 6 *Fillet of veal.* 7 *Beef silverside.*

EQUIPMENT
There are several different types of equipment which may be used for covered roasting.

Covered roasting dishes
Covered roasting dishes may be made of enamelled metal, ovenproof glass or ceramic. They usually have a handle at each side to make lifting out of the oven easier. The lid on a covered roasting dish should always be domed to enable you to get a fairly large piece of meat in the dish and also to encourage the formation of steam which helps to tenderize the meat.

Some covered roasting dishes are sold with a removable rack and can also be used for open roasting. If the lid is fairly deep and has a flat top so that it stands steadily, it can be used separately on other occasions for roasting or baking vegetables and for making pies.

Roasting bricks
Roasting bricks are often known by the name romertopf or diable. Meat roasted inside these clay dishes without the addition of any liquid is very tender.

Roasting bricks are, however, rather limited in use as they can only be used for roasting meat and poultry, baking fish or potatoes and not for anything requiring liquid, such as a soup, stew or casserole.

Aluminium foil
Aluminium foil is an excellent cover for roasting meat as its metal content gives good heat distribution and retention. It is inexpensive and generally available.

Cooking wrap and bags
Transparent cooking wrap and bags are cheaper than foil and have the advantage that you can see what is taking place inside the cover. In their early days there was a certain amount of alarm generated about their use, because they sometimes caused minor explosions. Technological development has now overcome this, and they are safe provided they are used correctly.

Cooking wrap and bags are made of a transparent nylon or polyester film that will stand oven temperatures of up to 200°C [400°F] gas mark 6. They become brittle when heated.

Electric casseroles and multi-cookers

Electric casseroles and multi-cookers of various sorts with closing lids can be used for covered roasting. They are especially suitable for very tough cuts which need long, very slow cooking. Full instructions on using these appliances for covered roasting are given in the manufacturers' handbooks.

SUITABLE CUTS

All the prime and medium cuts, as well as some of the coarse cuts of both red and white meat can be cooked by the covered roasting methods. So can chops and cutlets, which are best roasted individually wrapped.

Meat cooked in this way lacks to some extent a true 'roast' flavour and does not brown or crisp as does open-roasted meat, so there is usually little point in roasting the very best cuts, such as beef sirloin or saddle of lamb, under cover. The leaner prime and medium cuts, however, which tend to dry out unless basted frequently when open roasted—particularly veal—can benefit from covered roasting as much as the coarser cuts. If you have no time for preparations such as larding or barding, or need to let the roast cook without attention (ie without basting), then the covered method is a useful alternative, even for best prime cuts.

Obviously most prime and medium cuts can be successfully open-roasted in the oven in the normal traditional way.

Beef

Fore rib, top and back ribs, topside and aitchbone, which are medium cuts, all roast well under cover. A small roast such as topside, retains its full weight, and so emerges from the oven larger than if it had been open roasted. A large roast such as an aitchbone weighing 4.5 kg [10 lb], cooks right through without the outside becoming overcooked and tasteless.

Brisket and silverside, which are coarse cuts, can both be cooked by the covered-roasting methods as they are not really suitable for open roasting.

Silverside is a coarse cut from between flank and leg. It is sold both fresh and salted.

Brisket has a certain amount of bone and comes from between the flank and shin. It may be sold on or off the bone and is either fresh or salted. The cut tends to be rather fatty.

Lamb and mutton

This is one meat where even the prime cuts taste as good covered roasted. Leg, shoulder, best end of neck, loin, chump, and breast all do well cooked in this way.

Pork

As with beef, prime cuts such as leg and loin are rather wasted when covered roasted and any cut cooked for its crisp, crunchy crackling should, of course, be open roasted. Blade and hand and spring are good cuts for covered roasting. Fillet (or tenderloin) which has no outer fat is also successful cooked this way, as it benefits from the steamier atmosphere.

Veal

There are two kinds of veal sold by butchers. Milk-fed veal comes from calves reared in special housing units and the meat is pale, very tender and expensive. Grass-fed veal comes from smaller-sized calves reared outdoors; it is darker in colour, less tender, but has more flavour and probably benefits most from slow, covered roasting. Because the calves are slaughtered when very young, veal has no coarse cuts. All the prime cuts such as leg, fillet, loin, best end of neck and shoulder can be covered roasted.

CHOOSING AND STORING

Always go to a reputable butcher's shop or supermarket to ensure good quality meat and butchering. Store the meat in a cool place, or if you have a freezer, pack in freezer bags and follow instructions for freezing.

QUANTITIES

As a rough guide, allow between 125-225 g [4-8 oz] of boneless meat per person, depending on appetite, and about 175-275 g [6-10 oz] of meat with an average amount of bone.

PREPARATION

The preparation of meat for covered roasting is similar to that for open roasting. Some people prefer to remove all the fat as, unlike open roasting, it is not essential to keep the meat basted. The rind from pork should be removed.

Herbs and spices can be patted into the meat or you can make tiny slits in the meat with the point of a knife and press, for example, garlic slivers or parsley stalks into them. Because of the steam the flavour will penetrate more deeply.

The flavour and texture of any meat is usually better if it has been left at room temperature prior to roasting, from 30 minutes for pork and veal to about 2 hours for larger cuts of beef and lamb. Frozen meat should thaw in a refrigerator for at least 48 hours if possible.

However, if you haven't time to let it thaw out first, it is possible to cook meat straight from the freezer for any of the covered methods as long as you allow extra cooking time to compensate.

Marinades

A clever way of tenderizing and adding flavour to meat, particularly to the coarser cuts, is to marinate the meat for one to two days before roasting.

To make the marinade you need oil—plus flavourings such as herbs, spices, garlic and onions. Pepper is included but not salt as this would draw the juices from the meat. The inclusion of an acid such as wine, cider, wine vinegar or lemon juice helps to break down tough meat fibres.

If you intend to marinate the meat for longer than 24 hours, the vegetables in the marinade should be cooked first (soften them in a little olive oil), because uncooked vegetables could turn sour in the marinade if left too long. The wine is then added to the cooked vegetables.

The quantity of marinade is just sufficient to form a pool for the meat to stand in. The meat is not immersed and must therefore be turned occasionally to soak all sides.

The marinating meat should not be kept in the refrigerator, as the oil will solidify if too cool. Cover the meat lightly and keep it in a larder or other cool place. Drain before roasting and reserve the marinade for basting the meat.

Step-by-step to making marinade

1 medium-sized onion
1 garlic clove
1 medium-sized carrot
60 ml [4 tablespoons] olive oil
250 ml [½ pt] wine
150 ml [¼ pt] wine vinegar
1 bay leaf
bouquet of herbs
12 peppercorns

1 Peel and chop the onion and garlic clove. Wash and chop the carrot.

2 Cook the vegetables over gentle heat in the olive oil until soft.

3 Add the wine, vinegar, bay leaf, herbs and peppercorns.

4 Put the meat into a gratin dish and spoon marinade mixture over.

5 Turn the meat twice a day, spooning the marinade over the meat.

COVERED ROASTING METHODS

Basically, in all covered roasting methods, it is the steam that collects in the cover while the meat roasts which helps to cook it. This also helps to preserve the flavour and stops the meat from shrinking, but it does prevent it from browning in the same way as open-roasted meat. To achieve some crispness and colour on the outside of the meat, you can take away the cover for the last half hour of cooking. At this stage the meat is virtually cooked, so there is no shrinkage.

Covered roasting dishes

These are very versatile and can also be used for casseroles, soups and stews. Many models can be used on top of the stove as well.

For roasting, the meat is seasoned with pepper and herbs and put in the dish. The leaner cuts are rubbed with dripping or butter, the amount depending on how much outer layer of fat they have. The meat is then roasted with the cover on. Use a covered dish rather than any other form of covering if you intend to uncover the meat for the last half hour to brown. A dish is also easiest if you wish to baste, for example a very lean cut, during cooking.

Roasting bricks

Basically, the roasting brick is first soaked well in water to create steam during cooking, which tenderizes the meat. The seasoned meat is then put into the brick and roasted in the oven. Roasting bricks always come with instructions, which differ slightly with different makes, and these should be followed carefully.

Aluminium foil

Foil is a good medium for wrapping large or awkwardly shaped cuts which would not otherwise fit into a roasting pan. When wrapping meat in foil, leave enough space around the meat for steam to form, and crimp the edges of the foil firmly.

In theory, a foil parcel of meat can be placed directly on the oven shelf but, in practice, it is much better to place the parcel on a trivet in a roasting pan. All the juices will then fall into the pan when the meat is unwrapped and there will be no danger of dropping the roast on the floor when you lift it out of the oven.

The best way to wrap the meat in

foil is to cut a piece large enough to cover the whole cut and allow extra for overlapping folds. Place the foil, shiny side up, on a trivet in a roasting pan. Put the seasoned meat in the centre, then bring the longest two sides up over the meat and hold them together. Check for protruding bones and cover these, if any, with a double patch of foil. Fold the foil together in a neat seam, about 1.2 cm [½"] deep above the meat. Fold both end corners down towards you, then fold the foil up either side from the bottom of the pan.

Cooking wrap and bags
When using cooking bags or wrap, always put the wrapped meat in a roasting pan. Because the bag

A marinade both tenderizes and flavours meat. The liquid can be used for basting.

becomes brittle on heating, it is otherwise impossible to remove the bag from the oven without it bursting and pouring hot meat juices all over your hands and the floor.

Before the meat is enclosed, the surface of the bag or wrap should be sprinkled with about 15 ml [1 tablespoon] plain flour and, after the meat is wrapped, about six tiny slits made in the bag above the meat. The flour prevents sudden splashing inside the bag which could cause the bag to burst, and the slits prevent high-pressure steam building up, which could cause an explosion. The bags and wrap are sealed by twist ties which can be undone towards the end of roasting to allow the meat to brown.

Temperature chart for covered roasting

	low temperature	high temperature
Beef	160°C [325°F] gas mark 3 35 mins per 450 g [1 lb] plus 35 mins	220°C [425°F] gas mark 7 15 mins per 450 g [1 lb] plus 20 mins
Lamb	180°C [350°F] gas mark 4 27 mins per 450 g [1 lb] plus 27 mins	200°C [400°F] gas mark 6 20 mins per 450 g [1 lb] plus 27 mins
Pork	180°C [350°F] gas mark 4 30 mins per 450 g [1 lb] plus 30 mins	200°C [400°F] gas mark 6 25 mins per 450 g [1 lb] plus 25 mins
Veal	160°C [325°F] gas mark 3 35 mins per 450 g [1 lb] plus 35 mins	200°C [400°F] gas mark 6 25 mins per 450 g [1 lb] plus 25 mins

Step-by-step to roasting in foil

1 Heat oven, check weight and calculate cooking time. Season, add herbs and fat if using.

2 Cut foil to cover meat completely plus overlap, using serrated foil dispenser or kitchen scissors.

3 Put foil, shiny side up, in pan. Put meat in the centre on a trivet. If using marinade, spoon over.

5 Fold side foil up from pan bottom. Check that there is space for air to circulate and for holes.

6 Put pan in centre of oven and roast for calculated time. If browning, open foil 30 minutes early.

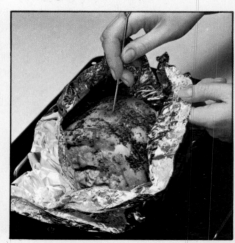

7 Test if meat is done with skewer in thickest part. Juices should be colourless for well-done roast.

TIME AND TEMPERATURE

Low-temperature roasting is usually preferable for all covered roasts and is essential for the coarser cuts. The higher temperatures also given here are for prime and medium cuts only: those for beef and lamb are calculated for a rarer roast. High-temperature cooking times for pork and veal are given only for when time is short. Use the chart as an approximate guide as the cooking time also depends on meat quality and thickness, and ovens can differ.

Check the meat is cooked, either with a meat thermometer, or by pushing a skewer into the thickest part of the meat. The juices should be colourless for well-done, rosy for rarer roasts.

4 Bring long sides of foil over meat. Fold together to make 1.2 cm [½"] seam. Fold corners down.

8 Transfer meat on to hot dish, keep warm. Remove trivet. Pour juices from foil into pan and make gravy.

Step-by-step to roasting in a bag

1 Heat oven, check weight of meat and calculate cooking time. Season meat and add herbs, etc.

3 Put meat in bag. Seal with twist tag. With sharp knife cut six 1.2 cm [½"] slits spaced over the top.

5 Take out of oven and remove twist tag or slit bag open. Check meat is cooked with skewer.

2 Put 15 ml [1 tablespoon] flour in roasting bag and shake to distribute flour over surface.

4 Put bag of meat in roasting pan and roast in centre of oven for calculated time.

6 Put meat on to hot dish and keep warm. Pour juices from bag into pan and make gravy.

LOIN OF PORK WITH CABBAGE

▨▨▨ *This recipe is based on loin of pork alsacienne, substituting cabbage for the sauerkraut. It is a delicious way of serving pork and the apples and lemon give an added tang to the cabbage.*

SERVES 4-5
loin of pork, chined, weighing 1.1 kg [2½ lb]
salt
freshly ground black pepper
½ medium-sized white cabbage
1 onion
25 g [1 oz] butter
4 eating apples
1 lemon
15 ml [1 tablespoon] flour
250 ml [½ pt] stock
freshly chopped parsley
2 hard-boiled eggs

1 Heat the oven to 180°C [350°F] gas mark 4. Calculate the cooking time, at 30 minutes to 450 g [1 lb] plus an extra 30 minutes.

2 Remove the rind from the pork, by cutting between the rind and the meat.

3 Season the meat with salt and pepper and put it into a covered roasting dish.

4 Insert meat thermometer, if you have one. Roast in the centre of the oven for 1 hour 45 minutes.

5 Meanwhile, shred the cabbage, then blanch it by submerging in boiling water for 1 minute. Drain it and refresh in a large bowl of cold water.

6 Peel and slice the onion. Melt the butter in a pan and cook the onion in it over a low heat until the onion is soft but not coloured.

7 Drain the cabbage thoroughly in a colander and add to the onion. Stir.

8 Peel and quarter the apples and arrange them at the bottom of a flameproof casserole.

9 Peel zest and all the white pith off the lemon. Slice the peeled lemon with a sharp knife and remove the pips. Add the slices to the cabbage and mix in.

10 Spoon the cabbage mixture on top of the apples one hour before the pork is due to be cooked. Put the dish in the oven on the shelf below the meat.

11 Thirty minutes before the pork is due to be cooked, take the lid off the roasting dish to allow the meat to brown.

12 Check that the meat is cooked from the thermometer reading which should show 85°C [185°F], or by inserting a skewer into the thickest part; the juice should be colourless.

13 Peel and slice the hard-boiled eggs into quarters lengthways.

14 Transfer the meat on to a hot dish and keep warm.

15 Stir the flour into the meat juices in the pan. Then cook over a low heat until lightly brown. Remove from heat and add stock. Return to heat and bring to boil stirring all the time. Check seasoning.

16 Carve the pork into slices, arrange on top of the cabbage on a hot dish and garnish with eggs.

OR turn out the cabbage mixture—like a cake—on to separate dish and garnish with parsley and the quartered hard-boiled eggs.

LAMB AND CHOPPED LIVER

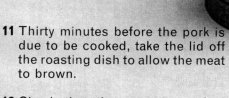
Liver, herbs and rice make a good stuffing for lamb. The weight given for the rice is for cold, cooked rice.

SERVES 6
shoulder of lamb, boned and rolled, weighing 1.1 kg [2½ lb]
1 onion
1 clove garlic
100 g [¼ lb] lamb's liver
25 g [1 oz] dripping
40 g [1½ oz] cooked long grain rice
5 ml [1 teaspoon] mixed herbs
salt
freshly ground black pepper
15 ml [1 tablespoon] flour
250 ml [½ pt] stock

1 Heat oven to 180°C [350°F] gas mark 4.

2 Peel and chop onion. Peel and crush garlic. Chop the liver into small cubes and shake the cubes in kitchen paper to remove excess moisture.

3 Melt dripping in a pan and fry onion and garlic until soft and beginning to change colour.

4 Add liver to pan and fry for 5 minutes. Stir in the cooked rice and season to taste. Add mixed herbs and allow to cool.

5 Unroll the lamb. Spoon the stuffing down the middle, pressing it into place. Roll up again and tie with string. Season the outside with salt and pepper.

6 Weigh the stuffed shoulder and calculate the cooking time at 27 minutes to 450 g [1 lb] plus 27 minutes extra.

7 Cut foil to size. Place it, shiny side up, on a trivet in the roasting pan, and place the meat on it.

8 Bring the longest two sides of foil up over the meat. Fold together into 1.2 cm [½"] seam and turn corners down towards you.

9 Fold sides up from the bottom of the pan. Check for holes and make sure you have left enough space for air to circulate.

10 Roast in the centre of the oven for 1 hour and 35 minutes.

11 Remove from oven. Undo foil and check the meat is cooked by piercing with a skewer; the juice should be colourless. Keep warm on a hot dish.

12 Remove the trivet and pour the juices out of the foil into the roasting pan. Add flour and stir.

13 Stir over low heat until mixture is lightly browned. Remove from heat and add stock.

14 Return to heat and bring to the boil stirring all the time.

15 Check seasoning and strain into sauce-boat.

Rosemary-flavoured veal (left) and brisket
with horseradish sauce are appetizing dishes
roasted under cover.

ROAST VEAL WITH ROSEMARY

☒☒☒ Veal is a lean meat with very
little fat and tends to get dry if
open roasted, so this is a good way of
keeping it moist and tender. The
rosemary adds extra flavour and the
wine gives a lift to the gravy. Serve with
creamed potatoes and new broad
beans.

SERVES 6

loin of veal, trimmed and
   boned, weighing 1.4 kg [3 lb]
salt
freshly ground black pepper
3 sprigs rosemary, crushed or
   10 ml [2 teaspoons] dried
   rosemary, crushed
50 g [2 oz] butter
400 ml [¾ pt] white wine

1 Heat the oven to 160°C [325°F] gas
   mark 3. Calculate the roasting
   time, at 35 minutes per 450 g [1 lb]
   plus an extra 35 minutes.

2 Wipe meat with a clean damp
   cloth. Season with salt, pepper

and the crushed rosemary, patting
it well into the surface. Spread the
butter over the whole outside of
the meat.

3 Cut foil to cover all the meat. Place
   it, shiny side up, on a trivet in the
   roasting pan.

4 Put the meat in the centre of the
   foil. Bring the two longest sides
   together in 1.2 cm [½"] seam. Turn
   the corners down towards you.

SERVES 4-6
**rolled and boned brisket
weighing 1.4-1.8 kg [3-4 lb]
6 cloves
freshly ground pepper
15 ml [1 tablespoon] flour**

**For the horseradish sauce:
45 ml [3 tablespoons]
 fresh horseradish
15 ml [1 tablespoon]
 lemon juice
15 ml [1 tablespoon]
 caster sugar
2.5 ml [½ teaspoon] English
 mustard powder
225 ml [8 fl oz] thick cream**

1 Heat the oven to 160°C [325°F] gas mark 3. Check weight of meat and calculate cooking time at 40 minutes per 450 g [1 lb] plus 40 minutes extra (slightly more than chart).

2 Tie the brisket up with string in four places to make a neat parcel. Stud the top with the cloves, and season with pepper.

3 Put flour in a roasting bag and shake it so that all the bag is coated.

4 Put the meat in the bag, seal it with the twist tag and place it in a roasting tin.

5 Roast in the centre of the oven for from 2 hours 40 minutes to 3 hours 20 minutes, according to weight.

6 Meanwhile make the horseradish sauce. Grate the horseradish into a bowl. Add the lemon juice, sugar and mustard powder and mix together.

7 Whip the thick cream to the piping stage—when the whisk leaves a mark on the cream. Fold it into the horseradish mixture.

8 At the end of cooking time, remove the brisket from the oven. Untie the twist or slit the bag open and check, with a skewer, that the meat is done: the juice should be colourless.

9 Put the meat on to a hot dish and remove the cloves.

10 Warm the horseradish sauce over a low heat if wished, but on no account let it boil.

skewer that the meat is cooked through: the juices should be colourless. Transfer meat on to a hot dish and keep warm.

8 Empty the juices from the foil into the roasting pan, removing the trivet. Add the wine to the roasting pan and stir until the gravy comes to the boil.

9 Continue to boil until liquid has reduced by about half. Check seasoning, and strain into sauceboat.

PIQUANT BRISKET

⬚⬚⬚ *This is a simple way of cooking an inexpensive cut of beef to its best advantage. For a mid-week meal you could substitute bought horseradish sauce to economize, but a home-made one is much nicer. The sauce can be served chilled or warmed gently. This roast can also be cooked in foil or in a covered roasting dish.*

5 Fold the sides upwards from the bottom of the pan. Check for holes, but make sure you have left enough space for air to circulate inside.

6 Roast in the centre of the oven for 2 hours 20 minutes.

7 Take out and open foil. Check with

True sautés

Sautéing is a method of shallow frying suitable for all tender meat, poultry, game and offal. True sauté dishes are completed in a sauté pan and the food is tossed and turned in hot fat until browned and sealed on all sides. A characteristic of a sauté dish is the particularly flavoursome sauce, made by deglazing the pan, which is served with the meat.

Although the word 'sauté' is very familiar to all who use written recipes, its precise meaning is not so clearly understood, simply because it is used in connection with a wide range of cookery processes. Sautéing is an important frying technique which has two basic applications.

Small, very tender pieces of food may be completely cooked by sautéing. Alternatively sautéing may be a preliminary browning technique for food that needs slightly longer cooking. In the second case, a further, short, period of cooking is carried out in the same pan, and the meat is often briefly reheated in a sauce. Dishes prepared by either of these techniques are correctly named sautés, and there are examples of each in the recipes that follow.

In either case, an essential operation in the sauté technique is to deglaze the pan with a small amount of liquid. This is later incorporated in a sauce or used to moisten the meat.

The term 'sauté' is also used to describe the quick preliminary browning given to tougher meats which are subsequently tenderized by long slow cooking, as in the case of stewing or braising. Such recipes are not classed as sautés as the meat is not fully cooked by the sauté method.

THE METHOD

The word itself comes from the French 'faire sauter' meaning 'to make (something) to jump', which exactly describes the way a chef tosses or flips over the pieces of food in a sauté pan, instead of turning them one by one as you generally do when shallow frying. Tossing the food rather than turning it requires a fairly strong wrist movement, and is only practicable when cooking relatively light pieces of food. It is possible to toss food in an open pan

but for obvious reasons it is easier (and safer!) if you cover the pan first.

Grasp the pan by the handle, pressing the lid on firmly with the other hand, and move the pan sharply—forward, up and back, with a jerky, circular movement. This should cause the contents of the pan to flip over and expose another surface to the hot fat.

When cooking relatively substantial pieces of food, such as chicken joints or noisettes of lamb, you will find it easier to turn each piece with tongs or a palette knife and spoon.

Preliminary browning

All true sauté dishes start with a quick initial browning of the food in a small amount of very hot fat. As in open frying, the object is to coagulate the surface proteins, which helps keep the juices and flavouring inside the food. Quick browning is only possible if the fat is sufficiently hot and the food is as dry as possible. Food to be sautéed is not usually coated with flour, so it is essential to pat it thoroughly dry with absorbent

kitchen paper, immediately before frying.

It is also important not to overcrowd the pan, otherwise the food will tend to steam rather than brown. Leave about 6 mm [$\frac{1}{4}$"] space between the pieces, but if this is not possible, cook in batches or use two pans rather than overcrowd one. On the other hand, it is equally important not to cook too few pieces of food in too large a pan, as the exposed surfaces of the pan will tend to dry up and burn.

Deglazing the pan

This is another important characteristic of a true sauté dish. The method is discussed in detail on page 30 and this describes shallow frying uncoated meat in an open frying-pan. This method of frying is essentially the same as sautéing, but is commonly used for red meat which can be served with or without the deglazed sauce, unlike a sautéed dish which always requires the sauce.

After the meat is cooked, remove it and pour away surplus fat, if any, leaving about one tablespoonful in the pan. Add the liquid stated in the recipe which may be red or white wine, a well-flavoured stock, dry white vermouth, mushroom cooking liquor or something similar. Boil rapidly to reduce and concentrate the liquid, at the same time stirring to dislodge and dissolve the solidified juices from the base of the pan. In some recipes the sauce is completed by thickening and enriching this small amount of liquid with pieces of butter or with thick cream. In others, a well flavoured, previously prepared and thickened sauce is added.

EQUIPMENT

The best pan to use is a sauté pan (sautoir or sauteuse). It has a flat heavy base, designed to spread the heat evenly. To facilitate the tossing process, it has straight sides of about 6 cm [2½"] depth, an easily grasped handle and a lid.

A heavy frying-pan can be used for the initial browning but is not so convenient for the rest of the cooking and making the sauce.

The small equipment listed on pages 26–28 are very useful in all the methods of shallow frying, including sautéing.

INGREDIENTS

Sauté dishes are always prepared from small pieces of tender meat or offal, or jointed game or poultry. Tough foods of any kind are not suitable for the sauté technique.

Red meat

Only tender steaks, liver and kidneys are suitable for sautéing. The method of sautéing steaks, deglazing the pan and serving them with a small amount of pan sauce poured over them is fully discussed on pages 28–33. Recipes for veal kidneys and

chicken livers are given here, and a recipe for liver Venetian-style appears on page 120 where liver is discussed in detail.

Pink meat (lamb, veal and pork)

Only the very tenderest cuts, such as escalopes of veal, can be cooked as a true sauté by frying briefly in an open pan. The classic method of sautéing less tender cuts, such as shoulder, is to cube the meat and give it a preliminary browning. To make the sauce, drain the fat from the pan, add wine and boil rapidly to reduce it. Then add a previously prepared sauce, such as espagnole or chasseur and then complete the cooking by simmering the sauce in a covered pan on top of the cooker, or in the oven.

The same technique is widely used for cooking chops and is discussed in this context on pages 35–40.

Poultry and game

Among chefs, sautéing is a favourite way of cooking poultry and game. In his 'Guide to Modern Cookery', Escoffier gives no less than fortyseven different ways to present sautéed chicken. Any type of poultry or game is very suitable for sautéing provided it is young and tender, but at the same time plump and meaty. According to size it should be cut into four, six or eight portions. After the preliminary browning, the cooking continues gently, with a lid on the pan, so that the meat is tenderized and kept succulent by the moist steam while it cooks through to the centre. Simmer on the top of the stove at a low heat and, if necessary, stand the pan on a wire or asbestos mat to spread the heat evenly. Alternatively, transfer the meat to an ovenproof pan and place this in a moderately hot oven 190°C [375°F] gas mark 5 to complete the cooking. With either method of cooking, the white meat, that is to say the breast and wings, will be cooked before the dark meat. Ideally, the white meat should be removed from the pan and kept warm while the dark meat continues to cook for another seven to eight minutes.

Sautéed chicken is deliciously succulent to eat and should be served as soon as possible after cooking, otherwise much of the charm of this method of cooking is lost. Rabbit can also be sautéed like chicken, although game is generally cooked by other methods.

Fat and oil for sautéing

Butter, fat and oil are the best mediums for sautéing meat, and are discussed in relation to frying meat on page 28.

The flavour of butter is an important element in many sauté recipes, but butter alone is not suitable because it burns at a relatively low temperature. Use either clarified butter, olive oil or a mixture of unsalted butter and oil.

Flavourings and garnishes

Sauté dishes lend themselves to an infinite variety of presentations. Vegetables such as shallots, spring onions, mushrooms and tomatoes are often softened in the fat after the meat has been fried and before the liquid is added.

In some recipes, the meat is flamed with brandy or another spirit such as whisky, before being removed from the pan.

Spices and herbs are frequent additions to the sauces (see recipe variation for chicken sauté with tarragon) and the dish can be garnished with croûtons of fried bread, fleurons of pastry or colourful vegetables.

SAUTÉED CHICKEN

This is the basic sauté method in which the jointed chicken is cooked entirely in the pan without additional liquid. After dishing up the chicken, the pan is deglazed with wine and a small amount of pan sauce is prepared to pour over the chicken. Use a fresh rather than a frozen bird, as the latter tends to contain more water. The stock may be made using a cube.

SERVES 4
1.6 kg [3½ lb] chicken,
   oven-ready weight
salt
freshly ground black pepper
50 g [2 oz] unsalted butter
15 ml [1 tablespoon] oil
2 shallots or 3 spring onions
60 ml [4 tablespoons] dry
   white vermouth
180 ml [⅓ pt] chicken stock
5 ml [1 teaspoon] soy sauce or
   mushroom ketchup
20 ml [4 teaspoons] freshly
   chopped parsley

1 Using a sharp knife, cut the chicken into 8 joints.

2 Dry the pieces of chicken thoroughly with kitchen paper. Season the skin lightly with salt and pepper.

3 Heat 25 g [1 oz] butter and the oil in a sauté pan over medium heat.

4 When the foam subsides put in the chicken pieces, skin side down, in a single uncrowded layer. If necessary, fry in two batches rather than overcrowd the pan.

5 Sauté over slightly higher heat, and when the chicken has browned on one side (about 2-3 minutes) turn and brown another surface. Repeat every two minutes or so until all the surfaces are golden. During this time regulate the heat so that the chicken sizzles and browns but the fat does not burn. If by chance the fat burns, lift out the chicken pieces, discard all the fat and heat fresh butter and oil before proceeding.

6 Peel and chop the shallots or onions. When the chicken has browned, add to the pan. Put on the lid and reduce the heat so that cooking proceeds at a gentle simmer.

7 After 15-20 minutes, test the white meat joints by piercing with a fine skewer. If the juices run clear, remove to a serving dish and keep hot. Continue cooking the dark meat joints for a further 7-10 minutes. When cooked, add these to the white meat joints.

8 Skim off any surplus fat leaving about 15 ml [1 tablespoon] in the pan, with the chopped onion and any juices that may have run from the chicken. Add the vermouth and stock.

9 Increase the heat and boil rapidly, uncovered, scraping up the coagulated juices from the base of the pan until the liquid is reduced to about 75 ml [5 tablespoons].

10 Remove the pan from the heat, add the soy sauce or ketchup and the parsley. Cut the remaining 25 g [1 oz] butter into small pieces and beat into the sauce to enrich and

thicken it. Check the seasoning, pour over the chicken and serve at once.

Variations

●Try chicken sauté with tarragon. Follow the instructions for the basic sauté recipe, adding a large sprig of fresh tarragon when deglazing the pan. After reducing the vermouth and stock remove the tarragon, add 60 ml [4 tablespoons] thick cream and 15 ml [1 tablespoon] chopped fresh tarragon. Simmer for a minute or two, check seasoning and pour over the chicken.

●For poulet sauté Georgina, first brown the chicken. Substitute, 12 peeled button onions and a small bouquet garni for the shallots or spring onions. When the chicken is cooked and dished up, discard the bouquet garni and deglaze the pan with 60 ml [4 tablespoons] mushroom cooking liquor and 60 ml [4 tablespoons] dry white vermouth. Boil rapidly to reduce by half, add 12 cleaned and trimmed button mushrooms and 150 ml [¼ pt] thick cream. Simmer gently until the sauce begins to thicken, check the seasoning and pour it over the chicken pieces.

VEAL KIDNEYS TRIFOLATI

This is a true sauté and a fresh-tasting Italian way of cooking sliced veal kidneys. If the kidneys are sliced thinly, the cooking is completed in five minutes and there is no danger of their overcooking and becoming tough. If you like a strong flavour of garlic, add it finely chopped with the herbs instead of using it subtly to flavour the fat. Before starting to sauté the kidney, fry small cubes of bread to make croûtons for a garnish.

SERVES 4
550 g [1¼ lb] veal kidneys, suet removed
1 large garlic clove
15 ml [1 tablespoon] oil
25 g [1 oz] butter
30 ml [2 tablespoons] chopped fresh parsley and/or chives
1 lemon
salt
freshly ground black pepper

1 With a sharp knife, carefully peel off the thin membrane covering each kidney and cut away the exposed fat and core.

2 Cut the kidneys crossways into very thin slices of between 3-6 mm [⅛-¼"] thick.

3 Peel the garlic clove and cut in half.

4 Put the oil, butter and garlic into a large sauté pan and heat very gently over low heat for about 2 minutes while the garlic flavours the fat. Remove and discard the garlic.

5 Increase the heat to medium and, when the foam subsides, add the kidney slices. Cook briskly, tossing or stirring constantly, for about 2 minutes until they change colour from pink to grey.

6 Stir in the herbs and continue cooking and stirring for another 2 minutes.

7 Squeeze the lemon. Add the juice to the pan and allow to bubble for a minute. By this time the kidneys should be tender but very slightly pink when cut, and the juices should be syrupy.

8 Finally, add salt and pepper to taste. Serve immediately, garnished with fried bread croûtons.

Sautéed chicken is cooked entirely without liquid. The pan is deglazed to make the sauce.

VEAL PIECES FRIED IN OLIVE OIL

This simple little dish of fried veal (vitello all'uccelletto) is a great favourite in Liguria. Italian gourmets explain patiently to their guests that the ingredients for success are just good quality veal, speedy cooking and fresh, fruity olive oil. A few suggest adding one or two fresh sage leaves to give the veal a gamey flavour, others tell you this spoils it. This all goes to show that flavourings are very much a matter of personal taste. Ask the butcher to slice the veal very thinly and to beat it out as if for escalopes, so that it is about 3 mm [⅛"] thick. Serve with French beans.

SERVES 4
550 g [1¼ lb] fillet of veal
2 garlic cloves
60 ml [4 tablespoons] olive oil
3 bay leaves
salt
freshly ground black pepper
75 ml [5 tablespoons] dry white wine or dry white vermouth

1 If the butcher has not done this already for you, slice the veal very thinly and beat it out as if for escalopes (see page 44).

2 Just before you are ready to cook, pat the slices of veal dry and cut them into small pieces, about 2.5 cm [1"] across.

3 To avoid overcrowding the pan, divide the meat into 2 or 3 batches, depending on the size of your pan.

4 Peel the garlic cloves.

5 Put 45 ml [3 tablespoons] olive oil into a heavy-based frying-pan, add the garlic cloves and bay leaves and warm over low heat so that the oil becomes impregnated with their flavour.

6 Off the heat add one batch of veal pieces and stir well so that the meat is well coated with the oil.

7 Increase the heat, replace the pan and cook briskly for 3-4 minutes, stirring frequently until the veal turns pale and is just cooked. Remove from the heat.

8 Using a slotted spoon, lift out the veal, allowing the surplus fat to run back into the pan, and transfer it to a hot serving dish. Season with salt and pepper.

9 Cook the rest of the veal in the same manner, adding more oil to the pan only if necessary.

10 After cooking the last batch of meat discard the garlic and bay leaves. Add the wine to the pan and heat briskly, scraping up the coagulated juices from the base of the pan, until reduced to a syrupy consistency.

11 Spoon the sauce over the meat and serve at once.

Frying with finesse

Some of the most delectable dishes imaginable emerge from the frying-pan, but frying is a process that demands suitable ingredients and the full attention of the cook. Here we outline the different ways of shallow frying meat and the basic techniques needed to master the art of open frying.

Opponents of frying describe it as an invention of the devil and the cause of innumerable digestive disorders. It may be true that badly fried food is greasy and indigestible, but, on the credit side, the cook who learns to wield the frying-pan with skill and panache has at her command a considerable repertoire of quickly prepared meat dishes, ranging from the everyday to the haute cuisine.

There is nothing intrinsically difficult about frying. The different methods are discussed here and on pages 20–24, and pages 34–50.

Success or failure depends primarily on the following factors:
- selecting suitable cuts of meat
- preparing the meat carefully
- choosing the correct method of frying
- controlling the cooking temperature and time.

With all methods of frying the initial heat must be sufficiently high when the meat goes into the pan to coagulate the surface proteins and seal the cut surfaces of the meat.

This helps the meat retain its juices and flavour. If the fat is not hot enough the surface of the meat will not be sealed. Instead, an unnecessary amount of fat will be absorbed, resulting in greasy instead of well-browned or crisp food. On the other hand, if the fat is allowed to become too hot, the surface of the meat will become inedibly charred before the centre has had a chance to cook. So careful control of temperatures is a vital factor in successful shallow frying—and is even more crucial in deep fat frying.

After the initial sealing and browning, the method of frying will vary according to the type of meat being cooked. Prime beef steaks are quickly sautéed (open fried) over high heat throughout but pork, lamb and veal chops, once sealed, are cooked at a reduced temperature, to allow the heat to penetrate and cook the meat through to the centre.

Fillet steak is briefly fried in butter and oil for perfect flavour.

METHODS OF SHALLOW FRYING MEAT

There are several basic methods of shallow frying meat. A synopsis of each method is given here; details of the different methods are given on pages 20–24 and 34–50. Here we discuss in detail the open frying of uncoated meat.

Open frying

This is true shallow frying and is what most people think of when you say 'fried meat'. It is a process of rapid cooking in a heavy-based pan containing from 3–12 mm [⅛–½"] depth of fat, depending on the nature of the meat being fried. It is essentially the same as sautéing, but the process is always quick and more suitable for red meat. Only relatively thin cuts of expensive prime quality meat is tender enough to be cooked successfully by this method. Some cuts are better fried uncoated (as demonstrated here), but some others are better first coated with egg and breadcrumbs. The frying of coated meat is discussed in detail on pages 41–50.

Sautéing

This is a generic term used to describe a method of tossing and browning pieces of food in a very small amount of hot fat in a shallow-sided pan. Very tender meat can be sautéed until fully cooked, while food that needs longer and slightly slower cooking can be finished in a sauce made in the same pan. This method of shallow frying is discussed on pages 20–24.

Steam frying

This is a method of frying where the meat is first browned in a small amount of hot fat, the heat is then reduced and the pan covered so that the meat completes its cooking in a moist atmosphere. All types of chop, cutlet and less tender steak can be cooked beautifully by this method. Variety is introduced by adding small amounts of flavoursome liquids and vegetables until, in some cases, the process is very similar to braising meat. Steam frying is discussed on pages 34–40.

Dry frying

This method has developed for food naturally rich in fat, such as bacon rashers and sausages. The pan is greased lightly to prevent the meat sticking when first put into the pan, but no further fat is added. This method is also called pan grilling. The pan used must always be heavy based (a ridged iron pan is a good example) for this method, but the temperature and timing vary quite considerably according to the type of meat. Sausages, for instance, need to be cooked over gentle heat to prevent their skins bursting; large sausages need 15–20 minutes to cook through. For more details, see opposite.

Fillet steak, on the other hand, can need as little as 4 minutes, but over a higher heat.

EQUIPMENT
The pan

Different types of frying-pan can be used for frying, but bear in mind the following: the first essential is a heavy, well-balanced, flat-based pan made of a material that conducts and holds heat evenly. Such materials include cast iron, heavy gauge aluminium or black wrought steel. The last mentioned is popular with chefs, but will rust unless kept dry and oiled when not in use. Handles must be heat resistant and reasonably long. Avoid a light-weight unbalanced pan with a metal handle—it would stick, buckle, tip over, burn your hands and generally be a hindrance rather than a help. A 25 cm [10"] diameter pan is ideal for frying four steaks or chops simultaneously, but a 20 cm [8"] pan is large enough when cooking for two people.

A sauté pan is useful for sautéing meat as well as vegetables. The lid allows it to be used for steam frying as well, making it a generally versatile pan.

A ridged iron pan is particularly useful for dry frying and gives a professional finish to steaks by making criss-cross burns on the meat.

An electric frying-pan has a lid and is thermostatically controlled, making it ideal for open or steam frying as well as stewing, braising and, even, baking. When cooking facilities are limited, the electric frying-pan is a versatile piece of equipment.

'Proving' a new pan. This seasoning of the pan makes it non-stick. Remember never to scour the pan once it has been seasoned.

Small equipment

When frying, there are several small

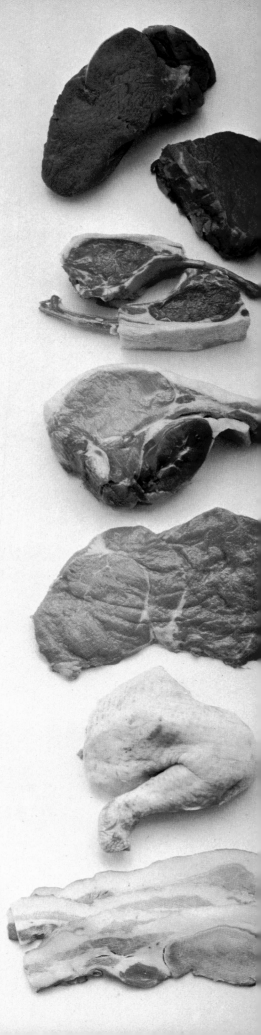

SUITABLE WAYS AND TIMES FOR SHALLOW FRYING MEAT

Meat	Frying method and time	Comments
Beef fillet steak 2.5 cm [1"] thick sirloin steak 2.5 cm [1"] thick minute steak 6 mm [$\frac{1}{4}$"] thick rump steak 2.5 cm [1"] thick	open fry for 6-8 minutes open fry for 8-10 minutes open fry for 4-5 minutes fry open or covered for 8-12 minutes	All these times are for medium rare. Only the very tender rump should be open fried. If in doubt, steam fry.
Lamb chops 2.5 cm [1"] thick cutlets 2.5 cm [1"] thick noisettes 2.5 cm [1"] thick	fry covered for 12-15 minutes fry covered for 12-15 minutes fry open or covered for 8-12 minutes	
Pork chops 2-2.5 cm [$\frac{3}{4}$-1"] thick spare ribs 2.5 cm [1"] thick thin escalopes cut from fillet	fry covered for 18-20 minutes fry covered for 14-18 minutes open fry for 6-10 minutes	Pork must always be thoroughly cooked right through.
Veal chops escalopes	fry covered for 18-20 minutes open fry for 6-10 minutes	Veal should be well cooked, but not overcooked, so the meat does not become dry.
Poultry chicken portions chicken /turkey escalopes	fry covered for 20-25 minutes fry open or covered for 10-15 minutes	
Bacon rashers chops or steaks 6 mm [$\frac{1}{4}$"] thick	dry fry for 3-5 minutes open fry for 10-15 minutes	Overlap, fat edge to pan.
Kidneys lamb's halved calf's, sliced 1.25 cm [$\frac{1}{2}$"] thick	dry or open fry for 6-8 minutes open fry for 6-8 minutes	
Liver calf's, lamb's or pig's, sliced 6 mm-1.25 cm [$\frac{1}{4}$-$\frac{1}{2}$"] thick	open fry for 5-8 minutes	Avoid overcooking which hardens and toughens liver.
Sausages pork or beef, thick pork or beef, chipolata pork or beef, skinless	dry fry for 18-20 minutes dry fry for 10-12 minutes dry fry for 8-10 minutes	Always fry sausages slowly to prevent skins bursting. Turn frequently to ensure even cooking and browning.
Minced meat patties 1.25 cm [$\frac{1}{2}$"] thick	open fry for 8-12 minutes	

items that make the job easier and safer. These include a slotted metal spoon for lifting and draining food, a heat-resistant plastic or fish slice for turning and lifting food, a pair of tongs for turning sausages and other firm food and absorbent kitchen paper. The paper is essential for patting food dry before frying, and also as a crumpled base for absorbing excess fat after frying.

CUTS OF MEAT FOR OPEN FRYING

Open frying is a short, sharp method of cooking suitable prime cuts of meat, especially red meat, or offal. Speaking generally these are the same expensive cuts used for grilling for example, all the beef steaks, lamb, pork and veal chops, cutlets, noisettes and escalopes. Most of these cuts are juicy slices of meat averaging 2.5 cm [1"] in thickness.

Because frying is a moist method of cooking, it is also suitable for very thin slices of meat, such as escalopes and 'minute' steaks which are not so satisfactorily cooked by the dry heat of grilling.

The timing of the cooking (see chart) is directly related to the thickness of the cut, and whether the meat is required (in the case of beef) rare, medium rare or well done. The times given in the chart are for meat at room temperature, and not for meat taken directly from the refrigerator.

It is important that the meat be of an even thickness throughout, and cut across the grain to encourage tenderness. Do remember that if the meat is cut thinner than 2.5 cm [1"] the time needed is appreciably less than the time given in the chart and vice versa.

OILS AND FATS FOR SHALLOW FRYING

When shallow frying, it is the job of the fat to prevent the food from sticking to the pan. Fat also conducts the heat from the pan to the food.

Raw meat is firm enough to be fried without a protective coating. When frying uncoated meat, relatively little fat is absorbed. The prime requirement therefore is a fat capable of being heated efficiently, without burning, to seal the surface of the meat when this is first added to the pan. Butter, fats and oils are used for all different methods of frying meat.

Oils

Vegetable oils are very satisfactory for shallow frying. When buying oil look at the label to see what it is made from. A blended vegetable oil is virtually flavourless and will not add taste to the meat. Flavour can be added by serving the meat garnished with pats of savoury butter such as parsley, or any complementary herb.

Butter

Butter alone is not a suitable frying medium, unless it has been clarified (melted and then strained). The milk solids contained in butter darken and burn long before frying temperature is reached. However, a half and half mixture of butter and oil is ideal, because the oil reduces the tendency to burn while the butter adds its own flavour. The residue in the pan after frying can be deglazed and used to make a small amount of flavoursome sauce to serve with the meat. Always use unsalted in preference to salted butter, as the salt residue encourages the fat to burn.

Fats and drippings

Other fat, such as lard or white cooking fat, fry very satisfactorily but contribute nothing in flavour to the food.

On the other hand, the dripping which results from roasting or grilling beef, pork or bacon adds delicious flavours to any food fried in it. Dripping needs to be used with care because such fat contains moisture and solids which can cause spitting and catching. As with butter, this can be avoided if the dripping is clarified before using. However, you will also lose much of the meaty flavour.

To clarify dripping put it into a large saucepan and cover with cold water. Heat very gently, uncovered, until the water starts to boil. Simmer for 3–5 minutes. Remove from the heat and strain through a sieve into a clean bowl. Leave to go cold and solidify. Lift the solid fat off the top of the water and scrape away any sediment from the underside.

Before using the dripping for frying, heat it very gently until all bubbling ceases, indicating that any water has been driven off.

Quantity of fat

The quantity of fat needed depends on the method of frying to be used. It ranges from the minimum of fat to grease the pan to prevent sticking when dry frying, to sufficient fat or oil to give a depth in the pan from 1.5–12 mm [$\frac{1}{16}$–$\frac{1}{2}$"]. In a 20 cm [8"] pan this will be up to 100 ml [3½ fl oz] and in a 25 cm [10"] pan 200 ml [7 fl oz].

Coated portions of meat require more fat, as some will be absorbed by the coating. A general guide for coated meat is that the fat should reach half-way up the sides of the food, which in practice means about 6 mm [$\frac{1}{4}$"] or 90 ml [6 tablespoons] in a 20 cm [8"] heavy-based pan. In fact, only irregular-shaped portions such as chicken joints are likely to need more fat, when 8–12 mm [$\frac{1}{3}$–$\frac{1}{2}$"] depth is necessary. The less fat you use, the better, but be sure to use sufficient to keep the food from sticking to the pan.

4 beef steaks, each weighing
175–225 g [6–8 oz], cut
2.5 cm [1"] thick
25 g [1 oz] unsalted butter
15 ml [1 tablespoon] oil
freshly ground black pepper
salt

4 Fry for 3–6 minutes, according to taste, over fairly high heat. Turn steaks, one by one.

OPEN FRYING UNCOATED MEAT

Preparing the meat

Wipe the meat with a damp cloth and cut off any excess fat.

Steaks: cut small incisions around the outer edge wherever there is a layer of gristle between the fat and the lean. This will help prevent the steak curling as it cooks.

Chops and cutlets: remove skin, if any, from outer edge of fat. Chops and cutlets can also be boned, then rolled and tied with fine string to form noisettes.

Although chops and cutlets can be open fried, they are more tender and succulent if just browned in an open pan and then covered to complete the cooking in a moist atmosphere. This method of frying is discussed on pages 34–40. If it is boned, beat the meat with a rolling pin or cutlet bat to bruise the fibres and help tenderize the meat. Beating also helps to flatten the meat to an even thickness.

Moist meat will not brown effectively, so it is important that immediately before frying you pat the meat dry on both sides, using kitchen paper. Never salt meat before frying, as this will cause the juices to flow.

Heating the fat

Put the fat into the pan and heat steadily over medium heat until frying temperature is reached. The method of judging the temperature differs a little according to the fat being used.

Oil and butter mixed: heat until the butter ceases to foam but has not started to turn brown.

Oil, clarified dripping or lard: heat fat then drop in a small cube of dry bread. When it sizzles and turns golden brown in 15 seconds, then the fat is ready to use.

Adding the meat

Raise the heat and gently lower the meat, one piece at a time, into the fat using tongs or a fish slice and spoon, to avoid splashing the fat or piercing the meat. Allow a few seconds between adding each piece, for the fat to regain frying temperature. Do not overcrowd the pan; there should be enough space between the pieces to allow them to be turned—about 6 mm [¼"] should be ample.

Browning and turning the meat

Fry over fairly high heat until the side of the meat touching the pan is sealed and browned. This quick sealing is necessary to help imprison the juices and flavour. Once browned, turn each slice, starting with the

Step-by-step to open frying meat

1 Prepare the steaks by wiping clean, trimming excess fat and nicking edges. Pat dry carefully.

2 Heat the butter and oil steadily in a 25 cm [10"] heavy-based pan, over medium heat. Add pepper.

3 When butter ceases to foam but has not coloured, put in the steaks, one at a time. Raise heat.

5 Fry second side for same time. Test by nicking with a knife to see colour of the meat inside.

6 Drain the steaks by holding over the pan with tongs, to allow excess fat to drip off.

7 Transfer to a hot serving dish. Season and arrange a garnish.

first one put into the pan, and continue cooking over the same heat until the second side is sealed and browned.

By this time thin pieces of meat such as minute steaks, escalopes and liver slices will be cooked, as will steaks required rare and medium. For pork, lamb, veal or beef which is required well done, lower the heat and continue cooking to the desired degree, turning the meat as necessary.

Needless to say, roly-poly shapes such as sausages need frequent turning for even cooking and browning, and irregular-shaped pieces such as chicken joints may also need turning more than once. When turning use tongs or a slice and avoid using a fork which might puncture the meat and allow juices to escape. The chart gives average cooking times.

Testing the meat
Steak is cooked to the medium-rare state when little beads of red juice begin to appear on the cooked surface or when, if you press it with the flat of a knife, it feels firm but has a definite 'give'. For well-done steak, continue cooking until the meat feels quite firm and no red juices can be pressed out with the flat of a knife. If you are in doubt, nick the steak with a knife so that you can see the condition of the inside.
Lamb should feel firm when pressed, but unless you like it well done, it need not be cooked to the point where no pink juices are visible.
Pork and veal need to be well cooked right through and should feel very firm when pressed.

Draining the meat
Remove the pieces of meat in the order in which they went into the pan, using a fish slice or tongs. Hold each piece in turn over the pan for a second or two to allow surplus fat to drain back, or lay on a bed of crumpled absorbent kitchen paper. Transfer the meat to a very hot dish and either garnish and serve immediately, or keep hot while deglazing the pan.

DEGLAZING THE PAN
One of the delights of shallow frying is that you are left with delicious meaty juices in the pan. With very little effort these can be made into a really delicious sauce or gravy to pour over the meat.

If there is more than 15 ml [1 tablespoon] or so of fat remaining in the pan, spoon the surplus out and reserve for frying other food. If the fat has become overbrowned, discard it all and replace with 25 g [1 oz] fresh butter.

Add 150 ml [¼ pt] good stock, consommé, red wine, dry white wine or dry vermouth to the pan and place over high heat. Stir and scrape the meat juices from the bottom of the pan and boil until the liquid is reduced to about 45 ml [3 tablespoons] and is of a syrup consistency. Spoon the sauce over the meat and serve immediately.

For a richer and thicker sauce, add 25 g [1 oz] butter. When the sauce has reached the syrupy consistency, remove the pan from the heat. Have ready the butter, cut into small pieces and beat these into the sauce, one by one. Return the pan to medium heat, warm through and pour over the meat.

FRYING FROZEN MEAT
Commercially frozen products, such as beefburgers, steaklets and sausages, usually carry full instructions and cooking times on the pack. Generally speaking, all these products retain their maximum succulence and flavour if cooked from the near-frozen state. The best method is to take them from the freezer and expose them to room temperature about half an hour before cooking. This allows any surface ice crystals to evaporate, and should avoid undue spluttering when the products are put into the hot fat. Cook over low to medium heat in the minimum amount of fat consistent with the depth of the product, turning as necessary (once for beefburgers, frequently for sausages).

Frozen chops, cutlets and steaks are also best cooked from frozen and, although they will benefit from being cooked by the steam-fry method, can be open fried. Again exposing them to the air for half an hour to allow surface ice crystals to thaw is best. Pat them dry with kitchen paper immediately before putting into the hot fat to prevent unnecessary spluttering.

The process is different from that of frying fresh meat. Place in the hot fat and cook over low to medium heat until completely thawed, then increase the heat towards the end of the cooking period to brown the surface. Allow half as long again as when cooking fresh meat, to allow for the thawing and cooking time combined. Season, drain and serve in the usual way.

Handy hints
Safety first frying
Hot fat, even in small amounts needs to be handled with great care. A frying-pan that is allowed to overheat, or spilled fat can catch fire very readily. Make sure that anyone in your home handling hot fat is aware of the potential danger and follows these rules.
●Never allow fat or oil to overheat. This is the cause of many fires that start in the kitchen.
●Keep pan handles turned inwards to avoid accidental overturning by the cook or an inquisitive child.
●See that food to be fried is patted dry or coated before being put into the hot fat. Moisture can cause hot fat to spit fiercely.
●Also see that there is no boiling kettle or pan near enough to splash water into the pan.

Putting out a fire
This should not be necessary if you have followed the rules just given, but if it does become necessary, immediate action is called for.
●Don't move the pan.
●Turn off the heat if you can reach the dial easily.
●Smother the flames. Use a lid or a flat baking sheet or, failing that, something thick and damp such as a towel or oven cloth. Never use anything dry and cottony like a tea towel which could act as fuel for the fire.
●Of course the simplest thing is to have a fire extinguisher. If you do have one make sure that it is maintained in serviceable order and that you know how to use it. There will be no time for reading instructions once a fire has started.

BEEFSTEAK GARNI

This is the simple basic method for cooking and serving a classic fried steak. The quality of the dish depends entirely on the quality of the meat, so use only a prime cut of well-hung fillet, rump or sirloin steak. Garnish with watercress and halved tomatoes and serve with a savoury butter.

It helps to have the garnishes and accompaniments ready before you cook the steaks, so that the meat can be served immediately it is cooked.

SERVES 4
4 beef steaks, each weighing 175–225 g [6–8 oz] and cut 2.5 cm [1"] thick
25 g [1 oz] unsalted butter
15 ml [1 tablespoon] oil
freshly ground black pepper
salt

1 Wipe the steaks with a damp cloth and trim any excess fat. Cut small incisions at 1.25 cm [½"] intervals around the edge of the steaks, especially where you see a layer of gristle between the fat and the meat.

2 Pat the steak dry with kitchen paper.

3 Place the butter and oil in a heavy-based pan large enough to hold the meat in a single uncrowded layer and heat steadily over medium heat. Pepper the steaks.

4 When the butter foam begins to subside, indicating that the fat is hot enough, put in the steaks one by one and cook for 3–4 minutes for medium rare or 6 minutes for well done, regulating the heat under the pan to keep the fat at frying temperature.

5 Turn the steaks with tongs and fry the other side for a similar length of time.

6 Remove the pan from the heat, season the steak with some salt and arrange on a hot serving dish. Add the garnish, top each steak with a pat of chilled savoury butter and serve immediately.

BEEFSTEAK MARCHAND DE VIN

This recipe dresses up a plainly fried steak with a simple red wine sauce, made by deglazing the pan when the steaks are removed. Choose a robust red wine for this simple sauce. If you cannot find any shallots or spring onions use some mild onion, finely chopped and blanched in boiling water for 1 minute. Refresh it under cold water and pat dry before frying.

SERVES 4
4 beef steaks, each weighing 175–225 g [6–8 oz] and cut 2.5 cm [1"] thick
50 g [2 oz] unsalted butter
15 ml [1 tablespoon] oil
salt and pepper
1 shallot or 4 spring onions
150 ml [¼ pt] red wine

The simplicity of beefsteak garni belies its succulence. A simple garnish and a savoury butter complete the presentation.

1 Prepare the steak for frying, as described in the step-by-step instructions.

2 Over medium heat melt 25 g [1 oz] of the butter plus the oil in a large heavy-based frying-pan.

3 When frying temperature is reached raise the heat and lower in the steaks one by one.

4 Cook the steaks as described in the step-by-step instructions and to your liking.

5 Remove the pan from the heat, season the steaks with salt and pepper on both sides and move to a hot serving dish.

6 Discard the cooking fat and replace with 15 g [½ oz] butter.

7 Chop the shallot or onions and put the pan with the butter over low heat. When melted, stir in the chopped shallot or onions and cook slowly for 2 minutes.

8 Pour in the wine, raise the heat and boil rapidly, stirring up the meat juices from the bottom of the pan, until the liquid has reduced to about 45 ml [3 tablespoons].

9 Remove the pan from the heat and beat in the remaining butter, in pieces, until it amalgamates and thickens the sauce. Season to taste and spoon over the steaks.

Variation

●For beefsteak à la Bercy, substitute dry white wine or dry vermouth for the red wine and stir in 30 ml [2 tablespoons] freshly chopped parsley before spooning the sauce over the steaks.

STEAK AU POIVRE

There are many variations of this simple but famous recipe, so alternative methods of serving it are given. Needless to say prime quality, well-hung beef is a prerequisite, but you can buy individual steaks or use two larger pieces of steak for portioning at the table. Begin preparations at least an hour before the meal to give the meat time to absorb the piquant pepper flavours. If possible use a mixture of black and white peppercorns, black for spice and aroma and white for strength.

Vary the quantity of peppercorns depending on how peppery you like the steaks. Serve with sautéed potatoes piled at either end of the dish, watercress sprigs between the steaks and lemon wedges on top of them. Have these ready before starting to fry the meat.

SERVES 6
900 g–1.1 kg [2–2½ lb] rump steak, cut into two slices 2 cm [¾"] thick
30 ml [2 tablespoons] black and white peppercorns, mixed
45 ml [3 tablespoons] olive oil
65 g [2½ oz] unsalted butter
salt
half a lemon

1 Wipe the steaks with a damp cloth. Trim off excess fat, beat vigorously with a rolling pin to help break down the fibres, and nick the fat edges at 1.25 cm [½"] intervals.

2 Crush the peppercorns using a mortar and pestle, or a stout bowl and the end of the rolling pin. Spread out evenly on a flat board or tray.

3 Press first one side of the meat into the crushed peppercorns and then the other, pressing the meat down firmly so that the peppercorns adhere.

4 Sprinkle the meat lightly with 30 ml [2 tablespoons] olive oil, cover with a piece of greaseproof paper and leave in a cool place for ½–2 hours.

5 When ready to cook, heat 40 g [1½ oz] butter and the remaining oil in a large 25 cm [10"] frying-pan. When the foam subsides, put in the pieces of steak, one by one, and fry for about 3 minutes on each side for medium rare, longer for well done. Adjust the heat to maintain frying temperature throughout the cooking time, but watch that the fat does not become too hot and burn.

6 Lift the pieces of steak on to a hot serving dish sprinkle with salt and garnish.

7 Pour the fat and the peppercorns out of the pan. Put the remaining butter in the pan and heat over medium heat while scraping up the coagulated juices from the base of the pan with a wooden spoon. Squeeze the lemon into the pan, stir and pour over the steaks. Serve immediately and portion at the table.

Variations

●After taking the steaks out of the pan, pour out the cooking fat and loose peppercorns and pour in 150 ml [¼ pt] dry white wine, dry white vermouth or robust red wine. Boil briskly until reduced to 45–60 ml [3–4 tablespoons] stirring to release the coagulated juices from the base of the pan. Off the heat stir in the remaining 25 g [1 oz] butter in small pieces, and pour over the steaks.

●A traditional cream sauce contrasts with the piquancy of the pepper steaks. After taking the steaks out of the pan, pour away the cooking fat and loose peppercorns. Add 60 ml [4 tablespoons] brandy to the pan and heat. Then, taking care to keep your face well averted from the flames, ignite the brandy. When the flames die down stir in 150 ml [¼ pt] thick cream. Stir to release the coagulated juices from the base of the pan and allow the sauce to thicken and mellow by simmering gently for a minute or so before seasoning. Spoon over the steaks.

Steak au poivre has a very pleasant piquant dash. It is impressive, and unusually delicious.

MINUTE STEAKS WITH MUSHROOMS

A minute steak is a chef's rather than a butcher's name for any type of very thin, tender steak. If your butcher does not normally supply minute steaks, ask him to cut sirloin into steaks about 9 mm [⅓"] thick from well-hung beef, and to beat them to about 6 mm [¼"] thick. Each steak should weigh about 175 g [6 oz].

SERVES 2
2 minute steaks, weighing 175 g [6 oz] each
225 g [½ lb] button mushrooms
1 large garlic clove (optional)
freshly ground
**   black pepper**
15 ml [1 tablespoon] oil
50 g [2 oz] butter
half a lemon
salt

15 ml [1 tablespoon] freshly chopped parsley or chives

1 Wipe the mushrooms and trim the stalks. Slice fairly finely and set aside.

2 Wipe the steaks, trim off excess fat and dry on both sides with paper towel.

3 Peel the garlic clove (if used), cut in half and rub the cut halves liberally over both sides of each steak. Season with pepper.

4 Put the oil and 25 g [1 oz] butter in a heavy-based frying-pan. Put over medium heat until the butter ceases to foam.

5 Put in the steaks, one by one, and cook over brisk heat for about 2 minutes each side, or a little longer if you prefer them well cooked.

6 Lift out, holding them over the pan to drain for a few moments, then arrange on a hot serving dish and season with salt. Reserve and keep hot.

7 Add the remaining butter to the pan and, as soon as it has melted, put in the mushrooms. Lower the heat and cook gently, stirring frequently, until the mushrooms soften and exude their moisture.

8 Increase the heat, season with salt and squeeze the lemon into the pan. Cook briskly for a couple of minutes until most of the moisture has evaporated, stirring occasionally.

9 Spoon the mushrooms over the steaks and sprinkle with the parsley or chives. Serve immediately.

An undercover job

Steam frying comes into its own when the less tender cuts of meat are being used. The moist atmosphere that is created when the lid is placed over the pan keeps the meat juicy while it is gently cooking. Vegetables and flavourings can be cooked with the meat. Dishes are both easy and quick to cook.

Open frying and sautéing are discussed on pages 20–33 and 41–50 and, as emphasized there, are successful only for relatively thin pieces of prime quality and tender meat, offal and poultry.

Put a lid on the pan and you can fry chops, cutlets, cheaper cuts of steak and chicken joints, all of which will produce particularly succulent and flavoursome meals.

THE METHOD
The basic principles are similar to those for all methods of shallow frying meat. The meat is given an initial brief open frying in hot fat to seal and brown the surfaces and help enclose the juices and flavour. The method of frying then proceeds according to the meat being cooked. In steam frying, the heat is reduced, the lid placed over the pan and the meat cooked very gently until it is tender.

Trim any skin and excess fat from the meat, wipe over with a damp cloth and then pat dry carefully with absorbent kitchen paper. Heat a small quantity of fat in a lidded pan large enough to take the meat in a single layer. When hot, fry the meat briefly, turning once. Regulate the heat, if necessary, so that the meat sizzles but the fat does not burn.

Add the vegetables or liquid stated in the recipe and bring to simmering point. Reduce the heat, put the lid on firmly and simmer gently until the meat is tender.

The beauty of this method of frying is the moist, steam-filled atmosphere that is created once the lid is placed over the pan. In this humid atmosphere, it is quite impossible for the meat to dry out—even pork, which often needs twenty minutes' cooking.

THE MEAT

Steam frying is undoubtedly the best method of frying for any cut of meat, if you have any doubts about its tenderness. This method is also better for thicker cuts of meat which need a longer time in the frying-pan; if open fried, these have a tendency to dry out. The cuts of meat in the following section will all benefit from this tender treatment and provide many dishes for family fare and entertaining.

Chops and cutlets

You need 12-15 minutes to fry thick, meaty pieces of veal or lamb, and as long as 18–20 minutes for a pork chop. Open frying for this length of time is apt to dry out, as well as cook, the meat. Once the lid goes on, however, the cooking continues in moist heat and the meat is thoroughly cooked yet remains beautifully moist and succulent. With chops and cutlets that are past their springtime best, the denser fibres are softened and any gristle gelatinized.

Poultry portions

Although you can depend on the youth of a chicken these days, the flesh is very lean and also needs a reasonably long cooking period to ensure that it is cooked right through. Chicken joints can be open fried, but the results are more succulent if the cooking is finished in a moist atmosphere. When a lid is put on the pan, you have an opportunity to add a variety of vegetables and liquid flavourings which can produce a range of interesting flavours.

Steaks

Prime quality steaks have no need of the undercover treatment (see on pages 28–33), but less prime beef will benefit in the same way as will chops.

Bacon chops and cooked gammon

The meat of bacon chops is usually very dense and covered frying helps to counteract any tendency to dryness. It is also an excellent way to reheat, and at the same time add a sauce to, slices of cooked gammon.

Sausages

The charm of plain-fried or grilled sausages is apt to pall. Adding a sauce to the frying-pan provides both variety and succulence.

VEGETABLES AND FLAVOURINGS

The moist atmosphere that is so important in covered frying is created firstly by placing the lid on the frying-pan and secondly by adding vegetables or liquid as well. Covered frying allows you to add a range of exciting flavours and textures and thus introduce variety and interest especially to bland meat, such as chicken.

Vegetables, such as onions, garlic, shallots, mushrooms, spring onions, celery, peppers, aubergines and tomatoes, are added for flavour, texture or moisture, or for all three.

Red and dry white table wines are popular additions and very successful as are smaller quantities of fortified wines, such as Marsala, Madeira and sherry. Cider is particularly good with pork and poultry, especially when it has been reduced to intensify the flavour.

Condiments, including mustard and piquant sauces such as soy, Tabasco and Worcestershire, provide individual flavourings. Spices such as ginger and paprika can add a sometimes necessary fillip to a dish.

When rich sauces are called for, cream has no peer and fillet of pork with prunes amply demonstrates this. For a rich, creamy sauce with a piquant flavour use sour cream.

BEEF STROGANOFF

When this celebrated Russian dish is made very quickly in an open frying-pan you have no option but to use tender, but expensive, fillet steak. But, if you cover the pan and cook it more gently, you can get very good results using less expensive topside, as in this recipe. If sour cream is not available, stir one teaspoon of lemon juice into double cream. To make an extra creamy stroganoff, increase the amount of cream.

Garnish the stroganoff with freshly chopped parsley and serve on a bed of boiled rice.

SERVES 6
700 g [1½ lb] topside, sliced 12 mm [½"] thick
freshly ground black pepper
2 medium-sized onions
175 g [6 oz] button mushroom caps
50 g [2 oz] unsalted butter
15 ml [1 tablespoon] flour
15 ml [1 tablespoon] tomato purée
1.25 ml [¼ teaspoon] French mustard
250 ml [½ pt] beef stock
salt
150 ml [¼ pt] sour cream

1 Cut away any fat or skin from the meat and discard. Lay the meat flat and beat it well with a wooden rolling pin or cutlet bat. Cut it into 6 mm [¼"] wide strips and then cut the strips into 2.5 cm [1"] lengths. Sprinkle with pepper and rub in lightly.

2 Peel and slice the onions thinly. Wipe, de-stalk and thinly slice the mushroom caps.

3 When ready to cook, heat the butter in a wide sauté pan over low heat and fry the onion gently for five minutes.

4 Add the mushrooms and continue frying gently for another 3-4 minutes, stirring from time to time.

5 Add the meat strips, increase the heat to medium and fry, stirring frequently, for about 5 minutes, until the colour of the meat changes from red to grey.

6 Sprinkle in the flour, stir and fry for another minute.

7 Stir the tomato purée and mustard into the stock and add to the pan, stirring to mix in smoothly. Bring to simmering point, cover tightly and simmer very gently for 30-35 minutes or until tender.

8 When the meat is cooked, check seasoning, stir in the sour cream and heat gently, without boiling.

9 Arrange the boiled rice in a shallow serving dish, ladle the stroganoff over the rice, garnish with parsley and serve immediately.

CHICKEN MARENGO

This dish is said to have been invented by Napoleon's chef and cooked for the first time on the battlefield, where the only ingredients to hand were chicken, eggs, wine, oil and mushrooms. Several garnishes have become traditional with this dish and can be used, or not, as you wish. The original was crayfish but also choose from freshly chopped parsley, croûtons or fried eggs.

If you do not have a bottle of white wine open, use dry vermouth diluted half and half with water. The stock may be made with a cube.

SERVES 4
**4 chicken quarters, each weighing 225 g [8 oz]
salt
freshly ground black pepper
1 medium-sized onion
1 garlic clove
100 g [¼ lb] button mushrooms
45 ml [3 tablespoons] oil
30 ml [2 tablespoons] flour
150 ml [¼ pt] dry white wine
250 ml [½ pt] chicken stock
20 ml [4 teaspoons] tomato
    purée
bay leaf**

1 Wipe the chicken joints with a damp cloth and sprinkle the skin generously with salt and pepper. Rub the seasoning in with your fingers.

2 Peel and chop the onion. Peel and crush the garlic clove. Wipe but do not peel the mushrooms.

3 Heat the oil in a wide saucepan (one with a lid) over low heat and, when hot, put in the chicken joints, skin side down. Fry gently, uncovered, for about 5 minutes until golden brown, then turn and fry the other side for a minute or two.

4 Add the onion and garlic and continue frying very gently for a further 5 minutes.

5 Now sprinkle in the flour, stirring into the fat and cook for a minute or two.

6 Add the wine, stock and tomato purée and bring to the boil, stirring continuously. Season to taste and add the bay leaf.

7 Cover the pan tightly and simmer very gently for 20 minutes. Add the mushrooms, re-cover the pan, and continue cooking for another 20 minutes.

8 Lift out the chicken joints, arrange on a serving platter and keep warm.

9 If the sauce is too thin, boil rapidly, uncovered, stirring frequently until reduced to a coating consistency. Check the seasoning and pour over the chicken.

PIQUANT LAMB CUTLETS

This recipe is an attractive way of adding piquancy to lamb that is past its springtime best. Marinating the cutlets briefly in seasoned oil and completing their cooking in a covered pan helps to

ensure both flavour and tenderness. If fresh marjoram is not available, use 5 ml [1 teaspoon] dried marjoram. The cooked cutlets look attractive arranged around a pile of golden sautéed potatoes, and garnished with thin wedges of lemon.

SERVES 4
8 lamb cutlets
2 garlic cloves
75 ml [5 tablespoons] olive oil
salt
freshly ground black pepper
15 ml [1 tablespoon] freshly chopped marjoram
30 ml [2 tablespoons] drained capers
1 lemon

1 Prepare and trim the fat from the lamb cutlets.

2 Peel and crush the garlic.

3 Prepare the marinade by putting 45 ml [3 tablespoons] oil, the garlic and a seasoning of salt and pepper into a shallow baking tray into which the cutlets will fit fairly snugly.

4 Put in the cutlets, baste with the marinade, cover loosely and leave in a cool place for 1-2 hours.

5 When ready to cook, lift the cutlets from the marinade, scrape the garlic back into the marinade and pat the cutlets dry with kitchen paper.

6 Heat the remaining oil in a large shallow frying-pan. When hot, fry the cutlets over high heat until

Lamb cutlets, with a piquant marinade, go well with sautéed potatoes and spinach.

lightly browned, about 2-3 minutes on each side.

7 Lower the heat, add the marinade, the marjoram and the capers. Cover the pan and cook very gently for 12-15 minutes, turning the cutlets once.

8 Squeeze the lemon, add the juice to the pan and cook for a further minute.

9 Arrange the cutlets on a large serving dish around a pile of sautéed potatoes. Spoon the pan juices over the cutlets and garnish with lemon wedges.

PORK CHOPS WITH WINE

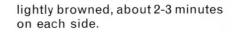 *This simple recipe is typical of those used by French families for cooking pork chops with a little local wine to help tenderize the meat. You do not need to buy the best quality pork chops—in fact, reasonably lean, spare rib chops would be quite suitable. The same method, but without the mustard and capers, is popular in Tuscany, where the dish is made with a young chianti and known as drunken or intoxicated pork chops.*

SERVES 4
4 pork chops
salt
freshly ground black pepper
50 g [2 oz] plain flour
10 ml [2 teaspoons] oil
150 ml [$\frac{1}{4}$ pt] dry white or rosé wine
15 ml [1 tablespoon] strong, made mustard, French or English
20 ml [4 teaspoons] capers
60 ml [4 tablespoons] stock

1 Trim the skin and excess fat from the chops and discard. Wipe the chops with a damp cloth. Sprinkle each side lightly with salt and pepper and dust with the flour.

2 Heat a large heavy-based frying-pan over medium heat and smear it with oil. When very hot, put in the chops and cook over fairly high heat until lightly browned on one side, about 2-3 minutes. Turn the chops and brown the other side.

3 Pour off any fat that has run from the chops (there may not be any if the chops are lean), then add the

wine and let it bubble briskly for a minute or two.

4 Lower the heat, cover the pan tightly and cook the chops very gently for 15-20 minutes, until the meat is quite tender.

5 Lift out the chops, arrange on a serving dish and keep warm.

6 Raise heat to medium and stir the mustard, capers and stock into the pan juices. Simmer for several minutes until well reduced. Check the seasoning.

7 Pour the sauce over the chops and serve immediately.

SAUSAGES WITH FRESH TOMATO SAUCE

◪ *This colourful family dish of sausages in a fresh tomato sauce comes from Rome. It relies upon a combination of open and covered frying to brown the sausages and achieve a pleasantly rough textured, fresh tasting sauce. If available, use coarsely chopped pure pork sausages, and serve them with spaghetti tossed in garlic-flavoured oil. If fresh sage is not available, use 1.25 ml [¼ teaspoon] dried sage.*

SERVES 4
450 g [1 lb] thick pork
    sausages
15 ml [1 tablespoon] oil
3 fresh sage leaves
450 g [1 lb] fresh tomatoes
15 ml [1 tablespoon] tomato
    purée
5 ml [1 teaspoon] sugar
salt
freshly ground black pepper

1 Heat the oil, and fresh sage leaves if used, in a sauté or frying-pan (with a lid) over medium heat. When hot, reduce the heat to low, put in the sausages and fry, uncovered, turning several times, until lightly browned all over. This will take about 8 minutes.

2 Meanwhile, drop the tomatoes into boiling water for a few seconds, then drain and skin them. Chop them roughly discarding any bits of really hard core.

3 When the sausages have browned, drain off any surplus fat that

has run from them. Add the tomatoes, tomato purée, sugar and salt and pepper to the sausages, and also dried sage if used instead of fresh. Cover the pan, bring to simmering point and simmer for 15 minutes.

4 Remove the sausages and keep hot in a serving dish. Continue simmering the tomatoes, uncovered, stirring frequently, until reduced to a rough-textured sauce. Remove sage leaves.

5 Check the seasoning of the sauce and spoon over the hot sausages.

FILLET OF PORK WITH PRUNES

◪◪◪ *Although fillet of pork is tender enough to cook by open frying, it is particularly delicious when the initial frying is followed by a gentle simmering in wine. The tender meat and succulent prunes are finally combined in a luscious wine and cream sauce. This is a simplified version of a famous speciality of Tours where, of course, a Loire wine such as a dry white Vouvray would be used. After the prunes have been soaked, the dish can be prepared in under an hour.*

SERVES 6
1 kg [2¼ lb] pork fillet
18 large prunes
425 ml [¾ pt] dry white wine
75 g [3 oz] seasoned flour
50 g [2 oz] unsalted butter
30 ml [2 tablespoons] oil
30 ml [2 tablespoons]
    redcurrant jelly
175 ml [6 fl oz] thick cream

1 Wash the prunes in cold water, drain and put into a bowl. Pour in 250 ml [½ pt] wine and leave to soak overnight.

2 Next day, tip the prunes and wine into a saucepan and simmer very gently until the prunes are tender—for 10-15 minutes, depending on the size of the prunes. Remove from heat, leave the prunes in the wine and keep warm.

3 Meanwhile, trim any skin and excess fat from the pork and wipe with a damp cloth. Holding a sharp knife on the slant, cut the fillet across into pieces about 2.5 cm [1"] thick.

4 Lay the pieces on a board and flatten them slightly by beating with a damp rolling pin.

5 Put the seasoned flour on a large piece of greaseproof paper, turn the pieces of pork in it until lightly coated, shaking off surplus flour.

6 Heat 25 g [1 oz] butter and 15 ml [1 tablespoon] oil in a wide sauté pan over medium heat and, when hot, fry a single uncrowded layer of pork slices fairly briskly for 2-3 minutes, until lightly browned. Turn the slices and brown the other side. Reserve in a warm place. Fry the rest of the pork in batches, adding more butter and oil to the pan as necessary.

7 When all the pieces of pork are fried, return them to the pan, add the remaining wine, bring to the boil and allow to bubble for a minute.

8 Lower the heat, cover the pan tightly and simmer gently for about 20 minutes, or until the meat is very tender.

9 Lift out the meat with a perforated spoon, allow it to drain momentarily over the pan, and then arrange in the centre of an oval serving dish. Keep hot.

10 Drain the wine from the prunes into the sauté pan and boil furiously, uncovered, stirring and scraping the juices from the base of the pan, until the liquid has reduced to about 150 ml [¼ pt].

11 Add the redcurrant jelly and stir until dissolved.

12 Add the cream, stir, and continue heating gently, shaking the pan now and then, until the sauce thickens sufficiently to coat the meat.

13 Check the seasoning of the sauce and pour it over the meat. Arrange the warm prunes, unstoned, on either side of the dish and serve immediately.

TURKEY BREAST ITALIENNE

Turkey breast meat is often available in supermarkets and this Italian method of cooking gives the meat character, as well as making it deliciously tender and succulent. Because of its piquant flavour, freshly grated parmesan is the best cheese to use, but if not available, substitute a finely grated, mature dry Cheddar. Braised celery or chicory goes well with this dish.

SERVES 4
450 g [1 lb] turkey breast meat
1 lemon
50 g [2 oz] seasoned flour
100 g [4 oz] button mushrooms
65 g [2½ oz] unsalted butter
20 ml [4 teaspoons] oil
60 ml [4 tablespoons] Marsala
45 ml [3 tablespoons] grated parmesan
60 ml [4 tablespoons] chicken stock

1 With a sharp knife, cut the turkey breast into 4 thin slices, across the grain of the meat if possible.

2 Lay the slices between pieces of damp greaseproof paper and beat with a rolling pin to flatten them slightly.

3 Cut the lemon in quarters and rub each piece of breast with lemon. Dip in seasoned flour to coat lightly on both sides. Reserve one quarter of lemon.

4 Trim and wipe but do not peel the mushrooms. Cut them into very thin slices.

5 Melt 25 g [1 oz] butter in a medium-sized frying-pan over low heat and fry the mushroom slices for 3-4 minutes until soft. Increase the heat to evaporate the moisture that has run from them, and season lightly with salt and pepper and a squeeze of lemon juice. Remove from the heat.

6 In a large pan with a lid, heat the remaining butter and the oil over fairly low heat and, when hot, fry the turkey slices gently for 5 minutes until golden. Turn the meat and brown the other side.

7 Pour the Marsala over the turkey and allow to bubble for a minute or two.

8 Spoon the musnrooms on top of the turkey slices and sprinkle thickly with parmesan cheese.

9 Spoon the chicken stock over each portion, cover the pan tightly and cook over very low heat for another 10-15 minutes, until the cheese has melted and the turkey is tender.

10 Lift out each portion carefully, arrange on a hot serving dish and keep warm.

11 Boil the pan juices rapidly, un-covered, until reduced and syrupy, then spoon over the portions. Serve immediately.

ROSY BACON CHOPS

Mild- and sweet-cured bacon chops or slices are widely sold, ready trimmed and vacuum packed. They need fairly gentle cooking and are well suited to covered frying. As they are usually rather lean, this rosy-coloured cream sauce suits them well. They look and taste especially good served with leaf spinach. This recipe is equally suitable for thick slices of cooked ham, and medium sweet sherry may be used in place of the Madeira. If you have no ready-made stock, a stock cube may be used.

SERVES 4
**4 bacon chops, each about
  6 mm [¼″] thick
25 g [1 oz] butter
15 ml [1 tablespoon] oil
1 shallot or 4 spring onions
15 ml [1 tablespoon] flour
200 ml [7 fl oz] ham or chicken
  stock
60 ml [4 tablespoons] Madeira
10 ml [2 teaspoons] tomato
  purée
freshly ground black pepper
150 ml [¼ pt] thick cream
salt**

1 Remove the bacon from the packet and pat dry with kitchen paper.

2 Heat the butter and oil in a wide pan with a lid and, when hot, fry the bacon chops, uncovered, over moderate heat until golden brown on each side. Lift out and reserve.

3 Skin and chop the onion and add to the pan. Reduce the heat and fry gently for a minute or so. Stir in the flour and cook, stirring, for a further 2 minutes.

4 In a separate pan, bring the stock, wine and tomato purée to the boil and add, little by little, to the first pan, blending it in smoothly. Season with pepper and bring to simmering point.

5 Stir in the cream and check the seasoning. Add salt if necessary. Bring to simmering point again and simmer gently for several minutes until reduced to a thin coating consistency.

6 Return the chops to the pan, cover and heat gently, without boiling, for 10 minutes.

7 Lift out the chops and arrange in a shallow serving dish. Check the seasoning of the sauce again and spoon over the chops.

Crispy coatings

The time-honoured custom of giving food a crisp overcoat does more than make it appear attractive. A coating embraces the food, enclosing the natural juices and flavour and generally acts as a protective skin. It is also an economical way of extending meat. It gives a crisp golden crust too!

Coating meat as a preliminary to frying may seem a fiddly extra step but this is an extremely useful technique. The many different kinds of coating can add a great deal of variety to simple, everyday fare, as well as to more exotic dishes.

The coatings can be light, for example seasoned flour, or of a more substantial and protective nature, such as egg and breadcrumbs, batter or pastry. A coating can also be simply the means of adding texture to a piece of food with, for example, chopped nuts or crushed cornflakes. The choice of coating will depend on its purpose, the cut of meat and the method of frying.

Coatings help to prevent too much fat being absorbed by the meat and, at the same time, they help to retain the meat's natural juices and flavour. Soft mixtures, like those used for rissoles (and fish balls), need a substantial coating to hold the mixture together during frying and to prevent the shapes breaking up in the hot fat. In fact, very soft mixtures need to be coated more than once.

From an economic point of view, coating and frying is an attractive way of disguising leftovers and of making the food go further. From the eater's point of view, the sheer pleasure of biting into a crunchy golden crust is sufficient reason to justify the time and trouble taken in the preparation.

MEAT CUTS FOR COATING

The cuts that benefit from a coating are those that do not form a natural seal when put into hot fat. Cuts of firm-textured meat, such as beef steak, form a natural seal and can be shallow fried without coating (see pages 25–33). The following cuts of meat will benefit from a coating to a greater or lesser degree.

Soft-textured mixtures: croquettes and rissoles, which are shaped and coated before frying, need a substantial coating to hold them together and to prevent them breaking up in the hot fat. These are more often deep-fried.

Medium-textured cuts: liver or portions of fish gain from the addition of a light, crisp coating. The preparation of liver for frying is discussed on pages 112–113.

Slices of meat: escalopes of veal, pork and chicken, which are sliced thinly, are made more substantial by the addition of a coating and can be prepared in a variety of ways. Here we explain in detail how to cut, prepare and cook escalopes.

Pieces of meat or fish: can be coated in batter and deep fried.

This technique is used mainly for pieces of chicken and fish.

THE COATINGS AND HOW TO USE THEM
Flour or fine oatmeal

Flour or fine oatmeal make a simple, quickly applied but light coating which absorbs surface moisture from the meat, and gives a slightly crisp surface after frying. The coating is suitable for any fairly firm-textured meat, such as chicken joints and liver slices, and also for whole or filleted fish. It is not suitable for soft-textured mixtures.

The flour, which should always be plain, or oatmeal is seasoned with salt and pepper in the proportion of 10 ml [2 teaspoons] salt and 2.5 ml [$\frac{1}{2}$ teaspoon] pepper to every 100 g [$\frac{1}{4}$ lb] plain flour or fine oatmeal. Additional powdered flavourings such as paprika or curry powder can be added to taste.

It is not possible to calculate exactly how much flour you will need. If you allow 25 g [1 oz] flour plus the seasoning for 225 g [$\frac{1}{2}$ lb] meat, this will be ample.

This coating is suitable for shallow frying but is not sufficiently protective for deep-fat frying.

Methods: there are two methods for applying this coating. The first is the polythene bag method. This is illustrated in step-by-step to fried liver on pages 118–119. The flour and the seasonings are placed in a polythene bag and shaken. The meat, which has been patted dry with kitchen paper, is then added, a few pieces at a time, and shaken in the flour until well coated. The coated pieces are carefully removed, shaken to release excess flour over the bag or a spare plate and reserved on a clean plate.

This is the most convenient method for coating all fairly small irregularly shaped pieces of meat. However, as it is not possible to calculate the exact quantity of flour needed, any remaining flour may be wasted if it cannot be used immediately, for example, for thickening a sauce.

The second method is the dredger method—more economical, and particularly suitable for sliced meat. Lay the meat (or fish) on a piece of greaseproof paper. Fill a dredger with flour and the appropriate quantity of seasonings, and sprinkle evenly over the flat surfaces of the meat. Pat the flour on firmly with a palette knife. Turn the meat and repeat on the other side. Lift the slice and shake gently to remove any excess flour and reserve on a dry plate. Very little flour is wasted by this method but remember to label the dredger 'seasoned flour' so that you do not use if for sweet food.

Egg and breadcrumbs

Egg and breadcrumbs make a firm, protective and moisture-proof coating, which provides a really crisp covering. It is used in addition to a light coating of seasoned flour. The coating is suitable for many kinds of meat and other food, including shapes made from soft mixtures such as croquettes and rissoles, escalopes of veal, pork and chicken and portions of fish. One use of this coating is for chopped lambs' breasts where a very cheap cut of meat is completely transformed. This is a particularly good coating for foods that are to be eaten cold (for example, Scotch eggs).

The breadcrumbs which are best to use are fine, white well-dried crumbs, which give a crisp and delicate golden crust. The making and drying of breadcrumbs is a very easy procedure indeed. The crumbs must be thoroughly dried or they will absorb too much fat and will not become crisp. It is not necessary to measure out the breadcrumbs because any that are left over can be sifted and reserved.

Herbs and grated cheese can be added to the breadcrumbs for extra flavour. The addition of a small proportion of finely chopped nuts adds not only flavour but texture as well.

The egg is used for sticking the crumbs securely to the food. The proteins in the egg coagulate rapidly when in contact with hot fat, forming a moisture-proof barrier, protecting the food and enclosing the natural juices and flavour. The egg is beaten and can be diluted with 15 ml [1 tablespoon] water. It will adhere to the food more readily when diluted, but do not dilute further, as this would spoil the moisture-proofing qualities.

This coating is suitable for shallow frying and deep-fat frying.

Alternatives to egg: in the absence of egg, evaporated milk is a useful and successful substitute, but if fresh milk is used the coating will not be so firm or crisp.

Sauces to accompany egg and breadcrumbed meat should always be served separately. A little melted butter and lemon juice can be served with the meat for added moisture, if wished.

Method: first assemble the food to be coated, an egg, a flour dredger containing plain flour seasoned with salt and pepper, and a pile of dried white breadcrumbs on a large sheet of greaseproof paper.

Break the egg into a shallow plate (a soup plate or saucer), add 15 ml [1 tablespoon] cold water and beat with a fork until the white and yolk are well mixed and running freely. Pat dry the pieces of meat with absorbent kitchen paper. Lay the meat on greaseproof paper and sprinkle evenly with seasoned flour. Pat the flour on firmly with a palette knife and then turn the meat and repeat. Lightly shake off excess flour and set aside.

When all the pieces have been coated with flour, dip each piece in turn into beaten egg; you can use a pastry brush to coat all the surfaces. Lift the meat out with a palette knife or with tongs and hold over the plate for a few seconds to allow surplus egg to drain back into the plate.

Immediately transfer the pieces of meat to the centre of the pile of breadcrumbs. Lift the corners of the paper in turn, so that all surfaces of the meat are covered generously with crumbs.

Lift the meat out and lay flat on clean greaseproof paper. When all the pieces of meat are coated, press the crumbs on firmly with the palette knife. If possible, leave the coated meat in a cool place for half an hour, covered lightly with another sheet of greaseproof paper, for the coating to firm up.

Sift the remaining breadcrumbs to remove any damp ones and return dry crumbs to the container for future use.

Miscellaneous coatings

There are a variety of coatings which are used in the same way as breadcrumbs and which provide a pleasant change. In each case the food to be coated should be patted dry, floured and brushed with beaten egg or evaporated milk before being coated and fried.

Rolled oats: these are rough textured with a nutty flavour, especially suitable for meat cakes and rissoles (and oily fish).

Packet stuffings: these contain a high proportion of dry breadcrumbs, together with seasonings and herbs and make very useful instant savoury coatings. These crumbs are particularly useful for meat (or fish) cakes and chicken joints.

Potato crisps: these provide a very crunchy savoury coating, especially good for chicken and fish. The crisps must be absolutely fresh and crunchy and crushed fairly finely with a rolling pin before being used.

Cornflakes: these are used crushed in the same way as potato crisps. This is a good way of using up the broken cornflakes from the bottom of the packet, but crushed cornflakes are also available commercially, in packets.

Matzo meal: this meal is prepared from crushed unleavened bread and is much used in Jewish cookery.

Nuts: chopped nuts make an extra crunchy and nutritious, if expensive, coating for bland meats such as chicken, veal or sweetbreads, or for fish fillets. Use walnuts, hazelnuts or almonds, very finely chopped.

There are also several coatings which are suitable only for deep-fat frying. These include the very popular batter coating, and pancakes and pastry which are used to wrap the food rather than to coat it. Fish and chicken pieces lend themselves well to deep frying.

MAKING ESCALOPES
Escalopes of veal
Fried escalopes of veal is one of those seemingly simple dishes that needs quite a lot of 'know-how' to get just right.

Tender, milk-fed veal is needed for good escalopes and, although expensive, the meat is firm and solid and under 100 g [¼ lb] is required for an average portion.

A true escalope is a thin slice, cut on the bias, from the long shaped muscle forming the topside of the leg. The slice should be free of seams, gristle and skin and cut about 9 mm [⅓"] thick which, after gentle flattening, will be reduced to about 6 mm [¼"] thick.

When buying prepared escalopes from a butcher, you may need to explain exactly what you want. A problem arises in some countries because butchers often divide a leg of veal into roasting joints by cutting straight across the grain. This means any escalope cut immediately above this will be straight across the grain. An incorrectly cut escalope (ie not cut on the bias) may have been bashed into submission by the butcher's mallet, but you can recognize it by the tell-tale seams and bits of skin and gristle running through it. The moment you put it into the pan it will buckle and shrink out of shape.

Cutting escalopes: buy the weight you require of seamless topside of leg. Failing that, buy either a piece of best end of neck or loin, on the bone, depending on the size of the calf. It is not difficult, with a sharp knife, to cut the meat from the bones and free the seamless eye of meat which you can then slice into escalopes. The process is similar when preparing cuts of lamb for noisettes, only once freed from the bone, the eye meat is then cut away from the thin flat piece of meat. The size of these eye meat escalopes will vary greatly according to the size of the calf. Although the average escalope is just under 100 g [¼ lb], you can serve several 25–50 g [1–2 oz] thin escalopes which, in Italy, are known as scaloppini or piccata. The trimmings can be minced or used in a pie and the bones used for making stock.

Once cut from the bone and trimmed, wipe the eye meat with a damp cloth and hold firmly on a board. Slice thinly with a very sharp, heavy knife towards the end on the diagonal to get good-sized escalopes. The trimmings can be used in another dish.

Preparing and flattening the escalopes: separate out the escalopes and remove any fine skin, fat and tissues that may be surrounding the escalopes. Place each escalope flat between two pieces of waxed paper or dampened greaseproof paper. Beat firmly, but not too heavily, with a rolling pin, cutlet bat or milk bottle until each one is reduced to an even thickness of about 6 mm [¼"]. These are now ready for cooking, but if you wish to keep them a few hours, store them in the refrigerator, still between the sheets of paper.

Cooking the escalopes: the escalopes can be cooked without any coating, with a light coating of flour or with a contrasting crisp coating of breadcrumbs. Cooking time is brief, ranging from 2 minutes each side for thin scaloppini to 4–5 minutes each side for 6 mm [¼"] escalopes.

When fried uncoated or with a light flour coating, a simple pan sauce is usually served with them. When coated with egg and breadcrumbs, sauces other than melted butter should be served separately, so that the escalopes retain their crisp coating.

Escalopes of pork
Unlike escalope of veal, pork escalopes are not part of the classic cuisine tradition, but are a relatively new idea for using fillets of pork.

Although a fairly expensive cut, the fillet is solid meat with very little waste and flattened into escalopes it goes quite a long way.

Cutting escalopes: buy the weight of meat that you will actually serve, allowing 100 g [¼ lb] per person, plus 25–50 g [1–2 oz] for trimmings. Lay the fillet on a board and, using a sharp knife, trim away any fat, skin or sinew on the outside of the fillet.

Holding the knife on a diagonal slant, cut the meat across into 2.5 cm [1"] thick slices.

Flattening the escalopes: flatten the escalopes in the same way as the veal escalopes, to a thickness of not more than 6 mm [¼"].

Escalopes of chicken
Chicken is a very lean meat, ideally suited to frying. Pan-fried and deep-fried chicken in a basket are among America's favourite recipes.

Because of their great leanness, chicken portions benefit from a coating. For shallow frying, use either a light coating of seasoned flour or a crisper coating of egg and breadcrumbs. However, chicken joints remain more succulent if, after the initial browning, the pan is covered. This technique is discussed on pages 34–40.

Chicken breasts, though, can be flattened into escalopes and cook quickly enough to be shallow fried in an open pan.

Cutting escalopes: it is often possible to buy packs of fresh or frozen chicken breasts. If you wish to cut your own, for four portions buy two 1.4 kg [3 lb] chickens (oven-ready weight). Cut off the whole breast from each bird.

Divide the breasts in two by cutting down the centre of the breast-bone, using a sharp knife.

Preparing and flattening the escalopes: free the portions of skin by pulling it away gently. Remove the bones with a sharp knife, cutting between the rib bones and the flesh. Then divide each piece of chicken as they separate naturally into two long escalopes. The two make one portion.

Flatten the escalopes in the same way as the veal escalopes, to an even thickness of about 6 mm [¼"]. Season with salt and freshly ground white pepper. Cover the escalopes, having removed the waxed paper or dampened greaseproof paper, and store in the refrigerator until ready to cook. Use the escalopes the same day.

Step-by-step to egg and breadcrumbing

1 Have ready the pieces of meat, an egg, a dredger of seasoned flour and the dried breadcrumbs.

2 Break the egg into a shallow plate. Add 15 ml [1 tablespoon] water and beat with a fork to mix.

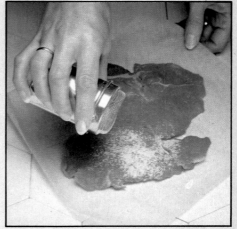

3 Pat meat dry with kitchen paper. Lay it on greaseproof paper and sprinkle with seasoned flour.

4 Pat the flour on both sides with a palette knife. Lift the meat and shake off excess flour.

5 Dip the meat, piece by piece into the egg, drain over the plate and transfer to the breadcrumbs.

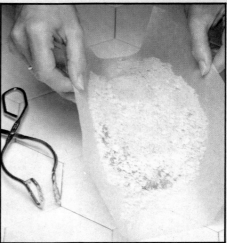

6 Lift the corners of the paper in turn so that the meat is coated generously on all surfaces.

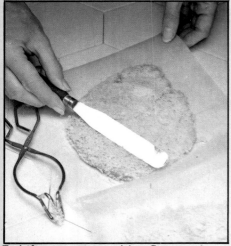

7 Lift out meat and lay flat on clean greaseproof paper. Press the crumbs with a palette knife.

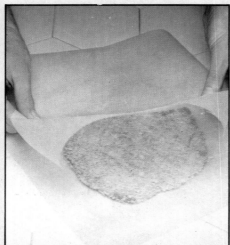

8 Leave the coated meat in a cool place, covered with greaseproof paper, for half an hour.

9 Sift the remaining breadcrumbs. Remove the damp ones and reserve dry ones for future use.

Step-by-step to cutting escalopes

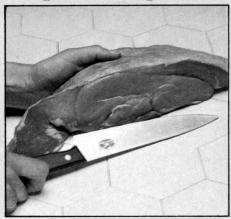

1 Wipe the fillet of veal with a damp cloth. Put it on a surface, length parallel to you. Hold firmly.

2 With a sharp knife, cut diagonally across the meat cutting good-sized escalopes on the bias.

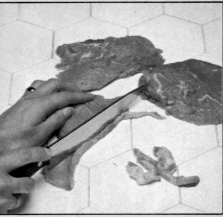

3 Remove all skin, fat or tissue surrounding the escalopes. Reserve veal trimmings.

4 Place each escalope on grease-proof paper and cover with another sheet of paper.

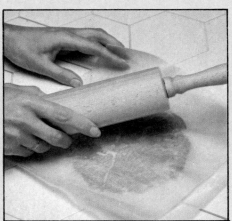

5 Beat firmly but not too heavily with a rolling pin or cutlet bat until 6 mm [$\frac{1}{4}$"] thick.

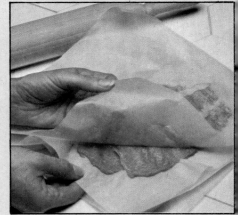

6 Store the escalopes, still between the paper, for a few hours until required or use immediately.

Step-by-step to chicken escalopes

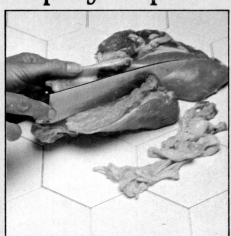

1 Peel the skin from the chicken breasts, then cut down with a sharp knife between the flesh and ribs to remove bones.

2 Divide each piece of chicken into two with your fingers. The flesh parts naturally giving two escalopes which is one portion.

3 Flatten the escalopes between two layers of greaseproof paper to a thickness of 6 mm [$\frac{1}{4}$"]. Season with salt and pepper.

CHICKEN ESCALOPES PARMESAN

☒ *In this recipe the bland flavour of the chicken is beautifully contrasted with a crisp crumb coating, well flavoured with cheese. Freshly grated parmesan is the ideal cheese to use, but if not available use a matured dry Cheddar. If served with a moist vegetable such as sautéed courgettes or ratatouille, no sauce is required.*

You can either buy two whole chickens and divide each whole breast into two and then into escalopes, or buy four single breast portions.

SERVES 4
**4 chicken breasts
salt
freshly ground black pepper
seasoned flour
1 medium-sized egg
50 g [2 oz] dried white
    breadcrumbs
40 g [1½ oz] parmesan cheese
oil**

1 Make escalopes from the chicken breasts as described. Season and leave in the refrigerator, until required.

2 When ready to cook, dust each escalope lightly with flour from a flour dredger and shake off the surplus.

3 Break egg into a shallow plate, add 15 ml [1 tablespoon] water and beat with a fork until lightly mixed.

4 Grate the cheese finely. Mix the breadcrumbs and cheese together and pile in the centre of a large piece of greaseproof paper.

5 Dip each escalope in turn into beaten egg, lifting out and allowing surplus egg to drain back on to the plate.

6 When drained, place each escalope in turn in the breadcrumbs and cheese mixture, and coat thickly.

7 Lift out, lay flat on greaseproof paper and press the coating on firmly with a palette knife.

8 Cover lightly and, if possible, leave for half an hour for the coating to firm.

9 Pour the oil into a sauté pan and heat until a cube of firm bread sizzles gently when put into the fat and turns golden in 20 seconds.

10 Lower 4 escalopes one at a time into the hot fat and fry until golden, about 5 minutes. Turn and fry the other side for a similar length of time.

11 Lift out, draining each piece in turn over the pan for a second or two, then lower on to crumpled paper to finish draining. Keep hot in the serving dish while frying the remaining escalopes. Serve immediately.

CHICKEN ESCALOPES A LA CREME

☒ *In this recipe the chicken escalopes are lightly coated with flour, fried in oil and butter and served with a simple but luxurious cream sauce. The stock may be made with a stock cube. Keep the vegetable accompaniments very simple, boiled rice or new potatoes and French beans, for example.*

SERVES 4
**4 chicken breasts, cut into
    8 escalopes
30 ml [2 tablespoons] flour
5 ml [1 teaspoon] salt
1.25 ml [¼ teaspoon] white
    pepper
40 g [1½ oz] unsalted butter
30 ml [2 tablespoons] olive oil
60 ml [4 tablespoons] chicken
    stock
150 ml [¼ pt] thick cream
half a lemon**

1 Prepare the chicken escalopes as described.

2 Mix the flour, salt and pepper thoroughly and spread on a flat plate.

3 Coat each escalope in turn with the seasoned flour, shaking off the surplus.

4 Heat 25 g [1 oz] butter and the oil in a heavy-based frying-pan, and when the foam subsides put in half of the chicken pieces.

5 Fry gently for 4–5 minutes until golden, then turn and fry the other side for a similar time. Regulate the heat so that the chicken is sizzling very gently but the butter does not burn.

6 Lift out the chicken pieces, drain on crumpled paper and keep hot on a serving dish.

7 Add the remaining butter to the pan, and when the foam subsides fry the rest of the chicken. Transfer to serving dish.

8 When all the chicken is cooked, add the stock to the pan and boil briskly, scraping up the coagulated juices from the base of the pan.

9 Stir in the cream and continue to boil until the sauce thickens enough to lightly coat the chicken. (It will be a pale beige colour.) Squeeze the lemon and stir in 5 ml [1 teaspoon] juice. Check the seasoning.

10 Serve the chicken with a little sauce spooned over each portion.

VEAL SCALOPPINI WITH MARSALA

☒ *This recipe can be made with standard size escalopes but is more delicate if made with smaller, thinner escalopes weighing from 25–50 g [1–2 oz] each, allowing two or even three per portion. The escalopes are lightly dusted with flour which gives them a warm, golden sheen. For an authentic Italian flavour use a medium dry Marsala, but failing that use a medium dry Maderia or sherry and a few drops of lemon juice. The stock can be made with a stock cube.*

SERVES 4
**450 g [1 lb] small escalopes
seasoned flour
65 g [2½ oz] unsalted butter
15 ml [1 tablespoon] olive oil
60 ml [4 tablespoons] chicken
    stock
125 ml [4 fl oz] Marsala**

1 Prepare and flatten the escalopes as described in the step-by-step instructions. Coat them lightly with the seasoned flour, shaking off the surplus.

2 Heat 25 g [1 oz] butter and the oil in a large, heavy-based pan, and when the foam subsides put in several escalopes, but do not overcrowd the pan.

3 Fry fairly briskly for about 2 minutes, or until golden on each side. Adjust the heat to keep the escalopes sizzling but do not let the butter burn.

4 Lift out, drain over the pan, arrange on a serving dish and keep hot whilst frying the rest of the escalopes in batches. Add a little more butter (reserving 25 g [1 oz]) to the pan between batches as necessary.

5 When all the escalopes are cooked, pour the stock and Marsala into the pan and boil briskly for at least 1 minute, scraping up the coagulated juices from the base of the pan.

6 Off the heat, stir in the remaining butter, bit by bit, to enrich and lightly thicken the sauce. Check the seasoning and pour over the escalopes. Serve immediately.

VEAL ESCALOPES VIENNOISE

This is a classic dish, but once you have acquired the knack of preparing, coating and frying escalopes of veal, there is nothing more complicated to deal with than arranging the garnish.

SERVES 4
4 escalopes of veal, each weighing 90 g [3½ oz]
seasoned flour
1 medium-sized egg
up to 75 g [3 oz] dried white breadcrumbs
75 g [3 oz] unsalted butter
30 ml [2 tablespoons] oil
half a lemon

For the garnish:
2 medium-sized eggs
4 anchovy fillets
half a lemon
4 pimento stuffed green olives
45 ml [3 tablespoons] freshly chopped parsley
15 ml [1 tablespoon] capers (optional)

1 Prepare and flatten the escalopes as described in the step-by-step instructions.

2 Dust the escalopes lightly with the seasoned flour and shake off any surplus.

3 Break the egg on to a shallow plate, add 15 ml [1 tablespoon] cold water and beat to mix.

4 Pile the breadcrumbs in the centre of a large piece of greaseproof paper.

5 Dip each escalope into the egg, brush the egg all over it, then lift out, draining briefly as you do so.

6 Transfer them to the breadcrumbs and coat thoroughly all over.

7 Lay on a flat surface and press the coating in place with a palette knife. Cover lightly and, if possible, leave for half an hour for the coating to set.

8 Meanwhile, prepare all the garnishes. Hard boil the eggs, cool rapidly and separate the whites from the yolks. Chop the whites finely and press the yolks through a metal sieve; keep separate.

9 Roll up the anchovy fillets and cut four thin slices from the lemon.

10 When ready to fry, heat 25 g [1 oz] butter and the oil in a large frying-pan. When the foam subsides put in two escalopes and cook over moderate heat for 3–5 minutes (depending on thickness) on each side. Adjust the heat so that the fat does not burn but the escalopes become crisp and golden.

11 Lift out the escalopes, drain on crumpled absorbent paper and keep hot on the serving platter. Add a little more butter to the pan, as necessary, and fry the two remaining escalopes.

12 When all are cooked wipe out the frying-pan. Squeeze the lemon,

add the remaining butter to the cleaned pan. Heat until just beginning to smell nutty and turn brown. Stir in 15 ml [1 tablespoon] lemon juice and remove from the heat. Trickle over the escalopes.

13 Garnish the centre of each escalope with a slice of lemon, a curled anchovy fillet topped with an olive, and sprinkle with capers (if used). At either side of the dish arrange small piles of egg white, parsley and egg yolk. Serve immediately.

Varations

●For veal Holstein serve the escalopes topped with a fried egg and garnished with anchovy fillets.

●For veal zingara, fry the escalopes as described. For the garnish, cut ham, tongue and mushrooms into matchsticks, lightly toss in melted butter and moisten with a Madeira sauce.

●For veal milanaise, fry the escalopes as described. Serve with boiled spaghetti which has been tossed in butter with matchsticks of ham and tongue, flavoured with grated Cheddar cheese and moistened with a tomato sauce made with fresh tomatoes.

ESCALOPE OF PORK WITH APPLE AND LEMON

Pork, being a richer meat than veal or chicken, is best given a slightly sharp contrasting flavour, as in this recipe with apple rings and lemon juice. The apple also adds succulence, and no sauce is required. Garnish with sprigs of watercress.

SERVES 4
450 g [1 lb] pork fillet
2 large cooking apples
salt

seasoned flour
1 medium-sized egg
up to 75 g [3 oz] dried white breadcrumbs
65 g [2½ oz] unsalted butter
30 ml [2 tablespoons] oil
1 lemon

1 Prepare, cut and flatten the escalopes of pork as described in the step-by-step instructions.

2 Peel, core and cut the apples into 6 mm [¼"] thick rings. Drop into salted water, 15 ml [1 tablespoon] salt per 550 ml [1 pt] water, to prevent discolouration.

3 Coat each escalope in turn with seasoned flour, diluted egg and breadcrumbs, as described. If possible, leave for 30 minutes for the coating to firm.

4 Heat 25 g [1 oz] butter and the oil in a heavy-based pan, and when the foam subsides fry half of the escalopes gently for 4–5 minutes each side, until golden and cooked through.

5 Lift out, drain on crumpled kitchen paper and keep warm while frying the rest of the escalopes. Use a little extra butter if necessary, reserving 25 g [1 oz] for frying the apple rings.

6 Meanwhile, drain the apple rings, pat dry with kitchen paper and dust lightly with seasoned flour shaking off the surplus.

7 When all the escalopes are cooked, pile them in the centre of a serving dish and keep hot.

8 Add the remaining butter to the pan and, when the foam subsides, fry the apple rings gently in a single layer until golden. Turn carefully, one at a time, and fry the other side.

9 Lift out the rings, one by one, and arrange around the escalopes.

10 Squeeze the lemon and add the juice to the fat remaining in the pan. Heat while stirring to scrape the coagulated juices, and pour over the escalopes.

11 Serve immediately, garnished with watercress.

LAMB CUTLETS A LA DORIA

Lamb cutlets coated with egg and breadcrumbs and fried until crisp and golden brown outside, but still slightly pink and juicy inside, are always popular. Served hot, they make an excellent main course as in this recipe, but left to get cold they are excellent for picnics or cold buffets. If for eating cold, fry everything in oil. Make sure the cutlets have good meaty 'eyes' and are trimmed of all excess fat. Allow 2 cutlets per person. Prepare and trim the fat from cutlets. Have some cutlet frills ready for the presentation.

SERVES 6
12 lamb cutlets
25 g [1 oz] flour
salt
freshly ground black pepper
2 medium-sized eggs
up to 100 g [¼ lb] dried white breadcrumbs
1 large cucumber
10 spring onions
25 g [1 oz] butter
60 ml [4 tablespoons] oil
15 ml [1 tablespoon] finely chopped mint

1 Wipe the cutlets with a damp cloth.

2 Put the flour on a flat plate, add generous seasonings of salt and pepper, mix and spread evenly over the plate.

3 Holding each cutlet in turn by the shank bone, dip into the flour and coat both sides evenly.

4 Crack the eggs on to a flat plate, add 30 ml [2 tablespoons] cold water and beat with a fork to mix. Pile the breadcrumbs on a large piece of greaseproof paper.

5 Dip each cutlet into the egg and coat all over, drain for a second or two over the plate, then roll in the breadcrumbs.

6 Lay flat and press the coating on firmly. Leave the cutlets in a cool place, lightly covered, until ready to fry.

7 Top and tail the cucumber but do not peel. Quarter it lengthways, then cut into 4 cm [1½"] pieces.

8 Wipe the spring onions with a damp cloth and cut into 1.25 cm [½"] lengths.

9 Bring a large saucepan of water to the boil, add the cucumber and spring onions and cook for 5 minutes. Drain very thoroughly.

10 Melt the butter in a saucepan over low heat, add the cucumber and onions and season with salt and pepper. Cover, and cook very gently until tender, about 10 minutes, shaking the pan frequently. Remove the pan from heat when cooked.

11 Meanwhile, pour the oil into a large frying-pan and heat until a cube of bread dropped into it sizzles and turns golden in 15 seconds.

12 Place cutlets gently in the hot fat, taking care not to overcrowd the pan (you will need to fry in two or three batches). Fry gently for 4–6 minutes until golden brown, then turn carefully and fry the other side for 4–6 minutes. Lift out and drain on crumpled kitchen paper. Keep hot in a serving dish. Repeat with remaining batches.

13 When all the meat is fried and drained, slip a cutlet frill on the end of each shank bone and arrange the cutlets around the outside of the serving dish.

14 Stir the chopped mint into the cucumber and onions. Lift the vegetables out with a perforated spoon and arrange in a pile in the centre of the cutlets. If serving hot, serve immediately.

15 If serving cold, leave the cutlets draining on the paper until quite cold. Pack into shallow plastic boxes between layers of grease-proof paper. Store in the refrigerator. Eat within 24 hours and slip on the cutlet frills before serving.

Into the pot

Casseroles and stews are made with tougher cuts of meat, which require long and slow cooking to tenderize them. Here we discuss both the ingredients and the principles common to all stews and casseroles, and explain in detail the cold-start method—the easiest method, and the one which is essential to transform really tough cuts of meat into remarkably tender and tasty dishes.

COLD-START STEWING AND CASSEROLING

Today the words casseroling and stewing are used to describe meat that is cut up and cooked very gently in liquid with other ingredients to provide a meal in a pot. But, strictly speaking, stewing means that the food is cooked in a saucepan on top of the stove, while casseroling implies cooking in an ovenproof dish in the oven so that heat circulates all around the dish.

From the cook's point of view, casseroles and stews are among the most useful meat dishes. They are cheap and warming and, once the initial preparation is done, they can be left to look after themselves except for an occasional, but important,

check on the rate of cooking.

The same basic principles of preparation apply to both casseroles and stews—an immensely versatile method of cooking that can be used for many different kinds and qualities of meat.

Described here is the cold-start method—which is virtually the only method by which really tough meat can be tenderized.

The fry-start method which is suitable for the not-so-tough stewing meats is covered on pages 61–72, and the casserole theme is developed even further by using wine, beer and cider as the cooking liquid on pages 85–94.

51

BEEF 2nd grade

Shin

Approximate cooking time   4 hours

Description

Lean, sinewy meat from the foreleg. Muscles are very elongated in shape and must be cut across the grain into small pieces. Usually sold off the bone, but some butchers will sell you a piece on the bone.

Method

Needs very slow cooking in unthickened liquid, starting from cold. In this way sinews are gelatinized, meat tenderized and gravy acquires a rich flavour. In more affluent times shin was valued for making beef tea and gravy soup, rather than for the meat itself.

Leg

Approximate cooking time   3½-4 hours

Description

From the hind leg; similar to shin, but less sinewy and therefore better quality meat—especially from the top of the leg rather than the more muscular lower part.

Method

Requires the same treatment as shin, but has a better appearance. If cooked long and slowly has an excellent flavour.

Clod and sticking

Approximate cooking time   3 hours

Description

Coarse-grained lean meat from the non-muscular neck and chest area.

Method

Can be cooked by either the cold-start or fry-start method. Add extra flavouring ingredients for best results.

LAMB or MUTTON

  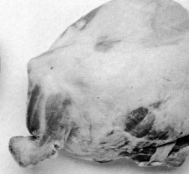

Middle-neck and scrag

Approximate cooking time   2-3 hours

Description

Very bony cut, but tender with good flavour. Makes rich flavoured gravy. Usually cut into chops by the butcher. Mutton may be rather fat.

Method

Traditional cut for hot-pots and Irish stew, which needs slow gentle cooking by the cold-start method. Young lamb is sometimes cooked by the fry-start method. Always rinse off splintered bone in cold water before cooking. Trim fat from mutton.

Breast

Approximate cooking time   2 hours

Description

Economical long thin strip of meat containing rib bones, skin and fat. Larger, meatier breasts are better value than those from very young lambs.

Method

Can be cooked by cold-start or fry-start method. It is essential to remove fat before or after cooking. Additional flavourings are necessary. Can be used with a less fatty cut.

Shoulder

Approximate cooking time   1½-2 hours

Description

A better quality cut, more often used for roasting or braising, which can also be boned and skinned, then cut into large cubes for stewing.

Method

Cook by the fry-start method. Use skin and bones for making stock. Trim away excess fat from meat.

and stewing

1st grade

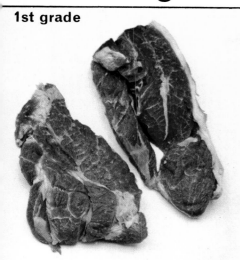

Chuck and blade
Approximate cooking time 2½-3 hours
Description
Good quality, lean stewing meat from between the fore rib and neck area. Medium grained. Can be cut into fairly large pieces.
Method
Among the best cuts for casseroling, with good flavour and texture. Can be cooked by the fry-start method. Chuck is sometimes braised in a piece.

Skirt
Approximate cooking time 2-2½ hours
Description
Thin pieces of meat from inside the rump, flank or rib area. The meat is made up of long fibres so it is important to cut across the grain.
Method
Don't be put off by the appearance; this well-flavoured, lean cut can be cooked by the fry-start or cold-start method. A favourite cut for pies and puddings

PORK

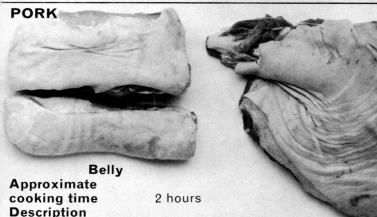

Belly
Approximate cooking time 2 hours
Description
The thick end of the belly consists of coarse but fairly lean meat. Rib bones may be included. The streaky end is interleaved with fat.
Method
For an all-pork stew use the leaner thick end. A proportion of streaky, especially pickled streaky, is often added to casserole of lean beef or poultry. Can be cooked by the cold-start or fry-start method.

Hand
Approximate cooking time 2 hours
Description
Coarse-grained but lean shoulder cut. Ask the butcher to bone it for you.
Method
A good cut for stewing usually cooked by the fry-start method. Additional flavouring ingredients are necessary.

CASSEROLES AND STEWPANS
The first essential for all casseroles and stewpans is a tight-fitting lid to minimize the evaporation of the liquid during cooking. If you have any doubts about the effectiveness of the lid, use a piece of cooking foil under it.

For cold-start stews cooked on top of the stove any heavy-based saucepan or stewpan can be used. The thick base is important, as otherwise the heat is distributed unevenly and it may be difficult to keep the stew simmering only gently. For oven casseroling earthenware, ovenproof glass or ceramic casseroles are all equally suitable.

CUTS OF MEAT
The cheaper, coarser-grained or sinewy cuts of meat which are unsuitable for cooking by fast, dry-heat methods (such as roasting, frying or grilling) are ideal for stewing or casseroling. Long, slow cooking in moist heat will tenderize the meat and the resulting dish will be just as nutritious as expensive grilled meat.

Just how long the cooking will take depends on the meat. The cheaper, more muscular and sinewy it is, the longer it will need.

Beef
There are really two grades of beef commonly used for stewing, the very muscular shin and leg, sometimes referred to as second grade stewing beef, and the coarse-grained but less muscular cuts, referred to as first grade stewing beef, such as chuck, blade and skirt.

The difference in the stewing time needed for grades one and two can be as much as two hours, so be sure to ask your butcher for a specific cut rather than just 'stewing beef'. If meat is labelled 'stewing beef' the chances are it will be a second grade cut, because the tendency these days is to label the first grade cuts 'braising steak'. To make sure, ask what cuts you are buying.

You can of course use the traditional braising cuts such as topside, brisket or top rump of beef for special occasion casseroles, but to use relatively tender cuts for stews and casseroles is on the whole unnecessarily extravagant.

If bones are included, use these in the casserole to enhance the flavour, even if you remove them after cooking.

In traditional French cookery a piece of pork rind (couenne) is often put in the bottom of a beef casserole to add body to the sauce, or a pig's trotter can be used for the same purpose.

Lamb and mutton
The most economical stewing cuts of lamb and mutton are middle neck, scrag and breast. Middle neck, cut into chops and cooked slowly from a cold start, makes an excellent tender hot-pot. Shoulder is a better quality meat used for roasting or braising, but it can be boned and cut up for a casserole or stew, cooked by the fry-start method. It has the advantage of needing less time to cook, but is of course more expensive.

Some cuts, particularly of mutton, have rather a lot of fat and any excess fat should be removed.

Pork
Belly and hand are both good stewing cuts of pork. Belly has a thick end and a streaky end; the streaky end can be stewed together with other meats or chicken.

Veal
Cuts of veal used for stewing and casseroling are similar to those of lamb—middle neck, scrag, breast and shoulder. Boned shoulder or knuckle are often used for a blanquette of veal.

Another cheap cut of veal, the shin, is used to make osso buco, and the recipe is on pages 90–91.

Poultry
Fast-reared or frozen chickens can be greatly improved in flavour by stewing or casseroling. Boiling fowl should be cooked by the cold-start method. Poultry is jointed before casseroling and it is often more economical, particularly if you are cooking for only one or two, to buy individual joints rather than a whole bird.

OTHER CASSEROLE INGREDIENTS
Seasoning and liquid are essential ingredients of a casserole. Vegetables add flavour and bulk to make the meat go further. The choice is enormous and means you can create infinite variety.

Seasoning
Next to the indispensable flavouring of freshly ground black pepper and salt, garlic is the most common addition to a casserole. Paprika, chilli and curry powders and many other spices are also used to create character. Herbs make a valuable contribution to flavour, with bay leaves, thyme, marjoram, basil and rosemary heading the list.

Liquid
The amount of liquid used should always be small, so that the gravy or sauce becomes rich and full of flavour. Too much liquid weakens the flavour. About 275 ml [½ pt] per 450 g [1 lb] meat should be the maximum. For simple stews the liquid can be water or a light stock. For richer recipes the liquid can include wine, beer or cider.

Vegetables and cereals
Because of the long slow cooking, root vegetables such as carrots, parsnips and swedes are most suitable for casseroles. Onions, celery, peppers, leeks and tomatoes are invaluable for flavouring. Bear in mind that during cooking all these vegetables tend to add a little liquid to the casserole.

On the other hand, pulse vegetables, rice and other cereals, absorb liquid and make a very substantial dish. Potatoes can be used to thicken the gravy as in a classic Irish stew.

Delicate vegetables, such as mushrooms, courgettes, peas or fresh beans are usually added towards the end of cooking so that they don't lose their colour and texture. Do not forget to check carefully exactly how long each different vegetable takes to cook.

GENERAL PRINCIPLES
Whatever method of stewing or casseroling you use—whether it is a simple cold-start or something more elaborate—the meat, especially second grade beef, should be cut into chunks or thin strips so that a large percentage of the surface area is exposed to the liquid.

The cheaper and tougher the meat, the smaller the pieces should be. When using second grade, sinewy meat the pieces should be cut into 1.2-2.5 cm [½-1"] cubes to maximize the surface area, but when using first grade stewing meat the

dish is more attractive if the pieces are slightly larger. Middle neck and scrag of lamb are often cut into chops; poultry is cut into joints.

Greasy stews are unattractive, so excess fat should be cut off the meat before cooking begins, and fat on the surface of the cooked casserole should be removed before serving. This can be done by drawing a piece of absorbent kitchen paper or a slice of firm bread across the surface to absorb the fat. When time allows, a better method is to let the casserole become quite cold, so that the fat solidifies and can be scraped or lifted off.

Temperature control
Careful heat control is crucial to successful stewing and casseroling. The cheaper and tougher the meat, the longer it will need to cook to tenderize it (for times, see previous page). Whatever the cut, with the exception of poultry, it should never be allowed to cook at more than a gentle simmer—and this means using far less heat than most people imagine. In fact the easiest way to ruin a casserole or stew is to try to speed things up by cooking too fast and too fiercely.

Bring the stew or casserole to simmering point slowly, then maintain a gentle simmer to complete cooking. If you go above a gentle simmer and allow the liquid to bubble in a constant state of movement, it will evaporate and, worse still, the meat will shrink and toughen instead of being reduced to melting tenderness.

When stewing on top of the stove, lift the stewpan lid occasionally to check that only an occasional bubble is breaking the surface liquid.

Sometimes it is difficult to reduce the heat sufficiently to achieve this state of gentle simmering, for instance in the case of cookers on certain types of gas. If so, move pan so it is only partly over the source of heat, or reconsider and cook the dish in the oven.

Casseroling is easier, because oven thermometers are usually simpler to control. Ovens vary, so be guided by knowledge of your particular oven. Generally speaking a temperature of 150°C [300°F] gas mark 2 is ideal to start with as it allows the casserole to reach simmering point slowly.

After 30 minutes, check to see

whether the casserole is bubbling and, if so, reduce the thermostat to 140°C [275°F] gas mark 1 to maintain a gentle but steady simmer. Check simmering from time to time (oven-proof glass casseroles score here because you can see without lifting the lid). If you are in doubt as to whether it is cooking too fast, reduce the oven temperature still further. In fact, if you have to be away from the kitchen for several hours, you can safely turn the thermostat down to 120°C [250°F] gas mark ½ on most ovens.

Poultry does not need to be tenderized in the same way as coarser cuts of meat. Because it takes a comparatively short time to cook, there is a danger that the heat might not reach the centre of the joints if the oven is on too low a heat, which could cause salmonella poisoning. It is therefore better to cook poultry at 180°C [350°F] gas mark 4, depending on your oven, unless you intend to cook it for a longer time.

Reheating

Unlike roasted or fried meat dishes, casseroles and stews reheat extremely well. If anything, flavours tend to intensify and mellow, so it makes good sense to cook at least enough for two meals at one time, and if you have a freezer, a good deal more. Always cool the casserole as quickly as possible before refrigerating or freezing. This means moving the quantity to be frozen straight into the foil-lined container(s) or freezer box(es) of appropriate size. It will cool quicker in a smaller container. When cold, cover and put in the freezer. Always leave 1.2 cm [½"] head space to allow for expansion.

Reheating should be done slowly. Taking the casserole straight from the refrigerator and subjecting it to fierce heat will toughen the meat, however tender the original cooked results. Reheat over gentle heat or in a medium-low oven, bringing the casserole slowly back to simmering point. Then maintain a gentle simmer for 10 minutes or so before serving.

THE COLD-START METHOD

As the name cold-start implies, this method of stewing or casseroling involves long slow cooking starting from cold, and it cannot be hurried.

It is the only method which successfully tenderizes the coarsest, muscular cuts of meat and is therefore essential for cooking shin and leg of beef, and middle neck and scrag end of lamb. If you attempted to cook these cuts by the fry-start method, the rapid heat involved in browning the meat would cause the sinews to contract and harden so much that no amount of subsequent gentle simmering would produce really tender results.

For all other stewing cuts you have a choice—use the cold-start method described here or the fry-start method given on pages 61–72.

Cold-start stews and casseroles are usually unthickened—except where potatoes disintegrate during cooking and naturally thicken the liquid. The omission of flour means that the liquid can penetrate meat fibres more easily so reducing tough sinews to a jelly-like texture and tenderizing the meat muscle. During this process the flavoursome juices are drawn from the meat into the small amount of added liquid, to produce a rich meaty gravy.

Step-by-step to cold-start stewing or casseroling beef

1 Wipe the meat. Cut away excess fat and tough outside skin. If cooking in oven, turn heat to 150°C [300°F] gas mark 2.

2 Cut meat across the grain into cubes—1.2-2.5 cm [½-1"] for sinewy meat, slightly larger for less tough cuts.

3 Peel or clean onions, carrots, turnips or other hard vegetables. Cut into even-sized slices or cubes, or leave whole.

4 Place the meat in stewpan or casserole. Add vegetables, herbs and cold liquid—not more than 275 ml [½ pt] per 450 g [1 lb] meat.

5 Season, cover tightly and bring slowly to simmering point, over gentle heat on top of the stove or in the oven.

6 Maintain a gentle simmer. If oven cooking, check liquid is barely moving. Reduce heat if necessary.

7 Check periodically that only an occasional bubble. breaks the surface liquid. If necessary, reduce heat further.

8 When meat is quite tender (for times see chart) skim off the surface fat with a slice of bread or with kitchen paper.

OR if time permits, allow the dish to become quite cold, then scrape or lift off the solidified surface fat with a knife.

SHIN OF BEEF CASSEROLE

⊠⊠⊠ *This recipe illustrates how slow and gentle cooking really can turn cheap and sinewy beef into an extremely tasty dish. Shin needs a minimum of 3½-4 hours. The addition of tomatoes gives the gravy a rich colour as well as flavour, and disguises the ragged appearance of the meat. They also supply the necessary liquid. This dish can also be cooked on top of the stove. It freezes and reheats well. Serve with boiled potatoes or buttered noodles.*

SERVES 6
900 g [2 lb] shin of beef
6 small onions
1 garlic clove (optional)
400 g [14 oz] canned
 tomatoes
15 ml [1 tablespoon] tomato
 purée
salt and pepper

1 Heat the oven to 150°C [300°F] gas mark 2.

2 Wipe the meat with a damp cloth and cut away any outside skin.

3 Cut across the grain of the meat into 1.2 cm [½"] cubes.

4 Peel the onions. Peel the garlic clove, if using, and chop up small.

5 Put the meat into a casserole, add the onions, and garlic, and the tomatoes including their juice.

6 Blend the tomato purée into 275 ml [½ pt] cold water and add to the casserole with a little salt and a generous seasoning of black pepper.

7 Cover tightly, and cook in the centre of the oven for about 4 hours. Check the rate of cooking from time to time and reduce oven temperature if necessary, so that the casserole just simmers and no more.

8 Check the seasoning, skim off surface fat and serve from the casserole.

LAYERED LEG OF BEEF CASSEROLE

⊠⊠⊠ *Begin this casserole in good time to allow at least the minimum 3½ hour slow cooking time needed to tenderize the meat. Let it take its time and you will be rewarded with deliciously tender meat in a richly flavoured gravy. Serve with boiled or mashed potatoes, a green vegetable and perhaps some crusty bread for mopping up the gravy.*

SERVES 6
900 g [2 lb] leg of beef
2 large onions
2 carrots
2 celery sticks
1 garlic clove (optional)
salt
freshly ground black pepper
30 ml [2 tablespoons] tomato
 purée

1 Heat the oven to 150°C [300°F] gas mark 2.

2 Wipe the meat with a damp cloth, trim away any skin and cut across the grain into 2.5 cm [1"] cubes.

3 Peel the onions. Scrape the car-rots. Wash the celery. Cut all the vegetables into thick slices. Peel and chop garlic clove, if using.

4 Arrange alternate layers of meat and vegetables in an ovenproof casserole, starting with a layer of vegetables, and season lightly between layers.

5 Mix the tomato purée with 550 ml [1 pt] cold water and pour over the meat and vegetables.

6 Cover the casserole tightly and cook in the centre of the oven.

7 After about 30 minutes, when simmering point is reached, reduce heat if necessary to maintain a gentle simmer. Cook altogether for 3½-4 hours until tender.

8 Before serving, skim fat off surface. Check seasoning. Serve from the casserole.

Layered leg of beef casserole makes a substantial meal.

LAMB AND KIDNEY HOT-POT

If you are inclined to dismiss neck of lamb as 'too bony to bother with' you are missing a dish of flavour and character. You can use the less bony, but more expensive, best end of neck if you prefer. The traditional Lancashire hot-pot often included 8-12 oysters in the ingredients.

Use a straight-sided brown earthenware hot-pot, or deep casserole. Leftover gravy can be strained into any vegetable or meat soup.

This casserole reheats well so you could double the quantities to allow for another meal. It is cooked at a slightly higher heat because lamb is basically not a tough meat; this also helps to brown the potatoes.

SERVES 4
700 g [1½ lb] middle neck of lamb cut into pieces
2-4 lambs' kidneys
225 g [½ lb] onions
700 g [1½ lb] potatoes
salt
ground black pepper
275 ml [½ pt] chicken or veal stock, or water plus chicken stock cube
25 g [1 oz] butter

1 Heat the oven to 160°C [325°F] gas mark 3.

2 Trim the pieces of meat of any surplus fat and rinse off any loose splinters of bone (sometimes the bones splinter when the butcher chops them).

3 Peel away the fat surrounding the kidney. Nick the skin on the rounded side of each kidney and draw it back on each side until it is attached by the core only. Draw out as much core as possible and then cut off skin and core close to the kidney. Cut each kidney in half horizontally.

4 Peel the onion and cut into thin slices.

5 Peel the potatoes and cut into 6 mm [¼"] thick slices.

6 Fill a hot-pot or deep casserole with alternate layers of potato, meat and kidney, and onions, starting with a layer of potatoes. Season lightly between each layer.

7 Pour on the cold stock. Top with a layer of potato, arranging the slices so that they overlap each other like roof tiles to completely cover the meat. Dot the potatoes with tiny pieces of butter, and put the lid on tightly.

8 Cook in the centre of the oven for 1½ hours, reducing heat if necessary.

9 Uncover the hot-pot and cook for a further ½ hour to allow the potatoes to brown. Serve from the pot.

Variations
● Add 100 g [¼ lb] mushrooms sliced or halved, to the meat.
● Add layers of celery, carrots or other vegetables to the onions.
● Instead of small pieces of meat, have the neck cut into chops. Trim off surplus fat. Lay half the potato slices in the bottom of the pot. Put the chops and kidney halves on top, then the onions. Add the liquid and finish with the rest of the potatoes overlapping as above. Season between layers.

IRISH STEW

⊠⊠⊠ *This is a traditional recipe in which potatoes thicken the liquid. Although water is stipulated in the original recipe, in this version a chicken stock cube is used to improve the flavour.*

SERVES 4
700 g [1½ lb] middle neck of mutton, cut into chops
1 chicken stock cube
225 g [½ lb] onions
900 g [2 lb] medium-sized old potatoes
salt
freshly ground black pepper
freshly chopped parsley and chives

1 Dissolve the stock cube in 425 ml [¾ pt] boiling water and allow to become cold.

2 Cut off and discard all excess fat. Rinse the chops under the cold tap to remove any bone splinters.

3 Peel and thinly slice the onions.

4 Peel the potatoes and cut half into slices. Put the remainder into a

Colourful pollo con peperoni is a delicious dish from Italy.

basin, cover with cold water and reserve.

5 Put the meat into a stewpan, put the onions and sliced potatoes on top, sprinkle generously with salt and pepper and pour on the cold stock.

6 Cover tightly and bring slowly to simmering point over low heat.

7 Immediately reduce heat and simmer gently for 1 hour.

8 Drain the whole potatoes and arrange on top of the stew. Cover and continue simmering gently for a further hour, or until meat and potatoes are tender.

9 To serve, lift out the whole potatoes and arrange around the edge of a serving dish. Then lift out the meat and pile in the centre.

10 Skim surface fat off the liquid. Using a wire whisk beat the mushy sliced potatoes into the gravy to thicken it, then check the seasoning and pour over the meat.

11 Sprinkle with the parsley and chives and serve very hot.

PORK AND HERB CASSEROLE

⊠⊠⊠ *The onions in this casserole create enough moisture to make extra liquid unnecessary. Be sure to ask for the thick end of the belly as it is much meatier and less fatty than the streaky end. Serve with boiled rice.*

SERVES 6
900 g [2 lb] thick end of belly of pork
450 g [1 lb] large Spanish onions
30 ml [2 tablespoons] oil
salt
freshly ground black pepper
10 ml [2 teaspoons] freshly chopped marjoram or 2.5 ml [½ teaspoon] dried marjoram
1 thyme sprig
15 ml [1 tablespoon] freshly chopped parsley

1 Heat the oven to 150°C [300°F] gas mark 2.

2 Peel and finely slice the onions.

3 Heat the oil in a wide flameproof

casserole and fry the onions gently for about 10 minutes, allowing them to become pale gold in colour. Take the pot off the heat.

4 Meanwhile wipe the meat with a damp cloth. Remove the rib bones by holding the knife close to the bones and cutting along underneath until they are freed from the meat. Reserve.

5 Cut the pork into rough cubes about 4 cm [1½"] square. Add to the onions in the pan with generous seasonings of salt and pepper, fresh or dried marjoram and the sprig of thyme. Stir well, lay the bones on top, and cover the casserole tightly.

6 Transfer to the centre of the oven and cook for 2 hours.

7 Skim off surface fat, remove the sprig of thyme and the bones, check the seasoning and stir in the chopped parsley.

8 Pile in the centre of a hot dish and surround with boiled rice.

POLLO CON PEPERONI

⊠⊠ *This is a good example of a simple unthickened stew, using chicken joints. It is a useful and versatile recipe which cooks over a single burner. If using frozen chicken make sure it is completely thawed. The tomatoes supply the necessary liquid.*

SERVES 4
4 chicken portions
salt and pepper
1 medium-sized onion
1 garlic clove
1 large green pepper
400 g [14 oz] canned, peeled tomatoes
1 chicken stock cube
12 black olives (optional)

1 Cut off all loose skin, rinse the joints under cold water and pat dry with kitchen paper. Sprinkle all surfaces with salt and pepper and rub in with your fingers.

2 Peel the onion and garlic, and slice very thinly.

3 Skin the pepper. Either spear it with a long-handled fork and hold over a gas flame, or put under a hot

Sea pie stew is topped with suet pastry and cooked over a gentle heat.

grill, turning until blistered and lightly charred all over. Peel off skin and cut pepper into 1 cm [⅓"] wide strips.

4 Open the can of tomatoes. Drain the liquid into a wide, heavy-based stewpan, chop the tomatoes roughly and add them to the pan, with the onion, garlic and pepper.

5 Crumble the stock cube into 45 ml [3 tablespoons] boiling water, dissolve and pour into the stew-pan. Bring to the boil.

6 Add the chicken pieces, skin-side down, and spoon some of the sauce over them. Cover tightly, and simmer gently, basting occasionally for 30-40 minutes, or until tender.

7 When cooked, lift chicken pieces on to a serving dish and keep warm.

8 Add the olives, if used, to the pan and bring the sauce rapidly to the boil. Boil until well reduced.

9 Check seasoning and pour over chicken pieces.

SEA PIE STEW

◫◫◫ *Judging by the name, this dish originated in a ship's galley. It is a useful recipe when camping or caravanning, or whenever a substantial meal has to be cooked over a single burner. Although prepared by the cold-start method, the stew is slightly thickened by tossing the raw meat in seasoned flour. A first grade stewing meat which cooks in 2-2½ hours should be used.*

SERVES 3-4
450 g [1 lb] chuck or blade steak
salt and pepper
25 g [1 oz] plain flour
75 g [3 oz] carrot
75 g [3 oz] turnip
75 g [3 oz] onion
275 ml [½ pt] light stock
15 ml [1 tablespoon]
mushroom ketchup or
tomato purée

For the suet pastry:
100 g [¼ lb] self-raising flour
pinch of salt
50 g [2 oz] shredded or grated suet

For the garnish:
freshly chopped parsley or chives

1 Wipe the meat with a damp cloth, trim away excess fat, and cut the meat into 2.5 cm [1"] cubes.

2 Season the flour generously with salt and pepper and toss the meat in it.

3 Peel the carrot and turnip and cut into 1.2 cm [½"] dice. Peel and slice the onion.

4 Put the meat and vegetables into a heavy-based stewpan.

5 Stir the ketchup or tomato purée into the cold stock and pour it into the stewpan.

6 Bring slowly to simmering point, cover and then allow to simmer gently for 1¼ hours, reducing heat as low as necessary.

7 Meanwhile make the pastry. Sift the flour and salt into a basin, add the suet and mix to a dough with 75 ml [5 tablespoons] of water.

8 Knead for a minute on a lightly floured surface, then roll into a circle slightly smaller than the stewpan.

9 Lay the pastry on top of the stew, pressing it down on to the meat. Cover the pan tightly, and continue simmering for another 1-1¼ hours.

10 When cooked, lift out the pastry on to a plate and cut into triangles.

11 Skim off surface fat from the stew. Check the seasoning of the gravy, then turn the meat, vegetables and gravy into a hot serving dish.

12 Arrange the pastry on top of the meat and sprinkle lightly with chopped parsley or chives. Serve immediately.

Fry-start stews and casseroles

Described here is the fry-start method of stewing and casseroling meats. The meat is first browned in hot fat to seal the surfaces and then given a long gentle simmering. This way of cooking meat and poultry is common to many countries; it produces succulent meat and rich savoury flavours and is the basis of a large number of exciting recipes.

Casseroles and stews made with the less tough cuts of stewing meat are usually begun by frying the pieces of meat quickly in hot fat to seal in the juices before adding liquid and vegetables. They are then slowly simmered in the oven or on top of the stove. This frying is called browning and gives the dish a rich savoury flavour. Where onions are used, these are also browned first.

The frying process does not invariably render the casserole brown, however, despite this name. The colour of the finished casserole depends partly on the type of meat used. The extent to which the meat is browned and the cooking of the roux

(flour and fat) before the liquid is added will finally determine the colour.

Recipes using chicken, veal, rabbit or pork are usually pale in colour, while beef stews and casseroles are generally a rich brown—hence the terms brown stews and white stews. For brown stews, the roux is cooked to a nut-brown colour before the liquid is added, but it is important not to overbrown it as burnt flour gives the dish an unpleasant bitter flavour. Tomato purée, mushroom ketchup and red wine also help to enrich the colour.

BEST CUTS

A detailed description of the most suitable cuts of meat for casseroles and stews cooked by the fry-start method are given on pages 51–60.

The better quality cuts of beef, such as chuck, blade and skirt, can be deliciously tender cooked in this way. So can breast and shoulder of lamb and mutton, belly and hand of pork, and all stewing cuts of veal. It is also extensively used for poultry and game. Second-grade cuts of beef should be cooked by the cold-start method.

OTHER INGREDIENTS

Described here are fry-start stews and casseroles thickened by a roux and using non-alcoholic liquids. However, the fry-start method can be used for a variety of types of casserole. For convenience and handy future reference, here is a guide to the thickenings, liquids and other ingredients used in all types of stews and casseroles.

Fats

Good dripping or oil is the most generally used fat in fry-start casseroles and stews. Fat is needed both to brown the meat and to make the roux with added flour, which thickens and can colour the casserole or stew. The flavour of the dripping is important because it lends character to the dish. Olive oil, very popular in Mediterranean countries, equally gives dishes a distinctive taste. Ordinary oil can also be used but, because it is tasteless, it will not add anything in the way of flavour to the dish.

Butter is sometimes used for fry-starting chicken, usually with the addition of a little oil to prevent burning. Butter is also used when a sauce is thickened at the end of cooking; a liaison of two parts butter to one part flour mixed into a paste is called a beurre manié. This is then dropped into the hot liquid, a little at a time, and has the effect of thickening the sauce without forming any lumps at all.

Flours

Always use plain white flour for the roux as it blends with and absorbs the liquids best. The raising agent in self-raising flour makes this type of flour unsuitable.

If a stew is thickened at the end of cooking, a beurre manié may be used, as described above, or alternatively the sauce may be thickened with cornflour. The thickening agent is added to the liquid, rather than the liquid to the thickening agent.

The cornflour is mixed with a little cold stock or water in a cup. A few spoonfuls of the hot liquid are then added and blended in. This mixture is stirred into the stew and cooked for a few minutes longer until it thickens.

Liquids

As already described on page 54, the amount of liquid should be in proportion to the amount of meat: 275 ml [½ pt] per 450 g [1 lb], or less if the vegetables used have a high moisture content.

White or brown stock, wine and water are the most frequently added liquids. Beer and cider, and sometimes orange or other fruit juice, can also be used. Tomato purée is often added with the liquid to colour and enrich the sauce.

Details of cooking alcoholic stews and casseroles are on pages 85–94.

Cream and sour cream are also used to enrich but, unlike other liquids which are added at the beginning of stewing or casseroling, they are added just before serving because long cooking causes them to thin or curdle. Usually, single cream is used for the enriching but double cream can also be used.

Other additions

The most common additional ingredients in a meat casserole or stew are onions and root vegetables such as carrots, parsnips and turnips. Many other vegetables, including leeks, celery, courgettes, tomatoes, and peppers can also be used to alter the character of the stew. You can use a small quantity—just for the flavour—in which case the casserole will be served with another vegetable as a separate accompaniment. Alter-natively, you can add a lot of vegetables for a meal-in-a-pot, which only needs an accompanying salad or hot crusty bread to mop up the delicious sauce.

Dried beans, particularly haricot beans, can help to turn a little meat into an inexpensive but substantial nourishing meal. There are also some less usual recipes which include fruit such as pineapple, apricots or oranges, or dried fruit.

Remember that more delicate vegetables such as peas or fresh beans should be added towards the end of cooking time to avoid over-cooking. Everything must be ready and perfectly cooked at the same time.

As well as garlic, salt and pepper, the inclusion of herbs, paprika, mustard, chilli or curry powder, and various spices all help to give each dish an individual flavour.

EQUIPMENT

The best cooking pot for fry-start stews and casseroles is a flameproof casserole attractive enough to take to the table. The meat can then be browned on top of the stove, transferred to the oven for slow simmering and served all in the same dish.

If, however, you don't own a flameproof casserole, an oven-proof one can be used for the oven cooking and the meat browning can be carried out first in a frying-pan on the stove. If you do this, be sure to scrape the base of the pan well when transferring the contents to the casserole, because the sticky sediment is as rich in flavour as it is in colour.

If the stew is simmered, as well as browned, on top of the stove, then a heavy-based stewpan can be used for all the cooking process. Whichever kind of pot you use, make sure that the lid fits tightly, as otherwise the

liquid will evaporate. If it does not, place a piece of aluminium foil across the top of the pot under the lid. As the liquid evaporates it will form droplets on the inside of the lid and drip back into the stew, keeping it moist.

Use a really sharp knife and a flat chopping board to cut the meat and vegetables. You also need a perforated spoon to turn the meat when browning and a wooden spoon to stir the roux.

PRINCIPLES OF FRY-START

After the removal of skin and/or surplus fat, the meat is cut into equal-sized pieces—4-5 cm [1½-2"] cubes. It is important that as much fat as possible is cut away, otherwise the casserole will be very greasy. Poultry and game are most often jointed and, in the case of poultry, the skin is usually left on.

There are several variations on the method of browning the meat, flour and vegetables. The meat can be tossed first in seasoned flour and then browned in fat, or it can be browned on its own without flour. The advantage of flouring is that the meat is really dry and so browns easily. When not using flour, therefore, make sure the meat cubes are thoroughly dry first.

The slow browning of onions until they are slightly caramelized is very important to the colour and flavour of a nut-brown stew. Sometimes sugar is added and caramelized in the same way.

Some recipes brown the root vegetables as well, others add them half way through the cooking so that they retain their texture and do not become too soft.

Flouring the meat

In the step-by-step casserole, which is a classic recipe for beef, the meat is first tossed in flour that is seasoned with salt and pepper. A simple way to do this is in a polythene bag. Put some of the seasoned flour and about 100-225 g [¼-½ lb] of the meat cubes in the bag and shake well. Empty the coated cubes on to a plate. Surplus flour will then fall off the cubes. Do not tip them straight into the hot fat. Repeat the process until all the meat cubes have been coated. The surplus flour on the plate is reserved for use in the roux.

Browning

Dripping or oil is heated in the flameproof casserole or frying-pan. When the fat is hot and almost smoking add the meat—a few pieces at a time to give them plenty of room all round—and brown on all sides over a high heat to seal the surface. When browned, remove them with a perforated spoon, so that fat remains in the pan, and keep them warm. Continue until all the meat has been browned.

Reduce heat to medium and fry the sliced onions in the fat; garlic can also be added at this stage. When the onions are golden brown, the pan is removed from the heat and the flour stirred in. The pan is then returned to a lower heat and the roux stirred and cooked to the desired colour. For a rich brown stew this should be nut brown without being burnt. For a white stew, the onions are only lightly fried, or sweated, and the roux stirred just long enough for the fat and flour to blend before liquid is added.

The onions must be left in the pan while making the roux because they have absorbed a good deal of the fat. If they were to be removed, more fat would be needed for the roux. This would result in an unnecessarily greasy stew.

Adding liquid

The pan is now removed from the heat and the liquid added slowly, starting with a trickle. Stir continuously. Return to the heat and cook gently until the flour and liquid have thickened into a smooth sauce. This blending is easier if the liquid is hot or warm when added to the roux. Bring to boiling point.

At this point the pan is taken off the heat again. If it is a flameproof casserole, the meat is returned to the casserole and herbs and seasoning are added. If you are using a frying-pan, the meat and liquid should be transferred at this point to an ovenproof casserole.

Simmering

The casserole is covered tightly, and then transferred to the centre of the heated oven (see times and temperatures overleaf). Simmer slowly for the required time. Root or other vegetables can be added half way through cooking, if wished. As an alternative to cooking in the oven, the stew can be simmered on top of the cooker. In this case it is important to adjust the heat to very low, so that the stew is barely simmering.

Degreasing

All fat should be removed from the meat before frying and no more oil or fat should be added to the pan than is necessary for browning the meat and the onions. If, however, at the end of cooking there is a layer of liquid fat floating on top of the casserole, this can be removed with a skimmer from the surface. Alternatively, remove this fat by absorbing it with a slice of bread or kitchen paper.

Cooking ahead and reheating

Most casseroles and stews can be reheated, some are even improved in flavour. Cooking large enough quan-

tities for two meals or for storing in the freezer can be a useful time saver. If the recipe calls for the addition of cream or sour cream, remove the portion of the stew to be kept for future use before stirring in cream, as otherwise this could curdle on reheating. When the reserved portion of the casserole is reheated, cream or sour cream can be added before serving, off the heat, in the usual way.

TIMES AND TEMPERATURES

A fry-start casserole is already at simmering point when it is put in the oven, so it is only a question of maintaining this gentle simmering throughout the cooking time. The oven must therefore be preheated so that it is ready to receive the browned meat.

Casseroles and stews are generally best cooked at 150°F [300°C] gas mark 2. Because ovens differ, it is important to check that the casserole is only barely simmering and to turn down the heat if necessary—or turn it up if the casserole contents do not seem to be cooking at all.

When vegetables are added half way through, you may have to increase the oven temperature briefly to bring the casserole back to simmering point. The addition of cold vegetables causes the temperature of the liquid to drop.

Poultry is an exception to the general rule that the casserole should be barely simmering. Chicken does not need the slow treatment to tenderize it; it also takes a much shorter time than other meat to cook. There is a danger that a very low heat may not thoroughly cook the centre of the chicken joints, which could lead to salmonella poisoning. A chicken casserole should cook at about 180°F [350°F] gas mark 4.

The length of cooking time depends largely on the type of meat used—the better the quality of cut, the less time it needs—and the size of the pieces. On average, a casserole of under 1.4 kg [3 lb] of beef takes three and a half hours to cook. Pork may take two and a half to three hours, but a lamb shoulder can take only two hours to become tender.

Cooking the stew on top of the stove takes approximately the same time as in the oven and, again, it must be only simmering.

Step-by-step to fry-start brown casserole

SERVES 6
900 g [2 lb] chuck, blade or skirt of beef
60 ml [4 tablespoons] plain flour
salt
freshly ground black pepper
2 onions
2 carrots
1 parsnip, turnip or small swede
40 g [1½ oz] beef dripping or 45 ml [3 tablespoons] oil
550 ml [1 pt] light beef stock or water
15 ml [1 tablespoon] tomato purée
a bouquet garni (a thyme sprig, parsley sprig and a bay leaf tied together)

1 Trim fat and skin from meat. Cut into 4 cm [1½"] squares. Heat oven to 150°C [300°F] gas mark 2.

5 Heat fat in flameproof casserole. When hot, brown a quarter of meat, lightly and quickly all over.

6 With perforated spoon, remove meat on to plate; keep warm. Repeat until all meat is browned.

10 Return the pan to the heat. Bring to the boil and cook stirring, until smooth.

11 Remove from heat. Add meat and bouquet garni. Cover tightly and simmer in oven centre for an hour.

2 Mix flour with seasoning. Put 100-225 g [¼-½ lb] meat in polythene bag with some flour. Shake.

3 Turn out floured cubes on to plate. Repeat until all the meat is coated. Reserve excess flour.

4 Peel vegetables. Slice onions and carrots. Cut parsnip, turnip or swede into 2.5 cm [1"] cubes.

7 Turn heat down slightly. Fry onion slices until golden brown, stirring occasionally.

8 Stir in reserved, seasoned flour. Cook over low heat, stirring until roux is nut brown.

9 Heat liquid, mix in tomato purée. Add slowly to roux in pan off the heat. Blend until smooth.

12 Add root vegetables, pushing them into sauce. Simmer for 1-1½ hours.

13 If casserole has a surface layer of fat, skim off with skimmer or blot with bread or kitchen paper.

14 Check meat is cooked. Check seasoning and adjust if necessary. Serve from the casserole.

Variations on simple fry-start brown casserole

●For a simple brown stew, follow the step-by-step recipe for a casserole, but use the hotplate instead of the oven in step 11 to simmer the ingredients. Make sure the flame-proof casserole or heavy-based pan is tightly covered, stir the stew from time to time, and watch that it doesn't cook too quickly or stick to the bottom of the casserole.

●For beef stew with dumplings, make eight small suet dumplings (or four large dumplings). Cook on the top of the stew for the last 25-30 minutes of cooking time. Keep the lid tightly covered and maintain a steady simmer.

●For a beef casserole with prunes, omit the parsnip, turnip or swede from the ingredients. Soak 8 prunes in warm water for 20 minutes. Add them to the casserole together with a thin strip of orange rind for the last 45 minutes of cooking time. Remove the rind before serving.

●For oriental beef, omit the parsnip, turnip or swede given in the basic recipe. Use only 400 ml [¾ pt] stock and replace the tomato purée with 60 ml [4 tablespoons] oyster sauce. Add 2 large green peppers (seeded and pith removed) cut into fine slivers, and 100 g [¼ lb] button mushrooms 30 minutes before the end of cooking time. As oyster sauce is salty, extra salt is probably unnecessary.

WHEN IS A STEW NOT A STEW?

In addition to the words 'stew' and 'casserole', many other names are given to dishes cooked by long slow methods, either on top of the stove or in the oven. Some of these names, strictly speaking, have fairly specific meanings, although in practice they are often used interchangeably.

Here is a brief description of the most important stews and casseroles, giving the various distinctive details of each.

Blanquette: a white stew based on veal, lamb or chicken, simmered in an unthickened liquid which is enriched just before serving with a liaison of egg yolk and cream. In other words it is served in a sauce velouté.

Blanquette de veau is one such famous stew.

Carbonnade: a stew of Flemish origin. The name is now applied to meat stewed in ale or beer.

Civet: this is the French name for what is usually a stew or casserole of rabbit, hare or other game in which the blood is added at the end of the cooking to enrich and thicken the sauce.

Daube: the name comes from the French daubière, meaning a covered casserole. It can be applied to all kinds of meat, poultry and game, cut up or in a piece, cooked very slowly in a covered pot with wine and aromatic flavourings. These stews are often marinated first.

Estouffade: the name comes from the French étouffer, to smother or stifle. It is applied to meat cooked very slowly with a minimum, if any, liquid, in a hermetically sealed pot.

Fricassée: strickly speaking, this is the correct word to use for any dish in which meat is first browned and then simmered. But nowadays the word usually refers to white meat (chicken, rabbit or veal) cooked in a sauté pan.

Goulash: a stew of Hungarian origin characterized by the addition of paprika and often, just before serving, sour cream. It can be made from beef, pork, veal or chicken.

Haricot: according to modern linguists the word haricot is a corruption of the French halicoter, to cut up. It does not, therefore, necessarily mean a lamb or mutton stew with haricot beans—but, nevertheless, this is often what it turns out to be!

Navarin: a stew or casserole usually but not necessarily cooked by the fry-start method and specifically of lamb or mutton.

Ragoût: a generic term applied to any type of stew or casserole of meat, poultry, game or fish.

NAVARIN PRINTANIER

 *This springtime version of lamb or mutton casserole is made with young lamb and early season vegetables. The combination of shoulder and breast gives a balance of lean and fat meat. Ask the butcher for a piece of shoulder big enough to give you 450 g [1 lb] of boned meat.*

The recipe can be adapted to use neck of lamb or mutton, also a favourite cut for a navarin, but allow an extra 30 minutes' initial cooking time.

The sugar is used to give the dish a good amber colour and does not make it taste sweet. Because lamb is a fatty meat, some of the liquid fat is spooned off in step 4 and more is skimmed off in step 11; you may also need to degrease after cooking. Frozen peas can be substituted for the fresh ones. This dish can also be cooked on top of the stove.

SERVES 6
450 g [1 lb] boned shoulder of lamb
450 g [1 lb] breast of lamb
30 ml [2 tablespoons] oil
1 garlic clove
10 ml [2 teaspoons] granulated sugar
salt and pepper
22 ml [1½ tablespoons] plain flour
30 ml [2 tablespoons] tomato purée
550 ml [1 pt] chicken or beef stock
1 bouquet garni
12 button onions
450 g [1 lb] small new potatoes
6 baby carrots
225 g [½ lb] shelled peas

1 Wipe the meat with a clean damp cloth. Remove the bones from the breast and reserve. Trim off excess fat or skin.

2 Cut all the meat into 4 cm [1½"] cubes and blot on kitchen paper. Heat oven to 150°C [300°F] gas mark 2.

3 Heat the oil over a medium-high heat in a flameproof casserole large enough to hold meat and all the vegetables. You will need one that holds about 3.4 L [6 pt].

4 When the hot fat is almost smoking, put in the meat, a few pieces at a time, and fry quickly, stirring frequently, until lightly browned.

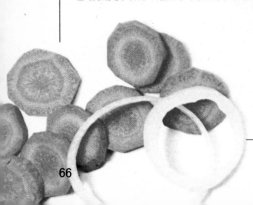

Spoon off the excess fat. Reduce heat slightly.

5 Sprinkle on the sugar and continue frying and stirring for several minutes until lightly caramelized.

6 Away from the heat, sprinkle on the flour and a generous amount of salt and pepper. Stir, then cook, still stirring, over a low heat for 2-3 minutes until the flour is pale fawn.

7 Heat the stock and mix the tomato purée into it. Pour into the casserole, stirring, away from heat. Bring to simmering point, still stirring.

8 Peel and crush the garlic and add to the casserole.

9 Add the lamb bones and bouquet garni to the casserole. Cover tightly and cook for an hour.

10 Meanwhile, prepare the vegetables; peel the onions and scrape the potatoes and carrots. Shell the peas.

11 Remove the bones and bouquet garni from the casserole. Skim off excess fat from the surface with kitchen paper or a slice of bread.

12 Add the onions and carrots to the casserole, pushing them down into the sauce. Cover and simmer in the oven for a further 30 minutes.

13 Add the peas and cook for another 15 minutes.

14 If there is a layer of surface fat on top of the casserole, skim again with a skimmer or blot the fat off with bread or kitchen paper.

15 Check all the meat and vegetables are tender. Check seasoning. Serve from the casserole.

Variations

●For winter navarin omit the new vegetables. At step 12 add to the pot with the onions 225 g [½ lb] dried haricot beans, soaked overnight and then simmered for an hour before adding to the casserole.

●For extra flavour, use pork dripping instead of oil to brown the meat. Replace some of the stock with canned tomatoes and their liquid, plus a crumbled stock cube.

BEEF GOULASH

▨▨▨ *This is a typical goulash using paprika and sour cream. There are various types and grades of paprika pepper, which is the ground seeds of the sweet pepper or pimento. The kind generally sold for cooking is fairly mild and sweet, valued as much for its colour as its flavour, and this is the one allowed for here. It does not keep well, so buy it in small quantities.*

The caraway and paprika are cooked with the roux because it helps to bring out their flavour. This dish can also be cooked on top of the stove.

Serve the goulash with boiled noodles tossed in butter.

SERVES 6
900 g [2 lb] chuck or blade of beef
450 g [1 lb] onions
30 ml [2 tablespoons] oil
1 garlic clove
5 ml [1 teaspoon] caraway seeds
30 ml [2 tablespoons] paprika
15 ml [1 tablespoon] plain flour
400 g [14 oz] canned, peeled tomatoes
250 ml [½ pt] stock
salt
freshly ground black pepper
45-60 ml [3-4 tablespoons] sour cream

1 Wipe meat with a damp cloth and remove excess fat. Cut into 4 cm [1½"] cubes. Blot these with kitchen paper to remove excess moisture.

2 Peel and slice the onions. Heat the oven to 150°C [300°F] gas mark 2.

3 Heat the oil in a flameproof casserole over a high heat. When the oil is almost smoking, add meat a few pieces at a time and brown on all sides, stirring frequently.

4 Remove meat from the pan with a perforated spoon on to a plate and keep warm.

5 Reduce heat to medium. Add the onions to the casserole and fry over a low heat for 8-10 minutes until soft and golden, stirring occasionally.

6 Peel the garlic clove and chop finely. Crush the caraway seeds with a pestle in a mortar or put them into a plastic bag and crush with a rolling pin.

7 Add the garlic and crushed caraway seeds to the onions.

8 Away from the heat, stir in the paprika and flour. Then cook gently for 1-2 minutes, stirring continuously.

9 Add the canned tomatoes—including the juice—the stock and salt and pepper to taste. Stir well and bring to the boil.

10 Return the meat to the casserole. Cover tightly and simmer gently in the oven for 2 hours or until tender, stirring occasionally.

11 Just before serving degrease with a skimmer or blot up excess fat with a slice of bread or kitchen paper.

12 Check the seasoning and, off the heat, stir in the sour cream. Serve.

PORK SWEET AND SOUR

Pork fillet (also called tenderloin) can be used in this recipe for a special occasion. The less expensive hand and spring of pork is just as good for a family meal, when the irregular pieces of meat won't matter. The casserole can be cooked on top of the stove with less fear than usual of sticking because this dish is thickened at the end of the cooking time instead of by the roux method. It should be served with boiled or fried rice.

SERVES 6

900 g [2 lb] boneless lean pork (tenderloin or hand and spring)
225 g [½ lb] onions
2 celery sticks
1 large green pepper
30 ml [2 tablespoons] oil
415 g [15½ oz] canned pineapple chunks
60 ml [4 tablespoons] wine vinegar
15 ml [1 tablespoon] soy sauce
75 g [3 oz] soft brown sugar
salt
30 ml [2 tablespoons] cornflour

1 Wipe the meat with a damp cloth. Remove any fat or gristle. Cut into neat chunks, about 2.5 cm [1"] square and blot these on kitchen paper.

2 Peel and slice the onions. Wash and slice the celery. Wash, remove pith, de-seed and slice the pepper.

3 Heat the oil in a large flameproof casserole or heavy-based stewpan over a high heat.

4 Add the meat and in batches fry stirring frequently, until the meat surfaces are sealed. As this happens, the colour changes from pink to grey.

5 Remove the meat from the pan with a perforated spoon and keep warm. Reduce the heat to medium and gently fry the onions in the pan for 2-3 minutes.

6 Return the meat to the pan.

7 Drain the pineapple chunks. Make the juice up to 250 ml [½ pt] with water.

8 Add the liquid and the pineapple chunks to the pork, together with the green pepper, celery, wine vinegar, soy sauce, sugar and salt to taste. Stir to mix.

9 Bring to boiling point, cover tightly and simmer gently until tender. This will take about an hour for tenderloin or 1½ hours for hand and spring.

10 If there is a layer of surface fat on the casserole, remove this by skimming or blot with a slice of bread or kitchen paper.

11 Blend the cornflour in a cup with 30 ml [2 tablespoons] cold water. Stir in 30 ml [2 tablespoons] hot liquid from the casserole.

12 Stir this mixture into the sauce in the casserole and bring back to boiling point. Cook for 2-3 minutes. By this time the sauce should be thick and clear.

13 Check the seasoning and serve.

68

2

1. Heat the fat in a flameproof

1 Rinse the chicken pieces in cold water then dry thoroughly with kitchen paper. Heat oven to 180°C [350°F] gas mark 4.

2 Sprinkle chicken all over with salt and pepper and rub in well with your fingers.

3 Heat the fat in a flameproof casserole over medium heat. Fry the chicken joints slowly, skin side down first, until golden on both sides. This will take about 10 minutes.

4 Meanwhile, peel and chop the onion. Wash and slice the celery. Derind the bacon rashers and cut into narrow strips.

5 Plunge tomatoes into boiling water for a minute. Remove, cool and peel off the skins. Cut into quarters.

6 Remove the chicken pieces on to a plate.

7 Add the onion, bacon and celery to the pot and fry gently for 5 minutes, stirring occasionally.

8 Heat the stock.

9 Away from the heat, sprinkle the flour into the pot, then cook gently stirring for 1-2 minutes until the roux is pale fawn.

10 Away from the heat, add the hot stock slowly, stirring continuously. Bring to the boil, still stirring. Cook until the sauce is smooth and slightly thickened.

11 Return the chicken to the casserole and add the prepared tomatoes.

12 Cover the casserole tightly and cook in the centre of the oven for 40 minutes.

13 Ten minutes before serving, add the cooked peas to allow them to heat through.

14 If there is a layer of fat floating on top of the casserole, skim this off, or blot up with a slice of bread or kitchen paper.

15 Check the seasoning. Serve from the casserole.

COUNTRY CHICKEN CASSEROLE

This is a simple casserole, the kind made by a busy farmer's wife with little help and many jobs to do. You can use a chicken stock cube for the stock and substitute frozen peas for the fresh ones. The chicken can either be simmered gently on top of the stove in a flameproof casserole or in the oven.

1. Beef Catalan
2. Beef goulash
3. Country chicken casserole
4. Pork sweet and sour

SERVES 4
4 chicken quarters
salt and pepper
40 g [1½ oz] bacon fat or 25 g
 [1 oz] butter plus 15 ml
 [1 tablespoon] oil
1 small onion
1 celery stick
2 rashers streaky bacon
15 ml [1 tablespoon] plain flour
250 ml [½ pt] chicken stock
3 ripe tomatoes

For the garnish:
150 g [5 oz] shelled and cooked
 peas

LAMB AND TOMATO CASSEROLE

The tomato purée and paprika in this recipe give the dish a rich tasty flavour. Instead of the fresh tomatoes and tomato purée you can substitute a 400 g [14 oz] can of peeled tomatoes, including the juice.

The tomatoes provide all the liquid element that is needed and thicken the sauce so that flour is unnecessary. Add yoghurt when serving. Serve with creamy mashed potatoes or boiled rice.

SERVES 4-5
700 g [1½ lb] boneless shoulder of lamb
salt
freshly ground black pepper
5 ml [1 teaspoon] paprika
25 g [1 oz] butter
15 ml [1 tablespoon] oil
225 g [½ lb] onions
450 g [1 lb] ripe tomatoes
15 ml [1 tablespoon] tomato purée
45-60 ml [3-4 tablespoons] yoghurt
15 ml [1 tablespoon] freshly chopped parsley

1 Wipe the lamb with a clean damp cloth. Trim away excess fat and /or skin. Cut into equal pieces, about 2.5 cm [1"] square and blot excess moisture on kitchen paper.

2 Heat the oven to 150°C [300°F] gas mark 2.

3 Sprinkle the meat with salt, pepper and paprika.

4 Heat the butter and oil in a flameproof casserole over a high heat. Put in some of the meat, but do not overcrowd the casserole. Fry fairly quickly, turning it to brown all the surfaces.

5 Remove pieces of meat to a warm place and continue putting in meat cubes until all the meat has been fried and removed.

6 Peel and slice the onion. Reduce the heat and fry slowly in the pot until soft and golden.

7 Meanwhile prepare the tomatoes. Immerse in boiling water for a minute, cool and skin. Cut into quarters.

8 Add the tomatoes to the casserole, together with the tomato purée thinned with 15 ml [1 tablespoon] water. For canned tomatoes, omit purée and water.

9 Return the meat to the casserole. Stir and bring to boiling point.

10 Transfer the casserole to the oven and cook at a gentle simmer for 1½ hours.

11 Check after 20 minutes that the casserole is just simmering and alter the oven temperature up or down as may be necessary.

12 If there is a layer of surface fat on top of the casserole, skim this off with a skimmer or blot with a slice of bread or kitchen paper.

13 Away from the heat, check the seasoning. Cover with yoghurt, sprinkle with parsley and serve.

BEEF CATALAN

This hearty, warming casserole is flavoured with onions, tomatoes and cheese. The rice is cooked in the casserole towards the end of cooking time and will absorb all the rich liquid. No flour is therefore needed to thicken the casserole. If preparing the casserole in advance, cook up to step 15 only. To reheat, place the covered casserole in a roasting tin with enough hot water to come halfway up the sides of the casserole, and place in an oven heated to 160°C [325°F] gas mark 3 for 40 minutes. The reason for using a water bath is that direct heat might dry out the rice too much. Stir in the olives and cheese only when ready to serve.

Shoulder of lamb is boned and diced for this casserole. Tomatoes and paprika give it a distinctive colour and flavour. The yoghurt is added when serving and gives the dish an attractive mottled appearance.

SERVES 6
900 g [2 lb] beef blade, chuck or thick flank, boned weight
225 g [½ lb] onions
60 ml [4 tablespoons] olive oil
225 g [½ lb] long grain rice
2 garlic cloves
2 bay leaves
5 ml [1 teaspoon] fresh thyme or 2.5 ml [½ teaspoon] dried thyme
pinch of saffron (optional)
salt
freshly ground black pepper
400 g [14 oz] canned, peeled tomatoes
400 ml [¾ pt] beef stock
12 black olives
75-100 g [3-4 oz] grated Parmesan cheese

1 Wipe the meat with a clean damp cloth. Trim away excess fat and cut into 4-5 cm [1½-2"] cubes. Blot cubes on kitchen paper to remove excess moisture.

2 Heat the oven to 150°C [300°F] gas mark 2. Peel and slice the onions. Peel and crush the garlic.

3 Heat half the oil in a flameproof casserole over a medium-high heat until almost smoking. Brown a proportion of the meat on all sides. Do not overcrowd the casserole. Remove with a perforated spoon and set aside on a plate.

4 Brown the rest of the meat cubes in batches.

5 Add another 15 ml [1 tablespoon] oil and reduce the heat slightly. Cook the onions until lightly browned. Remove with a perforated spoon and set aside with the reserved beef.

6 Add the remaining oil and the rice to the casserole and cook, stirring, for 2-3 minutes until it looks milky. Remove from the pan and reserve on a separate plate.

7 Add the garlic, bay, thyme, saffron (if using), tomatoes and stock to the casserole. Stir well to get the tasty sediment off the base of the casserole. Bring to the boiling point, still stirring.

8 Return the beef and the onions to the casserole, cover and transfer to the oven. Cook in the centre.

9 Cook for 3-3½ hours. After 20 minutes check that the casserole is at simmering point and adjust the oven temperature, up or down as necessary, so that only an occasional bubble breaks the surface of the liquid.

10 Remove the casserole from the oven and increase the oven temperature to 180°C [325°F] gas mark 3.

11 If there is a layer of surface fat on the casserole, skim this off with a skimmer or blot it up with a slice of bread or kitchen paper.

12 Place the casserole over medium heat on top of the stove. Stir in the reserved rice, together with salt and pepper to taste. Bring the contents back to simmering point.

13 Cover and return the casserole to the oven. Cook for 20 minutes, by which time most of the liquid should be absorbed by the rice and the grains should be tender.

14 Fifteen minutes after putting the rice into the oven, check on its progress. Remove the casserole briefly from the oven, take off the lid and eat a couple of grains of rice to check whether they are cooked. Do not stir the rice.

15 If the test grains are still some way off being tender, and the rice looks like drying out, pour on a little boiling beef stock. Cover and return the casserole to the oven.

16 When the rice is ready, sprinkle over and lightly stir in the olives and the grated Parmesan cheese, a spoonful at a time. Serve immediately.

Variations
●For pork Catalan substitute pork spare rib or the fillet rump part of the chump end for the blade of beef. Cook for 2½ hours then remove the bones and the rind. Add the rice and finish as before.
●For lamb Catalan, use an equal weight of lamb half and half made up of the boned shoulder and breast. Cook for about 2 hours then remove the breast bones. Add the rice and finish cooking as before.

CHICKEN FRICASSEE

◩◩ *Although the chicken meat is white, this is a tasty brown stew. Chicken and vegetables are sautéed to give rich colour and flavour, and the addition of tomato purée heightens colouring.*

SERVES 4
4 chicken portions
salt and pepper
40 g [1½ oz] butter
30 ml [2 tablespoons] olive oil
2 large onions
1 large garlic clove
1 large green pepper
15 ml [1 tablespoon] plain flour
60 ml [4 tablespoons] tomato purée
400 ml [¾ pt] well-flavoured chicken stock

1 Rinse the chicken pieces in cold water then dry thoroughly with kitchen paper.

2 Sprinkle chicken all over with salt and pepper and rub in well with your fingers.

3 Heat the butter and oil in a flameproof casserole over medium heat. Fry the chicken joints slowly, skin side down first, until well browned all over. This will take about 15 minutes.

4 Meanwhile, peel and chop the onions and garlic. Wash the pepper, remove the stalk, seeds and pith and slice thinly.

5 Remove the chicken from the casserole with a perforated spoon and set aside.

6 Reduce heat slightly, add the onion and garlic to the fat in the casserole. Cook for 10 minutes, stirring occasionally until softening.

7 Increase heat slightly, add the sliced pepper and fry, stirring, for a further 2-3 minutes.

8 Away from the heat add the flour and stir into the vegetables. Return to the heat and cook, stirring, until a rich nut brown.

9 Stir the tomato purée into the stock and pour the mixture into the casserole. Stir well to release all the sediment from the base of the casserole and bring to the boil, stirring all the while.

10 Return the chicken pieces to the casserole.

11 Cover the pan, reduce heat to the lowest possible simmer. Stew gently for one hour.

12 Skim off surface fat. Check the seasonings and serve.

Variation
●For veal fricassée, use 900 g [2 lb] lean mean cut into 4 cm [1½″] cubes and increase cooking time to 1½ hours. Suitable cuts are shoulder of veal, or half shoulder and half breast. Replace half the stock with dry white wine.

Beautiful boiled dinners

Boiling is an old method of cooking meat. It is highly practical too because, for the one expenditure of time and fuel, your cooking pot will produce sufficient for two meals—a substantial meat and vegetable dish plus a good quantity of stock for nourishing soup—or three meals or more if you choose a large joint.

Domestic cookers as we know them today are a very recent innovation. For many hundreds of years only the grandest establishments were sufficiently equipped to enjoy any real choice of cooking methods. The majority of people took their pies to the local baker to cook in his oven after the bread had been removed. Roasting and grilling were restricted to occasional communal feastings when a big fire and hand-turned spit would be built on open ground.

For daily cooking at home, the housewife relied on boiling: one large pot would be placed over the single source of heat and the whole evening meal would be cooked in it. Seasonal vegetables were the main ingredients and they went directly into the bubbling water together with meat, usually bacon. A suet pudding might be carefully tied in a clean cloth and lowered into the pot to cook along with the rest of the meal.

Perhaps many people spurn boiling today in favour of the newer, more fancy cooking methods, because it is such a basic cooking method. It is a misconception, however, that boiling produces boring stereotyped foods in an intolerably steamy kitchen.

Boiling is a good plain cooking method and it is important to rec-ognize that plain cooking does not mean dull dishes, but simply ones that are not rich: a carefully prepared plain dish can be just as good and interesting as a creamy rich one. Just how good it can be, depends largely on how much care you take in its preparation. Paying attention to seemingly small and insignificant details pays dividends and can raise the quality and status of the final dish from commonplace to memorable.

All sorts of different meats can be boiled and all sorts of vegetables too, so tastes, colours and textures can be very varied. If the foods are cooked with proper care, arranged decoratively and accompanied by an imaginative sauce, the results can be extremely handsome as well as very tasty—certain to tempt the appetite of even the most sophisticated gourmet.

A breast of lamb, stuffed with mushrooms and watercress, is rolled and then boiled. The accompanying mustard sauce counteracts the fattiness of the meat.

79

Boiling has other advantages:

1 Admirably lacking in greasy richness, boiled dishes are ideal for the calorie-conscious as well as for children or anyone with digestive problems.

2 Any flavours that escape from the meat and vegetables into the cooking liquid will form a fine stock for soups—so you are, in effect, producing food for two meals in one cooking operation, thus saving on fuel costs, cooking time and effort.

3 Large joints usually work out cheaper per kilo [pound] than small ones, so it makes sense to buy twice as much boiling meat as you need for one meal. Serve half hot and save the remainder for a cold meal or réchauffé dish later in the week. Theoretically a double-sized joint will require twice as much fuel and cooking time but in practice this need not be so. Cutting your double-sized joint in half, then cooking both pieces of meat simultaneously in the same pan will keep costs and effort down to the minimum.

SUITABLE MEATS FOR BOILING

The prime aim when boiling meat is to produce a good meaty meal, so choosing suitable cuts is important. The fact that you get stock at the same time is a bonus by-product.

Salt beef and bacon are the traditional and most popular joints for boiling in Britain, but many other meats (both fresh and salted) and chicken are equally good cooked by this method. Suitable cuts and cooking times are given in the chart.

The larger the joint the better the results will be. This is because if the cut surface area is small in proportion to the joint as a whole, the meat is better able to retain its full natural flavour. Birds are boiled whole for the same reason.

The following specific points are worth noting:

Breast of lamb makes a highly economical boiled dinner but, it is not worth the effort involved unless the breast is large and really meaty. It is also important that the breast is all in one piece, carefully boned and then rolled before cooking.

Boiling fowl are elderly birds which, while acceptable for stock-making, cannot be relied upon to provide good meat to eat. If in doubt, it is always safer to opt for a roasting chicken and to pay a little more for successful results.

Boil-in-the-bag bacon is useful when you want a small joint. Sealed cooking has the advantage of keeping the flavour intact and it also keeps the joint in neat shape, but remember that you won't get any stock.

Fresh pork is rarely used for boiling, except in Italy where the liquid used is milk.

OTHER INGREDIENTS

Apart from meat the only other essential ingredient is liquid. But one or more other optional ingredients are usually included in the boiling pot.

Liquid

As a general rule, meat is completely covered by liquid throughout the cooking process. By the end of cooking time this liquid should be so flavoured as to have become stock, but its flavour may be fairly weak. Fast boiling is needed, after the meat has been removed, to evaporate excess liquid and to concentrate flavour before it is used as stock or for soups and sauces. Alternatively, you can bolster flavour by adding a stock cube.

Water is almost always the liquid used (the only true exception being

MEAT BOILING CHART	
Timing always starts when boiling point is reached	
Meat	**Boiling time**
BEEF Silverside Brisket Topside Rump	If salted: 30 minutes per 450 g [1 lb] If fresh: 20 minutes per 450 g [1 lb] plus 20 minutes for joint weighing less than 2.25 kg [5 lb]
MUTTON AND LAMB Leg Shoulder	15-20 minutes per 450 g [1 lb]
Breast of lamb (boned and rolled)	1-1½ hours total
VEAL Leg Shoulder	20-25 minutes per 450 g [1 lb]
Breast (boned and rolled)	1-1½ hours total
BACON Half gammon Middle gammon Slipper Collar	20 minutes per 450 g [1 lb] plus 20 minutes for joints weighing less than 2.25 kg [5 lb]
PORK Loin Leg Hand Belly	If salted: 25-30 minutes per 450 g [1 lb] If fresh: boned and rolled: 25-30 minutes per 450 g [1 lb]
CHICKEN Roasting chicken Boiling fowl	20 minutes per 450 g [1 lb] 35-45 minutes per 450 g [1 lb]

when milk is used for the Italian method) but sometimes a small amount—no more than a glass or two—of wine, cider or beer is included. This produces a better-flavoured stock and is often specified when the stock is required for immediate use—for example to make a sauce to accompany the meat, or to make a soup to serve at the same meal as the meat.

Vegetables
To make the liquid more tasty a few traditional stock-making vegetables, such as celery, onion and carrot, are often added to the cooking pot at an early stage. By the end of cooking time, most of their flavour will have been given to the liquid, so these vegetables are too limp and tasteless to serve as accompaniment to the meat.

If you think it wasteful to throw them away, use them to add bulk to soup or some other (preferably spicy) dishes such as curry. Alternatively they can be used, as illustrated in the recipe for prosciutto al marsala, to give colour and body to the sauce which accompanies the hot meat.

You will save on fuel as well as washing-up if vegetables to accompany the meat are cooked in the same pot. Add them (either dropping them directly into the liquid or placing them in a steamer basket over the pan) when the meat is nearly cooked. Calculate timings so that both the meat and the vegetables will be ready at the same time.

Other flavourings
Herbs and spices are valuable for adding flavour to both meat and stock. Salt, peppercorns, bay leaves, bouquet garni and cloves are the most frequently used but citrus peel, fresh herbs, coriander seeds and others may be used too. Simply choose what you think appropriate but don't add so much as to dominate or detract from the flavour of the meat you are cooking.

Never add salt to the cooking pot when boiling salted meat!

Gelatinous ingredients
These are very optional extras but the inclusion of a split pig's trotter or calf's foot will produce a marvellously jellied stock. The rind from a joint of pork and bacon rinds can be used too but are less effective and will not produce quite same result.

PREPARATIONS
Before actually boiling the meat, there are two important preliminary steps—soaking salted meat and choosing the right pan.

Soaking salt meat
Meat was originally salted for two reasons: primarily to preserve it for the winter months and, secondly, to flavour it. In today's world of refrigeration, meat is salted solely because we enjoy the flavour. But, in practice, most people like only mildly salted meats and, therefore, often find it necessary to soak before cooking to wash out some of the salt.

To soak a joint, place it in a very large pan or bowl and completely cover with cold water. Change the water every few hours.

The big question is how long to soak the meat? This can range from 1 hour to 8 hours or even longer, depending on the saltiness of the cut. For the correct timing, rely on advice from the butcher and your personal taste.

The degree of saltiness depends on the strength of the brine used, the size of the joint and how long it was immersed. Your butcher should be able to answer these questions and give you his estimate for soaking time. But, because taste is such a personal thing, it is a good idea to double check by testing yourself. Take a sip of the soaking liquid after the meat has been in it for an hour or so. If it tastes very salty to you, change the water, leave the meat to soak for a few hours longer, then test again.

On balance it is better to oversoak than to undersoak. Oversoaking does little harm other than to make the meat so mild it loses some of its character (and this can be somewhat rectified by adding salt to the dinner plate). Undersoaking cannot be altered once the meat is cooked and it is disappointing, not to mention wasteful, if the resulting joint is too salty to eat with pleasure.

Selecting a boiling pan
Choosing the right pan can make all the difference to the final dish. The pan must have a heavy base or the meat touching the bottom of the pan could scorch; it needs a tightly fitting lid or liquid will evaporate during cooking and need constant topping up; and, ideally, it should have two handles to make it easier to lift when heavy and full.

The size of the pan is also vital, particularly when boiling fresh meat. It doesn't matter how deep the pan is, but it should not be much larger in diameter than the meat. This is because the less liquid you use, the better the flavour of both meat and stock will be. If the joint is swimming in a vast sea of liquid it will take so long to reach boiling point that more than necessary meat flavour leaks into the liquid—and the liquid itself will remain weak in flavour because there is so much of it. If the joint fits snugly into the shape of the bottom of the pan, with just enough room to tuck a few flavourings round it, you will need relatively little liquid to cover the meat and the resulting dish will be vastly superior. The water will also come to the boil sooner, requiring less fuel as a result.

GETTING OFF TO THE RIGHT START
There are four different methods by which you can start the boiling process. Which you should use, depends on the type of meat you are cooking and how you intend to serve it.

Cold start
This is a cooking method which encourages a certain amount of leakage from meat to liquid and is therefore a useful way of washing excess salt out of salted meats. It is also used for boiling fowl as the slowness minimizes toughening of the bird's already sinewy flesh.

Place the meat in the pan, pour on enough cold liquid to completely cover, place over low heat and bring slowly to boiling point.

Blanch start
This is a refinement on the cold-start method and is advisable if the meat is very salty or you had insufficient time to soak it properly. This method can also be used to replace soaking for bacon or other mildly salted meats.

Place the meat in the pan, pour on enough cold water to completely cover, place over low heat and bring slowly to boiling point. Immediately remove the pan from the heat, pour off the boiling water and wash scum off the joint. Return the joint to the cleaned out pan, pour on fresh cold liquid to completely cover the meat and again bring slowly to boiling point.

Hot start
Starting fresh meat in cold water encourages the leakage of juices and flavour. Plunging meat in boiling water, although advocated in many cookery books is too fierce. It causes sinews to contract which can toughen the meat as well as distort its shape. The method given here offers the happy medium and is advised for all fresh meats as well as roasting chicken that is to be served cold. This method also prevents excessive

Step-by-step to boiling meat

1 Immerse salted meat in cold water and soak for as long as necessary. Change water at intervals and sip to test for saltiness.

2 Choose a heavy-based pan that is only slightly larger in diameter than the joint so that it will fit snugly with flavourings.

OR to fry start roasting chicken, heat fat, sear the skin, turning to colour all over, pour on hot liquid and bring to the boil.

4 Add flavourings, skim, reduce heat to very low, cover pan and start timing. Cook at a gentle simmer. On no account boil.

leakage of meat juices from any cut surfaces on the meat.

Place the meat in the pan, pour on enough hot liquid to completely cover, place over medium heat and bring to boiling point.

Fry start

This method is recommended when boiling a roasting chicken that is to be served hot (unless you plan to use a coating sauce), as it colours the skin in an appetizing way. It is also used for the Italian method of boiling fresh pork. It should never, ever be used for a boiling fowl.

Melt a little clarified butter or a mixture of butter and oil in the pan. When hot, add the meat and cook, turning, to sear and lightly colour all over. Pour on enough boiling liquid to completely cover and bring back to boiling point.

COOKING

As soon as boiling point is reached, add to the pan any herbs, spices and/or vegetables you wish to flavour the liquid. The addition of vegetables will briefly cause the liquid to go off the boil. As it returns to boiling point, skim off any scum as it forms on the surface.

Immediately the liquid returns to boiling point, reduce the heat to very low, cover the pan and start timing the meat. Irrespective of starting method used, cooking time always begins at this point.

The term boiling is, in fact, something of a misnomer because, once boiling point is reached, temperature should always be reduced so that the liquid barely simmers throughout cooking time. It is because of this some cookery books refer to this cooking method as poaching or simmering. If necessary use an asbestos mat or move the pan half-on half-off the source of heat in order to maintain the correct temperature.

Boiling is not only an unnecessary waste of fuel but, more importantly from a gastronomic point of view, fast movement of the liquid will coarsen the texture of the meat making it stringy and tough. It will also have the effect of making the joint difficult to carve neatly and economically.

Towards the end of cooking time, you can add to the pan any vegetables that you plan to serve with the meat. Alternatively, ladle some of the stock into a seperate pan and cook the vegetables in it (or over it if steaming). The latter method is preferable, particularly if cooking dumplings. Although less economic on fuel, dumplings should be added to a liquid at a fast boil.

3 For a cold start, completely cover the joint with cold liquid, place the pan over low heat and bring slowly to boiling point.

OR for a blanch start, bring to boil. Empty pan, rinse joint, cover with fresh cold liquid and again bring slowly to the boil.

OR for a hot start, cover the joint with hot (but not boiling) liquid, put the pan over medium heat and bring to boiling point.

5 Near the end of cooking time, add vegetables to serve with the meat. Or cook them in another pan using stock from the boiling pan.

6 Turn off the heat as soon as cooking time is up. To serve hot, remove lid, add cold water and leave to rest for 10 minutes.

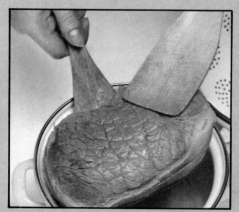

OR to serve cold, cool meat under cold tap then place in a clean pan, cover completely with cold liquid and leave until quite cold.

COOLING AND SERVING

As soon as the cooking time is up, turn the heat off.

To serve hot

If the joint is to be served hot, leave it to rest in the pan for 10 minutes or so. This will give it a chance to set, which makes for easier carving. Remaining immersed in the liquid will help keep it moist and succulent. Take the lid off the pan, however, and add a ladleful of cold water as a precaution against continued cooking.

To serve cold

Many cookery books advocate leaving the joint in the cooking liquor until it is quite cold and it is certainly true that this practice prevents the meat from drying out. Unfortunately, it also involves a health hazard, particularly for large joints as the cooling period is liable to be very long.

For safety's sake cooked meat should always be cooled rapidly and should always be allowed to become quite cold within a maximum of one and a half hours after the end of cooking time.

To comply with these standards yet enjoy a moist joint, the following practice is recommended. Lift the meat out of the pot as soon as it is cooked, place it in a colander under a running tap for a minute or two to reduce temperature quickly, then place the joint in a clean cold pan or dish, pour on enough cold liquid to completely cover and set aside. When the joint is quite cold, drain and dry it, wrap and refrigerate until required.

Handy hints

Chicken know-how

●If chicken is to be served hot immediately after boiling, it can either be carved into slices or divided into joints. Carving can be done at table but jointing is better done in the kitchen. Use a sharp kitchen knife or jointing scissors. A roasting chicken, boiled by the fry-start method, tastes best. Boiling fowl can be used too, of course, but its skin looks rather anaemic.

●When boiled chicken is to be served cold, it is always best to remove the skin (irrespective of whether roasting or boiling fowl is used) as chicken skin doesn't taste very pleasnt when cold. Skinning is easier to do if you halve or joint the chicken first. Then lift a cut edge of skin with the point of a knife, pull gently and the skin should peel away quite easily.

●Cooked, skinned and boned chicken meat is called for in many hot and cold dishes. These dishes usually involve coating the chicken (and often other ingredients too) with a sauce of the mayonnaise, béchamel or velouté family. When hot, these dishes are known as réchauffé, meaning reheated. You can use leftovers or chicken specifically cooked for the purpose.

●Many recipes specify boiled or poached chicken meat and it is certainly preferable to use this because boiled chicken meat is inclined to retain more moisture and succulence than chicken which has been cooked by a dry-heat method such as grilling or roasting.

●Once the chicken is jointed and skinned, use your hands to ease the meat off legs and wings. With gentle pulling the meat will divide itself naturally into fairly neat, bite-sized slivers and there is no need to cut it any smaller but do remove and discard gristle and fat. Only large pieces of thigh and breast meat will need slicing. Cut into neat shapes following the grain of the meat. Do not cut the pieces too small—it looks mean and the final dish will lack eye appeal.

●Never joint, skin or bone a chicken further ahead than necessary. Chicken meat is naturally lean and dry and, once the moisture-protecting skin and bones are removed, it tends to become sawdusty quite quickly.

●The approximate yields of chicken meat after boning and skinning are given in the chart. The wings of a 2.25 kg [5 lb] chicken will yield about 25-40 g [1-1½ oz] meat after skinning and boning. The drumsticks will yield about 50-75 g [2-3 oz] and the pickings from a carcass which has been carved at table will yield about 25-40 g [1-1½ oz] of meat.

Yield of cooked meat from chickens

1.4 kg [3 lb] chicken	= 600 g [1¼ lb] meat
1.5 kg [3½ lb] chicken	= 700 g [1½ lb] meat
1.8 kg [4 lb] chicken	= 800 g [1¾ lb] meat
2.0 kg [4½ lb] chicken	= 950 g [2 lb 2 oz] meat
2.25 kg [5 lb] chicken	= 1.15 kg [2½ lb] meat

●When you eat boiled roasting chicken, save the bones and skin. Return them to the liquor in the boiling pan, cover and simmer for 2 hours. Because initial cooking time was so brief they still retain much goodness which will boost the flavour of your stock.

CHICKEN POT-AU-FEU

The breast meat of a roasting chicken is tender enough to cook in steam only the thighs need to be immersed in liquid—and the use of less liquid than normal ensures stock with a concentrated flavour. The fry-start also gives the chicken skin good colour. Choice of vegetables can be varied according to season and pocket and, if more vegetables are used than specified here, the dish could be stretched to feed 5 or 6.

Other meats or mixture of meats can be used for pot-au-feu as shown in the variations below, but roasting chicken is the only meat for which a fry-start and partial immersion in liquid is suitable.

SERVES 4
1.4 kg [3 lb] roasting chicken
30 ml [2 tablespoons] fresh
chopped tarragon (optional)
a small strip of lemon rind
salt and pepper
1 large carrot
2 or 3 celery sticks
1 large onion

25 g [1 oz] clarified butter or
   15 ml [1 tablespoon]
   olive oil plus
   15 ml [1 tablespoon] butter
bouquet garni
350 g [¾ lb] new potatoes
450 g [1 lb] young leeks
225 g [½ lb] French beans
225 g [½ lb] mange-tout
275 ml [½ pt] vinaigrette
   à l'oeuf

1 Place the chopped tarragon and lemon rind inside the body cavity of the chicken together with a good seasoning of salt and freshly ground black pepper. Rub the outer skin with salt and pepper too.

2 Scrub the carrot, wash and chop the celery and peel and cut the onion into quarters.

3 Choose a heavy-based pan into which the chicken will fit snugly, and melt the fat in it over medium heat.

4 When melted and hot add the chicken and fry briefly, turning as necessary, until the skin is pale gold on all sides.

5 Lift the chicken out of the pan and add the carrot, celery and onion. Put the chicken back on top of the vegetables, add the bouquet garni and pour on enough hot water to cover the chicken thighs.

6 Bring to the boil quickly, then reduce heat, cover the pan and leave to simmer gently for 1 hour.

7 Meanwhile prepare the other vegetables and make the vinaigrette.

8 About half an hour before the chicken is ready, start steaming the new potatoes. They will take

about 30 minutes. Add the whole leeks about 10 minutes later, the beans after a further 8 minutes, and the mange-tout 4 minutes after that. They can all be cooked in the same steamer basket and steaming will keep them in better shape than boiling.

9 When the chicken is ready, switch off the heat but leave it in the boiling pan.

10 Arrange the steamed vegetables around the edge of a large, warmed serving dish and moisten them with a few spoonfuls of stock from the boiling pan.

11 Drain the chicken and cut into four portions with a sharp knife. Place in the centre of the serving dish and serve with accompanying vinaigrette in a sauce-boat.

Variations

●For chicken pot-au-feu using a boiling fowl, always use the cold-start method, increase cooking time and be sure that the bird is totally immersed in liquid.

● Serve with sauce poulette—velouté sauce made with veal stock with parsley and lemon juice added.

●Another delicious but more expensive alternative is sauce nénette: simmer 275 ml [½ pt] thick cream for 10 minutes or until reduced by one third. Meanwhile blend together 15 ml [1 tablespoon] English mustard powder, 30 ml [2 tablespoons] tomato purée, 30 ml [2 tablespoons] chopped tarragon or chives, 30 ml [2 tablespoons] chopped parsley and a good seasoning of salt and pepper. Away from the heat, gradually blend in the hot cream.

●Bacon joints and fresh beef also make delicious pot-au-feu. Starting methods and cooking times must be

altered according to type of meat used.

●Potée normande is a pot-au-feu on the grand scale for a party of 12 or more people. Chicken, fresh beef and lightly smoked Polish-type sausage are all included, each being added to the pot according to how long it takes to cook. A choice of sauces accompanies the dish—fresh tomato sauce and herb-flavoured mayonnaise are usually among them.

●Bollito misto, a Piedmontese speciality, is an Italian version of the potée normande. Again a variety of meats are used, usually including fillet of veal and, on special occasions, a small turkey. Accompanying vegetables nearly always include boiled white haricot beans and cabbage.

BOILED MUTTON WITH FENNEL

Boiled mutton is a traditional British dish and a large joint is usually used. For a small family meal use shank end of leg of lamb weighing about 1.4 kg [3 lb] and adjust cooking time accordingly. The hot-start method is used for this fresh meat recipe and partially cooking the fennel in the boiling pot saves on fuel and gives a delicate flavour to the stock.

SERVES 8
**shank end leg of mutton or
   whole leg of lamb weighing
   2.25 kg [5 lb]
salt
6 black peppercorns
4 medium-sized Florentine
   fennel
90 g [3½ oz] butter
freshly ground black pepper
40 g [1½ oz] plain flour
575 ml [1 pt] milk
15 ml [1 tablespoon] French
   mustard
15 ml [1 tablespoon] wine
   vinegar**

1 Wipe the joint with a clean damp cloth and trim away excess fat.

2 Choose a heavy-based pan into which the joint will fit snugly. Place the joint in it and pour on enough warm water to completely cover the meat. Place over medium heat and bring to the boil.

3 As soon as boiling point is reached, add 10 ml [2 teaspoons] salt, the peppercorns and skim away scum.

4 Reduce heat to low, cover the pan with a well-fitting lid and simmer gently for 1 hour 15 minutes to 1 hour 40 minutes depending on how well cooked you like the meat.

5 While the joint is cooking, prepare the fennel. Cut off feathery fronds, chop finely and reserve. Scrub and trim the bulbous roots leaving them whole.

6 Thirty five minutes before the end of cooking time, add the fennel to the boiling pan, pushing them well down into the liquid.

7 When cooking time is up, remove boiling pan from the heat. Lift out the fennel with a perforated spoon and ladle out and reserve 275 ml [½ pt] of the stock for making the sauce.

8 Pour a ladle of cold water into the pan and leave the joint in the uncovered pan to rest for 10 minutes or so.

9 Heat the grill and melt 50 g [2 oz] butter in a small pan. Use half the melted butter to coat the base and sides of a large gratin dish.

10 Pat the fennel dry, cut each bulb into 4 thick slices, lay them in the gratin dish, season with pepper and brush the remaining melted butter on top.

11 Cook under the hot grill until lightly coloured, turning the fennel slices and basting them with the buttery juices as necessary.

12 Meanwhile make a white sauce, using 40 g [1½ oz] butter, the flour, milk and reserved stock. Stir in at least 60 ml [4 tablespoons] chopped fennel fronds and leave to simmer, uncovered, for 5 minutes.

13 Away from the heat, stir the mustard and vinegar into the sauce and pour into a warmed sauce-boat.

14 Drain the joint, transfer to a warmed dish and serve together with the grilled fennel and accompanying sauce.

Variations

● For mutton with caper sauce, omit the fennel. Flavour the stock with a few carrots, celery stalks and an onion studded with cloves if wished. Accompany the meat with caper sauce.

● For mutton with onion sauce, make a basic white sauce and mix 225 g [½ lb] sautéed onions. Purée with 25 g [1 oz] butter and 25 ml [1 fl oz] thin cream.

● Watercress and walnut sauce can be added to left-over cold mutton or lamb. Grind 75 g [3 oz] shelled walnuts in a mill or pound them in a mortar. Strip the leaves from 2 bunches of watercress, wash them then blanch in boiling water for 30 seconds. Drain well, squeeze dry and chop finely. Beat together 150 ml [¼ pt] each of sour cream and natural yoghurt, blend in the nuts and watercress and season generously with salt and pepper.

SALT BEEF AND DUMPLINGS

◪◪◪ *Soaking the meat before cooking and using the cold-start method will remove excess saltiness from salt beef. Silverside is an English speciality, fine and lean in texture and well flavoured.*

Brisket makes a good alternative as it is well flavoured and quite a bit cheaper but it is only really economical if a joint of 2.25 kg [5 lb] or more is used as small joints are usually taken from the fatty end.

The inclusion of cider produces a stock which can be used for making beetroot or French onion soup.

SERVES 6-8
1.4 kg [3 lb] salted silverside
15ml [1 tablespoon] soft brown sugar
150-275 ml [¼-½ pt] dry cider
1 small onion
4 cloves
4 black peppercorns
2 bay leaves
900 g [2 lb] carrots

For the dumplings:
100 g [¼ lb] self-raising flour
50 g [2 oz] fresh brown breadcrumbs
75 g [3 oz] shredded suet
salt and pepper
5 ml [1 teaspoon] dried thyme
1 large egg
25 g [1 oz] plain flour

Salt beef with dumplings is served hot. The meat can be served cold, with balls of avocado pear and beetroot, as beefeaters' salad. The mustard should never be far away when serving hot or cold salt beef.

1 Trim excess fat from the joint, place it in a large bowl or pan, cover completely with cold water and leave to soak. Change the water occasionally and sip it to judge correct length of soaking time.

2 Drain and dry the meat, then rub the sugar into the flesh.

3 Place the joint into a heavy-based pan into which it fits snugly. Pour on the cider and enough water to cover completely. Set over low heat and bring slowly to boiling point.

4 Meanwhile peel the onion and stud it with cloves.

5 As soon as boiling point is reached, add the studded onion, peppercorns and bay leaves to the pan. No salt!

6 Skim away scum as the liquid returns to the boil, then immediately reduce heat to low.

7 Cover the pan and simmer gently for 75-90 minutes.

8 Meanwhile make the suet pastry for the thyme dumplings (see ingredients). These are made using part flour, part breadcrumbs, for extra lightness and an egg instead of the more usual water to bind the dough well. Divide the dough into 12 pieces and roll each firmly into a small ball. Dredge in plain flour and set aside.

9 Scrub the carrots and trim them. If they are large, cut lengthways into halves or quarters.

10 When cooking time is up, remove the meat pan from the heat. Ladle some of the stock into a seperate pan and pour a ladle of cold water into the meat pan. Leave the joint in the uncovered meat pan to rest while you cook the vegetables and dumplings.

11 Bring the stock pan to boiling point. Add the prepared dumplings and carrots and bring rapidly back to the boil.

12 Reduce heat to simmering point, cover the pan and leave to cook for about 10 minutes or until tender.

13 Drain the dumplings and carrots (keeping stock for later use in soups) and arrange them at either end of a warmed serving dish.

14 Drain the meat thoroughly, place it in the centre of the dish and serve.

Traditionally prosciutto al Marsala is made with raw ham. The recipe here has been adapted to bacon which is more readily available and equally tasty.

Variations

●Mustard is the traditional accompaniment to this dish but for a special occasion serve mustard cream—cream mixed with a little English mustard, milk and lemon juice.

●Fresh beef is also suitable for this method, in which case omit soaking and use of sugar. Use a hot water start and include a seasoning of salt. Serve with horseradish cream, using fresh horseradish instead of mustard.

●Both boiled fresh and salt beef are delicious cold. For beefeaters' salad, boil beef as described but, when cooking time is up, cool the meat under a cold running tap for a few minutes then place it in a dish and pour on enough vinaigrette to coat it. The vinaigrette should be well flavoured with mustard (but no salt should be included if salt beef is used). After 30 minutes, lift the joint out of the dressing, carve into thin slices, return to the dish and leave to marinate until quite cold. Drain to serve and accompany with seperate dishes of each of the following: balls of avocado, balls of beetroot, and diced but unpeeled cucumber. Sprinkle each dish with chopped chives and pour on a little of the vinaigrette in which the meat was marinated.

PROSCIUTTO AL MARSALA

▨▨▨ *Gammon is used here for an adaptation of an Italian recipe. Bacon is usually boiled by the blanch-start method. This is replaced here by brief soaking and the joint is then marinated before cooking. The delicious accompanying sauce is a clever combination of the reserved marinade plus the vegetables that have been used to flavour the stock. These vegetables are browned for rich colour and flavour.*

If you have some home-made chicken or beef stock which is only very lightly salted, use this instead of water to cook the bacon in. It will give the sauce even more flavour.

Steamed broccoli or courgettes are good vegetables to serve with this dish.

SERVES 6
1.15 kg [2½ lb] lean middle cut gammon
150 ml [¼ pt] cooking Marsala
60 ml [4 tablespoons] olive oil
1 large onion
2 large carrots
2 celery sticks
2 parsley sprigs
1 bay leaf
3 black peppercorns

salt and pepper
chicken stock (optional)

1   Soak the gammon in cold water for about 3 hours if wished. Drain and dry.

2   Place the gammon in a large bowl, pour on the Marsala and leave to marinate for 3-4 hours, turning at intervals.

3   Choose a heavy-based pan into which the gammon will fit snugly, and warm the oil in it over low heat.

4   Meanwhile slice the vegetables.

5   Add the vegetables to the pan and cook, stirring occasionally, for about 7 minutes to soften and faintly colour them.

6   Drain the gammon, reserving the Marsala. Add the gammon to the saucepan together with the herbs and peppercorns. Pour on enough cold stock or water to cover the gammon and bring to boiling point.

7 Immediately reduce heat, cover the pan and leave to simmer gently for 1 hour 10 minutes.

8 When cooking time is up, transfer vegetables from the pan to a liquidizer.

9 Ladle 425 ml [¾ pt] of the cooking liquor into a separate saucepan and concentrate flavour by fast boiling until reduced by nearly half.

10 Add a ladle of cold water to the boiling pan and leave the joint, uncovered, in it to rest.

11 Add the reduced stock to the liquidizer and reduce the mixture to a smooth purée.

12 Return to a saucepan, add the reserved Marsala, bring back to the boil and simmer for a few minutes. Thin with more stock if necessary. Adjust seasoning.

13 Meanwhile, drain the gammon, remove rind, carve into slices and arrange on a warmed serving dish.

14 Check the sauce for seasoning, pour it over the gammon, cover and place in a cool oven or plate warmer for 5-10 minutes before serving so that the gammon becomes impregnated with sauce.

BREAST OF LAMB WITH MUSHROOM AND WATERCRESS STUFFING

Here is a good and inexpensive dish but two things are vital to its success. First and foremost, the breast of lamb must be large and really meaty. This is particularly important because boiling, unlike grilling and other dry-heat cooking methods, does not crisp or dry out (and therefore reduce) the fattiness. Ask the butcher to bone and skin the breast and to remove the cartilage but to leave the breast in one piece.

The second important point is to drive off as much moisture as possible from the mushrooms and watercress. If this is not done, the stuffing will lack concentrated flavour and its texture will be so sloppy as to leak even as you roll the joint before cooking.

SERVES 4
1 large, meaty breast of lamb
100 g [¼ lb] mushrooms
15 ml [1 tablespoon] butter
1 garlic clove
salt
freshly ground black pepper
1 bunch watercress
50 g [2 oz] lean ham
30 ml [2 tablespoons] fresh breadcrumbs (optional)
150 ml [¼ pt] dry white wine (optional)

1 Wipe the mushrooms and trim the stems if necessary. Chop the mushrooms finely.

2 Melt the butter in a small pan over low heat.

3 Meanwhile, peel, slice and crush the garlic with a little salt.

4 Add the mushrooms and garlic to the pan. Increase heat to medium and cook, stirring, for 3–4 minutes or until most of the moisture has been driven off and the mushrooms are considerably reduced in bulk.

5 Remove the pan from the heat and season well with freshly ground black pepper.

6 Wash the watercress and strip the leaves of the stems. Blanch the leaves by boiling for 30 seconds. Drain and refresh in cold water. Squeeze dry with paper towels and chop the blanched leaves finely.

Add them to the mushrooms.

7 Chop the ham into small strips and add to the stuffing mixture.

8 If the stuffing still appears too moist, place over medium heat and stir until excess liquid is evaporated.

9 If using stir in fresh white breadcrumbs.

10 Trim excess fat from the breast meat and lay it flat on the work surface with the meatiest side facing upwards.

11 Spread the stuffing on the meat, tucking some under the flap. Do not place any of the stuffing very close to the edge of the meat. It will naturally spread to the edges when you roll the meat up.

12 Roll the meat into a short fat bolster, rolling from the thick end towards the flap end. Secure the bolster by tying it neatly with string in several places.

13 Choose a pan into which the bolster will fit snugly. Place the joint in it. Add just enough hot, but not boiling, water or water and white wine to cover the meat. Place over medium heat and bring to boiling point.

14 Skim away any scum that rises to the surface, reduce heat to very low, cover the pan and leave to simmer gently for 1–1½ hours.

15 When cooking time is up, switch off the heat. To serve hot, add a ladle of cold water to the pan and leave the meat in the uncovered pan for 10 minutes or so while you make a hot mustard sauce (English mustard, white wine vinegar and sugar mixed with white sauce).

16 To serve cold, transfer the cooked joint to a colander and place under a cold running tap for a few minutes, then put the joint in a large bowl, cover with cold water and leave until cold.

Variation
● Breast of veal can be cooked by the same method and timings using the same or other stuffings of your choice.

Eventful casseroles

The simplest way of turning an everyday casserole into an event is to add a little wine, beer or cider. The long slow cooking drives off the alcohol and leaves the essence of the liquor to enrich and round out the flavour of the dish. Here the basic principles of adding alcohol to casseroles are explained and recipes are given to illustrate them.

All the basic principles already covered on pages 51–72 regarding stewing and casseroling, remain unchanged—the cuts of meat to use, quantities of liquid and suitable equipment are all the same. In general terms by using alcohol in stews and casseroles you can add a new dimension in flavour. Replace up to half the liquid in any standard casserole or stew with either table wine, cider or beer. Naturally the wine, cider or beer you choose, and how you use it, will have a significant effect on the flavour and quality of the final dish.

COOKING WITH WINE

There is no mystique about cooking with wine. In wine-growing areas wine is a natural local ingredient which cooks through the ages have used to add an 'extra' quality to their dishes. It rounds out the flavour of a dish, adding a richness, mellowness or fillip according to the wine used and the method of adding it. It has a quality that is easier to taste and recognize than to describe in words.

Naturally, you don't slosh wine into any and every recipe, but only where it harmonizes with the other ingredients. The type and quality of the wine used is also an important factor. Cooking with wine is an art rather than a science, and like all good artists you must be prepared to experiment and, above all, to taste, as you go along.

CHOOSING WINES FOR COOKING
Table wines
Table wine is a generic name given to the unfortified wines you drink with food. Generally speaking any medium-dry wine you enjoy drinking can be used for cooking provided it is of sound quality and has both strength and flavour. It would be very extravagant to use a fine vintage wine unless it has gone past its prime and needs using up. But you will be very disappointed with the result if you use a thin, excessively dry wine that lacks body and flavour. Obviously you should never use a wine that has turned to vinegar, except in very small quantities as 'wine vinegar'.

When only a small amount of red wine is needed in a recipe, it is often possible to take it from the bottle to be served with the meal, because it is usual to open the bottle an hour or two before it is to be drunk. Similarly, small quantities left in the bottom of a bottle can be used for the next day's casserole. Most wines will keep for a day or so if transferred to a smaller bottle, which is of a size to allow only a minimum of air space between the wine and the cork. Tightly cork it and keep it in the refrigerator.

If you buy table wines specially for cooking bear the following points in mind.
Red wine: strong, full-bodied, youngish and flavoursome wines are best, for example, Beaujolais, Mâcon, St Emilion, Chianti, Barbaresco, Rioja, or wine of similar robust quality.
White wine: strong, medium-dry wines such as those from the Mâcon, Graves or Loire areas. Avoid very dry or thin wines. Reserve sweet wines for syllabubs, sweet wine sauces and puddings.

Fruit and home-made wines: many of these are excellent for cooking provided they have the qualities outlined above. But as everyone's home brew is likely to be different, be prepared to experiment.

Fortified wines
Fortified wines are, in general, the wines you drink before or after a meal rather than with it. Most have been 'fortified' with spirit and many have added flavouring ingredients. They range from very dry to very sweet and have many, many uses in the kitchen, but not necessarily in casseroles. They include sherry, Madeira, port, Marsala, liqueurs, and aperitif wines such as vermouth.

EVAPORATING THE ALCOHOL
A basic point to remember about cooking with wine is that you must allow it to cook sufficiently to evaporate all the alcohol, thus removing the 'raw' flavour. Then allow the residual essences to mellow and mingle with the other ingredients.

When wine is used in casseroles the alcohol evaporates naturally by virtue of the long slow cooking. If you have any doubt about this fact, taste the gravy of a wine casserole soon after preparing it and again after several hours' cooking—you can then taste the difference.

Of course you also use wine in quick cooking dishes, but there the technique is very different because you drive off the alcohol by rapid boiling, as opposed to the long slow cooking method described here.

METHODS OF REDUCING TABLE WINES
The purpose of reducing the volume of a table wine is to concentrate and strengthen its flavour, and at the same time drive off the alcohol. There are several ways of achieving this end, and the various methods also constitute the different ways of adding wines to casseroles.

Reduction before cooking
Pour the wine into a wide saucepan (so that the maximum surface area is exposed) and boil rapidly, uncovered, until the wine is reduced by the required amount, usually by a third or a half. When a reduced wine is added to a dish it is able to

A wine marinade imparts extra flavour to meat to be casseroled.

impregnate the other ingredients with a more concentrated flavour. This is especially useful when the cooking period of the dish is of relatively short duration, for example in a recipe for coq au vin rouge.

Reduction after cooking
After the cooking is completed, the meat may be removed and the cooking liquids, which include wine, remain behind in the pan. Alternatively, they may be strained off into another pan. The liquids are then reduced in volume by rapid boiling in the open pan. This method is frequently used for concentrating and strengthening flavour and improving the texture of a sauce. At the outset, season any sauce which is to be reduced only very lightly, otherwise the sauce may become too salty. The sauce should be tested and then seasoned after the reduction. An example of this method is given in the recipe for boeuf à la bourguignonne.

Reduction during initial stages
It is customary in Italian cookery to reduce wine immediately after it is added to a recipe. Time and time again an Italian recipe for stewed, braised or casseroled meat or poultry will direct you to add the wine to the fried vegetables and meat and then to 'allow it to bubble briskly until almost evaporated'. By this means the wine is forced to penetrate the meat or poultry and improve the flavour. Only after this fierce reduction is the other liquid, such as stock, added. An example of this method of reduction is shown in the recipe for abbacchio brodettato.

MARINATING IN WINE
A different but very effective way of strengthening the flavour of a meat casserole is to marinate the meat in the wine before cooking. This is particularly successful with stewing and braising cuts as it is popularly thought to help tenderize as well as flavour the meat.

A marinade usually consists of red or white wine, a small quantity of olive oil, herbs, seasoning, sliced onion, carrot and garlic. The addition of a tablespoon or so of wine vinegar, brandy or gin helps to strengthen a marinade, while spices such as coriander seeds and juniper berries impart a gamey flavour.

The marinating process can take a few hours or can be continued for a few days depending on the strength of flavour required. The meat is stirred or turned frequently to ensure that all surfaces are exposed to the marinade. Marinades that are to last for several days are always cooked then allowed to become quite cold before the meat is added. This is to ensure the vegetables do not become sour. Marinating must be carried out in a china, glass or earthenware container or some other non-corrosive material. Similarly the container and its contents must be kept lightly covered, in a cool and preferably airy place or in the refrigerator in hot weather.

In most recipes the marinade itself, or the strained liquid, is used as the basis of the liquid element for the casserole. This strengthens the flavour still further during the long, slow cooking. A marinade is used in the recipe for manzo stufato.

Handy hints

Reheating wine casseroles

It is a fact that the flavour of all casseroles containing wine is enriched and strengthened by reheating. So when convenient it is a good plan to cook them, at least partially, the day before they are to be eaten. However do remember the health hazards of reheating meat. Be sure to cool the casserole down as rapidly as possible by standing it in a bowl of cold water, and when cold leave it in a cool place or, better still, in the refrigerator. Having skimmed off any surface fat reheat very slowly, and very thoroughly, bringing the casserole to simmering point and maintaining this temperature for several minutes.

The same remarks are true of casseroles containing beer or cider.

COOKING WITH BEER

A full-flavoured mild beer or sweet stout is the most generally used for cooking purposes. If you use a bitter beer or stout a small amount of sugar may be added, or plenty of onions may be needed, to balance the flavour. All beers, except the very light, give casseroles a naturally brown colour. This means you have no need to make a brown roux to colour the casserole.

The big difference between beer stews and wine casseroles is that beer is not reduced during cooking as is wine. Beer stews can therefore be conveniently cooked on top of the cooker and thickened in the final stages of cooking.

COOKING WITH CIDER

In Normandy and Brittany cider is considered a natural alternative to white wine and has always been used for cooking in the same way and for the same purposes as local wine. Traditional British cider-making counties such as Somerset, Hereford and Devon have been slower to appreciate the potential of their local 'brew', but the habit of tipping cider into the cooking pot is catching on fast. Cider adds a mild piquancy to many everyday dishes without adding alarmingly to the cost. So never throw away left-over cider even if it is flat; use it for cooking instead! Like wine, cider loses its alcohol content when boiled, so the dish can safely be served to children and teetotallers.

Cider varies in alcoholic content and flavours range from very dry to sweet. Bottled ciders, both still and sparkling, are available at liquor shops and supermarkets, and in parts of Britain you may find draught cider on tap in local bars. Sadly 'scrumpy', the traditional farm-brewed strong dry, still cider from the West Country is now very scarce.

The type of cider you choose for cooking is a matter of personal taste and preference. Strong, dry ciders are usually best because they contribute more flavour to the dish and are generally used with fish, poultry and meat. Mildly pickled or smoked meats such as bacon, gammon and ham, can be cooked in a medium-dry cider. Medium-dry cider is also good for 'cutting' the richness of fat meats such as goose, mutton, sausages and belly pork. Medium-sweet ciders can be used for poaching apples, pears or prunes, for sweet cider sauces and for puddings, but are not really suitable for meat and fish dishes.

Reducing cider
If boiled rapidly in a wide, uncovered pan, cider can be concentrated and the alcohol driven off. Reduce the liquid by about half and the apple flavour will be greatly strengthened. When cold the reduced cider will keep for weeks in a screw-topped bottle in the refrigerator. Reduced cider is particularly useful as a base for sauces, for sousing oily fish, for marinating meat, and as a baste when roasting meat, ham, poultry or fish.

COOKING WITH SPIRITS
Spirits are distillations of wine or grain, and those with distinctive flavours (eg brandy, whisky, rum and sometimes gin) are used in very small quantities for flavouring purposes, especially for pâtés and rich puddings. They are also important as agents for flaming casseroles and other dishes. For both flavouring and flaming a rough spirit is more suitable than the expensive liqueur grades.

Spirits are not used as the basis of the liquid content of a dish as wines are.

STORING WINES AND SPIRITS
Table wines. The great enemies of wine are air and warmth. If sealed with a cork, keep unopened bottles lying horizontally (so that the cork remains moist) in a cool, dark place. A wine rack is not essential as bottles will stack neatly on top of one another provided you arrange 'stoppers' to prevent the end bottles rolling away. Once opened, a bottle of wine should be used up within a few days. Keep it cool and tightly corked until finished (spare plastic bottle caps come in useful here). Small amounts of left-over wine are best transferred to small bottles to reduce the air space which causes them to go vinegary. The storage life of a white wine can be extended a little by keeping it in a refrigerator.

Fortified wines and vermouths. Store unopened bottles upright in a cool place. For cooking purposes opened bottles will keep for a month or two, but they do not remain in good condition indefinitely, especially pale sherries or vermouths.

Spirits and liqueurs. Store upright in a cool place. Spirits and liqueurs do not deteriorate for a long time after the bottles are opened. Do not expose the contents to air more than necessary and keep the bottles tightly stoppered to prevent evaporation.

FLAMING WITH ALCOHOL
A dish may be flamed in the kitchen during the early stages of cooking. Alternatively, it may be flamed (flambéed) immediately before serving. The purposes of dousing food with alcohol and setting it ablaze are twofold. In the first place the burning alcohol consumes all excess fat and thus refines and 'degreases' the food. Secondly, the flavour of the dish is greatly enhanced by the concentrated essences of the spirit which are left behind when the flames die. It follows from this that the best spirits to use for flaming are those which have a concentrated flavour combined with a high proof spirit, to ensure that it catches alight readily.

'Cooking' brandy was always considered the classic spirit for all general purpose flaming, while rum was a favourite for certain fruits and puddings. But nowadays the residual flavour of whisky and gin is gaining both spirits a valued place in the

88

kitchen for certain dishes. When available, calvados is the traditional spirit for flaming dishes of Norman origin, but as it is seldom easy to find, brandy or whisky are common substitutes. Orange-flavoured liqueurs with a high proof spirit are especially successful for flaming fruits and puddings. But there are really no hard and fast rules, so don't be afraid to experiment with different spirits.

If a recipe is to be flamed either during cooking or at table, for safety's sake it is essential to use a flameproof container of stainless steel, aluminium, enamelled cast iron, copper etc. Avoid china or ordinary glass which might crack under the intense heat.

Make sure there is nothing inflammable around you when you prepare for flaming.

If a dish fails to blaze when a flame is applied it is usually because the spirit is cold. So, before flaming always release the alcohol by warming the spirit over a low heat in a soup ladle or tiny saucepan. When the

Add extra flavour to the dish and degrease your meat by flaming in brandy.

flame is applied, it will then catch fire readily. In some cases, when the bottle is nearly empty the alcohol may have evaporated from the remaining spirit, and it will then not catch alight. Remove the very ends of bottles and keep for flavouring purposes.

The spirit may be ignited in the ladle or pan and then poured, flaming, over the dish. Alternatively it may be poured over the meat and then flamed. If one large piece of meat is being served the second method is effective. However if there are several pieces of meat or if there is a certain amount of liquid already present the first method is more likely to be effective.

The ladle or pan of alcohol can be ignited either by exposure to a gas flame or with a lighted taper. If the alcohol has already been added to the dish it should be ignited with a lighted taper. Always light the alcohol at arm's length (that's why a taper is recommended in preference to a match), and avert your face. The flames leap high and engulf the whole pan while they last, and if the pan contains much surplus fat or sugar the blaze can be surprisingly fierce.

Once alight, the flames on a casserole will blaze steadily for several minutes. The flames will then gradually subside and finally burn out altogether.

BOEUF A LA BOURGUIGNONNE

◨◨◨ *This is a classic example of a slowly simmered wine casserole in which the flavours of the braising beef, red wine, onions, garlic, herbs and seasoning join together to make a richly harmonious dish. Although its origins are thought to be Burgundian, its fame has spread throughout France and it is now affectionately referred to as 'le bourguignon'. There are many versions of the recipe—some involve marinating the meat for several hours before cooking, and others flame the sautéed meat with brandy before adding the wine. This recipe is typical of that made in French homes. As it is a dish which improves with reheating and also freezes excellently, it is worth making in double quantities.*

If it is more convenient, steps 1–11 can be done one day, the dish rapidly cooled and any surface fat removed. The following day the casserole should

be placed over a low heat and brought to simmering point very gently; then continue from step 12. Serve the beef accompanied by plain boiled potatoes, tossed in butter and parsley.

SERVES 8–9
1.4 kg [3 lb] topside of beef or braising steak
225 g [½ lb] sliced, pickled pork belly
225 g [½ lb] button onions
1-3 garlic cloves (according to size and personal taste)
40 g [1½ oz] dripping or lard
50 g [2 oz] flour
400 ml [¾ pt] robust red wine
30 ml [2 tablespoons] tomato purée
400 ml [¾ pt] meat stock
2 bouquets garnis
salt
freshly ground black pepper
225 g [½ lb] button mushrooms
25 g [1 oz] butter
10 ml [2 teaspoons] oil
15 ml [1 tablespoon] chopped, fresh parsley

1 Heat the oven to 150°C [300°F] gas mark 2.

2 Wipe the meat with a damp cloth. Cut away and discard any gristle or excess fat. Cut the meat into neat pieces about 4 cm [1½"] square and pat dry with kitchen paper.

3 Cut the rind from the pork belly and discard. Cut the pork into 8 × 25 mm [⅓ × 1"] strips. Peel the button onions. Peel and crush the garlic.

4 Melt the dripping or lard in a flameproof casserole about 4.5 L [8 pt] capacity, over medium heat. When the fat is hot fry the strips of pork and the onions over moderate heat, stirring frequently, until both begin to turn golden. Remove with a slotted spoon to a plate and reserve.

5 Increase the heat to high and fry one-third of the beef briskly, stirring frequently, until lightly browned and sealed on all sides. Remove with a slotted spoon to a second plate and reserve.

6 Repeat twice more with the remaining two-thirds of the meat. After the last batch is sealed return all the beef to the casserole.

Osso buco is a traditional dish of Italian origin. The marrow inside the bones is a delicacy enjoyed by many and is the key feature of the dish.

7 Sprinkle in the flour. Reduce the heat to medium and cook, stirring, for 2 or 3 minutes.

8 Stir in the wine, bring quickly to the boil and allow to bubble briskly for a couple of minutes to evaporate some of the alcohol.

9 Dissolve the tomato purée in the stock and add to the casserole with the garlic, bouquets garnis and salt and pepper.

10 Bring to simmering point, stir well, cover tightly and transfer to the centre of the oven to cook for 2½ hours. Check the rate of cooking from time to time and adjust the oven temperature to maintain a bare simmer.

11 Add the reserved strips of pork and the onions and return to the oven for a further 30 minutes, or until the meat is very tender when pierced with a fork.

12 Wipe the mushroom caps. Heat the butter and oil in a shallow pan over medium heat and, when hot, sauté the mushrooms for 3–4 minutes. Shake the pan frequently until the mushrooms have disgorged their liquid and become dry.

13 Add the mushrooms to the casserole and cook for 5 minutes.

14 Check the quantity and consistency of the sauce and adjust if necessary. If the sauce is scant and too thick, stir in a little extra stock. Reheat gently.

15 If, however, there is a lot of liquid and the sauce is too thin, lift the meat, onions and mushrooms from the pan with a slotted spoon on to a dish and keep warm. Boil the liquid rapidly to reduce and concentrate the sauce. Stir from time to time to release the coagulations from the pan bottom. Then return the reserved meat and vegetables to the pan.

16 Check the seasonings and, if necessary, skim any fat from the surface of the sauce.

17 Serve sprinkled with chopped parsley.

OSSO BUCO (or OSSI BUCCHI)

The basis of this great dish of Milanese origin is leg of veal cut across the bone into 5 cm [2"] thick pieces. Literally translated, ossi bucchi means bones with holes and each portion should consist of the bone surrounded by meat, complete with marrow in the central hole. During cooking take great care to keep the marrow in place inside the bone, because devotees of osso buco like to dig out the marrow and eat it spread on a chunk of bread. Another special characteristic of an authentic osso buco is the 'gremolata', a mixture of lemon rind, garlic and parsley, sprinkled into the sauce just before serving. Being of Italian origin, this dish is normally cooked on top of the cooker. However, there is nothing to prevent you using the oven if this is more convenient and the oven should be heated to 150°C [300°F] gas mark 2. Osso buco should be served with a risotto.

SERVES 4
4 pieces shin of veal, each weighing about 275 g [10 oz]
15 ml [1 tablespoon] flour
1 small onion
1 small carrot
1 celery stick
45 ml [3 tablespoons] olive oil
1 bay leaf
150 ml [¼ pt] dry white wine
400 g [14 oz] canned, peeled tomatoes
salt
freshly ground black pepper

For the gremolata:
1 garlic clove
half a lemon
30 ml [2 tablespoons] chopped, fresh parsley

1 Wipe the pieces of meat with a damp cloth, taking care not to dislodge the marrow. Pat dry with kitchen paper.

2 Sprinkle each piece lightly with flour and rub in with your fingers.

3 Peel the onion and carrot and chop finely. Wash and finely chop the celery.

4 Heat the oil over a moderate heat in a wide sauté pan or flameproof casserole large enough to accommodate the pieces of meat in a single layer.

5 When the oil is sizzling hot put in the pieces of meat, increasing the heat to high. Quickly seal the meat, lightly browning each side, turning the pieces once.

6 Using a fish slice remove the pieces of meat to a plate and reserve.

7 Add the chopped vegetables and the bay leaf to the oil remaining in the pan and reduce the heat to low. Cover the pan and 'sweat' for 5–6 minutes, stirring or shaking the pan occasionally.

8 Pour in the wine, increase the heat to bring to the boil and allow to bubble briskly until the wine is reduced to about 30 ml [2 tablespoons].

9 Reduce the heat to low. Add the canned tomatoes and their juice, mashing them into the other vegetables, and season generously with salt and pepper.

10 Bring to simmering point and carefully replace the pieces of meat. These should stand on the cut edge of the bone, the other cut edge facing upwards, side by side. Take care not to dislodge the marrow.

11 Cover the pan tightly and simmer very gently for about 1½ hours, or until the meat is tender when pierced with a skewer.

12 Meanwhile prepare the gremolata. Peel and crush the garlic, finely grate the lemon zest and finely chop the parsley. Mix together and reserve.

13 Carefully lift out each osso buco and arrange them side by side in a warm, shallow heatproof dish. Cover and keep hot while the sauce is being prepared.

14 Pass the vegetables and cooking liquor through a food mill or sieve into a saucepan where they should form a fairly thick sauce. If the sauce is too thin, reduce it by boiling rapidly, uncovered, over a high heat. If the sauce is too thick, stir in a little stock or water and bring to the boil gradually, over a medium heat.

15 Check the seasoning. Stir in the gremolata and simmer for 3 minutes.

16 Pour over the veal and serve at once.

ABBACCHIO BRODETTATO

Baby lamb is considered a great delicacy in Italy, and this simple, fresh tasting dish from the Rome area is a great favourite. Relatively inexpensive shoulder of young lamb is the best cut to use, but leg of lamb could be used if preferred. The boned and cubed meat is stewed gently in stock and white wine, and the sauce thickened with egg yolks and flavoured with lemon juice and fresh herbs just before serving. To arrive at the correct boneless weight of the meat, the joint purchased should weigh 1.3 kg [2¾ lb] before boning. White pepper is specified in this recipe as the dish is pale coloured and black pepper grains would be visible.

SERVES 4
700 g [1½ lb] lean shoulder of lamb, boned weight
50 g [2 oz] slice of unsmoked streaky bacon or pickled pork belly
1 small onion
25 g [1 oz] lard
25 g [1 oz] flour
salt
white pepper
60 ml [4 tablespoons] dry white wine
300 ml [11 fl oz] stock
1 bay leaf
2 medium-sized egg yolks
15 ml [1 tablespoon] lemon juice
10 ml [2 teaspoons] chopped fresh parsley
5-10 ml [1-2 teaspoons] chopped marjoram

Two familiar meats, beef and pork, in two very different dishes. The beef is served in a rich, succulent wine-flavoured gravy while cider adds a punch to the pork.

1 Cut away and discard any gristle or coarse skin from the meat. Wipe with a damp cloth and cut the meat into rough 2.5 cm [1"] cubes.

2 Remove the rind, if any, from the bacon or pork and cut into small 8 mm [⅓"] dice. Peel and chop the onion.

3 Heat the lard in a flameproof casserole over medium heat. When sizzling hot put in the bacon or pork and onion. Fry for a minute and then add the lamb. Cook for 6-8 minutes, stirring frequently, until the onions are beginning to turn golden.

4 Sprinkle in the flour and season with salt and pepper. Cook, stirring, for another minute or so.

5 Add the wine and allow to bubble briskly until almost evaporated, then stir in the stock. Add the bay leaf.

6 Bring to boiling point and then immediately reduce heat to very low. Cover the pan tightly and simmer very gently for 45 minutes, or until the pieces of meat are tender when pierced with a fork. Stir occasionally.

7 Remove from heat and skim off any surplus fat by drawing a piece of kitchen paper across the surface of the stew.

8 If the liquid has evaporated considerably, make it up to 300 ml [11 fl oz] by adding a little extra stock. Check the seasoning, and remove the bay leaf.

9 When ready to serve beat together in a small basin the egg yolks, lemon juice, parsley and marjoram. Stir in 30 ml [2 tablespoons] of the hot lamb stock.

10 Stirring continuously, return this mixture to the brodettato and cook over very low heat until the egg has lightly thickened the sauce. On no account allow it to boil, or the sauce will curdle. Serve at once.

MANZO STUFATO

Traditional Italian cooking is done on the top of the stove rather than in the oven. This fact probably explains the Italian fondness for meat stews containing only a small amount of thick, richly flavoured gravy. This recipe is intended for lean first grade stewing meat such as chuck, blade or skirt. It is equally good with lean stewing veal. The recipe illustrates the use of a red wine marinade.

SERVES 5–6
1 kg [2¼ lb] lean stewing beef
1 large onion
45 ml [3 tablespoons] olive oil
100 g [¼ lb] sliced unsmoked streaky bacon or pickled pork belly
200 ml [7 fl oz] stock (optional)

For the marinade:
1 onion
3 garlic cloves
6 peppercorns
1 bay leaf
1 sprig thyme
1.5 ml [¼ teaspoon] salt
250 ml [½ pt] coarse red wine

1 Wipe the meat with a damp cloth and cut into large pieces about 12 mm [½"] thick and 5 cm [2"] square.

2 Prepare the marinade. Peel and slice the onion and garlic cloves, lightly crush the peppercorns and put all into a deep china basin. Add the bay leaf, thyme, salt and wine.

3 Put the meat into the marinade and stir to mix thoroughly. Cover lightly, and leave in a cool place for 5–6 hours, or overnight.

4 When ready to cook, peel and slice the onion. Heat the oil in a flameproof casserole over a medium heat. Fry the onion for 5 minutes.

5 Meanwhile lift the pieces of meat from the marinade and pat them dry with kitchen paper.

6 Add the meat to the onion and continue frying, stirring frequently, until the pieces of meat are sealed on all sides.

7 Cut the bacon into small cubes and stir into the pan.

8 Strain the marinade on to the meat

3 Sparingly grease a large frying or sauté pan with a bare minimum of oil and place over medium heat. When hot fry half of the meat, stirring frequently, until the fat begins to run from the pork and the flesh takes on a gold colour.

4 With a slotted spoon lift the meat from the fat and transfer to a large casserole, about 3.9 L [7 pt] capacity. Fry the rest of the meat and transfer to the casserole. Remove the pan from the heat.

5 Peel and slice the onions. Wash and finely slice the celery. Peel and crush the garlic. Wash, drain and shred the cabbage.

6 Return the pan to a low heat and fry the onions and celery in the fat that has run from the pork until the onions are beginning to soften. This will take about 10 minutes. Add the garlic and fry for another minute.

7 Sprinkle the flour over the vegetables in the pan. Fry, stirring, for a minute or two, then stir in the cider. Bring to the boil.

8 Pour the contents of the pan into the casserole, add the shredded cabbage and a generous seasoning of salt and pepper.

9 Crush the juniper berries (if used) and add to the casserole. Stir to mix the ingredients thoroughly. Lay the reserved bones on top.

10 Bring the casserole to simmering point over a low heat. Cover tightly and transfer to the centre of the oven. Cook for 2–2½ hours, until the pork is tender when pierced with a fork. Check the rate of cooking occasionally and adjust the oven temperature to maintain a bare simmer.

11 Remove the bones and check the seasoning, stir in the parsley and serve straight from the casserole.

and add the stock or the same amount of water.

9 Bring to simmering point, then reduce heat to very low. Cover tightly and simmer very gently for 3 hours, or until the meat is soft and tender when pierced with a fork. Check the rate of cooking from time to time, and if necessary use a wire or asbestos mat under the pan to maintain a bare simmer.

10 The liquid should be thick and of just sufficient quantity to cover the meat. If it has not reduced sufficiently by the time the meat is tender, transfer the meat to a shallow serving dish and keep warm. Reduce the liquid by boiling in the uncovered pan.

11 Skim off any surface fat and check the seasoning. Pour over the meat and serve immediately.

PORK, CABBAGE AND CIDER CASSEROLE

◨◨◨ *This is not a classic dish but a substantial family meat and vegetable casserole. It uses cider to add flavour to one of the cheaper cuts of pork. Extra flavour can be added if* wished by using double the quantity of cider specified and reducing this by half by boiling before use. The cider should be cooled before it is added to the casserole.

This dish can be served covered with lots of crisply fried croûtons or be accompanied by potatoes.

SERVES 6
900 g [2 lb] lean belly of pork, in a piece
5 ml [1 teaspoon] oil
225 g [½ lb] onions
2 celery sticks
1 large garlic clove
450 g [1 lb] white cabbage
30 ml [2 tablespoons] flour
275 ml [½ pt] dry cider
5 ml [1 teaspoon] salt
freshly ground black pepper
12 juniper berries (optional)
30 ml [2 tablespoons] chopped fresh parsley

1 Heat the oven to 150°C [300°F] gas mark 2.

2 Wipe the meat with a damp cloth. Slip a knife under the rib bones and remove them in one piece. Reserve. Cut the meat roughly into 2.5 cm [1"] cubes.

CARBONNADES A LA FLAMANDE

◨◨◨ *Using local ingredients is a natural instinct of all good cooks. It is therefore not surprising that this Flemish national beef casserole contains beer. Beer and onions have a* natural affinity, so traditional recipes contain a high proportion of onion and a noticeable flavouring of garlic. The slight bitterness of the beer is balanced by the addition of a little sugar and a piquancy is added with a dash of vinegar at the end. Both the beer and the stock help to give a natural brown colour, so it is not necessary to make a brown roux. The casserole can be very simply thickened with cornflour shortly before serving. For this reason there is little danger of the casserole sticking when slowly simmering on top of the cooker.

If you do not have any home-made beef stock to hand, a can of beef consommé may be used instead. This dish is particularly suitable for freezing. It should be very gently and thoroughly reheated over low heat and the result will be a full flavoured casserole with a beautifully smooth sauce.

SERVES 6
**900 g [2 lb] lean chuck
   or blade beef steak
450 g [1 lb] onions
3 garlic cloves
40 g [1½ oz] dripping or
   45 ml [3 tablespoons] oil
salt
freshly ground black pepper
150 ml [¼ pt] strong beef
   stock
400 ml [¾ pt] light ale or
   lager
15 ml [1 tablespoon] brown
   sugar
bouquet garni
15 ml [1 tablespoon] cornflour
25 ml [1½ tablespoons] wine
   vinegar**

1 Peel and thinly slice the onions. Peel the garlic cloves and crush them with the blade of a knife.

2 Cut away and discard any sinew or excess fat on the meat, wipe with a damp cloth and cut into slices about 8 mm [⅓"] thick and then into 5 × 7.5 cm [2 × 3"] strips.

3 Heat the fat or oil over a high heat in a wide, heavy-based frying-pan. When sizzling hot add half the meat and brown quickly on all sides. Remove with a slotted spoon and transfer to a flameproof casserole or large heavy-based saucepan.

4 Fry the rest of the meat and

transfer it to the casserole.

5 Reduce the heat to medium, stir the onions into the fat remaining in the pan and cook for 6–8 minutes, stirring frequently, until they are beginning to soften and brown slightly.

6 Add the garlic, a good seasoning of salt and pepper and cook for 1 minute. Then transfer onions and garlic to the casserole.

7 Pour the stock and beer into the frying-pan and heat, stirring with a wooden spoon to scrape up the coagulated juices from the base of the pan.

8 Add the beer and stock to the casserole. Stir in the sugar and bury the bouquet garni in the centre of the casserole.

9 Bring the casserole to simmering point, cover tightly and reduce the heat to maintain a bare simmer. Cook for 2¼–2½ hours until the meat is very tender when pierced with a fork.

10 Skim off any surface fat.

11 Blend the cornflour smoothly with the vinegar in a cup. Add a few spoonfuls of the hot liquid and blend thoroughly. Add to the casserole, increase heat slightly and simmer, stirring, for several minutes until thickened.

12 There should be about 300 ml [11 fl oz] of sauce. If there is much more than this, ladle off as much of the sauce as you can into a small saucepan. This is safer than trying to pour the liquid from the hot, heavy casserole. Put the saucepan over a high heat and boil rapidly, uncovered, to reduce the sauce. When the quantity is correct, return it to the casserole. Check the seasoning and serve from the casserole.

SPICED BACON CHOPS
Although not strictly a stew or casserole, this is an interesting dish because it is so simple, quick and practical. The cider provides a rich sauce for mildly cured bacon. The pineapple adds a refreshing contrast in flavour, and the spices can be changed

or adjusted to suit individual tastes. The cornflour is just sufficient to lightly and smoothly thicken the sauce and is added in the early stages of cooking which is unusual. Plain boiled rice makes an appropriate accompaniment.

SERVES 4
**4 mildly cured lean bacon
   chops
275 ml [½ pt] strong, dry
   cider
2 cloves
15 g [½ oz] butter
15 ml [1 tablespoon] cornflour
75 g [3 oz] Demerara sugar
2.5 ml [½ teaspoon] dry
   mustard
1.5 ml [¼ teaspoon] ground
   ginger
1.5 ml [¼ teaspoon] grated
   nutmeg
50 g [2 oz] firm button
   mushrooms
4 pineapple rings, fresh or
   canned and drained**

1 Heat the oven to 180°C [350°F] gas mark 4. Pour the cider into a wide saucepan. Add the cloves and boil, uncovered, until reduced to 150 ml [¼ pt]. This will take about 8 minutes. Allow to cool.

2 Remove the rind, if any, from the chops.

3 Butter a shallow baking dish large enough to hold the chops in a single layer.

4 Arrange the chops in a single layer in the centre of the baking dish.

5 Into a small bowl measure the cornflour, sugar, mustard, ginger and nutmeg (or other spices of your choice).

6 Mix thoroughly and spoon evenly over the chops.

7 Wipe the mushrooms with a damp cloth and trim the stalks. Slice finely and arrange around the edge of the chops.

8 Lay a pineapple slice on each chop and pour the reduced cider gently over the whole dish.

9 Cover tightly with foil and cook in the centre of the oven for 25–30 minutes.

Mincing matters

Minced meat is universally popular and forms part of many traditional dishes throughout the world. The process of mincing improves the texture of cheaper cuts of meat by breaking up the tough connective tissue and significantly reduces the cooking time. Mince mixes well with other ingredients to provide dishes for snacks and meals. Tasty pies and patties from mince abound.

Mincing meat is unquestionably the key to making many interesting low-cost meals. Although good quality meat can be used, the great advantage of mincing is that it is a means of making tough meat tender, without the inconvenience of long, slow cooking. The mincer breaks up the connective tissue and makes the meat easy to chew. The heat is able to penetrate between the particles so that the meat cooks relatively quickly.

Meat can be minced coarsely or finely, but the tougher the meat the more finely it needs to be minced. Coarsely minced meat retains more of its natural flavour and produces dishes with a fairly rough texture. Finely minced meat is, obviously, more smooth and more tender but loses more flavour during the mincing process. It binds and holds together more readily than coarse mince and the loss of flavour can be compensated by adding spices and herbs and piquant sauces.

Binding and shaping minced meat are discussed on pages 101–110.

BUYING MINCED MEAT

Always buy minced meat the day you intend to use it, never before. The meat comes into contact with so many different surfaces that the danger of bacterial infection is greatly increased when it has been minced.

Away from major towns, the only minced meat likely to be regularly on sale is beef, although veal and lamb can sometimes be bought.

There is no recognized standard for minced meat and it is a product that varies from shop to shop. Each butcher prepares his mince to suit his trade so one mince may be finer or coarser, leaner or fattier than the one next door. There are also, nearly always, at least two grades of mince on sale in each shop. The only answer, therefore, is to shop around to find the mince which suits your purpose best.

Beef mince should, of course, be a healthy red colour and veal and lamb, pink: beware of brownish or greyish coloured mince. The fineness of the mincing is easily discernible and, as the fat shows up in little white pieces, the meatier looking the mince the more lean it is likely to be.

A more reliable method of buying mince is to select the cut of meat you want and to ask the butcher to mince it for you. Most butchers will be happy to do so, provided you pick a convenient time. In this way, you can have veal, lamb and pork minced, as well as beef. Remember to allow a few grams (ounces) extra for trimmings and be sure to state whether you want fine or coarse mince.

MINCING MEAT

If you have an efficient electric or hand mincer it is a simple matter to make your own mince. Always leave mincing the meat until the last possible moment and if you have had to buy the meat the day before you intend to use it, store it in the piece, never minced. Mincing meat by hand takes some time and it is rather inconvenient not being able to do this in advance. However, it really is important from a health point of view.

MEAT FOR MINCING

BEEF

Butcher's mince	Varies from butcher to butcher according to cuts and trimmings available. Use for general purposes.
Leg and shin	Well-flavoured lean mince. Difficult to mince in hand mincer, owing to sinews. Mince shin finely.
Neck (clod and sticking)	Easy to mince and makes good gravy. Good choice for meat sauces or pie fillings.
Chuck or blade	More expensive mince for special meat balls or hamburgers.

LAMB

Shoulder	The meat must be lean or mince will be too fatty. Use for general purposes.
Middle neck and scrag	Good value. Mince the meat and use the bones to make good broth.

PORK

Boned hand/spare rib/shoulder	Relatively lean, general-purpose mince.
Belly (streaky)	Rich mince for pâtés and faggots.
Back fat	Sometimes minced with very lean meat to provide fat.

VEAL

Stewing/pie veal, breast	Difficult to judge quality owing to variation in size and type of carcasses—ask butcher's advice.

Equipment

Follow the manufacturer's instructions when assembling your machine and make sure that you fit the appropriate mincing plate. Electric machines are heavy enough to stand unsupported but hand machines must be firmly secured in place, either with a clamp or by suction pads.

When secure, consider the quantity of the ingredients to be minced and put a suitable-sized bowl under the mincing plates to catch the mince. Use a wooden spoon to push the mince down into the spiral grinder in the mincer.

The meat

Cut any skin, gristle and excess fat from the meat. Wipe the meat with a damp cloth and cut it into small pieces of a convenient size to feed into the mincer. Feed the meat in, a few pieces at a time, pushing it down with the wooden spoon. If you want very fine mince, or if the meat is particularly tough, put it through the mincer twice. The mince will accumulate tidily in the bowl with any bread, vegetables or other ingredients that are to be minced.

Cooked meat is minced in exactly the same way. The only preparation necessary is to cut away any bones and to cut the meat into cubes.

USING COOKED MEAT

Now that the large Sunday roast is virtually a thing of the past, the problem of thinking up interesting ways of using the left-over meat does not arise very often. When you do have meat left over, mincing it is a good way to convert it into another appetizing, hot meal. A little meat can go a long way when minced and used with other filling ingredients. It is also a good method from a health point of view, as the meat is thoroughly reheated and not just warmed up, which is inadvisable.

When using cooked meat there are a few points to remember. Firstly, the meat will have lost much of its natural juiciness and may be rather dry. Add plenty of moisture to the dish in the form of gravy, sauce or moist vegetables. The meat will also have lost some of its flavour and taste rather flat. Flavourings, such as herbs, spices, garlic, vegetables, bacon, wine and piquant sauces are easily added. Raw ingredients can be minced with the meat, which is minced in exactly the same way as raw meat, and cooked vegetables and liquids can be added during cooking.

Cooked meat can be stored, loosely covered with cling film or foil, in the refrigerator for 2-3 days. The sooner it is minced the juicier it will be but, once minced, it must be used the same day.

STRETCHING MINCE

The problem of making meat go further is not a new one. One of the reasons for the everlasting popularity of mince is that generations of housewives all over the world have found that mince can be extended in attractive ways, so that a relatively small amount of meat can feed and nourish a large family.

Many traditional extenders also contribute extra protein which increases the nutritive value of the dish. These include bread, pulse vegetables, pasta and pastry. Recently, the desire to extend meat without reducing the protein value of the meal has prompted the development of a meat substitute in the form of soya protein.

Bread can be used in various ways, either fresh, toasted, fried or crumbed. Fresh bread or rusk is minced with the meat and, as long as it is not used in too high a proportion, it blends in and becomes indistinguishable from the meat. Stale or dried bread is soaked in milk or water before being forked into the meat. Fried or toasted bread is used either to line the dish or to form a crisp topping. Breadcrumbs are mixed with the mince, used in layers, used as a coating around mince shapes, or fried and used as a topping.

Pulses are cooked with minced meat to produce nourishing and filling main dishes. Pre-cooked haricot beans are probably the most popular but red kidney beans, butter beans and split peas can all be used.

Potatoes are nearly always used mashed. Their main contribution is starch and bulk. They are combined with the meat to form meat and potato cakes, used as a topping or piped around the mince as a decorative border. Sliced, parboiled potatoes can be layered into the meat in dishes which do not use mashed potato.

Grated or finely chopped vegetables not only extend the meat but add flavour and vitamins too. Grated carrots are popular because they mix unobtrusively with the mince. There is no reason why the vegetables should always be indistinguishable. A more flavoursome mixture is the classic Italian one of gently sautéing finely chopped onion, carrot and celery together before adding the meat. This is used for a sauce, a pie filling or as a stuffing for vegetables.

Pasta, rice and polenta (maize flour) are the traditional extenders in Italian cooking. In the south of Italy, combinations of meat and pasta predominate to produce dishes of international popularity but in the north, rice and polenta are much favoured. There are many varieties of pasta, differing greatly in shape and size, from long thin spaghetti to tiny shells.

Pastry is one of the most successful and attractive ways of extending any food. Meat pies, both single crust and double crust are popular and shortcrust, flaky and puff can be used. Pastry can also be used as a casing, wrapped around the cooked mince.

Milk, with a little flour, combines to stretch minced pork. The meat absorbs the liquid before it is cooked and is then made into little patties and fried (see recipe for frickadeller on page 107).

Soya substitutes are becoming popular. Several brands of either textured or spun soya protein are now available in granule or 'chunky' form. They are sold either plain, seasoned or flavoured with beef or chicken. Although it is possible to make a dish from soya alone, most people find it far more useful and acceptable when used with meat to make this go further. For using with mince, you need the granule form. Used according to the packet directions it can be virtually undetectable, as well as a very convenient and nutritious way of making meat go further. The proportion of soya you use is a matter of personal preference and it is worth experimenting with different brands. The product is light and easy to store. In a dry cupboard it should have a shelf life of at least a year.

COOKING MINCE

Fresh minced meat always includes a certain proportion of fat. This is unavoidable but has the bonus of keeping the meat tender. It means, though, that very little extra fat is needed to cook the mince.

Minced meat, when used unshaped, is generally fried to give it a light browning. It can be fried after it has been formed into shapes but can also be grilled, simmered in a sauce, baked or poached in water. Better quality mince is used when it is to be shaped, and this is discussed on pages 101–110. General-purpose type mince and the cheaper cuts are best browned and then cooked gently in moist heat for as long as necessary to become tender.

The pan is merely greased with fat and frying is brief and is carried out over a high heat. The best fat to use for flavour is dripping but oil and margarine are also perfectly acceptable. Onion, garlic or herbs can be fried in the fat first to add flavour (for an onion use a little more fat). The mince is then added and stirred over the heat until it turns from red to brown. The stock or other moist vegetables are added and cooking continues at a gentle simmer, on top of the cooker or in the oven, until the meat is thoroughly cooked. This takes no longer than half an hour.

Cooked mince does not need to be browned, but it does need to be thoroughly heated. The raw vegetables, such as onions and peppers, are cooked first until soft. The moist ingredients are then added and are simmered with the vegetables for a moment before the meat is added. In this way, the meat goes straight into a moist atmosphere and there is no danger of it drying out. Cooked mince is particularly useful when the mixture has to be cooked before it can be used, for example for stuffing vegetables. It reduces the cooking time considerably and is an excellent way of using up a small amount of leftover meat.

SHEPHERD'S PIE

Well made, this classic British way of using up cold cooked meat is a perennial favourite with young and old alike. The secret is a moist and well-flavoured meat layer topped with buttery creamed potatoes which have been allowed to acquire a richly browned surface—even if this means finishing it off under the grill.

Use butter and cream (not milk) to purée the potatoes with. Do not include the optional herbs as herbs are included with the meat. If possible, make and serve the pie in a brown earthenware casserole.

Cottage pie is believed by some to be exactly the same mixture, made with cooked beef instead of lamb.

SERVES 4
350 g [¾ lb] cold cooked lamb
1 medium-sized onion
4 tomatoes
25 g [1 oz] dripping
10 ml [2 teaspoons] flour
150 ml [¼ pt] thin gravy or meat stock
5 ml [1 teaspoon] dry mixed herbs
15 ml [1 tablespoon] Worcestershire sauce
salt
freshly ground black pepper

For the topping:
450 g [1 lb] creamed potatoes
15 g [½ oz] butter

1 Heat the oven to 190°C [375°F] gas mark 5.

2 Cut any skin or gristle from the meat and cut into rough 2.5 cm [1"] cubes. Pass once through the coarse blades of a mincer.

3 Peel and finely chop the onion; peel and quarter the tomatoes.

4 Heat the fat in a saucepan over low heat and fry the onion gently for about 8 minutes, until soft and beginning to turn golden.

5 Sprinkle in the flour, stir and cook gently for a minute. Off the heat, stir in the gravy or stock. Return to the heat, stir until boiling and simmer for a minute or two.

6 Add the minced meat, tomatoes, herbs and Worcestershire sauce and salt and pepper to taste. Turn into a deep ovenproof dish and smooth the surface.

7 Spread or pipe the creamed potatoes over the layer of mince. If spread over, roughen the surface by drawing a fork across it, first in one direction and then the other.

8 Dot with butter and put in the oven. Bake for 20–30 minutes, until heated through, bubbling and well browned. Remove from the oven and serve immediately.

MOUSSAKA

This is the shepherd's pie of Greece. The succulent combination of fried aubergines, delicately spiced minced lamb and rich cheese sauce is irresistible and well worth the rather lengthy preparation. It is always popular at informal parties and can be prepared earlier in the day for final cooking and browning in the evening. There are many variations—for instance minced beef is sometimes used instead of lamb, and courgettes are very successful in place of aubergines. Some recipes include layers of sliced potatoes or breadcrumbs to make a more substantial pie. The recipe requires 425 ml [¾ pt] béchamel sauce of coating consistency, that is of medium thickness. Serve the moussaka with a green salad.

SERVES 6
700 g [1½ lb] shoulder of lamb, boneless weight
700 g [1½ lb] aubergines
salt
175 g [6 oz] onions
225 g [½ lb] tomatoes
150 ml [¼ pt] olive oil
5 ml [1 teaspoon] ground allspice

15 ml [1 tablespoon] freshly
  chopped parsley
freshly ground black pepper
425 ml [¾ pt] béchamel sauce,
  coating consisting
1 large egg
large pinch grated nutmeg
75 g [3 oz] Cheddar cheese

1 Wipe, top and tail, but do not peel the aubergines. Cut them into slices about 6 mm [¼"] thick. Put into a colander with a light sprinkling of salt between the layers and leave to drain for half an hour.

2 Prepare the meat for mincing and mince once, coarsely. Peel and slice the onions; peel, de-seed and chop the tomatoes.

3 When ready to cook, pat the aubergine slices dry with paper.

4 Heat 45 ml [3 tablespoons] oil in a frying-pan over low heat and, when hot, fry the aubergine slices gently until tender, in batches and turning once. Lift out and drain on absorbent paper. Add extra oil between batches as necessary.

5 When all are fried, make the oil in the pan up to 30 ml [2 tablespoons] again. When this is hot, fry the onions gently for about 5 minutes, until soft and pale gold.

6 Add the meat and fry, stirring, until lightly browned. Add the tomatoes, allspice, parsley and salt and pepper to taste. Stir well, cover, and cook very gently for 15 to 20 minutes.

7 Heat oven to 180°C [350°F] gas mark 4.

8 In a deep, ovenproof dish, arrange alternate layer of aubergines and meat, finishing with aubergines.

9 Warm the sauce over low heat. Separate the egg and, off the heat, stir the yolk, nutmeg and salt and pepper to taste, into the sauce. Reserve the egg white for use in another dish.

10 Pour the sauce evenly over the surface of the dish. Grate the cheese over the sauce.

11 Bake in the oven for 45 minutes, until the topping is golden and bubbling.

The popularity of moussaka has deservedly spread. It is a delicious combination of meat, vegetables and a thick, rich sauce.

CHILLI CON CARNE

Here is a dish for a hungry family which enjoys bold flavours.

SERVES 4

175 g [6 oz] red kidney beans,
  soaked
3 medium-sized onions
4 cloves
4 garlic cloves
bouquet garni
6 large dried chillies
450 g [1 lb] chuck steak
1 red pepper
20 ml [4 teaspoons] oil
15 ml [1 tablespoon] tomato
  purée
7.5 ml [1½ teaspoon] salt

1 Put the kidney beans and the water in which they have been soaking into a saucepan. Add more water if necessary, to cover the beans by at least 1.25 cm [½"].

2 Peel one onion and stick the cloves into it. Peel 2 garlic cloves and add these, the onion and the bouquet garni to the beans. Bring the pan to simmering point over medium heat, reduce heat to very low, cover pan and simmer very gently for 1½ hours or until tender.

3 While the beans are cooking, soak the chillies in a mug of hot water for an hour.

4 Lift the chillies out of the mug and reserve the, by now, cold water. Pull the stalks from the chillies, slit down the length of each chilli and flush away the seeds from inside, under cold running water. Chop chillies very finely. Mince meat.

5 Peel and finely chop the remaining onions and garlic. Halve, de-seed and chop the pepper.

6 Heat the oil in a large heavy-based frying-pan over medium heat. When hot, fry the onion and garlic for five minutes until beginning to soften and then add the meat, the chillies and the red pepper.

7 Stir the meat around, breaking it up with a fork, until it turns from red to brown. Then add a little of the reserved chilli water and reduce the heat.

8 After about ten minutes, drain the kidney beans and reserve the liquor. Stir the beans into the pan.

9 Dissolve the tomato purée in about 30 ml [2 tablespoons] kidney bean liquor and add to the pan. Add salt and check seasoning.

10 Simmer for 15 minutes.

100

Shaping up to mince

Minced meat can be bound into all shapes and sizes from marbles to bolsters. The recipes originate from all over the world, from the American hamburger to the Moroccan kefta and the flavours are as different as the countries of origin. Snacks and supper dishes predominate but, with a few accessories, dinner party dishes emerge from surprisingly cheap ingredients.

Minced meat undoubtedly provides value-for-money dishes. A little goes a long way and cheap cuts of meat are often used. Mincing meat, the best cuts to use, extending the mince with added nourishing and filling ingredients and recipes for many delicious pies are discussed on pages 95–100 in detail. Here we continue with the story of mince, visiting many countries to find recipes where the mince is bound and shaped before being cooked.

Minced shapes make the most of small amounts of meat. The meat is prepared and minced, and can also be stretched, in the same way as when it is used in pies. Raw minced beef, pork, lamb and veal can be used for preparing shaped mince dishes and practically every method of cooking can be utilized.

SHAPING THE MINCE

The mince is generally shaped with the hands and usually on a very lightly floured or dampened surface. This prevents the mixture from sticking. The shapes themselves are varied, ranging from balls, patties, croquettes and hamburgers to larger quantities of mince which are shaped into bolsters or cooked in loaf tins, cake tins or ring moulds.

The method of binding varies according to the texture required, as does the mincing of the meat.

When a loose texture is required, eg American hamburgers, the meat is coarsely ground and the only binding agent is the meat juices which coagulate on cooking and hold the particles of meat together.

When a smooth texture is required, as for meat balls, the meat is finely minced and sometimes even pounded almost to a smooth paste. The particles of finely minced meat hold together more readily than coarsely minced meat and smaller shapes will stay intact during cooking without an added binding agent.

The mixture may also be prepared and baked in a tin, which enforces a shape on it as with meat loaves.

Methods of binding

The most common method of binding minced meat is to use beaten egg. The egg proteins, like those of meat, coagulate on contact with heat and hold the ingredients together. Egg is needed when other ingredients, such as breadcrumbs or rice, have been mixed with the meat before shaping.

Another sure way of binding mince

is to use a protective coating. An egg and breadcrumb coating is the most efficient and this and other coatings and their application are discussed on pages 42–43.

Cooked mince is more difficult to bind. The meat is drier than fresh mince and does not hold together readily. A strong binding agent is needed and a thick paste of fat, flour and liquid is used. The shapes can then be coated with egg and bread-crumbs, for example, and deep fried to seal them completely.

HAMBURGERS

Few recipes are more typical of present-day America than hamburg-ers, which take their name from the German city of Hamburg. Yet by no means all English-speaking people know what a real hamburger should look and taste like. For a start, anything that contains ham is not a hamburger and nor are mixtures made from pre-cooked mince or general-purpose mince.

A true hamburger is made from good quality, lean beef, coarsely ground and, when cooked, it is thick and juicy. The average size is 100 g [¼ lb] which, when served in a warm bun, is sufficient for all but the most insatiable appetites.

The surest way of getting the right meat is to buy boneless chuck steak and to mince it at home, coarsely and only once. This way, the mince will be absolutely fresh and will retain more juice, flavour and texture. Hamburger mince should always be coarse and should just be able to hold together when shaped. When mixing and shaping, the meat should be handled as little as possible, to avoid com-pacting it. The juices coagulate during cooking and hold the burger in shape without the addition of any other binding.

It is also common, but not in America, to see hamburgers made from a mixture of good quality, lean beef and breadcrumbs which are bound together with beaten egg. Herbs are included and the result is equally tasty but less meaty fla-voured than the all-beef American -type hamburger which is described here (see below).

Cooking hamburgers

All-beef hamburgers can be grilled or fried rare, medium or well done, just like steak. The meat can be seasoned with pepper before it is shaped and should also be salted as this encourages the juices to run. This is contrary to the usual tech-nique of frying meat.

Grilling: heat the grill until very hot and cook hamburgers on a grid about 7·5 cm [3"] below the heat. Grill turning once, for 2–3 minutes each side for rare, 3–4 minutes each side

Step-by-step to making hamburgers

1 Trim any skin or gristle from the meat. Cut the meat into cubes and mince once, coarsely.

2 Then salt and pepper the mince. Turn on to a flat surface and divide into 100 g [¼ lb] piles.

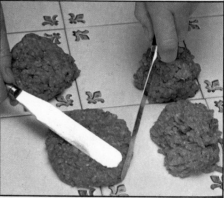

3 Using two palette knives, lightly flatten the piles and shape into rounds 1·25 cm [½"] thick.

4 Heat 15 ml [1 tablespoon] oil in a heavy-based frying-pan. When hot, add hamburgers, one by one.

5 Fry for 3–4 minutes for medium. Turn once with a fish slice and a palette knife.

6 Fry second side for 3–4 minutes. Lift from the pan, add topping and sandwich in a hot bun.

for medium and 5 minutes each side for well done.

Frying: grease a heavy-based frying-pan with oil and heat until sizzling hot. Lower in the hamburgers, one by one, and fry in a single layer over medium heat until browned on each side and cooked to your liking. The cooking times are the same as for grilling.

Flavourings for hamburgers

The mince for hamburgers can be flavoured before it is shaped. This is a particularly good idea if you wish to serve the hamburgers plain. Any of the following can be added to 450 g [1 lb] minced meat:

●50 g [2 oz] grated raw onion
●15 ml [1 tablespoon] each chopped parsley, chopped chives and Worcestershire sauce
●30 ml [2 tablespoons] finely chopped mixed pickles and 5 ml [1 teaspoon] French mustard
●a finely chopped garlic clove
●15 ml [1 tablespoon] cumin seeds, heated and pounded before adding.

Serving hamburgers

Serve the hamburgers in warm sesame seed buns. If you cannot find this particular type of bun, any variety of soft roll will do. Crusty rolls are not suitable. The rolls can be split and warmed in the oven if you are cooking for a large number, or lightly toasted under the grill.

Hamburgers are particularly succulent and tasty when served with a topping or with a selection of relishes. The topping is sandwiched between the hamburger and one half of the bun while relishes can be served separately and people can help themselves. American-type relishes are available in this country.

Hamburger ideas

●Try Spanish bolero hamburgers. Cream 40 g [1½ oz] butter with 30 ml [2 tablespoons] finely chopped stuffed olives and 10 ml [2 teaspoons] tomato ketchup. Spread over lower half of bun before adding cooked burger. Spear top of bun with a cocktail stick threaded with 2 or 3 stuffed olives.

●For blue cheese burgers, cream 40 g [1½ oz] butter with 50 g [2 oz] crumbled blue cheese plus a large pinch of dry English mustard. Spread over cooked burger before sandwiching in a hot bun.

●To make bacon burgers, wrap raw hamburgers in very thin rashers of streaky bacon and grill, turning once, until meat is cooked to your liking and the bacon crisp.

●For cheese and bacon burgers, top a cooked bacon burger with a slice of cheese and grill until cheese is bubbling. Choose a cheese that melts readily such as Bel Paese, Gruyère or processed cheese.

●Try cheese and tomato burgers. Top each freshly cooked burger with a thick slice of tomato and a thin slice of a cheese that melts readily. Put under the grill until bubbling, then sandwich in a hot roll.

●To make a salad topper, layer a bun with a lettuce leaf, thin slice of raw onion and thick slice of tomato. Put in the hot burger and top it with sliced dill cucumber.

MEAT BALLS

While hamburgers are an American dish, meat balls hail from the Middle East. The meat balls can be made from beef or lamb or from a combination of beef, lamb, pork and veal. The important thing to remember is that whatever meat is used, it needs to be fairly lean and it must be very finely minced so that the ground meat clings together and holds its shape.

Meat balls are made smaller than hamburgers and are rolled more firmly. The meat is minced up to three times through the fine blades of the mincer and is then divided into portions with a spoon. The meat balls can be as small as a marble. The portions are then shaped into balls with the hands or by rolling under the palm of the hand against a flat surface. The surface should be dampened or floured to prevent the mixture from sticking.

The meat balls will hold their shape without a binding agent but, when extending ingredients such as rice, bread, cracked wheat or potatoes are added to the meat, an egg can be used to hold the mixture together.

Flavouring meat balls

Meat balls are often served highly spiced. This is, of course, due to their Middle Eastern heritage where spices are used abundantly. Allspice, cinnamon, cumin, ginger, coriander and nutmeg are among the spices used. Grated onion, garlic, herbs, pine nuts, seedless raisins and tomato purée are other favourite additions.

Cooking meat balls

One reason for their popularity must be their versatility. Meat balls can be fried, grilled, baked, simmered in a sauce or poached in water and then finished in a sauce or fried or grilled.

Meat balls are fried or grilled in the same way as hamburgers and other minced meat shapes. The heat should be high and a minimum of cooking fat is used. The balls should, however, be turned frequently to ensure even browning. Cooking time is brief as the shapes are small, but they should be cooked through. Ten minutes is the average time needed.

When the meat balls are simmered or poached they are added to hot sauce or water. The heat is reduced to simmering point or just below and the meat balls are cooked for about ten to twenty minutes, according to their size.

MEAT BALLS IN SWEET SOUR SAUCE

This is a recipe which will soon become a family favourite. The meat balls are first browned in fat and then left to finish their cooking in a sweet sour sauce, thick with crunchy vegetables. It is delicious served with buttered tagliatelle. Use beef alone or a mixture of beef and lean belly of pork.

SERVES 4
450 g [1 lb] lean beef
50 g [2 oz] fresh breadcrumbs
1 medium-sized egg
salt
freshly ground black pepper
25 g [1 oz] flour
45 ml [3 tablespoons] oil

For the sauce:
1 small onion
1 medium-sized carrot
1 large leek
2 celery sticks
50 g [2 oz] button mushrooms
10 ml [2 teaspoons] cornflour
10 ml [2 teaspoons] sugar
15 ml [1 tablespoon] tomato ketchup
15 ml [1 tablespoon] wine vinegar
10 ml [2 teaspoons] soy sauce
salt and pepper

1 Trim the meat and mince very finely, two or three times through the fine blades of a mincer. Beat the egg lightly.

2 Put the mince, breadcrumbs, egg, and seasonings in a bowl. Add 15 ml [1 tablespoon] water and beat firmly with a wooden spoon until thoroughly mixed.

3 Turn the mixture on to a lightly floured board and divide into 16 portions.

4 Flour your hand and roll each portion firmly between the palm of your hand and the board to form a ball.

5 Cover the meat balls with grease-proof paper and refrigerate while preparing the other ingredients.

6 Peel and chop the onion. Peel the carrot, slice lengthways and then across into strips. Trim, wash and slice the leek into thin rounds, wash and slice the celery and wipe and halve or quarter the mushrooms, according to size.

7 Heat the oil in a large sauté pan with a lid over medium heat and, when sizzling hot, fry the meat balls, in two batches if necessary, until browned all over. Shake the pan gently so that the balls turn over and cook evenly. Lift out, drain on crumpled kitchen paper and reserve.

8 Put all the vegetables into the pan, lower the heat and fry gently uncovered, stirring from time to time, for about 10 minutes.

9 Meanwhile, put the cornflour and sugar in a bowl and gradually stir in 250 ml [½ pt] water. Stir in the ketchup, vinegar and soy sauce.

10 Pour this mixture over the vege-

Step-by-step to shaping meat balls

1 The meat must be very finely minced. Trim and cube the meat and mince finely, 2 or 3 times.

2 Add the flavourings and extending ingredients stated in the recipe. Lightly beat an egg and add.

tables in the pan and stir until it comes to boiling point.

11 Return the meat balls to the pan, season to taste with salt and pepper, cover, and simmer gently for 30 minutes.

12 Serve hot with buttered tagliatelle.

Variation
●For Swedish meat balls, make the meat balls steps 1–4 but, before shaping them, beat in 15 ml [1 tablespoon] onion, which has been very finely chopped and sautéed in butter until soft. Fry the balls gently until completely cooked, shaking the pan frequently. When cooked, re-move to a hot serving dish. Add 150 ml [¼ pt] water or stock to the pan, and scrape up the coagulated juices from the base. Blend 15 ml [1 tablespoon] flour with 150 ml [¼ pt] thin cream, add to the pan and stir until boiling. Simmer for 10 minutes, check the seasoning, and pour over the meat balls. Serve with sautéed potatoes, creamed root vegetables and pickled gherkins.

LYON-STYLE MINCED BEEF CAKES
The French bring their own inimi-table style to preparing and serving minced beef cakes. They sound more elegant as bifteck haché à la Lyonnaise, and they taste more lavish because the frying-pan is deglazed to make a little sauce to moisten the cakes. Wine is preferable, either red or dry white, but beef stock can be used. Select your herbs from those available, choosing

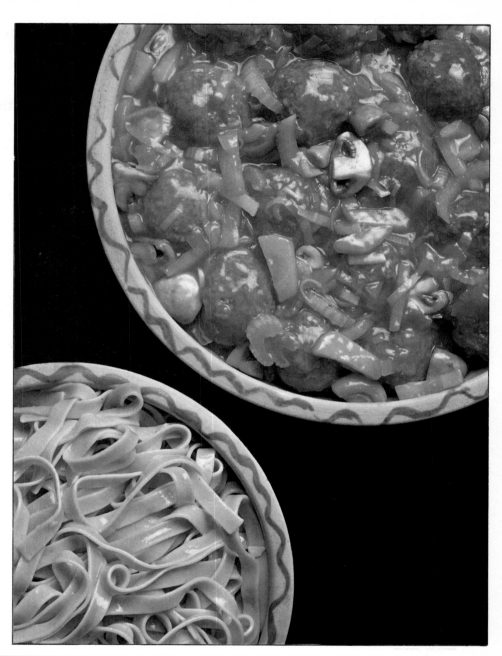

3 Pound the mixture well with a wooden spoon to bind. Turn on to a lightly floured surface.

4 Taking a spoonful of the mixture at a time, roll it into a ball between the palms of your hands.

OR roll the ball with one hand against the floured surface. Cover and refrigerate until needed.

from parsley, chives, tarragon and chervil, and use a good-quality lean beef, not too finely minced.

SERVES 4
450 g [1 lb] chuck steak
1 small onion
50 g [2 oz] butter
1 medium-sized egg
salt
freshly ground black pepper
45 ml [3 tablespoons] flour
15 ml [1 tablespoon] oil
150 ml [¼ pt] wine
15 ml [1 tablespoon] chopped
  fresh herbs
sprigs of watercress to garnish

1 Prepare the meat and mince finely once.

2 Peel the onion and chop very finely. Melt 25 g [1 oz] butter in a saucepan over low heat and fry the onion very gently for about 10 minutes, until soft but not coloured.

3 Add the minced beef, the egg and salt and pepper to taste. Beat until thoroughly mixed.

4 Divide into 4 and, on a board, shape each portion into a round cake about 2 cm [¾"] thick.

5 Put the flour on a plate and turn each meat cake in it to coat lightly. Shake gently to dislodge surplus flour.

6 Put the oil into a large frying-pan, place over medium heat and, when sizzling hot, put in the meat cakes.

7 Fry for 3 to 4 minutes each side until the surface is browned but the inside juicy and still a little pink— cook longer if you like beef well done.

8 Arrange on a serving dish and keep hot.

9 Pour any fat out of the pan. Add the wine and boil rapidly, stirring to scrape up the coagulated juices, until reduced to about half the quantity.

10 Off the heat, beat in the remaining butter in pieces until it is absorbed. Check the seasoning, add the herbs and pour the sauce over the meat cakes.

11 Garnish with the watercress and serve immediately.

MEAT BALL BROCHETTES

⊠ *For these meat balls, grilled on a skewer, good quality lean minced beef is essential. Ideally, buy chuck or blade steak, and mince at home. Grind it really finely by putting it two or three times through the fine blades of a mincer. The addition of grated cheese gives it a wonderfully rich flavour, and grilled with mushrooms and tomatoes this is a dish to set before a king. If you cannot get very small tomatoes, buy medium-sized ones and halve them.*

SERVES 4
450 g [1 lb] chuck or blade steak
150 g [5 oz] medium-sized button mushrooms
45 ml [3 tablespoons] oil
45 ml [3 tablespoons] grated parmesan cheese
salt
freshly ground black pepper
8 very small firm tomatoes

1 Trim the meat and cut into cubes. Put through the finest blades of the mincer two or three times.

2 Wipe, but do not peel, the mushrooms. Put into a bowl with 15 ml [1 tablespoon] oil and stir gently to film each mushroom with oil.

3 Put the minced meat, cheese, 15 ml [1 tablespoon] oil, and salt and pepper to taste, into a bowl. Beat with a wooden spoon until thoroughly mixed and sticking together.

4 Divide into 12 portions and roll each one firmly between lightly floured hands to form a compact ball.

5 Set the grill to a high setting.

6 Thread the skewers with a tomato then alternately, 3 meat balls and 3 mushrooms, finishing with another tomato. Push the ingredients closely together.

7 Brush the brochettes thoroughly with the remaining oil. Lay them on the grid in the grill pan and place the pan about 7.5–10 cm [3–4"] from the heat.

8 Grill the brochettes for 7 to 8

minutes, turning every 2 minutes, until well browned and cooked. Serve very hot.

POLPETTE

⊠ *This is the Italian housewife's way of making an interesting meal with a little minced meat. Cooked meat can be used up in this way but polpette are tastier, and more frequently, made with fresh minced veal. Fresh leg of beef could also be used. If you mince the meat at home, most of the other ingredients can go through the mincer at the same time. Polpette are delicious served with a mixed green salad and sautéed potatoes.*

SERVES 5–6
50 g [2 oz] white bread
a little milk
450 g [1 lb] pie veal
2 garlic cloves
4 parsley sprigs
25 g [1 oz] parmesan cheese
2 medium-sized eggs
2 thin strips lemon rind
large pinch grated nutmeg
salt
freshly ground black pepper
50 g [2 oz] plain flour
90 ml [6 tablespoons] oil
4 large lettuce leaves for garnish

1 Break the bread into pieces, put into a bowl, barely cover with milk and leave to stand for 10 minutes or until soft.

2 Trim any skin and gristle from the meat and cut the meat into small pieces. Peel the garlic cloves and cut any stalks from the parsley.

3 Grate the cheese and lightly beat the eggs.

4 Squeeze the bread free of liquid and put the bread, meat, garlic, parsley and lemon rind through the mincer, twice, collecting it in a large bowl.

5 Stir the eggs, cheese and nutmeg into the mixture and add salt and pepper to taste. Mix well.

6 Flour a board and your hands. Using a teaspoon, take one spoonful of the mixture at a time, roll lightly into a ball with your fingers, then roll in flour on the board and flatten slightly with a palette knife.

Handle the meat balls as little as possible so that they remain light. Continue until all the mixture is shaped.

7 Heat the oil in a large, shallow frying-pan over medium heat. When hot, fry the polpette in batches, cooking them for about 3 minutes each side, until crisp outside and cooked through.

8 Lift out with a perforated spoon, drain on crumpled kitchen paper and keep hot until all are fried.

9 Serve very hot on a bed of lettuce leaves.

Variation
● For Sicilian polpette, prepare and shape the polpette as above, then put into a pan, cover with a home-made tomato sauce (using fresh tomatoes) and simmer for 15 to 20 minutes. Serve hot in a dish surrounded by sautéed potatoes.

FRIKADELLER

⊠⊠ *This is an excellent Danish way of stretching minced pork, at the same time making it lighter and less rich. For a leaner meat mixture use a combination of half veal and half pork. Traditionally, the mixture was 'extended' with flour and milk, but modern Danish housewives use sparkling mineral water instead of milk to make the mixture even lighter. The flavouring can be either a little onion or a hint of sage. Serve with boiled potatoes, and cabbage which is chopped and cooked and well moistened with a basic white sauce.*

SERVES 4–5
450 g [1 lb] shoulder or spare rib of pork
1 small onion or 2.5 ml [½ teaspoon] dried sage (optional)
1 medium-sized egg
15 ml [1 tablespoon] flour
150 ml [¼ pt] milk or sparkling mineral water
salt
freshly ground black pepper
40 g [1½ oz] unsalted butter
15 ml [1 tablespoon] oil

1 Trim any skin and gristle from the meat and put twice through the fine blades of a mincer into a large bowl.

2 Peel and finely chop the onion if used, and add the onion or the sage to the meat.

3 Beat the egg and using a wooden spoon, work the flour, followed by the egg, into the meat.

4 Little by little, beat in the milk or mineral water until it is absorbed by the mixture. Season generously with salt and pepper.

5 Cover the bowl loosely and leave to stand in a cool place for about an hour.

6 Dampen a work surface with water, set out the mixture in large spoonfuls and flatten a little with a large metal spoon, which has been dipped in water.

7 Heat the butter and oil in a large shallow frying-pan and fry several meat patties (as many as the pan will hold flat with small spaces between) for about 3 minutes. Turn carefully and fry the other side for another 3 minutes, or until golden and cooked through.

8 Lift out, drain on crumpled kitchen paper and keep hot until all are cooked. Serve very hot.

MINCED VEAL PATTIES

Imported veal is always expensive, but home-produced veal is sometimes available at an economical price. Combined with a little cooked ham for flavour and pork for richness, minced veal makes delicious patties. Fried in butter and moistened with a little Marsala or white wine, veal patties become a dinner party dish.

SERVES 6
350 g [¾ lb] pie veal
1 thick slice of bread
a little milk
50 g [2 oz] lean cooked ham
75 g [3 oz] belly pork
1 small onion
1 medium-sized egg
15 ml [1 tablespoon] freshly
    chopped parsley
2.5 ml [½ teaspoon] dried thyme
salt
freshly ground black pepper
25 g [1 oz] flour
25 g [1 oz] butter
30 ml [2 tablespoons] oil
75 ml [5 tablespoons] Marsala

1 Trim any hard crusts from the bread, break the bread into pieces, cover with milk and leave to soak for 10 minutes. Then squeeze out as much milk as possible.

2 Cut away any skin, gristle or bone from the veal, ham and pork and cut into small cubes.

3 Peel and quarter the onion.

4 Put the prepared meats, the drained bread and the onion through the fine blades of a mincer, twice.

5 Beat the egg lightly and add it, the parsley and thyme to the meat with salt and pepper to taste. Beat with a wooden spoon until thoroughly mixed. Divide into six portions.

6 On a lightly floured board, flatten each portion with palette knives and shape into a thin oval patty. Turn to coat each side with flour. Shake gently to dislodge excess flour.

7 Heat the butter and oil in a large sauté pan and, when hot, put in the patties and fry for 2–3 minutes on each side or until golden.

8 Pour in the Marsala and spoon it over the patties. Cover the pan tightly and cook over very low heat for 15 minutes.

9 Lift the patties on to a serving dish, boil up the juices to reduce slightly, check the seasoning and spoon a little over each patty.

A simple meat loaf, cooked in a ring mould and garnished with cooked vegetables makes a tasty family meal.

SIMPLE MEAT LOAF

If you have an electric liquidizer, this quickly prepared loaf is an excellent way of feeding a family of six from 450 g [1 lb] minced beef extended with vegetables, eggs and bread-crumbs. If you have no liquidizer, grate the onion and carrot, chop the parsley and mix with the beaten eggs. Serve the loaf on a large plate surrounded by diced and cooked root vegetables and green peas. Hand round a brown or tomato sauce (use fresh tomatoes) separately if wished. Any leftovers are useful for packed lunches.

SERVES 6
450 g [1 lb] minced beef
15 g [½ oz] margarine
75 g [3 oz] bread
1 small onion
1 small carrot
2 medium-sized eggs
parsley sprigs

150 ml [¼ pt] beef stock
5 ml [1 teaspoon] dried oregano
5 ml [1 teaspoon] Worcestershire sauce
salt
freshly ground black pepper

1 Heat the oven to 180°C [350°F] gas mark 4. Thoroughly grease a ring mould or loaf tin with margarine.

2 Trim any hard crusts from the bread, cut into cubes and feed into the liquidizer to make crumbs. Tip into a mixing bowl.

3 Peel and slice the onion and the carrot.

4 Break the eggs into the liquidizer, add the onion, carrot and parsley and switch on until the vegetables are finely chopped.

5 Add to the mixing bowl, with the minced beef, stock, oregano, Worcestershire sauce and seasonings of salt and pepper. Mix lightly but thoroughly. The mixture will have a fairly soft consistency.

6 Press into the greased tin, leaving no air spaces, and smooth the surface. Cover the tin loosely with greaseproof paper or foil.

7 Cook in the centre of the oven for 50–60 minutes. When cooked, the loaf will feel firm when pressed with the finger.

8 Ease the loaf away from the sides of the tin with a palette knife. Turn out on to a hot dish and surround with diced, cooked root vegetables and green peas. Serve in thick slices.

AMERICAN MEAT LOAF

This is a popular American family recipe. The meat loaf can be shaped as a bolster and baked in a flat baking tin, or pressed into a greased loaf tin or ring mould. The mixture of minced meat can be varied according to what is available or good value at the time. The flavourings can be altered to include more spices, different herbs or piquant sauces. Texture can be soft-ened by increasing the bread content, or roughened by including finely chopped green pepper or more celery. The mixture is bound with eggs and the meat is finely ground. Serve a home-made tomato sauce (using fresh tomatoes) separately.

SERVES 8–9
450 g [1 lb] chuck steak
225 g [½ lb] pie veal
225 g [½ lb] pork
1 large onion
2 celery sticks
2 garlic cloves
30 ml [2 tablespoons] oil
25 g [1 oz] butter
150 ml [¼ pt] beef stock
3 slices of bread
2 bay leaves
5 ml [1 teaspoon] salt
2.5 ml [½ teaspoon] ground black pepper
5 ml [1 teaspoon] allspice
2.5 ml [½ teaspoon] dried thyme
2 medium-sized eggs
30 ml [2 tablespoons] tomato ketchup

1. Trim the meat, cut into pieces and pass once through the fine blades of a mincer, collecting the mince in a large mixing bowl.

2. Heat the oven to 180°C [350°F] gas mark 4.

3. Peel the onion and chop it finely; wash and finely chop the celery; peel and crush the garlic cloves.

4. Heat the oil and butter in a heavy-based saucepan over low heat and fry the onion, celery and garlic very gently for 5 minutes.

5. Add the stock and simmer for several minutes, then remove the pan from the heat.

6. Cut the bread into dice, add to the pan and leave to stand until soft, about 5 minutes. Then beat smooth with a wooden spoon.

7. Crumble the bay leaves as small as possible and add to the meat with the salt, pepper, allspice, thyme and contents of the saucepan.

8. Beat eggs and add to mixture.

9. Mix the ingredients lightly but well, and check that the mixture is well seasoned.

10. Grease a shallow baking dish, turn the meat mixture into the centre and shape into a thick oblong bolster.

11. Spoon the tomato ketchup along the top.

12. Bake in the centre of the oven for 1¼–1½ hours. Towards the end of cooking time, baste with the pan juices.

13. Serve the loaf cut in thick slices.

MOROCCAN KEFTA

Moroccan meat balls are very highly spiced and are usually made with lamb or mutton. The meat in this case should include some fat, so shoulder is a good cut to use. Allow time for shaping the balls because they should be small, about the size of a large marble. After shaping, the meat balls are poached in water, drained, allowed to cool and finished in various ways. They can be grilled, cooked on skewers ('en brochette'), *fried or, as in this recipe, simmered in a rich, thick tomato sauce. Make the sauce in advance. Some Moroccan cooks fry the balls before simmering them in sauce, which makes a richer dish. Serve with boiled rice.*

SERVES 4
450 g [1 lb] boneless shoulder of lamb
1 small onion
3 fresh mint leaves
4 fresh marjoram leaves
6 parsley sprigs
1.5 ml [¼ teaspoon] ground cumin
1.5 ml [¼ teaspoon] paprika
pinch each of cayenne pepper, ginger, cinnamon and nutmeg
salt
freshly ground black pepper
275 ml [½ pt] well-flavoured home-made tomato sauce

1. Cut away any skin and gristle from the meat and cut the meat in cubes.

2. Peel and quarter the onion.

3. Pass the meat, onion, mint, marjoram and parsley through the fine blades of a mincer 3 times, collecting the minced ingredients in a mixing bowl.

4. Add all the spices and the salt and pepper to the mince and, with a wooden spoon, stir and pound the mixture until thoroughly blended and smooth. Check that the mixture is very well flavoured. Bring a saucepan of water to simmering point.

5. With slightly wetted hands, take a teaspoon of meat at a time and roll into a ball the size of a large marble. Continue until all the meat is shaped.

6. Lower the balls into the pan of gently simmering water. Poach for 10 minutes.

7. Lift out with a perforated spoon and leave on a plate until cold.

8. Shortly before serving, bring the tomato sauce to simmering point, lower the kefta balls into it, and simmer for 10 minutes until heated through. Serve in the sauce.

FLAKY MINCE ROLL

Encasing minced meat in pastry is always an attractive way of making the meat go further and gives the dish a rather more interesting appearance. Use coarsely minced meat for preference and either all beef, or part beef and part lean pork. You can add flavourings of your choice to the meat in this basic recipe and serve the roll hot with vegetables or cold with a salad. Remember to thaw the pastry in advance.

SERVES 4
350 g [12 oz] lean minced meat
225 g [½ lb] frozen puff pastry
1 large egg
50 g [2 oz] fresh white breadcrumbs
15 ml [1 tablespoon] tomato ketchup
7.5 ml [1½ teaspoons] Worcestershire sauce
5 ml [1 teaspoon] salt
freshly ground black pepper

1. Heat the oven to 220°C [425°F] gas mark 7.

2. On a lightly floured board, roll out the prepared pastry to an oblong at least 25 × 20 cm [10 × 8"].

3. Beat the egg lightly in a bowl to mix the white and yolk. Reserve a little for glazing the pastry.

4. Thoroughly mix the meat, breadcrumbs, ketchup, sauce, salt, pepper and the egg.

5. Shape the mixture into a thick roll about 22.5 cm [9"] long and place in the centre of the pastry.

6. Brush the edges of the pastry with water and wrap around the meat, pressing the edges together and tucking the ends in so that the meat is completely enclosed.

7. Place the roll on a baking tray with the pastry join beneath. With the back of a knife make criss-cross lines over the top of the pastry, forming a diamond pattern. Brush with the reserved egg.

8. Bake in the centre of the oven for 20 minutes then reduce the heat to 190°C [375°F] gas mark 5, and continue cooking for 25 to 30 minutes until the pastry is golden brown.

Quick and inexpensive

Banish any squeamishness you may have about cooking and eating offal. Liver and kidneys are superb value for money—both cheap and nutritious. Cooked with care, they provide truly gastronomic treats, and if you don't tell the family what they are eating, the chances are they will ask for more.

In the traditional farmhouse kitchen, when an animal was slaughtered, almost all of it was cooked and eaten. As much care was given to making delicious dishes from offal, as was given to cooking the prime cuts of meat, and many of these offal dishes now rank among the world's great classic recipes.

Offal, or as the Americans prefer to call it, variety meats, is the organs of a slaughtered animal, plus the extremities which have little meat on them. This includes liver, kidneys, heart, brains, sweetbreads, tongue and tripe, as well as the head, ears, tail and feet. All these can be turned into tasty meals, although other parts of a slaughtered animal, such as the blood and lights, are usually only used in the making of commercial meat products.

Offal is inexpensive and packed with vitamins and minerals. It has a different taste and texture from other meats, and can add interest and variety to weekly meals.

Unfortunately falling demand and the decline of private butchery has meant that some types of offal are fast becoming rare delicacies. However it is well worth the effort of ordering offal which is not easily available, or hunting around for it, as the carefully cooked results are so cheap, tasty and different.

Explained here are details of choosing and preparing of liver and kidneys, and how to cook them by the quick and simple methods of frying and grilling. Braising and casserol-

ing of these meats is covered on pages 123–134.

CHOOSING LIVER

Liver is crammed with vitamins, especially those in the B group, and is rich in iron and other essential minerals, so it should figure in everyone's menu at least once every two weeks.

Types of liver

Different types of liver are shown in the illustrated chart. Lamb's or calf's liver is best for frying or grilling. Calf's liver is delicate and delicious, but expensive. Lamb's liver is cheaper, similar in flavour, and can be used for the same recipes. Pig's liver can be fried or grilled, but it has a rather

CALF'S
Allow 75-100 g [3-4 oz] per portion
Description
The best and most expensive kind, very tender, of excellent flavour and fine texture. Pale reddish in colour.
Notes on cooking
Excellent fried or grilled but care is necessary not to overcook. It should remain slightly pink in the centre.

LAMB'S
Allow 75-100 g [3-4 oz] per portion
Description
A good second best to calf's liver. Flavour a little more pronounced and more variable. Choose paler rather than darker coloured liver, as the flavour of the former will be more delicate.
Notes on cooking
Cooked like calf's liver. Also good for sauté dishes and casseroles.

PIG'S
Allow 75-100 g [3-4 oz] per portion
Description
Cheaper than calf's or lamb's liver. Usually darker in colour, softer, and stronger in flavour. Rather variable.
Notes on cooking
The best liver to use for pâtés and terrines or faggots. If to be fried or grilled the flavour is improved if liver is first soaked in salted water for a couple of hours, or overnight.

strong flavour for these methods of cooking. The flavour is improved if pig's liver is soaked in salted water for a couple of hours, or overnight if possible, before cooking. Add 5 ml [1 teaspoon] of salt to 550 ml [1 pt] of water for soaking.

The cheapest type of liver is ox liver; as this is coarser and more strongly flavoured, it is best used for braising and stewing. This is best soaked overnight in salted water.

Chicken livers are a rich tasting and relatively inexpensive delicacy mainly used in pâtés, or to make savoury fillings and snacks. They are dealt with separately.

Buying liver
Liver is always eaten fresh and is never hung to age like other meat. When buying fresh liver, avoid any that is dry, dull or tired-looking. Also beware of liver that has a bluish tint or an unpleasant smell.

Most butchers will usually give you liver cut down the length of the lobe into slices 6-12 mm [¼-½"] thick. Liver bought in supermarkets may well be cut into thick, uneven slices. By far the best thing, however, is to buy liver all in one piece (as it will be fresher),

and cut it yourself just before cooking. It is absolutely vital that liver for frying and grilling should be sliced very thinly and so it is preferable to do it yourself. Some recipes also call for liver cut in a different way.

Quantities
Because liver is rich, and because there is so little wastage, you need only allow 75-100 g [3-4 oz] per serving. This is considerably less than the amount needed for other meats, and is another reason why learning to serve beautifully cooked liver will help keep your household budget within reasonable limits.

Storing
Fresh liver will not keep in good condition for very long and should always be eaten on the day of purchase, unless it is to be soaked in salted water. Store it in the refrigerator, lightly covered with transparent film or kitchen foil, until time for cooking. Always remember to take it out of the butcher's wrapping or the supermarket's packaging as meat will not keep cool enough if it is stored in these ways.

Frozen liver
Frozen liver may keep for slightly longer than fresh liver but, like fresh liver, should ideally be eaten on the day of purchase. Store in the same way as for fresh liver, and thaw by leaving in the refrigerator for about 6 hours, or at room temperature for about 3 hours. Wash well after thawing, pat dry and use promptly.

One advantage of frozen liver is that it can be more easily sliced into the very thin slices when still in its frozen, or semi-frozen state.

PREPARING LIVERS
All livers are prepared in the same way, whatever the animal or the intended cooking process. Wash the liver well under cold running water, drain on crumpled kitchen paper, and pat dry. Slice the meat according to the recipe you will be using; the usual method is to cut the liver lengthways, down the length of the lobe, into even slices no more than 6 mm [¼"] thick. It is particularly important to cut thin slices, so that the liver can be cooked really rapidly and not lose its succulence and flavour. Equal-sized slices allow even cooking.

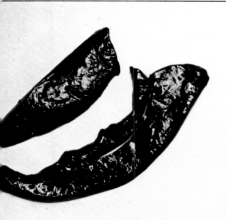

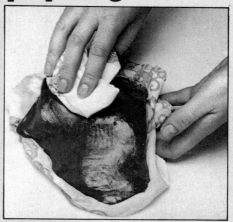

Step-by-step to preparing liver

OX
Description
Larger, coarser and stronger in flavour than other livers, but considerably cheaper.
Notes on cooking
Not recommended for frying or grilling. Best soaked in lightly salted water for several hours or overnight and then casseroled, braised or stewed.

Carefully remove any thin outside skin. If this is not removed the liver may curl up during cooking. Cut out any large veins running through the liver.

CHICKEN
Description
Small and soft with a rich distinctive flavour. Dark reddish-brown in colour.
Notes on cooking
Usually used for savoury snacks or fillings, or to make pâtés. Care is needed not to overcook.

1 Wash the liver well under cold running water, place on crumpled kitchen paper and pat dry.

2 Slice the liver down the length of the lobe into slices 6 mm [¼"] thick with a sharp knife.

CHICKEN LIVERS
Chicken livers are, of course, giblets rather than offal, because they come from poultry. For convenience they are included here as the method of preparation and frying is much the same as for animal livers.

Chicken livers are something of a delicacy and, because they are very rich, they are usually used in small quantities as savoury fillings or teamed with other ingredients to make savoury snacks, which are served with drinks, as an hors d'oeuvre, or at the end of a meal. They are also used to make very delicious pâtés.

At one time chicken livers were not widely available, but now cartons of frozen chicken livers are easily obtainable. Consequently they are less expensive than most other livers. Only small amounts are needed for many recipes where chicken livers are grilled or fried.

Storing
Like other types of liver, chicken livers do not keep well and should ideally be used on the day of purchase, unless they are to be stored in their frozen state. To thaw, leave the livers in the refrigerator for several hours, lightly covered with transparent film or kitchen foil, or leave them, covered, at room temperature for about 1-2 hours.

Preparation
When the chicken livers are completely thawed, carefully separate them and wash very thoroughly under cold running water. Drain them on crumpled kitchen paper and pat dry. Gentle handling is needed as the livers are small and often very soft—they are delicate and can be awkward to cut the trim.

Cut each liver into its two distinct lobes and discard the tough skin that holds them together. Frozen livers should be free of gall sacs, but inspect all chicken livers, whether fresh or frozen, very carefully and cut away any gall sacs and pieces of liver which have been stained dark green from the gall. If this is not done, the livers will taste bitter.

3 Remove any thin surrounding skin and cut away any large veins from the slices of liver.

Grilling and frying

Chicken livers are grilled and fried in the same way as other types of liver but, because they are small and fine-textured, extra care must be taken not to overcook them. When cooked, they should be nicely seared on the outside but still pink on the inside. They should feel pliable and spongy to the touch, not hard and rigid which indicates overcooking.

CHOOSING KIDNEYS

Like liver, kidneys are richer in the B group vitamins than most other meats, and are also rich in iron and other minerals.

Also, like liver, they must be cooked very briefly under or over a very high heat to prevent them becoming tough and leathery. This happens very easily, so careful timing and immediate serving is vital when frying or grilling kidneys.

Types of kidney

Different types of kidney are shown in the illustrated chart. Ox, veal, lamb's and pig's kidneys are all good to eat, but are very different from each other in appearance and their eating quality. They therefore require different cooking techniques.

Ox kidney is the largest, coarsest and strongest. It is also the cheapest, but because of its strong flavour it is not usually served on its own. Veal kidney, a miniature of the ox kidney, is relatively tender and something of a delicacy, therefore quite expensive.

Lamb's and pig's kidneys are smaller and have an entirely different shape to ox kidney. It is lamb's and pig's kidneys that give the traditional kidney shape. Pig's kidneys have a strong flavour and are best casseroled or stewed. However they can be fried or grilled. If you intend to do this, their flavour is much improved by soaking in salted water (add 5 ml [1 teaspoon] of salt to 550 ml [1 pt] of water) for two hours or more. Overnight soaking is best if this is possible.

Lamb's kidneys are more expensive than pig's kidneys, but have an excellent flavour when fried or grilled.

Buying kidneys

When buying fresh kidneys choose ones which are plump, firm and a good brown colour. Avoid any that have a greenish tinge, mottling, or an unpleasant smell. Lamb's, veal and ox kidneys are sometimes sold with their surrounding fat (suet), which should be firm and white; the thin covering skin (if any) should be unbroken. This fat can be used for suet pastry and suet puddings instead of the bought shredded suet you might normally use.

Kidneys which are sold with their surrounding fat are more expensive than those sold without, and are not always readily available from all butchers.

Quantities

The number of kidneys required per portion depends on the type of kidneys being cooked, and the recipe being used. For a main course 2-3 lamb's kidneys per portion is the normal serving. When cooking kidneys there is, of course, virtually no waste. Small veal kidneys around 150-175 g [5-6 oz] when weighed with their suet may make individual portions; a larger one will serve two. Amounts needed of other types of kidneys will depend on individual recipes.

Storing

Fresh kidneys should be eaten on the day of purchase as they do not keep well. Store in the refrigerator, lightly covered with kitchen foil or transparent film, until it is time for cooking. Always remember to take them out of the butcher's sealed polythene bag or the supermarket tray before storing.

Frozen kidneys

Like fresh kidneys, frozen kidneys do not keep well and should ideally be eaten on the day of purchase. They should be thoroughly thawed before preparing and cooking, by leaving in the refrigerator for about 5 hours, or at room temperature for about 2½ hours. Wash them well under cold running water and pat them dry with kitchen towels. They should be used promptly after thawing.

PREPARING KIDNEYS
Lamb's and pig's kidneys

Lamb's and pig's kidneys are prepared in a similar way. The suet, if any, is peeled off and set aside, unless the kidneys are to be cooked in suet. In this case the suet is trimmed to a thin layer all round the kidney.

Lay the kidney on a chopping board with the rounded side to the

LAMB'S
allow 2-3 per portion
Description
Small kidneys weighing from 25-50 g [1-2 oz] each. Flavour and texture are finest when kidneys are very fresh, so when available buy home-produced kidneys still encased in their surrounding fat. Imported kidneys are usually frozen and sold without surrounding fat. Choose light brown, firm kidneys, avoiding any that are dark or strong smelling.
Notes on cooking
Provided they are cooked quickly and not overcooked lamb's kidneys are excellent grilled or fried. When served they should still remain a little pink in the centre. If overcooked they toughen and harden. They are also good stewed and used in soup.

right, and with a sharp knife make a nick in the skin in the centre of the curved side. (If you are left-handed, this procedure is reversed.)

Draw the skin right back each side towards the core. Then carefully pull the skin away from the kidney, drawing out as much of the core as possible. Nick out the remaining core with scissors by cutting a V-shape in the kidney.

Lay the kidney on the board and, holding it flat with one hand, slice through horizontally from the curved side towards the core.

Pig's kidneys, because they are larger, are usually cut completely in two for frying or for grilling.

Lamb's kidneys are cut in two for frying, but for grilling they are almost severed, cutting from the round side leaving them still joined on the core end. Each kidney is then opened out

Types of kidney and uses

PIG'S
allow 1 per portion
Description
Similar in appearance to lamb's kidneys but wider and heavier, they average 100-150 g [4-5 oz] each. Flavour is not as attractive as lamb's kidneys, it is stronger and texture is firmer, especially when from an older pig.
Notes on cooking
To help modify the strong flavour soak in salted water for several hours or overnight. Best when sliced and casseroled or stewed, but can be grilled or fried in the same way as lamb's. Avoid over-cooking.

VEAL
allow 100 g [4 oz] per portion
Description
Larger than lamb's or pig's kidneys, light brown in colour and consisting of a group of segments joined to a central core. Can weigh from 150-350 g [5-12 oz] depending on the size of the calf. They have the mildest flavour of all kidneys and are considered the choicest. They are also the most expensive.
Notes on cooking
Excellent sautéed in butter and served in a sauce, or baked in the oven in some of their own sur-rounding fat. In either case it is important not to overcook, other-wise the kidneys harden and the delicate flavour is destroyed.

OX
allow 100-175 g [4-6 oz] per 450 g [1 lb] beef
Description
Similar to veal kidneys but larger in size, much darker in colour and stronger in flavour. It is usually bought by weight and is cut off the core by the butcher. Excellent for flavouring pies and puddings.
Notes on cooking
Soak large pieces of ox kidney in salt water before using. Because of its robust flavour, ox kidney is not usually eaten on its own but is used for flavouring dishes like steak and kidney pie or pudding, or stews and soups. It requires long slow moist cooking to tenderize it.

cut side uppermost, and the cut is extended a little, if necessary, to make sure the kidney lies flat, and is then opened up into a flat round shape. Kidneys tend to curl during grilling so lamb's kidneys, which are split open, are skewered through with a wooden or metal skewer to hold them flat. The skewer is stuck into the middle of one cut side of the kidney and brought out in the middle of the other side.

Veal kidneys
Veal kidneys are a different shape from lamb's kidneys and have a larger and thicker core. They are con-sidered a delicacy, and are often served whole, and so their prepara-tion is slightly different. They are peeled and cored in the same way as lamb's and pig's kidneys, but extra care must be taken that the initial cut

through the skin does not penetrate the flesh, and so make the kidney 'bleed' during cooking. Some of this preparation may have been done by your butcher.

Ox kidney
Ox kidney is normally bought by weight and skinned and cut off the core by the butcher. Large pieces are best soaked in salt water before using, to improve the flavour, but with small chunks this is not really necessary.

EQUIPMENT
To wash and prepare liver and kidneys, you will need kitchen paper for draining and drying and a sharp knife and board for slicing.

In addition, for preparing kidneys you will need a pair of small sharp

scissors—curved ones are ideal—for nicking out the kidney cores.
For grilling liver or kidneys you will need a grill pan or large, shallow, flameproof dish which will fit under the grill. A pastry brush can be used to brush the liver slices or kidneys with oil, melted butter or marinade. Tongs are also used to turn the liver slices over during cooking. Measur-ing spoons are also useful.

If kidneys are to be grilled you will need a medium length metal skewer for each kidney, to keep the two halves open.
For frying liver or kidneys you will need a large, heavy-based frying-pan with a thick, firm base and low sides—about 5 cm [2"] is best. The sides should rise straight from the base, sloping outwards at a slight angle, and the pan should have a long handle to prevent your hand being

Step-by-step to preparing lamb's kidneys

1 Cut through the suet encasing the kidney (if any) and pull it away. The suet may be rendered down.

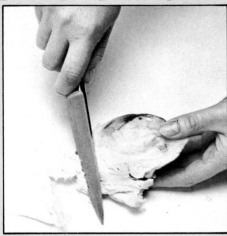

OR if cooking the kidneys in suet, trim the suet to a thin layer as this fat will be eaten.

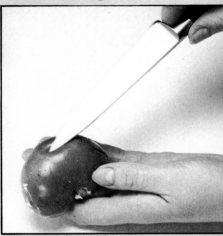

2 With a sharp knife, nick the skin in the centre of the rounded side being careful not to cut flesh.

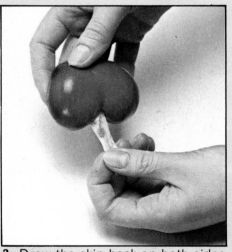

3 Draw the skin back on both sides until attached only by the core, then pull to draw out core.

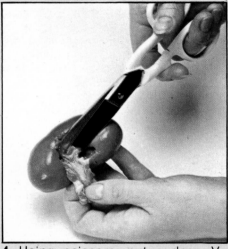

4 Using scissors, cut a deep V-shape in order to remove the skin and core completely.

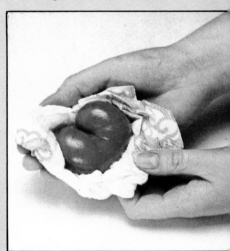

5 Rinse the kidney under cold running water for a moment, drain and pat dry.

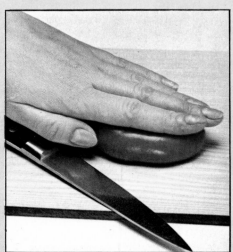

6 Place the kidney on a board with the rounded side to the right and hold the kidney flat.

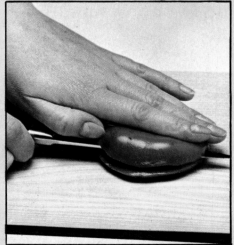

7 If frying, cut the kidney completely through horizontally into two separate halves.

OR if cooking the kidneys in suet, trim the suet to a thin layer as this fat will be eaten.

splashed by hot fat. Cast iron, stainless steel and heavy enamel are suitable materials for frying-pans. Make sure that your pan is not too large for your heat source, or the edges of the pan will not heat up sufficiently.

You will also need measuring spoons, a polythene bag or grease-proof paper, in which to shake the liver and seasoned flour, and two plates on which to turn out the floured meat. Kitchen tongs are used to turn the liver slices in the pan.

GRILLING LIVER

Quick cooking under or over a brisk heat is essential whether frying or grilling liver, otherwise the meat will harden and dry out. Nutritionally, as well as gastronomically, it is a question of the less cooking the better. In effect, the meat should merely be seared so that it is crusty on the outside and juicy pink (but not at all raw-tasting) inside.

Grilling seals and browns the surface of the meat, while trapping the flavour and juices inside. The basic rules of grilling any type of meat apply equally to offal and the important thing is to know how quickly your own particular grill heats up and cools down.

Before grilling the meat, turn the grill on fully and allow it to heat up for two minutes. Remove the rack from the grill pan.

Coating with fat

To prepare the liver, brush the slices with melted butter, or with oil, or marinade. Liver is a lean meat and does not supply its own cooking fat, so it is important both sides of the slices are well greased. Allow 5 ml [1 teaspoon] of fat per 100 g [4 oz] of meat.

Alternatively, put 30 ml [2 tablespoons] of oil, or 15 ml [1 tablespoon] of butter and 15 ml [1 tablespoon] of oil into the bottom of the grill pan or use a large, shallow, flameproof dish. The rack of the grill pan is not used because the fat will drip off the liver slices and the meat will harden and be less succulent when cooked.

Put the grill pan, or dish, under the grill and when the fat is sizzling, remove the grill pan and dip the liver slices in the fat. Using kitchen tongs, turn the slices so both sides are coated with oil, then arrange them

side by side with at least 6 mm [¼"] between them.

Cooking

Grill under high heat for 1-2 minutes until the surfaces are sealed and the liver changes colour and becomes greyish. Then remove from the heat and season lightly with salt and pepper. Turn each slice with kitchen tongs, season lightly with pepper and continue grilling for 2-3 minutes until the liver is just cooked—that is until it is pliable and yielding to the touch and the juices run pale pink when the liver is pricked with a fork. If the slices of liver are hard and rigid, they are overcooked.

Streaky bacon is a natural accompaniment to liver—it provides the fat which liver lacks. An excellent way to prevent liver from drying out during grilling is to cover it with bacon when it is turned over to grill the second side. The bacon fat then keeps the meat moist.

GRILLING KIDNEYS

Quick, speedy cooking is essential to keep kidneys succulent and to prevent them hardening and drying out. When frying or grilling, the aim is to seal the surfaces of the meat so the juices are kept inside. Kidneys are really ready as soon as the sides are seared, which must be done under a very fierce heat, or in very hot fat to prevent the juices 'bleeding' out. If you prefer kidneys well cooked, reduce the heat after searing and continue to cook for a little longer.

Kidneys are grilled in the same way as liver. There is no rule about which side of the kidney should be grilled first, but as with grilling liver, the surfaces must be moistened with fat to prevent them becoming dry and hard.

FRYING LIVER
Flouring the slices

Slices of liver must be well coated with seasoned flour before cooking to make them dry and crisp when cooked and to ensure they seal well and quickly when subjected to hot fat. Allow 15 g [½ oz] of flour, a large pinch of salt and freshly ground pepper for every 100 g [4 oz] liver. Put the flour and seasonings in a clean polythene or greaseproof paper bag and shake gently to mix well. Add the liver slices to the bag, shake, then

turn out on to a clean plate, to get rid of any excess flour. Shake the slices and put them on a clean dry plate. The liver is now ready to be cooked.

The fat

Butter, bacon fat, dripping or cooking oil can all be used to fry liver. If you are using butter, choose unsalted or clarified butter, as these are less prone to burning at high temperatures. Or mix equal quantities of butter and cooking oil together. To clarify butter, melt it then strain through a muslin-lined sieve to remove any sediment.

Cooking

Heat the frying-pan over moderate heat for about a minute, or until the pan is thoroughly hot, then add 15 ml [1 tablespoon] fat, or enough to just cover the base of the pan.

When the fat is hot and sizzling slightly carefully add the sliced liver. It is important not to crowd the pan with too many slices as this will cool the fat and make the meat greasy and heavy. Allow at least 6 mm [¼"] space between each slice. If your pan is small, or you are cooking a large amount of liver, cook the slices in batches, or use 2 pans at the same time.

Cook the liver over moderate heat for 2-3 minutes, or until beads of blood appear on the surface of the meat. This indicates that the liver should be turned over. Using kitchen tongs, turn over the meat, starting with the first slice that was put in the pan and working through to the last slice put into the pan.

The overall cooking time for liver varies according to the kind of liver being used, the thickness of the slices and the degree of heat. It should not take longer than 3-6 minutes in total.

When the meat is cooked it should be pliable and feel spongy if pressed. If it is rigid it is overcooked and will taste tough and leathery.

FRYING KIDNEYS

Kidneys are not dusted with seasoned flour before frying as their surfaces are relatively dry and will seal easily without a coating. Kidneys, in fact, are rarely fried as such, but are more commonly dry fried—seared in the frying-pan brushed with just enough oil to prevent the meat sticking.

117

Step-by-step to grilling kidneys

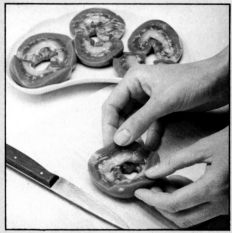 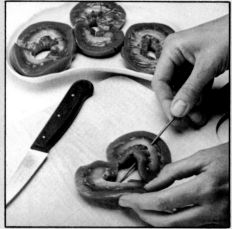 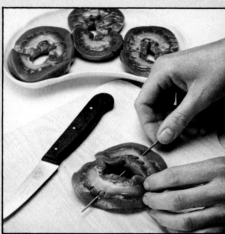

1 Prepare the kidneys as previously shown, cut through from the round side almost to the core end. Cut so that the kidney will lie flat.

2 Open the kidney out with the cut side uppermost and insert the point of the skewer into the middle of one cut side.

3 Take a big 'stitch' with the skewer so the point comes out in the middle of the other cut surface, keeping the kidney open.

Step-by-step to fried liver

350 g [12 oz] calf's or lamb's liver
45 ml [3 tablespoons] oil
40 g [1½ oz] plain flour
salt
freshly ground black pepper

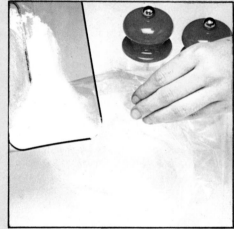 

1 Season the flour and place in a clean polythene bag. Shake lightly.

2 Add the liver slices, a few at a time, to the flour in the bag, and shake well until they are coated.

4 Put the oil in the frying-pan. Heat over moderate heat until it is hot and sizzling.

5 Lay liver slices flat in the pan. Cook for 2-3 minutes, or until beads of blood appear on the surface.

6 Turn the slices with tongs, starting with the first slice put in the pan, and cook for 1-2 minutes more.

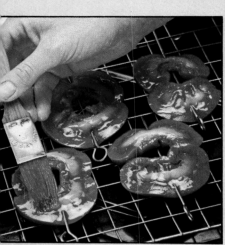

4 Brush cut side well with fat. Grill on a rack for 3 minutes. Turn, brush with more fat and grill for 3 more minutes.

3 Turn the liver slices on to a plate. Shake free of excess flour and put on a clean plate.

7 Lift the liver from the pan on to a hot dish, garnish if wished, and serve immediately.

FOIE AUX FINES HERBES

☒ *This is a delicious way of dry frying liver in a ridged grill pan, giving the slices of meat a lovely professional look. Alternatively grill the liver under high heat.*

Originally the term 'fines herbes' often meant fresh herbs with mushrooms, as in this recipe. The important thing is that all the herbs are fresh— dried ones cannot be substituted as they will not give the same taste.

SERVES 4
450 g [1 lb] lamb's liver, in one piece
100 g [¼ lb] mushrooms
30 ml [2 tablespoons] chopped parsley
15 ml [1 tablespoon] chopped chives
15 ml [1 tablespoon] chopped tarragon or 30 ml [2 tablespoons] basil
1 garlic clove
5 ml [1 teaspoon] oil
30 ml [2 tablespoons] clarified butter
15 ml [1 tablespoon] lemon juice
salt and pepper

1 Trim, wipe and finely chop the mushrooms. Trim and chop the herbs. Peel, chop and crush the garlic clove.

2 Wash the liver under cold running water and pat dry with kitchen paper.

3 Slice into 3-6 mm [⅛-¼"] slices. Trim away any outside skin and cut out any large veins.

4 Heat the grill pan over high heat until very hot and coat with a light film of oil, using a pastry brush.

5 Dry fry the liver slices for about one minute only on each side.

6 Keep the liver warm in a low oven (where it will continue cooking a little, hence the slight undercooking).

7 Melt the butter in a frying-pan over low heat. Add the garlic.

8 Add the mushrooms and herbs and cook, stirring continuously, for about 3 minutes.

9 Remove from the heat, stir in the lemon juice and add salt and pepper to taste.

10 Pour over the liver slices, scraping the pan well to collect all the juices. Serve immediately.

GRILLED LAMBS' KIDNEYS ON TOAST

☒ *This very simple recipe relies for its excellence on fresh, top-quality kidneys. Accurate timing is necessary to avoid overcooking the kidneys. The buttery pan juices give it maximum flavour and succulence. Have everything ready before you start to cook.*

SERVES 4
8 lambs' kidneys
4 slices of bread
100 g [¼ lb] butter
salt
freshly ground black pepper
4 sprigs of watercress (optional garnish)

1 Prepare the kidneys as shown in the step-by-step pictures, cutting them almost but not completely through.

2 Open the kidneys out in a round, flat shape and skewer them as shown in the second set of step-by-step pictures. Lay them cut side uppermost in a flameproof dish.

3 Heat the grill until it is very hot and toast the bread on both sides. Cut off the crusts, spread with half the butter and keep warm on a serving plate.

4 Put the remaining butter in a small heavy-based pan and melt it over low heat. With a pastry brush, liberally brush the kidneys with the butter.

5 Grill kidneys for just 3 minutes on each side turning once.

6 Season the kidneys to taste with salt and freshly ground pepper. Turn them over, brush with the rest of the butter and grill for another 3 minutes.

7 Test them by piercing with a fork. If the juices are pink but not too bloody, the kidneys are ready to serve. If the juice is bloody, continue grilling for another minute. Season lightly.

119

8 When cooked, use the prongs of a fork to slide the kidneys off the skewer and on to the toast.

9 Pour the buttery juices that have collected in the dish over the kidneys. Serve at once, garnished with watercress.

LIVER VENETIAN-STYLE

⊠ *This version of liver is fried with onions and is distinguished from other recipes by the use of olive oil—a very pure frying medium—and the cutting of the liver into small wafer-thin pieces. Ideally the liver should be calf's liver, in which case the cooking time will be no longer than a couple of minutes. If lamb's liver is used, the cooking time will be longer.*

The liver is not coated with flour in this recipe. Cooking time is very short and, together with the onions, this dish is moist and succulent rather than crisp.

SERVES 4
350 g [12 oz] calf's liver, in one piece
450 g [1 lb] onions
75 ml [5 tablespoons] olive oil
salt
freshly ground black pepper
15 ml [1 tablespoon] chopped fresh parsley
1 lemon, quartered lengthwise

1 Peel the onions and slice them very thinly.

2 Heat 45 ml [3 tablespoons] of olive oil in a sauté pan, add the onions, cover and sweat for about 20 minutes, or until they are soft and golden. Keep the pan covered and stir the onions, or shake the pan, from time to time to ensure they are cooking evenly, without sticking. Do this over a low heat to prevent the onions from over-browning and burning.

3 Meanwhile wash the liver in cold water, drain on crumpled kitchen paper and pat dry.

4 Cut away any outside skin and large veins while the liver is still in one piece, as the slicing method differs from the usual one.

5 With a very sharp knife cut the liver horizontally (rather than the more usual vertical) into wafer-thin

slices and then into 4 cm [1½"] squares. Trim away any remaining skin or large veins.

6 Lightly season the slices of liver with salt and freshly ground black pepper.

7 Heat a frying-pan over moderate heat for about a minute, or until hot, and add the remaining 30 ml [2 tablespoons] of olive oil.

8 When the oil is very hot, add the liver and fry briskly for a minute each side, turning the pieces with a kitchen slice.

9 Tip the contents of the frying-pan into the sauté pan and cook, stirring over moderate heat for a minute or until the liver is just perfectly cooked.

10 Turn on to a heated serving dish, sprinkle with parsley and serve immediately, garnished with lemon quarters.

LAMBS' KIDNEYS WITH HAZELNUT AND CHIVE BUTTER

⊠ *Kidneys are particularly good when dry-fried in a heavy, ridged grill pan. For a more substantial dish, substitute savoury rice for the toast, or serve on a bed of spinach with the toast.*

The butter pats take a little time to chill but once this is done, this is a very quick dish to finish.

SERVES 4
12 lambs' kidneys
50 g [2 oz] butter
40 g [1½ oz] unblanched hazelnuts
15 ml [1 tablespoon] fresh chives
5 ml [1 teaspoon] lemon juice
salt and freshly ground black pepper
15 ml [1 tablespoon] oil
4 slices of bread

1 Make sure the butter is at room temperature.

2 Chop the hazelnuts finely. Hold the chives in a bunch and snip them finely with a pair of scissors, into the nuts.

3 Put the butter into a bowl and cream with a wooden spoon until

soft. Stir in the nuts, chives, lemon juice and seasonings.

4 Shape the butter into a roll and put immediately in the refrigerator. Chill the butter while preparing the kidneys.

5 Prepare the kidneys as shown in the step-by-step pictures, cutting them completely in half.

6 Heat the ridged grill pan over high heat, then brush it with oil.

7 Remove the savoury butter roll from the refrigerator and cut into pats.

8 When the pan is thoroughly hot, put in the kidneys, cut side down. Fry over moderately high heat for 5 minutes, turning once.

9 Meanwhile make the toast, cut off the crusts and cut the slices into triangles.

10 Pile the kidneys into warmed small individual shallow dishes, arrange the toast triangles around the dishes and top each dish with a pat of the savoury butter.

11 Serve immediately with a crisp green salad.

Variation
● Serve the kidneys with other savoury butters such as maître d'hôtel butter or mustard butter.

Below: veal kidneys are unusual in that they may be roasted in their suet coating for veal en chemise.

VEAL KIDNEYS EN CHEMISE

This simple but delicious dish is good for a light main meal. It is essential to use small plump calves' kidneys of the correct weight, in order that the cooking can be perfectly timed. Each kidney should weigh between 150-175 g [5-6 oz] encased in its own suet, and must be bought and cooked in the suet. The recipe name means 'in a light coating'—literally 'in a night-shirt'!

Serve with creamy mashed potatoes, to absorb the natural juices, and a green vegetable.

SERVES 4
**4 small veal kidneys, 150-175 g [5-6 oz] each, encased in their own suet
salt
freshly ground black pepper
half a small lemon**

Below right: liver, Venetian-style, is a classic way of cooking calf's liver.

1 Heat the oven to 200°C [400°F] gas mark 6.

2 Trim the kidneys of any surplus fat and skin, leaving just a very thin covering of fat all over.

3 Place the kidneys side by side in an ovenproof dish and season with salt and pepper.

4 Cook in the centre of the oven for 20 minutes, turning several times and basting with the fat and juices that have collected in the dish.

5 Heat the grill until very hot.

6 Remove the baking dish from the oven and lift out the kidneys, reserving the juices. Arrange the kidneys, still in their suet, on the grill rack.

7 Grill rapidly, turning frequently, for 3-4 minutes, or until the fat is just crisp.

8 Serve immediately, with all the pan juices poured over them, and finish with a squeeze of lemon juice.

CHICKEN LIVER AND BACON ROLLS

These traditional savouries can be served as snacks with drinks, as an hors d'oeuvre, or as a savoury to finish a meal. The crispy bacon makes a superb accompaniment to the rich taste of the chicken livers. The savouries must be served piping hot.

SERVES 4
8 chicken livers
8 rashers of streaky bacon
5 ml [1 teaspoon] oil
8 bay leaves
freshly ground black pepper

1 Prepare the chicken livers. Wash well under cold running water and pat dry with kitchen paper. Carefully trim away any tough skin and greenish parts. Keep the livers whole.

2 Set the grill to its highest setting.

3 Remove rind and stretch bacon slices with a knife. Wrap the livers with the bacon.

4 Brush 2 metal skewers with oil and spear on the bacon and liver rolls. Thread a bay leaf between each bacon roll.

5 Sprinkle with pepper and place the skewers on the grill rack.

6 Cook under moderately high heat for 8 minutes, turning twice.

7 Ease the rolls off the skewers with the prongs of a fork. Spear each one with a cocktail stick and serve immediately.

Variation

● Add water chestnuts to these rolls by wrapping the bacon rashers round both a chicken liver and a water chestnut.

CRISPY CHICKEN LIVERS

This recipe makes a spicy and unusual hot appetizer. Serve the livers garnished with sprigs of watercress or parsley. Care must be taken not to overcook the small chicken livers.

SERVES 4
450 g [1 lb] chicken livers
15 ml [1 tablespoon] soy sauce
15 ml [1 tablespoon] dry sherry
5 ml [1 teaspoon] finely chopped fresh ginger
1 garlic clove, chopped
30 ml [2 tablespoons] finely chopped spring onions
50 g [2 oz] plain flour
salt
freshly ground black pepper
45 ml [3 tablespoons] oil

1 Prepare the chicken livers. Wash well under cold running water and pat dry with kitchen paper. Care-

fully trim away any tough skin and greenish parts. Cut each liver in half.

2 Put the soy sauce, sherry, ginger, garlic and spring onions into a shallow dish, just big enough to contain the livers in a single layer.

3 Put in the livers, stir to coat well with the marinade and leave for an hour.

4 Place the flour, salt and pepper in a clean polythene bag and shake gently.

5 Lift the livers from the marinade with a slotted kitchen spoon and drain on crumpled kitchen paper. Then pat dry.

6 Put one-third of the livers in the bag with the seasoned flour, shake well, and turn on to a plate. Repeat until all are coated.

7 Heat the frying-pan over high heat. Add the oil and when this is sizzling hot add the chicken livers, a few at a time being careful not to over-fill the pan. Cook for 4 minutes, turning once.

8 Reserve the cooked livers on a warmed serving plate in a low oven until all are finished. Serve immediately, garnished with parsley or watercress.

Crispy chicken livers can be garnished with croûtons.

Cheap and cheerful

Long slow cooking turns the tougher types of offal into a variety of rich and succulent dishes. Think of braised hearts stuffed with spicy seasonings or a thick meaty oxtail stew, and you will realize how delicious these inexpensive meals can be.

Many kinds of offal can be turned into deliciously tender dishes by long slow cooking. By varying the vegetables and the seasonings added to these dishes, you can extend your range of meat meals enormously, without hurting your purse too much.

Offal is the name given to the organs and the extremities of a slaughtered animal. Some kinds of offal, in particular the finer types of liver and kidney, are best suited to the quick cooking methods of frying and grilling, and these are described in detail on pages 111–122. But hearts, tripe and oxtail, as well as the tougher varieties of liver and kidney, need longer cooking. They can be braised or casseroled, or simmered in a savoury sauce, but whichever method is used, the dishes must be maintained at the barest simmer throughout the cooking time, to ensure that the meat becomes really tender.

Casseroled oxtail with a selection of vegetables makes a tasty family meal.

LAMB'S HEART
Allow 1 per portion

Description
The smallest of all the various hearts, averaging 175–225 g [6–8 oz], it is often fatty around the outside.

Method
Among the tenderest of hearts, it is best stuffed and braised, or may be slow roasted if kept well basted.

PIG'S HEART
Serves 1–2 portions according to size

Description
Very similar in appearance to lamb's but can be larger, ranging from 225–450 g [8–16 oz]. It is usually slightly paler in colour and leaner.

Method
Slightly less tender than lamb's heart, so cook a little longer. It has a good rich texture. Braise in a well-flavoured sauce or stuff as for lamb's heart.

CALF'S HEART
Allow 150–225 g [5–8 oz] per portion

Description
A larger heart ranging from 350–550 g [12–20 oz] depending on the size of the calf. Not always available on demand, and may need to be ordered specially.

Method
Usually tender and one of the best of the hearts. Very lean, so benefits from a rich, tasty stuffing. Cook as for lamb's heart, but longer according to size.

OX HEART
Allow 150–225 g [5–8 oz] per portion

Description
Very large, muscular, dark-coloured heart weighing up to 1.8 kg [4 lb].

Method
Rather large so always slice before cooking. Best braised or stewed with vegetables and herbs. Inclined to be tough, so needs extra long slow moist cooking.

TRIPE
Allow 175 g [6 oz] per portion

Description
The creamy coloured stomach lining of an ox, either deeply honeycombed or fairly plain in texture. Bought by weight.

Method
Always soaked, blanched and partially cooked by the butcher, so cooking times vary according to the length of pre-cooking. Soak in water with salt and vinegar then braise or casserole with vegetables and herbs.

OXTAIL
Allow 275 g [10 oz] per portion

Description
Rather dark meat with a high proportion of bone. Tails are sold whole or jointed into short lengths and sold by weight.

Method
Has an excellent rich meaty flavour but needs very long slow cooking to make it tender. Braise or casserole with vegetables and herbs.

CHOOSING OFFAL FOR SLOW COOKING

Hearts, tripe and oxtail are almost always cooked by long slow methods such as stewing, casseroling or braising or methods which combine elements of each. The coarser types of liver and kidney which are not quite tender enough for frying and grilling are best slowly cooked with other flavourings for a long period.

Hearts

Hearts have been a prized meat down the ages. At one time they were always eaten by hunters and warriors, who thought they built up strength and courage. In the eighteenth century it was the custom to serve a heart prepared in a special way, as a kind of visual joke. A calf's heart would be stuffed and braised, then rolled in coarse breadcrumbs and short lengths of cooked vermicelli to resemble prickles. The heart would then be browned in the oven, arranged on a platter surrounded with tomato-coloured gravy, and served as 'love in disguise'.

The meat of hearts is lean, close in texture and inclined to be rather dry. For this reason long, moist cooking is needed. Long cooking is also needed to tenderize the hearts. Since heart meat does not have a great deal of flavour, stuffing is often used to give the meat added taste and interest.

The hearts of lamb, calf, pig and ox all make nutritious and substantial meals. They are all inexpensive and rich in vitamins and essential minerals.

When buying hearts choose ones which are firm with a good colour and a fresh pleasant smell. Avoid any that are dull or dry-looking with an unpleasant smell.

Lambs' hearts are small and tender. They weigh about 175–225 g [6–8 oz] and one heart serves one person. They are often fatty round the outside.

Pigs' hearts are similar in appearance to lambs' hearts but slightly larger, paler and leaner. They are less tender and need longer cooking. Depending on size, one heart will serve 1–2 people.

Calves' hearts are very lean and tender but not always readily available and may have to be specially ordered from the butcher. They are larger than pigs' hearts and each one will make 2–3 servings.

Ox hearts are the largest of all the hearts and are usually sliced before cooking. They are large and dark coloured and need extra long slow moist cooking to tenderize them. Allow 150–225 g [5–8 oz] per serving.

Tripe

Tripe is the muscular stomach lining of an ox. It is always prepared before being sold, and has long been a firm favourite in the north of England where it is traditionally cooked and served with an onion sauce; Samuel Pepys was fond of tripe cooked in this way. It is also the basis of one of the world's great classic dishes—tripes à la mode de Caen—in which the tripe is casseroled for up to 10 hours with a calf's foot, salt pork, vegetables and calvados.

Tripe cooked with care and imagination makes a very cheap and tasty dish, so if you have never tried it you may be in for a very pleasant surprise. It is easily digested and rich in calcium.

Tripe is prepared by the butcher before being sold. This is a very long process which involves soaking it in lime, blanching it and partially cooking it. It is this process which gives the tripe its attractive clotted cream colouring.

The amount of cooking the tripe is given varies enormously. When buying tripe be sure to check with the butcher to find out how much further cooking the particular tripe needs. Check constantly when cooking to make sure it is not overcooking and spoiling. This is the only sure way of obtaining the right degree of tenderness as, due to this variation in the preparation of tripe, timings for tripe recipes can only be approximate.

There are various kinds of tripe. Tripe from the animal's first stomach is fairly plain and rather slippery in texture: it is known as 'thick seam' or 'blanket' tripe.

Tripe from the animal's second stomach is known as 'monk's head' or 'honeycomb' tripe and is deeply dimpled and honeycomb-like in appearance. In many tripe dishes it is customary to use a mixture of each kind of tripe, but if you are cooking tripe for the first time you may prefer to choose only the 'honeycomb' variety as this is usually more tender than the flat variety, and has a more interesting texture.

When buying tripe look for firm thick creamy-coloured tripe, and avoid any that is greyish, slimy or flabby-looking. Allow about 175 g [6 oz] per person—and remember always to check with the butcher about the amount of cooking the tripe has already had.

Oxtail

Oxtails weigh about 1 kg [2-2½ lb], just enough, with vegetables, for three to four portions. If you have a large family, you may prefer to cook two oxtails at once, as our forbears often did, using the large meaty end of the tails for the casserole and the thin ends for oxtail soup.

However, oxtail is more commonly jointed into short lengths and sold by weight. Because of the high proportion of bone to meat, and because oxtail tends to be rather fatty, allow about 275 g [10 oz] per serving.

Oxtail is available all year round, but the tails of animals slaughtered in autumn are likely to be larger and fattier because animals store reserves of fat in the tail ready for the cold months ahead.

When buying oxtail look for fresh red meat and white fat. Avoid any meat that is dark and discoloured or that has yellowing fat and smells.

Liver and kidneys

Types of liver and kidneys are discussed in detail on pages 111–122. The larger, coarser types are the ones best suited to longer, slower cooking. Pig's and ox liver can be cooked in this way, as can pig's and ox kidney. Lambs' kidneys are also good braised or cooked slowly in a flavoured sauce. Allow 100 g [4 oz] of liver, and 100–175 g [4–6 oz] of kidney per portion.

When buying liver look for firm, fresh meat and avoid any that is dry or dull, or has a bluish tint. Kidneys should be plump and firm.

STORING

Offal of all kinds is extremely perishable and should always be eaten on the day of purchase unless, as in the case of the stronger liver and kidneys, it is to be soaked overnight. This rule applies to both fresh and frozen meats.

Store in the refrigerator until time for cooking. Remove the meat from the butcher's sealed polythene bag or the supermarket tray, place it on a plate and cover lightly with kitchen foil so that a little air can circulate round the meat.

Step-by-step to preparing hearts

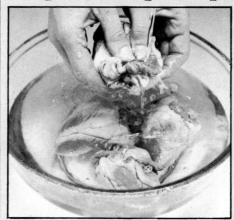

Wash the hearts thoroughly under cold running water, squeezing gently to remove congealed blood.

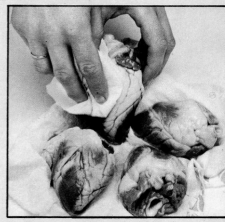

2 Drain on crumpled kitchen paper and pat dry. Place on a chopping board or firm work surface.

Step-by-step to stuffing a heart

1 Prepare the hearts up to stage 3 in the step-by-step to preparing hearts instructions.

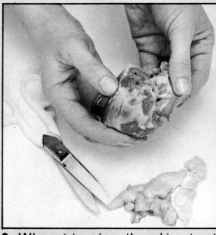

2 When trimming the skin, try to leave a flap of skin on one side to help enclose the stuffing.

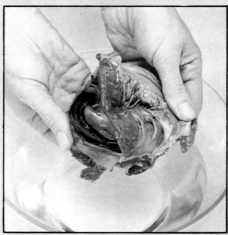

6 If washing a pig's heart, carefully turn inside out and wash away any persistent blood patches.

7 Soak the hearts for 30 minutes or more in lightly salted water. Drain and pat dry inside and out.

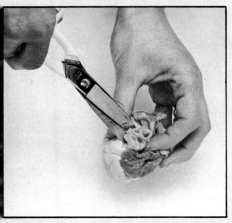

3 Using sharp scissors carefully snip away the muscular artery walls and any outside skin.

4 If preparing lambs' hearts, trim away any surplus fat from around the top of the heart.

5 Wash again under cold running water and soak for 30 minutes or more in lightly salted water.

3 Put each prepared heart on a board and, with scissors, snip down through the dividing wall.

4 Continue cutting down almost to the base, being careful not to cut the heart in two.

5 Wash the heart under cold running water to remove any remaining patches of congealed blood.

8 Using a teaspoon, fill the cavity in the middle of the heart with stuffing, pressing down firmly.

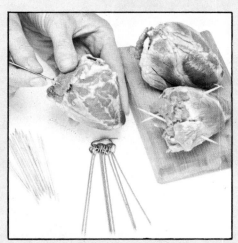

9 Close the heart and secure the stuffing in place with small skewers or cocktail sticks.

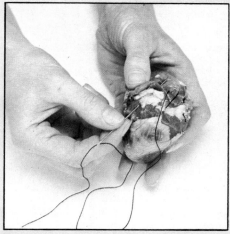

OR stitch across the hearts with a needle and coarse thread, pulling together the flaps on either side.

Step-by-step to preparing tripe

1 Put the tripe into a colander and wash thoroughly under cold running water.

2 Soak for up to an hour in cold water containing salt and vinegar.

3 Drain the tripe thoroughly, pat dry with kitchen paper and cut up according to the recipe.

PREPARING OFFAL FOR COOKING

Although there is very little waste on most kinds of offal, careful preparation is needed to get the best from these meats. It is well worth spending time on preparation, as it really does make a difference to the end results. Happily, once braised or casseroled offal is simmering, it needs little further attention.

Hearts

Wash the hearts under cold running water, squeezing gently to help remove any congealed blood. For easier handling, drain the hearts on crumpled kitchen paper and dry carefully. Use sharp scissors, trim away any muscular artery walls and any skin, although try to leave a flap of skin on one side if the hearts are to be stuffed. If you are preparing lambs' hearts, trim away any surplus fat there might be around the top of the hearts.

If the hearts are to be stuffed, try to leave a flap of skin on one side to help enclose the stuffing. With scissors snip through the central dividing wall, cutting down almost to the base, but being careful not to cut the heart in two. This deep cut provides a good space to fill with stuffing.

All hearts, whether they have been prepared ready for stuffing or not, should be washed again very thoroughly under cold running water to remove any remaining patches of congealed blood.

In pigs' hearts in particular, these blood patches can be persistent, so if the hearts have been cut through the centre ready for stuffing, carefully turn the entire heart inside out and wash thoroughly. Do this very carefully because if hearts are roughly handled, they are likely to split in two which, of course, then makes them unsuitable for stuffing.

Soak the hearts in lightly salted water—5 ml [1 teaspoon] of salt to 550 ml [1 pt] of water—for 30 minutes or longer. When ready to stuff or cook, drain the hearts and dry them very thoroughly inside and out with absorbent kitchen paper.

To fill hearts with stuffing, open them and with a teaspoon add the stuffing to the central cavity. Press the stuffing down firmly with your fingers. Close up the hearts and secure both halves with toothpicks or small metal skewers. When the hearts are cooking, some stuffing will inevitably escape into the sauce, but this will simply help to enrich the liquid. Hearts can be sewn together to make sure no stuffing escapes, but this procedure is rather time consuming and unnecessary.

Tripe

Tripe is very quick and simple to prepare, as so much preparation is done before it is sold. Put the tripe in a colander and wash it thoroughly under cold running water. Then soak in water containing 5 ml [1 teaspoon] of salt and 15 ml [1 tablespoon] of vinegar for every 2.5 L [4½ pt] of water. Drain the tripe thoroughly and pat dry with kitchen paper.

Tripe is cut up in different ways for different recipes. The most usual method is into pieces about 7.5 cm [3"] square, or alternatively into irregular-shaped pieces which resemble other stewing meats more closely.

Oxtail

Oxtail is best prepared by blanching as this is the simplest and most thorough way of cleaning the meat. Put the pieces of jointed oxtail in a large saucepan and cover them well with cold water. Bring the water slowly to the boil. Using a skimmer or slotted kitchen spoon, skim off the grey scum as it rises to the surface. Cover the pan and simmer the meat for 10 minutes, adjusting the temperature so a slow simmer is maintained. Drain the oxtail in a colander and dry the pieces with kitchen paper.

1 Put the pieces of oxtail into a large saucepan, cover with cold water and bring slowly to the boil.

Liver and kidneys

The preparation of liver and kidneys is described in detail on pages 111–122. Most stronger-flavoured livers and kidneys benefit from being soaked in lightly salted water (that is, 5 ml [1 teaspoon] of salt to every 550 ml [1 pt] of water) for several hours or overnight.

To prepare liver, first soak it then wash well under cold running water. Drain and dry thoroughly with absorbent kitchen paper. Slice into the required pieces. Trim away any outside skin or large veins using a sharp knife. When liver is being braised or casseroled it is usually cut into strips about 6 mm [¼"] wide down the length of the lobe, or else into pieces about 2.5 cm [1"] square. Ox liver must always be cut small as it is the toughest of livers.

To prepare kidneys, remove any suet, skin them carefully and then cut away the white core (as shown on page 116). Soak the kidneys in salted water for several hours or overnight. Wash them well under cold running water, drain and cut into the pieces required. When kidneys are casseroled or braised they are cut into halves if small or into strips about 12 mm [½"] wide, or alternatively into 2.5 cm [1"] cubes. Ox kidney must be sliced or cut into small pieces as it is tougher than the other kinds of kidney.

EQUIPMENT

Equipment for stewing and casseroling is discussed on pages 53 and 62–63, and equipment for braising is discussed on page 2. The single main essential is a heavy-based casserole with a tightly fitting lid. You will need a sharp knife, or scissors, and a board for trimming and preparing the offal, stuffing and vegetables, a colander to drain the offal and absorbent kitchen paper to dry it.

If you are stuffing hearts, you will need some small skewers or toothpicks to secure the hearts together again after the stuffing has been added.

A clean polythene bag is useful for shaking the meat in seasoned flour. A plate for floured slices, a slotted kitchen spoon for lifting the meat from the hot fat and a wooden spoon if you are making a roux will also be needed. You may also need a skimmer.

COOKING METHODS

When offal is to be cooked slowly it can be cooked by several different methods. It can be stewed or casseroled from a cold-start, or otherwise given a fry-start, depending on the toughness of the meat. Ox heart, for example, should always be cooked by the cold-start method, as it is tough meat.

Cold-start stewing and casseroling is dealt with in detail on pages 51–60, and is best suited to the toughest cuts. The offal must be cut up small, covered with cold water and simmered with any vegetables for a long period, 2½ hours or more.

Fry-start stewing and casseroling is described on pages 61–72. The offal is quickly fried to seal the surface, and vegetables are often fried too. This adds colour and flavour. These casseroles are usually flour thickened and take only slightly less time to cook than cold-start casseroles.

When the offal is casseroled it is important to maintain a slow simmer so that the meat will be really tender. At the end of cooking time skim as much fat as possible from a fry-start casserole.

Some types of offal can be braised, and instructions for braising are described on pages 1–8.

Braised offal is first browned fast and then cooked very slowly on a bed of chopped vegetables, which may be first sweated in hot fat. A very little liquid is used to create steam inside an almost sealed casserole.

Offal may also be cooked by a combination of these methods—to which no particular name is attached. A certain amount of simmering is required, but not the long cooking time of casseroling and braising.

Liver, kidneys and tripe can all be cut into pieces, fried quickly in hot fat, then simmered in a sauce over a low heat for between 15 minutes and 1 hour, depending on the requirements of the meat. Use a tightly covered pan, and maintain a slow simmer. Check the meat for tenderness regularly so that it does not overcook and spoil.

Step-by-step to preparing oxtail

2 Using a skimmer or slotted kitchen spoon, skim off the grey scum as it rises to the surface.

3 Simmer for 10 minutes, making sure that only one or two bubbles break the water's surface.

4 Drain the oxtail in a colander and carefully pat dry with absorbent kitchen paper.

Hearts

Lambs', pigs' and calves' hearts can all be stuffed and braised, or braised without stuffing. Lambs' hearts can also be roasted, provided they are kept well basted.

Stuffed lambs' hearts or small pigs' hearts take about 2½ hours to cook at a low simmer. Larger pigs' hearts and calves' hearts take proportionally longer according to size.

Unstuffed hearts cook more quickly. Lambs' hearts and small pigs' hearts take about 1½–2 hours at a low simmer, while larger pigs' hearts and calves' hearts take longer according to size. All these hearts are fry-started. They are ready to eat when they feel tender when pierced with a fork or skewer.

Ox heart is the toughest of all the hearts and is usually bought sliced. Its flavour is much improved if it is soaked in cold water for about 30 minutes before cooking. Because of its toughness, this meat is best braised or casseroled from a cold start for about 2 hours. If it were fry-started it could be tough and leathery.

Tripe

Tripe is usually cooked in one of two ways. It may be simmered slowly in a sauce for about an hour, until it is what the Italians call 'al dente', that is, tender but still slightly resistant to the teeth. Alternatively, it is stewed and casseroled for anything up to 10 hours until it is very soft and has taken on the flavours of the other ingredients.

The amount of cooking time needed varies according to the length of time tripe has been cooked before being sold, so any recipe times can only be very approximate. When stewed or casseroled, tripe can be either cold-started or fry-started, depending on the requirements of the particular recipe.

Oxtail

Oxtail always needs very long moist cooking to make it tender. Because the meat is often very fatty it is best, if possible, to cook it the day before it is to be eaten. Then the casserole can be cooled and the fat will rise to the surface. This can then be scraped off easily with a spoon.

If the oxtail is to be served immediately it is cooked, try to remove as much fat from the surface as possible. Use a spoon to skim it

off, or carefully blot it up with absorbent kitchen paper or a piece of bread.

Oxtail is usually fry-started to give the dish colour and flavour and to seal in the juices. It takes 3–4 hours of slow simmering to become really tender. When cooked, the meat should be coming away from the bone and almost soft enough to cut with a spoon.

To reheat, place the casserole or pan in a low oven, or over a low heat and allow to heat slowly but thoroughly. Sprinkle with chopped parsley before serving.

Liver

Pig and ox liver is almost always fry-started to seal in its juices when stewed or casseroled. It does not generally need a very long cooking time, but should be tender when pierced with a fork, after 1–1½ hours.

Very thin slices of pigs' liver can also be cooked by first frying them to seal in the juices, then simmering them in a sauce for just 15–20 minutes until tender. This method of cooking is neither, strictly speaking, braising or casseroling, but something between the two.

Pig's liver can be used to make the traditional British dish of faggots—literally 'a bundle' of partially-cooked minced ingredients wrapped round a small piece of well-flavoured fat.

Kidneys

Pigs' and lambs' kidneys need a relatively short simmering time, and like pig's liver, slices of these kidneys can be first fried to seal in the juices, then simmered in a savoury sauce for just 15–20 minutes until tender.

Ox kidney needs a long slow moist cooking to make it tender, and must be cut into small pieces. It can either be fry-started or cold-started and will take about 2–3 hours of braising or casseroling to become completely tender. When cooked, it should be easily pierced with a fork.

STUFFED BRAISED HEARTS

XXX *Lambs' or small pigs' hearts are used for this recipe, which makes a tasty lunch or supper. Allow one heart per person and serve with creamed potatoes and a green vegetable.*

SERVES 4
4 lambs' hearts
20 ml [4 teaspoons] oil
1 medium-sized onion
20 ml [4 teaspoons] flour
250 ml [½ pt] stock
10 ml [2 teaspoons] mushroom ketchup
salt
freshly ground black pepper
7.5 ml [1½ teaspoons] lemon juice

For the stuffing:
1 small onion
25 g [1 oz] butter
1 small lemon
40 g [1½ oz] fresh breadcrumbs
10 ml [2 teaspoons] chopped fresh marjoram or 4 ml [¾ teaspoon] dried marjoram
20 ml [4 teaspoons] chopped fresh parsley
salt and freshly ground black pepper

1 Prepare the hearts as shown in the step-by-step pictures. Try to leave a flap of skin on one side of the central division, to help enclose the stuffing.

2 Soak the hearts in lightly salted water for 30 minutes or longer.

Stuffed and braised lamb's hearts make a delicious lunch.

3 Meanwhile make the stuffing. Peel and finely chop the onion.

4 Heat the butter in a frying-pan and fry the onion gently over a low heat for 5 minutes until it is softened but not coloured. Grate the zest from the lemon.

5 Remove the pan from the heat and add the breadcrumbs, lemon zest, marjoram, parsley and salt and pepper to taste. Mix thoroughly.

6 Drain the hearts and dry them thoroughly with kitchen paper. Fill the cavities with the stuffing, pressing it down firmly into the hearts.

7 Secure the stuffing into place with small poultry skewers or tooth picks.

8 Heat the oven to 150°C [300°F] gas mark 2.

9 Heat the oil in a large flameproof casserole over a moderately high heat. When hot and almost smoking, fry the hearts briskly, turning them until they are browned on all sides. Remove to a plate and reserve.

10 Peel and slice the onion and add to the casserole. Reduce the heat and fry gently for about 10 minutes until it is beginning to colour.

11 Reduce the heat. Add the flour off the heat, stirring. Return to the heat, stirring continuously and cook until the flour turns fawn.

12 Remove the casserole from the heat and slowly add the stock, stirring it in until smooth.

13 Add the mushroom ketchup, return the casserole to the heat and bring to the boil, stirring continuously.

14 Add salt and pepper to taste, then replace the hearts. Cover the casserole and transfer to the centre of the oven.

15 Cook for 2½ hours, or until tender when pierced with a skewer. Adjust the oven heat, if necessary, to maintain a bare simmer.

16 Turn the hearts half way through the cooking time.

17 When cooked, skim off the surface fat, stir in the lemon juice and check the seasoning. Serve from the casserole.

OXTAIL CASSEROLE

This is a family dish, cooked and served in the same pot. In this method it is simmered on top of the stove, but it can also be cooked for the same length of time in a cool oven, heated to 150°C [300°F] gas mark 2. For a more elegant dish, arrange the pieces

of cooked oxtail in the centre of a hot, shallow serving dish, strain enough sauce over them to thoroughly moisten the meat, and garnish with freshly cooked vegetables such as baby carrots, button onions, new potatoes, diced turnips and green peas. Surplus sauce is always a bonus as, suitably extended and seasoned, it makes delicious oxtail soup.

SERVES 4

1.15 kg [2½ lb] oxtail, cut into pieces
100 g [4 oz] unsmoked streaky bacon
2 large onions
4 medium carrots
2 celery sticks
50 g [2 oz] dripping
45 ml [3 tablespoons] oil
15 g [½ oz] flour
700 ml [1¼ pt] meat stock
30 ml [2 tablespoons] tomato purée
1 bouquet garni
10 ml [2 teaspoons] lemon juice
salt
freshly ground black pepper
15 ml [1 tablespoon] chopped parsley

1 Put the pieces of oxtail into a large saucepan, cover with cold water and bring slowly to the boil, skimming off the grey scum as it rises to the surface. Simmer for 10 minutes.

2 Drain the oxtail and dry the pieces with kitchen paper.

3 De-rind and dice the bacon.

4 Peel and slice the onions. Scrape and slice the carrots. Wash and slice the celery.

5 Heat the dripping and oil in a large flameproof casserole over a moderately high heat. When it is hot and almost smoking, put in the pieces of oxtail, a few at a time, and fry them briskly, turning once, until browned on both sides. Remove with a slotted spoon and reserve.

6 Put the bacon in the pan and let it sweat for a minute or so. Then add the onion, carrot and celery and fry, stirring frequently, for about 5 minutes or until the onions are beginning to soften and colour.

7 Tilt the pan, push the vegetables to one side and spoon off all but about 15 ml [1 tablespoon] of the fat—the amount of excess fat will depend on the fattiness of the oxtail.

8 Remove the pan from the heat, sprinkle on the flour and stir until the remaining fat has been absorbed. Reduce the heat then cook for 1–2 minutes.

9 Remove the pan from the heat and stir in the stock, tomato purée, bouquet garni, lemon juice and salt and pepper to taste. Return the pan to the heat and bring slowly to simmering point, stirring continuously.

10 Add the pieces of oxtail to the pan, making sure they are covered with the liquid. Add a little water if necessary.

11 Cover the pan tightly, using a piece of foil under the lid if the fit is not close.

12 Simmer very gently for 3–4 hours, adjusting the heat to make sure a slow simmer is maintained. When cooked, the meat should be tender and coming away from the bone.

13 If for serving the next day, allow the casserole to become cold then spoon off the solidified surface fat. To serve, reheat gently but thoroughly, check the seasoning, sprinkle with chopped parsley and serve.

14 If the casserole is to be served immediately, skim off as much surface fat as possible, check the seasoning and sprinkle with chopped parsley.

HONEYCOMB TOSCANA

The Italians have many colourful and tasty ways of cooking tripe of which this Tuscan recipe is an example. The tripe is simmered in a tomato sauce lightly flavoured with marjoram, and served 'al dente'. The cooking method is not casseroling or braising, but something in between.

SERVES 4
700 g [1½ lb] honeycomb tripe
100 g [4 oz] onions
1 garlic clove
2 celery sticks
45 ml [3 tablespoons] oil
400 g [14 oz] canned tomatoes
15 ml [1 tablespoon] tomato purée
250 ml [½ pt] chicken or meat stock
5 ml [1 teaspoon] fresh marjoram or 2.5 ml [½ teaspoon] dried marjoram
2.5 ml [½ teaspoon] fresh parsley
5 ml [1 teaspoon] sugar
salt
freshly ground black pepper
50 g [2 oz] grated Parmesan cheese

1 Wash the tripe thoroughly, drain it and dry with absorbent kitchen paper.

2 Cut the tripe into strips 5 × 1.5 cm [2 × ½"].

3 Chop the parsley and fresh marjoram, if used.

4 Peel and chop the onion. Peel, chop and crush the garlic. Wash and chop the celery.

5 Heat the oil in a heavy-based casserole over moderate heat and when hot gently fry the onion, garlic and celery for 10 minutes, stirring frequently, until soft and slightly coloured.

6 Meanwhile, put the canned tomatoes into a basin and roughly chop them.

7 Add the tripe to the casserole and fry lightly for 1 minute, stirring continuously.

8 Remove the casserole from the heat, add the tomatoes, the tomato

purée, stock, marjoram, parsley, sugar and a light seasoning of salt and pepper. Stir well.

9 Return to the heat and bring slowly to the boil, stirring occasionally.

10 Cover the pan and reduce the heat to the point where the casserole maintains a slow simmer.

11 Cook for 1 hour, checking occasionally to ensure the casserole is only just simmering, until the tripe feels tender, but not soft, when pierced with a fork.

12 Lift out the tripe with a slotted serving spoon on to a hot serving dish and keep warm.

13 Return the casserole to the heat and boil vigorously until the liquid is reduced to a coating consistency. Check the seasoning and pour the sauce over the tripe.

14 Sprinkle thickly with Parmesan cheese and hand more Parmesan around separately.

SPICED KIDNEYS

This is an attractive way of cooking pig's kidneys, the least tasty of all the different types of kidney. The sauce is delicious as it is, but can be made more spicy by adding chilli powder to taste. However, go cautiously when adding chilli powder as it really is a 'hot' flavouring. Serve the kidneys on a bed of plain boiled rice.

SERVES 4
4 pigs' kidneys
450 g [1 lb] onions
1 garlic clove
45 ml [3 tablespoons] oil
350 g [¾ lb] ripe tomatoes
15 ml [1 tablespoon] coriander seeds
2.5 ml [½ teaspoon] cumin seeds
10 ml [2 teaspoons] turmeric
250 ml [½ pt] plain yoghurt
30 ml [2 tablespoons] meat stock
salt
a good pinch chilli powder (optional)

1 Peel the kidneys and snip out as much as possible of the white cores, as explained in detail on page 116.

2 Soak in lightly salted cold water (5 ml [1 teaspoon] salt to 550 ml [1 pt] of water) for an hour, then drain and pat dry. Cut across into 6 mm [¼"] slices.

3 Peel and slice the onions. Peel, chop and crush the garlic. Skin and chop the tomatoes.

4 Heat the oil in a flameproof casserole over a moderately high heat until the oil is very hot.

5 Add the kidney slices and fry the slices quickly, stirring them until they are brown on both sides. With a slotted spoon lift them out and reserve.

6 Reduce heat and add the onions to the pan. Fry gently for 10 minutes until they are softened and lightly coloured, then add the garlic and cook for 1 minute.

7 While the onions are cooking, crush the coriander seeds in a mortar with a pestle. Or put them in a polythene bag, seal this and roll with a rolling pin.

8 Place the cumin seeds in a saucepan without fat. Heat the seeds over a medium heat for 1 minute to release their aroma.

9 Remove the pan with the onions from the heat and stir in the coriander, the cumin seeds and turmeric.

10 Add the tomatoes, yoghurt and stock, and return the pan to the heat.

11 Bring slowly to the boil over a moderate heat, stirring continuously. Cover and simmer gently for 15–20 minutes.

12 Taste the sauce, add salt to taste and a small pinch of chilli powder. Taste again before adding more chilli powder, if you wish.

13 Return the kidneys to the sauce, cover the pan and simmer very gently for 15–20 minutes, until the kidneys are just cooked.

14 Serve immediately on a bed of rice.

PIGS' HEARTS A L'ORANGE

⊠⊠⊠ *In this recipe the rich texture of the pigs' hearts is emphasized by a full-bodied orange-flavoured sauce. The dish can be simmered on top of the stove, or casseroled in a low oven. The orange-flavoured liqueur is not essential but, if available, it helps make a memorable dish from inexpensive ingredients.*

Serve with buttered egg noodles and a watercress salad, or with new potatoes, buttered carrots and peas. For a decorative effect, pile the carrots in the centre of the serving dish, surrounded with halves of heart and spoon peas around the edges.

SERVES 4
4 pigs' hearts
225 g [½ lb] onions
1 garlic clove
1 orange
25 g [1 oz] butter
30 ml [2 tablespoons] oil
30 ml [2 tablespoons] flour
425 ml [¾ pt] meat stock
15 ml [1 tablespoon] tomato
  purée
1 bay leaf
1 sprig of thyme
30 ml [2 tablespoons] bitter
  marmalade
10 ml [2 teaspoons] lemon
  juice
salt and black pepper
15-30 ml [1-2 tablespoons]
  orange liqueur (optional)

1 Prepare the hearts, as shown in the step-by-step pictures. Wash under cold running water, removing any patches of congealed blood. Snip out the muscular artery walls and trim away any skin. Do not cut deeply down through the centre dividing wall.

2 Wash the hearts again under cold running water to remove all persistent patches of congealed blood.

3 Soak the hearts in lightly salted water for 30 minutes or longer.

4 Meanwhile peel and slice the onions and peel and chop the clove of garlic. With a swivel-type potato peeler, peel 2 strips of orange peel from the orange.

5 Drain the hearts and dry thoroughly with kitchen paper.

6 Heat the butter and oil in a heavy flameproof casserole over a moderately high heat until hot but not smoking.

7 Add the hearts and fry for several minutes until browned and sealed on all sides. Remove from the pan and reserve.

8 Reduce the heat, add the onions and garlic to the casserole and fry gently for about 5 minutes until they are slightly softened and beginning to brown.

9 Remove from the heat, sprinkle on the flour, stir in. Return to the heat and cook gently, stirring continuously, until the flour turns fawn.

10 Remove the pan from the heat and stir in the stock. Add the tomato purée, bay leaf, thyme, orange rind and marmalade. Return to the heat and bring slowly to the boil, stirring continuously.

11 Season with salt and pepper to taste and replace the hearts in the casserole. Cover, reduce the heat and simmer very gently for about 1½ hours.

12 Check during the cooking that the liquid maintains a very low simmer and adjust the heat if necessary. The hearts are tender when pierced with a fork.

13 Lift out the hearts, cut in halves lengthwise, and arrange in a circle in a warm shallow serving dish. Keep warm.

14 Skim off the surface fat from the cooking liquid, add the lemon juice and boil rapidly, uncovered, until the liquid is reduced to the consistency of a thick sauce.

15 Check the seasoning, add the liqueur if used, and strain over the hearts. Serve immediately.

Tongue-tied

Tongues may be small or large depending on which animal they come from. Tongues are equally tasty eaten hot or cold. They reheat well and can be enlivened by a wide variety of sauces. Here we tell you all you need to know about cooking and serving, including pressing, different types of tongue.

Buying a whole tongue and cooking it at home is much better value than buying ready-cooked and sliced tongue, especially when you plan to serve it in any quantity.

Once you have learned how, cooking a tongue is not nearly so daunting as people at first imagine. Tongues consist of very dense fibres and need long, slow, gentle cooking to tenderize them. When this is done, however, the meat is exceptionally tender, able, as Mrs. Beeton puts it, 'to be pierced with a straw'.

A glazed, arched tongue makes a stunning buffet dish while a cold, pressed tongue is a good and cheap alternative to cooked ham and, for a small family, may serve several meals.

BUYING TONGUES

Tongues are cut out of the heads of carcasses. Ox, calves', pigs' and sheep's or lambs' tongues are all sold for cooking. These may be sold either untrimmed or short-cut. An untrimmed tongue still has its root attached. If you buy an untrimmed tongue, the price per kilo [pound] should be lower but you will need to cut away the root after cooking. The root consists of gristle, fat and small bones. A short-cut tongue is trimmed to the best-quality tongue meat

Ox tongue is used for an arched tongue which is glazed with stock or consommé and then garnished.

and the price is therefore proportionately higher. Nowadays most ox tongues and nearly all sheep's and lambs' tongues are sold short-cut.

Tongues are sold in two ways: they may either be fresh (if specially ordered) or pickled in brine.

An unpickled tongue should be really fresh. When choosing a tongue or tongues avoid any that smell unwholesome. A thick, rough-textured skin encases all tongues; avoid any with sticky skins. Ox tongues are pink if fresh but the skin will be greyish if pickled. Lambs' tongues are reddish-brown when raw and creamy in colour when cooked. Some tongues have natural dark spots on the skin depending on the colouring of the animal. The skin is always peeled off and discarded after cooking.

A guide to tongues

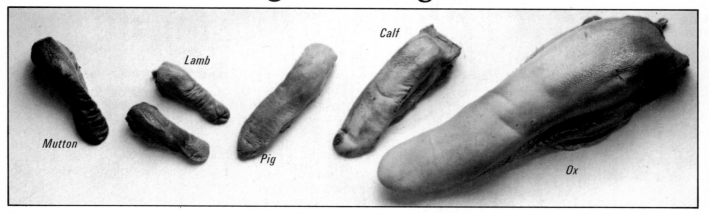

Mutton
Lamb
Pig
Calf
Ox

Kind and size

Ox: 1.4-2.7 kg [3-6 lb] per tongue. Allow 150-175 g [5-6 oz] raw tongue per portion (trimmed and unskinned). A 1.4 kg [3 lb] tongue should give 8 good portions.

Lambs' and sheep's: 100-275 g [4-10 oz] per tongue. Allow 175-225 g [6-8 oz] raw tongue per portion, depending on whether trimmed or untrimmed.

Calves': 275-700 g [10 oz-1½ lb] per tongue depending on age of calf. Allow 150-175 g [5-6 oz] raw untrimmed tongue per portion.

Pigs': 225-450 g [8-16 oz] per tongue. Allow 175-225 g [6-8 oz] raw untrimmed tongue per portion.

How sold

Nowadays usually short-cut (ie trimmed of root and bones) but occasionally untrimmed. Generally pickled by the butcher, it can be bought fresh if ordered. Pickled varieties are sometimes sold in sealed plastic bags with recommended soaking and cooking times.

Usually sold fresh. Imported frozen tongues are generally short-cut, but home-produced tongues may be untrimmed or short-cut. They are very variable in size. Sheep's tongues are naturally larger than lambs' tongues.

These tongues are usually sold fresh but can be bought pickled if required.

This type is usually sold as part of the head and used in pig's head brawn. Not generally sold separately, but there are exceptions.

Choosing and ordering

Look for a thick, short tongue rather than a long thin one. Avoid a tongue with yellowish fat around the root. Popular sizes often in stock are 1.4-1.8 kg [3-4 lb]; if you need a larger size you may have to order it. It is also advisable to discuss the degree of pickling you prefer.

Should be very fresh. Buy by weight rather than number as they are very variable in size. Remember to allow for waste factor if they are bought untrimmed.

Calves' tongues are in short supply and not generally available unless ordered specially. Cook exactly as for ox tongues but reduce the simmering time.

If available, they should be very fresh. Choose as for lambs' and sheep's tongues.

PICKLED OR FRESH?

There are no hard and fast rules, but generally speaking tongue to be eaten cold will have a more interesting flavour if it is lightly pickled in brine before cooking. For this reason, butchers normally pickle ox tongues unless you specifically order a fresh one.

Fresh ox tongues are usually served hot, and after initial boiling they are often simmered in a robustly flavoured sauce; but this is a lengthy cooking process, more popular with hoteliers than with home cooks. It can, however, be performed over two days and the tongue needs very little attention while boiling.

Calves' and pigs' tongues are generally eaten hot and so are sold unpickled. They are, however, excellent cold if salted in the same way as an ox tongue, but for proportionately less time.

Lambs' tongues are usually sold fresh and eaten hot. As they are small it is a simple matter to improve their flavour by salting them very lightly at home.

Pickling brine consists basically of water, salt, saltpetre and brown sugar. The pickle varies a little from butcher to butcher, so you may prefer tongues from one butcher rather than another. The length of time an ox tongue should remain in pickle

Step-by-step to preparing and pressing a tongue

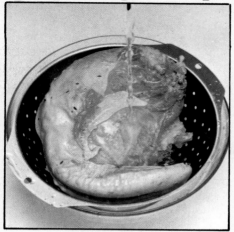

1 Leave the cooked tongue in the cooking liquid for thirty minutes after the heat has been turned off.

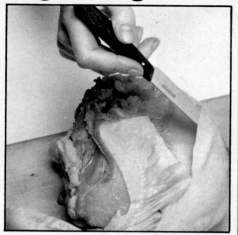

2 Place the tongue in a colander under cold running water to reduce temperature and loosen skin.

3 Place on a board and lift the skin at a loose point with a blunt knife. It should come away easily.

4 Holding skin between the knife and your thumb peel it carefully towards tip. Don't pierce the meat.

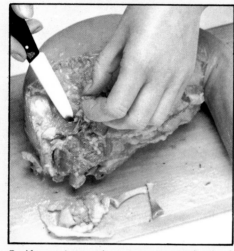

5 If untrimmed, cut out gristle and excess fat. Pull out the small bones from root.

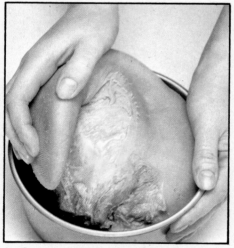

6 Curl the tongue to fit tightly inside a cake tin 7.5 cm [3"] deep and 15-20 cm [6-8"] in diameter.

7 Cover the tongue with a plate which fits exactly inside the rim of the tin. Press with a weight.

8 Leave overnight to set in a cool place. Juice will seep into spaces and form jelly.

9 To unmould, dip tin into hot water, cover with a serving plate and invert.

and soften the meat, lambs' tongues need slow, gentle cooking which can vary in length from 1½-2½ hours depending on the size and toughness of the tongues. As for ox tongues, allow for longer cooking and turn off the heat when the tongues are ready. They can be left to keep warm in the cooking liquor for up to one hour. As lambs' tongues are usually served hot, this may be a convenient time to make the sauce in which they are to be served.

You should allow plenty of time for skinning lambs' tongues as this is more fiddly and time-consuming than skinning a single, large ox tongue.

After skinning, lambs' tongues are usually split lengthways depending on their size. This is to make them easier to serve after any further cooking.

SKINNING AND TRIMMING TONGUES

Whether it is to be served hot or cold, a cooked tongue must be skinned and, if necessary, trimmed before serving. If possible leave the tongue in the cooking liquor for half an hour after cooking is complete. Then lift it out into a colander and rinse it thoroughly under the cold tap. This helps to loosen the skin so that it comes away more easily.

The skin should then be lifted with a blunt knife wherever it shows signs of coming free. This may be the side or the root end. Peel off by hand. Be careful not to spoil the beautiful surface of the meat under the skin.

If you are dealing with an untrimmed tongue, put it on a board after skinning and cut away all the gristle, excess fat and small bones from the root end. If the tongue is sufficiently cooked, any bones will be loose and easily dislodged.

PRESSING TONGUE

Because tongue is so soft when it is still warm from cooking, it is easy to mould into a shape which it will keep when cold.

An arched tongue, served cold is not pressed, except to keep it in shape. It is therefore slightly lighter in texture than a moulded tongue which is curled into shape and then pressed.

After skinning and trimming, the

Step-by-step to glazed arched tongue

⊠⊠⊠ *A glazed arched ox tongue takes some time and trouble but the result can look sensational for a special occasion. The stock in which the tongue has simmered should be used for making the glaze. However, you should taste the stock when cooking is complete. If it tastes very salty, substitute for it a jellied consommé with gelatine or commercial aspic jelly, made following the manufacturer's instructions.*

SERVES 8-10
1.6 kg [3½ lb] pickled ox tongue
2 onions
2 large carrots
1 celery stick
12 peppercorns
1 bay leaf
1 thyme sprig

For the glaze:
250 ml [½ pt] strained cooking stock
10 ml [2 teaspoons] gelatine
2.5-5 ml [½-1 teaspoon] meat or vegetable extract

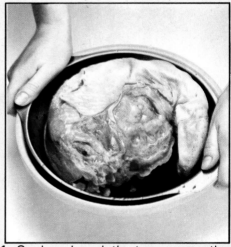

1 Soak and cook the tongue exactly as described in the recipe for boiled ox tongue.

2 While still warm, skin it and trim root end if necessary, as shown in the step-by-step pictures.

6 If stock is not too salty use it, with gelatine if necessary, for the glaze, otherwise use a can of consommé.

7 Stir in enough extract to give light brown colour, then set aside until glaze is almost at setting point.

warm. cooked tongue for pressing is curled to fit tightly into a round 7.5 cm [3"] deep cake tin. The diameter can be 15-20 cm [6-8"] depending on the size of the tongue.

A small plate or saucer is chosen to fit exactly inside the top of the tin and a heavy weight is placed on top. This can be old-fashioned kitchen weights but a kitchen canister will do as well. The tongue is then left in a cool place overnight. During the pressing enough liquid should seep into any small spaces in the tin to form a natural jelly.

To unmould the pressed tongue, dip the tin into hot water. Cover the top with a plate and then invert it. The tongue should slip out.

Cold pressed tongue is delicious served with a variety of sauces, for example salsa verde or Cumberland sauce.

CARVING TONGUES

Slice cold pressed tongues thinly across the top of the round. Each portion should consist of a full slice which includes some of the tip and some of the tongue base. About halfway down start gently slanting the knife, so making it easier to carve thin slices right to the last portion.

The texture of an arched cold tongue is much less dense than that of one which has been pressed and, consequently, much thicker slices of meat are necessary. Cut slices about 1·2 cm [½"] thick across the grain, taking the slices from the tip and the root end for each serving.

A hot tongue is carved against the grain of the meat into a series of rounds about 1 cm [⅓"] thick. Slices of pressed tongue which are to be reheated in a sauce are also carved like this.

SERVING OX TONGUE HOT

The preparation and cooking of ox tongue to be served hot is exactly the same as when serving it cold. Hot ox tongue does, however, open up the possibilities for serving the meat in one of a host of rich and deliciously flavoured sauces.

Tongue tends to be crumbly when hot so it is more economical to let it cool before attempting to carve. Slice the tongue into slices about 1 cm [⅓"] thick—not too thin—and arrange

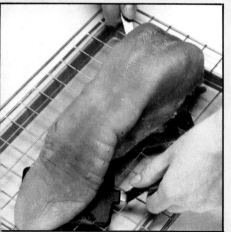

3 Cut a slice off the root end to enable the tongue to sit flat on a board with the tip stretched out.

4 Set two weights, covered with greaseproof paper, on either side of the tip to hold in position.

5 Cover lightly with greaseproof paper to prevent the surface hardening. Leave until cold.

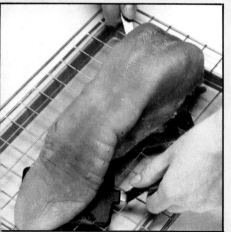

8 Place a tray beneath a wire cake rack to catch the glaze. Remove the tongue from the board and place it on the wire rack.

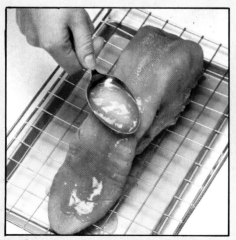

9 Spoon some glaze over the tongue, coating all exposed surfaces. Leave to set. Repeat once or twice for a thick, shiny glaze.

10 Transfer the tongue to a flat serving dish. Scrape remaining glaze from tray, reheat and pour round tongue.

them neatly in a shallow ovenproof serving dish. Coat with the sauce of your choice and reheat very gently in the oven at 150°C [300°F] gas mark 2 for about half an hour. If you are pressed for time, you may just as well slice the tongue while it is warm and coat it with the sauce. In this case it will need reheating for a shorter time.

Sauces to complement tongue should be full-bodied in texture and either richly flavoured or piquant. Sauce madère, sauce Romaine and sauce Robert are typical examples of suitable sauces to serve with a tongue.

SALSA VERDE

This Italian green sauce is like a strongly flavoured vinaigrette. It is a perfect accompaniment to cold tongue and also goes well with a variety of cold meats. This quantity is sufficient for serving with an ox tongue. For a smaller quantity, to serve four people, halve the quantities given.

MAKES ABOUT 250 ML [½ PT]
50 g [2 oz] spring onions or shallots
4 garlic cloves
90 ml [6 tablespoons] fresh parsley
60 ml [4 tablespoons] capers
8 anchovy fillets (optional)
60 ml [4 tablespoons] lemon juice
90 ml [6 tablespoons] olive oil
salt
freshly ground black pepper

1 Trim the spring onions or peel the shallots. Peel the garlic cloves and chop finely on a board.

2 Chop parsley finely.

3 Add parsley, drained capers and anchovy fillets, if used, to the board. Chop together with the spring onions or shallots as finely as possible.

4 Place in a mixing bowl and stir in the lemon juice and olive oil. Season with salt and freshly ground black pepper to taste.

5 Mix very thoroughly as for making a French dressing. A liquidizer is ideal; alternatively pour the sauce into a jar with a screw top and shake vigorously.

CUMBERLAND SAUCE

This is a traditional English sauce which goes well with tongue, ham, venison and lamb. It can be served with meat that is either hot or cold. It should be made with port; a substitute, such as red wine, changes the sauce's character. If not all of this sauce is immediately consumed, it will keep perfectly for several weeks.

SERVES 6
3 large oranges
90 ml [6 tablespoons] redcurrant jelly
15 ml [1 tablespoon] Dijon mustard
salt and pepper
150 ml [¼ pt] tawny port

1 Scrub the oranges. With a potato peeler pare off the rind very thinly and cut into thin matchstick-sized strips.

2 Bring a small saucepan of water to the boil, add the orange rind and boil for 5 minutes. Drain thoroughly.

3 Put the rind into a small bowl with the redcurrant jelly, mustard and a little salt and pepper.

4 Rest the basin over a pan of hot water and heat, stirring constantly, until the jelly melts and the ingredients blend.

5 If the jelly refuses to melt, press the jelly through a sieve and then continue heating.

6 Stir in the port and continue cooking for 5–6 minutes. Remove the basin from the water and leave in a cold place to cool and thicken.

7 Serve cold.

TONGUE IN SWEET-SOUR SAUCE

This recipe for sweet-sour sauce is an adaptation of the historic Italian salsa agrodolce. It is easy to make and is a popular Italian way of reheating sliced cooked tongue. Serve with carrots, cauliflower and plain boiled potatoes.

Salsa verde is a tasty Italian sauce which is a particularly good accompaniment to cold tongue as well as other cold meats.

SERVES 4
550 g [1¼ lb] thickly sliced cooked tongue

For the sauce:
50 g [2 oz] onion
30 ml [2 tablespoons] olive oil
400 ml [¾ pt] meat stock
25 g [1 oz] flour
30 ml [2 tablespoons] red wine vinegar
30 ml [2 tablespoons] brown sugar
15 ml [1 tablespoon] sultanas
15 ml [1 tablespoon] pine nuts
grated rind of half an orange
pinch of ground cloves

1 Peel and finely chop the onion.

2 Heat the oil in a saucepan and gently fry the onion over a low heat until it begins to soften.

3 Warm the stock in another saucepan.

4 Stir the flour into the onion off the heat. Cook over a low heat, stirring constantly, until the mixture is a pale fawn.

5 Remove the pan from the heat and gradually blend in the heated stock, stirring all the time.

Cauliflower is served with sliced tongue in a sweet and sour sauce. Fresh peas and baby carrots add colour and interest to farmhouse lambs' tongues.

6 Add the remaining sauce ingredients and bring to the boil, stirring. Cover and simmer gently for 30 minutes.

7 Heat the oven to 180°C [350°F] gas mark 4.

8 Arrange the tongue in overlapping slices in an ovenproof dish and, when ready, pour the sauce over it. Place in the oven for about 30 minutes so that the meat is impregnated with the sauce and thoroughly hot.

FARMHOUSE LAMBS' TONGUES

Fresh lambs' or sheep's tongues need long, slow cooking to tenderize them before serving piping hot in a well-flavoured sauce. The tongues are split in half lengthways before being coated with sauce. Allow 225 g [½ lb] per person if buying untrimmed tongues.

SERVES 4
700 g [1½ lb] trimmed lambs' tongues
1 small onion
550 ml [1 pt] meat stock
1 thyme sprig
4 peppercorns
225 g [½ lb] peas, shelled weight
225 g [½ lb] prepared baby carrots

For the sauce:
25 g [1 oz] butter
25 g [1 oz] flour
30–45 ml [2–3 tablespoons] medium dry sherry
squeeze of lemon juice
salt and freshly ground black pepper

1 Wash the tongues in cold water and, if fresh, cover and soak in cold water adding 15 ml [1 tablespoon] salt to every 1.15 L [2 pt] of water.

2 Leave to soak for 4 hours or overnight.

3 Drain and rinse the tongues, put into a saucepan and add the onion, stock, thyme and peppercorns.

4 Bring slowly to the boil, skim if necessary, cover the pan and simmer very gently for 1½ to 2½ hours, until the tongues are tender at the tip end when pierced with a skewer.

5 Transfer the tongues to a colander and rinse them in cold water. Strain and reserve 400 ml [¾ pt] of the stock.

6 With a sharp knife peel the tongues. If necessary trim away any gristle, small bones, loose skin or fat.

7 Simmer the peas and carrots for 10–15 minutes in salted water until cooked.

8 Cut the tongues in half lengthways, and put into a flameproof dish to keep warm.

9 Make the sauce. Melt the butter in a small heavy-based saucepan. Stir in the flour off the heat and then cook over moderately low heat, stirring continuously, until the flour turns a pale fawn colour.

10 Blend in the hot tongue stock and stir over a low heat until the sauce thickens.

11 Add the sherry, lemon juice and salt and pepper to taste, and pour over the tongues in the casserole.

12 Drain peas and carrots and add. Cover and heat together gently over a low heat for 15 minutes until ready to serve.

Under the skin!

The popularity of sausages has never waned and there are many reasons why. The first must be the enormous number of different types that are produced— each a reason in itself. Not only can sausages be cooked in many different ways but many are sold ready to serve. Here we describe the various groupings and the cooking methods, and give an identification parade of sausages most likely to be found. Serving suggestions are given for many varieties of raw and cooked sausages.

S ausages make good eating sense. The biggest bonus is the enormous selection that is available, which means that you need never be at a loss for a new flavour. Germany alone produces nearly 1500 varieties and while you may not be able to find all 1500 outside Germany, supermarkets and delicatessen everywhere offer a large selection. Do not be dismayed by the often rather daunting names or by lack of labels. Use the guidelines given here to help you interpret those which are labelled and ask the advice of your supplier whenever in doubt.

Sausages were invented to use up pork and although most still contain some pork, almost any meat can go into a sausage. The meat can be finely or coarsely minced and the sausages may be large or small, fat or thin, fresh or smoked, for cooking or ready to serve.

Sausages in the making. This is not as difficult as you might think and, with your own sausage meat, you can use as many herbs and flavourings as you like. Cook home-made sausages just as you would bought ones.

A type of sausage is often associated with a particular country but each region produces the sausages to its own recipe and many other countries will produce their own versions too. The variety, therefore, is virtually endless.

HISTORY OF SAUSAGE MAKING

Sausages, in the shape and form we know them, were developed by the ancient Romans to use up scraps of freshly killed pork. These could not be eaten at once and, therefore, had to be preserved. They became popular with everyone almost immediately. In fact, sausages became the most popular festival and fairground food. They became so closely associated, symbolically, with the wild feast of Lupercalia, that one Roman emperor tried to ban them from the empire completely, on the grounds that they were ruining public morals. He did not succeed!

Every country which came under Roman sway enthused over its sausages and copied them. When the Roman empire fell, people all over Europe went on making sausages in the Roman style—and still do. Italian Mortadella and some of the German sausages have scarcely changed since Roman times.

WHAT'S IN A SAUSAGE?

Originally, sausage meat consisted mainly of trimmings and coarse bits of pork and offal, minced with spices and a lot of pork fat. The latter was to help preserve the meat and to add extra flavour.

Most sausages, with obvious exceptions such as kosher sausages, are still made mainly of pork meat and all include some fat. Although the proportions vary in different kinds, sausages contain, on average, at least 225 g [½ lb] fat to each 1 kg [2¼ lb] meat.

However, even the Romans mixed other meat with their pork. Hundreds of different sausages have since been devised using different meat and offal, such as beef, veal, mutton, venison, liver, tongue, brains, and even just blood. The choice of meat depends mainly on local availability and tastes. Mutton sausages, for instance, are made in sheep-farming areas and in Canada, one can even find sausages that are made of bear meat!

British sausages

There are several differences between sausage making in Britain and the way sausages are made in other countries.

Whereas European sausages are nearly all made with a combination of different meat, in Britain most sausages are made with only one meat. They are usually pork or beef, although some mutton and some venison sausages are made too. The sausages can, and do, contain rusk

Handy hints

Home-made sausages

If you have a food mixer with a sausage-filling attachment there will be little difficulty, and a great deal of satisfaction, in making your own sausages. The bundles of casings sold by suppliers are usually far too big for household use, so your first step is to find a kindly butcher who will supply a small quantity from his stock. If your butcher cannot supply them, ask him to order some caul for you from his wholesaler.

Both natural and synthetic casings have to be soaked before use. Rinse the soaked casing and open it out with a strong jet of water. To do this, fit it over the end of the cold tap and turn on the water.

Attach the casing to your machine and feed in the minced meat mixture, being sure to leave no air pockets. Do not, however, pack the casing too full. When you have filled the length you require, stop the machine and tie off both ends of the casing tightly. Moisten the sausage and twist at intervals to make the links.

or other cereal: up to 50 per cent in beef sausages, 35 per cent in pork sausages. In other countries, this is illegal.

Another major difference between British and other sausages is that British sausages are always made of fresh raw meat and fat. These are minced together, so that the sausage meat has a crumbly texture which has the same appearance all through the sausage. Sausages made in other countries vary much more.

International sausages
The variety of sausages produced is, to put it simply, enormous. All are, by law, made only of meat and fat together with spices and, sometimes skimmed milk. No other ingredients may be added. There are, inevitably, some exceptions to this rule but any permitted extra ingredients have to be clearly shown on the label.

A mixture of meat is the general rule and the most usual mixture today is pork and beef, or pork and veal with pork fat added and, sometimes, ham or bacon. The sausages are sometimes made of fresh raw meat but many of them are made with cured meat salted in brine.

The texture of the sausages can also be very different. In some varieties, the sausage meat is minced very finely, almost as smooth as pâté, and in others it is coarsely ground. In either case, the basic mixture can be studded with small pieces of solid meat or fat to give a chunky or speckled appearance to the cut sausage.

Many of the sausages are treated before being sold. They can be sold raw, fully cooked, lightly smoked and fully or partly cooked, or smoked and semi- or fully dried.

Skinless (uncased) sausages
The first sausages were just patties made of minced or chopped meat and fat, without skins as we know them; they were wrapped in caul, which is the net-like membrane that covers an animal's internal organs. Sausages like these are still made a great deal in France where they are called crépinettes or gayettes.

There are various kinds of skinless sausage available commercially, some without any covering at all. Both pork and beef sausages are made without casings (the proper term for skins) and these are widely available in supermarkets. Sausage meat containing a percentage of cereal is also sold skinless, for use in stuffings and in other ways.

Besides the ordinary roll-shaped skinless sausages, there are other uncased meat products which can be described as sausages. Hamburgers and beefburgers are, in fact, flat, skinless sausages, while Jewish meat balls are small round ones. Faggots, which are made of pork innards, mixed with breadcrumbs or mashed potato, are very similar to the French gayette.

However, sausages with skins or casings are what we usually think of as sausages and they have many advantages over the skinless ones.

Sausages in skins
Good though all the skinless sausages are, adding a casing adds more than just a skin.

Casings were originally made from animals' intestines. The kind of animal they came from and, therefore, the size, determined the various standard sizes of sausage that could be bought, and these sizes are still used. Natural casings are still used but synthetic casings made from cellulose are becoming increasingly popular as they are generally easier to handle. Most of the mass-produced sausages with skins that you buy today have cellulose casings; they are made as very long tubes, which look just like the real thing. Some are colourless to let the natural colour of the sausage meat show through, others are brownish, to give the sausages a cured or smoked look.

Retail butchers who make their own sausages can choose whether to buy natural intestinal casings or synthetic ones. Both are used in the same way.

Casings make sausages usable in so many extra ways. Cased sausages can be boiled or steamed as well as fried and grilled; they can also be smoked (even at home if you have a home smoker).

Casings also make sausages look more attractive. Some European delicatessen sausages are given gaily-coloured coatings which show up well through the slightly glossy casing. The natural tan or russet of smoked sausages gets a sheen this way too, and they look very festive hanging in a row above a speciality shop's counter or in a delicatessen's chilled cabinet.

WHAT'S IN A NAME
It can be more than bewildering to be confronted by row upon row of sausages in a delicatessen, especially when the names are long and confusing. Before the various types of sausage are discussed, some meaning must be given to the numerous intricate names used. Here is a brief guide to interpreting the meanings of some of the names

Some British Sausages: faggots (below), white and black puddings in rings, haggis (behind), haslet (top right) and Cumberland sausage.

used on sausage labels. You can use these to help you work out others when you see them in the shop.

French names

It is useful to remember that the French call all small sausages saucisses and big ones saucissons. All liver sausages have the word foie (pronounced fwa) attached, so a 'saucisse de foie' simply means liver sausage. If it has another word attached, this specifies the kind of liver used, ie, calf's, pig's, chicken, goose and so on.

In the same way, all smoked sausages should include the word 'fumé' on the label and dried ones, 'sec', while the garlicky ones should have 'l'ail' (pronounced 'lie' as in 'lie down') attached to their names. A word beginning with a capital letter usually indicates the place of origin of that particular type of sausage, thus, saucisson de Lorraine, saucisson de Bourgogne and so on.

Italian names

Many of these, like French names, indicate place of origin. One of the best known sausages is probably Mortadella. Originating in Italy, this type of sausage is now made in other countries. Mortadella can, like many other sausages, have various extra natural ingredients and, therefore, extra explanatory words tacked on to the name. Concentrate on the principal name as the sausage always

keeps the same basic character whatever extra ingredients are added. The main word Mortadella describes the basic product you are buying.

Bologna is an Italian city which has given its name to a type of sausage. Again, concentrate on the main word, to identify the sausage.

You are much more likely to be confused by all the various names given to salami, a type of dried spicy sausage. Many varieties are made in Italy and the word will often be followed by the name of the locality in which it was made. The word salami used alone should indicate that the sausage is Italian. Salami-style sausage made in other countries should be prefixed with the name of the country, for example, Danish salami and German salami.

German names

Germany makes nearly 1500 kinds of sausage, exporting many of them. German names are the ones you are very likely to see in your supermarkets. The names are long and, when unfamiliar, are confusing. Luckily, however, they include some 'lead-in' syllables which are valuable clues to the character of the sausage.

For a start, remember that the word 'wurst' only means sausage, so you can ignore it and look at the rest of the name. You may also be able to

break the longer names down still further, by separating the syllables. 'Fleisch' means meat, 'Schinken' means ham and 'Kalbs' (calf's) shows that veal has been used in the sausage. Once you know this, you should be able to guess quite easily what 'Kalbsfleischwurst' or 'Schinkenwurst' means—and even 'Bierschinkenwurst' should not be too difficult!

This will not solve all your problems but it should make it a bit easier to ask for what you want.

TYPES OF SAUSAGE

From the manufacturer's point of view, sausages fall into three main categories: fresh raw sausages, cooked sausages, and dried sausages. Details are given here of the characteristics of each category of sausages and their treatment. Several specific names of sausages are also given.

From the cook's point of view, sausages fall into two categories: those that are ready to serve and those that need heating or cooking before serving. A chart is given of the various methods of cooking, followed by some delicious serving ideas.

1 *Jagdwurst*
2 *Bierwurst*
3 *Jagdwurst*
4 *Schinkensulzwurst*
5 *Kalbsleberwurst*
6 *Gutsleberwurst*

FRESH RAW SAUSAGES

Fresh raw sausages are made in tremendous numbers in Britain. The most popular of these are the fat 'bangers', each weighing about 50 g [2 oz] and packed eight to ten to 450 g [1 lb]. There is also a thinner sausage of 25 g [1 oz], known collectively as chipolatas in the south of England and as links or thins in the north. Cocktail sausages are also made and these are half the size of chipolatas.

The Germans and Italians prefer using precooked and smoked sausages on the whole, but the French make fresh raw pork sausages. These are mostly about the size of chipolata and are minced and spiced differently in each district of France. Toulouse, for instance, makes a very coarsely minced sausage which is used in the famous rich stew called a cassoulet; Alsace-Lorraine and the Perigord are well known for their more finely minced sausages.

Cooking: blanching is an essential preliminary to most cooking methods for all sausages from the European continent and is recommended, but is not essential, for British sausages.

All fresh raw sausages must be thoroughly cooked by whichever method you choose. The chart gives cooking methods with instructions.

Sausages should not, contrary to popular opinion, be pricked before cooking—this is the experts' view. If not blanched, the skin of the sausage should be moistened a little to allow it to stretch. Pricking merely encourages the sausage to burst.

Storage: raw sausages should always be stored, wrapped, in the refrigerator. Sausages do not keep well and are at their best eaten within a day of purchase. They will keep safely for 2-3 days but it is not worth the risk to store them for any longer than this.

COOKED SAUSAGES

There are two main kinds of cooked sausage that can be bought: the first has been made from fresh raw meat and is fully cooked before sale, usually by steam-heating. The sausages are nearly all ready to serve without any additional heating or cooking. The second kind of cooked

sausage has been lightly smoked as a rule, and has then been wholly or partly cooked by scalding. Some of these sausages can be served just as they are, but some of the best known ones are improved by reheating, and some others must be completely re-cooked before use.

Storage: most kinds of cooked sausage should be kept wrapped and refrigerated and be eaten within a week of purchase. Blood sausages are the exception: these must be eaten on the day of purchase. They should never be kept longer. Many brands of sausage are marketed with a date of sale on them. The sausages are best consumed well within this deadline.

Cooked fresh meat sausages

These are made of very finely minced meat and offal.

Ready to serve: probably the best known ones are the various kinds of liver sausage which can be smooth enough to spread like a pâté or contain puréed solid meat to give them body and make them sliceable. Most are pale, greyish, often with

7 *French cervelas*
8 *Knackwurst*
9 *Viennas*
10 *Frankfurters*
11 *Regensburger*

5

6

11

soft, white fat surrounding the liver mixture. They are sold in synthetic skins which should be removed after slicing or discarded once the contents have been scooped out. All varieties of liver sausage are eaten cold and are sold ready to serve. The French call liver sausage 'saucisses de foie', the Germans 'Leberwurst' or some more complicated name with 'Leber' in it. German varieties also come smoked and unsmoked.
Names to look for: German names with Leberwurst included, French names including the word foie.
Sausages needing re-cooking: blood sausages, including the British black puddings, are another kind of cooked fresh meat sausage. These are made from blood with bits of solid fat and cereal added. The sausage is sold either straight, or bent into a half-round with the two ends tied together. This is called a 'boiling ring'. These sausages must be kept refrigerated and cooked on the day of purchase. The French call their blood sausages 'boudins noirs' ('black pudding') and the German name is 'Blutwurst'. Unlike the varieties of

Cooking guide to sausages

Blanching before cooking
All sausages from the European continent should be blanched before cooking unless they are to be reheated, boiled or casseroled. Blanching is also recommended for British sausages.

Put sausages either whole or in large pieces, into boiling water. Reduce heat and simmer for 4 minutes. Take out with a slotted spoon and drain on kitchen paper.

Reheating
Reheating is more thorough than blanching and is used for frankfurters, Bockwurst, Knackwurst and other cooked, lightly smoked sausages which do not need to be completely cooked again.

Steam thin sausages and small pieces for up to 15 minutes. Put large pieces and thick sausages into boiling water, soup or stock. Reduce heat and poach for 8-12 minutes, or up to 18 minutes for very thick, whole sausages. Drain well.

Boiling
Boiled sausages are less rich and fatty than baked, grilled or fried ones. Grill them, without extra fat, to brown, after draining. Boil fresh raw sausages, blood sausages, boiling rings and cooked, lightly smoked sausages that need re-cooking before serving.

Put sausages, whole or in pieces, into boiling water, stock or soup. Reduce heat to just maintain boiling point and cook for 10 minutes (pieces and cocktail size), 15 minutes (thicker sausages), 20-30 minutes (boiling rings, depending on thickness). Drain well on kitchen paper.

Casseroling
Suitable for all sausages, whole if small, or in chunks or thick slices if large.

Add the sausages to any slow-cooking casserole, allowing 10-15 minutes cooking time.

Baking
Use baked sausages instead of fried or grilled sausages. This is a suitable cooking method for all fresh raw sausages. Use a moderate oven, 180°C [350°F] gas mark 4.

Put sausages in a greased roasting tin and cook for 25 minutes, turning once. (Cocktail sausages need only 15 minutes.) Drain on kitchen paper.

Barbecuing
All fresh raw sausages can be barbecued.

Barbecue the sausages over charcoal as for grilling. Cook on a greased grid or on a skewer, turning frequently.

Grilling
Suitable for all sausages after blanching.

Grill sausages on greased rack under medium heat, turning frequently. Allow 10 minutes for chipolata size, 15 minutes for thick sausages.

Shallow frying
Suitable for all fresh raw sausages and cooked sausages that need cooking again, whole, in pieces or sliced.

Fry in a hot, greased heavy-based frying-pan for 7-12 minutes, turning frequently. Fry slices for 2-3 minutes only, turning once.

liver sausage, blood sausages must be completely cooked again by boiling, grilling or shallow frying before eating.

Cooked, lightly smoked sausages
There are two sorts of sausage of this kind. Some are sold ready to eat and are eaten cold, others need reheating or cooking and are eaten hot or cold. It is not always easy at first to tell, simply by looking, which group a sausage comes in, so always ask the advice of your supplier if you are in any doubt.

Sausages for reheating/cooking
These sausages are nearly all finely minced, but are not as smooth as liver sausage. The most famous one, which everyone will know, is the frankfurter. Frankfurters come in various sizes and can be bought from a chilled counter or in cans. The most usual size is that of a chipolata. Austrian Wieners which English speaking countries call 'Viennas', are of course simply frankfurters by another name.

Frankfurters also vary in colour, according to local recipes and tastes. They are made of finely minced pork and beef except for kosher ones which, obviously, do not include pork. Frankfurters can be eaten hot or cold but in both cases need to be heated before use, either whole or in chunks, by steaming or poaching. After this they can be fried or grilled and served hot, while ones which are simply steamed or poached can be served hot or cold.

Other kinds of lightly smoked and cooked sausages which should be reheated or re-cooked include German Bockwurst and Bratwurst (or Rostbratwurst). These varieties are usually sold packeted, with a date of sale on them. They should be used well within the date given and must be thoroughly reheated as soon as the packet is opened. You will recognize Bratwursts by the darker outside colour; it is a frying or grilling sausage, which needs no other pre-cooking.

Bockwurst is equally easy to recognize because the sausages are extra long. In contrast to Bockwurst is the fat dumpy Knackwurst. When cut, you will see that it has the same close-knit, slightly spongy pink inside as a frankfurter. Both Bockwurst and this short, fat cousin should be treated like frankfurters.

Sausages from other countries which also have this light spongy texture should be treated in the same way. There are Polish, Italian, Hungarian, French and Danish varieties and many others on sale in delicatessen and supermarkets.

Names to look for: frankfurters, Bockwurst, Rostbratwurst, Munich Weisswurst (white skinned), Bratwurst and Knackwurst.

There are several varieties of cooked sausage that need to be fully cooked again rather than heated. Some of these sausages are shaped into 'boiling rings'. These should be fully cooked by boiling whole, and cut up afterwards for serving hot. Some straight sausages also need to be fully cooked. Among French ones, look out for the well-known Alsatian Strasbourg sausages and the paler cervelas sausage, meant for boiling. This sausage is often known as a saveloy. Once made of pig's brain, it is now made of minced pork, beef and bacon fat.

Names to look for: saveloys, Strasbourg and cervelas.

Ready-to-serve sausages
These cooked sausages are intended to be eaten cold, just as they are. They are sometimes sold packeted in thin slices, cut ready to serve.

Common sense will often tell you which sausages are ready to serve. If they are yielding, pasty sausages with a texture like liver sausage, they can be eaten without cooking. Clearly, any sausage with aspic jelly between the pieces of meat mixture is not meant for reheating, since the aspic jelly would melt. Likewise, ready-to-serve sausages contain solid pieces of meat between the sausage mixture, or other flavouring ingredients such as mushrooms, pimentos, pistachio nuts etc; if these were to be reheated, the solid pieces would fall out as the minced mixture softened.

Names to look for: Jagdwurst, Bierwurst, Bierschinken, Schinkensulzwurst (containing aspic and mushrooms) and saucisse Viennoise.

There are a few ready-to-serve cooked sausages that can be served hot as well. These are more finely minced, closely packed mixtures. Thin slices can be fried or the sausage can be diced and used in soups and stews.

Names to look for: Extrawurst, (fleischwurst) and lyoner.

DRIED SAUSAGES
Sausages are dried as a way of preservation. They are either semi-dried, which means that less than 20 per cent of their moisture is lost during curing or fully dried, which means that more than 20 per cent of their moisture is removed. Both types are smoked, either lightly or heavily, and can be finely or coarsely minced.

Fully dried sausages can be stored in a dry, cool place with a temperature between 15-18°C [60-65°F] and will keep well for up to three months. However, once the sausage has been cut it should be wrapped and refrigerated to maintain its storage life. Semi-dried sausages should be kept wrapped and refrigerated and will then keep well for up to three months. Most of the dried sausages on sale in Britain are the fully dried, preserved kind but, if you are in any doubt, keep the sausage refrigerated.

Every European country except Britain makes semi- and fully dried sausages and as each region makes differently flavoured ones, there are hundreds of varieties. Most are meant to be eaten just as they are. Best known of these is probably salami. There are a few that are cooked and eaten hot and this is usually when they are semi-dried and heavily spiced—chorizo and cabanos are examples.

Dried sausages are served thinly sliced. They look better sliced on the diagonal so that the slices are larger. Use a sharp knife and discard the skin or coating afterwards.

Salami is a well-known variety of dried sausage. The word 'salami' is Italian and the sausage originated in Italy. However, France, Germany, Hungary, Denmark and several other countries now make their own, although Italian salami is still the most highly flavoured. The following are names to look for, and some characteristics of each are given.

Salame Milanese: the most readily available Italian salami. Made of equal proportions of lean pork, beef, and pork fat, seasoned with garlic, pepper and white wine. Usually fully

A selection of dried sausages showing a Teewurst and a row of Italian salami. Below, Plockwurst, a ring of Mettwurst and some Zungenwurst followed by some French, Danish, Hungarian and Italian salami. In front, thin cabanos, chunky chorizos and a slice of Mortadella.

153

dried and sometimes called crespone.

Salame Napolitana: a stronger version of Milanese salami.

Salame Fiorentina: pure pork salami from Florence.

Salame Genoese: with home-made salami is considered the best Italian salami and best of all if made wholly with pork. Dried and usually sold sliced.

Salame Calabrese: from Sicily, a pure pork salami flavoured with hot peppers.

Salame Cremonese: a dried salami made from a mixture of pork, beef and skimmed milk. Like many salami it is gaily wrapped in foil.

Salame Ungherese: Hungarian salami made of pork and beef which is also very popular in Italy.

German salami: just called 'salami' made from a mixture of beef and pork and available with or without garlic. It comes in various sizes, fully dried, and is distinguished by a white jacket.

Kosher salami: an all-beef, semi-dried salami, available in many sizes.

French salami: there are many varieties which are made in different regions of France. Look out for the Corsican variety which is smoked over a chestnut fire.

Danish salami: made from a mixture of beef and pork mildly seasoned with salt, pepper and sometimes thyme. Fully dried.

Apart from salami, there are many other varieties of dried sausage that are sold ready to eat.

Cervelat (not to be confused with the precooked boiling sausage cervelas) is another excellent dried smoked sausage and a good choice if you want something less spicy than salami. The best known come from France but most countries produce their own varieties.

Mortadella is another, very well known dried Italian sausage. It has a close rubbery texture and is pink with chunks of pork fat and whole peppercorns in it. It sometimes also has pistachio nuts in it and can be very garlicky.

Plockwurst is a dark coloured German sausage with a lot of beef in it, marbled with solid white fat.

Mettwurst is a coarsely chopped, dried sausage. It is cold-smoked to a firm consistency and contains gobbets of pure fat. It is sold as a long straight sausage or in a ring.

Teewurst is German and there are several varieties made of pork and beef, including one which is spreadable; another is made only of pork and spare-rib bacon, smoked over beechwood. It is one of the most attractive sausages with an orange coating, a spicy yet mild flavour, and smooth yet not cloying consistency.

Tiroler ham sausage is made in both Germany and Austria. It is an attractive ham sausage of finely minced pink meat with darker red blobs of whole ham, and sometimes contains herbs or spices as green specks. It is smoked over resin-free beech and ash wood with juniper berries added.

Krakauer is a Polish dried slicing sausage of coarsely minced ham and pork, well smoked and firm.

Tongue sausage is sometimes called Zungenwurst. It is usually made in Germany and contains solid pieces of tongue which make it attractive when sliced.

Dried sausages for cooking

The following sausages can be eaten cold, sliced but are more usually served hot and always need to be recooked before serving.

Chorizo is originally Spanish, but is now made widely in other countries. It is strongly flavoured with cayenne pepper, juniper, red pepper and tomato. It is dark red in colour, made of pork and liver or beef coarsely sliced, with chunks of whole fat. It is available as straight sausages or in rings.

Cabanos is a 'little brother' of chorizo, made in several countries. It is much the same in looks as a chorizo but thinner and much less peppery.

SERVING IDEAS

All sorts of sausages from both the European continent and Britain can be used in many tasty ways. Here are a few to try.

●Turn tomato soup into something special by adding sliced frankfurters or another sausage from this group.

●For frankfurter salad, toss cold, sliced frankfurters in a mustard vinaigrette with a thinly sliced onion, chopped celery, cooked red kidney beans and finely chopped parsley.

●For a delicious toasted sandwich, toast bread on one side first. Butter the toasted side. Cover with a thick slice of cheese, two thinly sliced frankfurters and a liberal spreading of chutney. Re-assemble and toast both sides until the cheese has melted.

●For a filling meal on a winter's day, make a tatie pot. To serve four, you will need about 450 g [1 lb] scrag end of lamb, 225 g [½ lb] black (blood) pudding, a large onion, a large carrot, about 150 ml [¼ pt] good beef stock and 450 g [1 lb] potatoes, peeled and quartered. Seal the lamb in hot fat and place in the bottom of a heavy-based casserole. Slice the black pudding and put it on top of the lamb. Skin and slice the onion, scrub and slice the carrot and place over the black pudding. Pour in the stock and season to taste. Top with the potatoes and cook in the centre of an oven heated to 160°C [325°F] gas mark 3 for one hour, covered. Remove the lid and cook for two hours, until the potatoes are browned and crisp.

●Try frying black pudding and serving with bacon and eggs for breakfast.

●For a delicious sandwich, combine granary bread, sliced, cooked British sausages and apple sauce.

●Next time you make potato salad, include a few sliced frankfurters, bangers or a similar sausage.

●If you are serving cold sliced duck, serve some sliced salami with it. The combination is irresistible.

●For sausage layer, fry pork or beef thick sausages or chipolatas until lightly browned. Transfer to a deep casserole dish. Fry onions and mushrooms in the same fat and place over the sausages. Top with cheesy creamed potato and brown in a medium oven for 20 minutes.

●Give cauliflower cheese extra meal appeal by simmering chunks of chorizo or chipolata in the cheese sauce for about 5 minutes.

●Make an instant pâté by pressing liver sausage into little pots and covering with melted garlic and parsley butter. Allow the butter to set then serve as a dinner party first course, with toast.

●For traditional British bangers and mash, mix creamed potatoes with fried onions. Surround with fried or grilled pork or beef sausages.

●Try serving grilled or fried bangers or hot frankfurters or boiling sausage with mustard sauce and red cabbage or sauerkraut.

●For battered bangers, dip pork or beef sausages in batter. Deep fry until the batter is crisp and golden. A hot favourite with chipped potatoes.

Currying flavour

Full of Eastern promise, curries and korma are delicious dishes which range from lightly spiced to positively fiery. Here you will find out how to make many different types of curry and korma and how to prepare the traditional accompaniments favoured in Indian cuisine.

TRUE ASIAN FLAVOUR

Curries and korma are as important to Asian cookery as casseroles and stews are to European cuisine. Recipes for curries were first sent home to England when the British Raj was in control in India. British travellers in turn took the curry recipes to other countries and so these spicy dishes became known as far away from India as the United States of America.

Regrettably, however, the original Indian recipes often underwent considerable changes in British kitchens and, each time the recipes were passed on, further alterations were made to suit individual tastes and locally available ingredients. The resulting so-called curries and korma were frequently no longer recognizable as aromatic and delicious Asian stews. They were degraded to the status of a vehicle for leftovers—dried up meats masked by incendiary sauces.

If you have never tasted a true curry or korma, the flavour will be a revelation. True curries and korma are always made from fresh meat, poultry, fish or vegetables, lovingly combined with home-ground spices and cooked with care.

Curries are, in effect, stews and long slow cooking is essential to allow a rich flavour to develop, while korma are dishes made mild and creamy by the addition of yoghurt.

Don't think that all curries and korma have the same stereotype flavour. Just as casseroles and stews can vary widely in choice of ingredients and flavours, so too is the choice of curries and korma very varied.

In India alone, curries differ according to region. The curries of the south are hot and spicy while those from the central areas and northern India and Kashmir are mild.

It is thought that curries are exclusive to India. They are, in fact, found all over Asia and vary tremendously in flavour from country to country.

Burmese curries tend to be very hot and are cooked with a paste of ground chillis, garlic, onions, ginger and fresh turmeric. Western Sumatran curries are true spice-island fare with almost every edible herb, spice or leaf included. Thai curries have a unique lemony flavour. They are spiced with a selection of herbs indigenous to Thailand, and fish sauce called nam pla, plus lemon grass and lime leaves. Fresh red or green chillis are sometimes included to give a contrast in texture and colour.

The curries of Sri Lanka (formerly Ceylon), Bali and Malaysia are similar to those of southern India. Most have a coconut milk base, seasoned with fresh chillies and ginger, and they are coloured with turmeric. Lemon grass, a pungent shrimp paste called blanchan, ground nuts, shredded ginger and banana flowers make a curry sauce which is perfect with seafood, vegetables, chicken and some tropical fruits.

Different again are the curries of Java which are mild and sweet. A locally produced brown sugar from the aren palm is blended with herbs, cumin and coriander to make the sauce.

Here we concentrate essentially on the curries and korma of India as these are easier for the westerner to make. Apart from anything else, the spread of Indian groceries and specialist shops means that most of the ingredients are now easy to obtain. Even if you don't have a local Indian shop, most of the necessary ingredients can be obtained from the spice counter of a supermarket.

WHAT IS A CURRY?
A curry is a stew made from fresh meat, poultry, fish or vegetables. Like European stews, curries can be made with tough cuts of meat and long cooking will develop full flavour. Like any other type of stew, curries reheat well and can be made a day ahead. Curries always include plenty of sauce. This can vary in flavour from mildly aromatic to spicy and hot, depending on type. There are five basic types of curry.

Kashmiri: mild and slightly sweet, it contains fruit or nuts.
Kofta: mild meatball curry.
Molee: hot and uses a lot of coconut milk. Molee means coconut.
Madras: hot with thick, rich, spicy sauce.
Vindaloo: this is the hottest of all curries. The spices are made into a paste with vinegar.

Curries are always served hot and accompanied by rice. A range of other side dishes and accompaniments is also served. For details, see the list of accompaniments described under serving an Indian meal.

WHAT IS KORMA?
Korma is a stewed dish of meat or vegetables. As a good grade of meat is used, cooking time is slightly shorter than for curries which use inferior, tough cuts of meat requiring long, slow cooking.

The liquid element used in a korma is water or stock plus yoghurt or cream. Sometimes both cream and yoghurt are used to produce extra rich results. Korma is mild and creamy in flavour.

As well as the basic korma, there are two variations—bhogar and doh peeazah. Bhogar is finished by steaming. A doh peeazah involves the use of onions at two different stages of cooking to give a delicious mixture of textures and flavours. Twice as much onion as meat is used. Half the onions are added at the beginning of cooking; the remainder are grated or pounded and added close to the end. Sometimes half the raw onions are pounded with aromatics and added to the pan together with the raw meat. This makes the doh peeazah a dish of great character and gives it an extremely individualistic flavour.

EQUIPMENT
Very little special equipment is needed for making curries and korma. All these dishes are cooked on the top of the stove so the main requirement is a heavy-based pan. A flameproof casserole is ideal, especially if you want to keep the food hot in the oven after cooking.

A pestle and mortar, and electric blender, a pepper mill or a heavy rolling pin is essential to crush spices and pound ingredients to a paste where required. A pestle and mortar can be used for both pounding and crushing. A blender or grinder will only crush. A rolling pin can be used either to crush or pound.

You will also need a sharp knife for cutting up meat and vegetables, one or two bowls for mixing things, a measuring jug and a couple of large spoons for mixing.

Finally, you may need an asbestos mat to reduce heat and keep the pan at the merest simmer during cooking.

INGREDIENTS FOR CURRIES AND KORMA
Curries and korma are very individual dishes so it is impossible to list any general rules about quantities of ingredients used. Depending on type, different ingredients and varying proportions are used. Listed here are some of the ingredients most commonly used. For amounts, follow recipes carefully. There is no reason, for instance, why you should not use beef in a recipe calling for lamb providing that you use it in the same proportion to the other ingredients. But never be tempted to treat your curry as a convenient receptacle for anything you may have lying around. A careful balance of ingredients is essential for an authentic and truly delicious curry or korma.

Meat for curries
Meat for curries can be selected from the coarser cuts as the long, slow stewing in liquid breaks down the fibres. Suitable cuts are as follows.
Beef: shank, thick flank, flank steak, skirt, brisket, chuck or anything sold as braising or stewing steak.
Pork: shoulder, hand and spring, belly.
Mutton: shoulder, breast, leg, best end, scrag end, middle neck.
Lamb: shoulder, best end, scrag, middle neck, breast.
Offal: lambs', calves' or ox liver,

calves' or lambs' brains, tripe, calves' or lambs' tongues.
Poultry: duck, chicken, goose.

Meats for korma
Korma is made with younger, better quality meat because cooking is shorter. Usually only beef or lamb is made into korma, not pork or offal. Suitable cuts are as follows.
Beef: rump steak, good quality braising steak.
Lamb: best end, loin, leg, shoulder.

Fish
Fish is only used for curries, not for korma. Use fleshy fish for simmering in curry sauce. White fish are best. Oily fish do not respond so well to this treatment. Suitable fish are cod, halibut, coley, haddock, huss, hake and whiting.

Shellfish may also be used. This is the only ingredient in curry which is ever used pre-cooked and this is because it is rather difficult to obtain fresh, as most shellfish is boiled as soon as it is caught. Choose from prawns, shrimps, crayfish or crab. Lobster may also be used but it is, of course, rather expensive.

Vegetables
The only vegetable which is included in all curries and korma is onions. Onions are essential for flavour and the mild Spanish variety is best.

Other vegetables are rarely included in meat or fish curries but they are made into dishes in their own right. Vegetables which may be used are cauliflower, courgettes, aubergines, tomatoes, peas, potatoes, spinach, carrots, beans, cucumber, okra, red and green peppers.

Fruit
Fruit is always included in Kashmiri curries. The fruit used depends on the recipe. Fried apricots and bananas are popular choices, as are raisins, sultanas and currants. Sliced apple is often included when the meat is lamb.

Coconut
Coconut is an important ingredient in the hotter curries and it is also used in some of the milder ones. You will see that recipes call for coconut liquor, thin coconut milk or thick coconut milk. Always use the type specified as each is quite different.

Coconut liquor means the liquid found in the centre of the coconut—a substance somewhat confusingly called coconut milk by many westerners.

Thick and thin coconut milk are traditionally made by grating fresh coconut flesh.

Since fresh coconuts are not that easy to find in many countries, except at certain times of the year, and since coconut milk cannot be bought at many shops, the following substitutes are suggested.

To make 250 ml [½ pt] thin coconut milk—the average amount needed for making most curries—put 100 g [¼ lb] desiccated coconut in a liquidizer. Pour on 250 ml [½ pt] boiling water and leave to infuse for 10 minutes. Strain the liquid and discard any pulp. If you do not have a liquidizer, place 150 g [5 oz] desiccated coconut in a bowl. Pour on 250 ml [½ pt] boiling water and leave to soak for ten minutes. Place the mixture in a muslin-lined sieve over a bowl and allow it to drip through slowly. Towards the end, press with a wooden spoon to extract all the liquid.

To make thick coconut milk, mash and blend together commercial creamed coconut and enough boiling water to make a thick paste. The consistency should be creamy and quite smooth. Both thick and thin coconut milk should be used immediately.

Fat
The fat for cooking curries and korma is traditionally ghee (which is clarified butter) or coconut oil. Both have a distinctive flavour and are available from Indian delicatessens and some supermarkets. If you are unable to obtain ghee, clarify butter at home by melting then straining.

Alternatively, use sesame seed oil, but be sure to choose good quality—cheap peanut oil can be somewhat tasteless.

Yoghurt and cream

Yoghurt and cream are both used for cooking korma. Use only natural yoghurt, which is free from any sweetener or artificial flavouring. If you cannot obtain really sharp natural yoghurt, a useful but more expensive substitute is sour cream.

Cream should be thick; thin cream will separate too easily during the cooking.

Spices

The spices for curries and korma vary tremendously from recipe to recipe.

There is no magic powder which you can use for every recipe. Curry powder as we know it in the west simply does not exist in Indian cookery. Spices should be bought whole and ground and blended as and when needed. This way flavours are truly aromatic and blends are tailor-made to suit individual recipes and personal taste.

There are, however, a few basic mixtures used quite regularly so you may find it worth making up quantities for use throughout a week. These basic mixtures include garam masala, a powder which is sprinkled over curries or added towards the end of cooking to enhance flavour, plus molee and vindaloo pastes for which recipes are given.

When making these pastes or the spice blends used in curries and korma, always stick to the amount given in the recipe. Adding too much spice may upset the balance of the dish. Adding too little could also ruin results.

Other ingredients

Tamarind pulp is available dried in some shops and can be easily reconstituted. If you cannot obtain tamarind pulp, substitute lemon juice or omit completely. Where lemon juice can be used as a substitute, recipes usually give amounts.

Nuts such as almonds, brazils, hazelnuts and walnuts are often included in Kashmiri dishes: use type and amounts as given in recipes.

MAKING CURRIES

There are no basic rules for making curry as methods vary tremendously from type to type and recipe to recipe. In the step-by-step guide, you will find a simple Madras curry which can be adapted to any meat you choose.

For other curries, follow recipes carefully.

There are a few basic factors common to all curry making.

1 The meat must be sealed on all sides to keep in flavour and juices.

2 Onions, spices and garlic are always added early on so that they can flavour the fat. Onions are usually stirred into the pan immediately after the meat has been sealed. When they are translucent, the spices are stirred in so that they coat the onions and meat.

3 Liquid is added in two stages. First a little liquid is boiled quickly to thicken the sauce. The rest of the liquid is then added and the curry is left to simmer very gently to bring out the flavours and tenderize the meat.

VINDALOO PASTE

Vindaloo paste is used to make very hot, spicy curries. It is often used with pork—for obvious reasons in a hot country like India. A pork vindaloo is usually marinated before cooking, although this is not essential when adapting the recipe to beef and chicken. Vindaloo paste will only keep for a couple of days in the refrigerator so do not make too much.

SERVES 4
15 ml [1 tablespoon] coriander seeds
5 ml [1 teaspoon] ground turmeric
5 ml [1 teaspoon] cumin seeds
5 ml [1 teaspoon] chilli pepper
7.5 ml [1½ teaspoons] ground ginger
5 ml [1 teaspoon] black mustard seeds
pinch of fenugreek
7.5 ml [1½ teaspoons] black peppercorns
15 ml [1 tablespoon] white wine vinegar

1 Grind all the whole seeds using a pepper mill or electric grinder. Alternatively, crush finely with a pestle and mortar or place in a double thickness polythene bag and crush with a rolling pin.

2 Gradually blend in the vinegar to make a smooth thick paste. Store in an airtight container and moisten with an additional 5 ml [1 teaspoon] vinegar before use.

1 For 250 ml [½ pt] thick coconut milk place 100 g [¼ lb] creamed coconut in a bowl.

SERVES 4
450 g [1 lb] stewing steak
25 g [1 oz] plain flour
2 medium-sized onions
50 g [2 oz] clarified butter
5 ml [1 teaspoon] turmeric
5 ml [1 teaspoon] ground coriander
5 ml [1 teaspoon] cayenne
2.5 ml [½ teaspoon] ground black mustard seeds
2.5 ml [½ teaspoon] ground cumin
2 garlic cloves
50 g [2 oz] seedless raisins

4 Add the onion to the pan. Cook for a further 5 minutes, turning occasionally.

Step-by-step to coconut milk

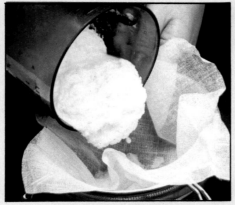

2 Add 150 ml [$\frac{1}{4}$ pt] boiling water, a little at a time and mix with a spoon or large fork to a smooth paste.

3 For thin milk, put 100 g [$\frac{1}{4}$ lb] coconut in a liquidizer with 250 ml [$\frac{1}{2}$ pt] boiling water. Soak for 10 minutes, blend then strain.

OR place 150 g [5 oz] coconut in a bowl with boiling water. Leave 10 minutes. Strain through muslin-lined sieve, pressing with a spoon.

Step-by-step to Madras curry

1 Cut the meat into 2.5 cm [1"] cubes. Toss the meat cubes in flour.

2 Skin and finely chop the onion. Place the fat in a heavy-based pan over medium heat.

3 When hot add the meat to the pan. Brown for 5 minutes, turning so that all sides are sealed.

5 Add the spices and cook for 3 minutes. Skin and crush garlic. Add and cook for 2 minutes.

6 Add 150 ml [$\frac{1}{4}$ pt] hot water and boil briskly, stirring all the time, for 5 minutes.

7 Add raisins and water to come just above the meat. Stew over low heat for 2$\frac{1}{4}$ hours.

LAMB KORMA

SERVES 4

450 g [1 lb] shoulder of lamb, boned weight
250 ml [½ pt] plain yoghurt
15 ml [1 tablespoon] ground coriander
15 ml [1 tablespoon] ground almonds
10 ml [2 teaspoons] ground cumin
5 ml [1 teaspoon] ground turmeric
5 ml [1 teaspoon] ground chilli
2.5 ml [½ teaspoon] ground black pepper
50 g [2 oz] ghee or clarified butter
1 small onion
2 garlic cloves
12 mm [½"] piece of fresh ginger
5 ml [1 teaspoon] ground cloves
5 ml [1 teaspoon] ground cardamom
piece of cinnamon about 5 cm [2"] long
30 ml [2 tablespoons] ground almonds
250 ml [½ pt] thick coconut milk

MAKING KORMA

Korma, unlike curries, has a set pattern which you can follow.

The meat is always marinated in the korma mixture, which is made up of spices and yoghurt. The composition of the mixture varies from recipe to recipe, but the marinating period is usually about one hour—just enough to lightly flavour the meat.

Before adding the meat to the pan, the onions are sealed in fat and the spices lightly cooked to bring out their flavour. This usually takes 8 minutes.

The meat and its marinade are then added. They are simmered for 5 minutes to amalgamate flavours before other ingredients (if any) are added.

The korma is cooked over very low heat for about 1½ hours until the sauce is thick and the meat tender. The pan is covered during this braising. Stir from time to time. If the sauce looks as though it might dry out before the end of cooking, add a

Step-by-step to lamb korma

1 Cut the lamb into 2.5 cm [1"] cubes and set aside. Stir the coriander, almonds, cumin, turmeric, chilli and pepper into yoghurt.

2 Add the cubes of lamb to the spiced yoghurt mixture. Cover and leave to marinate in the refrigerator for 1½ hours.

4 Add the onions and garlic to the pan and cook, stirring from time to time for 4 minutes. Chop the ginger and add to the pan.

5 Add cloves, cardamom and cinnamon to the pan and cook stirring for a further 4 minutes. Add the meat and marinade.

7 Stir occasionally to prevent sticking. If the sauce begins to dry up, add a few spoonfuls of water, blending it well into the mixture.

8 Stir in the coconut milk. Simmer uncovered, for 5 minutes, stirring occasionally so the coconut milk blends with the sauce.

160

Skin and finely chop the onion. Skin and crush the garlic cloves. Place the butter or ghee in a heavy-based pan over medium heat.

Simmer, covered, for 5 minutes. Stir in almonds. Lower heat still further, cover and cook for 1¾ hours until meat is tender.

Carefully remove the cinnamon stick. Serve immediately with boiled rice or chappati, sambals and vegetables of your choice.

little water, stirring well to blend.

Fat will rise to the surface of the korma during cooking. This is nothing to worry about, as it will be mixed into the sauce when the coconut milk is added.

If coconut milk is used it is stirred in at the end of cooking and cooked for about 5 minutes so that it blends evenly with the sauce. This is the point at which cinnamon sticks or any other solid spices should be removed from the pan.

SERVING AN INDIAN MEAL

Indian meals do not follow the pattern of a first course, main course and dessert that Europeans know so well. Instead, all the dishes appear on the table at once.

A traditional Indian meal used to consist of one large dish of meat or fish, five or more cooked vegetable dishes, a selection of about six sambals and chutney, some rice or bread, poppadoms, yoghurt and a sweet dish. The diners made up their meal from what they liked best and ate them in whatever order they pleased: if someone's preference was to have sweet first, he could do so.

Today it is more usual to serve one meat or fish dish, two vegetable dishes, some bread or rice, poppadoms, three to five sambals, and some yoghurt or a sweet dish.

Indian sweets tend to be very sweet, perfumed lavishly with rose-water and almonds. For western tastes, fresh fruit would probably be more appreciated.

Rice

Boiled rice is the best known of all the accompaniments to curry. Usually coloured rice (tinted yellow with turmeric) is served. Allow about 100 g [¼ lb] of cooked rice per person. Serve the rice in small individual bowls to be really authentic. Rice which has been spiced or a pilau, is also sometimes served with a curry.

Bread

Indian cuisine offers a wide range of bread. Bread is served as an accompaniment to the main course. The thicker type of bread is used to mop up the juices and is served as an alternative to rice. It is always served hot.

Many types of Indian bread are unleavened and most of them are made with wholemeal flour. This means they are very filling.

Chappati is about the size of a dinner plate. It is made from wholemeal flour and is chewy in texture. Serve one per person.

Phulka is a smaller version of chappati. Serve 1-2 per person.

Nan is a thickish, leavened bread made from white flour. Serve one per person.

Paratha is a crisp, wholemeal bread rather like a chappati in appearance. Serve one per person.

Stuffed paratha is filled with a spicy meat or vegetable mixture. Serve one per person.

Samosas are deep-fried triangles of dough filled with a spicy meat or vegetable mixture. Serve 2-3 per person.

Poppadoms are paper-thin circles of bread made from pea flour. They are available plain or spiced and look like enormous potato crisps. Poppadoms may be served with rice to provide a contrast in texture. Diners can eat poppadoms like bread or crumble them with their hands and sprinkle the crumbs over their rice, curry or korma. Before serving, poppadoms must be heated to make them crisp and light. Serve 2-3 per person.

Pickles and chutneys

It is traditional to offer small dishes of pickle or chutney with curry. Best known of all the Indian chutneys is mango chutney, a spicy, sweet chutney which goes well with all curries. Another favourite is lime pickle—but go cautiously with this, it is extremely hot. Pumpkin, tomato and coconut chutneys are also popular. All of these can be bought from Indian grocers. Mango chutney can be bought from almost any supermarket.

Sambals

Sambals are tiny bowls of sharp, freshly made pickle. They are made up usually of vegetables, spices, herbs, fruit and a sharp element, such as lime or lemon juice and vinegar. Sambals must be made about 2 hours in advance so that the ingredients can absorb the acid. They are served in little bowls and guests help themselves. The sambals given here all provide enough to serve 4-6.

●For coriander sambal, chop 30 ml [2

tablespoons] fresh coriander leaves. Mix with 1 plump garlic clove, skinned and crushed, a thin slice of fresh ginger, pounded, pinch of salt, 5 ml [1 teaspoon] sugar and 60 ml [4 tablespoons] fresh lemon or lime juice. This is very good with chicken and lamb curries and with fish molees.

● For mint sambal, combine 30 ml [2 tablespoons] freshly chopped mint leaves, 1 small onion, skinned and finely chopped, 1 fresh chilli finely chopped, 5 ml [1 teaspoon] sugar, a pinch of salt and 60 ml [4 tablespoons] lemon juice.

● For coconut sambal, combine 15 ml [1 tablespoon] grated fresh coconut, 5 ml [1 teaspoon] crushed black poppy seeds, 15 ml [1 tablespoon] freshly chopped mint, 1 chopped fresh chilli and 45 ml [3 tablespoons] lemon juice. This is good with fish curries.

●For tomato sambal, combine 3 tomatoes, skinned, de-seeded and chopped with 15 ml [1 tablespoon] chopped chilli, a pinch of salt, 5 ml [1 teaspoon] sugar and 45 ml [3 tablespoons] white wine vinegar. This is good with hot meat curries.

● For banana sambal, slice 3 bananas, combine with 30 ml [2 tablespoons] freshly chopped mint and 90 ml [6 tablespoons] lemon or lime juice. This is good with fish and poultry curries.

● For carrot sambal, grate 2 large carrots. Mix with ½ large onion, skinned and finely chopped, 30 ml [2 tablespoons] freshly chopped coriander or parsley leaves, 5 ml [1 teaspoon] minced fresh ginger, a pinch of salt and 90 ml [6 tablespoons] lime or lemon juice.

● For orange and coconut sambal, mix together 100 g [¼ lb] grated fresh coconut, 25 g [1 oz] crushed sesame seeds, 2.5 ml [½ teaspoon] cayenne pepper, 30 ml [2 tablespoons] grated orange zest and 90 ml [6 tablespoons] orange juice.

● For cucumber sambal, peel and chop half a large cucumber. Salt for 30 minutes, refresh and drain. Blend in a liquidizer with 2 plump garlic cloves, skinned, 2 fresh green chillies, 2.5 ml [½ teaspoon] sugar, a pinch of fenugreek and 90 ml [6 tablespoons] lime or lemon juice. Sprinkle with 30 ml [2 tablespoons] freshly chopped coriander or parsley leaves.

Vegetables and salads

Side dishes of vegetables are served with Indian meals in the same way as in the west. All the following will serve four.

● For alu bhoone (Indian sauté potatoes), peel, wash and dry 450 g [1 lb] potatoes. Cut into slices. Heat 25 g [1 oz] clarified butter in a large, heavy-based pan and put in the potatoes with 5 ml [1 teaspoon] turmeric and a bay leaf. Stir fry over medium heat for 5 minutes. Add a

1 Pour oil into a heavy-based frying pan. When the oil is very hot, di the poppadom in it, holding th poppadom by the edge.

pinch of salt, a pinch of onion salt and a pinch of cayenne pepper. Stir fry for a further 5 minutes so that all sides are browned. Dust with 10 ml [2 teaspoons] garam masala. Add another 15 g [½ oz] clarified butter and stir. Reduce the heat to low, cover and leave for 4 minutes, shaking the pan from time to time. Uncover, increase heat to medium and cook for another 2 minutes to crisp the outside. Serve immediately.

A simpler version is to sauté the potatoes with 15 ml [1 tablespoon] freshly chopped mint and 15 ml [1 tablespoon] crushed cardamom seeds. Serve alu bhoone instead of rice.

● For alu badam (smothered potatoes), prepare and boil 450 g [1 lb] potatoes until tender when pierced. Mix together 5 ml [1 teaspoon] turmeric, 2.5 ml [½ teaspoon] garam masala, 150 ml [¼ pt] natural yoghurt to a paste. Spread over the potatoes. Melt 75 g [3 oz] clarified butter in a heavy-based pan over medium heat. Add 2 fresh chillies, chopped. Cook until just translucent (about 4 minutes). Add the potatoes with 15 ml [1 tablespoon] freshly chopped parsley. Cover and cook in an oven heated to 160°C [325°F] gas mark 3 for 20 minutes. The yoghurt forms a crust over the potatoes, hence the name smothered. Serve instead of rice with meat curries.

● For alu bhurta (Indian puréed potatoes) mix puréed potatoes with 30 ml [2 tablespoons] minced pimento, 30 ml [2 tablespoons] freshly chopped chives, 30 ml [2 tablespoons] melted butter, 15 ml [1 tablespoon] freshly chopped coriander leaves and a pinch of turmeric dissolved in 15 ml [1 tablespoon] hot milk. Serve instead of rice.

● For dhali dum (steamed beans) prepare 450 g [1 lb] green beans for steaming. Finely chop one small onion and a thin slice of fresh ginger. Place 25 g [1 oz] butter in a heavy-based pan over medium heat. Add 45 ml [3 tablespoons] water and bring to the boil. Add the beans, ginger, onion and a pinch of ground fennel seeds. Mix well, cover and cook for 7 minutes, shaking the pan from time to time. Serve with meat or fish dishes.

● For khumbi sukhe (Indian sautéed mushrooms) wipe 350 g [¾ lb] button mushrooms and slice thinly. Place in a single layer in a shallow dish. Mix together 2.5 ml [½ teaspoon] onion salt, 2.5 ml [½ teaspoon] freshly ground black pepper, 2.5 ml [½ teaspoon] freshly chopped basil, 60 ml [4 tablespoons] lime or lemon juice and pour over the mushrooms. Turn to cover all sides and marinate for 2 hours. Place 50 g [2 oz] clarified butter in a heavy-based pan over medium heat. When it melts, add the mushrooms plus 5 ml [1 teaspoon] crushed cardamom seeds, a pinch of turmeric and a crushed garlic clove. Cook, stirring from time to time for 3 minutes. Goes well with all meat and fish dishes.

● Raita is another popular accompaniment for curries and korma. Raita is a mixture of natural yoghurt, diced cucumber and finely chopped onion.

Step-by-step to cooking poppadoms

2 As soon as the poppadom puffs up (about 2 seconds) lift out of the oil. Tap against the edge to shake off excess fat.

3 Dip the uncooked part of the poppadom in the fat. Cook for 2 seconds then tap against the edge to shake off excess fat.

OR cook the poppadoms in a very hot oven—230°C [450°F] gas mark 8, placing them in a single layer directly on the oven shelf.

HOT BEEF CURRY

[XXX] *This is a very hot curry and should never be served to anyone who has never tasted curry before.*

SERVES 6-8

900 g [2 lb] stewing steak
45 ml [3 tablespoons] seasoned flour
5 ml [1 teaspoon] ground cumin
30 ml [2 tablespoons] ground coriander
15 ml [1 tablespoon] ground cloves
15 ml [1 tablespoon] ground cinnamon
5 ml [1 teaspoon] ground fenugreek
5 ml [1 tablespoon] crushed dried chillies
5 ml [1 tablespoon] crushed fennel seeds
1 whole bulb of garlic
2.5 cm [1"] piece of fresh ginger
45 ml [3 tablespoons] white wine vinegar

75 ml [3 tablespoons] ghee
2 small onions
550 ml [1 pt] beef stock or water

1 Cut the meat into cubes and toss in seasoned flour.

2 Mix the ground and crushed spices. Peel and crush the garlic cloves and mince the ginger. Add them to the spices, then blend in the vinegar to make a paste.

3 Put the ghee in a heavy-based flameproof casserole over low heat. When hot, add the spice paste and cook for 2 minutes, stirring all the time. Lower the heat and cook for a further 2 minutes.

4 Peel and chop the onions. Add to

the casserole and fry over a medium heat for 4 minutes.

5 Add the meat and cook, stirring for 5 minutes.

6 Pour on the beef stock or water, stir and bring to boiling point.

7 Reduce heat to simmer, cover the casserole and stew gently for 2-2½ hours until the meat is tender.

Variation

● For hot curry pork, make spice paste as for hot curry beef. Cut about 900 g [2 lb] boneless shoulder of pork into small pieces. Mix thoroughly with the spice paste and marinate for 2 hours. Omit flour. Proceed as from step 4. Use chicken instead of beef stock.

164

Special spreads

Perfect for a party, both for entertaining a crowd or for a smaller, more formal occasion, pâtés and terrines are equally good for light meals, snacks, picnics and packed lunches. They are always nourishing, but can be as luxurious or as economical as you choose and can soon become a firm favourite not only in the cook's repertoire but with diners as well.

Pâtés and terrines rank among the most delicious and the most useful creations to emerge from the kitchen. They are very nutritious, can be made in bulk and do not need to be expensive.

A cooked pâté or a terrine can be made from a mixture of any meats or from fish. The main ingredient is enriched and preserved with plenty of fat and seasoned and flavoured to your taste. Once mixed and turned into its dish it can be left in the oven to cook slowly, demanding no attention from the cook. It keeps well and

can be served as a first course, main course, in sandwiches or as a snack on biscuits.

The different mixtures of meats and the consequent varieties in flavour are positively endless. The basic mixture can also be dressed up quite considerably to be served as a luxurious dinner party pâté: it can be layered with other ingredients, wrapped in pastry or covered in aspic. Here we deal basically with making, cooking and serving of the many different basic pâté mixtures.

As well as the cooked pâtés and terrines there are the uncooked pâtés. This is a slightly misleading

term, as the ingredients are precooked rather than eaten raw. However, they are not cooked as a pâté, but are briefly cooked separately and then pounded together. In this respect they are more like potted meats and pastes and, as the ingredients are more tender than those used in cooked pâtés, the results are usually particularly rich and creamy. Most fish pâtés are uncooked pâtés, because fish does not need the long slow cooking as do the cheaper cuts of meat used in cooked pâtés.

Cooked pâtés and terrines are worth making in quantity as they take some time to prepare and cook, regardless of their size. If you are looking for a quickly made alternative, then try the uncooked version.

PATE OR TERRINE?

There is little point in trying to make distinctions between two words which nowadays are used interchangeably. Any meat or fish mixture which is baked in the oven in an ovenproof dish can be called a pâté or a terrine.

The only distinction that is made, and it is not strictly speaking a true one, is that smooth mixtures are generally called pâtés and firmer, coarser mixtures, terrines. When the dishes were originally created there were, of course, several clear distinctions.

Pâté

To be absolutely accurate, the word pâté should be used only to describe a meat or fish mixture which is completely enclosed in pastry and baked in the oven. In other words, a pie. Nowadays, this dish or type of pâté is termed 'pâté en croûte'.

Pâtés, as we know them, are very well-flavoured meat or fish mixtures, not enclosed in pastry, which have been baked in the oven, usually in a dish lined with bacon or pork fat. The name also applies to pâtés made from previously cooked ingredients which are then pounded until smooth. The latter are never called terrines.

Terrine

A terrine takes its name from the oblong ovenproof dish (a form of tureen) in which it was cooked. The dish is now used to bake pâtés as well and, of course, both products can be baked in any suitably sized ovenproof dish of any shape.

A terrine is always made from raw ingredients and baked in the oven, and is traditionally decorated with bay leaves laid in a trefoil pattern (a group of three leaves) on top. The term terrine has come to be used for coarser types of pâté mixtures which is a useful distinction, although not terminologically correct.

Smooth or coarse

The consistency of pâtés and terrines can vary from the velvety smooth to the coarse and crumbly. A smooth pâté mixture must be exactly that: as smooth as velvet and rich and creamy. These pâtés are the luxurious ones, made with ingredients such as chicken livers or smoked salmon, enriched with cream and bound with eggs. Such pâtés are best served as a first course. Like uncooked pâtés they are too rich to be served as a main course.

Crumbly pâtés are like those traditionally made by the busy housewife who cannot afford to spend a long time pounding the ingredients. These are the main coarse pâtés, nourishing yet not so rich as to be indigestible in larger quantities. They are, therefore, worth preparing in bulk: bake in a large terrine and store for future use. They can be sliced or spooned out and served with plenty of salad and fresh bread for a deliciously nourishing lunch or supper.

Uncooked pâtés

Uncooked pâtés are a different dish altogether. They are more like potted meats and pastes, being quick to make, demanding little effort and emerging smooth, rich and creamy. They are best served with canapés for a party, or as a first course for a meal.

INGREDIENTS FOR COOKED PATES AND TERRINES

Cooked pâtés and terrines were originally created to use the offal and various other parts of a carcass of a pig or game animal which were not needed immediately and which, if not cooked straight away, would go to waste. Nowadays, we make cooked pâtés and terrines from any kind of meat and poultry and from fish too. Plenty of fat is still used because this moistens the food and preserves the dishes for a day or two. This brief rest before serving greatly improves the flavour.

The main ingredient

The main ingredient may be just one kind of meat, poultry, game, fish or offal but is more often a mixture. Pork, in some form, is still included in

most meat pâtés: sausage meat is the most popular way.

The cuts of meat used, except in luxury pâtés made from small amounts of expensive ingredients, are the cheaper cuts which are not suitable for the fiercer cooking methods. Cuts suitable for stewing are excellent and the cheaper varieties of liver can be used successfully.

Fat

Fat is always blended into a pâté mixture, as well as being used to line the dish in which it is cooked. In a mixture of red meat, game or liver, pork fat is the kind most often used. When the pâté is being made from white meat or poultry, butter, cream or chicken fat is more usual. With fish, use cream or oil.

The proportion of fat to the main ingredient in a pâté varies with the quality of the meat or fish. A lean meat, such as liver, can have as much as an equal quantity of pork fat, in the form of belly of pork, streaky bacon or sausage meat. Duck, on the other hand, being a rich meat will need very little extra fat added.

If the pâté is to be turned out, the dish must be lined with fat before the mixture is put in for cooking. The fat can either be rashers of streaky bacon or pork fat cut into strips and sliced to 6 mm [¼"]. The fat forms a jacket and is turned out with the pâté.

Flavourings

The flavourings are chosen to complement the main ingredient of the pâté mixture. Herbs and spices vary widely but in meat mixtures there is almost always a hint of onion or garlic, which can be strong or subdued.

Brandy is a popular flavouring ingredient for pâtés. It not only has a pleasantly distinctive flavour, but also helps to preserve the mixture. It can be used with other liquid flavourings to marinate the meat for extra flavour.

167

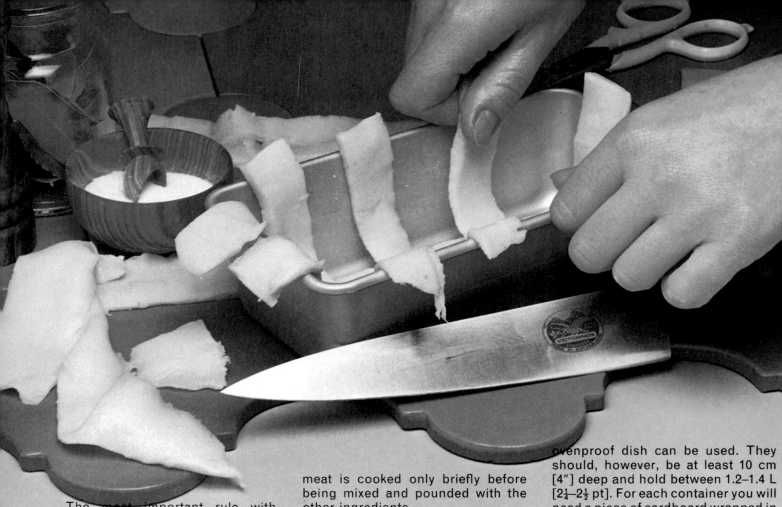

The most important rule with flavourings and seasonings is to be generous. Cold foods need more seasoning and flavouring than hot dishes. If you are not sure whether you have added sufficient flavourings, fry or grill a spoonful of the mixture before you pack it into its dish. Allow it to cool and then test the flavour; add more if necessary.

A binding agent

A binding agent is sometimes used to firm up a crumbly or soft mixture which is to be served turned out and sliced. Common binding ingredients are breadcrumbs, flour or beaten egg which bind the greasy meat and fat particles together. Hard-boiled eggs are popular, too, because they mash to a smooth paste very easily. Jellied stock or aspic can also be used.

INGREDIENTS FOR UNCOOKED PATES

Uncooked pâtés are made with similar ingredients though a different method of preparation. The principal ingredient must be either fish, or a meat that needs little cooking—the most popular being chicken livers. Meat that needs long, slow cooking is totally unsuitable, because the fish or

meat is cooked only briefly before being mixed and pounded with the other ingredients.

Fat is used in the form of butter, oil or cream cheese. The fish or meat is usually fried in butter or oil and is then pounded with this fat. Alternatively, it may be added to extra butter or cream cheese and pounded until smooth. Since the added fat makes the mixture very smooth and soft, it is unnecessary to line the dish with additional fat.

As with cooked pâtés and terrines, uncooked pâtés nearly always contain onion, garlic or similar flavourings and need to be well seasoned because of the high quantity of rather bland fat or cream cheese.

EQUIPMENT

You will find it considerably easier and quicker to make pâtés with the help of a liquidizer, which will produce a well-blended, smooth paste in a few seconds. Without a liquidizer you will need a mincer and a heavy mortar and pestle and must be prepared for some heavy elbow work, pounding and blending the ingredients to the required consistency.

Oblong tins (such as loaf tins) or dishes are best for cooking pâtés and terrines that you wish to serve in slices. Otherwise, any attractive

ovenproof dish can be used. They should, however, be at least 10 cm [4"] deep and hold between 1.2–1.4 L [2¼–2½ pt]. For each container you will need a piece of cardboard wrapped in aluminium foil which fits just inside the rim of the dish. This is put on top of the cooked pâté (foil side down) and weights, such as cans of food, are placed on top to press the mixture.

Uncooked pâtés can be served in any small decorative container. Because they are not cooked the dishes do not need to be oven- or flameproof, and as they are not pressed, neither the cardboard nor weights are needed.

QUANTITIES
Cooked pâtés and terrines

When considering making a cooked pâté or terrine it is wise to think in terms of large quantities for a number of reasons. It is, in any case, very difficult to calculate accurately how much will be needed at one sitting, especially if the guests are helping themselves. Although 450 g [1 lb] might be more than sufficient for your purpose, it is worth doubling and trebling the quantity to justify the effort and the fuel consumed. A 450 g [1 lb] pâté would serve 8–10 as a first course and 4–5 as a main course with bread.

The best reason for making a large

quantity is that cooked pâtés and terrines keep perfectly for up to 4 weeks in the freezer. It is always nice to have something to hand in case of emergencies or for 'spur of the moment' invitations, and especially something home-made. If the emergency never comes, you will have a cheap but nutritious filling for sandwiches or a family meal ready to hand.

All the ingredients you are using are inexpensive, so it is inappropriate to buy a small quantity and process this, when a larger quantity could be processed in the same time and for little extra cost.

Because cheap cuts of meat are being used, they need long slow cooking to tenderize and mature properly. A small quantity of pâté in a small container would heat through too quickly and toughen, shrink and dry out. It also consumes almost as much fuel as a large quantity in a larger container.

Uncooked pâtés
For a quickly made, rich and nourishing dish, nothing can beat an uncooked pâté. Because they are so quick to make and demand little effort, it is practical to make them in very small amounts 225 g [½ lb] meat or fish mixed with the other ingredients will make more than enough pâté for 4 people, if served as a first course at supper.

Once the pâté has been refrigerated, it will only keep for up to 48 hours. For this reason, it is obviously better to calculate roughly how much you will need, allow a little extra for large appetites and any left over can be used in sandwiches or on biscuits the next day.

MAKING COOKED PATES AND TERRINES
There are two clear processes in making cooked pâtés and terrines: making the mixture and cooking it. Uncooked pâtés are made in an entirely different way.

Mixing a cooked pâté or terrine
The main ingredient must be completely freed from any sinews, gristle, skin and bones. It should then be chopped if you are using a liquidizer or chopped and then finely minced if you are not. You can, at the same time, chop or mince any flavouring ingredients that are solid, such as onion, bacon and garlic.

In recipes for smooth pâtés it is quite common to sauté the solid flavouring ingredients and the main ingredient before pounding. This makes them softer and easier to blend. This is not done with a mixture that is designed to be coarse and crumbly.

Mix together all the solid and dry ingredients. If using a liquidizer, add any liquid flavourings and process a small amount at a time. If using a mortar and pestle, pound the minced ingredients with any dry flavourings and seasonings until the desired consistency is achieved. Then add any liquid flavourings and mix in well.

Taste the mixture and add extra seasoning or flavouring if required.

Lining the dish with fat
If the pâté is to be turned out and sliced—and sometimes when it is not—the dish in which it is to be made must first be greased and then lined with fat. This fat layer acts as a preservative and moisturizer when it is on the serving plate. There are two suitable fats for lining—streaky bacon, which gives a particularly pretty pink and white marble effect when cooked and cold, and pork barding fat. The dish can either be lined across in straight rows, or a lattice pattern which shows when the pâté is turned out.

Pork fat is cut into strips for lining rather in the same way as for larding (see page 524). Chill it first to firm it up then cut downwards towards the rind with a warm knife. Cut the fat lengthways, according to its width, in strips of about 4 cm [1½"] wide. Turn each strip on to the side and split it at 6 mm [¼"] intervals.

For a plain lining, in a single layer, you will need bacon rashers or strips of pork fat slightly longer than the measurement down one side of the dish or loaf tin, across the width and up the other side. This means that when a slice is cut from the pâté it will have a single piece of fat around 3 sides.

Fit the strips neatly into the mould or loaf tin across the width, overlapping slightly and leaving no gaps. The ends should slightly protrude above the rims on each side. If you are using bacon rashers, which do not have straight edges, you will find them easier to fit together and more malleable if they are at room temperature when used.

For a lattice effect when turned out, lay the strips across in one direction leaving small gaps between them. Lay more strips across in the other direction. These will give you a double layer of fat, while the meat mixture should show through at intervals.

Filling the dish
If the dish is not lined with fat, it must be well greased before filling. Turn the pâté mixture into the prepared dish. Press it down with the back of a spoon and smooth the surface. Whether the dish is lined or not, add more rows of fat or bacon to completely cover the top of the pâté. The traditional decoration for a pâté or terrine to be served from the dish is a pattern of bay leaves. These should be laid on top of the fat covering if you intend to serve this, or underneath it if you intend to remove the fat before serving. A pâté that is to be turned out and sliced will not need this decoration.

Cooking a pâté or terrine
The oven should be heated to 180°C [350°F] gas mark 4. The dish of pâté is cooked in a bain-marie. The dish is placed in a roasting tin or similar container and this is filled with hot water until it reaches halfway up the sides of the pâté dish. The dish is closely covered with foil. The pâté is baked for the time stated in the recipe, which will vary according to the quality of the main ingredient. A hearty solid pâté mixture, made from stewing meat, may need up to 2½ hours, while a smoother mixture of the same weight made from more tender ingredients might need less than 1½ hours. This browning improves the appearance of the pâté.

About 15–20 minutes before the end of cooking time, remove the pâté from the oven. Take off the foil and, if you wish to serve the pâté from the dish without the fat covering, remove this as well. Return the pâté to the oven in its roasting tin, so the fat covering, or the surface of the pâté may brown.

After the browning, remove the pâté from the oven—it should have shrunk in slightly from the sides of the dish—and check to see if it is cooked. If you are not certain, run a hot skewer into the mixture; it should come out clean if the mixture is cooked. Lift from the roasting tin and finish the pâté.

Step-by-step to liver pâté

MAKES 1.2 KG [2½ LB]
450 g [1 lb] pig's liver
175 g [6 oz] rindless streaky bacon
350 g [¾ lb] fresh belly of pork
175 g [6 oz] hard pork fat
garlic clove
75 ml [3 fl oz] medium-dry white wine
15 ml [1 tablespoon] brandy
salt and pepper
pinch of ground mace
1 large egg
30 ml [2 tablespoons] plain flour
15 g [½ oz] lard
400 g [14 oz] barding fat

1 Wash liver and pat dry. Chop or mince the liver and bacon. Chop the belly of pork and the fat and mince finely.

2 Mix the chopped and minced ingredients. Add chopped garlic. Pour over the wine and the brandy and leave overnight if wished.

6 Lay the strips across the greased tin, overlapping them slightly and pressing them against the greased surfaces.

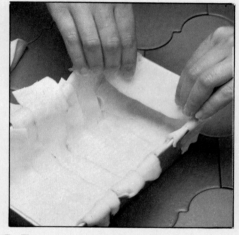

7 The strips should stretch right down and across the dish and up the other side to completely surround the pâté mixture.

8 Turn the mixture into the lined dish. Cover the surface with the remaining barding, cut to fit. Cover tightly with foil.

10 Remove from the oven and from the tin of water when cooked. If uncertain, pierce with a hot skewer. It should come out clean.

11 Remove the foil and lay a piece of foil-wrapped cardboard, cut to size, over the surface of the pâté. Weight down with cans.

12 Put the dish into cold water and leave overnight. Remove weights and cardboard, cover with cling film and refrigerate for 24 hours.

Season well with salt and pepper and add the mace. Beat the egg into the flour and add to the mixture. Mix well with your hands.

4 Heat the oven to 180°C [350°F] gas mark 4. Lightly grease a 1 kg [2¼ lb] loaf tin or an oblong dish with the lard.

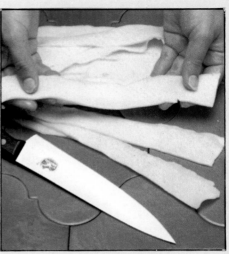

5 Slice the barding fat into 4 cm [1½"] strips and cut into slices 6 mm [¼"] thick. Reserve some strips for the topping.

OR if not turning out the pâté, simply turn it into the greased dish, cover the surface with fat and cover dish tightly with foil.

AND bake as described in step 9 but, after 2 hours, remove foil and fat too if wished, and brown in the oven for the remaining time.

9 Put the dish into a roasting tin and pour in water to come halfway up the sides of the dish. Bake for 2½ hours or until juices run clear.

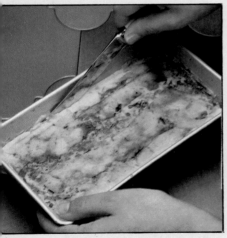

3 To serve, remove the cling film and all the surface fat. Run a knife around the dish to loosen the pâté and jacket of fat.

14 Place a plate over the top of the dish and invert smartly to dislodge the pâté and its jacket. Serve in slices with crusty bread.

OR to serve the pâté from the dish, either cut it into wedges with a knife or spoon it out if the mixture is very loose and crumbly.

Finishing the pâté or terrine

A few pâtés are eaten while still hot but most are meant to be eaten cold. They should be allowed to mature, to allow the flavours to blend and mellow. A cooled pâté should wait for at least 24 hours before being eaten.

A pâté to be served cold must first be cooled and then chilled. If you are serving the pâté from its dish, simply cover tightly with clean aluminium foil, put in a pan of cold water and leave until quite cold. Then refrigerate until needed.

Pressing: a pâté that is to be turned out must be firm and sliceable. To ensure this it must be pressed while cooling. Place a piece of foil-covered cardboard, cut to fit inside the rim, on the surface of the pâté. Stand the dish in a pan of cold water. Weight the pâté down with either kitchen weights, or cans of fruit or vegetables or other suitable articles. Leave the pâté until quite cold, then remove from the pan of water and refrigerate. Leave the weight in place if there is room in your refrigerator.

Serving a cooked pâté or terrine

If the pâté is to be turned out and sliced, run a knife around the dish to loosen the pâté and its jacket of bacon or fat. Lay a plate over the dish and invert sharply. The turned-out pâté needs no further garnish, except maybe a sprig of parsley or watercress on top to add a touch of colour.

A pâté to be served from its dish can be decorated in several ways. It can have the traditional three bay leaves which must be added before cooking. Alternatively, a cooled pâté which has had the covering fat removed and its surface browned can be covered with a small amount of melted consommé before it is refrigerated. Decorations, such as orange slices, a fanned gherkin and juniper berries, can be set in the consommé.

MAKING AN UNCOOKED PATE

Any sinew, gristle, skin or bones must be removed from the fish or meat. This is cooked for a brief period, normally by frying, and flavouring ingredients which need cooking, such as onion, are added. The meat or fish and other ingredients are then mashed or minced finely. A liquidizer can be used,

which will speed up the process still further, but this is not so invaluable as for cooked pâtés and terrines. Alternatively, pound the ingredients together until well blended and completely smooth. Taste the mixture and add any further seasonings and flavourings that may be needed.

Turn the mixture into a decorative pot, tapping the surface while filling to remove any air bubbles. Wipe the rim of the pot clean, cover with cling film and refrigerate until required. The pâté must be used completely within 48 hours. It needs no garnish, since it is very rich. Serve it in spoonfuls from the dish.

PATE MAISON

This household recipe uses rabbit, pork and liver. The ingredients are coarsely chopped and, being cheap, make a quick-to-make yet delicious family pâté.

MAKES ABOUT 1 KG [2¼ LB] PATE
100 g [¼ lb] pig's liver
100 g [¼ lb] belly of pork
225 g [½ lb] cold, cooked rabbit
225 g [½ lb] pork sausage meat
lard for greasing
8-10 rindless streaky bacon rashers
1 onion
25 g [1 oz] soft white breadcrumbs
1 medium-sized egg
15 ml [1 tablespoon] milk
75 ml [3 fl oz] brandy
salt and pepper

1 Grease a 1.2 L [2¼ pt] oblong or round ovenproof dish with a little lard and line with bacon rashers, keeping 2 or 3 aside to cover the pâté. Heat the oven to 180°C [350°F] gas mark 4.

2 Remove any sinew, skin, gristle or bones from the liver, pork and rabbit. Coarsely chop the liver and pork and shred the rabbit.

3 In a large bowl, mix the liver, pork, rabbit and sausage meat thoroughly. Skin and chop the onion and add to the meat with the breadcrumbs.

4 Mix together the egg, milk and brandy. Pour this over the meat. Mix in well, and season to taste.

5 Turn the mixture into the lined dish. Cover with the reserved bacon rashers.

6 Cover the tin tightly with foil. Stand it in a roasting tin of hot water which comes halfway up its sides. Bake for 1½ hours. Check to see if it is cooked. Remove from the oven when done.

7 Remove foil. Cover the pâté with a piece of foil-wrapped cardboard, cut to fit, inside the rim. Stand a weight on top. Stand the tin in a pan of cold water. Leave in a cool place for 24 hours.

8 Take off the weight and cardboard. Scrape off any excess fat round the top of the pâté. Refrigerate for at least 12 hours.

9 Remove the top bacon rashers. Turn the pâté out on to a dish for serving.

SMOOTH LIVER PATE

Use any good quality liver for this pâté, which has no bacon lining. It is not meant for long keeping. Cream gives the pâté extra smoothness and richness in place of the fat. Its texture will depend on how thoroughly you pound or process it. Serve with dry biscuits for a snack meal.

MAKES ABOUT 700 G [1½ LB]
PATE
**500 g [18 oz] calf's, pig's or
    poultry livers**
**100 g [¼ lb] rindless streaky
    bacon**
1 small onion
50 g [2 oz] butter
**2 finely chopped hard-boiled
    eggs**
pinch of dried mixed herbs
10 ml [2 teaspoons] brandy
**20 ml [4 teaspoons] thick
    cream**
salt and pepper
butter for greasing
watercress sprig

1 Chop the liver and bacon finely. Skin and chop the onion. Mix the liver, bacon and onion together. Heat the oven to 180°C [350°F] gas mark 4.

2 Melt the butter in a heavy-based frying-pan. Fry the liver, bacon and onion gently for about 4 minutes, turning them over to brown all the pieces of liver.

3 Take the pan off the heat, and add the chopped hard-boiled eggs.

4 Either mince and pound the mixture to a smooth paste, or process it in a liquidizer, a small amount at a time, until it is smooth.

5 Mix in the herbs, brandy and cream and season to taste. Blend thoroughly.

6 Grease a 1 L [1¾ pt] ovenproof dish with butter. Turn in the mixture, pressing it down into the corners so as not to leave air pockets. Cover the dish securely with foil.

7 Stand the dish in a tin of very hot water. Bake it for 40-50 minutes.

8 Remove it from the oven, check to make sure it is cooked and remove from the pan of water. Take off the foil and cover with a sheet of greaseproof paper.

9 Stand the dish in a pan of cold water in a cool place. Leave until quite cold.

10 Re-cover with foil or cling film and refrigerate for at least 24 hours. Use within the following 24 hours.

11 To serve, garnish the pâté with a sprig of watercress. Slice or spoon from the dish.

HERB PATE

Since it has several less fatty ingredients than most pâtés, this garden-lover's coarse-cut one is cooked in a jacket of pure fat instead of bacon. It is unusual, and useful, because you can serve it hot or cold. When it is sliced for serving, each person removes the thin strip of fat from around his portion.

MAKES ABOUT 1.7 KG [3¾ LB]
PATE
1 kg [2¼ lb] spinach
salt and pepper
50 g [2 oz] ham
**225 g [½ lb] rindless streaky
    bacon**
2 onions
2 garlic cloves
1 sprig parsley
1 sprig rosemary
4-6 chives
**2.5 ml [½ teaspoon] dried
    marjoram**
**2.5 ml [½ teaspoon] dried
    savory**
2 medium-sized eggs
700 g [1½ lb] sausage meat
lard for greasing
**700 g [1½ lb] thinly sliced pork
    barding fat**

1 Wash the spinach very thoroughly. Put the spinach in a saucepan, season with salt and pepper and cook with no added water over low heat for 8-10 minutes. The pan must be well sealed.

2 When the spinach is cooked, drain it. Squeeze it to get rid of as much water as possible. Heat the oven to 180°C [350°F] gas mark 4.

3 Chop the spinach roughly. Then finely chop the ham and bacon, onion, garlic and fresh herbs. Sprinkle with the dried herbs.

4 Mix all the chopped ingredients in a bowl. Beat the eggs and mix them in. Then mix in the sausage meat and season.

5 Grease two 1.2 L [2¼ pt] oblong ovenproof dishes and line with strips of sliced pork fat, reserving some for the top.

6 Put in the pâté mixture. Press it down and smooth the surface. Cover it with more slices of fat.

7 Cover the dishes securely with foil. Stand them in a roasting tin of hot water. Bake for 1-1¼ hours. Remove from the oven. Test that the pâtés are cooked.

8 Remove the foil, take off the top layer of fat and serve the pâtés hot. Alternatively, weight the pâtés, cool and then chill. To serve, remove the top covering of fat, turn out of the dishes and slice.

DANISH LIVER PATE

Liver pâté is a very popular everyday food in Denmark where it plays an important part in the nutrition of the people. It is low in carbohydrates and rich in iron and vitamin B. This recipe is for a smooth textured pâté, and is one which is typically Danish.

Pig's liver is especially ideal for use in pâtés, as it has a strong robust flavour.

The choosing and preparing of liver is discussed on pages 111–113.

MAKES 700 G [1½ LB]
450 g [1 lb] pig's liver
1 small onion
275 ml [½ pt] milk
1 bay leaf
300 g [11 oz] streaky bacon
1 garlic clove
15 g [½ oz] lard
6 anchovy fillets or 10 ml [2 teaspoons] anchovy essence
25 g [1 oz] butter
25 g [1 oz] flour
2 small eggs
salt
freshly ground black pepper
grated nutmeg

1 Peel the onion and slice into thin rounds.

2 Put it into a saucepan, add the milk and bay leaf and bring slowly to the boil. Remove from the heat, cover and leave to infuse for 15 minutes. Strain through a fine strainer and reserve the milk

3 Trim any rind or bones from the bacon. Set aside 4 rashers and cut the rest into medium pieces using a sharp knife.

4 Wash and dry the liver, remove any skin or connective tissue and cut into pieces.

5 Peel the garlic clove.

6 Heat the oven to 180°C [350°F] gas mark 4. Grease a 1.2 L [2¼ pt] capacity dish, casserole or loaf tin with lard.

7 Mince the liver, bacon, garlic and anchovy fillets (if used) finely, three times. If anchovy essence is used, add to the ingredients after mincing. Pound the mixture until it is smooth.

8 Melt the butter in a saucepan, add the flour and cook gently for a minute, without browning. Stir continuously. Off the heat, add the strained milk all at once and blend smoothly with a wire whisk. Bring to the boil, stirring, and boil for a minute or two.

9 Off the heat, stir in the liver mixture.

10 Beat the eggs lightly and add to the mixture, stirring until it is smoothly blended. Season by adding more salt, pepper and nutmeg, according to taste.

11 Turn into the greased dish, lay the reserved bacon lightly over the top and cover with foil. Stand the dish in a roasting tin containing hot water to reach half-way up the sides of the dish.

12 Bake the pâté in the centre of the oven for 1 hour, or until it is firm.

13 Remove from the heat, take off foil and replace with foil-wrapped cardboard and a weight. Leave in a bowl of cold water, preferably overnight and then refrigerate for 24 hours.

14 Serve the pâté straight from the dish.

GAME PATE

Good for using up the less attractive bits of game meat, this makes another main-course dish. You can use hare, or meat from the wings and legs of game birds not wanted when the animal or bird was first served. If you have no game leftovers already, you can buy some stewing venison. The pâté can be as smooth or as coarse as you like. Simply pound it to the consistency you prefer.

SERVES 8
450-500 g [16-18 oz] game meat without bone
15 rashers rindless streaky bacon
1 slice bread, 1.2 cm [½"] thick without crusts
30 ml [2 tablespoons] milk
50 g [2 oz] button mushrooms, sliced
25 g [1 oz] unsalted butter
50 g [2 oz] softened salted butter
1 medium-sized egg
90 ml [6 tablespoons] medium-sweet sherry
good pinch of grated orange zest
salt
freshly ground black pepper
lard for greasing

1 Mince or shred the game meat and 5 of the bacon rashers. Put the bread in a bowl, and pour the milk over it.

2 Wipe the mushrooms, trim the stalks and slice. Melt the unsalted butter, and sauté the mushrooms gently until tender. Heat the oven to 180°C [350°F] gas mark 4.

3 Squeeze the bread dry. Mix or pound together the meat, mushrooms and bread to the texture you want. It can be a smooth paste, or a coarse one with fragments of mushroom in it.

4 Add and mix in the salted butter, egg, sherry, and orange zest. Season generously.

5 Grease a 450 g [1 lb] loaf tin or a similar sized dish and line with the remaining bacon rashers. Keep 3 rashers aside to cover the pâté. Fill the tin with the mixture.

6 Smooth and level the surface of the pâté. Cover with the remaining 3 rashers. Cover the tin tightly with foil.

7 Stand the pâté in a roasting tin of hot water. Bake for 1½ hours or until the meat shrinks slightly from the sides of the tin. Check with a skewer if necessary.

8 Remove the pâté from the oven and from the water. Remove the foil and top bacon rashers. Spoon off any excess fat.

9 Stand the tin in a pan of cold water. Cover the pâté with foil-wrapped cardboard, then with a weight. Leave for 24 hours.

10 Remove cardboard and weights. Refrigerate for another 24 hours, then turn out for serving. Serve with rye bread or pumpernickel.

Star recipe
Loin chops
with sauce Robert

175

Star recipe

LOIN CHOPS WITH SAUCE ROBERT

These grilled pork chops are lifted from the ordinary and made dinner party fare by the sharp-tasting sauce, made from a demi-glace sauce. If you have sauce espagnole stored in the refrigerator, you can start at step 8 and the recipe will take you three-quarters of an hour. Serve with new potatoes.

SERVES 4
4 loin pork chops
30 ml [2 tablespoons] oil

For the demi-glace sauce:
40 g [1½ oz] butter
1 small carrot

1 celery stick
1 small onion
25 g [1 oz] mushroom stalks
50 g [2 oz] streaky bacon
1 bouquet garni
675 ml [1¼ pt] good brown stock
10 ml [2 teaspoon] tomato purée
salt and black pepper
150 ml [¼ pt] jellied brown stock

For the sauce Robert:
1 small onion
25 g [1 oz] butter
125 ml [4 fl oz] white wine
25 g [1 oz] gherkins
20 ml [4 teaspoons] French mustard
5 ml [1 teaspoon] chopped parsley

1 Wash the carrot and celery, pee[l] onion, chop with mushrooms Remove bacon rind and chop.

5 Remove from the heat and trickle in the brown stock, stirring continuously. Bring to the boil.

6 Add the bouquet garni, cover and simmer for 1 hour. Skim off any fat that rises with a skimming spoon.

7 Add a spoonful of cold stock. Le[t] the fat rise to surface and skim off Do this again. Add tomato purée

11 Turn grill to highest heat and arrange the chops in single layer in gratin dish.

12 Continue the sauce. Peel and chop onion. Melt butter in small heavy-based pan; cook onion till soft.

13 Add the wine and simmer t[o] reduce by half. Add to demi-glace simmer for 20 minutes.

2 Melt butter in a medium-sized heavy-based pan. Add the bacon and sweat for 2 minutes.

3 Add the vegetables and cook over low heat until onion softens. Stir occasionally.

4 Add flour off the heat, then cook, stirring all the time, until the roux is a rich nut brown.

8 Strain the sauce through a sieve, into a small saucepan, pressing all the juices from the vegetables.

9 Add the jellied stock. Simmer until the sauce has reduced to 250 ml [½ pt] about 30 minutes.

10 Brush the loin chops on both sides with a little of the oil. Set aside till ready to cook.

14 Grill chops 1 minute each side. Lower heat or dish and grill 5-7 minutes each side, basting.

15 Chop gherkins. When sauce is ready, stir in mustard, gherkins and parsley. Do not reheat.

16 Dish pork chops on to warmed serving dish. Spoon a little sauce over each portion of meat.

Star recipe
Mediterranean lamb

⊠⊠ *If in your book, cold roast lamb is synonymous with washday dinner, then here is a recipe so tasty and different it will dispel that unfortunate image for ever. The roast lamb in this case is a joint of best end of neck which has been boned and rolled. The butcher may do this for you or you can fillet the joint yourself. Allow a little extra time if you intend to do the job yourself. If you are filleting the joint yourself, take the opportunity to sprinkle the seasoning on the meat before rolling it up so that you gain a subtle flavour on the inside of the joint and not just on the outside as with a pre-rolled joint.*

The accompanying richly coloured and flavoured tomato sauce is not unlike a cold ratatouille but with a different combination of vegetables—olives and herbs in place of courgettes and aubergine. By removing children's portions of sauce before these sophisticated ingredients are added, you can turn this into a dish to suit younger members of the family as well. The quantities given serves 4 adults and 2 children.

Serve with hot, crusty French bread and lots of butter.

SERVES 6
1 best end of neck of lamb boned and rolled
salt
freshly ground black pepper

For the sauce:
450 g [1 lb] onions
1 garlic clove
90 ml [6 tablespoons] olive oil
900 g [2 lb] tomatoes
pinch of sugar
10 ml [2 teaspoons] lemon juice

Additional ingredients for adults:
1 medium-sized red pepper
1 medium-sized green pepper
1 garlic clove
10 ml [2 teaspoons] coriander seeds
15 ml [1 tablespoon] chopped fresh basil
75 g [3 oz] black olives

For the garnish:
sprig of parsley

1 Heat the oven to 180°C [350°F] gas mark 4.

2 Rub the surface fat of the joint with a mixture of salt and pepper. Do not rub the mixture into the flesh.

3 Stand the joint on a rack in a roasting pan and roast for 45 minutes to each 450 g [1 lb].

4 Meanwhile prepare the sauce. Peel and chop the onions and crush the garlic.

5 Heat the oil in a frying-pan and lightly sauté the onion and garlic—about 5 minutes.

6 Skin, de-seed and chop the tomatoes and add them to the pan, together with the sugar and lemon juice. Simmer, uncovered, until tomatoes begin to pulp down—about 10 minutes.

7 Spoon half the sauce into a separate pan for the children and simmer it for 30 minutes, stirring occasionally to prevent sticking.

8 Prepare the additional ingredients. Rinse and de-seed both peppers and cut into thin strips; crush the second clove of garlic. Add peppers, garlic and basil to the adult pan and simmer for 30 minutes, stirring occasionally.

9 When the cooking time is up, the liquid in both pans should have evaporated, leaving a rich, juicy stew. Season both pans with salt and pepper. Leave junior sauce in saucepan to cool.

10 Crush the coriander seeds and stir into adult sauce with the olives. Adjust seasoning if necessary. Transfer to bowl.

11 When cool, transfer to the refrigerator to chill.

12 When the meat is ready (when the flesh pierced with a thin skewer gives out slightly rosy juices) remove the joint from the oven and leave in a cold place to cool rapidly.

13 When the joint has cooled, wrap in foil or cling film and refrigerate.

14 Shortly before serving, unwrap the joint and carve into thin slices, removing string as necessary. If adults are not eating at this stage, leave carving their portions until later because cut meat tends to dry. Re-wrap joint until needed again.

15 For children, serve meat on individual dinner plates with their special sauce on top.

16 For adults, arrange their carved slices of meat in an overlapping circle round a serving dish, with the sauce spooned into the centre and garnished with a sprig of parsley.

Star recipe

LAMB AND APRICOT POLO

Lamb and apricot is a combination as popular in the East as in the West. Dried apricots are always used. They are cheaper and have a better flavour than the canned variety. This dish is economical as it makes a small amount of lamb go a long way. Shoulder of lamb has the best flavour. Ask the butcher to bone it for you. He will know how much to allow for the weight of the bone so that you end up with the correct amount of usable meat.

There is no need to soak the apricots first as they absorb liquid during cooking.

SERVES 6
175 g [6 oz] long grain rice
1 medium-sized onion
100 g [¼ lb] butter
350 g [¾ lb] boned shoulder of
** lamb, cubed**
salt
freshly ground black pepper
2.5 ml [½ teaspoon] ground
** cinnamon**
25 g [1 oz] seedless raisins
100 g [¼ lb] dried apricots

1 Boil the rice in salted water for 8 minutes. Drain and rinse with cold water. Leave until cold.

5 Cover with warm water and simmer gently, covered, for about 1½ hours until the meat is tender.

9 Place the tea-cloth over the top of the rice so that it is all covered and then cover with the lid.

2 Skin and finely chop the onion. Melt half the butter. Add the onion. Fry slowly until soft.

3 Add the meat, turning the pieces so that all sides of the lamb are coated with butter.

4 Add the fruit, turning the pieces so that all sides are coated with butter.

6 Use the remaining butter to grease a heavy-based casserole or flame-proof dish with a well-fitting lid.

7 Make a layer of rice about 1.25 cm [½"] thick in the base of the dish. Cover with a layer of meat.

8 Continue layering in this way, finishing with a layer of rice. Fold a clean tea-cloth into four.

10 Place over very low heat and steam gently for 20 minutes until rice is tender and has absorbed sauce.

11 When cooking time is up, remove the lid and the cloth. If wished, remove from the dish.

OR turn the polo into a warmed serving dish and mix the rice and meat together before serving.

Star recipe

★

NOISETTES JARDINIERE

The attraction of this party dish lies in the garnishes which must be prepared and arranged carefully to look really effective. Canned asparagus spears were used here but you can use fresh, steamed asparagus. Be sure to choose small spears with tight heads and a good colour.

Use very firm tomatoes and place them under the grill just long enough to warm through, not to cook them. The butter must be soft when used to fill the tomatoes so do not chill it.

Tarragon butter is used here, but any savoury butter can be served.

SERVES 4
4 noisettes of lamb
2 large tomatoes
olive oil
50 g [2 oz] unsalted butter at
room temperature
a sprig of fresh tarragon or
5 ml [1 teaspoon] dried
salt
freshly ground black pepper
1 x 425 g [15 oz] can asparagus
spears.

1 Plunge the tomatoes into boiling water for 1 minute to loosen skins. Cool in cold water.

2 Using a sharp knife, nick the tomato skin near stalk base. Peel away and discard the skin.

6 Place the butter in a bowl. Beat (stir vigorously) with a wooden spoon to soften.

7 If using fresh tarragon, snip leaves and chop them finely, using small scissors in a mug or glass.

11 Meanwhile, heat the canned asparagus, following manufacturer's instructions.

12 Brush the tomatoes with oil and add them to the grill for the last minute of cooking time.

13 Remove the tomatoes from the grill and fill each half with 5 ml [1 teaspoon] tarragon butter.

14 Arrange the noisettes on a hot serving dish. Garnish with tomatoes and asparagus.

3 Using a sharp knife, make zig-zag cuts around the middle of each tomato.

4 Cut through the centre of the tomatoes and gently pull the halves apart.

5 Scoop out the seeds using a spoon. Discard. At this point, turn the grill to its highest setting.

8 Add the tarragon to the butter. Stir until well blended. Add salt and pepper to taste.

9 Brush the noisettes on both sides with olive oil. Grill under fierce heat for 1 minute each side.

10 Reduce heat. Grill for 4 minutes on each side for medium-rare 6 minutes for well-done.

Star recipe

ORIENTAL SPARE RIB CHOPS

Spare rib chops are lean but less tender than loin or chump chops. They grill best if liberally basted with a sauce. Do be sure to buy English cut or spare rib chops—American cut or Chinese spare ribs are not suitable.

SERVES 4
4 spare rib chops
45 ml [3 tablespoons] oil
1 small onion
1 x 225 g [½ lb] can peeled tomatoes
60 ml [4 tablespoons] wine vinegar
50 g [2 oz] soft brown sugar
30 ml [2 tablespoons] tomato sauce
10 ml [2 teaspoons] soy sauce

1 Brush the chops on both sides with a little of the oil. Set aside until ready to cook.

2 Chop onion finely: peel, cut in half, slice towards root, slice downwards then slice across.

6 Add the tomatoes, their juice, vinegar, sugar, tomato sauce and soy sauce to the saucepan.

7 Bring to the boil and simmer (cook below boiling point) for 10 minutes, stirring occasionally.

8 Meanwhile turn grill to highest heat and arrange the chops in a single layer in a gratin dish.

9 When heat is fierce, place dish under it. Cook chops for 1 minute on each side, turning with tongs.

10 Pour sauce over chops. Reduce heat to low or lower dish as far away from heat as possible.

11 Grill chops for 7-8 minutes on each side, turning and basting with sauce from time to time.

Pour the remaining oil into a small saucepan and set over low heat to warm gently.

4 Add the chopped onion and cook very gently for about 5 minutes until beginning to soften.

5 Turn tomatoes into a sieve over a bowl to reserve juice. Chop the tomatoes roughly.

Star recipe

ROAST FILLET OF PORK WITH WALNUT STUFFING

⊠⊠ *Crunchy walnut stuffing is a delicious accompaniment to pork and helps to make a fillet go further. The onion is grated to make the pieces very tiny, however, chopping finely in a mezzaluna is equally successful. The streaky bacon keeps the fillet moist while cooking and also adds flavour to the meat. Do not use nylon string to tie up the meat.*

The larding bacon is sliced with the fillet and forms a crisp edge to each slice. Each portion shows an attractive pattern of meat and stuffing. Serve with new potatoes and braised celery or a green vegetable.

SERVES 4
450-500 g [16-18 oz] fillet of pork

For the stuffing:
1 small onion
1 celery stick
40 g [1½ oz] shelled walnuts
15 g [½ oz] seedless raisins
50 g [2 oz] white breadcrumbs
1.5 ml [¼ teaspoon] nutmeg
salt and pepper
1 medium-sized egg
3 long rashers of streaky bacon
15 ml [1 tablespoon] flour
250 ml [½ pt] stock or vegetable water

1 Heat oven to 180°C [350°F] gas mark 4. Remove any skin and fat from the fillet.

5 Add the onion, celery, walnuts and raisins to the breadcrumbs. Add nutmeg, salt and pepper. Mix.

6 Break the egg and stir with fork. Add to the mixture. Stir until the stuffing binds together.

7 Spread the stuffing on the fillet, pressing firmly between the meat layers along the whole length.

11 Pierce to check that the meat is cooked and juice is colourless. Transfer to a heated dish. Keep warm.

12 Pour off all but 15 ml [1 tablespoon] of fat. Add flour then stir over gentle heat till lightly brown.

13 Add stock away from the heat and bring to the boil. Simmer for 2-3 minutes. Check seasoning and strain to serve.

186

2 With a sharp knife cut lengthways down the centre of the fillet two-thirds through the meat.

3 Open out. Make a further lengthways cut on either side, half way between centre and outside.

4 Peel the onion and grate (or chop finely). Finely chop the celery stick and the walnuts.

8 Roll the fillet up lengthways. De-rind the bacon rashers and bard the meat on top and both sides.

9 Tie with string several times along its length. Make sure all the stuffing is enclosed.

10 Place on a rack in the roasting pan and roast in centre of oven for 55 minutes to 1 hour.

14 Remove the string then carve the stuffed pork into round slices with the stuffing in the centre.

Star recipe

SPICY MINCE PIE

This economical family pie has a topping made from 'yoghurt crust'—a quickly made and economical alternative to pastry. If wished, the filling may be made in advance. Use yoghurt thickened by adding cornflour.

SERVES 4
350 g [¾ lb] minced beef
1 medium-sized onion

1 large garlic clove
1 celery stick
25 g [1 oz] beef dripping
75 g [3 oz] mushrooms
15 ml [1 tablespoon] plain flour
125 ml [¼ pt] beef stock
30 ml [2 tablespoons] tomato purée
10 ml [2 teaspoons] curry paste

For the topping:
275 ml [½ pt] thickened natural yoghurt
2 large eggs
25 g [1 oz] plain flour
30 ml [2 tablespoons] grated Cheddar cheese
salt
freshly ground black pepper

1 Skin and finely chop the onion. Skin and chop the garlic clove. Scrub and chop the celery stick.

2 Melt the dripping in a heavy-based pan over low heat. Add the mince and brown gently.

3 Add the chopped vegetables and cook, stirring until soft but not coloured.

4 Stir in the flour. Cook for 2 minutes and then stir in the stock. Stir in tomato purée and curry paste.

5 Simmer gently for 5 minutes until slightly thickened. Wipe the mushrooms, slice and add.

6 Transfer to a 1·15L [2 pt] ovenproof pie dish. Heat oven to 190°C [375°F] gas mark 5.

7 Stir the yoghurt until smooth. Beat the eggs. Beat in the flour and add to yoghurt.

8 Stir in the cheese. Season to taste. Pour mixture over the filling. Place in the centre of oven.

9 Cook for 30 minutes until the topping has set and is golden-brown in colour.

Star recipe

LASAGNE BOLOGNESE

This is the most popular lasagne of all, as the meaty filling combines deliciously with the cheese and the creamy sauce. If you are unable to obtain Mozzarella cheese, it's better to omit cheese completely than to use a substitute which would not give the dish the true flavour or texture.

Make béchamel like white sauce, but infuse some vegetables in milk first. Both the sauce and the bolognese filling may be made in advance. Cover the sauce with a circle of greased greaseproof paper to prevent a skin forming if you make it in advance.

Lasagne bolognese is almost a one dish meal, since it contains both meat and filling pasta. Serve it alone or with a salad or green vegetable.

SERVES 4

75 g [3 oz] streaky bacon
1 medium-sized onion
1 medium-sized carrot
half a celery stick
225 g [½ lb] lean beef mince
100 g [¼ lb] chicken livers
25 g [1 oz] butter
15 ml [1 tablespoon]
  concentrated tomato purée
150 ml [¼ pt] white wine
200 ml [7 fl oz] beef stock
250 ml [½ pt] béchamel sauce
salt
225 g [½ lb] lasagne
15 ml [1 tablespoon] oil
freshly ground black pepper
225 g [8 oz] Mozzarella cheese
75 g [3 oz] grated parmesan
  cheese

1 Select a dish for the lasagne, grease liberally with butter and set aside.

2 Remove the rind from the bacon and cut bacon into small pieces. Skin and finely chop the onion.

3 Scrub and chop carrot and celery. Fork over mince to break it down. Wash and dry the chicken livers.

4 Remove and discard any greenish parts from the chicken livers then chop them into small pieces.

190

5 Heat the butter in a heavy-based saucepan over medium heat. Cook the bacon pieces until just brown.

6 Add the onion, carrot and celery. Fry until tender and turning brown. Mix in the mince.

7 Stir the mince until it browns all over. Add the chicken livers and cook for a further 3 minutes.

8 Mix in the tomato purée and the wine. Add the stock and bring to the boil. Season to taste.

9 Reduce heat and simmer, covered, for 30 minutes. Prepare the béchamel sauce.

10 Cover the béchamel sauce with a round of greased greaseproof paper to prevent a skin forming.

11 Bring a large pan containing at least 4.5 L [8 pt] water to the boil. Add 10 ml [2 teaspoons] salt.

12 Add the oil to the water in pan. Add the lasagne to the pan a few pieces at a time. Boil 3-4 minutes.

13 Drain the lasagne. Spread out on a clean, damp cloth in a single layer to cool.

14 Heat the oven to 200°C [400°F] gas mark 6. Place a shelf in the centre.

15 Line the base of the dish with pasta so that it comes slightly up the sides.

16 Cover the pasta with half of the bolognese sauce. Cut the chees into slices.

17 Place half of the cheese slices over the sauce. Cover with another layer of pasta.

18 Pour about half the béchamel sauce over the pasta and sprinkle with one-third of parmesan.

19 Repeat the pasta, bolognes sauce and Mozzarella cheese layers. Cover cheese with pasta.

20 If the sheet of lasagne is too large, trim with scissors. If it is too small, add another piece.

21 Pour the rest of the béchamel sauce over the pasta and sprinkle with remaining parmesan cheese.

22 Bake in the centre of the oven fo about 15 minutes until golden an bubbling.

Finger lickin' chicken

Now that chicken is always available, pennywise cooks are constantly on the look out for new ways of cooking it. Grilling is often thought to be a rather dull way to cook chicken but if tangy herbs and spicy sauces are added it becomes deliciously interesting. Here you are shown how to choose for flavour, divide into portions and grill to perfection.

Thanks to agricultural progress chicken, once a luxury food reserved for high days and holidays, is now cheap enough to eat for everyday meals. There are sceptics who say that today's intensively reared birds taste just like cardboard but, cooked with flair, modern chickens are just as good and tasty as those of days gone by.

With suitable young birds, grilling is the simplest and most variable method of cooking. It enhances the flavour, retains the natural succulence of the bird and results in crisp, golden brown skin. Fresh birds can be grilled simply with herbs or a delicate basting sauce, while frozen birds can be given extra flavour with a robust sauce or topping.

Here we show how to divide both large and small birds. Small, young

The marinade used for Devilled chicken Delmonico is thickened with breadcrumbs and spooned over chicken before final cooking

birds are best for grilling. If serving, say, 8 people, it is better to buy two small birds and to cut each into 4 portions rather than to cut one large bird into 8 pieces.

CHOOSING CHICKEN

Chickens for cooking by methods other than boiling or long casseroling are all specially reared so that they will put on the maximum of tender flesh at minimum cost to the producer. Almost all chickens sold in poulterers, butchers and markets are reared indoors under controlled conditions. Outdoor or free-range chickens are rarely seen these days, partly because they are uneconomic, but mainly because their quality is difficult to control and it is hard to guarantee that the customer will always get a tender, tasty bird. It is in fact something of a myth that these free-range birds taste better. Because outdoor chickens run around and eat at will, they are prone to disease and liable to develop rather more muscle and sinew than is desirable for a tender grilling or roasting bird.

It is the processing method after killing, not the rearing, that most affects the quality of the chicken you buy and, for this reason, it is important to go to a butcher or poulterer if you want a really well-flavoured bird. There are several types and sizes of chicken available. These are described in the chart. Chickens are processed in four different ways: fresh, farm fresh, chilled and frozen.

Fresh chickens

Fresh chickens are seen in butchers' and poulterers' shops either feathered or plucked out with head and feet left on (known as New York dressed). These chickens come to the butcher with their feathers on. He then hangs them for about three days

Types of chicken suitable for grilling

Type	Description	Method
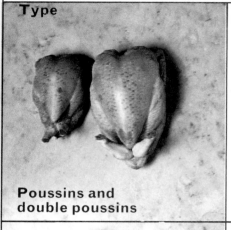  **Poussins and double poussins**	Both available fresh, farm fresh, chilled or frozen. Poussins are killed when 4 weeks old and usually weigh about 450 g [1 lb], which means they will only serve 1 portion as the ratio of bone to meat is rather high. Double poussins are killed when about 6 weeks old and weigh about 1 kg [2 lb]. They can be cut in half or spatchcocked to serve 2 portions. One double poussin between two is better value than a whole poussin each.	The most satisfactory way of cooking poussins is en cocotte or by pot roasting, although it is possible to spatchcock them, that is, opened out flat and skewered for grilling. Season, brush with butter or oil and grill for 10 minutes, skin side down, 12 cm [5″] away from medium heat. Turn and grill for another 8 minutes, basting occasionally. Double poussins are grilled as for a poussin but increase grilling time by 2-3 minutes on each side, depending on size.
 **Spring chicken**	Available fresh, farm fresh, chilled and sometimes frozen. Spring chickens are not reared in the spring as the name might suggest but are killed when 8 weeks old. They have an average weight of 1¼-1½ kg [2½-3 lb] and may be roasted or divided into portions for grilling.	Grill as for poussins, increasing the grilling time by 2-3 minutes each side, depending on the thickness of the pieces. Add the thinner breast portions to the grill 5 minutes after starting to cook the leg portions.
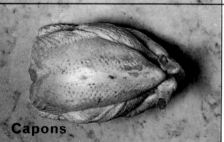 **Roaster**	Sometimes also called a broiler (not to be confused with a boiler which is a much older bird), these chickens are available fresh, farm fresh, chilled, frozen or cut into portions. A roasting chicken is killed when it is between 8 and 10 weeks old and usually weighs from 1½-3 kg [3-6 lb], and is suitable for roasting whole or grilling divided into portions.	Season, brush with butter or oil and grill for 12 minutes, skin side down, 12 cm [5″] away from medium heat. Turn and grill for a further 10 minutes, basting occasionally. Increase grilling time for very thick pieces and add thinner breast pieces 5 minutes after the legs.
Capons	Available fresh, farm fresh, chilled and sometimes frozen, capons are male birds which have been treated with female hormones to make them put on a lot of weight in a short time. Capons are usually killed when 8 weeks old and weigh from 3-4 kg [6-8 lb]. Capons are suitable for roasting whole or dividing into portions and grilling.	Grill as for roaster portions. Cook as above, depending on size.

to allow the maximum flavour to develop before preparing for selling.

Look for chickens with smooth, unbroken flesh, a slightly pliable beak and breastbone and pale yellow legs with small scales. All these factors indicate a young, tender bird.

If you buy a New York dressed or feathered chicken, the butcher will charge you for the total weight of the bird before he has removed the head, feet, feathers and innards (called drawing or eviscerating). These 'extras' can add up to 1 kg [2 lb] to the weight of the bird, depending on its size, so always take this into account when buying. If you are unsure of how much to buy, ask the butcher. Make sure you take the giblets and feet with you to use for stock or giblet gravy.

Because selling chickens in this way is a fairly labour-intensive process they tend to be expensive but hanging does mean that the flavour is good.

Farm-fresh chickens
Farm-fresh chickens are hung and prepared for selling on the poultry farm. They are usually sold whole, oven ready with the giblets in a little bag inside. Once again, this is a labour-intensive process so the chickens cost more but taste good. You are not, however, paying for unusable parts as when buying a New York dressed chicken as the head, feet and innards have been removed before selling.

Chilled chickens

Chilled chickens are usually seen in chain stores. They are factory-produced birds, reared by intensive methods, killed when a certain weight (usually 1.4-1.7 kg [3-3½ lb]) is reached, plucked, eviscerated, then air-chilled immediately without hanging. Air-chilling is a dry method so the bird does not take in water as with a frozen chicken. For this reason, chilled chickens are slightly more expensive than frozen chickens. Chilled chickens are available oven ready, halved or as portions. They are always marked as chilled on the wrapping.

Frozen chickens

Frozen chickens are reared and killed in exactly the same way as chilled chickens and are usually sold in supermarkets and chain stores. The only difference is that in the freezing process the bird takes in quite a lot of water. The chicken is weighed after freezing and, in some cases, you may be paying for rather a high ratio of water to flesh. It also has a slight effect on flavour though expert opinion says that, if thawed correctly, frozen chicken is as good in flavour as chilled. Frozen chicken is available oven ready with the giblets in a little bag (usually placed in the cavity), halved or divided into portions.

How much to buy

Knowing how much to buy is always a problem with birds as their odd shape makes it hard to judge. Below is a quantity guideline for serving chicken plainly grilled. If the recipe you are using has several garnishes or a sauce, this amount can be decreased. All weights are for oven-ready birds (plucked and drawn, with head and feet removed) so, if buying fresh chicken, ask the butcher for a bird of whatever weight you require after drawing.

For two people you will need two poussins weighing 450 g [1 lb] each or one 700 g-1 kg [1½-2 lb] double poussin or spring chicken cut in half.

For four people choose a 1¼-1½ kg [2½-3½ lb] broiler and cut it into portions as shown in the step-by-step instructions.

For six people choose a 2.75-3.6 kg [6-8 lb] capon and cut it into joints as shown in the step-by-step instructions.

When serving chicken joints allow 1 large quarter or 1 breast or 2 drumsticks or 2 thighs per person. Wings are not really substantial enough to serve unless they are cut with a large portion of the breast attached, as shown in quartering chicken step-by-step.

STORING

Chicken, like all meat, is perishable and must be stored carefully to preserve goodness.

Fresh and farm-fresh chickens and portions

Remove butcher's wrapping and put the chicken on a plate. If the giblets are in a bag inside the bird, remove them. Cover the chicken lightly with greaseproof paper or kitchen foil to allow a little circulation of air and store in the coldest part of the refrigerator under the frozen food compartment. Whole birds will keep for 2-3 days, portions for a maximum of 36 hours. Alternatively, you can store whole birds in a cool larder for 1 day but never do this in warm weather as the flavour will go 'off' very quickly.

Chilled birds

Store the chicken in the polythene wrapping in which you bought it but loosen the wrapping a little to allow circulation of air and remove the giblets. Store in a refrigerator or larder, as for fresh or farm-fresh chickens.

Frozen birds

These must be placed in the freezer or the freezer compartment of a refrigerator as soon as you get them home. Store for up to 3 months, depending on the star rating of your refrigerator.

Cooked chicken

Cooked chicken joints are excellent picnic and packed lunch fare, but go 'off' very quickly so they must always be stored in a refrigerator and should be eaten within two days. If you plan to eat chicken cold, drain off any liquid immediately after cooking then cool the meat rapidly. As soon as the chicken is cold, wrap it loosely (in polythene, kitchen foil or shrink wrapping) to protect against drying out, to prevent infection and the transfer of food flavours. Refrigerate.

PREPARING

If you are planning to serve chicken joints, it is much cheaper to buy a whole bird and divide it up yourself. Although this might sound a daunting prospect, it is really very easy.

Equipment

To portion a chicken you will need a really sharp, large cook's knife. A good sharp knife will cut easily through bones and flesh. A blunt or serrated-edge knife should be avoided as it will tear the flesh.

If you find a knife awkward it may well be worth investing in a pair of poultry shears. These are large scissor-like implements with strong curved blades. A useful alternative to poultry shears, and especially good for cutting through chicken backbones, is a strong pair of kitchen scissors. The kind which are nicked at the bottom of the blades are best because they make cutting up poultry easier.

You will need a chopping board on which to stand the chicken.

Thawing

Before a frozen chicken can be cut into pieces, it must be thawed. For health reasons, it is most important to thaw chicken very thoroughly. Chickens contain tiny bacilli called salmonella. These are quite harmless when the chicken is cooked right through. If the chicken is not thawed

fully there will be a cold spot at the centre which will not cook quite as well as the rest of the bird. The bacilli remain active in this undercooked portion and, if eaten, can cause an attack of a particularly unpleasant and virulent form of food poisoning.

Frozen whole birds and portions sometimes come with thawing instructions and these should always be followed meticulously. When thawing chicken, leave it in the wrapping to avoid loss of juices.

The best place to thaw is in the refrigerator. When thawing a whole bird in the refrigerator, allow 5 hours per 450 g [1 lb] of chicken. This means a 1.4 kg [3 lb] chicken needs 15 hours to thaw properly. Portions will take about 6 hours. Chicken can be thawed at room temperature but this is a quicker process and is not quite so kind to the flavour of the bird as gradual thawing. When thawing at room temperature, allow 3 hours per 450 g [1 lb] of whole bird. Portions will need about 3 hours.

In an emergency, chicken thawing can be hastened by immersing the bird (still in its polythene wrapping) in cold water. This makes the flavour extremely bland and is not really advisable. Never immerse chicken in hot water to speed thawing. It makes the flesh tough and does not thaw thoroughly.

Preparing for jointing
Before you start cutting up your chicken, make sure the giblets have been removed from inside.

To make cutting easier, it is a good idea to cut off the loose flap of skin at the neck end. Scissors are best for this job as the skin is rather awkward to cut with a knife.

You may also wish to remove the little oil sac situated above the parson's nose (the pointed end of the chicken where its tail feathers used to be). This little sac contains a rather strong oil which the chicken uses to lubricate its feathers. Some people feel it gives a fishy flavour. Removing the parson's nose itself is the subject of controversy. Some families have battles over who gets the parson's nose, while others regard it with horror, so this is very much a matter of personal taste.

There may be some little bits of feather left over after plucking. These are usually found on the legs and wings and are quite easily removed by pulling gently.

Removing the bony tips of the wings depends very much on what you are going to do with the chicken. If you are cutting large wing portions with a piece of breast attached, it is a good idea to leave the wing tips on as they help to make a neat shape. Leave the tips on, too, if trussing a whole bird for spit roasting or grilling. The wing tips can always be cut off after cooking. Cutting off after cooking is quick to do as the bones become very soft.

On a fresh chicken, there may be a piece of yellow leg left on the end of the drumstick. Cut this off before starting preparation.

GRILLING CHICKEN
One of the joys of chicken is that, after cutting it into halves or portions, it needs very little else in the way of preparation before being grilled.

Advance preparation
Because chicken is a fairly dry meat, portions and halves must be brushed liberally inside and out with melted butter or olive oil before grilling. Cut surfaces of chicken are small and, unlike other meats, raw chicken does not bleed when salt is applied so seasoning can be done before cooking. This is in fact quite a good idea because salt crisps the skin.

Grilling
Because chicken is dry and delicately flavoured, grilling must be carried out under gentle heat throughout. This is achieved by positioning the grill pan 12-15 cm [5-6"] below the grill and setting the heat at about medium. There is no need to start grilling under fierce heat to seal the cut surfaces. This is because chicken is not red meat and, therefore, does not lose blood and juice as is the case in pork, lamb and beef. Also, cut surfaces with portions and halves are rather small.

Start grilling the chicken skin side down. Grill large portions and halves for 12-15 minutes, small portions for 8-12 minutes. Turn skin side up and grill large portions and halves for a further 10 minutes, small portions for 8 minutes. Baste with melted butter throughout cooking to prevent drying.

SPATCHCOCK CHICKEN
◨◨ *This is a very simple dish and, in*
◪◪ *order to ensure its success, be sure to use a fresh, plump double poussin.*

Although it is usual to start grilling the chicken skin side down, here the order is reversed and the chicken is

Spatchcock chicken served with chips and garnished with lemon and watercress makes an appetizing main course.

Step-by-step to chicken portions

1 Lay the chicken on a board. Cut off the oil sac and the parson's nose if wished. Then cut off the loose skin at the neck.

2 To halve the chicken, cut through and along the breastbone. The breastbone is very soft, so a sharp knife will do this easily.

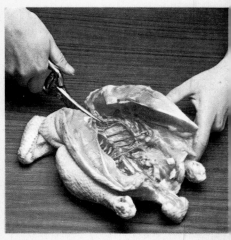

3 Then cut through the backbone. If the backbone is too hard to cut with a sharp knife, use poultry shears or kitchen scissors.

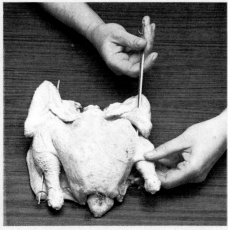

5 Now run a sharp, straight skewer through the leg and the fleshy part of the wing at one side. Repeat at other side.

6 To make chicken quarters, first cut the chicken in half. Lay the halves skin side up and cut diagonally between the leg and wing.

7 To joint a large chicken, first cut the leg away from the body. Pull the leg towards you so that the joint is exposed.

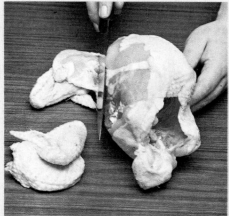

10 Cut through the joint to sever the wing and fold it into a neat shape with the attached breast meat tucked underneath.

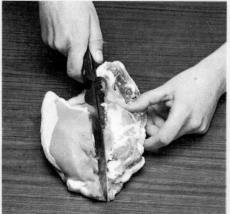

11 To remove the whole breast, first separate from the back by cutting through the rib bones along the side of the body.

12 Cut down the centre of the breast-bone to divide the breast into 2. Large breasts may be divided again to make 4 portions.

OR to remove the backbone completely, cut along each side of it with a sharp knife and then lift out. Save for stockmaking.

4 To spatchcock a chicken, first cut it in half through the backbone and open it out so that it lies flat on the board.

8 Now cut through the pink, moist part of this 'ball and socket' joint. Cut off the other leg. Set the two severed legs aside.

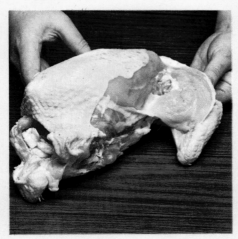

9 To remove the wing, first slice into the white breast meat to make a better portion. Pull the wings away to expose the joint.

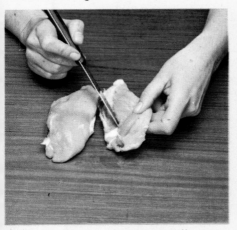

13 To skin the breast, pull away gently. To bone, insert a knife between rib bones and flesh and cut away gently. Save for stock.

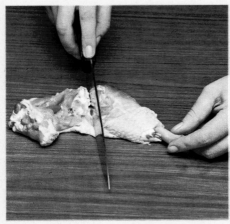

14 Large legs may be divided into thighs and drumsticks by cutting through the centre ball and socket joint.

SERVES 2
1 double poussin, about 700 g [1½ lb] in weight
salt and pepper
half a lemon
50 g [2 oz] butter
25 g [1 oz] grated Parmesan cheese
1 thick slice two-day-old white bread

For the garnish:
2 lemon quarters
1 small packet straw potatoes
bunch of watercress

1 Cut off the leg shanks, parson's nose and loose neck skin.

2 Cut the chicken open right along the backbone.

3 Open the bird and press it flat.

4 Secure the bird by running a fine skewer through from the lower thigh to the wing on each side.

5 Rub the chicken with the cut lemon, season with salt and pepper and leave for 30 minutes in a cool place.

6 Heat the grill to medium. Melt the butter in a small pan.

7 Brush the chicken all over with melted butter.

8 Place the bird skin side up on the grid. Grill 12 cm [5"] below the heat for 8-10 minutes. Brush with more butter once during this time.

9 Turn the chicken over and grill the cut side for 10-12 minutes, basting it during this time.

10 Meanwhile, remove crust from bread and grate the bread on a grater over a plate (or use a liquidizer) to make 15 g [½ oz] fine crumbs.

11 Mix the breadcrumbs and the Parmesan cheese together.

12 Turn over the chicken again and sprinkle the skin evenly with the breadcrumb mixture.

199

Milanese chicken consists of boned chicken breasts topped with ham and tomatoes.

13 Dribble remaining melted butter from the saucepan (or spoon it from the grill pan base) over the crumbs, moistening them as evenly as possible.

14 Grill for a further 5-10 minutes until crisp and golden. Run a skewer into the thickest part of the chicken to see that juices run clear. If juices are clear the chicken is cooked. Pink juices indicate that further grilling is required.

15 Remove skewers and serve garnished with warm straw potatoes, wedges of lemon and watercress.

MILANESE CHICKEN

◨◨◨ *This is an excellent dish for a dinner party. Once the preliminary cooking is done the dish continues cooking in a very low oven until you are ready for it.*

You can buy 2 chickens and cut the breasts off them (each chicken will give 2 portions) and save the rest of the meat for another dish. Alternatively, you can buy 4 portions of breast meat—the butcher will normally sell frozen portions.

SERVES 4
4 chicken breasts
4 slices ham
salt
2 medium-sized tomatoes
40 g [1½ oz] grated Parmesan cheese

For the marinade:
30 ml [2 tablespoons] oil
30 ml [2 tablespoons] lemon juice
5 ml [1 teaspoon] salt
freshly ground black pepper

1 Work a sharp knife along the bones to loosen and then pull the meat away by hand so that the breasts are boneless. Remove all the skin and any attached fat.

2 Lay the breasts flat, in a single layer and a small space apart, between 2 sheets of greaseproof paper. Beat hard with a rolling pin to flatten the meat.

3 Mix all the ingredients for the marinade and pour into a shallow,

200

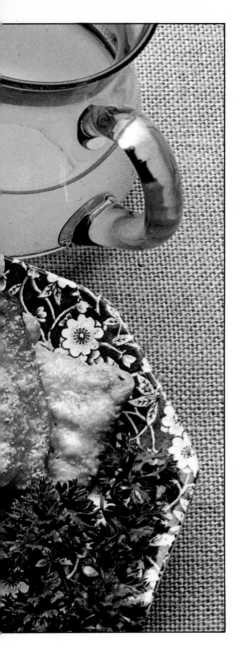

flame-proof dish large enough to hold the chicken pieces flat in a single layer.

4 Put in the chicken breasts, turn in the marinade, cover the dish and leave in a cool place for 2 hours.

5 One hour before serving time, heat the grill. Heat the oven to 150°C [300°F] gas mark 2.

6 Uncover the chicken and put the flame-proof dish 12 cm [5"] below the grill. Grill each side 5 minutes.

7 Meanwhile, plunge the tomatoes into boiling water for 1 minute, drain and refresh under cold water, then peel away the skins. Cut each tomato into 4 slices.

8 Remove chicken from under grill. Arrange a slice of ham on top of each of the chicken breasts. Top each with 2 tomato slices. Sprinkle on half of the Parmesan cheese and then cover the dish with foil.

9 Transfer to the oven and leave for 30-40 minutes. (They won't spoil at this low temperature if left a little longer.)

10 Five minutes before serving, heat the grill. Remove the dish from the oven, take off the foil, sprinkle the tops of the tomatoes with remaining Parmesan cheese and brown quickly under the grill.

11 Serve immediately.

DEVILLED CHICKEN DELMONICO

Frozen chicken quarters can be used for this dish as the spicy devilled sauce will keep the joints moist and enhance the flavour. The chicken must be completely thawed before cooking, of course, so allow adequate time for this if using frozen chicken quarters. Cooking is finished in the oven so it is a useful dish when you are entertaining. Served cold, it makes a piquant picnic meal.

SERVES 4
1 kg [2½ lb] chicken or 4 chicken portions
3 slices of two-day-old bread

For the devil spread:
65 g [2½ oz] butter
5 ml [1 teaspoon] mustard powder
10 ml [2 teaspoons] curry powder
10 ml [2 teaspoons] caster sugar
2.5 ml [½ teaspoon] salt
2.5 ml [¼ teaspoon] paprika
5 ml [1 teaspoon] Worcestershire sauce

1 If using a whole chicken, halve it by cutting along the breastbone. Open the chicken and cut along the backbone. Remove the backbone and cut the chicken into quarters.

2 Turn the wing tips under and run a fine skewer through the leg and backbone to hold the joints flat while cooking.

3 Prepare the devil spread by melting the butter in a small pan over low heat. Stir in the remaining ingredients.

4 Heat the grill to medium heat and warm the oven to 180°C [350°F] gas mark 4.

5 Brush the chicken pieces on both sides with half the devil mixture. Lay the pieces skin side down and side by side in a shallow flame-proof dish.

6 Place the chicken dish 12 cm [5"] below the heat and grill for 5 minutes on each side.

7 Meanwhile, remove crusts from the bread and reduce to crumbs on a grater or in a liquidizer to make 50 g [2 oz] fine crumbs.

8 Re-heat the devilled mixture remaining in the saucepan. Add the crumbs, remove from heat and stir until crumbs have absorbed the liquid.

9 Spoon the crumbs evenly over the chicken pieces and transfer the dish to the centre of the oven.

10 Cook for 30 minutes. Serve hot or cold.

CHICKEN IN SPICY TOMATO SAUCE

This is the type of dish that soon becomes a family favourite. It is colourful, tasty and simple—suited to fresh or frozen chicken joints.

SERVES 4
4 chicken portions
50 g [2 oz] butter

For the sauce:
60 ml [4 tablespoons] tomato ketchup
15 ml [1 tablespoon] finely grated onion
30 ml [2 tablespoons] water
30 ml [2 tablespoons] wine vinegar
10 ml [2 teaspoons] soft brown sugar
2.5 ml [½ teaspoon] mustard powder
2.5 ml [½ teaspoon] salt

For the garnish:
bunch of watercress

1 Heat the grill to medium heat.

2 Melt the butter in a small sauce-pan. Brush the chicken joints all over with butter.

3 Remove the grid from the grill pan and arrange the chicken pieces, skin side down and side by side, in the bottom of the grill pan, or in a large flame-proof gratin dish.

4 Grill the chicken 12 cm [5"] away from the heat for 5 minutes. Turn the chicken over and grill for another 5 minutes.

5 Meanwhile, grate the onion over a plate to catch the juice.

6 Put the onion into the saucepan containing the remaining melted butter. Stir in the other sauce ingredients and simmer for 5 minutes.

7 Brush the chicken with the sauce and continue grilling under mod-erate heat, turning and brushing with more sauce every 5 minutes until the chicken is cooked right through, a total of 30 minutes.

8 If the grill pan was used, turn the chicken pieces on to a hot serving dish and spoon the sauce on top. Garnish with watercress.

COUNTRY-STYLE CHICKEN

This is a simple but attractive way of cooking chicken. Fresh chicken is recommended. Use a whole chicken and divide it into portions yourself (it's probably cheaper too) but if you are in a hurry you can buy chicken joints. If you buy fresh chicken joints on your way home you can have this dish ready to eat within 45 minutes of arriving in the kitchen. The skewers are run through the chicken to prevent the joints 'flying akimbo' during grilling, in which case some parts would be cooked before others as they would be closer to the heat.

SERVES 4
1 kg [2½ lb] chicken
1 large lemon
75 g [3 oz] butter
salt
freshly ground black pepper
4 large rashers of streaky bacon
225 g [½ lb] button mushrooms

For the garnish:
bunch of watercress

1 Heat the grill to medium heat.

2 Divide the chicken into halves by cutting along the breastbone. Open the chicken and cut along the backbone. Cut the chicken into quarters.

3 Run a small skewer through each leg and out by the backbone. Tuck the wing tips under.

4 Rub the chicken with the cut lemon, squeezing the lemon to release plenty of juice as you do so.

5 Melt the butter in a small pan and brush generously all over both sides of the chicken.

6 Sprinkle both sides of the chicken liberally with salt and lightly with pepper.

7 Lay the joints skin side down in the grill pan with the grid removed.

8 Place the chicken 12 cm [5"] below the grill and cook for 12-15 min-utes.

9 Meanwhile, de-rind the bacon and cut each rasher in half crossways. Roll up and secure each piece with a cocktail stick.

10 Remove earthy ends, wipe but do not peel the mushrooms and brush over with some of the butter.

11 Turn the chicken skin side up, brush with remaining melted but-ter, or baste with the grill pan juices, and continue grilling for 5 minutes.

12 Add the bacon rolls and mush-rooms around the chicken under the grill. Baste with the pan juices.

13 Continue grilling and lower the heat if the chicken shows signs of overbrowning. Turn the bacon and mushrooms to cook them on both sides, basting them as you do so.

14 Cook until the chicken's skin is brown and crisp and the bacon and mushrooms are ready.

15 Arrange the cooked chicken on a serving dish. Arrange the bacon and mushrooms around it and pour over any remaining lemon juice and the juices from the grill pan. Garnish with the watercress and serve immediately.

Variations
● For almond chicken, omit the bacon and mushrooms and instead fry 40 g [1½ oz] flaked almonds in a little butter for 1 minute until golden brown. Do this just before serving the chicken. Use medium heat and shake the pan to turn the nuts frequently to prevent burning. Add the lemon juice and pour over the grilled chicken. Serve immediately.

● For pineapple chipolata, omit the bacon and mushrooms. Brush 4 pineapple rings with butter and grill until golden. Grill 4 chipolata saus-ages at the same time and thread them through the pineapple rings for the garnish. Arrange on top of the grilled chicken in the serving dish.

BROILED CHICKEN WITH LEMON BARBECUE SAUCE

Here is an American recipe which gives the chicken an unusual flavour. You need to start preparations a couple of hours ahead to give the chicken time to marinate in the sauce. Fresh chicken is best for this recipe but you could use frozen chicken because the marinade will add flavour. (Broiled is the American word for grilled.)

SERVES 4
4 chicken portions

For the marinade:
1 garlic clove
5 ml [1 teaspoon] salt
2.5 ml [½ teaspoon] freshly ground black pepper
45 ml [3 tablespoons] oil
45 ml [3 tablespoons] lemon juice
bay leaf

For the garnish:
watercress sprigs
1 lemon

1 Peel and slice the garlic clove and crush with salt under the blade of a knife.

2 Put the garlic into an earthenware or glass dish, add all the other ingredients for the marinade and stir well.

3 Put the chicken pieces in the marinade and spoon the marinade over the chicken. Cover and leave in a cool place for at least 2 hours.

4 Heat the grill to medium heat.

5 Place the chicken pieces skin side down in the grill pan. Cook 12 cm [5″] away from the heat for 15 minutes, basting frequently with

1 *Chicken with lemon barbecue sauce.* 2 *Country-style chicken is served with bacon and mushrooms.* 3 *Substitute pineapple and chipolata sausages for the bacon and mushrooms for an attractive variation.*

the remaining lemon marinade.

6 Turn the chicken skin side up and grill for 10 minutes, basting fre-

quently with the lemon marinade.

7 Test the chicken by piercing it with a fine skewer to see that the juices run clear. If the chicken shows signs of overbrowning, turn the heat down. The skin should be crisp when the chicken is cooked.

8 Serve on a hot dish and garnish with lemon quarters and cress.

TANDOORI-STYLE CHICKEN

Frozen chicken can be used for this spicy chicken dish as it is marinated overnight in a yoghurt mixture which tenderizes and flavours the meat. A smaller chicken can be used if it is fresh—the weight given here allows for loss of weight due to thawing and skinning.

If you like a hot dish add 5 ml [¼ teaspoon] chilli powder to the marinade. Powdered ginger is no substitute for fresh root ginger and it is not suitable for this recipe. Fresh root ginger is sometimes available from vegetable markets and always from Indian food shops. Sesame, cumin and coriander seeds, rather than the powdered varieties, are used because the crushed seeds are far more aromatic than powders.

Traditionally, tandoori chicken is red so you can use a few drops of food colouring or spoonfuls of tomato purée to colour the chicken.

SERVES 4
1.6 kg [3½ lb] chicken or 4 chicken portions
salt and pepper
30 ml [2 tablespoons] butter
15 ml [1 tablespoon] le.non juice

For the .narinade:
40 g [1½ oz] fresh ginger
2 garlic cloves
125 ml [4 fl oz] yoghurt
5 ml [1 teaspoon] sesame seeds

Rôtisseries are useful for controlled and even grilling whether for succulent whole chickens or exotic kebabs.

5 ml [1 teaspoon] coriander seeds
5 ml [1 teaspoon] cumin seeds
2.5 ml [½ teaspoon] red food colouring or 30 ml [2 tablespoons] tomato purée

For the garnish:
2 lemons
fresh coriander leaves or watercress

1 Peel and chop the ginger and garlic into very small pieces.

2 Crush the seeds in a mortar with a pestle or with a rolling pin in a small plastic bag.

3 Mix together the yoghurt, sesame, coriander and cumin seeds, ginger, garlic and red colouring or tomato purée.

4 If using a whole chicken, halve it by cutting along the breastbone. Open the chicken and cut along the backbone. Remove the backbone and cut the chicken into quarters.

5 Remove the skin and fat from the chicken portions and, using a sharp knife, make 3 or 4 incisions in the flesh of each portion.

6 Place the chicken pieces in a glass or earthenware dish and spoon the

If using frozen chicken for Tandoori-style chicken allow for weight loss due to defrosting and skinning.

marinade over. Cover and leave for 8 hours, turning occasionally and spooning over the marinade.

7 Heat the grill to medium heat.

8 Remove chicken from marinade and season with salt and pepper.

9 Remove grid and place chicken pieces in the grill pan with the bony side upwards. Pour over the lemon juice, dot with butter and grill 12 cm [5″] away from heat for 12 minutes, basting it two or three times during this time.

10 Turn over the pieces, baste with the pan juices and grill for 8 minutes, again basting the chicken two or three times. Test with a skewer to see that meat is cooked and tender.

11 Place on a warm serving dish. Garnish with coriander leaves and the lemons cut into wedges and serve. Use cress if no coriander.

ROTISSERIES

In rôtisserie cooking the meat is fixed to a spit which is either a long skewer-like pin which goes right through and out the other side or a pair of long 'forks' to grip the meat from either side. This spit is attached at both ends to a framework and is turned automatically. Heat may be from below or above according to the model used. The meat is then revolved slowly so that each side is in turn exposed directly for cooking. The big advantage of spit roasting or grilling is that all sides are quickly seared to seal in the natural juices. On a conventional grill you must hand-turn the meat several times to

just seal, and then cook it. The meat then continues to cook evenly without burning on any one side.

Lean meat should be lightly brushed with melted butter or oil, after fixing to the spit, to ensure that the outside does not brown too quickly. The meat needs no further basting because as it rolls the fat is distributed over the surface. Flavourings, such as herbs, in the cavity of a chicken are also distributed. It is an ideal method for cooking fatty meat if the heat is on top, as all excess fat drips away.

Most rôtisserie models come with a choice of spits. A single spit may be used with a chicken trussed as for roasting—or even two chickens with larger models. Several small game birds can be spit-roasted in a row, or boned and rolled roast meat. Some models have revolving baskets. Several spits can be used simultaneously to cook kebabs.

Barbecues burning both charcoal and gas are available with automatic spits fitted to them. Meat thus cooked is really grilled. Rôtisserie cooking is, in effect, a modern method of spit roasting—the ancient way of cooking meat over an open fire.

Electric models are available and these have heating elements at the top. Because there is a door which is shut, creating an enclosed, heated space, meat cooked in these is as much roasted as grilled. They have the advantage of a time switch, so there is no risk of the meat overcooking if you forget it. Without the spits they can also be used as small ovens—they heat quickly and are economical on electricity—or instead of a conventional grill for browning dishes finished off with cheese, breadcrumbs and other gratin toppings.

Perfect poultry

A good cook will roast a chicken so that it has a golden crisp skin and juicy flesh—a simple but real treat. To get these perfect results requires time and care. Because chicken meat is dry thoughtless roasting can easily reduce it to a tasteless, sawdusty texture. Here we describe the preparation, stuffing and roasting needed to produce a golden, succulent chicken and show you how to carve economically.

CHOOSING CHICKEN FOR ROASTING

There's an old saying 'choose the bird that roosts next to the cockerel', and although it is no longer possible to follow this sage advice literally, we can still pick out the plumpest bird, which is the one the cockerel would have singled out! Other signs of youth, such as a pliable tip to the breastbone and a thin skin, are no longer relevant as all chickens sold for roasting are under three months old.

Since chicken meat is lean, it is worth looking for a bird with a thin layer of fat beneath the skin. This fat helps to keep the bird succulent when cooking. You will only find it on larger birds.

All types and sizes of chicken (as described in detail on pages 193–196) are young and tender enough to be roasted. The bird you cannot roast is one labelled 'boiling fowl'. This is usually an old and fairly tough bird that has reached the end of its useful life as an egg producer.

Capon

This is a young cockerel treated by injection and then specially fattened for the table. Very few capons are reared nowadays so you may have difficulty finding one. Capons weigh between 2-3.6 kg [4½-8 lb] which is ideal when cooking for a large number of people. Prepare and cook the capon in the same way as a chicken, with the same stuffings and sauces.

INITIAL PREPARATION

Chicken is perishable and must therefore be stored carefully. Remove the butcher's wrapping and put the chicken on a plate. If the giblets are in a bag inside the bird, remove them and store separately. Cover the chicken only lightly with greaseproof

paper or kitchen foil, to allow a little circulation of air. Store it in the coldest part of the refrigerator at the top under the ice compartment.

It is most important to thaw frozen birds before cooking (see on pages 196–197), otherwise the centre may still be raw at the end of cooking time. Fresh or defrosted chickens should be removed from the refrigerator three quarters of an hour before cooking to bring the meat to room temperature. If the chicken is put into the oven straight from the refrigerator because of some emergency, allow an extra 20-30 minutes cooking time.

Most poultry is sold ready for cooking. But there are some preparations specific to roasting chicken which are as necessary to successful appearance and taste as actual roasting.

Look carefully at the bird's skin. If there are any unsightly stubbles where the bases of the feathers are still sticking in the skin remove them. Raise the skin at the point where the stubble occurs and grasp each stubble in turn between your thumb and a round-bladed knife, and tug sharply.

Rinse out the bird's body cavity by holding the tail end under a running tap. Lift the skin of the neck flap, so water runs through the bird. Drain the chicken thoroughly. Then pat dry inside and outside with kitchen paper. This is very important because if the chicken is left wet it will not acquire an attractively brown skin in the oven.

Season the inside of the bird. This is most important as flavours permeate more readily through the inner cavity walls than through the exterior skin.

Stand the bird up and grind salt and pepper into the body cavity through the tail end. You can use salt as well as pepper because there are no cut surfaces to bleed if salted. Chicken, being a white meat, can be salted before cooking.

It is a good idea to insert a moisture-creating ingredient, such as an apple, onion or lemon, inside the bird, as well as flavourings such as herbs or spices and garlic. A dessert apple, onion or lemon also adds a subtle flavour, and gives off juice as it cooks, which helps to keep this lean meat succulent and prevents it from drying out. Discard these additions before serving.

Step-by-step to stuffing a chicken

1 Stand bird up with its back to you. Open neck by holding skin back against the breast. Loosely pack the stuffing under the neck skin.

2 When the bird looks plump without being stretched, lay it breast side down. Fold neck skin over the back to enclose stuffing.

3 The neck skin is secured and held in position on the back of the bird by folding the wing tips over it on each side.

OR fasten the skin 'stitching' it to the back of the chicken with a small poultry skewer (which is removed when serving).

A walnut-sized piece of butter mashed together with salt, pepper and herbs is a valuable addition to the body cavity. The buttery juices can be used for the gravy at the end of cooking.

NON-STUFFY STUFFINGS

Stuffing the bird is another way of adding both moisture and flavour to the meat. A well-chosen stuffing can be the making of a simple roast chicken. It is also economical because it makes the meal more substantial.

Choose ingredients that will provide a stimulating contrast in flavour and texture. Stuffing can add the richness that lean poultry meat lacks. Mild bacon, bacon fat, butter, minced pork and pork sausage meat are all very suitable ingredients for stuffings.

Another important function of a stuffing is to help maintain the bird's moisture by generating steam during cooking. For this reason, stuffings themselves need to be fairly moist and should not be packed tightly but loosely into the neck end of the bird. Avoid stuffing the body cavity as this obstructs the circulation of heat (if you do increase the cooking time).

Although stuffings can be made the day before and refrigerated, they should not be put into the bird until shortly before cooking. The stuffing must be cold, or at least cool, when put into the bird. The quantities given in the recipes are sufficient for stuffing a 1.4-1.8 kg [3-4 lb] chicken. If there is too much stuffing for the neck cavity, the remainder can be cooked separately in a small covered dish on the shelf beneath the bird for the last 30-40 minutes of roasting time.

APRICOT AND HAZELNUT STUFFING

This is an unusual stuffing made with fruit and nuts. Allow the stuffing to cool before inserting it into the bird.

STUFFS 1.4-1.8 KG [3-4 LB] CHICKEN
75 g [3 oz] dried apricots
50 g [2 oz] onion
1 celery stick
40 g [1½ oz] butter
25 g [1 oz] shelled hazelnuts
50 g [2 oz] white bread
2.5 ml [½ teaspoon] finely grated lemon zest
salt
freshly ground black pepper

1 Put the apricots in a bowl and pour over enough boiling water to just cover. Leave to stand while preparing the other ingredients.

2 Peel and finely chop the onion. Wash and chop the celery.

3 Melt the butter in a medium-sized saucepan. Gently fry the onion and celery until soft, but not brown.

4 Meanwhile roughly chop the hazelnuts. Drain and chop the apricots, reserving the liquid.

5 Make the breadcrumbs by grating on a coarse grater. With the pan off the heat add the crumbs to the pan. Add hazelnuts, apricots and lemon zest, with salt and pepper to taste.

6 Mix thoroughly. The apricots should provide enough moisture to bind the stuffing loosely. If the mixture seems too dry to bind, add a little of the water in which the apricots were soaked.

SAUSAGE MEAT AND APPLE STUFFING

This is a quick stuffing to make and must be used immediately before the apple has time to discolour.

STUFFS 1.4-1.8 KG [3-4 LB] CHICKEN
1 cooking apple
225 g [8 oz] pork sausage meat
10 ml [2 teaspoons] dried herbs
salt and black pepper

1 Peel, core and chop the apple.

2 Put the sausage meat, herbs and seasoning into a bowl. Add the apple and mix thoroughly.

3 Use the stuffing for the neck cavity of a bird or cook in a dish underneath the roast for 30-40 minutes.

THREE HERBS STUFFING

This is a traditional parsley and lemon-flavoured stuffing with the addition of marjoram to give it an interesting new flavour. The stuffing should be crumbly in texture and very green.

STUFFS 1.4-1.8 KG [3-4 LB] CHICKEN
45 ml [3 tablespoons] fresh parsley leaves
15 ml [1 tablespoon] fresh marjoram leaves or 5 ml [1 teaspoon] dried marjoram
5 ml [1 teaspoon] fresh lemon thyme leaves or 1.5 ml [¼ teaspoon] dried thyme
1.5 ml [¼ teaspoon] grated lemon zest.
50 g [2 oz] white bread
40 g [1½ oz] butter
salt and pepper

1 Finely chop all the fresh herbs.

2 Make the breadcrumbs by grating on a coarse grater.

3 Melt the butter in a small saucepan.

4 With the pan off the heat, stir the breadcrumbs and herbs into the butter and season to taste.

BACON AND CELERY STUFFING

This stuffing uses the chicken liver that comes with the bird. The stuffing is cooked first so allow it to cool before using it.

STUFFS 1.4-1.8 KG [3-4 LB] CHICKEN
2 rashers smoked streaky bacon
2 small celery sticks
40 g [1½ oz] butter
1 chicken liver
50 g [2 oz] white bread
salt and pepper to taste

1 Remove the bacon rinds and cut the bacon rashers into pieces.

2 Wash the celery, split the sticks lengthways into 2 (or 3 pieces if broad). Cut into 1.2 cm [½"] dice.

3 Melt the butter in a small saucepan. Add the bacon and celery and fry, covered, for 5 minutes.

4 Wash and then blot the liver with kitchen paper. Remove any stringy parts. Chop and add to the pan.

5 Stir in the breadcrumbs and season to taste.

6 Allow the stuffing to cool then stuff into neck cavity of a chicken

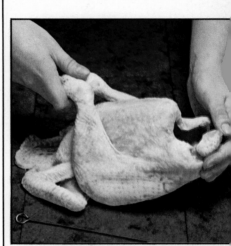

1 Laying the bird on its back lift the legs and pull them back towards the neck.

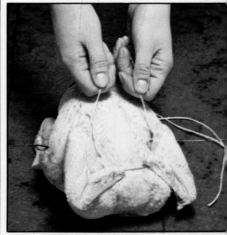

5 Cut a long piece of thin string and centre it, whilst placing it under the wings.

TRUSSING A CHICKEN

These days chickens and capons are usually sold drawn and trussed ready for the oven. Sometimes, however, you may need to truss a bird at home, or retruss one after stuffing it. The purpose of trussing is simply to hold the bird in a compact shape during cooking, so that it browns evenly and looks attractive when served. The joints of an untrussed bird would spread out in the oven and be very untidy. Parts like wing tips may also burn.

Trussing after stuffing is done either with a trussing needle, threaded with fine string, or very simply with a skewer and string as shown in detail in the step-by-step pictures below.

PRECAUTIONS AGAINST DRYING OUT

Chicken is a very lean meat and precautions both before and during roasting are essential to prevent it from drying out. The breast meat is especially susceptible to drying as it has no natural fat and, being at the top of the chicken, is more exposed to the heat.

The most usual precaution is to bard the breast. The breast is completely covered with thin rashers of mild fatty bacon, such as streaky, which are laid across it covering the top of the drumsticks as well. The barding bacon is removed just before the end of cooking to allow the breast to brown before serving. The bacon may be reserved and crumbled into the gravy if you wish.

Another method is to cover the breast loosely with a double thickness of well-buttered greaseproof paper, a butter wrapper, or buttered foil. The paper is discarded 20 minutes before the cooking time is up. The chicken should be painted all over with a generous coating of oil or softened butter.

A method much practised in France, is to rub the bird all over with softened butter and to roast it breast downwards for the major part of cooking time. This method encourages the juices to run down into the breast meat and keeps it beautifully succulent. The bird is then reversed, breast upwards, for the last 20 minutes of cooking. Baste it

Step-by-step to trussing a chicken

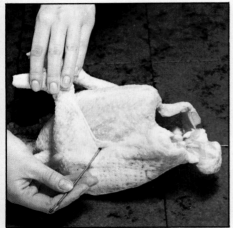

2 Pass a metal skewer through the body meat, inserting it in the angle of the thigh and drumstick.

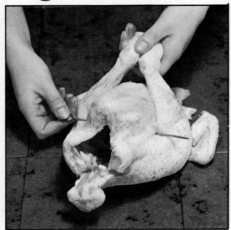

3 Push the skewer through the bird so that it emerges in the corresponding place on the other side.

4 Turn bird on to its breast. Fold the wing tips across the back to hold the neck skin in position.

6 Draw the ends of string under, up and over the skewer ends then cross them over the bird's back.

7 Turn the bird on to its back. Twist the string around the leg ends then under the parson's nose.

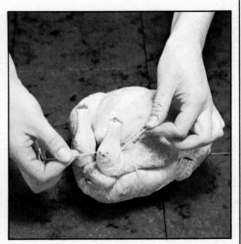

8 Tie the two ends of the string securely so that the legs and tail are firmly held together.

thoroughly to allow the skin to brown. Baste again after 10 minutes and complete cooking time. The chicken should be succulent and tender.

CAREFUL ROASTING

The following simple rules will help you achieve a successful roast—crisp and golden outside, succulent within.

Always heat the oven so that it is at the required temperature when the bird is put into it. A fairly hot oven, 190°C[375°F] gas mark 5 is effective and economical for a small bird. A slightly lower temperature of 180°C [350°F] gas mark 4 is used for a larger bird to ensure that it is cooked all the way through. If the body cavity is stuffed, allow an extra 20-30 minutes.

For a crisp skin, rub salt all over with your fingers, working it well into the cracks. The oil or butter may then be painted on with a brush afterwards.

Unless roasting in the French way, place the chicken on a rack, breast side upwards. There is no need to put fat in the tin unless the giblets are used. If bacon is used for barding, this will make a certain amount of fat. The moisturizing ingredients inside the bird, whether butter or fruit or vegetable, will also make a certain amount of juice. This can be used for basting the bird in the last 20 minutes to ensure a crisp, golden skin.

If the breast is to be covered by foil or paper, this must be well-buttered with 15 g [½ oz] of butter or margarine. It is wise also to put a little butter inside the bird to create enough fat for basting. Baste two or three times during the last 20 minutes when the chicken is uncovered.

The French method

This method of roasting uses more fat and gives the chicken a crisp golden skin all over in much the same fashion as a rôtisserie-cooked chicken. It takes longer than the English method of roasting given above, because frequent basting and turning of the bird are necessary.

Butter is always inserted in the bird's cavity after seasoning. Herbs may also be added, the most common one being tarragon. The outside of the bird is rubbed over with salt and pepper and then generously brushed all over with a mixture of butter and oil or butter and lemon juice.

CHICKEN ROASTING TIMES
Times for cooking fully thawed, room-temperature birds, stuffed at the neck end only.*

oven-ready weight	number of servings	oven temperature	cooking time
1 kg [2 lb]	2-3	190°C [375°F] gas mark 5	1 hour
1.4 kg [3 lb]	4	190°C [375°F] gas mark 5	1 hr 20 mins
1.8 kg [4 lb]	5-6	190°C [375°F] gas mark 5	1 hr 40 mins
2.25 kg [5 lb]	7-8	190°C [375°F] gas mark 5	2 hours
2.7 kg [6 lb]	8-9	180°C [350°F] gas mark 4	2 hrs 15 mins
3.2 kg [7 lb]	10	180°C [350°F] gas mark 4	2 hrs 30 mins
3.6 kg [8 lb]	12	180°C [350°F] gas mark 4	2 hrs 45 mins

*If the body cavity contains stuffing, allow an extra 20-30 minutes cooking time.

THE GIBLETS

The giblets contribute a considerable amount of flavour to a chicken and should never be discarded. They consist of the neck, gizzard, heart and liver. When you buy an oven-ready bird the giblets are usually wrapped separately and tucked inside the body cavity. As soon as you get a fresh bird home or, if frozen, as soon as it has thawed, remove the giblets from their wrapping and wash them under the cold tap. Check that the liver is free of gall. Look for any area that is stained green and cut away and discard it as gall is very bitter. Remove any thick yellow skin remaining on the gizzard.

● Make stock from the giblets. Put all the washed giblets except the liver, into a small saucepan. Add a slice or two of onion, carrot and celery, a small bay leaf, 3 peppercorns, 1.5 ml [¼ teaspoon] salt, and 250 ml [½ pt] of water. Bring to the boil, cover, and simmer for 30 minutes. Cool, strain and use the stock for the gravy.

● Add the cooked heart, gizzard and neck meat, all finely chopped, to the stuffing.
● Cook the washed giblets, excepting the liver, in the roasting tin beneath the chicken. You will need to add 15 ml [1 tablespoon] of fat to the roasting tin. This is a simple way of ensuring that their flavour will enrich the gravy.
● The raw liver can be chopped and added to the stuffing or roasted beside the bird for the last 15 minutes of cooking time. Remember to baste it well. It can also be used to make liver and bacon rolls.
● If you can't use the giblets immediately, freeze them until you have collected enough to make a rich giblet soup.
● Cooked chicken carcasses can be frozen for making stock later, but be sure to freeze them promptly while they are still fresh.
● Freeze the livers separately so they can be used for a special omelette filling or for making a pâté.

The chicken is not placed upon a rack or trivet but laid in the pan on one side of its breast. Be sure that the thigh in the highest position is well buttered. After 25 minutes the chicken is turned on to the other breast. Baste all the upper surface thoroughly with the pan juices. Finally after 25 minutes, the chicken is turned on to its back and the breast is thoroughly basted for browning.

To test when a chicken is cooked

Undercooked chicken is slimy and unpleasant to eat, pink at the thickest part round the thigh joints and it gives off a pink juice when pierced. It can also be a health hazard. It is important to cook chicken thoroughly, until a meat thermometer inserted into the fleshiest part of the thigh registers 80-82°C [175-180°F].

210

Step-by-step to roasting chicken

1 Remove the bird from refrigerator to reach room temperature. Weigh and calculate the cooking time.

2 Sprinkle cavity liberally with salt and black pepper. Insert stuffing or moisturizing ingredients.

3 Place chicken, breast upwards, on a rack or trivet in a roasting tin. The juices drain into the tin.

4 Bard or cover the chicken breast and thigh tops with thin rashers of bacon. Roast the chicken.

5 Remove and discard bacon 20 minutes before cooking ends, so that the skin can crisp.

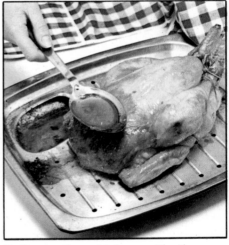

6 Baste the chicken with the pan juices two or three times to moisten and help crisp the skin.

7 Test the chicken by piercing it with a skewer. If the juices run clear the chicken is ready.

8 Twist the leg shanks to remove them. Remove any trussing string and the skewers if present.

9 As you lift the bird to transfer it, tilt it so that the juices run from the tail end into the pan.

An alternative reliable test is to pierce the chicken deeply in the thigh with a skewer and note the colour of the juices that run from it. When fully cooked the juices will be colourless or yellowish. If they are pink, return the roast to the oven and continue cooking a little longer before testing again.

Dishing up
Choose a serving dish large enough to accommodate the chicken and any garnishes such as bacon rolls, chipolatas or watercress. There should also be plenty of room for the chicken joints as the carver separates them from the carcass. It makes carving more difficult if the plate is crowded.

As you lift the bird to place it on the warmed serving dish, tilt the tail end (the end with the parson's nose) downward for a few seconds. The juices in the body of the bird will then drain into the roasting pan and improve the gravy.

Always leave the chicken to rest for ten minutes before carving, to allow the meat to set. This also gives you time to make the gravy.

Cut the trussing string and pull away from the bird. Remove the skewer if there is one. Using a piece of kitchen paper to keep your fingers clean, twist off the leg shanks, which are inedible and unsightly. Before serving, if you wish, you can use a cutlet frill to cover the ends of the legs, but this is not essential.

Cooked garnishes are then arranged round the dish. Salad garnishes must be added at the very last moment before serving.

CARVING A CHICKEN OR CAPON
It is easy to make a professional job of carving a chicken or capon. The flesh is very tender, and, once you have mastered the art of finding and severing the ball and socket thigh joint, there are no real problems.

Step-by-step to carving a large chicken

1 Drive the fork into the bird to hold it firmly and carve off the right leg and thigh.

2 Holding the knuckle joint, sever the thigh from the drumstick through the ball and socket joint.

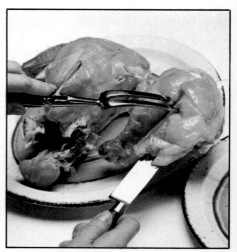

3 Turn the dish and carve the left side. Each of the four leg pieces with breast meat makes a portion.

5 Again turn the dish, so that the wishbone is to your right. Insert knife in front of breastbone.

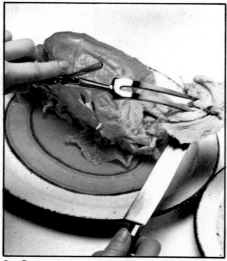

6 Cut down following curve of wishbone. With breast meat this makes one portion.

7 With front end facing you, carve the breast into thin slices using downward strokes of the knife.

The method of carving a large chicken or a capon is an extension of that used for a small bird, so if possible practise on a small bird first. As well as a sharp knife, and a carving fork with a finger guard, you will need a spoon for serving a crumbly stuffing. A napkin is also used for holding the leg tip when the thigh and drumstick needs to be divided.

CLASSIC ACCOMPANIMENTS
Classic accompaniments are chicken liver and bacon rolls, pork chipolatas and, of course, bread sauce.

4 Carve each of the wing joints. (Serve with some of the breast meat to make two more portions.)

8 Portions can be made up of breast meat and any remaining meat such as the oyster pieces on the back.

Step-by-step to carving a small chicken

1 The chicken should be allowed to rest before carving in order that the meat can firm up.

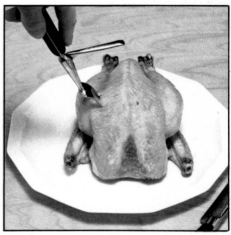

2 With the wishbone facing you, hold the bird firmly in place by driving the fork into left side.

3 Cut through the skin and around the right leg joint to free the leg from the body of the chicken.

4 Starting at the wishbone end of the breastbone, hold the knife close against the carcass.

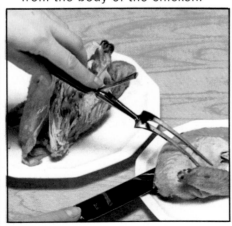

5 Carve away the whole breast and wing in one piece so that you have the second portion.

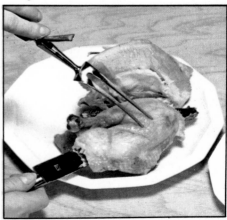

6 Repeat the carving on the other side until the bird is divided into four portions.

BREAD SAUCE

This essentially English sauce adds both piquant flavour and contrast to the texture of the chicken. The secret of well-flavoured bread sauce depends on a long enough infusion of the onion and spices in the milk to impart a really distinctive flavour. The consistency should be that of thick cream, neither thin nor stiff.

SERVES 6
1 small onion
2 cloves
250 ml [½ pt] milk
4 peppercorns
1 small blade mace
1 bay leaf
50 g [2 oz] stale white bread
salt
25 g [1 oz] butter or 15 ml
   [1 tablespoon] cream

1 Peel and slice the onion, stud it with the cloves.

2 Put the milk into a small saucepan and add the studded onion, peppercorns, mace and bay leaf.

3 Bring slowly to boiling point. Remove the pan from the heat, cover it and leave in a warm place to infuse for at least 30 minutes, preferably longer.

4 Make the breadcrumbs by grating the bread on a coarse grater.

5 Strain the milk and discard the onion, herbs and spices. Return the milk to the saucepan and stir in the breadcrumbs.

6 Leave to stand for 15 minutes while the crumbs absorb the milk.

7 Reheat gently before serving, add salt to taste and stir in the butter or cream.

FRENCH ROAST CHICKEN

The French method of open roasting a small chicken differs from the English in that the bird is cooked initially on its side and needs turning and basting. It is usually cooked without a stuffing, and is invariably served with a crisp green salad. Traditionally the quantity of gravy is very small, but is very well flavoured. Potato crisps can be warmed through in the oven and used as a garnish.

SERVES 4
1.4 kg [3 lb] chicken
salt and pepper
50 g [2 oz] butter
sprigs of fresh or dried herbs,
   such as rosemary, lemon
   thyme or tarragon
10 ml [2 teaspoons] oil
giblet stock

1 Heat the oven to 190°C [375°F] gas mark 5.

2 Wash, drain and dry the chicken.

3 Mash the salt and pepper into 15 g [½ oz] butter. If you are using dried herbs, these may be added to the butter. Put the butter and any fresh herbs into the body cavity. Retruss the bird if necessary.

4 Rub salt and pepper over the chicken skin. Melt the remaining butter with the oil and brush the bird liberally all over.

5 Rest the bird on one side of its breast in a roasting tin just large enough to hold it comfortably. Roast in the centre of the oven for 25 minutes.

6 Turn the bird on the other side, baste with the butter and oil, and roast for another 25 minutes.

7 Meanwhile prepare the giblet stock and leave to simmer.

8 Turn the chicken breast upwards and baste with the remaining butter and oil or drippings in tin.

9 Fifteen minutes before the end of cooking time, baste the chicken with the juices that have collected in the roasting tin.

10 Test if the chicken is cooked by piercing the thigh with a skewer. The juices should be colourless.

11 Tilt the bird to drain the juices from the body cavity into the roasting tin.

12 Transfer the chicken to a large warm serving dish. Remove the trussings, skewers and leg shanks and keep warm.

13 Tilt the roasting tin and pour off any surplus fat, leaving the drippings behind. Strain the giblet stock into the tin.

14 Bring to the boil over medium heat. Stir and scrape round the pan to release the scrapings from the bottom of the tin.

15 Simmer for 5 minutes until stock has reduced. Check the seasoning. Serve in a warm sauce-boat.

TRADITIONAL ROAST CHICKEN

A large chicken, or a capon, is the bird to choose when you plan to spend time preparing all the delicious trimmings. Instead of expensive bacon for barding, cover the bird with foil, and reserve the bacon for rolls to eat with the bird. It helps to prepare the breadcrumbs for stuffing and sauce in advance.

SERVES 7-8
2.25 kg [5 lb] roasting chicken
25 g [1 oz] butter
three herb stuffing (or any other
   stuffing)
salt and pepper
small dessert apple
giblet stock
the chicken liver
bread sauce
4 rashers streaky bacon
225 g [½ lb] pork chipolatas

For the garnish:
a few sprigs of watercress

The French roast a chicken by placing it on its side initially, turning and basting it and then completing roasting time in the usual position.

1 Remove the butter from the refrigerator. Uncover and leave to come to room temperature.

2 Prepare the stuffing and leave to cool.

3 Heat the oven to 190°C [375°F] gas mark 5.

4 Prepare, wash, drain and thoroughly dry the chicken. Sprinkle the body cavity and the skin with salt and pepper.

5 Peel the dessert apple and put it into the body cavity.

6 Fill the neck end of the bird with the stuffing, fold the skin over the back and secure with wing tips or poultry skewer. Retruss the bird if necessary.

7 Spread some of the butter on a piece of foil to cover the breast, then spread the rest all over the chicken.

8 Stand the chicken on a rack in a roasting tin and cover the breast loosely with the buttered foil. Roast in the centre of the oven for a total of 2 hours.

9 Meanwhile prepare the giblet stock (reserving the liver). Infuse the milk for the bread sauce.

10 Cut the rinds off the bacon, stretch the rashers with a knife, and cut in half. Place a portion of chicken liver on each piece of bacon, roll up and impale on a small skewer.

11 Separate the chipolatas and put in a lightly greased ovenproof dish.

12 Half an hour before the end of roasting time discard the foil and baste the chicken with the pan juices. Put the dish of chipolatas, uncovered, on the shelf beneath the bird.

13 Quarter of an hour before roasting time is up, baste the bird again and put the liver and bacon rolls on roasting tin base.

14 Finish making the bread sauce. Put it into a sauce-boat or serving bowl and keep warm.

15 Test if the bird is cooked by piercing the thigh with a skewer. If the juices are colourless remove the chicken from the oven.

16 Tilt the chicken to drain the juices from the body cavity into the roasting tin.

17 Place the bird on a heated serving dish. Remove the trussing strings and the skewer. Break off the leg shanks.

18 Arrange the chipolatas and bacon rolls round the chicken and keep warm.

19 Tilt the roasting tin and skim off the surface fat. Strain the giblet stock into the roasting tin. Put the tin over a medium heat and bring to the boil, stirring. Simmer for 5 minutes until the quantity of liquid has reduced. Check seasoning and transfer to a sauce-boat.

20 Just before serving, garnish the tail end of the bird with watercress.

ROAST TARRAGON CHICKEN

⊠⊠ *Chicken, cream and fresh tarragon are one of the great flavour combinations for the summer months. This chicken is roasted by the French method. Dried tarragon has its uses for flavouring but for this simple recipe fresh tarragon is essential.*

New potatoes, French beans and buttered baby carrots would make a perfect accompaniment.

SERVES 4
**1 oven ready chicken weighing
   1.4 kg [3 lb]
50 g [2 oz] butter at room
   temperature
salt and ground black pepper
3 tablespoons fresh tarragon
   leaves
1 small clove garlic
150 ml [¼ pt] thin cream
5 ml [1 teaspoon] flour
15 ml [1 tablespoon] cold
   chicken stock**

1 Remove the butter from the refrigerator to bring it to room temperature.

2 Heat the oven to 190°C [375°F] gas mark 5.

3 Wash and dry the chicken. Sprinkle the body cavity with salt and pepper and rub salt over the skin.

4 Chop the tarragon leaves roughly. Peel and crush the garlic. Reserve half the butter then cream 25 g [1 oz] with the garlic. Add half the tarragon leaves. Put this mixture into the body cavity of the bird.

5 Truss the chicken if necessary, then spread it all over with the remaining softened butter.

The pineapple rings left over from the stuffing are used as a garnish.

6 Place the bird on one side of its breast in a roasting tin just large enough to hold it comfortably. Roast in the centre of the oven for 25 minutes.

7 Turn the chicken on to its other breast and baste it thoroughly. Roast for 25 minutes.

8 Finally turn the chicken breast upwards. Baste it with the pan drippings and roast for another 25 minutes basting it two or three times.

9 Test the chicken, by piercing with a skewer. The juices should be colourless.

216

10 Tilt the chicken so that the juices run into the pan, then transfer the bird to a warmed serving dish. Remove the trussing strings, skewer and the leg shanks. Keep warm.

11 Add the cream and the rest of the chopped tarragon to the buttery juices in the roasting tin. Heat gently over a low heat. Stir round the pan with a wooden spoon to release the scrapings.

12 Put the flour in a small bowl and add the cold stock. Stir to a smooth paste.

13 Spoon a little of the hot cream on to the flour paste and incorporate it.

14 Transfer the flour paste back to the roasting tin off the heat. Stir to incorporate.

15 Return the baking tin to a gentle heat and bring to the boil, whisking continually with a small wire whisk. Simmer gently for 2-3 minutes to cook the flour. Check the seasonings.

16 Joint the chicken and pour a little of the sauce over it. Serve the rest in a sauce-boat.

ROAST CHICKEN WITH PINEAPPLE WALNUT STUFFING

Trying a new stuffing is a good way of ringing the changes on roast chicken. The flavours and textures of both pineapple and walnuts are in pleasant contrast with chicken, but it is essential to use top quality canned pineapple. The stock can be made with half a bouillon cube as the giblets are roasted in the tin with the chicken and will add their flavour at the end.

SERVES 4
1.4 kg [3 lb] chicken with giblets
salt and pepper
25 g [1 oz] butter
250 ml [½ pt] stock

For the stuffing:
350 g [12 oz] canned pineapple
**   rings**
50 g [2 oz] walnuts, chopped
40 g [1½ oz] butter
50 g [2 oz] dry white
**   breadcrumbs**

1 level teaspoon salt
half a lemon

For the garnish:
a few walnut halves
watercress

1 To make the stuffing, drain the pineapple rings, weigh out 100 g [4 oz] and chop them, reserving the rest for the garnish.

2 Chop the walnuts and grate the zest from the half lemon.

3 Melt the butter for the stuffing in a small saucepan, add the breadcrumbs and stir and cook for a minute or so.

4 Stir the chopped pineapple, chopped walnuts, salt, lemon zest and add enough pineapple juice to give the stuffing a fairly moist consistency.

5 Heat the oven to 190°C [375°F] gas mark 5.

6 Wash, drain and dry the chicken.

7 Sprinkle the body cavity with salt and pepper, and rub well into the skin. Insert 12 g [½ oz] of butter into the cavity.

8 Fill the neck end of the bird with the stuffing and retruss the bird.

9 Soften the remaining 12 g [½ oz] butter. Use some of it to grease a piece of kitchen foil. Spread the rest of the butter all over the bird. Cover the breast with foil.

10 Put the giblets, but not the liver, in the bottom of the roasting tin, and stand the chicken, breast up, on a rack, over them.

11 Cook in the centre of the oven for 1 hour.

12 Remove the foil, baste the bird with the pan drippings, and put the liver in the tin beside the bird and baste it. Cook for another 20 minutes.

13 Test the chicken by piercing the thigh with a skewer. The juices should be colourless.

14 Tilt the chicken to drain the juices into the roasting tin and transfer the chicken to a warmed serving dish. Remove the trussing strings and break off the leg shanks.

15 Add the stock to the roasting tin and bring to the boil, stirring and scraping to release the sediment from the bottom of the tin. Simmer for 2-3 minutes until slightly reduced.

16 Check the seasonings then strain the sauce into a sauce-boat and discard the giblets.

17 Halve the remaining pineapple rings, arrange them around the chicken, topping each half with a walnut. Tuck a few sprigs of watercress between the chicken legs.

Talking turkey

Gone are the days when only the rich ate turkey, and even they only once a year. Today's turkeys are such good value for money, they could well take the place of the traditional Sunday roast. Turkey is easy to roast and can be given extra flavour with tasty stuffings and sauces to make good value family meals the whole year round.

Turkey has been favourite fare for festive occasions since the time of the first Queen Elizabeth. Legend has it that when Columbus sailed the ocean blue, in the year of 1492, one of the things he brought back with him was the turkey. Because it was rare, turkey was looked on as a delicacy, though contemporary accounts suggest that the birds of those times were stringy compared to the plump, well-fed fowl that we know. Because turkey was a delicacy, it became linked with special days, such as Christmas and Thanksgiving. The fact that turkeys were difficult to rear and rather expensive also meant that roast turkey could not be served too often.

Modern rearing techniques which revolutionized our chicken-eating habits have now done the same for turkeys. No longer are we forced to face an 11.3 kg [25 lb] monster which will last for weeks. Turkeys today are specially bred to mature at different stages and are now available weighing from 2.2 kg [5 lb]— just right for a family Sunday lunch or a special

dinner. Modern turkeys are excellent value for money and if cooked and carved correctly, can prove cheaper than more everyday meats.

CHOOSING A TURKEY
There are several different types of roasting turkey available. With each type the points to look for are a plump breast and white flesh; smooth black legs indicate that the bird is young and therefore tender.

When considering what type of turkey to buy, consider also the size of the bird and the size of your oven.

New York dressed and traditional farm fresh
These are the fresh birds seen hanging in poulterers' windows at Christmas, plucked, but with the head and feet still attached. Fresh birds are still the choice of traditionalists who claim that they have a better flavour than chilled and frozen birds. Turkey producers, however,

claim that there is now no difference between the flavours of fresh, chilled and frozen turkeys. When buying a New York dressed bird, you pay for the weight of the head, feet and innards as well as the edible parts of the bird. It is estimated that these can weigh as much as 1.4 kg [3 lb]. New York dressed birds are more expensive per 450 g [1 lb] than other birds because the butcher has to dehead and eviscerate at the point of sale, unlike prepared birds which can just be handed over the counter. Only the larger birds weighing from 4.5–11.3 kg [10–25 lb] are sold New York dressed.

Chilled turkeys

Chilled turkeys are eviscerated and dressed for the oven on the farm and then air chilled rather than frozen. There is no intake of water in this process, unlike the deep-freezing process. Chilled birds are slightly more expensive than frozen and have the advantage that there is no thawing time to consider. They are available in sizes from 2.2–11.3 [5–25 lb].

Chilled birds are usually sold in chain stores, bagged and labelled with the giblets in a separate bag inside.

Frozen turkeys

The cheapness and ready availability of frozen turkeys have largely been responsible for moving the turkey away from the Christmas dinner table to other, less festive, times of the year. Frozen turkeys are sold oven ready with the giblets in a little bag inside. In the freezing process, there is quite a large intake of water which will add about 5% to the weight of the bird. Lengthy thawing is required to make the bird really tender. Frozen turkeys are available in sizes from 2.2–11.3 kg [5–25 lb].

Turkeys do not necessarily have to be enormous things that won't fit into the oven. Garnished with traditional accompaniments, a small bird is perfectly suitable for a Christmas dinner.

Self-basting turkeys

Self-basting turkeys are frozen birds which have vegetable oil or butter injected under the skin. This keeps the flesh moist during roasting and means that no basting is needed. Once thawed and prepared you literally put the bird in the oven and forget about it. Self-basting birds are slightly more expensive than ordinary frozen birds.

Turkey rolls

Turkey rolls are boneless turkey meat rolled up and are available fresh, chilled and frozen. They are rolls of breast meat only, dark meat (leg) only, or a mixture of breast and dark meat, wrapped in turkey skin or pork fat and tied with string or encased in a meat mesh. They are sold plain or stuffed. They are more expensive per 450 g [1 lb] than whole birds but as there is no waste, the actual price per 450 g [1 lb] of edible flesh works out at about the same as for a whole turkey. Turkey rolls are without doubt the best choice if you want to serve a large number of people with sliced turkey as, being boned, they are very easy to carve. They are particularly good for slicing cold and a 4.5 kg [10 lb] turkey roll would provide enough cold sliced meat for 40 people, working on the catering allowance of 100 g [¼ lb] meat per person.

STORING TURKEY

Fresh turkeys should be stored separately from their giblets, on a plate in the coldest part of the refrigerator. Covered loosely with greaseproof paper, a fresh turkey will keep safely for 2 days. The giblets have a shorter life and should, if possible, be used to make giblet stock for gravy on the day the turkey is bought. Reserve the liver for use in the stuffing if preferred.

Fresh turkey rolls should be stored as for whole birds.

Chilled turkeys should be stored according to the manufacturers' instructions. This varies from processor to processor so read the label carefully.

The same applies to chilled turkey rolls.

Frozen turkeys should be stored in a freezer or star marked frozen-food compartment if not immediately required for thawing.

Frozen turkey rolls should be stored in the same way.

THAWING TIMES FOR TURKEY

Thaw your frozen turkey on a rack over a tray, in the bottom of the refrigerator. Remove wrapping as soon as bird is sufficiently thawed to do so. Remove bag of giblets from the bird as well.

Weight	Thawing Time
2.2–3.6 kg [5–8 lb]	20–36 hours
3.6–5 kg [8–11 lb]	36–42 hours
5–5.9 kg [11–13 lb]	42–48 hours
5.9–9.1 kg [13–20 lb]	48–60 hours
9.1–11.3 kg [20–25 lb]	60–72 hours

TURKEY SIZES

Uncooked weight	No. of servings
2.2 kg [5 lb]	4
2.7 kg [6 lb]	5
3.1 kg [7 lb]	6
3.6 kg [8 lb]	7
4 kg [9 lb]	8
4.5 kg [10 lb]	10
5 kg [11 lb]	12
5.5 kg [12 lb]	13
5.9 kg [13 lb]	15
6.4 kg [14 lb]	17
6.8 kg [15 lb]	19
7.3 kg [16 lb]	20
7.7 kg [17 lb]	22
8.2 kg [18 lb]	24
8.6 kg [19 lb]	26
9.1 kg [20 lb]	28
9.5 kg [21 lb]	30
10.1 kg [22 lb]	32
10.5 kg [23 lb]	34
11 kg [24 lb]	36
11.3 kg [25 lb]	38

THAWING FROZEN TURKEY

Thorough, slow thawing of frozen turkeys and turkey rolls is essential for health and for flavour. They should be thawed in a cool place, where the temperature will not rise above 15°C [59°F]. Turkeys should always be thawed in their plastic wrappings: this helps to prevent drying out. Raise the bird on a rack or grid over a tray into which the water can drip. Never attempt to accelerate the defrosting process by placing the turkey in hot water. This toughens the flesh and can lead to insufficient thawing before cooking. If a turkey is not thawed thoroughly all the way through before cooking, it will not cook right through and the germs which cause food poisoning will not be destroyed. The chart given here indicates thawing times which will ensure your turkey is thoroughly thawed and safe. It is always best to cook the bird as soon as possible once it has been thoroughly thawed. When thawing turkey rolls, follow the manufacturer's instructions as these vary.

The neck cavity of a turkey is stuffed and not the body cavity. Stuffing ingredients can include the turkey liver, sausage meat, mushrooms, nuts, currants, herbs and spices.

HOW MUCH TO BUY

What size turkey you buy depends very much on what you want to do with it. If you want it only for one meal then it is likely that a smaller bird will be the best choice. If you have guests over several days, it would be more economical to buy a larger bird where there is a greater proportion of flesh to bone. The bird could be served roasted first, and then used for a number of réchauffé dishes. If these were made sufficiently varied (turkey pie, croquettes, curry, pilaf are just four you could choose from), your turkey could be used for several meals without anyone tiring of it. A large bird is also the best choice for a party, where it makes a splendid centrepiece.

For a buffet party or an occasion where cold sliced turkey will be served, a turkey roll is a better choice than a whole bird as it is quick and easy to carve and there is no waste.

The chart here is calculated to take into account the weight of the bones and to allow the professional caterer's portion weight of 100 g [¼ lb] meat per person. The weights are for oven-ready, raw, defrosted birds. When buying a New York dressed bird, remember to allow about an extra 1.4 kg [3 lb] for the weight of head, feet and entrails. On frozen birds allow up to 225 g [½ lb] extra for the weight of giblets and water. On chilled birds allow 100 g [¼ lb] for the weight of the giblets. With rolls there is no need to

make any allowance as there is no waste, and only minimal water intake as the flesh is so closely packed. When buying a roll, base your calculations on four portions per 450 g [1 lb]. When buying a whole bird, follow the chart given here.

PREPARING FOR ROASTING

First rinse the bird with cold water and pat dry carefully both inside and out. If the inside of the bird is damp

Step-by-step to trussing a turkey

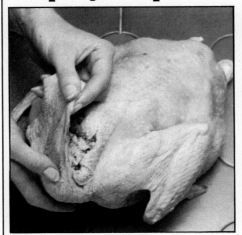

1 Lay the bird breast side down. Make sure the neck skin is flat to the back, enclosing the stuffing.

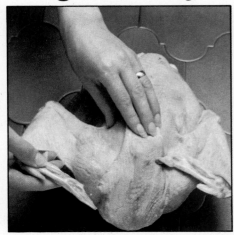

2 Fold the wing tips under to hold the neck skin in place and so that the wings are close to the body.

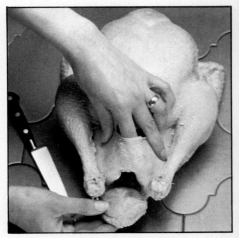

3 Make a slit in the skin above the vent. Push the parson's nose through this slit.

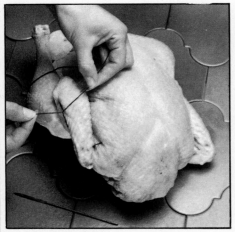

6 Push back through to secure wing tips and neck skin. Bring out at first joint of wing. Tie off.

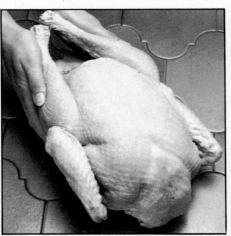

7 Using both hands press the legs to the sides so that the breast is plumped up.

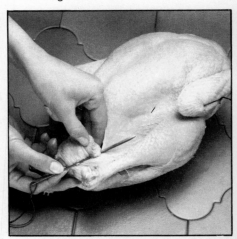

8 Turn bird round and insert the needle in the gristle at the right of the parson's nose. Make a stitch.

when cooking, the flesh will steam and inhibit the roasting. Season the bird liberally inside with salt and freshly ground black pepper. If you are roasting the bird plain without any stuffing, half a lemon and a couple of plump garlic cloves (peeled and left whole) or a sprig of fresh sage, thyme, basil or marjoram placed in the body cavity will delicately flavour the flesh.

If you have bought a fresh New York dressed bird, there may be a few quills remaining where the bird has been plucked. A sharp tug will bring these out without breaking the skin. Chilled and frozen birds are machine plucked and do not have quills left.

If you are roasting a turkey roll, it will be oven ready and there is no need to do any of the above.

Stuffing

You may see in older recipe books that turkeys are stuffed at both ends. This is not really a very good idea as stuffing the cavity can prevent the turkey being properly cooked, leading to an attack of what doctors call 'the Christmas collywobbles'. The neck cavity of a turkey will take quite a large amount of stuffing so there will be no shortage if you only stuff the neck end. As a rough guide, allow 25–40 g [1–1½ oz] of stuffing per 450 g [1 lb] raw oven-ready turkey.

The method is the same as for stuffing a chicken. (See step-by-step to stuffing a chicken on page 207). The stuffing used should not be put into the bird until shortly before cooking, nor should it be made in advance. The stuffing must be cold,

or at least cool, when put into the bird. Push the prepared stuffing into the neck cavity of the turkey, packing as full as possible. Stuffing mixtures should always be fairly damp and sticky so that they will pack in. When the cavity is full, fold the neck skin over to enclose the stuffing. Fold the wing tips over the skin on each side to hold it in place, or fasten the skin with a small poultry skewer.

If you wish to serve more stuffing than the bird can accommodate, it can be cooked in a greased baking dish covered with foil, on a lower shelf, for the last 30–40 minutes of roasting time.

Trussing

Although some turkeys are sold ready trussed (it usually says so on

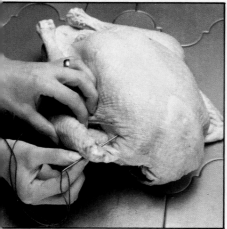

4 Thread a trussing needle with fine string. Insert at second joint of right wing and push into bird.

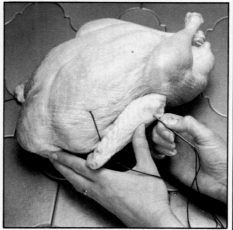

5 Pull out at second joint of left wing leaving an end. Re-insert at the first joint of this wing.

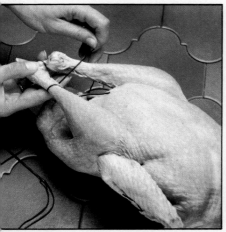

Pass the string around the right leg, over the body and over the left leg.

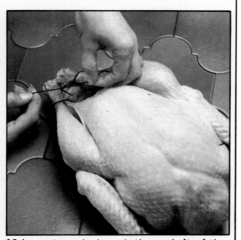

10 Insert again in gristle on left of the parson's nose. Bring under the parson's nose and tie off.

he packet), many are not. Trussing has rather gone out of fashion but for a large bird it is essential, otherwise egs and wings will fly akimbo in the oven and carving will be rather like a ussle with an octopus!

If trussing is new to you, it may vell take a few minutes. It is one of hose tasks that once familiar can be accomplished in no time. Because urkeys are usually quite large, they should be trussed with a trussing needle and string rather than with a skewer as described for chicken on ages 208–209. The trussing needle s rather like a large darning needle with an eye big enough to take fine tring. Always use natural rather han plastic coated or nylon string for russing. If you use plastic or nylon tring it will melt and ruin the turkey.

STUFFINGS

Stuffing adds flavour to the flesh of turkey and provides a pleasant contrast in texture. Never buy ready-made stuffing mix. It is mostly bread and is flavourless. Much tastier stuffings, which are also economical, can be made quite easily at home. Instructions on how to stuff are given in the section on preparing for roasting.

The stuffings given here are all to fill the neck cavity of a bird weighing 4.5 kg [10 lb]. An easy way to work out how much stuffing you will need is to allow roughly 25–40 g [1–1½ oz] for every 450 g [1 lb] of bird.

Sage and onion stuffing is the classic Christmas stuffing for turkey. It may be made with either fresh or dried sage. Fresh sage gives the stuffing a better flavour, as with any fresh herb. Dried sage can sometimes taste a little musty.

SAUSAGE FORCEMEAT

In the days when turkeys were always stuffed at both ends, the sausage forcemeat went in the neck end. You may, if you wish, stuff the neck end with another stuffing and cook this forcemeat separately. One of the traditonal ways to serve forcemeat is to make it into little balls and cook them under the turkey (which is raised on a rack) in the roasting tin. They are usually added to the tin about 1½ hours before the end of cooking time. Alternatively, place the forcemeat in a greased dish, cover with foil and cook in the bottom of the oven for the same length of time as the turkey.

FOR 4.5 KG [10 LB] BIRD
175 g [6 oz] sausage meat
50 g [2 oz] fresh white
**   breadcrumbs**
15 ml [1 tablespoon] freshly
**   chopped parsley**
1 small onion
1 streaky bacon rasher
1 large egg
salt and black pepper

1 Place the sausage meat in a bowl and stir in the crumbs and parsley.

2 Peel and finely chop the onion and add to the bowl.

3 De-rind the bacon rasher and mince or finely chop it. Add to the bowl. Break the egg into a separate bowl, beat and then stir into the sausage meat mixture so that a smooth paste is formed. Season to taste and use as required.

SPECIAL FORCEMEAT

This is a classic forcemeat which was a favourite of the Edwardians. It is rather expensive for modern tastes but is well worth making if you want to go the whole hog for Christmas dinner. Pounding the meat before adding the other ingredients gives a good contrast of rough and smooth textures.

FOR 4·5 KG [10 LB] BIRD
1 streaky bacon rasher
3 shallots
100 g [¼ lb] pie veal
50 g [2 oz] fresh white
**   breadcrumbs**

223

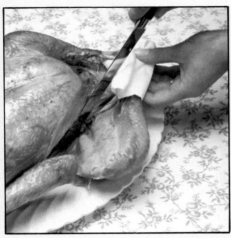

1 Cut through and remove trussing strings. Pull the leg away from the body and cut through the joint where it joins the body.

2 Cut through the centre joint of one leg to divide it into drumsticks and thigh. Slice the meat from the drumstick.

3 To slice thigh, hold firmly on a plate with a fork. Cut slices parallel to the centre bone. Divide other leg in the same way.

---

50 g [2 oz] butter
2 large mushrooms
15 ml [1 tablespoon] freshly chopped parsley
salt and black pepper
pinch of cayenne
pinch of mace
1 large egg

1 De-rind the bacon. Skin the shallots. Mince together the veal, bacon and shallots and place in a bowl with the breadcrumbs.

2 Cream the butter until light and fluffy then gradually pound into the mixture a little at a time. An easy way to do this is with either a pestle or the end of a rolling pin.

3 When all the butter has been amalgamated, wipe clean the mushrooms, trim the stalks and chop. Add to the mixture with the parsley and seasonings.

4 Beat the egg in a separate bowl and use to bind the forcemeat.

RAISIN AND NUT STUFFING
This stuffing is quick to make and has a delicious flavour. Salted peanuts give the best taste but you can use any other nuts in their place.

FOR 4·5 KG [10 LB] BIRD
100 g [¼ lb] fresh brown breadcrumbs

50 g [2 oz] seedless raisins
50 g [2 oz] salted peanuts
15 ml [1 tablespoon] freshly chopped parsley
freshly ground black pepper
1 large egg

1 Place the breadcrumbs in a bowl with the raisins. Roughly chop the nuts and add.

2 Add the parsley. Season to taste with pepper. Beat the egg in a separate bowl and stir into the stuffing mixture to bind it.

CHESTNUT STUFFING
This is the traditional stuffing for turkey. Chestnuts are extremely time consuming to boil and skin so it is quicker and easier to use canned chestnut purée for this dish, especially at the festive season when most cooks have enough to do anyway. Be sure to use the unsweetened variety.

FOR 4·5 KG [10 LB] BIRD
225 g [½ lb] unsweetened chestnut purée
1 small onion
25 g [1 oz] fresh white breadcrumbs
25 g [1 oz] butter

1 Place the purée in a bowl. Skin and finely chop the onion and add to the purée. Mix well.

2 Stir in the breadcrumbs. Melt the

butter in a heavy-based pan over low heat and add to the dry ingredients. Mix well and leave until cold before use.

STUART STUFFING
The original for this recipe may be found in an anonymous 17th century manuscript in London's Victoria and Albert Museum. It was originally intended for chicken but is very good indeed with turkey, especially when served cold. This stuffing uses the liver from the turkey.

FOR 4·5 KG [10 LB] BIRD
100 g [4 oz] sliced bread
150 ml [¼ pt] milk
1 lemon
15 ml [1 tablespoon] mixed finely chopped parsley, thyme and chives
1 shallot
15 ml [1 tablespoon] ground almonds
salt and black pepper
liver from the turkey

1 Place the bread in a shallow dish. Pour on the milk and leave to soak for 20 minutes.

2 Squash the bread to a pulp with a fork. Grate the zest from the lemon and squeeze the juice. Add the juice and zest to the bread with the herbs.

3 Peel and finely chop the shallot

a large turkey

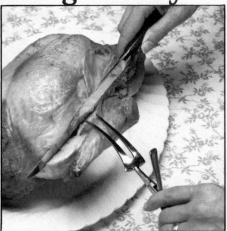

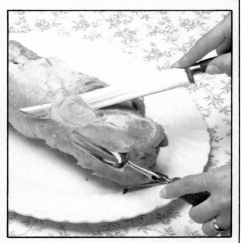

4 To slice the breast, place the knife parallel and as close to the wing as you can. Make a deep cut down the bone.

5 Now carve the breast downwards, ending at the deep cut. Do other side in the same way. Remove wings and set aside.

6 Turn the bird over and slice off meat from the base and from the oyster as for chicken.

and add to the mixture with the almonds and seasoning, to taste. Mince the liver and add. Stir well before use.

ROASTING TURKEY

Everyone wants to roast turkey to be a special treat, regardless of the occasion, with crispy golden skin and moist, tender flesh. There are few rules to observe and with a little care you will be guaranteed success every time.

The methods for roasting small and large turkeys vary slightly. All times given here are for stuffed birds. For unstuffed birds, cook for about 5 minutes less per 450 g [1 lb]. When cooking self-basting birds, follow the manufacturer's instructions.

Barding

Both large and small turkeys must be barded to prevent the skin drying out and becoming tough. Do not bard self-basting turkeys as they already have sufficient fat or oil to keep them moist. Either spread the skin of the breast and legs generously with softened or melted butter, and sprinkle with salt to encourage crispness, or lay bacon rashers over the bird. Streaky bacon is best as it has the most fat.

Small birds

Small birds are best cooked at a high heat. This ensures that the flesh is cooked right through but is still moist. This method is suitable for birds weighing up to 3.6 kg [8 lb]. Bard the turkey then place on a piece of foil on a roasting rack in a roasting tin. Roast in the centre of an oven heated to 230°C [450°F] gas mark 8 for 22 minutes per 450 g [1 lb] or until the juices run clear when the flesh is pierced near the thick part of the leg. About 20 minutes before the end of cooking time, open the foil to allow the breast to brown. Baste frequently with the juice in the foil during this time.

When roasting small self-basting birds, follow the manufacturer's instructions.

Large birds

Set the oven to 160°C [325°F] gas mark 3. Bard the bird and then place it on a rack in a large roasting tin in the centre of the oven. Cook, following the times given in the chart. Baste frequently during cooking. Turn the bird every hour to make sure that the skin browns evenly. If the turkey has been barded with bacon rashers, remove these 20 minutes before the end of cooking time. If the breast skin looks as though it will be over browned, cover with a piece of foil. Remove this 5 minutes before the end of cooking time to complete crisping the skin.

If the bird is very large and only just fits into the oven, it may be rather too large for the roasting tin. In this case place the bird on the rack on the centre shelf and the roasting tin on a surface of foil (to catch any stray drips) on the shelf below. Baste with the melted fat caught in the roasting tin.

However large the turkey and long the cooking time, never part-cook the bird the day before. This is a great health hazard as there is a danger that the bird will not be properly heated through and salmonella germs will multiply.

When cooking time is up, test the meat with a skewer in the fleshy part of the leg. If the juices run clear, the bird is cooked. Remove from the oven and leave in a warm place for at least 10 minutes (30 minutes for very large birds) to allow the flesh to set. This makes carving easier.

Turkey rolls

Manufacturers usually recommend that rolls be roasted at 160°C [325°F] gas mark 3 for 15 minutes per 450 g [1 lb]. Always check the label carefully though, as this may vary.

COOKING TIMES FOR LARGE TURKEYS
At 160°C [325°C] gas mark 3

Weight	Hours
4–4.5 kg [9–10 lb]	4–4½
4.5–5.5 kg [10–12 lb]	4½–5
5.5–6.8 kg [12–15 lb]	5–5½
6.8–7.7 kg [15–17 lb]	5½–6
7.7–9.1 kg [17–20 lb]	6–6½
9.1–11.3 kg [20–25 lb]	6½–7½

CARVING A TURKEY

The three essential requisites for carving a turkey are a sharp knife, a stout carving fork and a spiked carving plate to hold the bird steady while you cut.

Small birds

If you are roasting a small turkey, you will probably want to carve it at the table following the time-honoured family method of a leg or a wing each, and some breast meat.

This is an excellent way to carve a turkey for a small family and is fairly fully understood by every cook. Do remove the stuffing first though—something which is often forgotten when carving by this method.

Large birds

If you have spent a lot of money on a large turkey, you will want it to go as far as possible. This is achieved by clever carving. It is best to carve a large turkey in the kitchen as the process is quite time consuming. As you carve the meat, place it on a warm plate in a warm place then it will not go cold before it gets to the table. When carving turkey in this way, it is customary to give everyone portions made up of some light and some dark meat (ie, breast and leg). Once again, remember to remove the stuffing first and serve it in a separate dish.

COLD TURKEY

If you are roasting turkey to serve cold, it must be cooled as rapidly as possible and then stored, covered, in a refrigerator. When the turkey is cooked, remove from the oven and place on a cold plate. Leave until cool then cover lightly with foil and store in the refrigerator. It will keep for two days. Do not cut the turkey before required or the meat will dry out. To serve left-over turkey hot, it must be completely cooked again—in a stew, curry or casserole, for instance, or brought slowly just up to boiling point in a sauce, to destroy the germs which cause food poisoning. If you have cold sliced turkey left over, wrap it in foil or greaseproof paper and store in the refrigerator.

ACCOMPANIMENTS FOR TURKEY

As befits such a splendid bird, turkey has a wide range of traditional accompaniments.

Chipolata sausages may be cooked in the bottom of the roasting pan and arranged around or at one end of the bird. Be sure to get the real spicy, small chipolatas to serve with turkey.

Forcemeat balls may be made from the forcemeat described in the stuffings section and cooked underneath the turkey. An alternative to making balls is to place the prepared forcemeat in a greased dish, cook in the bottom of the oven for the same time as the turkey but, in the case of a big bird, for no more than 1½ hours. Serve with the bird.

Cranberry sauce has a sharp flavour that contrasts agreeably with the taste and texture of turkey. You can, of course, make your own cranberry sauce if you have the time, but the bottled varieties now on sale are mostly very good.

Bacon rolls are another traditional and tasty accompaniment. Try them stuffed with prunes which have been stoned and soaked overnight in strained cold tea. Drain thoroughly before stuffing.

Bread sauce is to chicken and turkey what mint sauce is to lamb. It's rather strange savoury sweet flavour and creamy texture marries well with both hot and cold turkey. A recipe for a traditional bread sauce is given on page 214.

Gravy for turkey should be thin and brown. For best flavour use giblet stock and follow the recipe given here for turkey gravy.

TURKEY GRAVY

The stock from giblets makes a well-flavoured gravy to accompany turkey. You cannot, however, make a good giblet gravy if the liver is being used for stuffing the bird. If this is the case, use chicken stock to make the gravy instead. Preparation of the giblets must be done carefully otherwise the stock will have a very strong flavour and a cloudy grey appearance. This gravy is traditional but if your family does not like it there is no reason why you should not thicken turkey gravy in the usual way by adding plain flour to the pan juices.

MAKES 250 ML [½ PT]
turkey giblets
half an onion
1 carrot
1 bay leaf
15 ml [1 tablespoon] cranberry jelly

1 Cut away the greenish gall bladder and any green patches on the liver as these will be bitter.

2 Cut up the gizzard as far as the crop. Peel off the flesh and discard the rest.

3 Place the giblets in a pan with the peeled and halved onion, scrubbed and halved carrot, bay leaf and about 250 ml [½ pt] water.

4 Bring gradually to boil and then skim off any scum. Cover and simmer for 2 hours.

5 Strain the stock through a muslin-lined sieve. Leave until cold and then remove any fat which has set on the surface.

6 Bring slowly to the boil while the turkey is roasting.

7 Remove the cooked turkey from the roasting tin and keep in a warm place. Pour the fat away from the tin leaving the sediment behind.

8 Pour the hot giblet stock gradually into the roasting tin, stirring and scraping the bottom of the tin to lift the sediment.

9 When the gravy is a rich brown, set the roasting tin over low heat and bring slowly to the boil.

10 Remove from heat, stir in the cranberry jelly and serve hot.

ROAST TURKEY WITH ORANGE CURRANT STUFFING

◩◩◩ *A small turkey can be made into a family treat if you use an interesting and tasty stuffing. The stuffed apples which accompany this dish make it look especially festive. Red-skinned eating apples look nicest and their flavour contrasts pleasantly with that of the stuffing.*

SERVES 4-6
2.2 kg [5 lb] turkey
100 g [¼ lb] butter
salt
100 g [¼ lb] fresh white breadcrumbs
75 g [3 oz] shredded suet
1 orange
50 g [2 oz] currants
1 small onion
pinch of nutmeg
freshly ground black pepper
1 medium-sized egg
4 red-skinned eating apples

1 Set the oven to 230°C [450°F] gas mark 8. Grate the zest from the orange and squeeze to extract the juice.

2 Place the breadcrumbs, suet, orange zest and juice and currants in a bowl. Skin and finely chop the onion and add to the bowl.

3 Add the nutmeg and pepper to taste. Break the egg into a separate bowl, beat it and add to the stuffing ingredients.

4 Wash and season the inside of the turkey. Stuff the neck end, leaving 60 ml [4 tablespoons] stuffing for the apples. Truss if necessary.

5 Spread the breast and legs liberally with 50 g [2 oz] butter.

Sprinkle with salt. Wrap in foil.

6 Cook in the centre of the oven for 2 hours. About 25 minutes before the end of cooking time, core the apples and stuff with remaining stuffing. Melt the remaining butter over low heat and brush over the apples. Place the apples in a dish in the oven.

7 About 20 minutes before the end of cooking time, unwrap the turkey to allow the breast to brown.

8 To serve, arrange the stuffed apples around the turkey.

Roast turkey with orange currant stuffing is garnished with baked apples. Cranberry sauce is a traditional accompaniment with roast turkey.

SPICY ROAST TURKEY

⊠⊠*Rubbing the skin of turkey with spiced butter gives an unusual flavour which contrasts pleasantly with the bacon and olive stuffing. If you wish, soaked prunes may be substituted for stuffed olives as they go equally well with bacon.*

SERVES 4
2.2 kg [5 lb] turkey
salt
freshly ground black pepper
25 g [1 oz] white breadcrumbs
50 g [2 oz] streaky bacon
25 g [1 oz] stuffed green olives
25 g [1 oz] walnuts
3 garlic cloves
1 small egg
50 g [2 oz] butter
5 ml [1 teaspoon] ground cinnamon
2.5 ml [½ teaspoon] ground cloves

1 Wash the turkey and season inside with salt and freshly ground black pepper.

2 Set the oven to 230°C [450°F] gas mark 8.

3 Place the breadcrumbs in a bowl. De-rind the bacon, cut into small pieces and add to the bowl. Chop the olives and walnuts and add to the bowl.

4 Skin and chop the garlic cloves and add to the bowl. Beat the egg in a separate bowl and stir into the mixture.

5 Stuff the neck of the turkey with the mixture and then truss if necessary.

6 Beat the butter in a bowl until soft and creamy. Mix in 5 ml [1 teaspoon] freshly ground black pepper, the cinnamon, the cloves and a pinch of salt.

7 Spread the turkey breast and legs liberally with the spiced butter. Wrap in foil.

8 Cook in the centre of the oven on a rack for 2 hours. About 20 minutes before the end of cooking time, unwrap the foil to brown the breast. Baste frequently with the juices during this time. When cooked transfer to a serving plate to rest before carving.

BUFFET TURKEY WITH CAMBRIDGE SAUCE

⊠⊠*If you have a large number of people to feed, a turkey roll is the perfect choice. Turkey rolls are easy to carve and economical because there is no waste. Turkey meat served alone can, however, be rather uninteresting, so choose a sharp sauce to offset the blandness of the meat. Cambridge sauce, a favourite of 19th century dons and deans fits the bill perfectly. Its pale colour blends well with the meat.*

SERVES 12
1.4 kg [3 lb] turkey roll
50 g [2 oz] softened butter
salt

For the sauce:
4 medium-sized hard-boiled eggs
50 g [2 oz] anchovy fillets
15 ml [1 tablespoon] capers
15 ml [1 tablespoon] freshly chopped chives
15 ml [1 tablespoon] freshly chopped tarragon
10 ml [2 teaspoons] French mustard
30 ml [2 tablespoons] red wine vinegar
90 ml [6 tablespoons] olive oil
15 ml [1 tablespoon] freshly chopped parsley
2.5 ml [½ teaspoon] cayenne pepper

Buffet turkey with Cambridge sauce.

1 Set the oven to 160°C [325°F], gas mark 3. Spread butter over the turkey roll and sprinkle with salt.

2 Place the turkey roll on a rack in a roasting tin. Place in the centre of the oven and cook for 1¼ hours, basting from time to time.

3 Remove the turkey roll from the oven. Allow to become cold before slicing.

4 Meanwhile, make the sauce. Cut the hard-boiled eggs in half and remove the yolks.

5 Place yolks in a mortar with the anchovies, capers, tarragon, chives and mustard. Pound with a pestle until you have a smooth cream. Alternatively, place the ingredients in a bowl and pound with the end of a rolling pin.

6 Stir the vinegar into the mixture. Now add the oil a drop at a time as for mayonnaise until the sauce turns thick.

7 When the sauce is thick, strain. Add the parsley and cayenne pepper.

8 Slice the cold turkey thinly and serve with the sauce.

Out for a duck!

Roasted correctly, duck and goose are delicious. Roasted badly, they are positively unpleasant. Duck is more readily available today than ever before while goose, pushed out of its traditional role as the Christmas bird by the turkey, deserves a come-back. Here you will see how to roast both birds to perfection, and how to make a number of classic dishes.

Duck is prized for its pronounced flavour and succulence. Unfortunately, it is not a very fleshy bird and consequently the meat does not go very far. Nor are the birds very large. You will never be able to feed more than four people from a single duck.

Geese are larger but, again, are not fleshy. When roasted, a goose will feed a maximum of eight people.

When it is to be roasted, the bird should always be young and tender. Strictly speaking, a duck which is less than three months old is correctly called a duckling but the terms duck and duckling are used fairly loosely. A young goose is called a gosling but older birds (up to about a year) are also suitable for roasting.

CHOOSING DOMESTIC DUCKS

Domestic ducks come prepared in four different ways — New York dressed, fresh oven-ready, chilled and frozen. A guide which applies to all, is to choose a bird weighing between 1.4–2.2 kg [3–5 lb]. Birds of this weight are still young and tender.

Duck has a distinctive flavour and its flesh is dark and rather rich. Fresh fruit complements the flavour particularly well.

Remember that frozen birds take up water and thus weight, during the freezing process, and that the weight of a New York dressed bird is increased by about a third by the head, feet and innards. When choosing any kind of duck, look for a plump breast and creamy white skin. The legs should be well rounded.

New York dressed
New York dressed birds are seen

229

hanging in butchers' shops, with head and feet attached. If the bill and feet are pale yellow and the bill is flexible, you will know you are buying a young bird. Like all New York dressed birds, ducks prepared in this way are quite expensive per 450 g [1 lb] because you are paying for the head, feet and innards. These can add up to one third on the weight. Flavour is not really that much better than chilled oven-ready birds, so the expense of a New York dressed bird is not really justified.

Fresh oven-ready
These are birds which have been completely prepared for the oven. Giblets are usually sold with the bird. They are slightly less expensive than New York dressed and a good buy if you are adamant about having fresh duck.

Chilled
Chilled birds are sold pre-packed and oven-ready. They are cheaper than fresh birds and a good buy because there is no uptake of water as with frozen birds.

Frozen
The large scale production and freezing of duck has been responsible for a greater interest in the bird. Frozen ducks are sold completely oven-ready. All you have to do is thaw the bird thoroughly. Some weight is lost when the duck is thawed because it will lose the water taken in during the freezing process. Frozen ducks are the cheapest and are an excellent buy if you plan to roast with a well-flavoured stuffing.

Also available are frozen duck portions. These are made up of leg and breast and are a good buy for a dinner à deux as they cut down on preparation and carving.

CHOOSING WILD DUCKS
Wild ducks are only available fresh and are limited by the game seasons. The main varieties of wild duck sold for eating in the United Kingdom are teal, widgeon and mallard. They are in season from late August to March. Wild ducks are small. Widgeon are the largest but rarely come in weights greater than 1.6 kg [3½ lb].

Wild ducks are almost always sold New York dressed or feathered: an expensive buy, as a lot of weight is lost once the inedible parts have

been removed.

If a sporting member of your family goes shooting and bags a duck, hang it head down for three days before plucking and drawing.

There is very little to choose between teal, mallard and widgeon. They all have rather coarse, strongly flavoured flesh. Usually you have to take pot luck on what is available when buying.

CHOOSING DOMESTIC GEESE
Because geese are temperamental birds (so fierce are they that Scottish distilleries use them instead of dogs to guard the whisky), they cannot be intensively reared. This means they are still farmed in a small way, so are always expensive. Consequently, the supply of domestic geese follows their natural life cycle and they are only readily available towards the close of the year.

The season for geese begins in late September with the traditional Michaelmas goose that was given as a tithe for hundreds of years. The season ends in March with the so-called green geese or goslings of Easter.

Geese are sold either New York dressed or oven-ready. As already explained, New York dressed means expensive. Up to half the weight of a goose can be lost once the head, feet and entrails are removed. Oven-ready birds are always sold fresh and work out to be marginally cheaper. It is not advisable to buy a goose over 4.5 kg [10 lb] as the flesh of an older bird can be very stringy. Nor is it advisable to buy a goose under 2.7 kg [6 lb] as you will be paying for more bone than flesh.

Wild geese
Wild geese are rarely sold commercially. They have a strong, gamey flavour and are inclined to be very stringy. Should a member of your family shoot one, casserole it or use it for pâté. Roast wild goose is not recommended.

HOW MUCH TO BUY
One of the sad things about duck and goose is that neither bird goes very far. They both have a very high proportion of bone to flesh and this means you have to allow quite a lot of bird per person to get a reasonable

portion. However, the bones make a very good gamey stock which can be used for soups and the fat is exceptionally flavoursome and is excellent for frying meat or sautéing or roasting potatoes.

Domestic duck is the fleshiest of the birds discussed but even so you will need to allow a minimum of 450 g [1 lb] oven-ready weight per person. In practice, allow a bit over so if you are serving four, count on a 2.2 kg [5 lb] bird (oven-ready weight), to allow good-sized portions.

Wild ducks are small and also bony. When buying teal, allow one plump bird (about 700 g [1½ lb] per person). When buying widgeon and mallard, allow at least 450 g [1 lb] per person, as for domestic duck.

Geese are even bonier than ducks. When buying a goose, you must allow 700 g [1½ lb] of dressed bird per person.

PREPARING FOR ROASTING
Duck and goose are prepared for roasting in similar ways. The main difference is the trussing and the removal of fat from inside a goose.

Duck
First thaw the bird thoroughly if frozen. Thaw it in the bag and allow 1½ hours per 450 g [1 lb] at room temperature or 2¼ hours per 450 g [1 lb] in the refrigerator.

Cleaning: remove the giblets if inside and rinse the bird under cold water inside and out. Pat dry carefully, both inside and out, and season the inside with salt and pepper.

Stuffing: domestic ducks are stuffed through the tail end, not the neck. A sharp, tangy stuffing is almost essential to contrast with the rich flesh. A suitable stuffing for duck is sage and onion. Also good are those given in the recipe section here. Allow 25 g [1 oz] stuffing per 450 g [1 lb] of duck. Do not stuff the duck until just before you roast it and do not make the stuffing in advance. Stuffing is such a mixture of ingredients that it can easily spoil and may even become a health hazard.

Trussing: after stuffing, ducks are trussed with string in exactly the same way as a chicken except that the wings are not pinned to the back. Trussing a chicken is discussed in detail on pages 208–209.

The skin: domestic duck has a thick

Handy hints

In the North of England, one of the more bizarre uses of goose fat was to spread it on the chest of anyone suffering from a cold and then wrap them up in a brown paper waistcoat. The unfortunate sufferer was then sent to bed with a hot water bottle and supposedly awoke cured, after a smelly night!

●The fat from duck and goose is exceptionally well flavoured and should be saved for use in fry-start casseroles, for sealing meat, for roasting and for making pâtés. It also makes delicious fried bread and sautéed potatoes.

●When you render down the solid fat from inside a goose, you will find little crisp pieces are left behind. These are called frittons d'oie. If you pound them to make a paste, they are a delicious spread for toast.

●Store your goose or duck fat in a jar in the refrigerator or freezer. Covered with cling film it will last for three months.

layer of fat under the skin so there is no need to bard the bird. Prick the skin lightly all over with a fork. This will encourage the fat to flow out during cooking. Then rub the skin generously with salt and freshly ground black pepper. This will give a lovely flavour and also help to crisp the skin.

Wild ducks are cleaned, then seasoned inside and trussed but not stuffed as they are too small for this. Prick the thighs to allow excess fat to run out and rub the skin with salt and pepper. The breast of wild duck is much drier than that of domestic duck, so it must be barded with strips of streaky bacon. The bacon is laid across the breast and is removed about 20 minutes before the end of cooking to allow the breast to brown and crisp.

Goose

A goose is cleaned and seasoned in the same way as a duck.

Removing fat: inside a goose, underneath and around the flap of skin at the neck end, there is a large amount of solid white fat. This must be removed before the goose is roasted or it would be impossibly greasy. To remove the fat, simply pull it away with your hands. Render the fat down and use it in the ways suggested.

Stuffing: like duck, goose needs a sharp stuffing to contrast with the rich flesh. When stuffing a goose, you will need 40 g [1½ oz] stuffing for every 450 g [1 lb] goose, dressed weight. Goose is, like duck, stuffed through the tail end.

Trussing: a goose is trussed with skewers rather than with string. You will need three long, plain metal skewers. First, press the wings close to the sides of the bird. Pass a skewer through the centre joint and out at the other side. Pass another skewer through the wing tips. Push the legs

Duck, roasted and served with some simply cooked fresh vegetables, makes a pleasant change from the usual Sunday joint.

1 Prepare the required quantity of stuffing for the bird. Heat the oven to 220°C [425°F] gas mark 7.

2 Rinse bird and pat dry. Remove solid fat from inside goose. Season inside the bird.

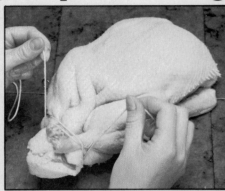

3 Stuff through the tail end. Truss a duck with string in the same way as a chicken.

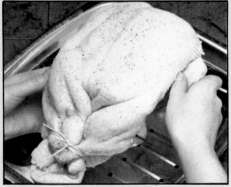

7 Place the bird on a rack in a roasting tin. Roast for 15 minutes. Reduce heat as specified in text.

8 Roast for 18 minutes per 450 g [1 lb]. Pour off excess fat from tin at regular intervals.

9 Turn the tin from time to time so that the bird browns evenly on all sides.

close to the sides of the bird. Push a skewer through the thickest part of the leg and right through the bird.
The skin: the skin of a goose is prepared in exactly the same way as domestic duck.

ROASTING

Duck and goose are roasted in the same way. Wild duck is roasted in a slightly different way which is given in a separate section.

Domestic duck and goose

Place the prepared bird on its back on a rack in a roasting tin. The rack prevents the bird from sitting in a pool of grease while in the oven. Set the oven to 220°C [425°F] gas mark 7 and when the temperature has been reached, place the roasting tin on the centre shelf. Cook for fifteen minutes at this temperature. This initial period at high temperature starts the fat flowing. After fifteen minutes reduce the heat to 180°C [350°F] gas

mark 4 for duck, 190°C [375°F] gas mark 5 for goose and roast for eighteen minutes per 450 g [1 lb].

During roasting, do not baste the bird at all but tip the excess fat out of the tin every fifteen minutes or so. Hold the bird securely in place by the legs, or remove it from the tin. The fat from the body cavity of a goose can be poured out into the tin by tilting the bird on to its tail end with a fish slice. Place a gloved hand on the body of the goose to prevent it slipping. Then tip the fat from the tin, holding the bird in place. If the goose is stuffed, it will not be possible to tip the cavity fat out at the tail end. The fat will remain in the cavity and some of it be absorbed by the stuffing. Turn the tin several times during roasting so that the bird browns evenly.

Twenty minutes before the end of roasting, turn the bird upside down to brown its back. Turn it breast side up again 5 minutes before the end of roasting, to give the breast skin a final crisping. The bird is cooked when the

juices run clear. To test this, pierce at the thick part of the leg with a skewer.

Wild duck

Because it is less fatty, the breast of wild duck is barded with bacon before roasting. The duck is then roasted at a constant temperature of 220°C [425°F] gas mark 7 for 10 minutes per 450 g [1 lb]. Half way through cooking, remove the bacon barding strips and pour 45 ml [3 tablespoons] port or fresh orange juice over the bird. Baste frequently, every five minutes or so after this. Teal is quickest to cook being smallest. An average teal will cook in twenty minutes. Mallard and widgeon take about 30 minutes.

CARVING DUCK AND GOOSE

Ducks and geese are rather an odd shape and because of this are not easy to carve. It is simpler, by far, to portion a duck, either in two or in

domestic duck and goose

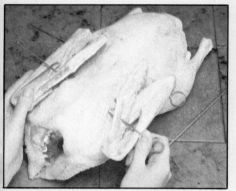

4 Truss a goose with skewers. Push one through the centre joint and one through the wing tip.

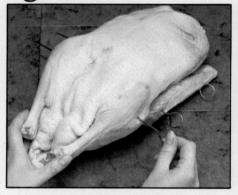

5 Turn the bird on to its back and press the legs to the body. Push the skewer through the thighs.

6 Prick the skin all over to allow fat to escape and rub with salt and freshly ground black pepper.

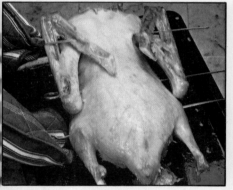

10 About 20 minutes before the end of roasting, turn bird upside down to brown the back.

11 Turn breast side up 5 minutes before the end of roasting for a final browning and crisping.

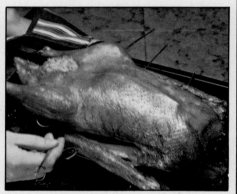

12 To test if cooked, pierce the thick part of the leg with a skewer. The juices should run clear.

four. However, a large duck can be carved in the same way as a goose. Either job is better completed in the kitchen, whenever possible. Carving takes some time and when done in the kitchen, the carved meat can be kept hot. Wild duck, which is served one per person, obviously needs no carving or portioning.

Portioning a duck
To portion a duck, place the bird on a board and remove the trussing strings. If stuffed, remove the stuffing and serve separately. Sit the bird upright and, with a very sharp knife, cut down through the breastbone and through the backbone and right along the length of the duck. This gives you two portions. Lay each half flat and make a slanting cut upwards over the leg to separate the leg and wing. Any rib bones sticking out can be snipped off with kitchen scissors. You now have four portions of approximately equal weight, each with some breast meat.

Carving a goose or duck
To carve a goose or duck, first remove the trussing and leave the bird to rest in a warm place for about fifteen minutes for the flesh to set. (This also gives you time to make the gravy.) A spiked carving plate will hold the bird steady and make carving much easier.

If the bird is stuffed, first remove the stuffing before you start carving and serve separately. This is best done with a spoon so that you can spoon out the surplus from inside the body cavity.

Begin carving by removing the legs. These are set differently to those of a chicken and join the body under the bird's back. Cut through at the joint and remove. Do not carve the meat from the legs but sever the thigh from the drumstick. Cut off the wings, slicing off a piece of breast with each.

To carve the breast, make the first cut along the breastbone, right down to the carcass. Carve the meat in thick

slices working down each side of the breast, cutting into the bird. The slices will still be attached to the bird at this point. Loosen the slices by cutting upwards, with the knife held flat against the carcass. You will then have long, narrow slices of breast meat.

To serve, lay the breast slices in the centre of the serving platter, place the legs at one end, wings at the other, and pour over a little gravy. Garnish with suitable vegetables, fruit or greenery.

ACCOMPANIMENTS FOR DUCK AND GOOSE
Duck and goose have similar accompaniments.

Giblet gravy
Make giblet gravy in the same way as for chicken on page 210. The addition of 45 ml (3 tablespoons) port or orange juice goes very well with both duck and goose. A little red-

Step-by-step to carving a goose

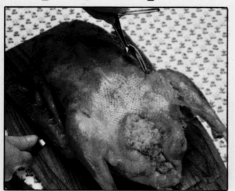

1 Remove trussing and leave bird to rest for 15 minutes. Place it on a spiked carving plate.

2 Remove the stuffing with a spoon before starting to carve. Keep hot while carving.

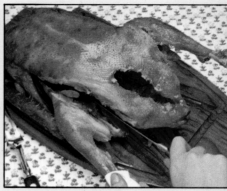

3 Ease each leg away from the body. Cut through at joint with body, under the back. Separate thigh.

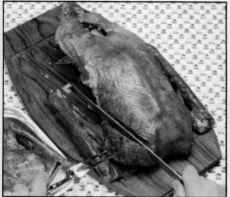

4 Ease each wing away from the body and cut off, slicing off some breast meat with each wing.

5 Cut down along the breastbone. Carve breast by cutting into the bird, parallel to the first cut.

6 Loosen the slices by cutting upwards, holding the knife flat against the body of the bird.

currant jelly stirred into the gravy also gives good flavour. If you can get them, crab apples sliced into rings and cooked in the pan below the duck or goose give the gravy a good flavour. If you cannot get crab apples, cooking apples may be used instead.

Other accompaniments
Redcurrant jelly offsets the rich flavour of duck and goose. Ready-made redcurrant jelly is widely available and perfectly presentable.
Sliced oranges and bunches of watercress make an attractive garnish which complements the flavour of duck and goose.
Vegetables to accompany duck and goose should always be very plain as the main interest of the meal lies in the meat. Julienne potatoes (strips) or game chips (crisps), grilled tomatoes, green peas or beans or boiled new potatoes are all suitable.
Stuffings should be slightly sharp and fruit is often included.

Fruit accompaniments are particularly good with plainly roasted duck or goose—try the stuffed spiced peaches given here.

Apple rings fried in butter are a traditional accompaniment for both duck and goose. To make, peel, core and slice the dessert apples. Fry lightly in butter until just browned.

Baked oranges are seldom seen today but they too deserve a revival for plainly cooked duck or goose. They are also good with pork.

BAKED ORANGES
Baked oranges are an old-fashioned accompaniment for duck, goose or pork and are cooked in the oven at the same time. Choose medium-sized oranges with brightly coloured skins. This usually indicates that they are juicy.

If being baked alone, the oven temperature required is 180°C [350°F] gas mark 4.

SERVES 4
4 medium-sized oranges
20 ml [4 teaspoons] brown sugar
50 g [2 oz] unsalted butter
20 ml [4 teaspoons] sweet sherry

1 Cut a thin slice off the top of each orange. Using a grapefruit knife, cut around inside the orange from the top, to loosen the flesh.

2 Remove the flesh from the skin shell. Holding the flesh over a plate to catch the juice, divide into segments, discarding membrane, pith and pips.

3 Return the segments of orange and juice to the shell. Place 5 ml [1 teaspoon] sugar in each shell. Divide the butter into four and place a piece in each shell.

4 Place the oranges in a dish. Pour

in enough hot water to come half way up the oranges. This prevents the skins drying out. Bake for 30 minutes on the floor of the oven while you are cooking your bird.

5 Just before serving, pour 5 ml [1 teaspoon] sherry into each orange.

SPICED PEACHES

Stuffed, spiced peaches are simplicity itself to make. Choose firm rather than very ripe peaches. Very ripe fruit may well disintegrate. The peaches are cooked in the oven at the same time as the meat. Spiced peaches can also be cooked under a moderate grill for 3–4 minutes until golden.

SERVES 4
4 medium-sized peaches
45 ml [3 tablespoons] brown
  sugar
50 g [2 oz] butter
pinch of ground nutmeg
pinch of ground cloves
45 ml [3 tablespoons] orange
  juice (optional)

1 Skin, halve and stone the peaches.

2 Mix together the sugar, butter and spices. Use about half of the mixture to fill the stone cavities in the peaches.

3 Place the peaches in a shallow baking dish. Dot the rest of the butter and spice mixture around them. Add 45 ml [3 tablespoons] of orange juice or water.

4 Bake on the floor of the oven while you are roasting your duck or goose, for 30 minutes. Spoon the juices over the peaches from time to time.

STUFFINGS

All the stuffings given here are for a 3.6 kg [8 lb] goose or for a 2.2 kg [5 lb] duck. Remember that you need 40 g [1½ oz] stuffing per 450 g [1 lb] goose and 25 g [1 oz] per 450 g [1 lb] duck. All stuffings should be cool before being put into the bird.

APPLE AND POTATO STUFFING

This rather filling stuffing is used mostly to extend goose which does

not go very far. If you can get them, crab apples have a sharper flavour and give the best results. For convenience the potatoes can be made in advance and allowed to cool. For this recipe there is no need to include an egg.

STUFFS 1 GOOSE
100 g [¼ lb] creamed potatoes
100 g [¼ lb] onions
2 sprigs lemon thyme
2 sprigs savory or parsley
1 orange
100 g [¼ lb] crab or cooking
  apples

1 Place the creamed potatoes (either freshly made or ready cooked) in a bowl.

2 Skin and finely chop the onions and add to the potatoes.

3 Chop the herbs and add. Grate the zest from the orange and add to the bowl. Squeeze, and add the

juice to the other ingredients.

4 Peel and chop the apples. Add to the stuffing. Leave to cool if necessary.

ORANGE STUFFING FOR DUCK

Duck and oranges are a well-known combination. This stuffing could be used for goose, in which case increase the quantity by half.

STUFFS 1 DUCK
2 medium-sized onions
2 celery sticks
50 g [2 oz] butter
50 g [2 oz] fresh brown
  breadcrumbs
2 lemons
3 oranges
pinch of mace
salt
freshly ground black pepper
1 large egg

Step-by-step to portioning a duck

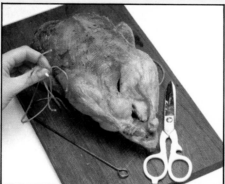

1 Place the bird on a board and remove the trussing strings. Spoon out stuffing, if stuffed.

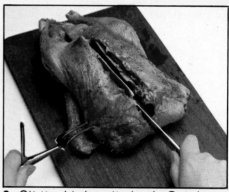

2 Sit the bird on its back. Cut down along the breastbone and through the backbone to halve the duck.

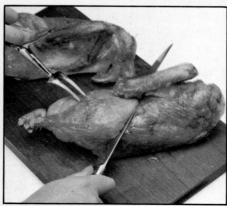

3 Lay each half flat on the board. Make a slanting cut, up over the leg, to separate leg from wing.

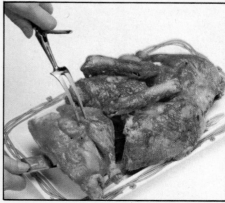

4 Tidy up any jagged bones with kitchen scissors. This gives you four portions, all with breast.

1. Skin and finely chop the onions. Scrub and chop the celery.

2. Melt the butter in a heavy-based pan over low heat. Add the onions and celery and cook for 2 minutes so that they are coated in butter but not coloured.

3. Transfer to a bowl and add the breadcrumbs. Grate the zest from the lemons and squeeze them to extract the juice. Add the zest and juice to the bowl.

4. Grate the zest and extract the juice from 1 orange. Add to the bowl.

5. Skin and divide the other oranges into segments. Chop the flesh and add to the bowl.

6. Add the spice and seasonings of salt and pepper.

7. Beat the egg separately and then mix in to bind the stuffing.

APPLE AND PRUNE STUFFING

This is the most famous of all the stuffings for goose. It can be used for duck as well, in which case reduce the quantity by about a third. For extra flavour, soak the prunes overnight in cold tea to which you have added a piece of cinnamon stick.

STUFFS 1 GOOSE
75 g [3 oz] fresh brown breadcrumbs
12 prunes, soaked
1 apple
25 g [1 oz] chopped hazelnuts
salt
freshly ground black pepper
1 lemon
15 ml [1 tablespoon] butter
1 large egg

1. Place the breadcrumbs in a bowl. Stone and chop the prunes and add to the bowl.

2. Peel, core and chop the apple. Add to the bowl with the nuts.

3. Season to taste. Squeeze the lemon and add the lemon juice.

4. Melt the butter over low heat and add to the mixture. Beat the egg separately and then use to bind the stuffing.

GOOSE WITH GARLIC STUFFING

This recipe comes from the Auvergne, an area famous for both its geese and its garlic. Although the quantity of garlic used looks frighteningly large, the resulting dish carries only a delicate aroma. In the Auvergne, geese are fed on a diet of chestnuts and fine wheat so they are plump and delicious. The goose should be taken to the table flaming and carved at the table.

SERVES 6
3.6 kg [8 lb] oven-ready goose
100 g [¼ lb] fresh brown breadcrumbs
12 stuffed green olives
1 cooking apple
24 garlic cloves
1 onion
1 lemon
1 medium-sized egg
60 ml [4 tablespoons] calvados

1. Clean the goose and prepare for stuffing as described. Set the oven to 220°C [425°F] gas mark 7.

2. Place the breadcrumbs in a bowl. Chop the olives and peel, core and chop the apple. Peel and chop the garlic cloves and the onion and add all these to the bowl.

3. Grate the zest from the lemon and squeeze to extract the juice. Add the lemon juice and zest to the bowl together with the egg. Mix well to bind.

4. Stuff the goose and complete preparation for roasting.

5. Roast the goose as described in the step-by-step instructions.

6. At the end of cooking, remove the goose to a serving dish. Warm the calvados in a ladle and pour over the breast of the goose. Flambé and take the goose to the table while the flames are still burning.

ROAST GOOSE WITH BEER AND CRANBERRY SAUCE

This is an old British recipe, traditionally served at Michaelmas when geese were given to landlords and squires as a tithe from tenants. Brown ale is best but if you cannot obtain this, use stout. Make stock with the giblets in advance.

SERVES 6
3.6 kg [8 lb] oven-ready goose
salt
freshly ground black pepper

For the stuffing:
100 g [¼ lb] fresh white breadcrumbs
150 ml [¼ pt] milk
2 celery sticks
50 g [2 oz] sultanas
50 g [2 oz] goose liver
1 small onion
15 ml [1 tablespoon] freshly chopped sage

For the sauce:
225 g [½ lb] cooking or crab apples
1 medium-sized onion
100 g [¼ lb] cranberries
150 ml [¼ pt] brown ale or stout
30 ml [2 tablespoons] brown sugar
5 ml [1 teaspoon] vinegar
30 ml [2 tablespoons] fresh brown breadcrumbs
pinch of dry English mustard
pinch of cinnamon

1. Prepare the goose for stuffing and set the oven to 220°C [425°F] gas mark 7.

2 Soak the white breadcrumbs in the milk for 15 minutes. Scrub and chop the celery sticks and add them together with the sultanas.

3 Mince and add the goose liver. Skin and chop the onion and add. Add the sage and season to taste.

4 Stuff the goose and complete preparation for roasting. Roast as described in the step-by-step instructions.

5 Meanwhile, prepare the sauce. Peel, core and chop the cooking apples or peel and core the crab apples. Skin and chop the onion and simmer with the apples and cranberries in the beer for 30 minutes until tender. Add the remaining ingredients, simmer for a further five minutes and set aside to keep warm.

6 When the goose is cooked remove the trussing and leave it in a warm place to rest. Make a giblet gravy in the same way as given for turkey on page 226.

The combination of goose, cranberries and beer produces a full-flavoured dish.

7 Carve the goose and arrange the meat on a warmed serving platter. Serve sauce and gravy separately.

ROAST DUCK WITH NUT SAUCE

Although this list of ingredients looks rather forbidding, this is not a time-consuming dish to make. Make the giblet stock before starting on the bird itself.

SERVES 4
2.2 kg [5 lb] oven-ready duck
salt
freshly ground black pepper

For the stuffing:
50 g [2 oz] fresh brown breadcrumbs
1 celery stick
1 small onion
1 orange
1 lemon
1 small egg

For the sauce:
250 ml [½ pt] duck giblet stock
2 shallots
100 g [¼ lb] walnut halves
5 ml [1 teaspoon] plain flour
half a lemon
150 ml [¼ pt] sweet sherry

2 dessert apples
1 bunch watercress
15 ml [1 tablespoon] freshly chopped parsley

1 Prepare the duck for roasting but do not truss. Heat the oven to 220°C [425°F] gas mark 7.

2 Place the breadcrumbs in a bowl. Scrub and chop the celery stick and skin and chop the onion and add. Grate the zest from the orange and lemon and squeeze the juice. Add the citrus zest and juice to the bowl. Crack the egg into the bowl and bind the mixture. Stuff the duck and complete preparation for roasting, as described.

3 Roast the duck, following the step-by-step instructions. Reserve any excess fat which is poured off.

4 When the duck is cooked, remove it to a serving platter and keep warm. Pour off the fat from the roasting tin and reserve. Add half the stock to the remaining pan juices.

5 Place 45 ml [3 tablespoons] of the reserved duck fat in a heavy-based pan. Skin and chop the shallots and add to the pan with the walnuts. Cook for 1 minute over medium heat then remove from heat and stir in the flour. Return to heat and cook for 1 minute.

6 Remove from heat again and add the remaining duck stock gradually. Return to heat and simmer for 5 minutes to thicken, stirring all the time.

7 Squeeze the juice from the half lemon. Add the sherry and lemon juice to the sauce. Pour the sauce into the roasting tin, mix with the stock and juices and simmer over low heat for 5 minutes, scraping the sediment from the bottom. Keep warm over very low heat.

8 Peel, core and slice the apples into rings. Fry for 2 minutes on each side in the remaining reserved duck fat.

9 Portion the duck and garnish with the parsley, apple rings and watercress sprigs. Spoon a little of the sauce over the apple rings and serve the rest separately.

Gamesmanship

Game birds, beautiful creatures both to look at and to eat, have a unique flavour. They are, however, not easily obtainable and are only available to cooks for a short period of the year. From the wild moors of Scotland and the peaceful lowlands of England come some of the world's best game birds, so roast game birds, described in detail here, may be considered something of a British speciality.

Game is the general term for any edible wild bird or animal which can be hunted. In the United Kingdom and many other countries most birds (with the exception of wood-pigeon and guinea fowl) are protected by law during certain times of the year so that they may breed. In the close season, as it is called, game birds may not be shot so you will never see them in a butcher's or poulterer's. As most birds come, like Christmas, but once a year, it is well worth sampling their unique flavour while the opportunity exists.

Game birds breed in the cool temperate areas of the northern hemisphere (and occasionally warmer temperate areas too), and a large selection is found in Britain. Traditionally, game birds lived a free and natural life on moorland, heath and pasture and dodged death when the sportsmen and their guns were in hot pursuit. Today, however, the rearing and shooting of game tends to be a much more controlled affair. This has become necessary in order to protect the species. Birds are now killed only under license at certain times of the year and are being bred on farms and in special hatcheries to be released during the season to keep shoots well stocked for the clients, who come from all over the world for the chance of taking a pot shot at a British game bird. Some game birds (quail and guinea fowl for instance) live all their lives on game farms and are killed in exactly the same way as chickens or other domestic fowl.

With the exception of wild ducks (see on page 230), British game birds come from the pheasant, partridge, grouse and wader families. Many are small birds and will serve one or at most two people. This means that game birds are not exactly family fare

but they do come into their own when something special is required for an intimate dinner party for perhaps four people, or for a romantic dinner for two. Although game birds are often thought of as very expensive, they are much cheaper than other luxury meats such as steak or the better cuts of veal—a good point to bear in mind when you want to put on the style without breaking the bank.

CHOOSING GAME BIRDS

The most important thing when choosing game for roasting is determining its age. With youth, comes tenderness: with age and extensive dashing around the countryside comes stringiness.

Determining age is easy when the bird is feathered, much harder when it is plucked, so for this reason it is better to buy feathered rather than oven-ready game.

Hanging is also very important as this develops the flavour of the bird. Most good poulterers (the best person to buy from) sell birds which have been hung for the correct length of time or, if you order in advance, the poulterer will hang a bird for you and prepare it for roasting.

Weight

Knowing how much to buy when you choose the bird feathered can be difficult as game birds have lush plumage which can hide a puny body. For this reason, it is wise to deduct 50 per cent from the weight of a large bird, 35 per cent from the weight of a smaller bird. Some game birds are not drawn before roasting. The list overleaf tells you which these are, and how many people each bird will serve. Generally speaking, you should allow 350–450 g [¾–1 lb] oven-ready bird per person.

Three braces of freshly killed game birds. On the left are a hen and a cock pheasant, on the right a hen and a cock capercaillie and below these a plover and grouse.

SEASONS FOR BRITISH GAME BIRDS

Black grouse	August 20th–December 20th (September 1st–December 20th in Somerset, Devon and the New Forest)
Capercaillie	As black grouse
Guinea fowl	All the year round
Partridge	September 1st–February 1st
Pheasant	October 1st–January 31st (England) October 1st–December 10th (Scotland)
Pigeon	All the year round
Plover	August 20th–December 10th
Ptarmigan	August 20th–December 10th
Quail	All the year round
Red grouse	August 12th–December 10th
Snipe	August 12th–December 20th
Woodcock	October 1st–December 20th

Grouse

Perhaps the best known of all game birds, red grouse has a subtle yet distinctive flavour of the Scottish heather on which it feeds. Red grouse is indigenous to the British Isles and has defied all attempts to transplant it elsewhere in the world.

The best Scottish grouse, perfect for roasting, are those shot in the same year in which they hatched. These young birds can be distinguished by their pointed flight feathers and soft down under the wings. The female has brownish plumage with dark bars, the male a dark back and a white breast. Both have little 'trousers' of white feathers down their legs. There is very little difference in flavour between the male and the female bird though the female tends to be a bit plumper. If you buy a brace, you will get one of each.

If the grouse is very small, allow one each. If larger, allow one between two. Grouse should be hung for seven days in summer, nine days in winter or in frosty weather.

Black grouse

The black grouse, sometimes called black cock or black game, is slightly larger than the red grouse but similar in flavour. The male is black with a lyre-shaped tail. The female is smaller than the male and is brown with darker bars. Not often seen in butchers and poulterers but the same rules as red grouse apply when choosing. Hang it for the same length of time as red grouse.

Capercaillie

Also called the cock o' the wood or wood grouse, this is the largest British grouse and has been mistaken for an airborne turkey! The male is dark grey with a long, broad tail. The female is similar to the female black grouse but is slightly larger and has a chestnut patch on its breast. Choose your birds as for red grouse. A male bird will serve two, a female one. Hang your birds as for red grouse.

Ptarmigan

Yet another member of the grouse family, the ptarmigan is rarely seen in poulterers. In winter, both male and female are all white. In summer, the upper parts are a greyish buff. Choose your birds as for grouse. A ptarmigan will serve one. Hang your birds as for red grouse.

Partridge

Partridge is the perfect introduction to eating game, as it has a more delicate flavour than many other birds. The flavour of a young partridge, fattened on stubble where they habitually feed, is not unlike that of a very superior chicken.

Both male and female birds have a greyish breast, barred wings and a chestnut coloured face. A young partridge will have pale yellow feet and fluffy down under the wings. The French draw a useful distinction between old and young partridges. The young partridge they call a perdreau, the older one a perdrix.

Perdreau become perdrix on 1st October and about three weeks after this date are better left for casseroling. A partridge will serve 1–2, depending on size. Partridge should be hung for only 3 days as prolonged hanging spoils the delicate flavour.

Pheasant

Pheasants are the most handsome of the larger game birds. The hen is small with muted brown plumage, the cock is larger with brilliant russet feathers, a long sweeping tail and a beautiful bright green head. Like partridge, pheasants feed on stubble fields and have a similar though rather stronger flavour.

A young cock pheasant will have short, rounded spurs on the legs. The flight feathers should be rounded and downy underneath. The hen is a small, plump bird. A young hen has pale feet and pale plumage. Pheasants are best in November/December. In cold weather, a phea-

sant should be hung for 10-14 days. In warm weather, 3-5 days. A pheasant will serve 3-4 depending on size.

Pigeon
Only wood-pigeons can be classified as game, although tame pigeons are also sold by some poulterers.

Like other young birds, young pigeons have downy feathers under the wings, soft, pliable legs and a supple breastbone. They may be bought ready prepared, but it is difficult to judge age unless you can feel the breastbone. Allow one bird per person. Pigeons should be hung for about two days.

Quail
Quail are the smallest of the British game birds. They are buff coloured with darker streaks. Quail are reared on game farms and are available all the year round. They are usually sold ready prepared. Because they are farm reared, you can be sure of

getting a young quail. Quail are eaten undrawn. You will need one bird per person.

Guinea fowl
Guinea fowl are also farm reared and are available all the year round. The guinea fowl can be regarded as a sort of wild turkey as it tastes rather like turkey in flavour. Once again, it is safe to buy guinea fowl oven ready. One bird will serve 2–3 people.

Snipe, woodcock, plover
Snipe is a small, long-billed bird of the wader family. It does not appeal to most tastes because it is served whole, complete with head and bill. The flesh has quite a strong flavour. Woodcock and plover are similar. You are very unlikely to see these in poulterer's shops as conservationists are urging that these birds should not be shot. Because of the limited appeal, they are perhaps, best avoided.

PREPARING GAME BIRDS FOR ROASTING
If you buy your bird from a poulterer, he will hang, pluck and draw it for you (where appropriate). If you are given a bird, most poulterers will hang it for you and prepare it for roasting for a fee.

It is essential that game birds are hung, otherwise the true game flavour does not develop. The birds are hung from 2-10 days, depending on the weather. Hanging times are given in the section on individual birds so you can tell your butcher or poulterer how long you want your bird hung for.

More game birds, easily recognizable when feathered by their distinctive plumage. The birds shown are, from left to right: a wood-pigeon, a woodcock, a snipe (with its long pointed beak), a golden plover, a partridge and a guinea fowl (identified by its speckled grey plumage).

A rich, fruity stuffing goes particularly well with roasted game. This cranberry stuffing, although shown with grouse, can be used with many other birds as well.

STUFFING

Because game birds tend to be dry, a rich stuffing which will add moisture or, at the very least, some butter is always placed in the cavity. The amount of stuffing varies from bird to bird because they are all different sizes. It is best to check with individual recipes.

Like all other stuffings, those for game birds should not be prepared until just before required. They must be allowed to cool before being put in the bird. Nor should the bird be stuffed in advance.

To stuff the bird, first prepare your stuffing. Put the stuffing into the bird through the vent end, using a large spoon to fill the cavity in large birds and a smaller spoon to fill smaller birds. The bird should be loosely filled. When all the stuffing is in place, pull down the flap of skin above the vent and close the opening with small, thin poultry skewers. The opening at the neck end should be closed in the same way. This will trap the moisture inside the bird.

As well as the stuffings given here, you can try the stuffings given for duck and goose (pages 235–236) and turkey (pages 223–224).

An alternative to stuffing is to use flavoured butter. Lemon butter and orange butter, watercress butter and maître d'hotel butter are some of the best. You will need about 50 g [2 oz] butter for smaller birds, 75 g [3 oz] for larger.

● To make orange butter, first soften the butter until light and creamy. Blend in the grated zest and juice of an orange. Form into a ball and chill before putting inside the bird. Lemon butter is made in the same way.

● For watercress butter, soften the butter as for orange butter. Select about three good sprigs of watercress. Discard yellowing leaves and tough stalks. Chop the watercress finely and combine with the butter, adding a generous squeeze of lemon juice. Chill before use.

LIVER PATE STUFFING

*The sherry added to this stuffing helps to bring out the flavour of the liver. This stuffing can also be used as a spread for toast. In the latter case, bake it in a buttered dish in a bain-marie in an oven set to 180°C [350°F] gas mark 4.*

FILLS ONE PHEASANT OR
TWO SMALL BIRDS
half an onion
50 g [2 oz] streaky bacon
15 g [½ oz] butter
150 g [5 oz] liver pâté
15 ml [1 tablespoon] sweet
    sherry or Madeira
salt
freshly ground black pepper
pinch of paprika

1 Skin the onion. Cut the rind off the bacon and mince or chop both finely.

2 Heat the butter in a small heavy-based pan. Fry the onion until soft and lightly coloured.

3 Add the bacon. Cook, stirring for a further 2 minutes. Drain off most of the fat.

4 In a bowl, cream the liver pâté with the sherry. Mix in the onion and bacon, plus the fat still remaining in the pan. Season to taste and stir in the paprika.

CREAM CHEESE STUFFING

This is a classic stuffing for pheasant. Always use full fat cream cheese to give a smooth, well-flavoured stuffing. If you do not have the bird's liver, a chicken liver may be used although the flavour will not be as good.

FILLS ONE PHEASANT OR TWO SMALLER BIRDS
half a small onion
1 pheasant or chicken liver
15 g [½ oz] butter
100 g [¼ lb] streaky bacon
15 ml [1 tablespoon] freshly
    chopped parsley
75 g [3 oz] full fat soft cheese
salt
freshly ground black pepper

1 Skin and chop the onion. Wash the liver and discard any greenish parts. Chop finely or mince.

2 Heat the butter in a small heavy-based frying-pan. Fry onion and liver until the onion is soft but not coloured. Drain off the fat. Set aside.

3 Cut the rinds off the bacon. Cut the bacon into small pieces. Put in a bowl with the parsley. Stir in the onion and liver.

4 Add the cheese to the bowl. Mix all ingredients together well and season before use.

CRANBERRY STUFFING

Fruit is a traditional favourite with game and goes especially well with the strong, heather flavour of grouse. This stuffing may also be used with capercaillie, black game and partridge or guinea fowl.

FILLS TWO GROUSE
175 g [6 oz] poached cranberries
25 g [1 oz] soft white
    breadcrumbs
15 g [½ oz] raisins
1.5 ml [¼ teaspoon] grated
    lemon zest
50 g [2 oz] butter
salt
freshly ground black pepper

1 Drain the cranberries. Mix with breadcrumbs, raisins and zest.

2 Melt the butter. Stir into other ingredients. Season to taste.

BROWN RICE STUFFING

Although wild rice is traditional with game, it is now so expensive that very few cooks can afford to use it. Brown rice provides a pleasant alternative. This stuffing is excellent with pheasant and pigeon.

FILLS TWO PHEASANTS OR SIX PIGEONS
175 g [6 oz] cooked brown rice
30 ml [2 tablespoons] finely
    chopped onion
60 ml [4 tablespoons] chopped
    celery
15 ml [1 tablespoon] chopped
    green pepper
25 g [1 oz] chopped walnuts
25 g [1 oz] butter
livers of 2 pheasants or
    chickens
5 ml [1 teaspoon] freshly
    chopped parsley
pinch of dried marjoram
freshly ground black pepper

1 Mix together the onion, celery, pepper and nuts.

2 Heat the butter in a heavy-based pan over low heat. Add the chopped vegetables and nuts and fry gently for 5 minutes.

3 Mix the contents of the pan into the rice. Chop the livers and add.

4 Stir in the parsley and marjoram. Add pepper to taste.

TRUSSING

After the bird has been stuffed, it must be trussed. Game birds may be trussed in the same way as described for chickens (see pages 208–209) with the exception of snipe and woodcock. These are skewered with their own long beaks through the back legs.

BARDING

Because game birds are naturally dry, extra fat must be added to prevent them drying out completely during roasting. The easiest way to do this is to wrap a sheet of pork fat or streaky bacon rashers, which you have stretched with the back of a knife, around the breast of the bird. Wrap the rashers around the bird, making sure they completely cover the breast and legs, then tie in place with string.

ROASTING

In order to prevent excessive drying out of the flesh, the barded game must be roasted at a high temperature. This means that cooking is fast.

Preparing the tin

To keep the bird moist and to help provide fat with which to baste during cooking, the tin in which the bird is roasted should be buttered generously. The tin should be quite a close fit round the bird—this will prevent the juices from spreading too thinly.

When the oven has reached the correct temperature (see chart), place the bird in the tin and position this in the centre of the oven. Cook for the time given on the chart, basting frequently with the pan juices or with extra melted butter if the pan juices are a bit sparse.

Frothing

About 5 minutes before the bird is ready, remove the bacon from the breast. Do not discard these crisp, pieces of bacon. They are useful for crumbling into soups or salads. Dredge the breast of the bird with flour. This will make the skin golden brown and crisp.

CARVING

Because game birds are small and often only serve one or two people, they are usually sold whole or halved. To halve a bird, simply cut down through the breastbone with a sharp

Step-by-step to roasting game birds

Bird	Temperature	Time per bird
Black grouse	220°C [425°F] gas mark 7	40 minutes
Capercaillie	as black grouse	40 minutes
Grouse	as black grouse	40 minutes
Guinea fowl	as black grouse	40 minutes
Partridge	as black grouse	25-30 minutes
Pigeon	230°C [450°F] gas mark 8	15 minutes
Plover	as black grouse	15-20 minutes
Pheasant	as black grouse	30 minutes
Ptarmigan	as black grouse	40 minutes
Quail	as black grouse	15 minutes
Snipe	as black grouse	15-20 minutes
Woodcock	as black grouse	15-20 minutes

1 Stuff the bird through the tail end with your chosen stuffing.

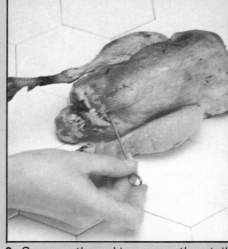

2 Secure the skin over the tail opening with a small poultry skewer.

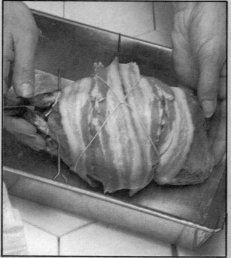

5 Butter the roasting tin generously and place the bird in it.

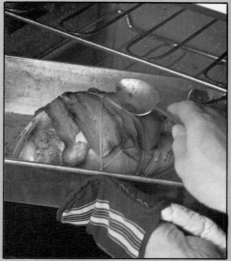

6 Cook the bird in the centre of the oven for the time given on the chart, basting often.

knife and then chop through the backbone with a cleaver or cut with poultry shears.

ACCOMPANIMENTS FOR ROASTED GAME

Fruit sauces are a traditional and delicious accompaniment to game. Cranberry is perhaps the best known but apple, gooseberry and apricot are also good. Crab-apple jelly, if available, is excellent. Bread sauce (see page 214) may also be served.

Gravy for game is traditionally thin and has a base of giblet stock (see details on page 210). There are two suitable gravies given in the recipe section.

Bread in the form of croûte or fried crumbs is a well-known accompaniment for game. A croûte is usually served with small birds, while fried crumbs are served with larger birds such as pheasant or guinea fowl.

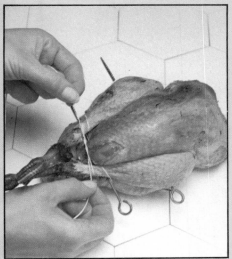

3 Truss the bird in the same way as you would truss a chicken, using small skewers.

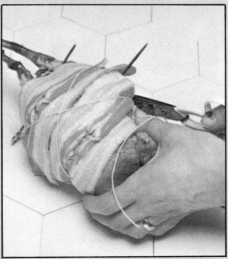

4 Tie thin sheets of pork fat or stretched streaky bacon rashers over the breast and legs.

Making a croûte

A croûte is a slice of toasted or fried white bread about 2.5 cm [1"] thick. The bird is served on top of the croûte.

To make a croûte, remove the crusts from a thick slice of bread. Toast or fry in butter until pale golden. If you are serving a croûte with a bird, remove the tin from the oven about 10 minutes before the end of roasting. Lift the bird and slip it on to a roasting rack. The croûte then goes under the rack and juices from the bird drip down on to it. If wished, the liver of the bird may be minced and spread on the croûte before it is placed under the bird.

Fried crumbs

Fried crumbs are the other popular alternative to serve with roast game. They are usually served separately. To make fried crumbs, simply fry soft, fresh white breadcrumbs in butter until golden brown.

Other accompaniments.

The traditional vegetable accompaniment for game birds is game chips. Peel and cut potatoes into very thin rounds and deep-fry in hot oil. Drain and serve sprinkled with salt.

Roast potatoes are good with all game. Other suitable vegetables are Brussels sprouts, braised celery, turnips, swede, carrots or parsnips.

Watercress is frequently used to garnish a roast bird.

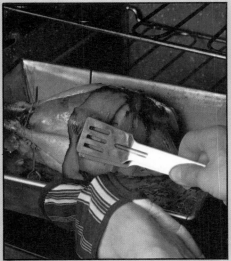

7 About 5 minutes before the bird is ready, remove the bacon from the breast.

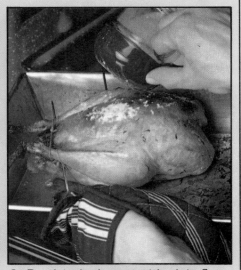

8 Dredge the breast with plain flour. Return the bird to the oven and allow breast to brown.

THIN GRAVY FOR GAME

This basic gravy makes good use of the tasty pan juices and of giblet stock. When you are making giblet stock, set the livers aside for use in making stuffings or for spreading on croûtes.

MAKES 575 ML [1 PT]
giblets of 2 game birds or
    chickens
feet of 2 game birds or
    chickens (optional)
1 carrot
1 onion
bouquet garni
salt
freshly ground black pepper
2.5 ml [½ teaspoon] plain
    flour

1 Wash the giblets. Scald the feet for 4 minutes in boiling water.

2 Put feet and giblets into a large saucepan. Scrub and slice the carrot. Skin and chop the onion and add both to the pan.

3 Just cover the ingredients with cold water and bring to the boil. Skim. Add bouquet garni and seasoning and simmer for 40 minutes.

4 Strain the stock. There should be about 700 ml [1¼ pt]. Remove the bird from the roasting tin and pour off the fat, leaving juices and sediment behind.

5 Sprinkle the flour into the tin. Stir into the sediment. Place over low heat and cook gently for 2–3 minutes, scraping the sediment from the bottom of the tin.

6 Remove from the heat and gradually stir in the giblet stock. Place over high heat and boil for 2–3 minutes. Season to taste if wished. Strain and serve.

RICH GRAVY FOR GAME

This very rich gravy makes game into a really special dish. It can very well be made in bulk and frozen if wished. It will keep for 3 months.

MAKES 275 ML [½ PT]
450 g [1 lb] game or chicken
    giblets
225 g [½ lb] shin of beef
1 medium-sized onion

1 small carrot
15 g [½ oz] beef dripping
150 ml [¼ pt] beef stock
bouquet garni
salt
freshly ground black pepper

1 Wash the giblets and set the livers aside for other use.

2 Blanch the giblets for 2 minutes in boiling water. Drain and rinse under cold water. Pat dry.

3 Cut the giblets and shin of beef into small pieces. Place in a heavy-based saucepan.

4 Skin and slice the onion. Scrub and chop the carrot. Add to pan.

5 Add the dripping to the pan. Melt slowly over low heat, turning the meat and vegetables so that they are coated in fat. Cook for about 5 minutes, until the onion is soft but not coloured.

6 Add the stock. Cook, stirring from time to time for about 15 minutes until the liquid has almost reduced to a glaze.

7 Pour in 700 ml [1¼ pt] cold water. Add the bouquet garni. Stir. Bring to the boil then reduce heat so that the liquid is just simmering. Half cover the pan.

8 Simmer for 40 minutes until well reduced. Season to taste with salt and pepper.

9 Strain into a bowl and leave until cold. Lift off the fat. Heat before serving until throughly warmed through.

GROUSE WITH APPLE AND RASPBERRIES

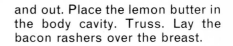*The tart flavours of apples and raspberries provide an excellent contrast to the heathery tang of grouse. Frozen raspberries are fine for this dish but not canned ones as they are too sweet. Make lemon butter as shown on page 242.*

SERVES 2
1 grouse weighing about 900 g [2 lb]
salt
freshly ground black pepper
25 g [1 oz] lemon butter
2 rashers streaky bacon
25 g [1 oz] butter
2 crisp dessert apples
100 g [¼ lb] frozen raspberries
15 ml [1 tablespoon] caster sugar
15 ml [1 tablespoon] melted butter
25 g [1 oz] plain flour
275 ml [½ pt] giblet stock

1 Wipe the grouse. Season inside and out. Place the lemon butter in the body cavity. Truss. Lay the bacon rashers over the breast.

2 Heat the oven to 220°C [425°F] gas mark 7. Butter a roasting tin.

3 Place the grouse in the tin. Cook in the centre of the oven for 40 minutes.

4 Peel and core the apples. Cut into thick slices. Toss raspberries in sugar and leave to thaw.

5 Place the apples in a baking tin. Pour the melted butter over them. About 20 minutes before the grouse will be ready, place the apples in the bottom of the oven.

6 Five minutes before the end of cooking, remove the bacon from the birds. Dredge with half of the flour and leave to brown.

7 Remove bird from the oven. Make gravy using pan juices, giblet stock and remaining flour.

8 Arrange the apple slices around the bird. Spoon on raspberries.

ROAST BRANDIED GUINEA FOWL

Guinea fowl is milder in flavour than other game birds because it is farm bred. The addition of brandy gives it the extra flavour needed. Serve it with buttered crumbs, watercress and apple sauce.

SERVES 4
2 guinea fowl weighing about 900 g [2 lb] each
salt and pepper
25 g [1 oz] chilled butter
2 streaky bacon rashers
25 g [1 oz] softened butter
275 ml [½ pt] giblet stock
30 ml [2 tablespoons] crushed juniper berries
30 ml [2 tablespoons] brandy
15 g [½ oz] plain flour

1 Wipe the birds. Season inside and out with salt and pepper. Put half the chilled butter inside each bird. Truss. Place bacon over the breasts.

2 Set the oven to 220°C [425°F] gas mark 7. Use the softened butter to grease the roasting tin.

247

3 Pour half the stock into the roasting tin. Place the birds in the tin. Roast for 10 minutes.

4 Add the crushed juniper berries, scattering them over the birds. Baste the birds with the stock.

5 Roast the birds for the time given in the roasting chart, basting frequently. Remove the bacon 5 minutes before the end of cooking.

6 When the birds are ready, warm the brandy. Pour over the birds and set alight.

7 When the flames have died down, remove the birds from the tin to a heated serving dish.

8 Make the gravy using the remaining stock, flour and pan juices as given in thin gravy for game birds (see page 246).

TRADITIONAL ROAST PHEASANT WITH GRAPES

◻◻*It is traditional to garnish a pheasant with its own tail feathers just before bringing it to the table. Obviously if you do this, you cannot portion the bird in the kitchen. In this recipe, the breast of the bird is buttered to make it extra rich.*

SERVES 2–3
pheasant weighing about 1.15 kg [2½ lb]
175 g [6 oz] white grapes
5 ml [1 teaspoon] grated lemon zest
salt
freshly ground black pepper
15 g [½ oz] softened butter
1 large rasher streaky bacon
425 ml [¾ pt] cold giblet stock
15 g [½ oz] plain flour

For the garnish:
fried breadcrumbs

1 Skin, halve and de-seed the grapes. Mix with the grated lemon zest. Set the oven to 220°C [425°F] gas mark 7.

2 Sprinkle the pheasant inside and out with salt and freshly ground black pepper.

3 Fill the pheasant with grapes, reserving any surplus for garnish.

4 Truss the pheasant as shown in step-by-step to roasting game birds. Cover the breast with butter. Tie the bacon rasher over the breast. Place in a roasting tin.

5 Pour all but 150 ml [¼ pt] of the cold stock over the pheasant.

6 Put the roasting tin in the centre of the oven. Roast for 30 minutes, basting frequently.

7 Five minutes before the end of cooking, remove the bacon and dredge the flour over the bird. Allow to brown.

8 Place the bird on a heated serving dish. Make the gravy as given for thin gravy, using the remaining stock and the sediment from the pan.

9 To garnish the bird, tie the quill ends of the feathers with fine thread. Insert a small poultry skewer into the bundle. Stick the skewer into the bird where the tail feathers should be so that they stick up.

ROAST PARTRIDGES WITH JUNIPER STUFFING

◻*The delicate flesh of these small birds is delicious combined with juniper, which is the classic spice for game. If you select very small birds, you can serve one per person. This always looks more attractive than portions, however neatly carved.*

Because there is stock in the pan there is no need to butter it to keep the birds moist.

SERVES 4
4 young partridges about 275 g [10 oz] each
4 streaky bacon rashers
50 g [2 oz] melted butter
350 ml [12 fl oz] giblet stock
25 g [1 oz] plain flour
salt
freshly ground black pepper

For the stuffing:
6 juniper berries
40 g [1½ oz] white bread
50 g [2 oz] cooked ham
1 medium-sized onion, skinned
5 ml [1 teaspoon] grated orange zest
pinch of marjoram

50 g [2 oz] melted butter
1 large egg
salt
freshly ground black pepper

For the croûtes:
4 slices white bread at least 2.5 cm [1"] thick
50 g [2 oz] butter
livers of the birds

1 Heat the oven to 220°C [425°F] gas mark 7.

2 Make the stuffing first. Crush the juniper berries. Mince together the bread, ham and onion.

3 Mix the minced ingredients with other stuffing ingredients, blending thoroughly.

4 Stuff and truss the birds. Lay the bacon rashers over the breasts.

5 Put the birds in a roasting tin. Trickle melted butter over them then pour over three-quarters of the stock.

6 Roast in the centre of the oven for 20 minutes, basting frequently with the stock.

7 When you have put the birds in the oven, start preparing the croûtes. Melt the butter in a heavy-based frying-pan. Cut the crusts off the bread and fry until golden.

8 Mince the livers and spread over the slices of fried bread.

9 Ten minutes before the end of roasting, raise the birds on to a roasting rack. Place the croûtes underneath.

10 Five minutes before the end of roasting, remove bacon and dredge the birds with some of the flour.

11 When the birds are cooked, place each on a croûte on a heated serving dish.

12 Use remaining giblet stock and flour to make thin gravy as given in thin gravy for game birds. Season to taste before serving.

A traditional roast pheasant and, in the background, a plate of stuffed partridges.

Flavour of the wild

Game was man's first meat and although we no longer depend on it for survival, it can make a delicious change to the farmed meat to which we have become accustomed. Cooks in castles and cottages have, throughout the ages, developed dishes of excellence which make good use of a source of meat still plentiful in season but often neglected.

Game is a meat that tends to be ignored, thanks to the swift transport and freezing that has made farmed meat so easy to obtain. Not only is this a waste of a natural source of food that has served man for many centuries, but the meat has a distinctive flavour which, with a little careful preparation, can be brought out to the full by roasting, braising, casseroling or stewing. Any leftovers can be used to make pies and pâtés and the bonier parts used for soups and stock.

Explained here are techniques of roasting game. The stages of preparation which can be easily carried out at home are the marinating, stuffing, trussing and barding. The preliminary stages of preparation, that is hanging, paunching and skinning may be done at home, but will also be done by a kindly butcher, on request, if you buy a whole, unprepared animal. Many are available which have been completely prepared before sale.

TYPES OF GAME ANIMAL

The types of game animal most commonly found and cooked are rabbit, hare and venison. Several other animals such as hedgehog, squirrel and boar, are eaten as game meat on the European continent and in other parts of the world, and bear and beaver are eaten in the colder parts of North America and in Canada.

Rabbit

There are two types of rabbit, wild and tame (farmed), both available from suppliers of game. The meat of each is quite different.

Wild rabbit has been popular with cooks throughout history, proof that the meat makes better eating than it is now given credit for. The flesh is dark with a noticeable game flavour, which is affected by its diet. A rabbit that has fed in a cornfield will be particularly plump and well flavoured.

Tame rabbits (so-called) are now farmed in quantity, both for their pelts and their meat. They have white flesh, are a good deal larger than wild rabbits and are more expensive.

Hare

Hare is found all over the world and has been associated with folk tales since ancient times. The Romans maintained that eating hare made one beautiful! In most parts of Europe and the Far East, hare is valued as a luxury meat. The British are almost alone in treating it as fit only for everyday eating. It is in season from the beginning of August to the end of February in the northern hemisphere.

There are two types of hare. The larger, and the tastier, is the lowland brown hare of central and southern Europe, introduced into Australasia. The second type is the Scottish blue hare, which may be the same creature as the Arctic hare found in North America. Other types of American hare are known as snow-shoe and jack rabbits.

The flesh of hare becomes darker the older the animal is. A young hare, with lighter coloured and less game flavoured flesh, is called a leveret.

Venison

In days gone by, any wild animal used for food was called venison; in English-speaking countries the term is now only used for the flesh of deer and similar animals, such as the reindeer, moose, elk, buck and caribou.

Three types of deer are commonly found in Great Britain: red deer, roe deer and fallow deer. The three varieties are treated for cooking in the same way.

The red deer is the most noble British game animal but the meat of fallow deer is held by gourmets to have the finest flavour. Roe deer meat is whiter in colour and less game flavoured. Buck meat is considered to be better than that of the doe (the female). As with game birds, venison has a close season, when the animals may not be shot. Fresh venison is available in the northern hemisphere from June–September (bucks) and October–December (does). The animals are at their best for eating between 18 months and 3 years old.

CHOOSING AND BUYING GAME ANIMALS

Although deer, rabbits and hares are shot in the wild, most people have to buy their game meat. If you buy a joint, the animal will have already been paunched (that is, the innards removed) and skinned and the meat hung. A whole rabbit will have been paunched and hung but may still be in its skin. A hare will have been hung but will not necessarily have been skinned and paunched. Although

these tasks are not difficult, they are not appealing to everyone, are time consuming and take some care and attention. The butcher from whom you purchase the game will skin and paunch the animal for you.

It is most important though to be able to assess what you are buying, at whatever stage of preparation it has reached. You also need to know the further treatment which may be necessary before cooking, which differs with the age of the animal and its condition.

Rabbits, wild and farmed

Rabbits can be bought whole or jointed. If you are roasting, which is the subject of this course, you will need to buy a whole animal. Wild and farmed rabbits can be bought already prepared, that is paunched, hung and skinned, or simply paunched and hung, but not skinned.

If you buy the wholly prepared rabbit, the hints as to age and condition, which are obvious in an animal still in its skin, will not be here. Look for plump flesh, plenty of fat around the kidneys and a bright red liver. These giblets will be left in the carcass with the heart, as with a chicken.

Wild rabbits, still in their skins and hanging by their hind legs, are a common sight in the window of a game butcher. If you buy one of these animals you will be better able to judge its age and condition. Look for a pliable lower jaw, small, even white teeth, a narrow lip cleft and thin soft ears which would tear easily. The feet should be flexible with smooth, sharp claws and the pads underneath well developed. All these are signs of a young rabbit. A rabbit with thick haunches, rough blunt claws and dry ears is probably too old for anything but stew or stock.

A wild rabbit is a fairly small animal, the average weight after preparation for cooking being 1 kg [2¼ lb] which will serve 4–5 people. Its handling and cooking is like that of a young hare. The average weight of a farmed rabbit after preparation is about 1.4 kg [3 lb] serving 4–6 people and the big Ostend type is even larger and may weigh up to 2.9 kg [6½ lb]. Farmed rabbits, although their meat is less delicate than that of chicken, are handled and can be cooked in most of the ways suitable for chicken.

Joints of both wild and farmed rabbits are sold fresh and frozen. Fresh saddle and hindquarter joints, with their fleshier meat, may be more expensive than the bonier forequarter joints. You can buy a joint for each member of the family, as you would chicken joints.

Frozen rabbit is quite widely available; most of it is imported, farmed rabbit, pale pink in colour. You can buy frozen rabbit not only as joints, but also in blocks of boneless rabbit meat. This frozen boneless meat seems solid when you buy it still frozen, but do not expect to be able to cook it 'in the piece' like a frozen fish steak. It breaks up into small pieces when thawed.

Frozen rabbit needs some care in preparation and cooking; otherwise it can be tasteless and tough. The boneless meat in particular is better used for making stews and casseroles.

Hares

Like all game, hares make better eating when young. A hare is at its best for the table between 3–6 months old, although a female (doe) may still be tender at 18 months.

Hares are sold like rabbits, whole and unprepared, whole and completely prepared or in joints. A hare is

hung to tenderize it before its head, feet and fur are removed and before it is paunched. Many game butchers then sell the animals as they are, and will prepare the animal as requested. This is the best buy as you can really see what you are getting. The following signs will help you to choose well, if you are buying a whole, unprepared hare.

A young hare can be identified by its short stumpy neck, long slender joints, smooth sharp claws hidden by fur and its small white teeth; its coat is smooth, its ears soft and its lip cleft narrow. As the animal ages, its claws project and become rounded and rough, the lip cleft widens, its teeth become long, irregular and yellow and its coat coarsens. Grey flecks appear in the coat, white hairs appear around the animal's muzzle and its ears become dry and tough.

Hares that are sold unskinned are generally sold at a fixed price, regardless of weight. The animal will lose up to 40 per cent of its weight by the time it is ready for cooking. The lowland brown hare will weigh about 2.2–4 kg [5–9 lb] when prepared and the smaller Scottish blue, 1.4–2.7 kg [3–6 lb]. A whole brown hare, stuffed will serve 8–10 people and a Scottish blue or a leveret, 5–6 people.

If you buy a hare already skinned it may be whole or in joints. A good reason for buying the whole animal is that the liver, heart and kidneys are left in place when the animal is paunched. These are valuable for making rich stock, or can be used in a grilled supper dish. Another very good reason for buying the whole animal is the blood. The blood collects in a membrane under the ribs while the animal is hanging and makes a rich thickening for the gravy, or a sauce. You can ask the butcher to partially joint the animal for you at purchase. As well as asking for the blood (which will come sealed in a separate bag and will not be poured in on top of the joints) also ask for the head and trimmings. You will have paid for these and be entitled to them. You can then use the body, in a piece, for roasting and use the other joints in a stew.

If you buy joints of hare you are obviously not entitled to the trimmings and the blood. The saddle and the hindquarters (the rabble) are the best parts of the animal for roasting and are roasted in the piece. The forelegs, or wings as they are called,

are best made into a civet (hare stew), although in a young leveret may be tender enough to be roasted. The flesh of the animal gets darker with age and in an old animal may be almost purple.

Venison

Venison is sold already hung, skinned and jointed. It is very important, for tenderness and flavour, that venison is properly hung and then marinated before cooking, or it will be flavourless, dry and tough. If you buy from a game butcher who buys his meat privately, he will willingly tell you how long it has been hung and its probable degree of game flavour. He will tell you how long you should marinate it before cooking to complete the tenderizing and flavouring process. The meat of a fawn, up to about 18 months old, is more tender but the game flavour is virtually undetectable. However, if you buy from a large store you will have to choose the meat just by its appearance. Stewing meat is usually sold chopped into small pieces and can also be bought frozen. Take no chances when buying a roasting joint. Even if it is sold as ready for roasting, it is always wise to marinate it, as shown here, before cooking it.

The flesh of venison should be dark, fine-grained, with thick, firm, clear white fat. The best joints are, in order, the haunch, the saddle, the loin and the shoulder. The remaining joints should not be roasted but used for stewing. If possible, choose a joint not damaged by shot, because torn or ragged meat deteriorates quickly.

A haunch is the classic roasting joint but will probably be too large for the average family. Part of the loin is a good buy; have some of it cut into chops. When buying, calculate the weight required by allowing 175–200 g [7–8 oz] per serving.

STORAGE

Do not try to store newly-killed game or fresh game bought from a shop. The only game that can be stored successfully is the rabbit and venison bought frozen. The meat can be stored for up to 6 months.

Fresh game from a game butcher, market or shop which has been bought already hung, paunched and skinned, should be put into a marinade immediately. The outer flesh on

Rabble of hare—a succulent dish of roasted meat served with a creamy sauce.

all the animals will harden otherwise and will dry out. Hare, with its valuable blood can be particularly messy and must be dealt with immediately.

Frozen rabbit or venison should be thawed slowly in the refrigerator taking between 12–24 hours. Once defrosted, venison should be put into a marinade straight away; rabbit should be soaked and then marinated.

Cooked game, although it can be used in other dishes, is not worth storing. The meat does not keep well and becomes dry and stringy. The best use for leftovers is to make them, fairly promptly, into one of the excellent traditional pâtés to which game lends its flavour so well.

PREPARING GAME ANIMALS FOR ROASTING

The meat of game animals, particularly venison, tends to be dry and for this reason is greatly improved by being marinated before being cooked. This is not necessary for farmed rabbit but is very important if venison or wild rabbit is to be roasted. The meat must be protected from the dry heat of the oven and the marinating,

barding and frequent basting all help to do this.

In addition to marinating, rabbits, both wild and farmed, must be rinsed and soaked as soon as possible after skinning. This neutralizes any very strong flavour and lightens the colour of the flesh.

The first thing to do with a hare is to carefully transfer the blood into a bowl. The blood will most likely have been sealed in a plastic bag by the butcher. If not, and it is still inside the animal, puncture the membrane under the ribs which encloses the blood and drain it into a bowl.

Once the game has been marinated, rabbits and hares can be stuffed and trussed ready for cooking. Venison is not stuffed but must be trimmed of fat and all the joints must be well barded.

Soaking a rabbit

As soon as you get the skinned rabbit home, remove the giblets and rinse the animal several times in lightly salted water. Then fill a bowl with clean salted water and leave the rabbit to soak, completely immersed, for at least 30 minutes. Pat the rabbit dry after removing it from the water and then marinate it.

Marinating game animals

All game meat is improved by a period of marinating before cooking as this continues the tenderizing process which has been started by the hanging, and adds moisture to the meat. For venison, marinating is an essential part of the preparation for roasting.

The most usual marinade used is one made with red wine, which has been cooked. Basic marinade including wine and vinegar is adapted by replacing the vinegar with extra wine and it can be made with red or white wine. The marinade must be cooked before use if it is to be used for longer than 24 hours. The marinade should include 15–30 ml [1–2 tablespoons] wine vinegar, the only concession to a great size being an increase in the quantity of vinegar used. Use a non-corrosive vessel and one that is large enough to allow the meat to be turned in the marinade, from time to time.

Wild rabbit: if it is young and has been soaked properly it may not necessarily need marinating. However, as marinating can only

253

improve the meat, it is worth the very small amount of work. Put a young animal to soak in red wine to which you have added 15 ml [1 tablespoon] vinegar, or in white wine with 15 ml [1 tablespoon] lemon juice, according to your recipe. For example, do not soak the animal in red wine if white wine is used during cooking, and vice versa.

An older, probably more tough, animal and frozen rabbit meat which can be rather flavourless can be marinated with a marinade made up of wine as suggested above and made with white wine and used uncooked. Marinate the animal for 2 hours and this will greatly improve the flavour of a frozen rabbit and the quality of a tougher animal.

Hare: a hare should, like venison, always be marinated before cooking to ensure tenderness and flavour. Use a recipe, suitably adapted making it with red wine. Cook the marinade before soaking the animal and use 20 ml [4 teaspoons] vinegar Leave the animal to marinate for 12 hours, or longer if the hare is rather old and stringy.

A young hare (leveret) does not need to be soaked in a liquid marinade. Sprinkle the animal with dried herbs, selecting them to complement those used in the recipe for cooking. Then sprinkle the animal with 75 ml [3 fl oz] oil and equal quantities (30·ml [2 tablespoons]) water with either vinegar, red wine, white wine or brandy. Leave the leveret to absorb the flavours for 3–4 hours.

Venison: even the better joints of venison which are used for roasting must always be marinated before cooking. Correct hanging is also essential for tenderness and flavour and although your meat will already have been hung by your supplier, this may not have been sufficient for your liking. Marinating is a continuation of the hanging process and the longer the meat is marinated the stronger the game flavour and the more tender the meat. A marinade also prevents the meat from deteriorating.

Cover the venison with a cooked, red wine marinade following a suitable recipe which is adapted, using 30 ml [2 tablespoons] vinegar. Leave the joint to soak for 24–48 hours, turning from time to time. After 24 hours the meat will be tender and the longer that it is left after this, the greater the game flavour will be. It is perfectly

safe to leave the meat for a further 24 hours (72 hours in total) if you wish a really distinctive game flavour.

Stuffing

Hare and rabbit can be roasted with or without stuffing. If not stuffed, the stuffing mixture can be shaped into balls and served as an accompaniment. Several stuffings are used with hare and rabbit: those used with chicken (see page 208) and for game birds (see page 242). The stuffings often contain fat meat or fruit to enrich and flavour the rather dry meat.

The animals are stuffed in the body cavity created by paunching. Spoon the stuffing into the cavity until it is full but not packed too tightly. Then draw the edges of the cavity together and sew up with strong thread (not nylon or plastic coated). Leave a long end to the thread so that it can be pulled out after cooking, without touching the hot meat.

You will need about 175 g [6 oz] stuffing for a rabbit to serve four people. A hare, which will serve six, will take about 350 g [¾ lb] stuffing.

Venison is not stuffed. The joints are large and the meat solid so extra bulk is unnecessary. Nor does the savoury flesh require the extra flavour that stuffing provides.

Trussing and barding

Game animals can be roasted in joints or whole. When roasted whole, stuffed or unstuffed, they need to be trussed in order to hold their shape.

Rabbit and hare: a whole rabbit or a hare is trussed in the same way, except for the head, and the process is very straightforward.

In both animals, the forelegs are pulled backwards along the side of the body. The hind legs are then pulled forward which necessitates cutting through the sinew in the thigh. The legs should overlap slightly and can be held in place by a poultry skewer. This is all that is necessary with an animal that is served without its head.

If you are trussing an animal with the head in place, there are two methods of securing it. One is to turn the head sideways and twist it so that it can be skewered to the breast or shoulder. Alternatively, with a young hare that is being trussed in the traditional style, the head is held

upright. Push a poultry skewer down through the lower jaw and into the front of the neck. Then tie a string to the leg skewer on one side of the animal, pass it through the skewer in the jaw and tie off at the leg skewer on the other side. This will hold the head securely in place.

A hare can also be roasted with the forequarters removed. This makes a good-sized roast for six people and the rest of the hare is used for another dish. The forequarters are cut off just behind the shoulder and the saddle, haunches and hind legs are roasted in a piece.

The backbone of a hare is very tough and if you are removing the forequarters you will need a very sharp heavy knife or a pair of poultry shears in order to cut through the backbone. The forequarters can be kept and used for a stew or stock. The hind legs are trussed in the same way as with a whole animal and are secured to the side of the animal with poultry skewers.

Rabbits and hares need to be well barded before being put in the oven. Use plenty of fat bacon and lay the rashers over the animal to cover the body. If the head is still in place, cover this with several layers of greased foil and do the same with the legs if the bacon does not cover them completely.

Venison: joints of venison should be trimmed, and then barded or covered with foil before being roasted. Trim any ragged ends from the meat and all fibres and fat. The taste of deer fat is unpleasant and affects the flavour of the meat. The meat is, however, dry so the lack of fat must be compensated for by generous barding. Use plenty of fat bacon laid across the whole joint or cover the surface of the joint with softened fat and lay a double thickness of foil over the top. If a haunch joint still has the hind leg attached, wrap the latter in several layers of greased foil.

This generous barding or the fat and foil covering, combined with frequent basting will keep the joint moist during cooking.

ROASTING GAME ANIMALS

The most important point to remember when roasting rabbit, hare and venison is that the meat must be kept moist throughout cooking. The meat must be well barded or protected with foil before being put in the oven.

Roasting rabbit and hare

Wild rabbit and hare are roasted in exactly the same way, for the same length of time, despite their difference in size. A farmed rabbit should be trussed and barded like a wild rabbit and then roasted in the same way as a chicken (see pages 210–211).

Sit the prepared hare or rabbit on a roasting rack. Place it in a roasting tin with any fat or liquid that your recipe includes. Roast the animal at 220°C [425°F] gas mark 7 for 10–15 minutes. Reduce the oven temperature to 180°C [350°F] gas mark 4 and continue roasting the animal for a further 35–40 minutes. Baste the meat frequently and generously and after 30 minutes total cooking, remove the barding bacon or foil to allow the meat to brown. Continue basting the meat frequently. Test the meat to see if it is cooked after 40 minutes. Push a thin skewer into the thickest part of the haunch above the thigh, and if it comes out clean and no blood seeps from the flesh, the meat is cooked.

If you are roasting only the saddle and haunches of a hare, it will still take the same time to cook as a whole animal. Roast it at the same temperature, basting frequently and test for readiness after 40 minutes.

Roasting venison

Venison is the driest of all game animals and must be very thoroughly barded and protected from the dry heat of the oven. Venison can be fast or slow roasted but the fast roasting method can only be recommended for properly hung, tender animals, when the results will be excellent. If you do not know for certain for how long the animal was hung or have any doubts about its quality, it is better to slow roast the meat.

If you are fast roasting, set the oven to 220°C [425°F] gas mark 7 and roast your joint for 12–15 minutes per 450 g [1 lb]. Roast it on a rack in a roasting tin and baste generously throughout cooking. Remove the barding or foil 15 minutes from the end of cooking and allow the surface to brown. Continue basting while browning.

The slow roasting method is obviously a rather lengthy process but it will ensure that the meat is tender and juicy when cooked. Roast the meat for 40 minutes per 450 g [1 lb] at 160°C [325°F] gas mark 3. Baste the meat frequently and remove the barding or foil about 20 minutes before the end of the calculated cooking time to allow the surface to brown. This final browning can be increased by dredging the joint with plain flour before returning it to the oven. The flour will 'froth' and brown.

CARVING GAME ANIMALS

Game meat cools quickly, particularly venison, and the flavour of the meat is affected. The joint, or animal should not, therefore, be rested in the normal way but served immediately.

Venison can be carved in exactly the same way as a similar type of joint of lamb or mutton. Venison meat is close knit and will carve thinly even without the 'resting' period.

Both hare and rabbit are awkward to carve and jointing is the most efficient and satisfactory way of portioning the meat. This can be done in the kitchen or at table, although if done behind the scenes it allows you to keep the portioned meat hot while dealing with the rest. If dealing with a hare, have a pair of poultry shears handy to deal with the very tough backbone. If the animal was roasted with a stuffing, remove this by pulling out the thread by the long end and spooning out the stuffing. Serve it on a separate dish if serving from the kitchen, or in spoonfuls with each portion of meat at table.

First, cut the forequarters, with the legs attached, from the rest of the animal cutting through just behind the shoulders. With a rabbit, simply divide in half, but with a hare, cut the

legs from the forequarters, cutting round the shoulder joint and taking some of the flesh with the leg. This gives you two leg portions and a forequarter portion.

You are now left with the saddle and the haunches with the hind legs attached. In a rabbit, this is three or four portions. Cut the saddle from the haunches and cut the haunches in two, down the middle. For four portions, cut the saddle in half. A hare, being larger, is divided into six portions. The saddle is divided in half to make two, then the hind legs are detached from the haunches, at the joint (two portions), and the haunches are cut in half with poultry shears (two portions).

TRADITIONAL ACCOMPANIMENTS

Prepare your accompaniments for roasted game either before cooking or while the meat is roasting. It is important to serve the meat, especially venison, while still really hot and juicy.

Roasted meat is always served with gravy or some variety of moistening sauce. Both rabbit and venison are served with an unthickened gravy in the same way as a traditional turkey (see page 226), but not so hare. Hare is traditionally served with a thick gravy which is made by adding the blood of the hare. This is why it is important to ask the butcher for the blood when buying the animal.

Thick or thin gravy is, however, a matter of personal taste and gravy can always be thickened, as when you serve a gravy with lamb. If you wish to serve something rather more adventurous than gravy with your meat, try a fruit sauce. Oranges and redcurrants in particular, go well with game, but any sweet-sour or tart fruit can be used for a sauce.

If you serve gravy with the meat, provide a bowl of redcurrant or any other sharp fruit-flavoured jelly as well.

If hare or rabbit is roasted without stuffing, the stuffing mixture can be shaped into balls, fried briefly and then cooked with the meat for the last 30 minutes of roasting.

Bacon rolls can be served with hare and rabbit. Also delicious are onions roasted with hare during cooking. Roast potatoes are a traditional accompaniment to all roast meat as are green vegetables or a salad.

FORCEMEAT STUFFING

Old in history, but reliable and tasty, this recipe comes from a cookery book of 1860. Use it either to stuff your hare, or to make into forcemeat balls. Fry the balls in lard until lightly browned on all sides or put in the roasting tin with the animal for the last 30 minutes of cooking. Baste well.

FOR A MEDIUM-SIZED HARE OR TWO RABBITS
50 g [2 oz] lean rindless bacon or cooked ham
100 g [¼ lb] shredded suet
grated rind of half a lemon
5 ml [1 teaspoon] freshly chopped parsley
5 ml [1 teaspoon] freshly chopped mixed herbs or 2.5 ml [½ teaspoon] dried mixed herbs
salt
small pinch of cayenne pepper
pinch of ground mace
175 g [6 oz] soft white breadcrumbs
3 medium-sized eggs

1 Cut the bacon or ham into small pieces and shred or mince.

2 Put the bacon or ham, suet, grated lemon rind, parsley, herbs, salt, pepper and mace in a bowl.

3 Mix thoroughly with a fork, breaking up any lumps of suet.

4 Stir in the breadcrumbs. Make sure all the ingredients are evenly mixed.

5 Beat the eggs lightly in a small bowl. Mix them into the dry forcemeat gradually. Use enough egg to make a light firm mixture which you can roll into balls. It should not be sloppy.

THICKENED GRAVY FOR HARE

The gravy that is traditionally served with hare is thickened with beurre manié, the hare's liver and the blood. Use the other innards to make a stock (see page 210) and this will form the basis of your gravy. Use as much or as little of the hare's blood as you wish, but do not use more blood than stock. If you use less blood or find the resulting flavour, having used 425 ml [¾ pt], too strong, add some extra stock.

SERVES 8–10
425 ml [¾ pt] giblet stock
50 g [2 oz] butter
1 hare's liver
40 g [1½ oz] plain flour
425 ml [¾ pt] hare's blood

1 Skim any fat from the surface of the cold strained stock. Put it to heat while the meat is still cooking.

2 When the meat is cooked, remove it and the rack from the roasting tin and keep hot. Pour the fat from the tin and put over a low heat.

3 Pour the hot stock into the tin, stirring and scraping any sediment from the bottom of the tin. Set aside.

4 Melt 15 g [½ oz] butter in a small frying-pan. Fry the liver gently over low heat, turning once, for a few minutes. It should be brown outside but still pink in the middle.

5 Tip the contents of the frying-pan into a bowl and mash the liver. Then pound it until smooth.

6 Bring the giblet stock in the roasting tin to the boil. While doing this use the remaining butter and the flour to make a beurre manié. Add this, in small pieces and over low heat, to the boiling stock. Stir to thicken and remove from the heat.

7 Stir in the pounded liver and as much blood as you wish. Heat gently without boiling and serve in a heated sauce-boat.

ROAST VENISON WITH APPLES

Young venison is so good for its price that it is well worth the treat of a roasted joint. The venison must be from either the saddle or the haunch and should be marinated before cooking. If you have no port, use the end of a bottle of medium-sweet red wine to make the gravy. Make the stock from a cube. Garnish with watercress.

SERVES 4

1 kg [2¼ lb] venison
45 ml [3 tablespoons] soft beef
   dripping
4 small cooking apples or
   Cox's orange pippins
juice of a lemon
15 g [½ oz] butter
45 ml [3 tablespoons]
   redcurrant jelly
10 ml [2 teaspoons] caster
   sugar
1 clove
175 ml [6 fl oz] beef stock
5 ml [1 teaspoon] salt
2.5 ml [½ teaspoon] freshly
   ground black pepper
2.5 ml [½ teaspoon] ground
   cinnamon
10 ml [2 teaspoons] cornflour
75 ml [3 fl oz] port

1 Heat the oven to 170°C [325°F] gas mark 3. Trim any ragged ends of the meat. Brush the meat all over with soft dripping and cover with a double thickness of foil.

2 Place the meat on a rack in a roasting tin and put in the oven. Baste about every 10 minutes while roasting, replacing the foil each time.

3 Prepare the apples. Peel and core them but keep them whole. Mix the lemon juice with 175 ml [6 fl oz] water and bring it to simmering point in a saucepan.

4 Put in the apples, and simmer very gently for 5 minutes. They should be tender outside but not broken. Drain and cool them.

5 Work the butter until soft with the back of a spoon. Work in 15 ml [1 tablespoon] jelly. Fill the mixture into the core holes in the apples. Top them with the sugar.

6 When the meat has been cooking for about 55 minutes, arrange the apples on the roasting rack beside the meat. Return to the oven and continue cooking.

7 For the final 20 minutes of cooking, remove the foil to allow the meat to brown. Baste well.

8 Crush the clove. Put the stock into a small saucepan. Scatter in the crushed clove. Add the remaining 30 ml [2 tablespoons] jelly, and the salt, pepper and cinnamon.

9 Bring the mixture slowly to the boil and stir until the jelly dissolves. Stir the cornflour into 15 ml [1 tablespoon] water, add a little hot stock and add to the pan. Simmer for 1 minute, stirring all the time. Put aside to keep warm.

257

10 When the meat is cooked, transfer it to a heated serving dish. Arrange the apples around it. Keep it hot while you finish the sauce.

11 Tilt the roasting tin. Skim off excess fat. Stir in the thickened stock. Mix well, scraping up and stirring in any sediment from the bottom of the tin.

12 Heat the sauce gently over low heat on top of the stove until very hot but not boiling. Stir in the port and serve in a heated sauce-boat.

ROAST STUFFED RABBIT

The lightly flavoured flesh of a farmed rabbit does not need a strong stuffing. The lemony flavour of the forcemeat in this course suits it well, if you use freshly ground black pepper instead of cayenne—use half the quantity in the recipe. The chicken stock can, if wished, be made simply with a cube.

SERVES 4–6
1.4 kg [3 lb] farmed rabbit, approximate weight when skinned and paunched
salt
20 ml [4 teaspoons] lemon juice
90 g [3½ oz] forcemeat stuffing
30 ml [2 tablespoons] French mustard
freshly ground black pepper
15 ml [1 tablespoon] cooking oil
4 rashers fat bacon
150 ml [¼ pt] chicken stock
freshly chopped parsley

1 Cut off the rabbit's head if still in place and take out the giblets.

2 Rinse the rabbit two or three times in lightly salted water. Then leave to soak, immersed in salted water with 5 ml [1 teaspoon] lemon juice added, for 30 minutes.

3 Wipe the rabbit and pat it dry. Stuff it with the forcemeat as described in this course.

4 Heat the oven to 190°C [375°F] gas mark 5.

5 Truss the rabbit with skewers, pulling the fore legs back and the hind legs forward.

6 Spread the mustard all over the rabbit. Sprinkle it with salt and pepper.

7 Place the rabbit on a rack in a roasting tin. Sprinkle it with the oil and the remaining lemon juice.

8 Cover the rabbit with the bacon. Trickle the stock over it.

9 Put the rabbit in the oven. Roast it for 40 minutes. Baste it frequently with the stock in the tin.

10 After 40 minutes, take bacon barding off the rabbit. Baste it with stock. Return it to the oven for 10–15 minutes or until lightly browned.

11 Place the rabbit on a heated serving dish. Pull or snip out the sewing thread. Keep the rabbit hot under buttered paper.

12 Tilt the roasting tin so that the juices run to one end. Skim off as much fat as you can. Scrape up and stir in any sediment from the bottom of the tin.

13 Put the tin over moderate heat, on top of the stove. Bring to the boil. Boil for 2 minutes. Check the flavour and seasoning.

14 Strain the gravy into a heated sauce-boat. Sprinkle the rabbit with chopped parsley. Serve at once.

GERMAN ROAST SADDLE AND RABBLE OF HARE

You get the best of all worlds when using this recipe. Marinating and roasting with wine in the pan will give you tender meat, even from an old hare. Yet the cooking method is as simple as plain roasting. You have the pleasure of a roast joint and, as a luxurious bonus, the richness of a cream-finished sauce and mushrooms to go with it. Prepare the meat by removing the head and forequarters, taking out innards and marinating.

SERVES 6
1 hare, weighing 2–2.25 kg [4½-5 lb] when skinned and paunched, marinated
6 rashers rindless streaky bacon
75 g [3 oz] dripping
275 ml [½ pt] red wine
225 g [½ lb] flat mushrooms
150 ml [¼ pt] soured cream
15 ml [1 tablespoon] cornflour
salt and pepper

1 Heat the oven to 220°C [425°F] gas mark 7.

2 Take the joint of hare from the marinade and pat dry carefully with kitchen paper. Truss the hind legs by pulling them forward and securing with skewers.

3 Place it on a rack in a roasting tin. Cover its back with the bacon rashers and the hind legs with some greased foil if the bacon does not cover them.

4 Heat the dripping gently until melted. Pour it over the hare.

5 Roast the hare for 15 minutes. Reduce the oven heat to 180°C [350°F] gas mark 4. Pour the wine into the roasting tin.

6 Continue roasting for another 40 minutes. Baste the joint with wine several times.

7 Add the mushrooms to the roasting rack, around the meat. Baste them well, remove the barding bacon and reserve. Roast the meat for another 10 minutes or until the hare is tender.

8 Put the joint, mushrooms and bacon on a heated serving dish. Keep hot. Blend cornflour with 30 ml [2 tablespoons] water.

9 Tilt the roasting tin, and skim off as much fat as you can from the sauce. Scrape up the sediment from the bottom of the tin. Stir in the soured cream.

10 Heat the sauce in the tin over low heat. Bring it to boiling point and add a little to the blended cornflour. Stir this mixture into the tin and boil for 1 minute. Season.

11 Portion the hare, making 2 portions from the saddle, 2 from the haunch and 1 each from the hind legs. Pour a little of the sauce over. Cut up the bacon and arrange this and the mushrooms on the serving dish. Serve the remaining sauce separately.

New rules for old game

As game gets older, it gets tougher, making the flesh totally unsuitable for roasting. This however, is not the end of the story. Using the tender techniques of casseroling and braising, you can turn even the toughest old bird or beast into a delicious meal.

Game, like other things (including people), gets tougher as it gets older. As every good cook knows, meat which is past the first tender flush of youth needs slow, persuasive cooking to make it tasty and succulent. Gentle casseroling and braising are ideal methods for this purpose and are excellent ways to cook end of season game birds, hare, rabbit and the tougher cuts of venison.

Long slow cooking will give these tougher beasts a new succulence. Casseroles provide more liquid whereas braises include more vegetables and less liquid.

Generally speaking, game is best when cooked with alcohol of some kind. Replace up to half the liquid with wine, cider or beer. The alcohol will evaporate during cooking leaving behind a subtle flavour. Wine and cider will reduce during cooking whereas beer will not, so casseroles made with beer are thickened at the end of cooking time.

GAME TO USE
All game can be braised or casseroled but this method is only worthwhile for older birds, hare, rabbit and the stewing cuts of venison.

Birds
With birds, it is fairly easy to detect age if they are sold feathered. The feathers under the wings will be fully formed rather than downy, cock pheasants will have pronounced spurs and the scales on the legs and feet of all birds will be larger and coarser than those of young specimens. The feet, beak and breastbone of old birds are rigid rather than pliable and in old partridges, the legs are red rather than yellow. If the birds are sold ready dressed, you can only take the butcher's word for their age but it is worth betting that any birds sold towards the end of the game season (see details on page 240 for

game seasons in the UK) will be beyond the age when they can be roasted successfully. With pigeons, it is hard to judge age anyway and they are almost always better casseroled or braised than roasted.

Rabbit and hare
It is difficult to judge the age of rabbit and hare. The only guideline that can be relied on is the ears. If the ears are soft and will tear easily, the animal is young. If they are tough, the animal is old. With cut rabbit it is impossible to judge age so here it is best to play safe and casserole or braise rather than roast.

Venison
Venison is sold ready-cut and is usually clearly marked if intended for casseroling. Joints of loin or haunch can be bought for braising.

HOW MUCH TO BUY

Many cooks find it difficult to judge how much game to buy, especially when it comes to birds as they look so puny. Bear in mind that game is a fairly rich food and therefore portions do not have to be too generous—serve an additional accompaniment if you feel the quantity of meat looks rather mean.

Pigeons: allow one per person.
Partridges: allow one per person.
Pheasant: allow one between two.
Grouse: allow one between two.
Capercaillie: allow one between two.
Rabbit: allow 225 g [½ lb] cut rabbit per person. One average-sized rabbit skinned and jointed by the butcher will serve 4-6.
Hare: hare can only be bought whole. An average-sized hare, skinned and jointed by the butcher will serve 6. Make sure that you get the hare's blood (usually sold in a plastic bag with the hare) for enriching casseroles and jugged hare.
Venison: allow 175 g [6 oz] boneless meat per person. If buying a joint with a bone, allow 225 g [½ lb] meat per person.

OTHER INGREDIENTS

Other ingredients for game casseroles and braises can be divided into marinade, fat, fruit and vegetables, liquid and thickening.

Marinade

All game tends to be dry and this is a tendency which increases as the bird or animal gets older. A marinade helps to break down tough fibres and moisturize the meat. A good marinade consists of an acid element to break down tough fibres and oil to moisturize the meat, plus herbs and spices to add flavour. There are two kinds of marinade for game, cooked and cold.

Cooked marinade: a cooked marinade is used hot and is good for large pieces of venison for braising. The ingredients for the marinade are assembled, brought to the boil and then poured hot on to the meat. Venison marinades always contain juniper berries which have a particular affinity with this meat. Make sure the berries are bruised (do this with a rolling pin or a meat hammer) before adding to the marinade or they will not give up their flavour. A cooked marinade for venison is given in the recipe section.

Cold marinade: for a cold marinade, the ingredients are simply mixed together and then poured over the meat. Once again make sure that spices and berries are crushed so that they will release their flavour. Although cold marinades are less effective than hot marinades they are successful especially if a less gamey flavour is required.

How long to marinade

Game should be marinated for at least four hours. The meat should be turned from time to time so that all sides are coated with the marinade. Most game marinades can be strained and added to the liquid or sauce for the braise or casserole.

Fat

Game must always be sealed in hot fat before you start casseroling or braising. This will seal in the scarce juices. Bacon dripping gives the best flavour. Alternatively, chop about two rashers of streaky bacon and sauté in the bottom of a casserole dish until the fat runs out. This fat can then be used as part of the mirepoix for a braise or in the ingredients for a casserole.

Fruit and vegetables

For braising, game is cooked on a bed of vegetables (and sometimes fruit) called a mirepoix. The classic mirepoix is made from onions, carrots and celery cut into fairly large diced pieces, with the addition of a few parsley stalks, a bay leaf and some thyme. For a game mirepoix fruit such as apples or quince may be included. There should be enough fruit and vegetables to make a good layer up to 5 cm [2"] deep in the bottom of the casserole dish. Some recipes use one vegetable only for the mirepoix (such as partridge with cabbage) and here the same rules apply unless the recipe states differently.

Vegetables are used in game casseroles in exactly the same way as for any other casserole, in that they are served with the meat.

Suitable vegetables to use with game are celery, red or white cabbage, swede, onions, mushrooms, carrots and parsnips. Apples go well with all game birds. Prunes go well with rabbit.

Liquid

The liquid for game casseroles and braises can be a combination of game or chicken stock and alcohol or can have liquid from the marinade added. The only exception where liquid is concerned is when jugged hare is made. Here the blood of the hare is also added.

When using alcohol, use in the proportion of $\frac{1}{4}$ alcohol to $\frac{3}{4}$ stock and marinade mixture if used. You will need about 275 ml [$\frac{1}{2}$ pt] liquid to every 350 g [$\frac{3}{4}$ lb] meat for casseroles and about half this for braises. In braising, the liquid should come about halfway up the sides of the meat.

Thickening

The liquid in game casseroles and braises can be thickened by either tossing the meat in seasoned flour before you fry it, adding a beurre manié to the juices after cooking or adding a velouté of egg and cream to the juices after cooking.

Flour

Always use plain flour and season it with salt and freshly ground black pepper. You will need just enough flour to thinly coat the meat, not to encrust it. During cooking, the flour dissolves into the liquid and thickens it.

Beurre manié

A beurre manié is a combination of two parts butter to one part flour which is mixed to a stiff paste. To thicken an average game casserole you will need a beurre manié made from 15 g [$\frac{1}{2}$ oz] butter and 15 g [$\frac{1}{2}$ oz] flour.

Velouté

A mixture of egg yolks and cream (known as velouté) is a traditional thickening for the liquid from game casseroles and braises. One large egg yolk beaten with 45 ml [3 tablespoons] cream is sufficient for a casserole or braise to serve 4–6.

PREPARING GAME FOR CASSEROLING

Preparation differs slightly for birds and animals.

Birds

Birds are best left whole for both casseroling and braising. They can be portioned afterwards (see step-by-step to portioning). Left whole, the birds retain maximum juice and flavour and the end results are much

better than casseroles where the birds are cut into portions.

The first thing to do when you get your plucked birds home is to see if the butcher has removed the innards. Quite often they are left in and unless you specifically ask, the butcher will not remove them. To remove the innards, enlarge the vent (the hole at the tail end) with a pair of scissors. Make a whole large enough to get your fingers in. Put your fingers inside the bird, grasp the windpipe (the only hard part in the intestines) and pull. All the intestines should come out at once. Separate the liver and windpipe, wash and use for game stock. The rest of the innards can be discarded.

Wash the inside of the bird thoroughly with cold running water. Pick any feathers off the outside and wash the body. The bird is now ready for casseroling or braising.

Rabbit and hare

Rabbit and hare are best bought ready jointed from the butcher. This spares you a great deal of messy preparation.

Venison

Venison is also sold ready to use. Stewing venison or venison chops are ready cut. Haunches for braising are sold whole so no further preparation is necessary.

CASSEROLING AND BRAISING

When you have prepared your game, marinate it, using one of the marinades given in the recipe section. Marinate for at least 4 hours, longer if possible, and turn the game from time to time.

Preparing the stock

While the game is marinating, make stock using the giblets from birds (or, if these are unavailable, chicken livers), a few bruised juniper berries, a scrubbed and halved carrot and a quartered onion. Making giblet stock is described on page 210.

Cooking

Game is braised or casseroled in exactly the same way as meat. The only difference is that cooking times and temperatures will not be exactly the same, so do be sure to follow the times given overleaf. The time and temperature are the same for both braising and casseroling.

Step-by-step to portioning cooked game bird

1 Lift the cooked bird out of the casserole dish. Place on a flat surface.

2 Using kitchen scissors or poultry shears, cut away the backbone and discard.

3 Divide small birds by cutting in half down the breastbone, using a sharp knife.

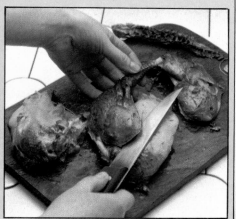

4 Cut larger birds in half again, cutting at the point where the leg joins the body.

BRAISING AND CASSEROLING TIMES FOR GAME

Oven temperature 180°C [350°F] gas mark 4

Game	Time
Pigeon	1½–2 hours
Partridge	2–2½ hours
Pheasant	2½ hours
Grouse	2½ hours
Capercaillie	2½ hours
Rabbit	2 hours
Hare	2½–3 hours
Venison	2½–3 hours

Portioning birds
After the casserole or braise has been cooked, birds will need to be portioned. Small birds, such as pigeon and partridge and grouse are best halved. Using kitchen scissors or poultry shears, cut away the backbone. Using a sharp knife, cut through the breastbone.

Larger birds can be cut into four portions. Halve as described above then cut in half again, cutting at the point where the leg joins the body. Keep the portions warm in a low oven while you thicken the liquid if necessary, or remove the mirepoix to finish the sauce.

Portioning animals
Animals will not need portioning as the pieces are ready cut. Venison braised in a piece should be sliced thickly and served as suggested (see right).

Reducing the sauce
If you have not tossed the meat in flour to thicken the braising or casseroling juices they will still be quite thin. They can be reduced in three ways.

Before reducing, strain the liquid and reserve the vegetables.

Rapid boiling: return the liquid to the casserole and boil rapidly uncovered until reduced to the desired quantity. Reducing by this method does not really thicken the juices.

Beurre manié: return the juices to the casserole. Set over low heat and add beurre manié a piece at a time, stirring until each piece has dissolved into the liquid. Cook for 2–3 minutes until thick.

Velouté: return the juices to the casserole. Beat together the yolk of a large egg and 45 ml [3 tablespoons] thick cream. Add a little of the hot juice to this mixture and blend. Add the mixture to the liquid in the casserole and cook gently for 2–3 minutes until thickened.

Serving
To serve a game casserole, return the pieces to the sauce if necessary. To serve a braise, arrange the portions or sliced meat on a serving plate. Arrange the reserved mirepoix around it and spoon over some of the hot juice. Serve the rest of the juice separately.

MARINADE FOR VENISON AND HARE

This is a cooked marinade and should be poured on the venison hot. The meat should be marinated for at least 4 hours, overnight if possible. Turn from time to time so that all sides of the meat receive the benefit of the marinade.

MAKES 150 ML [¼ PT]
150 ml [¼ pt] dry red wine
30 ml [2 tablespoons] olive oil
1 small finely chopped onion
2 bay leaves
freshly ground black pepper
4 juniper berries, bruised

1 Combine all the ingredients in a saucepan.

2 Bring to the boil and pour over the meat while hot.

3 When the meat has been removed, the marinade can be strained and added to the cooking liquid or boiled down to add to the finished casserole.

MARINADE FOR RABBIT AND BIRDS

Pour the marinade over the meat while it is still hot. Leave for at least 4 hours, turning the meat occasionally.

MAKES 150 ML [¼ PT]
1 large onion, skinned and chopped
150 ml [¼ pt] brandy or medium sherry
5 ml [1 teaspoon] powdered thyme
1 bay leaf
4 chopped parsley stalks
30 ml [2 tablespoons] olive oil
4 bruised allspice berries

1 Combine all the ingredients. Pour over the meat. Turn from time to time.

2 If wished, the marinade may be strained and added to the cooking liquid for the braise or casserole.

Marinating game birds helps to tenderize their rather tough flesh and also prevents drying out when the birds are cooked.

PIGEONS WITH CHERRIES

You can use either fresh or canned cherries for this dish. Feuillitons, which are little squares of puff pastry, are traditional accompaniments to this dish. Marinate the pigeons in the marinade for birds given on page 263. Serve the pigeon with game chips and a green vegetable such as broccoli.

SERVES 4
4 pigeons
150 ml [¼ pt] marinade
50 g [2 oz] bacon dripping
2 shallots or large spring onions
25 g [1 oz] flour
550 ml [1 pt] game or chicken stock
bouquet garni

30 ml [2 tablespoons] soured cream
225 g [½ lb] stoned red cherries
25 g [1 oz] butter

1 Marinate the pigeons for 4 hours.

2 Heat the oven to 180°C [350°F] gas mark 4. Heat the bacon dripping in a large heavy-based casserole.

3 Brown the pigeons in the bacon dripping until all sides are sealed. Lift out.

4 Skin and chop the shallots or spring onions. Sauté in the bacon fat.

5 Stir in the flour. Cook for 2 minutes until just turning brown.

6 Return the pigeons to the dish. Pour on the stock and any strained left-over marinade. Add the bouquet garni.

7 Cook in the centre of the oven for about 1½ hours.

8 Remove the pigeons from the casserole and cut in half. Strain the sauce into a clean pan.

9 Set the sauce over low heat and allow to boil and reduce by about half.

10 While the sauce is reducing, melt the butter in a heavy-based frying-pan over low heat. Add the cherries and sauté for 3 minutes.

11 Stir the soured cream into the reduced sauce. Return the pigeons to the sauce to reheat.

12 Scatter the cherries over the meat before serving.

CASSEROLED PHEASANT WITH CELERY AND CREAM

▨▨▨ *Here is an example of how game casseroles can be thickened with egg yolk and cream. This is one of the best ways to serve a pheasant which is past its youth and is a method which can also be used with chicken, turkey, grouse and capercaillie. Marinate the birds using the marinade for pheasant given on page 263.*

SERVES 4
2 pheasants
150 ml [¼ pt] marinade
75 g [3 oz] bacon dripping
2 rashers middle cut bacon
250 ml [½ pt] game or chicken stock
bouquet garni
125 ml [4 fl oz] port
2 celery hearts
150 ml [¼ pt] thick cream
1 large egg yolk
salt and black pepper

1 Prepare and marinate the birds for at least 4 hours or overnight.

2 Melt the bacon dripping in a heavy-based casserole over low heat. Heat the oven to 180°C [350°F] gas mark 4.

3 Brown the birds in the fat, turning so that all sides are coloured.

4 Remove the rind from the bacon rashers and cut the bacon into strips. Remove the pheasants from the casserole.

5 Lightly fry the bacon strips. Return the pheasants to the casserole. Add the stock, port, bouquet garni. Place in the oven.

6 Cut the celery hearts into rounds. Add to the pheasant when it has been in the oven about 30 minutes.

7 Continue cooking for a further 2 hours or until the bird is tender.

8 Lift the birds and celery rounds out of the casserole. Cut birds into portions and arrange on a warmed serving dish. Keep warm.

9 Beat the egg yolk and cream together. Add a little of the hot liquid from the casserole dish.

10 Set the casserole dish over low heat. Gradually add all the egg and cream, stirring all the time. Heat gently but do not boil or the sauce will curdle. Season if necessary.

11 Spoon the sauce over the birds.

PARTRIDGE EN COCOTTE NORMANDE

▨▨▨ *End of season partridges become tender and delicious if braised with apples and cider. Pigeons can also be used for this recipe. Make sure that the cider is dry. Sweet cider will spoil the flavour of the partridges. This recipe is particularly suitable for partridges which have been hung until they are very gamey. Use the marinade for game birds given on page 263.*

SERVES 2
2 partridges
150 ml [¼ pt] marinade
2 rashers streaky bacon
1 medium-sized onion
1 cooking apple

150 ml [¼ pt] dry cider
150 ml [¼ pt] game stock
bouquet garni
salt and black pepper

For the garnish:
2 cooking apples
25 g [1 oz] butter
fresh parsley sprigs

1 Wash the partridges inside and out and remove any feathers. Marinate for 4 hours or overnight. Heat the oven to 180°C [350°F] gas mark 4.

2 Cut the rind off the bacon. Cut the bacon into strips. Place in the casserole over low heat.

3 Cook the bacon until the fat is running freely. Add the partridges and brown well on all sides. Remove from the dish and set aside.

4 Skin and chop the onion and add to the fat. Peel and chop the apple and add to the fat. Cook over low heat for about 3 minutes, turning from time to time.

5 Return the partridges to the dish. Add the cider, stock, strained marinade and bouquet garni.

6 Place in the oven and cook for 2–2½ hours, covered until the partridges are tender when pierced with a skewer.

7 Just before the partridges are ready, peel, core and slice the apples. Melt the butter in a heavy-based frying-pan over low heat and fry the apple rings until golden on both sides. Set aside.

8 Remove the partridges from the casserole. Cut away the backbone using kitchen scissors or poultry shears then halve the birds. Place on a serving dish. Arrange the apple rings on the dish and place in a low oven or warming drawer.

9 Strain the liquid. Return strained liquid to the casserole and boil rapidly for about 4 minutes until reduced. Check seasoning.

10 Spoon a little of the hot sauce over the meat and serve the remainder separately. Garnish with parsley just before serving.

RABBIT WITH PRUNES

■■■*Preparation for this dish must begin a day in advance as it is essential that the rabbit is marinated overnight. Use the marinade given for birds and rabbit on page 263.*

SERVES 4
1 rabbit, skinned and jointed
150 ml [¼ pt] marinade
225 g [½ lb] prunes
575 ml [1 pt] strained tea
50 g [2 oz] bacon dripping
15 g [½ oz] flour
150 ml [¼ pt] dry red wine
250 ml [½ pt] game or chicken stock
salt and black pepper

1 Marinate the rabbit and soak the prunes in the tea for 8 hours.

2 Lift the rabbit pieces out of the marinade. Pat dry. Heat the oven to 180°C [350°F] gas mark 4.

3 Gently melt the bacon dripping in a heavy-based casserole over low heat. Add the rabbit pieces and brown on all sides. Remove.

4 Sprinkle the flour into the casserole and allow to brown. Add the wine and stock.

5 Replace the rabbit. Add the prunes and any remaining soaking liquid.

6 Cover and cook in the centre of the oven for about 2 hours.

7 If there is more than 275 ml [½ pt] liquid remaining at the end of cooking, lift out the rabbit pieces, strain out prunes and reduce the sauce by rapid boiling. Check seasoning. Return rabbit pieces and prunes before serving.

RABBIT WITH LENTIL PUREE

■■■*Lentils and rabbit make a delicious combination, especially as the pulses are cooked with the rabbit, giving a delicious flavour. Start preparations the day before.*

SERVES 4
1 rabbit, skinned and jointed
150 ml [¼ pt] marinade
100 g [¼ lb] lentils
1 small onion
1 celery stick
bouquet garni
75 g [3 oz] butter
4 slices white bread

1 Marinate the rabbit for at least 8 hours. Pat the pieces dry. Soak the lentils, overnight, in enough water to cover.

2 Put the rabbit in a large casserole or stewpan with the lentils and any remaining soaking water.

3 Skin and chop the onion. Scrub and chop the celery and add to the pan. Add bouquet garni.

4 Add enough water just to cover. Cover the pan or casserole and simmer over low heat for 2½ hours until the rabbit and lentils are tender.

5 Lift the rabbit out of the liquid and keep warm.

6 Strain out the vegetables and

266

lentils. Rub through a sieve to purée. Put the purée in a clean pan.

7 Add enough of the rabbit cooking liquid to make the purée a coating consistency. Stir in 25 g [1 oz] butter, season to taste.

8 Return the rabbit to the pan and allow to reheat gently.

9 While the rabbit is reheating, melt the butter in a heavy-based saucepan over low heat. Cut the crusts off the bread and cut each slice into four triangles.

10 Fry the bread until golden on both sides. Serve the rabbit surrounded by croûtons.

GROUSE WITH CABBAGE

⧖⧖⧖ *Partridge is the classic favourite for this dish but grouse actually tastes much better. Use a firm, hearty green cabbage—not the white kind, it does not have such a good flavour and the finished dish will not look particularly attractive. Marinate the birds using the marinade given on page 263.*

SERVES 4
2 grouse
150 ml [¼ pt] marinade
2 medium-sized onions
2 medium-sized carrots
1 medium-sized cabbage
175 g [6 oz] streaky bacon in one piece
25 g [1 oz] bacon dripping
100 g [¼ lb] good pork sausages
bouquet garni
250 ml [½ pt] game or chicken stock
salt
freshly ground black pepper
freshly chopped parsley to garnish

1 Prepare the grouse and marinate for at least 4 hours using the marinade for birds given on page 263.

2 Skin and chop the onions. Scrub and dice the carrots. Trim the cabbage, cut into four, remove centre stalk and wash.

3 Blanch the bacon and cabbage in boiling salted water for about six minutes. Meanwhile heat the oven

to 180°C [350°F] gas mark 4.

4 Place the dripping in a large, heavy-based casserole. Pat the grouse dry and brown on all sides.

5 Take the grouse out of the dish. Add the carrots and onion and brown. Drain the cabbage, cut each quarter in half.

6 Cut the rind off the bacon. Cut the flesh into strips.

7 Remove the onion and carrot from the dish. Add the sausages and brown lightly. Remove.

8 Lay half the cabbage on the bottom of the dish. Place the birds on top of the cabbage, add the sausages and bacon.

9 Place remaining cabbage and other vegetables on top of the birds.

10 Add the stock and seasonings. Cover and cook in the centre of the oven for 2–2½ hours.

11 To serve, remove the birds. Halve. Place on a warmed serving dish.

12 Remove the sauages and slice. Arrange around the birds with the bacon strips and vegetables.

13 Pour a little of the liquid over the dish. Serve remainder separately. Sprinkle the grouse with chopped parsley just before serving.

BRAISED VENISON

⧖⧖⧖ *If you are in doubt about the origin or age of your venison, marinate it well and braise it. Its own good flavour enriched by the marinade needs no extras. Use the cooked marinade given on page 263, and marinate for at least 24 hours for maximum flavour.*

SERVES 6
1.4 kg [3 lb] haunch or leg of venison
150 ml [¼ pt] marinade
2 medium-sized onions
2 medium-sized carrots
2 sticks celery
1 small turnip
25 g [1 oz] bacon dripping
bouquet garni
275 ml [½ pt] good game or

beef stock
salt
freshly ground black pepper
15 ml [1 tablespoon] redcurrant jelly
15 g [½ oz] butter
15 g [½ oz] plain flour

1 Cut any membranes, gristle and ragged ends off the meat, and any fat. Marinate the joint for 24 hours. Turn it over several times.

2 Skin and chop the onions. Scrub and chop carrots and celery. Peel and chop turnip. Wipe and dry the meat. Heat the oven to 180°C [350°F] gas mark 4.

3 Heat the dripping in a large stewpan or flameproof casserole with a lid. Put in the meat. Brown it on all sides. Take it out.

4 Put the mirepoix into the same fat in the pan. Lower the heat. Cover the pan, and cook the mirepoix very gently for 6–7 minutes. Shake the pan from time to time to make sure that the vegetables do not stick to the bottom.

5 Uncover the pan, and put in the venison. Add the bouquet garni and the stock.

6 Cover and place in the centre of the oven. Cook for 2½–3 hours or until the meat is tender.

7 When tender, lift the meat with a carving fork. Hold it over the pan to let the juices drip off. Put it on a heated serving dish. Strain out the vegetables and arrange around the meat. Keep hot.

8 Skim excess fat off the braising liquid. Add the redcurrant jelly. Over moderate heat, stir the sauce until the jelly dissolves. Take the pan off the heat.

9 Mix the butter and flour together to a smooth paste. Stir it into the sauce in small pieces.

10 Return the pan to the heat, and stir until it boils and thickens to the consistency of thin cream. Check the seasoning.

11 Spoon a little of the sauce over the venison. Serve the rest in a heated sauce-boat, with the meat.

JUGGED HARE

This traditional English recipe is very rich indeed. Buy the hare ready skinned and jointed from the butcher. He will give you the blood which is used in the casserole in a plastic bag. Do not buy the hare until the day before you plan to serve the casserole as the meat can dry out very quickly. Marinate the hare using the hare and venison marinade given on page 263.

SERVES 6
1 large hare, jointed
150 ml [¼ pt] marinade
15 ml [1 tablespoon] bacon dripping
2 large onions
2 cloves
5 black peppercorns
1 celery stick
1 carrot
5 ml [1 teaspoon] bruised allspice berries
bouquet garni
pinch of salt
juice of 1 lemon
strip of lemon rind
850 ml [1½ pt] game stock
15 g [½ oz] butter
15 g [½ oz] plain flour
blood of the hare
150 ml [¼ pt] port
15 ml [1 tablespoon] redcurrant jelly
8 shallots
100 g [¼ lb] mushrooms

1 Marinate the hare for 4 hours or overnight, turning occasionally.

2 Pat the pieces dry. Melt the bacon fat in a large casserole over low heat. Add the hare pieces and fry until sealed on all sides. Heat the oven to 180°C [350°F] gas mark 4.

3 Remove from heat. Skin the onions and stick a clove into each one. Add to the casserole. Add peppercorns.

4 Scrub and chop the celery stick. Scrub and quarter the carrot. Add to the casserole.

5 Add remaining spices, lemon juice and rind. Pour in the stock.

6 Cover, place in the centre of the oven and cook for about 3 hours.

7 Set aside the hare. Strain the juices. Discard the vegetables. Trim the shallots and wipe the mushrooms. Brown shallots lightly in a pan and add mushrooms.

8 Combine the butter and flour to make a beurre manié. Set the gravy over low heat. Add the beurre manié a little at a time. The liquid should be thickened to the consistency of thin cream. Add shallots and mushrooms.

9 Allow the liquid to boil then remove from the heat. Add about 45 ml [3 tablespoons] of the gravy to the blood of the hare, stirring after each addition.

10 Gradually add the blood to the gravy, stirring well. Stir in the port and redcurrant jelly.

11 Place the hare pieces in a clean flameproof dish. Pour over the gravy. Reheat carefully, shaking from time to time. Do not stir as this may break up the pieces of hare.

A perfect setting

A galantine provides the perfect centrepiece for a cold table. It is an elegant dish which demands some careful preparation but no last minute attention. Being completely boneless and firmly rolled means that it is particularly easy to carve. It is versatile, too, in that it can be served with hot vegetables or with a salad and bread, as befits the occasion.

A galantine is a very clever way of extending meat that is to be served cold and making it more interesting. The idea has been around for a long time. Originally, only poultry was used but then other types of bird and eventually cuts of meat were turned into galantines. Nowadays, recipes can be found for chicken, turkey, game birds, veal, pork and beef galantines. The making of a galantine is a rather long and involved process but equally it is a decorative and rewarding skill to learn.

A galantine is a boned roll of uncooked meat, stuffed with a well-flavoured and substantial stuffing, poached in stock, cooled and finally coated with aspic or chaudfroid or a layer of each. The process sounds more complicated than it in fact is, but this is certainly not a quick dish to prepare. It is very sensible, and essential if using a turkey, to cook the galantine at least the day before it is needed so that it can cool at room temperature overnight. Once it is cold the bird can be stored in the refrigerator in its muslin wrappings until needed, but not for more than 2-3 days.

A galantine is an ideal dish for a summer party, especially if you have an awkward number to serve, such as five or seven. The stuffing can be relied upon to make a bird that, plain roasted, would serve four or six, stretch to serve the extra one with absolutely no difficulty. It is also a good dish for a party in that it is prepared in advance by necessity and there is no last minute preparation.

If the weather suddenly changes and you do not want to serve a completely cold meal, hot vegetables go with a galantine just as well as a salad. No accompanying sauce is needed as this is already coating the meat, in jellied form. The lack of bones and the shape and firm texture of the roll make it easy to carve, and no one can criticize its appearance. A delicate garnish of fresh fruit or vegetables is all that is needed to decorate the galantine and this again is arranged in advance.

INGREDIENTS
There are three principal ingredients in a poultry galantine: the bird, the stuffing and the coating. You will also need a quantity of stock in which to poach the bird, made from the carcass and giblets, and various fruit and vegetables to garnish the final result.

The bird
If you are serving a large number of people your first choice will obviously be a turkey. Once sliced a galantine will dry out, so calculate carefully the size of turkey required for the number of guests. If you are serving a smaller number you can choose between a chicken, a duck and a game bird.

A galantine is one dish where a frozen bird can be used very successfully. The stuffing adds plenty of flavour and, as the galantine is poached, there is no danger of the flesh becoming dry. This is also an excellent method for cooking birds which may no longer be in their prime. The cooking can be extended for an older and tougher bird to ensure tender results.

Frozen birds are always sold oven-ready with the giblets inside. Thaw the bird in the refrigerator in its wrappings for the calculated time (see on page 197). When completely thawed, remove and reserve the gib-

lets and rinse the bird inside with cold water.

The stuffing

The stuffing for a galantine is always substantial. It usually contains a large quantity of minced meat, seasoned and flavoured with herbs and a little onion, and moistened with a well-flavoured liquor such as Madeira, cognac or sherry.

The stuffing must be moist as meat that is left to become cold is usually drier than when it is hot. For this reason, pork or pork sausage meat is included. Veal is also used in quantity as the flavour is mild, and smaller quantities of ham or bacon are used for flavouring but not so that they overpower the flavour of the bird. The ham or other flavouring meat can be cut into strips and layered between two quantities of stuffing. This will give a decorative effect to the cooked galantine when it is sliced. Many variations can be added to the basic stuffing mixture.

The coating

A galantine can be coated with aspic alone, with a chaudfroid sauce alone or with a glazing of aspic over the sauce.

Aspic is a smooth, shimmering clear jelly made from consommé. It sets over the galantine to form a transparent, lightly coloured glaze. Consommé is made from the stock in which the bird is poached, and the consommé is then used to make the aspic. The stock for the consommé must be clarified with the white and shell of an egg. If it does not set when cold, some gelatine can be used. You will need 25 g [1 oz] of gelatine for every 575 ml [1 pt] of stock used. Aspic is also obtainable in powdered form.

Chaudfroid is a thick, flavoursome sauce which is jellied with a small quantity of aspic and when poured over the food sets to form a moist opaque coating. Both chaudfroid and aspic set firmly enough to be sliced with the meat.

The bird must be completely cold before it is coated and the aspic or chaudfroid is used while still unset but cool. If the chicken or the sauce were warm, the coating would not set. If you wish to use a combination of both coatings, a glazing of aspic can be added after the chaudfroid coating has been allowed to set firmly.

The garnish

A simple, fresh fruit or vegetable garnish is used to decorate the top of a galantine. There is a variety of pieces of fruit and vegetables that can be used and they should be chosen for their decorative qualities rather than their flavour. Strips and thin slices are best as they can be firmly secured to the bird. Larger pieces would be less secure and could make carving a little difficult. Strips of citrus peel, anchovies, cucumber, sliced radishes, cloves, capers, sliced gherkins, sliced olives and thin slices of celery are some of the garnishes that can be used to decorate a galantine.

If the coating is aspic alone, the garnish can be arranged by being dipped into the aspic and stuck on the galantine. When secure, the aspic coating can be poured over. With a chaudfroid coating, the garnish is arranged in the coating before it has been allowed to set and the two set together. Aspic shapes can be used here.

When using as aspic glaze over a chaudfroid coating, the cool aspic is poured over when the chaudfroid and the garnish are firmly set.

QUANTITIES

Galantines are a good way of stretching a single bird to serve a larger number of people. The stuffing is substantial as it is usually meat-based. This, combined with a boneless bird, means portions do not have to be too large.

Bear in mind that the larger the bird, the higher the proportion of meat to bone—small birds weighing up to 2.2 kg [5 lb] give about half this weight of meat when boned: larger, heavier birds yield meat in an increased ratio. However, birds over 4.5 kg [10 lb] are not really suitable. By the time they are stuffed, they will be so large as to make handling difficult. It will also be difficult to cook the bird through to the centre, and you probably will not have a pan large enough to take the galantine.

The weight of the stuffing used can be as much as half the weight of the boned meat, depending on the number of servings required. For example, a 2.2 kg [5 lb] chicken boned will yield about 1.1 kg [2½ lb] meat. This can be combined with up to 600 g [1¼ lb] stuffing: allowing 175 g [6 oz] per person, this will serve about 10.

METHOD

Making a galantine is rather a long and involved process though it can be effectively divided into several clear stages. You should allow at least six hours for boning, making the stock and cooking the galantine. The bird must then be allowed to cool at room temperature which, for a turkey, definitely means overnight. The final stage is the coating, which must be allowed to set firmly (2 hours in the refrigerator) before the galantine can be served.

Boning the bird

The first step in preparing a galantine is to bone out the bird so that you are left with the skin and flesh in one piece. This is not as difficult as it may sound but the first few attempts will undoubtedly be time-consuming. Detailed, step-by-step instructions are given here for boning a chicken. Always use a sharp knife and keep the bones and trimmings for stock.

A turkey, duck or game bird is boned in a similar way. The size and weight of a large turkey will make it more difficult to handle and for the same reason, small game birds will be more fiddly. The most important thing to remember is not to pierce or tear the skin during the process. If the skin remains whole, there will be no danger of the stuffing seeping out when the galantine is cooking.

When the bird is boned, cover it lightly and store it in the refrigerator until you are ready to stuff it.

Making the stock and stuffing

Once the bird is boned, the carcass and other bones are used with the giblets to make a well-flavoured stock.

The stock required will take quite some time to cook as the flavours from the bones, giblets and vegetables must be given up to the liquid. When it is cooked, the stock should be strained and degreased ready for use.

While the stock is simmering, and in order to save time, the stuffing can be prepared. Trim any skin and bone from the meat and mince the meat finely. If an onion is used, peel, chop and mince this as well. Mix the stuffing ingredients and keep in a bowl covered with a piece of damp greaseproof paper until you are ready to stuff the bird. Any stuffing ingredients that are to be used in layers can be sliced ready for use.

Step-by-step to boning a chicken

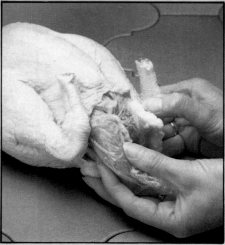

1 Remove the giblets and wipe the bird inside and out. Gently pull out any bits of feather.

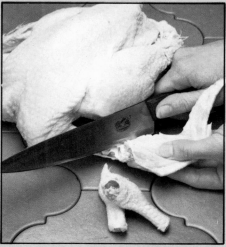

2 Lay the chicken on its back. Cut off the legs at the first joint and the wings at the second.

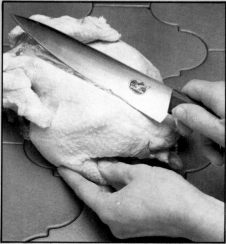

3 Turn the chicken on to its breast. Using a very sharp knife, make a cut along the backbone.

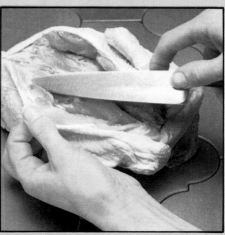

4 Work the skin and flesh away on both sides, holding the knife flat against the carcass.

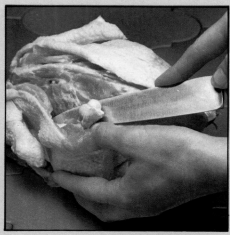

5 When you reach the legs, sever each thigh bone from the carcass and work the thigh flesh loose.

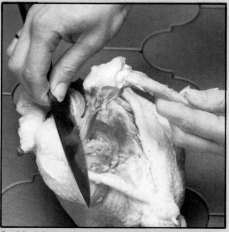

6 Holding the drumstick, loosen the flesh as far as the thigh. Draw out the complete leg bone.

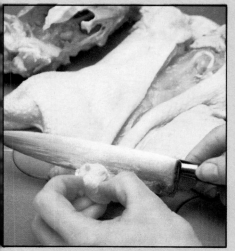

7 Loosen the flesh up each wing to the body. Sever wing bone from carcass and draw out the bone.

8 Work the flesh away from the ribs being careful not to cut the skin. Lift out the carcass.

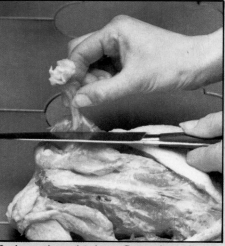

9 Lay the chicken flat, skin down. Cut off the parson's nose. Turn the legs and wings inside out.

Step-by-step to chicken galantine

SERVES 6-8
1 oven-ready chicken weighing 1.4 kg [3 lb]
salt
freshly ground black pepper

For the stock:
700 g [1½ lb] knuckle of veal, chopped and blanched
2 large carrots, quartered
2 Spanish onions, quartered
1 leek, sliced
1 celery stick, sliced
bouquet garni
6 white peppercorns

For the stuffing:
100 g [¼ lb] stewing veal
100 g [¼ lb] gammon
100 g [¼ lb] sausage meat

50 g [2 oz] fresh white breadcrumbs
30 ml [2 tablespoons] lemon juice
zest of half a lemon
large pinch of nutmeg
1 small egg

For the coating:
25 g [1 oz] gelatine (optional)
7 black olives
strips of cucumber skin

1 Bone the chicken following the step-by-step instructions. Cover the chicken and refrigerate.

5 Season the stuffing mixture generously and add the spice. Beat the egg, add and mix well.

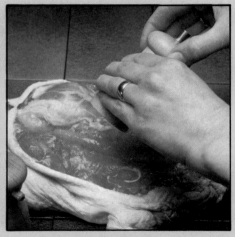

6 Spread the boned chicken out flat on a board, skin down. Season the flesh with salt and pepper.

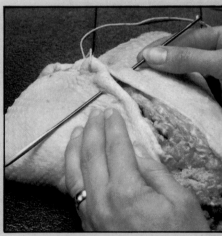

7 Spread the stuffing evenly over the centre of the chicken. Draw together into a roll and sew up.

11 When cool enough to handle, either tighten the muslin wrappings or renew and tie tightly.

12 Put the galantine between two plates and put a weight on top. Leave to become quite cold.

13 Remove muslin wrappings and cut away trussing. Put gelantine on cake rack with plate underneath.

2 Make the stock using the bones and giblets from the chicken and other stock ingredients.

3 While the stock is simmering, prepare the stuffing. Mince the veal, chop and mince the gammon.

4 Mix the minced meat with the sausage meat and breadcrumbs. Add the lemon juice and zest.

8 Wrap the galantine in a double layer of muslin and tie the ends together to make a tight roll.

9 Pour the strained stock into a saucepan. Immerse the galantine. Cover and simmer for 1½ hours.

10 When cooked, drain the galantine over the pan and set aside to cool slightly. Reserve the stock.

14 Make 575 ml [1 pt] apsic using some of the stock. Use gelatine if necessary. Leave to cool.

15 Halve and stone olives. Dip pieces of garnish into the aspic. Stick in place. Allow to set.

16 Pour the aspic along the top of the galantine and let it run down to completely coat the bird.

273

Stuffing and cooking the bird

Take the bird from the refrigerator and spread it out flat on a board, skin down. Season the cut surface with salt and pepper. Spread the stuffing evenly down the centre of the bird. Arrange any solid ingredients you may have, such as strips of ham and tongue or pieces of olives, etc between two layers of stuffing.

Thread a trussing needle with some fine string or strong cotton thread. Draw the edges of the bird together and stitch securely to form a roll. Wrap the roll in a double layer of muslin and tie the ends firmly.

Strain the prepared stock into a saucepan just large enough to hold the galantine. Immerse the galantine in the stock: it must be completely covered. Cover the saucepan securely and simmer the galantine for the time given in the recipe.

Cooling and pressing the galantine

Drain the cooked galantine over the pan for a few moments and then set it aside. Reserve the stock. When the galantine is cool enough to handle, either tighten the muslin wrappings or change them for clean ones and tie these tightly round the roll. Put the galantine between two plates and put a weight on top. Leave the galantine to cool at room temperature until it is quite cold. This may mean overnight depending on the size of the galantine.

At this stage the galantine can be stored in the refrigerator, in its muslin wrappings, until it is needed. It should not be stored for longer than 2-3 days.

Coating the galantine

Depending on the chosen coating, make a quantity of aspic and/or chaudfroid. For a medium chicken you will need about 575 ml [1 pt] of either sauce. The reserved poultry stock is used in the making of the aspic sauce, and it may not, in fact, require any additional setting agent.

Take the galantine from the refrigerator and take off the wrappings. Undo the trussing stitches. Put the bird on a rack and slip a plate underneath. If using chaudfroid, pour over an even coating of sauce, arrange the garnish and allow to set in the refrigerator for 2 hours. If using aspic, set the garnish in place with a dab of aspic and when firm apply an even glaze of aspic. Leave to set in

the refrigerator for 2 hours.

If wished, an aspic glaze can be applied over the chaudfroid coating once it has set firmly.

Alternatively, slice the cold, ungarnished galantine and arrange on a serving dish. Apply an even coating of aspic over the slices and leave in the refrigerator to set.

SERVING A GALANTINE

A whole galantine makes a marvellous centrepiece for a cold table and can be carved very easily after your guests are assembled. In this case it simply needs to be arranged on a serving dish with a plain garnish of lettuce, chopped aspic, watercress and other salad vegetables. You may wish to do the carving before the guests arrive so that you can forget the food and concentrate on them. In this case, the galantine can be coated and garnished in the normal way and sliced just before serving. Arrange the slices on a serving dish, garnish and serve fairly promptly.

The alternative is to serve aspic-glazed slices of galantine. Once the aspic has set a simple garnish can be arranged to suit the size and shape of the dish. This is a very practical idea if the slicing has to be done in advance, for example, for a wedding reception, as it keeps the meat moist very effectively.

GALANTINE OF PHEASANT

This is an excellent way in which to serve a pheasant if you have any doubts about its tenderness and do not want to casserole it. With a veal and ham stuffing, one pheasant will serve four with no difficulty. The galantine can be served whole but in this recipe the serving suggestion involves slicing the galantine and then coating the slices with aspic.

You will need 1.15 L [2 pt] previously made brown stock (homemade) in order to make a well-flavoured game stock. The other ingredients and directions for making the stock are given on page 210. Add the brown stock to the giblet stock with 700 g (1½ lb) game carcasses. If the clarified stock does not set firmly enough when cold, use 25 g (1 oz) gelatine.

SERVES 4
**1 pheasant weighing about 1.15 kg [2½ lb]
salt**

**freshly ground black pepper
850 ml [1½ pt] game stock**

**For the stuffing:
100 g [¼ lb] stewing veal
175 g [6 oz] ham
25 g [1 oz] fresh white breadcrumbs
1 small onion
10 ml [2 teaspoons] freshly chopped sage
15 ml [1 tablespoon] freshly chopped parsley
salt
freshly ground black pepper
45 ml [3 tablespoons] Madeira**

**For the garnish:
½ orange, peeled and sliced
fresh watercress sprigs**

1 Wipe the bird inside and out with a damp cloth. Bone the bird, following the step-by-step instructions.

2 Use the bones, giblets and carcasses to make the game stock as detailed on page 210.

3 While the stock is simmering, make the stuffing. Mince the veal and ham finely and mix with the breadcrumbs.

4 Peel, chop and mince the onion and add to the meat and breadcrumbs.

5 Add the herbs, season well with salt and pepper and pour in the Madeira. Mix well and check and adjust the flavour if necessary with a little more herbs and salt.

6 Spread the pheasant out on a flat surface, skin down. Season with salt and pepper. Spoon the stuffing mixture on to it and spread in evenly down the centre with the back of a spoon.

7 Draw the edges of the bird together to form a roll. Sew the edges together securely using strong cotton thread or fine string and a trussing needle.

8 Wrap the galantine in a double layer of muslin, tying the ends to make a neat shape.

9 Place the galantine in a pan just large enough to hold it. Pour over sufficient strained stock to cover. Cover the pan.

10 Set over a low heat and bring to simmering point. Simmer the galantine for 1 hour.

11 Remove the galantine, holding it over the pan to drain. Set it aside until it is cool enough to handle. Reserve the stock.

12 Either tighten the muslin wrapping or change them for clean ones. Then press the galantine between two plates, with a weight on top, until it is quite cold.

13 Store the galantine in its muslin wrappings, lightly covered, in the refrigerator if not needed immediately.

14 When ready to decorate, make 425 ml [¾ pt] aspic using the cold stock and some gelatine if necessary.

15 Unwrap the galantine and remove the trussing stitches. Using a sharp knife, carve the galantine in even slices and arrange these on a serving dish.

16 The aspic should be cool but not set. Using a spoon, pour the aspic over the slices, coating them generously. Transfer the dish to the refrigerator and leave to set for 2 hours.

17 When ready to serve, arrange the orange slices and watercress sprigs at one end of the dish or around the glazed slices, according to the size and shape of your dish. The rind can be left on the orange for extra colour.

CHICKEN GALANTINE EN CHAUDFROID

▨▨▨ *This recipe combines the use of chaudfroid sauce and aspic. Fresh tomatoes are added to the chicken stock to give the aspic a bold colour. The chaudfroid is based on a velouté sauce which is much richer, both in colour and texture than a béchamel sauce. A béchamel sauce could be used, if preferred, and the aspic coating could be omitted if you suddenly run short of time. Use homemade chicken stock if possible.*

SERVES 6–8

1 oven-ready chicken weighing 1.5 kg [3½ lb]
salt
freshly ground black pepper
1.15 L [2 pt] chicken stock
700 g [1½ lb] ripe tomatoes
150 ml [¼ pt] dry white wine

For the stuffing:
175 g [6 oz] lean veal
175 g [6 oz] lean pork
1 Spanish onion
100 g [¼ lb] fried mushrooms, cold
50 g [2 oz] fresh white breadcrumbs
30 ml [2 tablespoons] freshly chopped parsley
30 ml [2 tablespoons] drained capers
salt and pepper
large pinch of cayenne
large pinch of mace
50 ml [2 fl oz] dry sherry
1 large egg

For the coating:
400 ml [¾ pt] velouté sauce
5 ml [1 teaspoon] gelatine

For the garnish:
radish slices
cucumber skin and slices
orange peel and slices
cloves

1 Bone the chicken following the step-by-step instructions. Cover lightly and refrigerate until needed.

2 Make the stock following the instructions on page 18, and using the chicken bones and giblets.

3 While the stock is simmering, make the stuffing. Chop and mince the veal and pork. Peel, chop and mince the onion.

4 Put the minced meat and onion in a bowl with the cold cooked mushrooms and breadcrumbs. Add the parsley and chop and add the capers. Season well with salt and pepper and add the spices.

5 Pour in the sherry. Beat the egg lightly, add to the mixture and beat together well.

6 Season, stuff, roll and wrap the chicken as shown in the step-by-step instructions.

7 Roughly chop the tomatoes and put into a saucepan large enough to hold the galantine. Add wine.

8 Place the galantine in the pan. Pour over enough strained stock to cover the galantine. Cover the pan and simmer for 1½ hours. Drain the cooked galantine over the pan and set aside to cool. Reserve the stock.

9 When cool enough to handle, press the galantine as shown in the step-by-step instructions.

10 Make 700 ml [1¼ pt] aspic with the reserved stock, using a recipe or powdered aspic.

11 Make the chaudfroid sauce using the velouté sauce, 150 ml [¼ pt] aspic and the gelatine. Set the sauce aside and allow it to cool. When it will coat the back of a wooden spoon, the sauce is ready.

12 Set the chicken galantine on a cake rack with a plate underneath. Coat the chicken with the sauce, pouring it along the centre and allowing it to run down to completely coat the galantine.

13 Arrange the garnish in the sauce, making a pretty design.

14 Transfer the galantine, still on the

10 ml [2 teaspoons] freshly
   chopped sage
salt
50 ml [2 fl oz] brandy or sherry
1 medium-sized egg

1 Chop the veal, pork and ham and mince finely. Put into a large bowl with the breadcrumbs.

2 Peel, chop and mince the onion and add to the bowl.

3 Season the mixture generously with pepper and mix in the fresh herbs. Add salt to taste.

4 Pour in the liquor. Beat the egg lightly and add to the bowl. Mix the stuffing mixture very well. Cover with damp greaseproof paper until required.

Variations

●For a spicy stuffing, omit the herbs and add a pinch of nutmeg, a pinch of allspice, 30 ml [2 tablespoons] lemon juice and the zest of half a lemon.
●To make a sausage meat stuffing, replace the pork with sausage meat. Use with chicken, capon or turkey.
●For poultry stuffing for game birds replace the veal with the same quantity of chicken meat, marinated for 2 hours in 30 ml [2 tablespoons] Madeira and 30 ml [2 tablespoons] brandy. Use thyme instead of sage and omit the cognac or sherry, using the marinating liquor instead.
●Add 50 g [2 oz] coarsely chopped pistachio nuts and 25 g [1 oz] sliced stuffed green olives to the spicy stuffing variation above.
●A chequerboard effect is made by omitting the ham from the herbed stuffing mixture. Using 175 g [6 oz] ham and 100 g [¼ lb] cooked tongue, slice the meat and cut it into strips about 1.25 cm [½″] wide. Layer these, with 15 ml [1 tablespoon] drained capers and thin strips of pimento, between two layers of stuffing.
●To make a mushroom stuffing, add 100 g [¼ lb] fried mushrooms and 6 chopped black olives to the herbed stuffing mixture and omit the breadcrumbs.
●To make an orange-flavoured stuffing, use 30 ml [2 tablespoons] orange juice, and the zest of an orange. Use brandy rather than sherry.
●For a fruity stuffing, add 100 g [¼ lb] chopped dates, the pulped flesh of an orange and 50 g [2 oz] chopped walnuts to the orange stuffing.

rack, to the refrigerator to set for 2 hours.

15 When the chaudfroid coating is thoroughly set, bring the galantine out of the refrigerator. If the aspic has set firmly, warm it gently to melt it slightly and pour it over the coated galantine. Return to the refrigerator for a further 2 hours.

16 Serve the galantine on a large dish, from which it can be sliced.

Variation

●If you do not have time to apply an aspic coating and allow it to set, when you have made it turn into a baking tray to set while the chaudfroid coating is setting on the galantine. Serve the galantine in the chaudfroid sauce, garnished with bits of orange peel and radish and spoon the cold aspic around the galantine. Serve with a selection of salads.

HERBED STUFFING MIXTURE

The stuffing for a galantine is very quick to make as it involves no cooking. It should be made while the stock is simmering in order to save time. Weigh the boned meat to see how much stuffing you can make. You can have anything up to half the weight of the boned meat, depending on the number of people you wish to serve. Allow 175 g [6 oz] gross weight per portion.

FOR A 1.25 KG [2 LB 12 OZ]
CHICKEN,
BONED WEIGHT
225 g [½ lb] lean veal
225 g [½ lb] lean pork
75 g [3 oz] lean ham
**50 g [2 oz] fresh white
   breadcrumbs**
1 onion
freshly ground black pepper
**15 ml [1 tablespoon] freshly
   chopped parsley**

Chicken Kiev

❌❌❌ *The secrets of perfect chicken Kiev come in chilling the centre thoroughly beforehand, so that it melts gradually throughout the frying process; in using fresh, home-made breadcrumbs and not the ready-made ones to which busy restaurants so often resort; and in heating the oil to the exact temperature specified, in order that both the breadcrumb coating and the chicken within are fried to perfection and no more. If the oil is too hot, the outside browns while the chicken inside is still half raw; if the oil is not hot enough, it soaks right through the coating making the dish soggy.*

An infallible way of achieving the right oil temperature is by using a thermometer, unless you have an electric controlled-temperature deep frier.

For a stylish finished effect, bone chicken portions but do it in such a way that the end of the leg bone is left attached. If desired, this can be covered with a paper frill at the serving stage. For this effect, buy chicken portions made up of the leg and a piece of breast.

SERVES 6
6 chicken portions, weighing about 125-175 g [4-6 oz] each with bone
175 g [6 oz] unsalted softened butter
1 lemon
salt
freshly ground black pepper
4 garlic cloves
45 ml [3 tablespoons] freshly chopped parsley
30 ml [2 tablespoons] plain flour
freshly ground black pepper
4 medium eggs
275 g [10 oz] fresh white breadcrumbs
oil for deep frying

For the garnish:
lemon wedges
sprigs of parsley

1 Use a sharp knife to bone the chicken portions, leaving the small bone at the end of the leg attached to each of the pieces. Boning is not essential but as well as improving appearance it makes eating easier.

2 Place the butter in a bowl. Grate three-quarters of the zest off the lemon into it. Beat the butter and lemon zest together.

3 Squeeze the lemon and add the juice slowly to the butter mixture, beating all the time. Mix in the seasoning.

4 Skin and crush the garlic and add to the bowl. Add the parsley and stir well.

5 Transfer the butter mixture to a sheet of greaseproof paper. Form into a roll and chill in the refrigerator for at least 1 hour.

6 When the butter is firm, divide it into six. Take the prepared chicken portions and place a piece of the butter in the centre of each piece of chicken. Roll the chicken up round the butter and secure with a cocktail stick.

7 Season the flour and put in a polythene bag.

8 Beat the eggs and pour on to a large plate.

9 Tip the breadcrumbs into another polythene bag.

10 Lightly coat each piece of chicken by tossing in the bag of seasoned flour, then brush with beaten egg and finally toss in the breadcrumbs.

11 Repeat coating process. Chill in the refrigerator until required.

12 In a deep fat fryer, heat the oil to 180°C [350°F], or until it will brown a cube of bread in 60 seconds.

13 Place 3 of the chilled, coated chicken portions in the frying basket and lower into the oil. Fry for 15 minutes, until golden brown.

14 Take the basket out of the fat, remove cocktail sticks and transfer the chicken pieces to absorbent kitchen paper to drain, and then keep warm in a low oven while the other 3 chicken pieces are fried.

15 Arrange fried chicken pieces on a warm serving plate and garnish with lemon wedges and sprigs of parsley.

Star recipe

Avgolemono chicken with rice and lettuce

The name avgolemono shows that this dish includes eggs and lemon, a favourite combination in Greek and Turkish cooking. Tender chicken flesh and creamy lemon sauce are nicely offset by the nutty textured rice and an unusual lettuce garnish, producing a feast of a dish at relatively modest cost. This dish is an excellent example of just how good boiled chicken can be.

SERVES 6
1 roasting chicken weighing about 1.8 kg [4 lb]
1 large lemon
1 large onion
1 large carrot
bouquet garni
2.5 ml [½ teaspoon] whole peppercorns
60 ml [4 tablespoons] fresh chives
30 ml [2 tablespoons] fresh parsley
75 g [3 oz] walnut pieces
1 large egg yolk
150 ml [¼ pt] thick cream
250 g [9 oz] long grain rice
30 ml [2 tablespoons] butter
30 ml [2 tablespoons] plain flour
salt and pepper
half a lettuce

1 Wipe the chicken inside and out. Grate the lemon zest, skin and slice the onion. Scrub and slice the carrot.

2 Place the chicken in a pan or flameproof casserole into which it fits snugly. Add the lemon zest, onion, carrot, bouquet garni and peppercorns and pour on enough warm water to cover the chicken thighs.

3 Place over medium heat and bring to simmering point. Immediately reduce heat to the lowest possible simmer, cover and leave to poach gently for 1½ hours or until the chicken is quite tender.

4 Meanwhile prepare the other ingredients. Chop 45 ml [3 tablespoons] chives and all the parsley and mix together with the nuts. Beat the egg yolk into a paste with the cream. Squeeze the lemon juice.

5 Strain the poaching stock, discarding vegetables and seasonings, and let the chicken rest in a low oven.

6 Reduce 575 ml [1 pt] of the chicken stock to 450 ml [¾ pt] by fast boiling.

7 Put the rice into a jug to measure volume. Using the remaining stock—plus a little water if necessary—measure out twice the volume of the rice in liquid.

8 Pour this liquid into a large pan, and add the rice and some salt. Place over a medium heat and bring to the boil, stirring once.

9 When boiling point is reached, lower the heat so that the water is just simmering and cover the pan. Cook for 15 minutes.

10 Meanwhile, make a roux with the butter and flour. Blend in the reduced stock and the lemon juice. Bring to the boil and simmer for 2 minutes, stirring all the time.

11 Drain the cooked rice, fluff it with a fork and stir in most of the nuts, chives and parsley. Arrange the rice mixture on a warm serving dish. Keep warm.

12 Joint the chicken into six pieces (see pages 198–199), skin and arrange on rice. Keep warm.

13 Blend a few tablespoons of the hot sauce into the egg and cream liaison, then carefully stir this mixture into the saucepan. Reheat very gently without boiling.

14 Season to taste with salt and pepper and pour the sauce over the chicken. Garnish with remaining herb and nut mixture, cover and keep warm.

15 Wash and shred the lettuce. Place in a colander and pour boiling water over it. Drain, salt and arrange the lettuce garnish in a ring round the dish. Chop the remaining chives over the sauce to decorate.

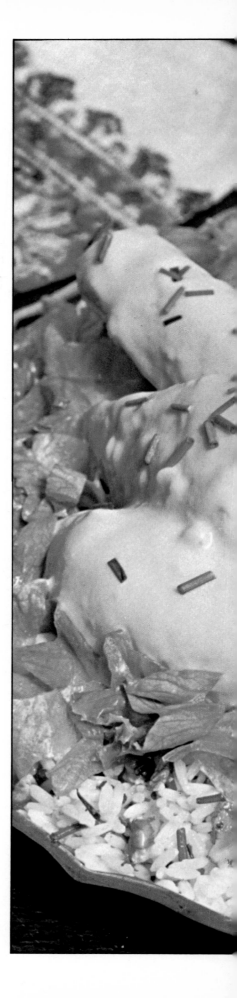

ROAST DUCK WITH ORANGE SAUCE

This is one of the most famous of all roast duck dishes, canard à l'orange. Unfortunately, it is also one of the most maligned. Too often the sauce is too sweet and marmaladey, ruining the flavour of the duck.

The giblet stock which is needed for the sauce should be made in advance, as the sauce is made while the duck is roasting. Madeira or red wine may be used in place of the port.

This is one instance where the duck must be served whole and portioned at table. Serve the duck surrounded by slices of orange and add some watercress or mint for colour. Garnish the breast with unpeeled, halved orange slices and serve the sauce separately.

SERVES 2
1.4 kg [3 lb] oven-ready duck
4 thin-skinned oranges

30 ml [2 tablespoons] granulated sugar
60 ml [4 tablespoons] red wine vinegar
300 ml [½ pt] giblet stock
15 ml [1 tablespoon] arrowroot
175 ml [6 fl oz] port
1 lemon
30 ml [2 tablespoons] orange flavoured liqueur or juice
25 g [1 oz] butter

1 Heat the oven to 220°C [425°F] gas mark 7. Prepare duck for roasting and roast as described.

2 Meanwhile, peel 2 of the oranges with a vegetable peeler. Cut the peel into julienne strips.

3 Place strips in a pan and cover with water. Bring to boil. Simmer for 15 minutes. Drain well.

4 Put sugar and vinegar in a pan. Bring to boil. Boil rapidly for 5 minutes to caramelize.

5 Remove from heat and add 150 ml [¼ pt] stock. Stir over low heat to release caramel from pan.

6 Add remaining stock, bring to the boil, reduce heat again and simmer for 2 minutes. Squeeze lemon.

7 Blend arrowroot with 30 ml [2 tablespoons] port. Add a little of the hot sauce and blend well.

8 Stir this into the sauce. Add lemon juice and reserved peel. Simmer for 3 minutes and set aside.

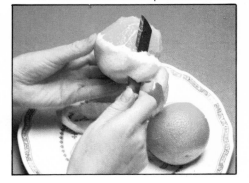

9 Keep half an orange for garnish. Peel, remove pith and slice other oranges across the segments.

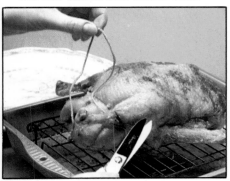

10 Remove the cooked duck from the oven. Remove trussing and leave in warm place on serving plate.

11 Tip fat from roasting tin. Add remaining port. Boil, stirring, to reduce to 45 ml [3 tablespoons].

12 Warm the sauce over low heat. Strain in port reduction and simmer. Stir in liqueur and butter.

Star recipe

CHICKEN DRUMSTICKS EN CROUTE

Encasing chicken drumsticks is one of the easiest and most attractive ways of wrapping food in pastry. Drumsticks do not take very long to cook, so they can be prepared and wrapped in the pastry well in advance. This means that drumstick parcels are the ideal choice for buffets, picnics and parties. To make them in advance, cook the meat and allow it to cool. Then you can wrap the pastry round and leave the parcels in the refrigerator until needed. Bake them immediately before eating. They do not, however, have to be served hot.

SERVES 6
6 chicken drumsticks
30 ml [2 tablespoons] vegetable oil
salt and pepper
30 ml [2 tablespoons] French mustard
225 g [½ lb] rough puff or flaky pastry
beaten egg to glaze

1 Skin and wipe drumsticks. Heat oil in a pan and add drumsticks. Fry for 5–10 minutes until browned.

2 Drain drumsticks and allow to cool. Using a small, sharp knife, slash flesh at 1.2 cm [½"] intervals.

3 Sprinkle drumsticks liberally with salt and pepper. Spread the mustard into the slashes in the flesh.

4 Heat oven to 220°C [425°F] gas mark 7. Roll pastry 3 mm [⅛"] thick to 25 × 33 cm [10 × 13"].

5 Trim edges and cut pastry into strips 2.5 cm [1"] wide, each about 30 cm [12"] long.

6 Brush edges with beaten egg. From thick end of each drumstick wind pastry strips pressing to join.

7 Continue winding the pastry strips, joining the ends if necessary, and pressing well.

8 Finish winding the pastry at the knuckle end on each drumstick and seal with egg if necessary.

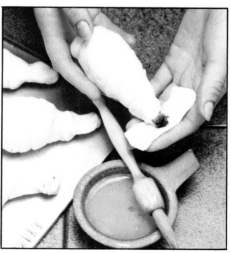

9 Use trimmings to cover knuckle ends. Place drumstick on baking sheet and relax 30 minutes.

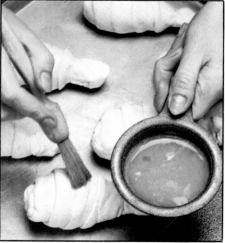

10 Brush chicken parcels with egg and bake in centre of oven for 25 minutes. Serve immediately.

Star recipe

COQ AU VIN ROUGE

The basis of this great classic dish is a richly flavoured glossy wine sauce embracing tender portions of chicken. The traditional garnish of tiny onions, button mushrooms, little pieces of fat bacon and crisply fried bread croûtons is an important feature of the dish.

This elegant dish needs a robust full-flavoured wine, preferably from the Burgundy, Mâcon or Beaujolais areas. When a particular wine is used the dish takes the name of the wine, thus Coq au Beaujolais, or, for a really splendid occasion Coq au Chambertin.

There are many versions of the recipe. The rich flavour of this one is achieved by reducing the wine beforehand so that its concentrated essences permeate and flavour the pieces of chicken more effectively during the relatively short cooking period. It is also

flamed in brandy to further enhance the flavour, and is finally thickened with a beurre manié.

The fried bread croûtons are decorated for an addition of colour by dipping one corner first into softened butter and then into finely chopped parsley.

The short cooking period makes it more economical to use the top of the cooker although the oven could be used for the simmering if it is already in use at the correct low temperature. Considerable preparation and attention to detail are necessary to make a really good coq au vin, but the results justify its reputation.

SERVES 4
1 roasting chicken weighing
   1.1–1.4 kg [2½–3 lb]
5 ml [1 teaspoon] tomato purée
half a chicken stock cube

1 small onion
salt
freshly ground black pepper
1 large garlic clove
1 bay leaf
1 sprig thyme
400 ml [¾ pt] robust red wine
100 g [¼ lb] sliced pickled
   belly pork
12 button onions
15 ml [1 tablespoon] oil
45 g [1¾ oz] butter
60 ml [4 tablespoons] brandy
175 g [6 oz] small button
   mushrooms

For the beurre manié:
15 ml [1 tablespoon] flour
20 g [¾ oz] softened butter

For the garnish:
12 triangles of white bread
freshly chopped parsley

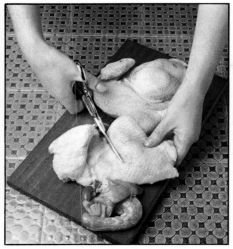

1 Wash the chicken and giblets in cold water. Drain. Quarter chicken. Cover it and refrigerate.

2 Cover chicken giblets and trimmings with water. Add the stock cube and tomato purée.

3 Peel and slice the onion and add to pan. Season and simmer for 30 minutes. Strain. Reserve liquid.

7 Heat oil and butter in frying-pan. Brown lardons and fry onions for 5 minutes. Remove and reserve.

8 Fry seasoned chicken in the pan, skin downwards, until gold. Turn and fry for 1–2 minutes.

9 Transfer chicken to flameproof casserole. Flame with warmed brandy. Add onions and lardons.

13 Remove the mushrooms, onions and lardons. Place around the chicken and keep hot.

14 There should be about 400 ml [¾ pt] sauce. Concentrate it, if necessary, by boiling, and season.

15 Skim off any surplus fat. In a bowl cream together the flour and the softened butter.

4 Meanwhile, peel and slice garlic and put in a pan with the bay leaf, thyme and red wine.

5 Simmer for about 15 minutes over a medium heat, uncovered, until the quantity is reduced by half.

6 Trim the rind from the pork and slice into lardons 6 × 25 mm [¼ × 1"]. Peel the onions.

10 Strain wine over chicken. Add the stock, cover, and simmer very gently for 40 minutes.

11 Wipe the mushroom caps and trim the stalks. Add to the casserole and simmer for 5 minutes.

12 With a slotted spoon remove the chicken and arrange in a warmed shallow serving dish.

16 Whisk this into the sauce over a low heat, piece by piece. Simmer the sauce for a few minutes.

17 While the sauce is simmering fry the bread triangles in very hot fat over medium heat.

18 Pour the thickened, glossy sauce over the chicken and garnish with oroûtons and parsley.

On the line

Flat fish, round fish, oily fish, white fish—a confusion of fish and full of bones. So why do we bother to eat fish? Well, think of a tasty, golden grilled fish fillet served with a wedge of lemon—tempting and good for you as it's absolutely full of protein with low-fat content. Whatever your preference there is a fish for you whether it is whole, boned and stuffed, cut into steaks and cutlets or filleted. Here we take away all the nonsense which is talked about round white fish.

Absolutely fresh, inshore white fish has such a marvellous delicacy of flavour that it is a pity to smother it with added flavours. If you are lucky enough to have such fish, simply grill and baste it with butter and lemon juice or a maître d'hôtel butter. Less tasty fish from distant waters, perhaps frozen after landing, respond excellently to additional flavours including such strong ones as cheese, onion, garlic, tomato and anchovy.

Although fish and frying are almost synonymous, in fact grilling is often a better way of cooking fish. Not only is it a quick, clean and convenient method but it also seals in the flavour and prevents the loss of salts and nutrients.

Small, oily fish are excellent grilled whole or split, and grilling is the tastiest way of cooking white fish fillets and steaks.

Apart from dividing fish into white and oily categories, fish are also flat or round shaped. All oily fish are round but white fish can be flat, such as sole, or round, such as cod. Strictly speaking, the term round fish applies to all cylindrical fish as opposed to flat fish, such as sole, plaice and skate.

A selection of white fish and oily fish includes mackerel, sprats, red monk fish, sole, John Dory and haddock.

1 Cod
2 Gurnard
3 Rock salmon
4 Haddock
5 Whiting
6 Monk fish
7 Hake

ROUND WHITE FISH

The term white fish is most commonly associated with the familiar cod, coley, haddock, hake and whiting. But, in effect, it is simply a generic term covering all fish containing less than 2 per cent. oil. This small amount of oil is usually concentrated in the liver of the fish and the flesh is very lean. White fish is excellent for people on a low-fat diet. It is easy to digest, hence its association with convalescent diets.

Round white fish include bass, bream and gurnard, the less familiar pollock, pout and ling, as well as the more familiar ones which are usually available all year round and include the following:

Cod is a large white-fleshed fish which can weigh as much as 34 kg [75 lb]. Small cod are sold whole, but most shoppers buy cod already cut up into fillets, steaks or cutlets. These are sometimes frozen and fillets are available smoked. Cod grills well but, because its natural flavour is rather bland, it is best to serve the grill with a well-flavoured sauce or cooked with herbs so that it becomes more interesting and raises its status.

Coley, also known as saithe, is a member of the cod family and as the price of cod rises it is being used more and more as an alternative. It has off-white flesh when raw, which deters some people, but it turns white when cooked. It is sold skinned and filleted and, like cod but even more than cod, it needs a sauce or the addition of herbs to make it more interesting.

Gurnard, also called gurnet, is a small, tasty fish with firm white flesh. It is sold whole or filleted, is more tasty than cod and therefore needs less help to improve its flavour. It can be grilled and baked and is also particularly good eaten cold with salads.

Haddock belongs to the cod family, it is popular smoked but is also sold fresh whole, filleted or as steaks. It can be used for grilling and baking as well as in made-up dishes.

Hake is a tender fish with few bones and is sold as fillets and cutlets. It is a very tasty fish with flaky flesh and lends itself to any method of cooking with the minimum of fuss.

Whiting is a member of the cod family and is available all year round. It can be purchased whole or in fillets and is suited to baking and grilling. It is particularly good with a savoury stuffing, in which case it can be boned although this is not essential.

CHOOSING FISH

Don't be put off buying fish because you are not sure how to prepare it. Fishmongers are pleased to advise you about buying and preparing and they will usually prepare the fish for you without further charge, that is they will scale, behead, skin and fillet fish or divide it into steaks and cutlets as you require. However, these jobs are not difficult and step-by-step instructions are given to make them even simpler.

The sooner fish is cooked after catching the better it will taste. So always look first for signs of freshness. Fresh fish is at its very best when in season and plentiful, and the price should be cheaper then too. Medium-sized fish are likely to have a finer flavour and texture than larger specimens which tend to become coarse. Choose plump thick fish or fillets in preference to thin ones.

The following guidelines will help you to spot the freshest fish on the fishmonger's slab. In general, a firm shining appearance and clean fresh smell is essential. Any sign of dullness or flabbiness is a sign of age.

Whole fish: gills should be bright red—they darken and brown with age. The eyes must be bright and clear—they become dull and sunken with age. The skin must be moist and glistening, with clear colours. Dryness is a sign of age.

Fillets, cutlets and steaks: the flesh should look firm and bright—spongy texture denotes poor quality.

Frozen fish: buy where you know the turnover is brisk. See that packs are fresh looking and unbroken. Transparent bags of separate fillets are very useful because you can take out the number of fillets needed for one meal and grill them from their frozen state without having to thaw them first. Cook frozen fillets under low heat and for a longer time than when cooking fresh fillets.

QUANTITIES

Fish vary greatly in size, but all round fish have a general similarity in shape. Not all cuts are suitable for every type of fish—cutlets, for example, require a larger fish. However, the fishmonger applies the same methods of cutting to all fish, whether large or small. For example, if fillets are required the filleting is done in the same way whether it involves a large cod or a small whiting.

Small fish are usually sold whole. If a fish weighs less than 450 g [1 lb] it can be grilled whole for one person. This may sound a lot but remember that the head, tail and bones account for quite a bit of the weight. Fish weighing 450-1 kg [1-2½ lb] are usually used for stuffing and baking, or they are filleted.

Medium-sized fish weighing about 1-2.3 kg [2½-5 lb] can be cooked whole and then be divided at table to serve several people but, for the purposes of grilling, a fish of this size is usually filleted before cooking to provide one long fillet from each side of the backbone. Each fillet, depending on size, can be divided into a number of portions. It is not necessary to buy whole fillets; the fishmonger will cut off as much as you require.

Large fish are usually cut crosswise to provide cutlets and steaks. The tail piece is sold for roasting or baking, or it may be filleted. The tail can also be poached, depending on the type of fish.

How much to buy

People's appetites vary enormously but, as a rough guide, any one of the following will provide enough for a main dish for one adult:

Fish fillets—150-175 g [5-6 oz] because every bit can be eaten.

Fish steaks or cutlets—175-200 g [6-7 oz]—slightly more than for fillets to allow for the bones.

One small whole fish—250-350 g [9-12 oz]. Additional weight here allows for head, tail and bones.

Large whole fish—allow 225 g [½ lb] per portion. This allows for the head and tail wastage and the weight of steaks or cutlets cut from a large whole fish should be as above.

PREPARATION FOR COOKING

When you get home after having bought the fish, unwrap it and rinse under cold running water, and drain thoroughly.

Lightly sprinkle the fish with cooking salt and lay it on a wire rack or on an inverted plate standing in a tray (this prevents the fish from standing in any liquid that drains from it). Cover loosely with polythene or foil and leave in a cold place, preferably the refrigerator under the frozen food compartment away from any other food that could possibly absorb the odour.

Keeping fish is not recommended; generally it should be cooked on the day of purchase and should never be kept for longer than 24 hours.

If the fishmonger has prepared the fish for you no further work is necessary; if not you will have to scale, gut, behead and fillet or bone the fish as required, depending on recipe.

Ideally, the fish should be prepared as close to cooking time as possible. However, this is not always convenient and if done a few hours in advance no harm will be done, but do cover the fish loosely with polythene and keep it chilled until it is required for cooking.

Scaling, gutting and boning or filleting a fish are messy jobs, but really very quick and easy to do once you know how.

If you want to stuff a fish and grill it whole, it is best to bone it (remove the backbone) so that the stuffing can be inserted into the cavity created. Removing the backbone is optional— the fish can be stuffed without boning—but it does give extra room so that you can use more stuffing, and it also makes eating easier. Boning is different from filleting in that the latter separates the fish into two halves, whereas boning removes the backbone without dividing the fish into two pieces. To bone a fish the initial preparation is the same as for filleting (see steps 1-5) although removing head and tail is optional, then proceed from step 11.

●The basic tools you will need are a sharp knife and a wooden or glass chopping board. The board must be clean and dry to prevent the fish from slipping.

●It is a good idea to rub both the working surface and your hands with a cut lemon afterwards to get rid of any fishy smells.

●Use the blunt side of the knife or a granton-edged knife for scaling.

●Have a roll of kitchen paper towels at the ready to blot up excess water after gutting and rinsing.

●Skinning fish is made easier if you first dip your thumb and forefinger in salt because this helps to give you a firm grip on the skin.

1 To scale, hold fish by tail and use blunt side of knife to scrape scales off towards the head.

5 To remove the tail, cut through the fish at its thinnest part. Cut off the head just behind the gills.

9 To skin a fresh fillet work a knife between the skin and flesh at tail end. Work skin away by hand.

Step-by-step filleting, boning and skinning fish

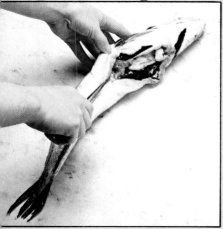

2 To gut fish, make a slit along the belly from below the gills along two-thirds of the body length.

3 Scrape out inside of belly. Rub cavity with salt and scrape away black skin inside cavity.

4 Cut off the gill covers (the little fins behind the head) on both sides of the fish.

6 To fillet, cut along the backbone down to the tail end. Cut into the flesh, not just through the skin.

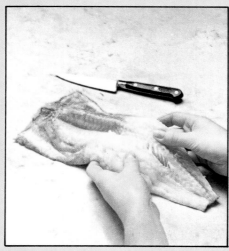

7 Cut the fish from belly cavity to tail and open it out flat by easing the belly cavity open.

8 Lift out the backbone from the head end. Ease the flesh from the backbone. Cut fillets in half.

10 To skin a frozen fillet lay the fish flesh side down and pull off skin from tail end.

11 To bone, press the fish, belly side down, along its backbone to open slightly without halving it.

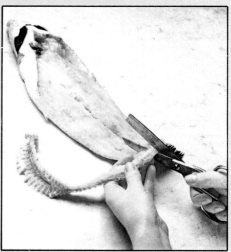

12 Cut through the bone at head end and ease away the backbone. Cut through at tail end and lift clear.

GRILLING WHITE FISH

Grilling is a particularly good method of cooking members of the round fish family. Because white fish do not contain much oil, for normal diets they should be grilled with added fat to prevent them from drying out during cooking.

There are various ways of adding extra fat when grilling fish.

1 Dot with butter and baste frequently during grilling time.
2 Marinate in flavoured oil before cooking and use the marinade as a baste when grilling.
3 Spread with a savoury topping containing fat and baste during grilling.
4 Use a savoury butter and baste during grilling time.

Salt is a great ally of white fish. This is not surprising as these fish come from the sea. The flavour of fish benefits enormously if the cut surfaces are liberally sprinkled with salt before cooking. Pepper can be added too if you like.

Temperature

Skinned fresh fish should be grilled under medium heat and skinned frozen fish under medium-low heat. Wet skin is unpleasant to eat and is a major reason why some people

dislike fish. Medium heat is not sufficient to cook the skin thoroughly. So, when grilling fish with its skin on, the secret recipe for really crisp and tasty results is to grill under fierce heat initially.

Fillets need not be skinned for grilling. In fact the skin makes the fillets easier to handle and less likely to break up. Grill fillets skin side up for a couple of minutes. Do this under fierce heat and do it first. Then reduce heat to medium, turn the fish carefully and cook the cut side. A fish slice and palette knife are the best implements for turning fish without breaking it.

Grilling times

Fish cooks extremely quickly, much quicker than many people imagine, and it is all too easy to overcook it. So do stay close to the grill when cooking fish and time things so that diners are ready to eat as soon as the fish is cooked.

It is always a pity to overcook fish because it dries out, becomes unappetizingly chewy and loses its delicate flavour— so good food goes to waste and all your labour has been in vain.

When grilling whole fish, steaks and cutlets, watch for the moment when the skin starts shrinking and then check that the flesh is opaque and comes cleanly away from the bone. This is a sure sign that the fish is cooked, so remove it from the grill immediately.

Fillets are cooked when the flesh is opaque right through to the skin. And if the fish is really fresh you will see a white creamy substance oozing out between the flakes.

Exact times vary depending on the size of the fish, but here is a guide for fresh fish. (Allow slightly longer for frozen fish.)

Grill fillets for a total 8-10 minutes, cutlets and steaks for 6-12 minutes each side depending on thickness, and 6-10 minutes each side for whole or stuffed round fish.

Turn cutlets, steaks and whole fish during grilling so that both sides will cook through. Also turn fillets which are cooked with the skin on. Skinned fillets do not need turning.

MONTE CARLO COD STEAKS

This is a colourful way of bringing a little Mediterranean flavour to any type of white fish steaks or cutlets, fresh or frozen. Garnish with chopped parsley.

SERVES 4
4 cod steaks
30 ml [2 tablespoons] oil
450 g [1 lb] ripe tomatoes
15 ml [1 tablespoon] finely chopped onion
1 small garlic clove, crushed
salt
black pepper
5 ml [1 teaspoon] sugar
2.5 ml [½ teaspoon] oregano or thyme
4 anchovy fillets

1 Put the tomatoes into boiling water for 1 minute, drain and refresh in cold water. Skin, cut in half and squeeze out the seeds. Chop the flesh into rough pieces.

2 Heat half the oil in a small saucepan, add the onion, cover and sweat over a low heat for about 5 minutes.

3 Stir in the garlic and cook for another minute.

4 Stir in the tomatoes, raise the heat and cook until the tomatoes are soft and most of their liquid has evaporated, about 5-10 minutes. Season to taste with salt, pepper and sugar.

5 Heat the grill to medium heat.

6 Choose a shallow flame-proof dish into which the fish will fit in a single layer. Heat the remaining oil in it.

7 Season the fish fairly liberally with salt and pepper on each side, place in the dish and turn so that each side is lightly coated with oil.

8 Grill the fish on each side for 4 minutes. Meanwhile, cut each anchovy fillet in half lengthways.

9 Spread each portion of fish with the tomato mixture and sprinkle a little oregano or thyme on top. Add the anchovy fillets, arranging them criss-cross fashion over the top of each fish steak.

10 Continue grilling for another 3-4 minutes until the fish is cooked through.

Handy hints

● Lemon juice, of course, is a perfect foil for all kinds of fish. It counteracts the richness of oily fish and heightens the flavour of white fish. Make it a golden rule when buying fish to buy a lemon at the same time.

● Glass working surfaces are excellent for fish as they do not retain the smell afterwards. The best type has a raised dimple surface to prevent the fish from slipping while you are working and to raise it up from the blood which escapes when the fish is gutted.

● When using a wooden chopping board cover it with several layers of paper (newspaper will do). This makes cleaning up afterwards easier and also prevents the chopping board from absorbing the fish flavour which could spoil other foods.

FISH FILLETS IN MORNAY SAUCE

Any fish fillets can be used for this dish and you can vary it by using fish steaks or cutlets instead of the fillets. Initial grilling time is slightly shorter than usual because the fish will continue cooking when it is covered with sauce and browned under grill.

SERVES 4
700 g [1½ lb] white fish fillets
15 ml [1 tablespoon] butter
salt and black pepper

For the Mornay sauce:
half a small onion
half a small carrot
quarter of a celery stalk
250 ml [½ pt] milk
bay leaf
62 g [2½ oz] butter
25 g [1 oz] flour
salt and white pepper
pinch of nutmeg
50 g [2 oz] Gruyère or
    Parmesan cheese

For the topping:
25 g [1 oz] Cheddar or
    Gruyère cheese

1 Prepare the vegetables, put into a pan and add the milk and bay leaf. Season and bring to the boil. Remove from the heat, cover and leave to infuse for 30 minutes. Then strain the milk and reheat gently.

2 Grate the cheese. Heat the grill to fierce heat and butter a flame-proof dish.

3 Melt 25 g [1 oz] of the butter in a pan over low heat. Remove from the heat and stir in the flour. Return to the heat and stir to a smooth paste.

4 Remove the pan from the heat and add the milk, stirring continuously. Bring to the boil, stirring, and then cover and simmer for 5 minutes.

Sprigs of parsley add a touch of green to fish fillets smothered under a lightly browned Mornay sauce.

5 Season the fish fillets. Place them in a single layer in the gratin dish, skin side up. Grill for 2 minutes to crisp the skin.

6 Carefully turn the fillets over with a fish slice, reduce heat to medium and continue grilling for 2 minutes.

7 Meanwhile, remove the sauce from the heat and stir into it 50 g [2 oz] cheese and the remaining butter.

8 Remove the gratin dish from under the grill and increase heat again to fierce.

9 Pour the Mornay sauce over the fish fillets. Sprinkle the remaining grated cheese on top.

10 Brown quickly under the grill and serve immediately.

CARNIVAL FISH KEBABS

Use thick fillets of firm white fish, such as gurnard, monk fish or rock salmon as well as coley and cod. Thick fillets are used so that they can be cut into the 2.5 cm (1") cubes required. A bed of boiled rice coloured with turmeric, or sweet corn topped with crumbled crispy bacon, goes well with this colourful dish. Serve the kebabs garnished with wedges of lemon.

SERVES 3
450 g [1 lb] fish fillets
1 large green pepper
100 g [¼ lb] cap mushrooms
1 garlic clove
6 bay leaves
6 small firm tomatoes

For the marinade:
45 ml [3 tablespoons] olive oil
30 ml [2 tablespoons] lemon juice
salt and black pepper
5 ml [1 teaspoon] dried oregano

1 Remove the skin from the fillets by easing it away from the flesh with a knife, then pulling gently with your fingers.

2 Cut the flesh into 2.5 cm [1"] cubes.

3 Cut the pepper in half, remove the stalk and seeds and blanch. To do this, put the pepper into a basin, cover with boiling water, leave for 5 minutes and then drain.

4 Cut the pepper into 2.5 cm [1"] squares.

5 Wipe the mushrooms clean with damp kitchen paper and trim stalks level with caps.

6 Mix all the marinade ingredients together in a basin and add the fish, green pepper and mushroom caps. Stir to coat the ingredients thoroughly. Cover and refrigerate for 2 hours. Stir once or twice during this time.

7 Rub kebab skewers with oil, then rub each skewer with a halved garlic clove to pick up the flavour.

Fish kebabs served on a bed of yellow rice and garnished with wedges of lemon makes a colourful and appetizing meal.

8 Drain the kebab ingredients from the marinade, reserving marinade. Thread pieces of fish, pepper and mushroom caps on to the skewers. Continue until all the ingredients have been used, including two bay leaves on each skewer.

9 Heat the grill pan with the grid in position to medium heat.

10 Put the kebabs on the grid and cook for 12 minutes, turning the skewers and basting with the marinade several times.

11 Slip the tomatoes on the ends of the skewers for the last 5 minutes of cooking time.

12 Heat any remaining marinade in a small pan.

13 Transfer the fish to a warmed serving dish and pour the heated marinade and pan juices over the fish. Garnish and serve immediately.

GOLDEN GRILL FISH FILLETS

A blanket of tangy creamed cheese keeps the fish beneath it beautifully moist and succulent, and is an excellent way to add zest to fish with a bland flavour. It is a good way of cooking any type of white fish fillets, steaks or cutlets—frozen or fresh—but remember to adjust temperature and timing accordingly if deviating from the basic recipe. Use equal quantities of Gruyère and Parmesan for a subtle flavour or Cheddar cheese to give a more robust flavour.

SERVES 4
4 cod fillets each weighing 150-175 g [5-6 oz]
salt and pepper
25 g [1 oz] butter
4 tomatoes
parsley sprigs

For the topping:
150 g [5 oz] grated cheese
15 ml [1 tablespoon] French mustard
30 ml [2 tablespoons] thin cream or top of milk

1 Choose a large, shallow flame-proof dish in which the fillets can lie side by side in a single layer, and in which they can be served.

2 Heat the grill to a fierce heat and melt the butter in the flame-proof dish.

3 Season the fish fillets by sprinkling them generously with salt and pepper.

4 Lay the fillets cut side down in the melted butter in the dish and grill under high heat for 2 minutes to crisp the skin.

5 Meanwhile put the cheese and mustard into a basin and beat in the cream to make a soft easily spread mixture.

6 Turn the fillets carefully with a fish slice and spread the cheese mixture evenly all over the cut side.

7 Reduce heat and grill under a medium heat (or lower the grill pan) for 6-8 minutes depending on the thickness of the fillets.

8 Cut the tomatoes in half and arrange, cut side up, around the fish for the last 5 minutes of grilling.

9 Do not let the dish overbrown. When cooked the surface should be a mottled golden brown all over. Garnish with parsley and serve immediately.

Variations

Substitute one of the following in place of the creamed cheese topping:
● For a caper grill, mix 45 ml [3 tablespoons] olive oil, 22 ml [1½ tablespoons] wine vinegar, 15 ml [1 tablespoon] drained and chopped capers, 15 ml [1 tablespoon] chopped pickled gherkins and salt and pepper to taste. Pour over the cut side of the fish and baste frequently while cooking. Sprinkle with chopped parsley just before serving.
● For a garden grill melt 50 g [2 oz] butter, add 30 ml [2 tablespoons] lemon juice and 45 ml [3 tablespoons] grated onion. Pour over the cut side of the fish and baste while cooking. Sprinkle with finely chopped chives before serving.
● For a devilled grill, melt 50 g [2 oz] butter, add 10 ml [2 teaspoons] curry powder, 15 ml [1 tablespoon] fruit chutney and 15 ml [1 tablespoon] French mustard. Mix the ingredients and spread over the cut side of the fish. Baste during grilling.

SERVES 4
2 whiting, each weighing
    350-450 g [¾-1 lb]
salt and black pepper
15 ml [1 tablespoon] butter

For the stuffing:
75 g [3 oz] butter, at
    room temperature
40 g [1½ oz] white breadcrumbs
30 ml [2 tablespoons] freshly
    chopped mixed herbs such
    as parsley, chives, balm
    and mint
salt
black pepper
1 lemon

1 Butter a flame-proof gratin dish.

2 Skin the fillets by easing a knife under the skin and gently pulling the skin away.

3 Cut each fillet in half lengthways so that you have a total of 8 fillets.

4 Heat the grill to medium heat and prepare the stuffing. First beat the butter in a small bowl until smooth and creamy.

5 Add the herbs and breadcrumbs.

6 Grate the lemon zest and add to the stuffing. Season with salt and pepper and mix well.

7 Squeeze the juice from the lemon and add a few drops to the stuffing, if required, to give it a spreading consistency.

8 Divide stuffing into 8 portions.

9 Using a round-bladed knife, spread each fillet lengthways with a portion of stuffing.

10 Roll up from the tail end and secure with a skewer or cocktail stick.

11 Place the rolled fish fillets in the buttered gratin dish, laying them flat in a single layer. Pour over the remaining lemon juice.

12 Grill under medium heat for 5 minutes and then turn each fillet over using a fish slice.

13 Grill for a further 5-8 minutes until the fish is cooked. Serve immediately.

PINWHEEL WHITING GRILL

Ask the fishmonger to clean and fillet the fish for you, or prepare them yourself following the step-by-step instructions given. The two fillets from each fish are divided lengthways into two and spread with stuffing before being rolled and grilled. Secure the pinwheels with poultry skewers or with wooden cocktail sticks. If using cocktail sticks, trim any protruding

Fillets of whiting are stuffed with a mixture of herbs, butter and breadcrumbs for a pinwheel grill.

ends or they may char when placed under the grill.

Fresh herbs are best for the stuffing. Use any that are available. The butter in the stuffing keeps the fish moist during grilling.

A fishy story

Oily fish include both sea and freshwater fish; they have darker flesh and are richer than white fish. They grill very well and have a great affinity with piquant sauces made from tart fruit such as gooseberries. Here we include details of oily fish and how to grill and serve them with sauces and savoury butters.

OILY FISH

The definition 'oily' is given to fish which have an oil content of between five per cent and 15 per cent. The oil is distributed throughout the flesh instead of being concentrated in the liver, as is the case of white fish (see pages 289–291). Oily fish include herring, mackerel, eel, salmon, sprats, sardines and mullet, among others. The flesh of all these fish is darker in colour than white fish and, as you might expect, they are richer to eat. In fact, some people have difficulty in digesting oily fish, so grilling is a better way of cooking.

Whereas white fish can be either flat or round, all oily fish are round. Some oily fish are seasonal but the more common and popular ones are available all year round, either fresh or frozen. Frozen oily fish should not be kept for more than 2 months.

Carp is a freshwater fish with a muddy flavour. To counteract this soak it in salted water for at least three hours before cooking it. There are different varieties and sizes—small fish can be grilled whole but a larger fish is better baked or poached, with or without stuffing.

Common eel is a freshwater fish. It can be smoked or jellied, and it is also available fresh. It is displayed at the fishmongers alive. The fishmonger will kill it for you on purchase or you can take it home alive—it should be cooked as soon as possible after killing. It is tasty and can be fried, grilled or poached and is also particularly suitable for fish soups and stews.

Grey mullet is not related to red mullet. It is fatty and can be grilled although large grey mullet is better baked, poached or fried rather than grilled.

Herring is a salt-water fish and is eaten by most people in the form of kippers. It is also available salted and as rollmops and buckling. Herring is sold fresh, usually whole, and is very tasty. This is a very versatile fish but it is at its best simply grilled and served with a savoury butter. Soft herring roes are sold separately and these too can be grilled or poached.

Mackerel is a salt-water fish. It may be smoked and, of all oily fish, it is probably the most popular for grilling (being cheaper than trout). Mackerel goes off very quickly and should therefore be bought as fresh as possible and cooked on the day of purchase. It can be served hot or cold.

Pilchards are small salt-water fish and are seldom available fresh as they do not keep at all well and are therefore canned.

Red mullet is a salt-water fish with a delicate flavour and distinctive for its close texture. Small fish are delicious grilled whole. Mullet can also be baked, poached or fried.

Salmon is a salt-water fish which spawns in fresh water. It is probably best known to most people in its canned form and also its smoked. Fresh salmon is available as steaks and cutlets. Tail-end pieces can be baked or poached whole. Salmon is of all fish the most highly prized. It is tasty and has a distinctive texture and appearance. It is also expensive, but a great treat for an occasional splurge.

Sea or salmon trout is smaller than salmon. Although no relation to the salmon, it is similar in appearance—hence its name. It is more delicate in flavour, and it is usually baked or poached, but may be substituted for salmon in salmon recipes.

Sprats are small salt-water fish related to the herring family. They are often fried but can be grilled for a light snack and are a cheap alternative to whitebait.

Trout is a freshwater fish which has become so popular that it is specially reared on fish farms. It can be smoked. Fresh trout is usually gutted and grilled or fried whole for one serving.

Whitebait is the fry (or young) of herring and sprats and is made up of a mass of these tiny silver fish. Whitebait is best deep-fried whole, complete with heads and backbones, and served as an appetizer.

CHOOSING FISH
Oily fish are sold in the same cuts as white fish: whole, as steaks or as cutlets or fillets, depending on the size of the fish. Always look for signs of freshness. Gills, eyes and skin should be bright. Any sign of dullness denotes poor quality and should be avoided. Scaly fish, such as herring, should have plenty of scales. Fillets, cutlets and steaks should look firm and bright. In addition to the above, oily fish should be 'stiff alive', as the fishermen say, and not floppy when picked up.

Quantities and preparation of oily fish are the same as for round white fish (see pages 291–293). Remember that it is always important to look for signs of freshness and to cook fish on the day of purchase. When grilling fish whole, it is optional whether you remove the head and tail but the fish looks better served with them; the diners then remove the flesh from the bones on the dinner plate. If, however, the fish is to be split open and laid out flat, the head should be removed. Most oily fish are cleaned, boned and filleted in the same way as round white fish.

You are more likely to find roes in herring and mackerel than in white fish. Leave the roe in the fish or combine it with a stuffing. If you have sufficient quantity, roes can be grilled separately.

Herring has a lot of scales and mackerel has none, but as mackerel has a larger belly than herring the overall cleaning time will remain the same.

GRILLING OILY FISH

Whole oily fish to be grilled must be given a few oblique slits along each side. These slits prevent the fish from splitting because the flesh contracts as it cooks, pulling away from the skin. It also allows the heat to penetrate for even cooking. Make three or four cuts 2.5 cm [1"] apart in the body on each side.

Apart from an initial brushing with oil to help crisp the skin and prevent the fish from sticking to the grid, no additional fat is needed. Oily fish are at their best well seasoned with salt and pepper plus, if you wish, a little lemon juice or wine vinegar. Serve with a tangy sauce to counteract the richness.

Grilling time depends on the size and therefore the thickness of the fish—do not overcook fish as they will dry out. Fresh fish cook slightly quicker than frozen fish. Generally fish are grilled under a medium heat but, to crisp the skin on fillets, grilling is started under a fierce heat which is then reduced after about two minutes or the pan is lowered.

Split fish, steaks and cutlets cook more quickly than whole round fish and can be grilled closer to the heat or under a slightly higher heat. Grill fillets for 3-5 minutes each side. The skin is left on as it does help to hold the fillet together. Grill the skin side first under a fierce heat for 2 minutes to dry it out. Reduce heat and continue grilling. Turn the fillet over with a fish slice and finish the cooking. Cutlets and steaks need to be cooked for 6-10 minutes on each side, depending on thickness.

Small whole round fish weighing up to 450 g [1 lb] need 6-12 minutes under a medium heat on each side.

Larger fish should be grilled at a slightly lower temperature long enough for the heat to penetrate the thickest part of the fish.

Ridged-pan grilling

Fish can be pan grilled or 'dry fried'. A very thick frying pan made of iron or cast aluminium is essential or, better still, is a ridged iron pan which gives fish a 'quadrilled' surface.

Heat the pan over a high heat for a few minutes until it is thoroughly hot. Grease the pan with a piece of hard fat impaled on a fork, or brush the pan with oil. Use just enough oil to give a thin film of grease. Pour off any surplus. When the oil is sizzling put the seasoned fish in the pan. Grill the fish but decrease the cooking time by about 1 minute on each side.

A variety of oily fish—1 Carp. 2 Herring. 3 Sprats. 4 Red mullet. 5 Eel. 6 Whitebait. 7 Trout. 8 Grey mullet. 9 Mackerel.

SAVOURY BUTTERS

These are an excellent way of adding both fat and flavouring to fish. Oily fish do not need the extra fat so much as white fish but the herbs or other flavouring in the butter make the fish more interesting, while the butter provides a little sauce at the same time.

Use chilled pats of butter to top the cooked fish, or use the savoury butter as a stuffing, or put it on the fish halfway through cooking time and, as it melts, use it to baste the fish. Be sure to pour the buttery juices from the pan over the fish just before serving.

The savoury butters mentioned in previous courses may be used but the following are particularly good with oily fish:
● For mustard butter, cream 50 g [2 oz] unsalted butter with 10 ml [2 teaspoons] French mustard. Season with salt and pepper.
● For mustard and watercress butter, add 15 ml [1 tablespoon] finely chopped watercress to a mustard butter. Use this for a topping only and not as a baste.
● For anise butter, cream 50 g [2 oz] unsalted butter with 10-15 ml [2-3 teaspoons] Pernod, pastis or Ricard. This is an interesting flavour with fish.

SAUCES

The best sauces for rich oily fish such as mackerel and herring are ones that contrast sharply in flavour and texture and reduce the richness of the fish.

GOOSEBERRY SAUCE

This is best made from early season cooking gooseberries which are still very sharp and fresh tasting. It is a perfect foil for grilled mackerel.

SERVES 4
225 g [½ lb] green gooseberries
15 ml [1 tablespoon] white sugar
10 ml [2 teaspoons] butter
pinch of grated nutmeg

1 Top and tail the gooseberries and rinse in cold water.

2 Put into a small heavy-based saucepan with 60 ml [4 tablespoons] water and leave uncovered. Stew gently for 10-15 minutes until all the gooseberries become soft. Then allow to cool a little.

3 Reduce to a purée in a liquidizer. For a rough-textured sauce, break up the gooseberries to release the juice by beating briskly with a small wire whisk.

4 Return to the saucepan, reheat and add the sugar, butter and nutmeg. Serve hot or cold.

Variations

Substitute one of the following for the gooseberries.
● For rhubarb sauce: use young rhubarb and, instead of nutmeg, a piece of finely grated orange zest.
● For damson sauce: use damsons and remove stones from the cooked fruit with a spoon before reducing to a purée.

APPLE AND HORSERADISH CREAM

This is a delicately sharp, uncooked sauce especially suited to grilled herring and is also good with mackerel.

SERVES 4
1 large cooking apple
15 ml [1 tablespoon] lemon juice
15 ml [1 tablespoon] horseradish sauce
45 ml [3 tablespoons] thick cream or sour cream

1 Quarter the apple, cut out the core and grate the flesh including the skin on the coarse side of a grater.

2 Immediately add the lemon juice and stir to mix thoroughly.

3 Stir in the horseradish and the cream and serve.

Grilled whole herring is accompanied by parsnips—a tasty Scottish custom. Apple and horseradish cream is an uncooked sauce.

GRILLED WHOLE HERRING

There is no better way of cooking herring than grilling. Vinegar is spooned into cuts in the fish to counteract the rich oiliness of the herring.

Eating parsnips with herring is a Scottish custom—the flavours do go together very well. Instead of boiling the parsnips as given in the recipe, they can be steamed; for this method chop them into pieces as steaming whole parsnips takes a long time.

Serve the grilled herring with apple and horseradish cream or a mustard sauce.

SERVES 4
4 fresh herring weighing 225-350 g [$\frac{1}{2}$-$\frac{3}{4}$ lb] each
700 g [1$\frac{1}{2}$ lb] parsnips
15 ml [1 tablespoon] cooking oil
salt and black pepper
15 ml [1 tablespoon] wine vinegar
2.5 ml [$\frac{1}{2}$ teaspoon] caraway seeds (optional)
30 ml [2 tablespoons] butter

1 Scrub the parsnips under cold running water.

2 If the fishmonger has not already done so, prepare the herring by scaling and gutting it. Wash outside and inside under running water, and blot dry.

3 Fill a large pan one-third full of water. Add salt and bring to the boil.

4 Add the parsnips to the boiling water. Cover and simmer for 20 minutes.

5 Cut 3 oblique slits on each side along the length of each fish.

6 Heat the grill pan to a medium heat with the grill pan and grid in position.

7 Brush the fish with oil and season with salt and pepper.

8 Lay the fish on the grid and spoon a few drops of vinegar into each of the exposed cuts.

9 Grill for about 6 minutes.

10 Turn the fish gently, spoon a few drops of vinegar into the cuts and continue grilling for 6-8 minutes until the fish is cooked.

11 Drain the parsnips as soon as they are cooked. Chop them into bite-sized pieces.

12 Melt the butter in the empty pan. Add the parsnip pieces and shake the pan so that they are covered on all sides with the butter. Grind over a generous quantity of black pepper.

13 Arrange the parsnips round the edge of a large serving dish and sprinkle over the caraway seeds. Put the herrings in the middle.

BROILED SPLIT MACKEREL

Serve gooseberry sauce with this dish as the sauce is the perfect complement to the richness of plainly grilled mackerel. If gooseberries are out of season, use another fruit such as damsons or, even, rhubarb.

SERVES 4
4 fresh mackerel weighing 225-350 g [$\frac{1}{2}$-$\frac{3}{4}$ lb] each
salt and pepper
15 ml [1 tablespoon] cooking oil

For the garnish:
gooseberry sauce
sprigs of parsley or watercress

1 If the fishmonger has not already prepared the fish, cut off the gill covers on both sides of each fish and remove the heads.

2 Make a slit along the belly cavity to two-thirds of the length and gut the fish. Remove any black skin inside the cavity.

3 Wash the body cavity of the fish under running water and blot dry.

4 Cut the fish open from the belly cavity to the tail end. Press it along its backbone to open it without actually halving the fish.

5 Turn the fish over, and working from the head end, ease away the backbone from the flesh. Cut it free where it joins the tail, lift it out with as many bones as possible.

6 Sprinkle with salt and pepper and brush both sides with oil.

7 Heat the grill to a high heat with the grill pan and grid in position.

8 Lay the mackerel open on the grid so that the whole skin is exposed to the heat. Cook for 2 minutes to crisp the skin.

9 Reduce heat to medium and carefully turn the fish over. Grill for 4-6 minutes until cooked through.

10 Heat the gooseberry sauce in a small saucepan.

11 Serve the fish flesh side up on a heated plate with a little hot fruit sauce spooned down the centre of each fish. Garnish with parsley or watercress.

MACKEREL MARINATA

Fresh mackerel, marinated then grilled and served cold make a substantial but elegant main meal dish to serve with a crisp salad. The mackerel can be boned or left whole.

SERVES 4
4 fresh mackerel weighing about 225-350 g [$\frac{1}{2}$-$\frac{3}{4}$ lb] each

For the marinade:
45 ml [3 tablespoons] olive oil
45 ml [3 tablespoons] lemon juice
5 ml [1 teaspoon] salt
black pepper
1 bay leaf

For the garnish:
2 seedless oranges
50 g [2 oz] black olives
watercress sprigs

1 If the fishmonger has not already gutted the fish, make a slit along two-thirds of the body length. Scrape out the inside of belly cavity and remove black skin.

2 Wash the belly cavity under running water and blot dry.

3 Cut off the gill covers on both sides of each fish.

4 Cut the fish open from the belly cavity to the tail end. Press it along its backbone to open it without actually halving the fish.

5 Working from the head end, ease away the backbone from the fish. Cut it free at the head and tail ends. Lift it out with as many bones as possible and discard.

6 Cut a few oblique slits along the body length.

7 Place fish side by side in a flameproof dish.

8 Mix all the ingredients for the marinade together; pour it over the fish and spoon it into the body cavity. Cover and refrigerate for 2 hours turning the fish occasionally.

9 Heat the grill to a medium heat.

10 Uncover the fish, baste again with the marinade and place the dish under grill.

11 Cook for 6-8 minutes depending on size. Turn over carefully and grill for a further 6-8 minutes until the fish is cooked. Baste with pan juices during grilling time.

12 Set aside in a cool place until completely cold, basting occasionally.

13 To serve, arrange the fish on a flat platter and spoon a little of the marinade over them. Slice the oranges thinly and arrange around the fish with the olives and watercress sprigs.

GRILLED SPRATS

Sprats are inexpensive and make a tasty grill. The problem of turning so many small fish is solved by skewering them in a row like clothes on a line. Serve sprats on their own for a snack allowing 450 g [1 lb] for 3 portions—this will give about 7-8 fish per portion.

Serve with lemon wedges and brown bread and butter. Children will also enjoy grilled sprats. This dish can be served as a first course to a meal.

Sprats are small and the bones are soft enough to eat. There is no need to remove the head or tail as they are edible. Grill the sprats under a high heat to crisp the skins—the flesh cooks quickly because the fish are so small.

SERVES 3
450 g [1 lb] sprats
15 ml [1 tablespoon] oil
salt and black pepper

1 Wash the sprats under running cold water, then pat dry with kitchen paper.

2 Put them into a basin, add the oil, salt and pepper, and stir gently so that each fish is lightly coated with oil and seasoning.

3 Heat the grill to a high heat.

4 Thread the sprats through the heads on two or three metal skewers, spacing them out so that each fish will lie flat on the grid without overlapping—the grid allows surplus fat to drain away.

5 Grill close to a high heat until the skin is crisp and golden then carefully lift each skewer and turn it over to present the uncooked side of the sprats to the grill.

6 Grill for another 2-3 minutes until crisp and cooked through.

7 Ease the sprats off the skewer with a fork on to a hot serving dish. Garnish with lemons and serve.

Left: mackerel marinata is a colourful and substantial dish which is served cold.
Right: grilled sprats cooked on skewers make an enjoyable tea-time treat.

SALMON STEAKS FLORENTINE

This superb dish tastes as magnificent as it looks—and it's easy and quick to prepare too!

SERVES 4
**4 salmon steaks about 2.5 cm
[1″] thick
50 g [2 oz] unsalted butter
1 kg [2 lb] spinach
50 ml [2 fl oz] thick cream
salt and black pepper**

**For the sauce:
175 g [6 oz] unsalted butter
juice of half a lemon
salt and white pepper
cayenne pepper**

1 Remove stems and discard any yellow leaves from the spinach.

2 Wash thoroughly and drain to remove excess water.

3 Heat the grill to a medium heat.

4 Season the salmon steaks.

5 Place the salmon on the grid of the grill pan and dot each steak with butter.

6 Grill for 8-10 minutes.

7 Meanwhile pack the spinach into a large pan and place it on a fairly high heat. Cover.

8 As soon as the spinach starts sizzling, turn it using a wooden spoon. Reduce the heat.

9 Turn the salmon steaks over and cook for 8-10 minutes, basting with the pan juices during this time.

10 Turn the spinach over in the pan; it will reduce in quantity as it cooks. Continue cooking for a total of 10-12 minutes.

11 Melt the butter for the sauce and add the lemon juice and seasonings.

12 Turn the cooked spinach into a colander and press with a spoon to extract any moisture.

Lemon twists add a decorative touch to salmon steaks which are served on a bed of spinach with a butter sauce.

13 Return to empty pan and add cream, salt and pepper. Mix together and transfer to a serving dish.

14 Transfer the cooked salmon steaks on to the spinach and pour the butter sauce over. Serve immediately.

KIPPERS GRILLED FACE TO FACE

Kipper cures vary a great deal from smoker to smoker so always ask the fishmonger the best method of cooking the particular brand he stocks. For mildly cured kippers grilling is best and the following way of cooking them in pairs keeps them especially moist and succulent. Allow 1 pair of kippers for 2 portions.

SERVES 2
**1 pair of kippers
25 g [1 oz] butter at room
temperature**

1 Heat the grill to a medium heat.

2 Cut the heads off the kippers. Spread the flesh side of one kipper with half the softened butter. Lay the other kipper, flesh side down, on top of it, like a sandwich.

3 Lay on the grid and cook for about 5 minutes.

4 Using a fish slice turn the pair of kippers over and grill the other side for 5 minutes.

5 To serve, separate the kippers and arrange the butter side uppermost, with a pat of the remaining butter on each.

HERRING ROE TOASTS

To grill herring roes use the grill pan without the grid. If the grill pan is large, use a flame-proof dish instead as the pan or dish should be only large enough to hold the roes in a single layer.

SERVES 4
**450 g [1 lb] soft herring roes
5 ml [1 teaspoon] curry powder
black pepper
2.5 ml [½ teaspoon] salt
15 ml [1 tablespoon] flour
65 g [2½ oz] butter
4 slices of bread**

**pinch paprika pepper
parsley sprigs**

1 Heat the grill to a moderate heat with the grill pan in position but remove the grid.

2 Put the roes in a colander and rinse under cold water. Remove any black or silver threads.

3 Drain the roes on kitchen paper and blot dry.

4 Add the curry powder, pepper and salt to the flour and mix well. Roll roes in the seasoned flour until they are thoroughly covered.

5 Melt 40 g [1½ oz] butter in the grill pan or dish and, when hot, put in the roes. Turn them carefully with a spoon to coat them with butter.

6 Grill gently for about 5-6 minutes, turning and basting them now and then.

7 Cut the crusts from the bread. Place the slices on the grid and place the grid over the roes in the grill pan. Toast the bread on both sides.

8 Spread the toast with butter, arrange the roes on the toast and sprinkle lightly with paprika.

9 Garnish with parsley and serve very hot.

RED MULLET WITH FENNEL

Herring, mackerel and sea bream can also be used for this recipe. The essential thing is that the fish must be fresh. The dried fennel stalks impart a smoky aniseed fragrance to the fish.

SERVES 4
**4 red mullet each weighing
about 350 g [¾ lb]
3 dozen dried fennel stalks
40 g [1½ oz] butter at room
temperature
15 ml [1 tablespoon] chopped
parsley
15 ml [1 tablespoon] lemon
juice
salt and black pepper
15 ml [1 tablespoon] oil
15 ml [1 tablespoon] brandy**

1 Remove heads from the fish, gut, and bone them if you wish. Wash

and dry the fish. Score each side of each fish with 3 or 4 cuts along the body.

2 Heat the grill to a medium heat.

3 Stuff each fish with 6 fennel stalks. Place the remaining fennel stalks on a flame-proof serving dish and keep warm.

4 Mix together the butter, parsley and lemon juice and season generously with salt and pepper.

5 Fill the cuts in the fish with the butter mixture.

6 Brush the fish with oil and place on the grid of the grill pan.

7 Grill the fish for 6-10 minutes (depending on size) until the skin is crisp and golden.

8 Carefully turn the fish over and brush with oil and continue grilling for 6-10 minutes until the fish is cooked through.

9 Place the grid with the fish on it over the fennel stalks in the flame-proof serving dish.

10 Heat a metal tablespoon and pour the brandy into it. Set fire to the brandy and pour it over the fish. The fennel stalks will catch fire giving off smoke which imparts its flavour to the fish. Let the fish stand over the smoking stalks for 10 minutes before serving.

Variation
If fresh fennel is available, it makes an interesting variation instead of the dried stalks and the brandy.
● Cut the fennel stalks from the top of the bulb, and insert one into each fish. Cut the bulb into paper thin slices, sprinkle with oil, lemon juice and salt, and arrange it as a garnish round the fish.

Small red mullet—a salt-water fish—is close textured and has a delicate flavour.

308

Full steam ahead

For many people steamed fish conjures up images of invalid meals with portions of anaemic white fish languishing in a pool of pale, insipid sauce. Here we introduce flat fish and explain the secret of steaming fish to retain all its original flavour and nutrients as well as the preparation of skinning and filleting.

ADVANTAGES OF STEAMING

Steaming is one of the most popular ways of cooking fish in Chinese and Japanese cookery, where the art of adding colour and flavour, and presenting the fish attractively is thoroughly understood. It is a method which uses an absolute minimum of fuel, and where the same fuel can be used to cook other small pieces of food at the same time. This makes steaming a very convenient method for campers, caravanners or people living in limited accommodation, as well as for everyone trying to keep down fuel bills. Another advantage of this cooking method is that all the valuable nutrients in the fish are retained.

Bear in mind the following to serve fish at its best.

1 Use really fresh fish—steaming is a method which retains all the natural flavour, so the fresher the fish the better the results.

2 Season the fish well. Even the freshest fish is improved if sprinkled generously with salt, lightly with white pepper (the colour of white pepper looks more attractive than black with most fish) and finally, adding a good squeeze of lemon juice. This seasoning is best done immediately after preparation (cleaning and filleting) so that the flavours have a chance to penetrate during the time the fish is kept in the refrigerator before it is cooked. Fine-flavoured fish, such as sole, halibut and John Dory need no other seasoning, but less tasty fish such as megrim or witch, benefit from more exotic seasonings, such as soy sauce and spices, which are added just before cooking.

3 Do not overcook fish. Fish cooks remarkably quickly so always time the cooking carefully (use a timer if necessary). Overcooking spoils the texture as well as the flavour. Steam fish in a single layer so that it cooks evenly.

4 Add tasty and colourful sauces and garnishes. For flavour use the juices that escape from the fish during steaming to make the sauce.

To give the fish eye-appeal as

well as flavour, counteract the whiteness of fish with colourful ingredients such as lemon or orange slices, tomatoes, mushrooms and strips of sweet pepper.

SUITABLE FISH FOR STEAMING

Steaming is primarily a method for cooking portions of fish or small whole fish, but it is not suitable for whole large fish. Use it for:
● thick fillets of round fish, cut in portions
● steaks or cutlets
● small whole white fish, such as dab or whiting
● thin fillets of flat fish which can either be folded or rolled.

FLAT FISH

All fish are hatched 'round' (as described on pages 289–308) with one eye on each side of the head. It is the habit of a flat fish to lie on the seabed, with the result that the eye that has no field of vision gradually works its way around towards the light to lie on the top side of the fish beside the other eye. The mouth, of course, remains in its original position. The body flattens to give the fish its characteristic shape. For camouflage the skin on the uppermost side becomes pigmented, but that on the underside remains pale. The skin on the unprotected side also becomes considerably thicker than that on the lower side.

The colour and marking of the dark skin varies considerably in tone, even within the same species, as this is nature's way of camouflaging the fish to make it as indistinguishable as possible from its natural background of pebbles, sand or mud. Which side of the fish becomes pigmented depends on the species, and results in some fish being known as 'right handed' and some as 'left handed'.

To decide the 'handedness' of a particular fish all you have to do is to hold it, dark side uppermost, with the gut cavity nearest to you. If the head then points to your left, the fish is left handed, and vice versa. In fact the only three left-handed fish commonly used for food in the United Kingdom are turbot, brill and megrim; the others are all right handed.

All flat fish are white fish (oily fish are all round). Flat fish only make up a small percentage of the white fish

landings but they include many different species of varying sizes. Depending on the catches, these fish are available all the year round, but are least plentiful, and not at their best, in spring, that is, during and immediately after spawning. For convenience the flat fish are divided into two groups.

Small flat fish include plaice and sole, the smaller specimens of which are often bought whole, while the larger ones can be bought either whole or filleted.

Large flat fish such as halibut and turbot, are usually cut up for sale by the fishmonger, but smaller specimens are sometimes sold whole. Sizes are very variable, depending on the age of the fish when caught.

CHOOSING FLAT FISH

Like round and oily fish, the sooner most flat fish are cooked after catching the better they taste. So look first for signs of freshness, for fish in season, and for small to medium-sized fish in preference to larger fish of the same species. Always look for plump, thick fish or fillets rather than thin ones. It is useful to know that the dark-skinned upper fillets of flat fish are usually thicker than those from the underside.

Whole fish. Look for a firm fish with bright, fresh colouring and a moist skin. Fish when just caught, and therefore very fresh, often has a positively slimy skin (especially lemon sole). This protects the fish from going stale, so do not wash it off until you are preparing the fish for cooking. Eyes should be bright and protruding, rather than dull and sunken. Dryness, floppiness or anything other than a clean, fresh smell are signs of staleness.

Fillets and cutlets. The flesh should have a bright, firm look. Avoid fish with a spongy texture or dull surface.

Frozen fish. Inshore fish (that is, caught near the shore), frozen on landing, or fish frozen at sea, can be fresher than so called 'fresh fish' bought inland. Generally speaking, however, with the exception of plaice, flat fish are not available in sufficient quantities for mass-market freezing.

Buy frozen fish where the turnover is rapid, because once in the distribution chain the recommended storage life of frozen white fish is up to three months.

1 Halibut
2 Brill
3 Turbot

Large varieties of flat fish

TURBOT

Turbot is a thick, left-handed, round-shaped fish. The darker skin is a dull grey-brown with lighter specks and darker blotches and occasional blunt, boney tubercles. Turbot is a fine-flavoured, firm-fleshed fish and relatively expensive.

How sold: the fish is cut up into cutlets and fillets. Small, or chicken turbot, is sometimes sold for cooking

and serving whole.

Ways of cooking: cook cutlets by any method. Whole turbot is sometimes poached in a specially shaped fish kettle. Turbot is very good served cold.

Brill
Brill is very similar to turbot, but with a smooth skin and slightly more oval shape. The dark skin is fawnish-brown, the underside white with pinkish markings. Only small quantities of brill are landed. Brill is usually less expensive than turbot.
How sold: as for turbot.
Ways of cooking: as for turbot. Brill is particularly good grilled.

HALIBUT
A long, right-handed, diamond-shaped fish with thickish body. The dark skin is seen in varying shades of dark green to grey, the underside is white. Potentially halibut is the largest of the flat fish. Small, immature fish are known as chicken halibut. A choice, firm-fleshed and fine-flavoured fish, halibut is relatively expensive.
How sold: halibut is usually sold in cutlets cut right across the fish. These are cut in half if from very large fish. The tail piece is sold as one cut.
Ways of cooking: cook cutlets by any method. Halibut is a substantial and satisfying fish. The tail piece is usually poached or braised. A good

fish for serving cold.

MOCK HALIBUT
(Greenland halibut, blue halibut)
This fish is rather similar to halibut but the dark skin is purple-brown and the underside is also pigmented. It is less expensive than true halibut but the flavour and texture are inferior to it.
How sold: rarely seen whole, this fish is usually cut into cutlets or fillets at the port and transported frozen.
Ways of cooking: cook this fish by any method, but good seasoning and sauces are needed to compensate for lack of flavour and texture.

1 Lemon sole
2 Dover sole
3 John Dory
4 Dab
5 Witch
6 Plaice

Small varieties of flat fish

PLAICE

This is a right-handed, 'pointed oval-shaped' fish. The tone colour of the dark skin is variable—speckled with many orange, red, yellow or chestnut spots—and also varies according to habitat. The underside is creamy white. This is a soft-textured fish with variable flavour.

How sold: small fish are sold whole or as cross-cut fillets, larger fish are sold whole or as quarter-cut fillets.

Ways of cooking: cook fillets by any method. Coating and frying helps to add crispness and texture. Plaice is best served with rich and tasty sauces.

DAB

Dab is a right-handed fish of ovoid shape. The dark skin is grey-brown with dark speckles (but no coloured spots), the underside is a broken white. This is an inshore fish, locally caught, with good landings off the English Channel. It can grow up to 42 cm [17"] long. Dab has a good flavour and firm texture.

How sold: usual landings of small fish, up to 350 g [¾ lb] are sold whole. The heads are usually left on but they can be removed if wished. Larger dab can be filleted.

Ways of cooking: dab is best cooked on the bone, whole, by grilling, frying or steaming. It can be cut crosswise into slices and fried. Fillets of dab can be cooked by any method.

FLOUNDER (fluke)

This is an ovoid fish, normally right handed (but can be found reversed). An inshore fish, it sometimes lives in fresh water inlets. The variable dark skin has reddish blotches, while the underside is opaque white. Landings of the fish are small.

How sold: flounder is usually sold whole, but if the fish is large enough the fishmonger will fillet it for you.

Ways of cooking: if caught in brackish water, the fish can have a muddy flavour which may be counteracted by sprinkling with salt and leaving overnight. Cook it by any method.

SOLE

Dover sole is considered the aristocrat of the sole family. It is a right-handed fish with a narrow streamlined shape. The upper side has dark grey blotched skin, with white underside. This firm-fleshed fish of fine flavour is expensive.

312

How sold: Dover sole: 225–700 g [½–1½ lb], slips: 175–225 g [6–8 oz], tongues: 100–175 g [4–6 oz]. Smaller fish are sold whole, but large fish of 450 g [1 lb] or over can be filleted. A whole fish usually has the head left on. It is usual to remove the dark skin only.

Ways of cooking: cook sole by any method. Small fish are best grilled, or fried à la meuniére, on the bone. Fillets are usually poached and used as the base for a vast range of classic fish dishes. Bones and trimmings should be used for making stock.

LEMON SOLE (smear dab)
A right-handed lemon-shaped plump fish. The darker side is a distinctive golden to sandy-brown colour with a creamy white underside. An excellent fish for eating, of fine flavour and medium-firm texture. In Scotland often referred to as 'sole'.

How sold: as for sole.
Ways of cooking: as for sole.

WITCH (Torbay sole, pole dab or grey sole)
A thin, right-handed fish of elongated oval shape. It is easily recognised by its almost transparent appearance and 'ragged' fins. The dark skin is mottled pale brown, the underside is greyish white. This is a cheaper fish of inferior quality and has a low yield of flesh to bones.

How sold: witch is usually sold whole, but could be filleted if it were large enough.
Ways of cooking: as for plaice.

MEGRIM (whiff, meg, Scarborough sole)
A thin, left-handed fish of oval shape. The dark skin is light brown in colour with yellow and dark brown blotches;

the underside is off-white.
How sold: megrim is usually sold whole, but could be filleted if large enough.
Ways of cooking: as for plaice.

JOHN DORY
This distinctive fish is not strictly a flat fish, but a round fish flattened sideways with an eye on each side of the head. The colouring all over is olive to brown with yellowish wavy bands. Its distinguishing features are a large black mark (St Peter's thumb mark) in the centre and a large head. Small landings make this an expensive fish, but one of fine flavour and texture.
How sold: John Dory is sold whole if small (allow for beheading and trimming) or in quarter-cut fillets if large enough.
Ways of cooking: grill, steam, poach or fry.

Step-by-step to cross-cut fillets of flat fish

1 To prepare cross-cut fillets, lay fish on board with head facing you. Cut off head and tail. Trim fins.

2 Place the knife with blade facing away from you at the head end. Push knife under flesh.

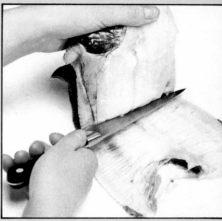

3 Work along backbone, and with a sawing movement work towards the outer edge to free fillet.

Step-by-step to skinning fillet of flat fish

1 To skin a fillet, lay the fillet with its skin down and tail end towards you.

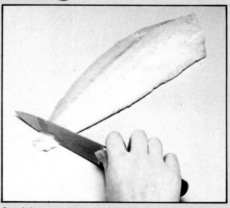

2 About 12 mm [½"] from the tail end cut through the flesh down to the skin.

3 Hold the tail of the fish firmly with fingers dipped in salt and, with the other hand, hold the knife.

Step-by-step to skinning a Dover sole

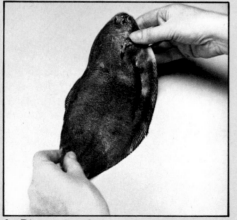

1 Place the fish with its dark skin facing upwards and tail end towards you.

2 Cut through the skin about 12 mm [½"] from the tail end and free enough skin to catch hold of.

3 Dip fingers in salt and hold the tail firmly with the one hand and grip skin with the other hand.

Step-by-step to quarter-cut flat fish

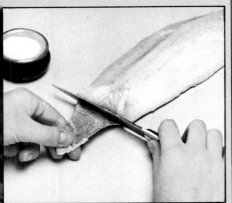

4 Don't turn the fish over but repeat on the other side of the backbone to free second fillet.

1 To prepare quarter-cut fillets, lay fish, dark skin up, on a board. Cut off head and tail. Trim fins.

2 Place the fish with its tail end facing you. Cut down to the bone along the length of the fish.

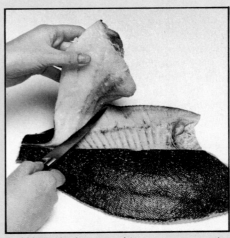

4 With the knife firmly against the skin, work the flesh up and away to free it completely.

3 To remove the first fillet, work the knife into the cut and gently lift the flesh.

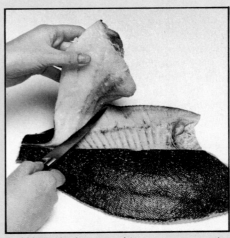

4 With light, stroking movements use the knife to free the fillet from the head end to the tail.

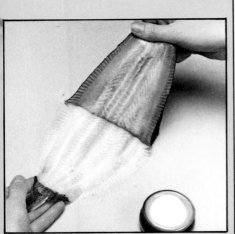

4 With a swift movement rip the skin off from tail to head. It should come away in one piece.

5 To remove the second fillet, turn the fish round and repeat the same action.

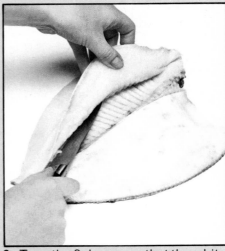

6 Turn the fish over so that the white skin is facing upwards. Remove two remaining fillets.

QUANTITIES

People's appetites vary enormously but, as a rough guide, any one of the following will provide enough for a main dish for one adult.

Fillets—150–175 g [5–6 oz].
Cutlets—175–200 g [6–7 oz]— slightly more than for fillets to allow for the bones.
One small whole fish—250–350 g [9–12 oz]. Additional weight here allows for head, tail and bones.
Large whole fish—allow 225 g [½ lb] per portion. This allows for the head and tail wastage. The weight of steaks or cutlets cut from large whole fish should be as given above.

PREPARING FLAT FISH FOR COOKING

Flat fish of not more than 450 g [1 lb] in weight is usually sold and cooked on the bone. To gut a flat fish make a semi-circular slit on the dark side behind the head and scrape out the entrails (flat fish have a relatively small amount of intestines). Fish with small heads, dabs for example, can be served with the head on, but if the fish has a large, unattractive head, such as John Dory, this must be removed. A good fishmonger will always fillet small flat fish for you without charge, and will also remove the skin if you wish. However, neither job is difficult to do yourself.

Cross-cut fillets. This means you get two fillets from each fish, one fillet taken right across the backbone on each side of the fish, making two good portions. This method is used for flat fish weighing 350–450 g [¾–1 lb]. Cross-cut fillets are naturally thin and are therefore not usually steamed.

Quarter-cut fillets. This method gives you four fillets from a fish, one fillet from either side of the backbone and two fillets from each side of the fish. This is the usual method for flat fish weighing 450–900 g [1–2 lb]. Quarter-cut fillets can be skinned or not according to preference. Often only the dark-skinned fillets, which are naturally thicker, are skinned.

STEAMING FISH

Keeping fish is not recommended. Generally fish should be cooked on the day of purchase and it should never be kept for longer than 24 hours.

Ideally, the fish should be pre-pared as close to cooking time as possible. However, this is not always convenient and if preparation is done a few hours in advance no harm will be done. Cover the fish when pre-pared and keep it chilled until it is required for cooking.

If the fish is to be steamed, it can be prepared as soon as you get it home. Skin and fillet the fish if you wish, season it with salt and pepper and a squeeze of lemon juice. It is a positive advantage to season fish a little ahead of cooking it, and not only when steaming. Then cover and refrigerate it until it is time to start cooking. If other seasonings and flavourings, such as soy sauce, are used, add these just before cooking.

Steaming is a method whereby fish is cooked in the vapour of boiling water. Fish should always be steamed by the closed method. This ensures that all the nutrients and flavour are preserved, either in the fish itself or in the juices which escape from the fish into the con-tainer. These juices can then be added to the sauce. This way all the food value and flavour is retained and nothing is lost.

The rate of cooking is fairly rapid, although slower than when fish is poached or cooked in an open steamer. Naturally it helps to speed things if a good heat conductor, such as an aluminium container, is used rather than one of thick china.

Equipment for steaming

There are many different types of steamer available but for fish the container must be a suitable size for the type of fish being steamed. Because fish should always be cooked in a closed steamer, it is often parcelled in foil or greaseproof paper and cooked in one of the improvised steamers.

Small pieces of fish, steaks and cutlets can be steamed on a plate covered with foil or sandwiched between two plates, in either case placed over a saucepan of boiling water. Soup plates, being slightly domed, are a good shape, although aluminium or enamelled plates are better heat conductors.

Large pieces of fish, rolled or folded fillets and small whole fish are securely parcelled in foil or grease-proof paper and placed in a tiered steamer, flower-shaped steamer, two-handled metal colander or a Chinese tiered steamer. This stands

in the container and the water should not reach to the level of the parcel. (The only exception to this is when a fish kettle is used; this does not use the closed method of steaming and is covered in a later course.)

The saucepan is then covered with a well-fitting lid or, when a colander is used, a sheet of foil may provide a more effective seal.

Points for successful steaming

Whatever type of steamer is used, observe the following points.
●Ensure that the container of fish does not touch the water but is completely surrounded by freely circulating steam.
●Cover the steamer really tightly with a well-fitting lid or foil, so that no steam can escape while cooking is in progress.
●Lightly grease the grid or foil in which the fish rests just sufficiently to prevent the fish sticking (fish skin tends to stick readily).

Step-by-step to steaming fish

1 If steaming on a plate grease it lightly to prevent the fish sticking to it.

OR if steaming in kitchen foil, lightly grease a piece large enough in which to wrap the fish securely.

2 Place fish on plate or foil in a single layer. Season well with salt, white pepper and lemon juice.

3 Cover the fish with another plate or with kitchen foil and refrigerate it until required for cooking.

4 Prepare a steamer and bring the water to the boil. The water must not touch the fish container.

5 Add any other seasoning or flavouring, such as soy sauce, to the fish parcel.

6 To steam the fish on the plate make sure that it is well covered. Place it over pan to cook.

OR to steam fish in foil make sure foil is secure and place on the steamer to cook. Cover pan.

7 Remove fish from steamer to serve and add cooking juices to accompanying sauce.

● Wait until the water is boiling and steam is rising before starting to cook the fish.

● Keep the water boiling. It is not usually necessary to top up with additional boiling water during cooking because fish steams quickly.

● Do not overcook the fish, as this affects the flavour and texture of the fish.

Steaming times

Fish cooks extremely quickly and it is all too easy to overcook. It would be a pity to do this as the fish loses its delicate flavour.

Steaming times differ, depending on the size of the fish, its container and the method of steaming. For example, fish steamed on a china plate will take slightly longer than fish steamed in greaseproof paper or in an aluminium or enamelled plate. A china plate can, of course, be heated before adding the fish but this is not always convenient.

Depending on the container small pieces of fish, such as thin fillets, will take about 8–15 minutes; thicker fillets, folded or rolled, will take 15–25 minutes. The longest time fish should be steamed is 25 minutes. A 2.5 cm [1"] thick cutlet or steak may well take 20 minutes, but always check towards the end of cooking time to make sure that the fish is not being overcooked.

Fish is cooked when the flesh becomes opaque and comes away from the bone. In the case of very fresh fish a white creamy substance oozes from between the flakes.

COOKING FISH TO SERVE COLD

Cold fish dishes can be most attractive to look at and delicious to eat. Colourful fish salads with creamy dressings make light and refreshing main dishes, while smaller portions of fish with piquant dressings make excellent first courses. The latter include simple pickled and soused fish (described on pages 349–355).

The very best white fish for serving cold are the more expensive ones, such as turbot and halibut. These can be served fairly plainly (as is shown in the star recipe). Excellent dishes can, however, be made from cheaper fish, provided you dress them up with sharp-flavoured creamy dressings and colourful garnishes. Use a sauce that is not only piquant but also colourful.

Steaming is a good way of cooking white fish for salads because there is no loss of nutrients or flavour. For serving cold the important point to remember is not to cook too far in advance. When cold, the sooner the fish is eaten the moister and tastier it will be.

Smoked whole fish for serving cold or reheating is probably better poached in milk and water. This method takes care of any excess saltiness.

When oily fish is to be served cold, it is best to grill, pickle or souse it. (Poaching and sousing are described on pages 329–339 and 349–355. For grilling only fish see on pages 299–308).

STEAMED FILLETS WITH CHIVE AND CUCUMBER SAUCE

These fillets of flat fish are cooked on a plate, covered with foil and set over a saucepan of simmering water. This is a very convenient method when cooking for 2 to 4 people only. It is also a very economical way of cooking, especially if you cook vegetables in the water beneath the fish. Any variety of small flat fish fillets can be used, but naturally the better the fish the better the dish. Unless it is being cooked for invalids, steamed fish is best served with a rich, well-flavoured sauce. This is especially true of the less interesting varieties of flat fish. If fresh chives are not available, use chopped spring onions, but sweat and then cook them with cucumber.

SERVES 4
4 flat fish fillets, about 150 g [5 oz] each
salt and white pepper
half a lemon
half a small cucumber
50 g [2 oz] butter
25 g [1 oz] flour
250 ml [½ pt] milk
30 ml [2 tablespoons] chopped fresh chives

1 Select a large, heatproof plate (aluminium is best) which is large enough to hold the fish in a single layer and will rest on the top of a large saucepan. Grease it very lightly with butter. Then butter a piece of greaseproof paper or foil large enough to cover it completely.

2 If the fishmonger has not already done so, skin any dark-skinned fillets.

3 Lay the fillets flat on the greased plate, putting unskinned fillets skin side up. Sprinkle well with salt and a little white pepper. Squeeze the lemon and add the juice.

4 Fold each fillet in three. Cover the plate with the greased covering. Secure the parcel firmly and refrigerate until ready to cook.

5 Half fill a saucepan with water and bring to boiling point. Set the covered plate on top and cover with the lid of the pan, being careful not to perforate the covering.

6 Steam for 10–15 minutes, depending on the thickness of the fillets.

7 While the fish is cooking, prepare the sauce. Wipe the cucumber and chop it roughly into very small dice.

8 Melt 25 g [1 oz] butter in a small heavy-based saucepan, put in the cucumber, stir well, cover and leave to sweat over low heat for 5 minutes.

9 Melt the remaining butter in another small saucepan. Add the flour off the heat and cook, stirring, over low heat for 1 minute to make a roux.

10 Off the heat blend in the milk smoothly, then return to the heat and stir until boiling. Cover and leave to simmer over low heat.

11 Check the fish; when cooked the fillets will look opaque. Transfer the cooked fillets with a fish slice to a hot serving dish and keep warm.

12 Stir the fish juices which have collected in the plate into the sauce. Add the cucumber, chives and seasoning to taste.

13 Stir and simmer for a moment or two then pour over the fish.

Steamed mackerel fillets served with a piquant sauce flavoured with capers, mustard and chopped parsley.

CHINESE STEAMED FISH

This makes a light main course for two people. Instead of the fillets of plaice you can use a whole dab weighing 700 g [1½ lb] or two whiting each weighing 250–350 g [9–12 oz].

If you have some white wine you can use it instead of the wine vinegar, in which case omit the sugar. Steamed rice and green beans are a suitable accompaniment.

SERVES 2
2 plaice fillets weighing about 175 g [6 oz] each
100 g [¼ lb] mushrooms
1 garlic clove
2 spring onions, finely chopped or 30 ml [2 tablespoons] chopped onions or shallots
5 ml [1 teaspoon] cornflour
30 ml [2 tablespoons] soy sauce
60 ml [4 tablespoons] sesame oil
15 ml [1 tablespoon] wine vinegar
1.5 ml [¼ teaspoon] sugar
salt and pepper

1 Select a plate large enough to hold the fish in a single layer and grease it lightly.

2 Place the fish on the plate and season. Slice the mushrooms very thinly and add to fish.

3 Peel and finely chop the garlic and add it to the finely chopped onions in a small mixing bowl.

4 Blend the cornflour with the soy sauce and add to the onions. Stir in the oil, vinegar, sugar and some pepper. Mix well.

5 Add to the fish. Cover securely with another lightly greased plate or foil.

6 Steam for 10–15 minutes. Serve immediately.

MACKEREL FILLETS WITH PIQUANT SAUCE

Oily fish, such as herring and mackerel, can be steamed too. Gutted whole fish can be wrapped in greaseproof paper or kitchen foil and steamed, or fillets can be steamed flat or rolled. For mustard sauce, mix 5 ml [1 teaspoon] each of English mustard, white wine vinegar and caster sugar into 250 ml [½ pint] basic white sauce. Oily fish for successful steaming must be fresh. If you cannot buy mackerel large enough for this recipe, buy four small ones instead. The steaming time here is slightly longer because the fillets are folded.

SERVES 4
2 mackerel, weighing about 500 g [18 oz] each
salt and pepper
15 ml [1 tablespoon] lemon juice

For the sauce:
250 ml [½ pt] mustard sauce
10 ml [2 teaspoons] capers
10 ml [2 teaspoons] freshly chopped parsley

For the garnish:
2 tomatoes
bunch of watercress

1 Wash and fillet the mackerel (see pages 292–293).

2 Lay the fillets on a piece of oiled greaseproof paper or kitchen foil. Sprinkle with plenty of salt, a little pepper and some lemon juice.

3 Fold each fillet into three.

4 Wrap the fish into a secure parcel.

5 Prepare the steamer and place the parcel over the boiling water. Steam for 20–25 minutes, depending on the size of the fillets.

6 Meanwhile prepare the sauce and let it simmer gently until the fish is cooked.

7 Transfer the fish on to a serving dish. Add the fish juices to the sauce. Crush the capers and add to the sauce with the parsley. Pour over the fish.

8 Garnish with tomato wedges and sprigs of watercress. Serve immediately.

Right out of water

Baking is one of the easiest ways to cook fish and often the best. Whole fish, steaks and fillets can all be cooked in this way. Since you cook them with little or no liquid except their own juices, none of their flavour or nutrients seep away. Baking is also a very good way to cook stuffed fish.

The term baking fish covers several simple methods of cooking fish in the oven. The amount of liquid or fat that is used is always small and this distinguishes baking from other oven-cooking processes, such as casseroling, braising and sousing. Liquid and/or fat are added to help keep the fish moist while it is cooking. These prevent it sticking to the dish and add extra flavour.

Baking is a very adaptable and trouble-free way to cook fish. No matter the shape, your fish will remain firm and appetizing. Even fish which breaks or flakes easily can be baked successfully as you can serve it straight from the dish in which it has been cooked. This saves on the washing up too!

There are five methods of baking fish: sur le plat, en papillote, au gratin, with a savoury topping and roasting. The first two methods, which are the simplest, are suitable for all varieties of fish. A gratin or savoury topping can be used with any fish except for a whole round fish (which can be egg and breadcrumbed instead). The roasting method is generally used for larger varieties of round fish which are to be cooked whole.

All the methods apply the principle of a minimum of added liquid or fat and with each method the fish is cooked in its natural juices, so all its flavour and goodness are contained. With a quality fish of fine flavour, the addition of a few herbs will be sufficient to bring the flavour out to the full. With a more modest fish the tasty coatings and stuffings which can be used will compensate for flavour which the fish may lack.

A fish can be baked, stuffed, as easily as it can be baked plain. The fish is cooked in exactly the same way, but for slightly longer if the fish is stuffed; the stuffing provides extra flavour and ekes out the fish.

When baking fish, a variety of effects can be achieved. The presentation can be impressive while little time-consuming effort is demanded of the cook.

EQUIPMENT

A baking dish and foil are all that are required in the way of cooking apparatus, though you will need the usual equipment for preparing the fish (listed on page 292) and also bowls and other equipment for preparing any stuffings.

Fish bricks

The one specialized piece of equipment you may come across and wish to use is the fish brick. This is designed to take round fish, fillets or portions, but not whole flat fish. The brick is prepared by lining the bottom with oiled or buttered greaseproof paper or foil. This makes the cleaning of the brick easier, as it can be scrubbed, but no detergent must be used in the water. The brick would absorb and hold the soapy flavour and the perfumed smell.

Unlike chicken bricks, a fish brick does not need to be soaked in water before use. It should, though, always be placed in a cold oven. The oven is then set at the required temperature. Small fish should be cooked at a high temperature, 230°C [450°F] gas mark 8 and will need about 25-30 minutes, timed from the minute the brick is placed in the oven. Larger fish or portions of fish require slower cooking at 180°C [350°F] gas mark 4. A fish or portion of fish weighing about 1.1 – 1.4 kg [2½–3 lb] will need an hour and

maybe longer at this temperature, depending on the thickness of the fish. Remember to allow a slightly longer cooking time (about 10 minutes) if cooking stuffed fish, to allow the heat to penetrate right through the stuffing.

PREPARING YOUR FISH

Fish does not keep well. It should be bought as fresh as possible and should preferably be cooked on the day it is bought. It should never be kept longer than 24 hours. Having bought your fish, unwrap it, rinse it under cold running water and drain it thoroughly.

Ideally, the fish should be prepared just before cooking but if this is not convenient no harm will be done if the preparation is undertaken a few hours beforehand. In fact, it is a positive advantage to be able to season the fish a little in advance as it helps the flavour. Keep the prepared fish covered and refrigerate.

If a fish is bought whole it must be scaled and gutted. Clean (scale and gut) the fish and fillet it if this is how you intend to serve it. These processes are fully discussed for round fish on page 292 and for flat fish on page 316. Reserve the roe and liver for possible use in the stuffing. Season the flesh with salt and pepper and a squeeze of lemon juice. The removal of the head and tail from the whole fish is a matter of personal preference, as is the skinning of a whole fish or fillets. A large expanse of dark skin on a flat fish or fillet can look very unappetizing to some people and can be quickly removed (see pages 314–315).

If you want to stuff a fish and bake it whole, the removal of the backbone will create a large cavity and make eating easier. However, this is optional, and is only possible with round fish (see pages 292–293).

OVEN TEMPERATURE AND TIMING

Once in the oven fish needs so little attention that it is easy to leave it there too long. If you are busy you may be tempted to think that a few moments' extra cooking will not matter; don't be misled. Fish cooks remarkably quickly in comparison to meat and once overcooked cannot be rescued. It may dry out and will then have a 'flannelly' texture, despite any

flavouring, wine or butter you may have added. It may be completely ruined and you will have wasted both time and money.

As a rule the oven temperature when baking fish is moderate: 180-190°C [350-375°F] gas mark 4-5. A higher temperature is needed initially for the roasting method, 230°C [450°F] gas mark 8, which is then reduced to 160°C [325°F] gas mark 3. When browning a gratin, the temperature will be raised during the last few minutes of cooking to 230°C [450°F] gas mark 8.

One cannot set fixed times for baking fish. Exact times vary according to the size and thickness of the fish, on whether it is fresh or frozen and on whether it is cooked plain or stuffed. Use the times given as a general guide only for baking fresh fish. (Allow slightly longer for frozen fish.)

Bake thin fillets for 8-12 minutes and for up to 20 minutes if stuffed. Bake thick fillets, steaks, cutlets and small whole fish for 15-20 minutes and for up to 30 minutes if stuffed. Bake whole large fish for 25-30 minutes and for up to 45 minutes if stuffed.

Testing for readiness

Baked fish is cooked when it is opaque right through and the fish comes away easily from the bone. The easiest way of testing to see if it is cooked is to pierce the thickest part of the fish with a thin skewer. The skewer will go in and come out without any resistance when the fish is cooked. It is advisable to test the fish before the recommended cooking time is quite completed. The fish can always be returned to the oven if it is not cooked, but overcooking cannot be remedied.

SUR LE PLAT

This method of baking is the simplest and most straightforward. It is suitable for whole flat fish, fillets, steaks and cutlets. Being a plain dish it is most important that the fish is absolutely fresh and that fine-flavoured ingredients are used. The fish that is classically associated with this method of baking is sole, but many other varieties of white fish, such as plaice, lemon sole and whiting, are perfectly acceptable.

Although margarine can be substituted for butter in many recipes,

the simplicity of this baking method makes it desirable to use butter.

Prepare the fish and season with salt and pepper and a squeeze of lemon juice. A whole fish should be skinned for this recipe but the removal of the head and tail is optional. Dark-skinned fillets may be skinned if preferred.

Choose a shallow, flameproof dish into which the fish will fit snugly in one layer. The dish needs to be flameproof as the cooking is finished off under a hot grill. Butter the dish well and lay the fish in it. Place thin fillets slightly overlapping each other. Pour in a very little liquid, not more than 15 ml [1 tablespoon] for four small fillets or 60 ml [4 tablespoons] for a whole fish weighing 900 g [2 lb]. Dry white wine or strong fish stock is frequently used but dry vermouth is very successful as only a small quantity is needed. Dry cider, thin cream or top of the milk can also be used. Dot the fish all over with a little butter (in small dabs) and cover the dish securely but not tightly with buttered greaseproof paper or foil. Bake at 180°C [350°F] gas mark 4 until the fish is tender.

Basting during cooking is not necessary as the dish is closely covered and all the juices are contained. When the cooking time is almost completed, turn on the grill to hot and test the fish to see if it is baked.

When the fish is cooked right through, remove the paper cover and baste the fish with some of the buttery juice. Pop the dish under the hot grill for a couple of minutes (no longer) to glaze the fish lightly.

If you wish to serve the fish cold, replace any butter in the recipe with oil. It is unnecessary to glaze a fish to be chilled after baking. Simply remove it from the oven; place the fish in a cold serving dish, cover loosely and allow to become cold. Then keep it chilled. Do make sure that there is sufficient liquid in the dish to keep it moist. The fish should be eaten on the day it is cooked.

EN PAPILLOTE

Cooking 'en papillote' means, literally in a paper case. Fish is wrapped in greased foil with fat, liquids and flavourings, then baked. Greaseproof paper can be used but it is harder to seal.

The main advantage of cooking en

The cleanest, and a very simple way to bake whole fish, fillets and steaks is in foil parcels.

papillote is that the added flavourings are easily adapted to suit the fish (and your purse) and are firmly sealed in with each parcel. There need be no fear of lost goodness or watering down of flavour, while this must surely be the cleanest way of cooking. The juices, being sealed in, do not even dirty the baking tray on which the parcels are cooked and these can be transferred unopened, directly on to plates.

This method of cooking is suitable for small whole fish; thick fillets, steaks and cutlets. Prepare the whole fish by cleaning and seasoning with salt and pepper and a squeeze of lemon juice. The skinning of the dark side of a flat fish is a matter of personal preference but the head and tail should not be removed. Darkskinned fillets can be skinned, if preferred.

Select your flavouring ingredients to suit your fish. A fine-flavoured fish can be treated simply (as sur le plat) while a cheaper, less flavoursome fish can be stuffed before cooking and/or be baked with a savoury topping.

Using savoury butters
Savoury butters, placed on the fish, will keep it moist during cooking and also improve the flavour. You will need about 50 g [2 oz] butter for four parcels.

Here are some ideas particularly suited to fish.

To make all the following butters start by mashing 50 g [2 oz] unsalted butter.
● To make anchovy butter add 3-4 crushed anchovies.
● For aniseed butter add 10-15 ml [2-3 teaspoons] Pernod, pastis or Ricard.
● For mustard butter add 10 ml [2 teaspoons] French mustard and a seasoning of salt and pepper.
● For orange butter add 10 ml [2 teaspoons] each of orange juice and grated zest.

The butters can be used with any species of fish but mustard butter and aniseed butter go particularly well with oily fish.

Making the case
The paper case for the fish could not be easier to make. It can, in fact, be made of greaseproof paper or aluminium foil. Foil is easier to handle as it is more malleable and forms a better seal when the edges are crimped together.

Cut a double thickness of foil or paper large enough to enclose the fish generously. Grease the foil or paper with melted butter if you intend eating the fish hot, or with oil if you plan to eat it cold. Season it lightly.

Wrapping the fish
Place a piece of prepared foil or paper on a baking tray. Place the fish in the centre and add the flavourings. Pull up the edges of the foil or paper and twist them together over the fish to make a baggy parcel. Crimp the ends together firmly too. Continue with the other pieces of fish and then place the baking tray in the oven. Bake the fish at 190°C [375°F] gas mark 5 until tender.

Serving the fish
To serve the parcels in style, open up the edges and fold them back to display the top of the fish. You can pinch or snip the edges into shapes such as petals and garnish each parcel with parsley or watercress.

If you wish to serve the fish cold, it must be removed from the foil (where it would continue to cook gently). Keep the fish moist and chilled and eat it the day it is cooked.

AU GRATIN
Gratin is the term given to the thin crust which forms on a dish which is 'browned on top'. The gratin is made by sprinkling the dish with fresh breadcrumbs, grated cheese or with a mixture of breadcrumbs and flavouring ingredients such as herbs, spices or cheese. You will need about 50 g [2 oz] gratin for a dish for four people. A gratin can be used to coat a whole flat fish, steaks and fillets and pieces of fish on top. Whole fish is more successfully treated by rolling in egg and breadcrumbs before baking.

Cooking the gratin with the fish
Clean the fish as usual and skin it; the head and tail may be removed if preferred. Season with salt and pepper and a squeeze of lemon juice. Butter a shallow dish and place the fish in it, either with extra butter, with a little liquid or in a coating sauce. Cover the surface with the gratin and dot with flakes of softened butter. Bake uncovered, in order that the gratin may brown, at 190°C [375°F] gas mark 5. If the gratin is not

sufficiently browned by the time the fish is cooked, either raise the temperature of the oven to 230°C [450°F] gas mark 8 for 2-3 minutes, or place the dish under a hot grill to get the same results.

Adding the gratin after cooking
If you are adding the gratin to a cooked dish, bake the fish, either sur le plat or with a coating sauce or savoury topping (see below). Add the uncooked crumbs, cheese and any other ingredients and pop into the hot oven for 2-3 minutes. Alternatively, sprinkle ready-fried or toasted crumbs over the dish and serve straight away. Bread that is a few days old and less moist is best for making breadcrumbs. Dark rye breadcrumbs in place of white add a bite to fish.

SAVOURY TOPPINGS
This is a particularly good method for baking the less glamorous types of fish. An added bonus—and one of the stimulating features of baking—is that you can completely change the flavour simply by changing the topping.

The method is suitable for all fish except whole round fish. The topping is added in the same way as a gratin, but in this case the topping is made from soft ingredients and is not browned.

Preparing the fish
Clean the fish and season it with salt and pepper and a squeeze of lemon. Remove the head and tail from the whole fish and skin it, or use skinned fillets if preferred. Butter an ovenproof dish well and lay the prepared fish in it.

Adding the topping
The quantity of topping needed is about 50 ml [2 fl oz] for portions for four people. Mix the topping and then spoon it over the dish, dividing it between the fish or portions of fish. Cover the dish securely but not tightly with buttered greaseproof paper or foil. Bake the fish at 190°C [375°F] gas mark 5 until tender. Remove the covering and serve straight from the dish.

If serving cold, remove the fish and the topping to a cold serving dish. Cover and keep chilled. Eat the day it is cooked.

Stuffing a flat fish is a simple process. Slit the fish down the backbone, lift the flesh and spoon in the prepared stuffing.

Suitable toppings
● For a cheesy cream topping mix 25 g [1 oz] grated Cheddar cheese and 5 ml [1 teaspoon] French mustard or 1.5 ml [¼ teaspoon] dry English mustard with 50 ml [2 fl oz] thick cream.

● For a crème fraiche topping add 25 ml [1 fl oz] sour cream to 50 ml [2 fl oz] thick cream.

● For a caper topping add 10 ml [2 teaspoons] capers to the crème fraiche.

● For a tomato cream add 5 ml [1 teaspoon] tomato purée and 1.5 ml [¼ teaspoon] dried basil to 50 ml [2 fl oz] thick cream.

● For a mushroom cream topping fry 100 g [¼ lb] mushrooms in a little butter, add the juice of a lemon to the pan, season with salt and pepper and turn the lemony mushrooms into 50 ml [2 fl oz] thick cream.

Two quick, easy toppings using readily available commercial products are:

● a small tin of condensed soup such as mushroom or tomato, well flavoured with herbs.

● a jar of cheese- or fish-flavoured baby food, well seasoned with salt and pepper; a 100 g [¼ lb] jar will serve four people, a 175 g [6 oz] jar will serve six people.

ROASTING
This open cooking method of baking is ideal for larger varieties of fish which will not fit comfortably under a grill, such as sea bass, grey mullet, large red mullet and hake.

Preparing the fish
Scale and clean the fish and season the belly cavity with salt and pepper and a squeeze of lemon juice. Do not skin the fish but slash or slit the skin with a knife at 2.5 cm [1"] intervals on both sides. This prevents the skin splitting under the fierce heat and allows the heat to penetrate for even cooking. Brush the fish all over with a little olive oil and place it on a grid in a baking dish. The fish should be roasted at 230°C [450°F] gas mark 8 for five minutes, turning once, to allow the skin to crisp. The heat is then reduced to 160°C [325°F] gas mark 3 to allow the fish to cook in its thickest part. The fish should be turned once during the slow cooking and basted frequently with olive oil. When it is cooked, place the fish in a serving dish on a bed of watercress and serve with wedges of lemon and a savoury butter.

STUFFING A FISH
Whole fish and fillets are as easy to bake with a stuffing as they are without one. Just remember to allow a little extra cooking time (about 10 minutes) to let the heat penetrate right through the stuffing.

If serving baked fish cold, it is advisable to make the stuffing on the moist side and to reduce any strongly flavoured ingredients, such as onion, to a minimum.

Round fish
You can stuff a round fish either in the cleaned belly cavity or you can remove the backbone and stuff the fish down its entire length. Removing the backbone is optional but it does give extra room so that you can use more stuffing. The fish is also easier to eat without the bones. The preparation and boning of a round fish is discussed on pages 292–293. Removing the head and tail is a matter of choice. When cleaning the fish reserve the liver and roe for possible use in the stuffing.

Make sure the cavity is quite clean by washing it under cold running water and remove any traces of blood

with salt. Season the inside of the fish with salt and pepper and a squeeze of lemon juice. Prepare your stuffing and stuff the fish, leaving room for the stuffing to swell. It may be necessary to stitch the opening together to contain the stuffing. Using strong thread (not nylon) and a large needle, oversew the edges with large stitches, or secure them with very small poultry skewers.

The fish may be baked lying on its side or upright with the cavity slit underneath. A round fish looks more dramatic upright, particularly when served this way, garnished with wedges of tomato and lemon and sprigs of parsley or watercress.

A smaller round fish can be prepared and boned, and rolled round the stuffing. Follow the directions for boning on pages 292–293 and remove the tail. Removing the head is optional. Spread the chosen stuffing all over the cut side, pressing it down if crumbly. Starting at the tail end, roll the fish up like a swiss roll. Secure the end with a couple of cocktail sticks or small poultry skewers. If the resulting roll is rather bulky and likely to be insecure, tie the roll with loops of fine string to prevent it unrolling. If you use string this limits you to baking the fish either sur le plat or en papillote

because it must be removed before serving. Cocktail sticks or skewers can be picked out fairly easily and you could bake fish, thus secured, with a savoury topping or egg and breadcrumbed.

Flat fish
Clean fish (as described on pages 314–315) and skin the dark side. Season it with salt and pepper and a squeeze of lemon. Place the fish on a board, skinned side up and make a slit with a knife along the length of the fish down the backbone. Work the knife into the cut and ease the flesh away from the bone, making a pocket between the flesh and the bone on each side. Season the inside of the pockets lightly with salt and pepper and a squeeze of lemon juice. Stuff the pockets loosely. The stuffing will swell; it will lift the flesh of the pocket making the fish look fatter, and will show as a line down the centre of the fish. If you do not object to the dark skin, lay the fish light side up and stuff without skinning.

Bake this stuffed fish either sur le plat or en papillote.

Fillets
Stuffing fish fillets is a good way to make them go further, especially thin ones. The stuffing can be done in any of the following ways.

Skin the fillets if preferred, season with salt and pepper and a squeeze of lemon juice and lay flat on a board (skinned side up if not skinned on both sides). Spread the surface of the fillet with the prepared stuffing and lay a second fillet (skinned side down) on top, making a sandwich.

Alternatively, having spread the fillet with the stuffing, roll it up, starting with the tail, and secure with a cocktail stick. A fillet roll can also be made by moulding the stuffing into little sausages and wrapping the fillet around. Again, start with the tail and secure the completed roll with a cocktail stick. These fillets can be baked sur le plat, en papillote, au gratin or with a savoury topping.

BASIC STUFFING
⊠ *This standard basic stuffing is a good 'extender' to use with any fish (or with meat or poultry). You can fill it into the belly cavity of a large fish, or spread it over a flat fillet and then roll the fish up round it. You can layer it between small fish fillets, or roll it into*

small balls and bake them with the fish, to garnish it. Assemble all the ingredients before starting the stuffing.

MAKES 200 G [7 OZ] STUFFING
1 lemon
100 g [¼ lb] fresh white breadcrumbs
50 g [2 oz] soft butter or margarine
15 ml [1 tablespoon] chopped parsley
2.5 ml [½ teaspoon] dried chopped mixed herbs
salt and pepper
pinch of grated or ground nutmeg
1 large egg

1 Grate the zest from the lemon. (The fruit and juice are not used.)

2 In a bowl, mix together all the ingredients except the egg.

3 In a small bowl, beat the egg and then add it to the other ingredients. Work it in until the mixture holds together lightly; it should not be a clogged mass. Check the seasoning.

Variations
● For ham stuffing, add 50 g [2 oz] minced cooked ham and a good pinch of ground allspice to the dry ingredients, and beat the egg with 30 ml [2 tablespoons] milk. Use for stuffing large coarse white fish.

● For orange stuffing, add 15 ml [1 tablespoon] grated orange zest plus 5 ml [1 teaspoon] grated lemon zest to the basic stuffing. Beat the egg with 10 ml [2 teaspoons] orange juice before mixing it in. Use the stuffing for whole sole or plaice, or for white fish fillets.

● For roe stuffing, poach 1-2 hard or soft roes from small fish in a very little salted water for 2-3 minutes. Chop them finely and add to the dry ingredients for the basic stuffing. Use this for any fish.

● For fresh mushroom stuffing, chop 100 g [¼ lb] mushrooms finely. Remove the rind from 50 g [2 oz] bacon, then chop the bacon and fry it for 2 minutes. Add the mushrooms and fry for 3 minutes. Mix the bacon, mushrooms and any fat in the pan with 100 g [¼ lb] fresh white breadcrumbs, 15 ml [1 tablespoon] softened butter, seasoning and a little grated nutmeg. Bind with 1 beaten egg. Use this to stuff any fish.

FILLETS OF SOLE BERCY

⬚ *This is an example of the sur le plat method, the simplest and the classic way to bake and serve whole flat fish or fish fillets, especially sole. But lemon sole, plaice or whiting fillets may also be used. The flesh of these fish flakes easily, so they are best left in the baking dish and finished under the grill.*

SERVES 4

**8 fillets of sole weighing in
    total about 700 g [1½ lb]**
salt and white pepper
half a lemon
30 ml [2 tablespoons] butter
½ shallot or 3 spring onions
**15 ml [1 tablespoon] chopped
    parsley**
**60 ml [4 tablespoons] dry white
    wine or dry cider**

1   Heat the oven to 180°C [350°F] gas mark 4.

2   Skin the fillets if preferred. Free the flesh from the skin with the blunt side of the knife and, holding the skin firmly, rip it off. Pat the fillets dry with kitchen paper. Season on both sides with salt, pepper and a squeeze of lemon juice.

3   Take 15 ml [1 tablespoon] of the butter and grease a shallow flame-proof dish which will just hold the fillets in one layer, and a piece of greaseproof paper or foil large enough to cover the dish.

4   Chop the onion finely and scatter over the bottom of the dish with the chopped parsley. Lay the fillets on top in one layer, slightly overlapping them, and pour the cider or white wine over.

5   Dot the fillets with the remaining 15 ml [1 tablespoon] butter. Cover the dish securely but not tightly with buttered greaseproof paper or foil.

6   Bake the fillets for 8-12 minutes, depending on their thickness. They should be milky white and tender when pierced with a thin skewer. While they are cooking, heat the grill to high.

7   Spoon some of the onion and the buttery liquid over the cooked fillets.

8   Place the dish under the grill for 2

minutes to glaze the fillets lightly. Serve immediately, from the baking dish.

MACKEREL 'EN PAPILLOTE'

⬚ *Use this recipe as a model when you cook any small whole fish, steaks or fillets in parcels. Serve the packages still closed, or with just the tops unfolded, each with its juices still sealed in it. Serve lemon wedges with the parcels, and place a spare plate on the table for the unwrapped foil or paper*

SERVES 4

**4 mackerel each weighing
    225-275 g [½-¾ lb]**
salt and pepper
half a lemon
1 small onion
75 g [3 oz] butter
**15 ml [1 tablespoon] chopped
    parsley**

1   Heat the oven to 190°C [375°F] gas mark 5. Cut off the fins and tails of the fish but leave on the heads. Slit open the fish along the belly cavity, clean and rinse the fish. Pat dry.

2   Squeeze the lemon and season the

A haddock, stuffed with some home-made stuffing and coated with rye breadcrumbs, makes a dinner party dish. Garnish with colourful vegetables.

fish with salt and pepper and a little of the lemon juice.

3 Peel and chop the onion roughly.

4 Cream 50 g [2 oz] butter in a bowl. Mix in the onion, parsley, the remaining lemon juice, salt and a pinch of pepper.

5 Divide the mixture and pack it into the belly cavity of each fish.

6 Cut out 4 double-thickness pieces of greaseproof paper or foil large enough to wrap each fish generously. Grease them with the remaining butter.

7 Wrap each fish in paper or foil, leaving some air space inside the parcel. Twist the top edges of the paper or foil together firmly, and twist the ends to prevent juices escaping.

8 Bake the fish parcels for 20 minutes. Test one to see if it is cooked. Serve them as they are, or with the tops of the parcels turned back and trimmed.

WHOLE STUFFED HADDOCK

Your fish will look dramatic, served upright, as if swimming on the dish. Skewered into an 'S' shape, it cannot fall over. Give it a crusty coat of browned crumbs.

Serve the fish with a sauce-boat of creamy smooth velouté sauce which will add richness to the white fish and herb stuffing.

SERVES 4
1 fresh haddock weighing about 900 g [2 lb]
salt and pepper
1 lemon
100 g [¼ lb] basic stuffing (see recipe)
1 small egg
35 g [1½ oz] dark rye bread
60 ml [4 tablespoons] butter

1 Prepare the breadcrumbs by grating the bread, then brown the crumbs in a warm oven, 160°C [325°F] gas mark 3 for 20 minutes. Make the stuffing as described.

2 Raise the oven heat to 180°C [350°F] gas mark 4 once the breadcrumbs have been removed.

3 Rinse and scale the fish but leave the head and tail on. Clean the belly, rinse and dry it. Season the cavity with a little salt and pepper and a squeeze of lemon juice.

4 Fill the cavity loosely with stuffing, leaving room for the stuffing to swell. Sew up the opening or skewer the sides together with small cocktail sticks.

5 Skewer the fish into an 'S' shape. To do this, bend the fish so that the side of the head almost touches the body. Drive a long skewer through the gills into the middle of the body. Use the same method to skewer the tail to the opposite side of the fish.

6 Set the fish upright on a sheet of greaseproof paper so that the cavity slit is underneath.

7 Beat the egg. Brush it all over the fish. Cover the fish with the browned crumbs and press them on to make a firm coating.

8 Use 15 ml [1 tablespoon] of the butter to grease a shallow ovenproof baking dish which will just hold the fish.

9 Place the fish in the dish, discarding the greaseproof paper. Melt the remaining butter, and sprinkle some of it over the fish. Reserve the rest.

10 Bake the fish for 25-35 minutes. Baste twice during baking with the reserved melted butter.

11 Test whether the fish is done by piercing the flesh with a skewer through the coating.

12 When the fish is tender, raise the oven heat to 230°C [450°F] gas mark 8 for 2-3 minutes, to crisp the coating.

13 Remove the skewers. Serve in the dish or on a warmed serving platter.

ROLLED STUFFED HERRINGS

⊠ *Serve this attractive yet economical dish hot for a substantial main course. For a summer lunch, chill it and serve it sliced on a bed of lettuce so that its 'pinwheel' circles of stuffing show. Remember to use oil for greasing the dish if serving cold. A salad of golden sweetcorn goes well with either dish.*

SERVES 4
**4 small herrings, each
    weighing 225-275 g [½-¾ lb]
salt and pepper
half a lemon
30 ml [2 tablespoons] freshly
    chopped parsley
200 g [7 oz] roe stuffing
1 medium-sized egg
50 g [2 oz] bread
75 g [3 oz] butter**

1 Heat the oven to 190°C [375°F] gas mark 5 and prepare the stuffing.

2 Cut off the fins, heads and tails of the fish, and scale them. Slit open along the length of the belly cavity. Rinse all the bones.

3 Lay the fish flat, cut surface down, and press along the backbone to loosen it. Turn the fish over, and remove all the bones.

4 Season the cut surface lightly with salt and pepper and a squeeze of lemon juice. Place the fish in a dish, cover and put aside.

5 Make the bread into crumbs. Melt 50 g [2 oz] of the butter over low heat and fry the crumbs, stirring constantly, until golden brown.

6 Cover the cut surface of the fish with stuffing and press it down firmly into an even layer.

7 Roll up each fish like a swiss roll, beginning at the tail end. Skewer the ends with wooden cocktail sticks, to fasten them.

8 Beat the egg. Brush the rolls with beaten egg, then coat them with the fried crumbs.

9 Butter a shallow baking dish with the remaining butter. (Use oil if serving cold.) Put in the herring rolls with the cocktail sticks tucked underneath.

10 Bake the rolls for 20-30 minutes, uncovered. Baste occasionally.

11 Remove the cocktail sticks and serve immediately.

12 Alternatively, remove the rolls to a cold dish and allow to become cold. Slice them across, then lay in overlapping lines on a bed of lettuce.

FISH FILLETS AU GRATIN

⊠ *This makes a lovely dish for a dinner party if you use fillets of plaice or whiting. To make a family dish which is still a great treat, use cod, haddock or coley fillet, but cut the fish into much smaller strips than the above fish. Serve the golden-topped fish garnished with slices of tomato and accompanied by crisp French fried potatoes and garden peas.*

SERVES 4
**8 thin fish fillets weighing in
    total about 700 g [1½ lb]
salt and white pepper
half a lemon
pinch of grated or ground
    nutmeg
50 g [2 oz] butter
100 ml [4 fl oz] white wine
2 shallots
100 g [¼ lb] button mushrooms
10 ml [2 teaspoons] freshly
    chopped parsley**

**For the sauce:
25 g [1 oz] butter
20 g [¾ oz] flour
salt and pepper
150 ml [¼ pt] thin cream**

**For the gratin:
15 g [½ oz] Gruyère cheese
25 g [1 oz] fried breadcrumbs**

1 Heat the oven to 180°C [350°F] gas mark 4. Skin the fillets if preferred. Pat them dry and season them lightly with salt, pepper, a squeeze of lemon juice and a pinch of nutmeg.

2 Use 25 g [1 oz] of the butter to grease a shallow baking dish and a piece of foil or greaseproof paper large enough to cover the dish.

3 Fold the fillets in half. Place them in the dish, side by side, with the tail end underneath. Pour the wine and the same quantity of water

round them. Cover the dish with the foil or greaseproof paper.

4 Put the dish in the oven and bake the fillets for 10 minutes.

5 Peel and chop the shallots. Melt the remaining butter in the pan. Add the shallots and fry them gently for 2 minutes.

6 Wipe the mushrooms with a damp cloth, trim the stalks and chop the mushrooms. Add them to the pan and fry for 3-4 minutes until just soft. Stir in the parsley.

7 Spread the mixture in the bottom of a warmed serving dish.

8 By now the fish fillets should be cooked. Turn the oven to its lowest temperature—110°C [225°F] gas mark ¼. Remove the dish from the oven. Lift the fillets out of the dish with a perforated spoon and lay them on the shallots and mushrooms. Reserve the liquid in the baking dish.

9 Cover the serving dish loosely with the buttered paper or foil, and put it in the oven while you make the sauce.

10 Melt the butter for the sauce very gently over low heat in a small saucepan. Stir in the flour off the heat. Make a white roux and cook briefly, stirring all the time. Do not let the flour colour.

11 Remove from the heat and stir in the fish cooking liquid gradually. Return to heat and cook, stirring all the time, until the sauce thickens, about 2-3 minutes. Season with a little salt and pepper.

12 Remove from heat and stir in the cream. Return the pan to the heat and cook gently until the sauce re-thickens. Check the seasoning.

13 Grate Gruyère. Mix the crumbs and cheese. Take the serving dish from the oven, remove the covering and pour in the sauce. Sprinkle on the grated cheese and the breadcrumbs evenly to form a gratin over the sauce.

14 Garnish the dish and serve immediately.

In the swim

Cooking fish in liquid can provide some of the finest, most delicious dishes. Poaching is often mismanaged: the fish is boiled rather than poached and most of its flavour thrown down the drain. Given the right cooking liquid for the type of fish, the right quantity and the correct temperature, you will produce fish dishes which are moist and firm with a subtle flavour.

Poaching is the correct way to cook fish in liquid. Poaching on top of the cooker is suitable for large whole fish, both round and flat, for fillets and for smoked fish. Poached fish make ideal meals for children, invalids or slimmers. More than that, fish is poached for many of the most delicious haute cuisine dishes; these are especially good when sauce is made from the poaching liquor—a far cry from soggy, tasteless boiled cod!

Poaching is not the same as boiling. Once the liquid has been brought up to simmering point, the heat must be reduced immediately. The temperature should not exceed 88°C [190°F], which is a very bare simmer. The liquid should quiver around the fish but not bubble.

The only time fish should ever be boiled is when you are making soup or stock. Cheap fish or trimmings are then boiled deliberately, so that all the fish flavour is given up to the liquid.

Poaching does not break up the fish as boiling does. Nor does it make the kitchen smell of fish. It keeps delicate fish flavour where it ought to be—trapped in the fish. Poaching leaves the cooked fish near to its natural state, letting the fish 'speak for itself'.

Truite au bleu is a classic dish and is best served simply with melted butter.

GOLDEN RULES FOR POACHING

The fish must be absolutely fresh. It goes stale quickly once out of water and any hint of staleness will be detectable when the fish is poached because the method shows up the fish's natural flavour. Apart from this, the fresher the fish the sweeter and more delicate its flavour. Moreover, fresh fish keeps its shape better.

The liquid should be chosen to suit the particular fish and should be used at the correct temperature. The chart gives the various types of liquid that can be used and the fish with which each is used.

Use as little liquid as you can for the size and shape of fish you are cooking. Use a pan which holds the fish snugly without unwanted space around it. Only just cover the fish with liquid—do not submerge it deeply. The less liquid you use the more flavourful your fish will be. If you are making sauce from the poaching liquor, this will also have a more concentrated flavour.

Do not overcook your fish. The timing begins from the moment the liquid reaches simmering point. Watch your clock or set your timer; do not risk wasting time and energy and, above all, the fish. Remember that it will go on cooking, if only very slightly, even after you have taken it off the heat. A chart of poaching times is given.

Presentation is particularly important with fish. Even perfectly cooked fish can be spoiled by poor presentation. Always remember to drain poached fish well. Lift small pieces out of the liquid with a perforated fish slice. Transfer larger pieces or whole fish to a board and pat dry before placing on a serving platter.

For most recipes, skin the upper-surface of a whole fish after it is cooked. This is done in much the same way as with a raw fish. Make a nick in the skin just above the tail, hold the skin firmly in one hand and with the other carefully loosen and lift the skin from the flesh with the blunt side of a knife. If it does not come off in one piece, simply scrape the remaining bits and pieces off gently with the knife. There is no need to skin the under-surface of the fish as a rule.

Garnishes should be colourful to overcome the blandness of the white fish flesh.

A fish kettle is a heavy piece of equipment not often seen nowadays.

PREPARING FISH

It is always easier to ask the fishmonger to clean and gut the fish for you but you can, of course, do this yourself if you prefer. Round fish are dealt with on pages 292–293 and flat fish on pages 314–315. Take the fish out of its packaging as soon as you get home, rinse it in cold running water and drain thoroughly. Keep the fish chilled, lightly covered with polythene or foil.

If the fishmonger has cleaned the fish for you, a little seasoning and a squeeze of lemon will improve the flavour and texture. If you are cleaning the fish yourself, this is better done as near cooking time as possible. However, no harm will be done if the preparation is done a few hours in advance. Add lemon juice and seasoning before chilling.

Clean the fish, rinse it, season it and keep covered and chilled until needed. Fillets may be simply wiped with a damp cloth, seasoned with salt, pepper and a squeeze of lemon and kept covered and chilled until needed. Smoked fish needs no preparation—simply keep refrigerated.

EQUIPMENT AND HOW TO USE IT

To poach the fish on top of the cooker you will need a large pan, preferably with some type of rack to keep the fish off the base of the pan, and also some means of getting the fish in and out of the poaching liquor.

Fish kettle. The classic way to poach a large whole fish such as a salmon or a chicken turbot is in a fish kettle. This is a large, deep pan, usually oval in shape with a flat perforated plate which fits inside. It is not elevated as in a steamer but supports the fish just above the base of the pan. Thus the liquid covers the fish (which is then poached) and is not below the level of the fish as it would be in a steamer.

The perforated plate is fitted with two tall handles so that the fish can be lowered in and lifted out easily, without burning your arms on the sides of the pan. When the liquid in the pan is ready for use the fish is laid on the plate and lowered into place. At the end of cooking time it is lifted out again, still on the plate, without risk of it breaking up. Any liquid drains back into the pan through the perforations.

Improvised fish kettles. If you have not got a fish kettle, don't worry. Few people have one these days as it is a

Fish can be poached on top of the cooker or in the oven. Poaching on the top of the cooker is suitable for large whole fish, fillets and smoked fish. Oven poaching, which is better suited to steaks and portions of fish and is also used for fillets, is discussed on page 349.

When poaching on top of the cooker, there is basically one method for large fish and one method for small fish and fillets. Smoked fish are treated in the same way as small fish and fillets, or they can be poached without additional heat by the 'jug' method.

The important difference between the method for large fish and the method for small fish is the temperature of the liquid at the point at which the fish is immersed.

Large fish

For large whole fish or a large portion of a whole fish the liquid must be cool to start with. If you were to immerse a large whole fish in near-boiling water, this would cause the skin to shrink and burst. The liquid is brought slowly to just below boiling point (simmering point) and this slow treatment allows the heat to penetrate right through the fish. If hot liquid were used, the outer part of the fish would cook too quickly while the inside remained cold and raw.

To poach the fish place it on the trivet, rack, oiled greaseproof paper or foil then pour in the liquid to barely cover the fish. It is important that the fish should be a good fit for the pan or an unnecessarily large amount of liquid will be needed. Cover the pan and bring slowly to simmering point. When the first bubble appears, reduce the heat to just below the simmering point. The liquid should quiver around the fish with not a bubble in sight. Poach for the time appropriate for the weight of the fish. Poaching times are given in the chart.

Small fish, fillets and smoked fish

If you are poaching small fish or pieces of fish it is not necessary to start with cool liquid. The liquid should be near simmering as heat is needed to seal the open surface of fillets. This prevents the flavour dispersing into the liquid. The gentle warming that is required for large fish is also unnecessary.

large piece of equipment for large fish, and large numbers. Improvisation is easy and successful. The bonus of the fish kettle is the supporting perforated plate. There are two quick and simple methods for improvising this plate, but you will need a pan large enough to hold the fish. Although it must be large it must not be unnecessarily so.

For the fish pan you can use a preserving pan, a solid roasting tin, casserole dish or any flameproof pan deep enough and long enough to hold the fish and the liquid. A lid can be made from foil or greaseproof paper, as it does not have to be airtight.

You also need something on which to lie the fish to make handling easier and, if possible, to raise it off the bottom of the pan. A small roasting trivet, cake rack or the grid from the grill pan is ideal if it will fit the chosen pan.

If you have none of these, cut a double thickness of foil large enough for the fish to lie on, grease it lightly with very little oil, and place the fish on it. Alternatively, wrap the fish in lightly oiled greaseproof paper and secure with string.

You will also need some help with lifting the fish in and out of the pan, to prevent it from breaking up. Cut a piece of muslin large enough to wrap round the fish and its support, including the rack or grid if either is being used, long enough for the ends to hang over the sides of the pan. Wrapping the fish in this way also helps it to keep its shape. If you have not got any muslin, a trivet, cake rack or grid can be lifted out fairly easily without it. A fish lying on foil or wrapped in greaseproof paper will have to be raised with the aid of fish slices or slings made of foil.

To make the slings of foil, cut two double-thickness pieces of foil long enough to go under the width of the fish and hang over the sides of the pan. Put one piece under the fish towards the head and the other towards the tail. When the fish is cooked, draw the ends of each sling together, take the pieces at the head in one hand and the pieces at the tail in the other (or however suits you) and lift the fish out on to a board.

Poaching small fish and fillets

Small fish and fillets, being light in weight, do not need a supporting base. The fish can be poached in a shallow pan covered with a lid, foil or greaseproof paper, or a flat baking tray. The fish is easily removed from the pan with the aid of a perforated fish slice.

331

Ingredients	Making the liquid	Using the liquid
BRINE 100 g [¼ lb] salt 1 bay leaf (optional)	Add the salt to 1.7 L [3 pt] water to make a strong brine. Use seawater if you can with less salt. A bay leaf floating on top is optional.	The brine should be cool. Poach fresh salmon for time given in recipe.
SIMPLE COURT-BOUILLON 8 black peppercorns 1 medium-sized onion 30 ml [2 tablespoons] white wine vinegar salt	Crush peppercorns coarsely. Peel and slice onion. Mix all ingredients with 1.2 L [2 pt] water, heat to simmering point and simmer, uncovered, for 30 minutes. Allow to cool and check seasoning before use.	Start with cool liquid for large fish, near simmering for small. Poach fish for time given in recipe. Discard liquid after use.
SIMPLE WHITE COURT-BOUILLON 550 ml [1 pt] milk 1 lemon slice salt and pepper	Mix all ingredients with 550 ml [1 pt] water.	Start with cool liquid for large fish or pieces. Heat and use at boiling point for jugging. Discard lemon and use liquid for sauce.
GENERAL-PURPOSE COURT-BOUILLON 10 black peppercorns 3 cloves bouquet garni 550 ml [1 pt] dry white wine or dry cider 1 large carrot 1 large mild onion 2 small leeks 7.5 ml [1½ teaspoons] pickling spice	Crush peppercorns coarsely. Tie herbs and spices in muslin. Peel and slice leeks. Mix all ingredients with 550 ml [1 pt] water. Heat to simmering point and simmer, uncovered, for 30 minutes. Allow to cool and check seasoning before use.	Start with cool liquid. Poach fish for time given in recipe. Strain liquid after use and use as basis for fish soups or mild sauces.
REDUCED COURT-BOUILLON Ingredients as for general-purpose court-bouillon.	Prepare and mix as above. Bring to boil and boil rapidly, uncovered, to reduce by half.	Start with near simmering liquid. (Put shellfish in boiling liquid.) Poach fish for time given in recipe. Strain liquid after use and use for sauces.
FISH FUMET (CONCENTRATED FISH STOCK) 900 g–1.4 kg [2–3 lb] fish bones, trimmings and heads, including those of turbot and sole if possible 700 g [1½ lb] cheap white fish 1 large onion 1 medium-sized carrot 1 leek 5 cm [2″] celery stick 8 black peppercorns 10 ml [2 teaspoons] white wine vinegar 200 ml [7 fl oz] dry white wine	Peel and slice onion and carrot. Clean and slice white part of leek, chop celery. Put all ingredients in a large pan with enough water to cover. Bring to the boil and skim. Lower heat and simmer, uncovered, for 20–30 minutes. Strain at once through muslin-lined sieve. Keep hot for small fish and fillets, cool for poaching large fish.	Use as for reduced court bouillon above.

Suitable fish

Fat, silvery early-season salmon, grilse, shellfish.

Mature, and thinner, reddish salmon, whole oily fish such as trout and mackerel.

Smoked white fish (haddock, cod), kippers, turbot, brill and halibut.

Any large whole fish or portions of fish.

Any small fish, fillets or shellfish.

Any fish recipe which needs fish fumet.

POACHING TIMES FOR FISH

Small thin fillets /portions shellfish	3–5 minutes
Smoked fish (jugged)	5–10 minutes
Medium /thick fillets	6–10 minutes
Steaks /cutlets /portions, according to thickness	8–15 minutes
Small whole fish (eg sole, whiting, plaice)	8–15 minutes
Whole fish or piece of fish, 700 g [1½ lb] to 900 g [2 lb]	8–15 minutes
Whole fish, 900 g [2 lb] to 1.8 kg [4 lb]	15–18 minutes
Whole fish, 2 kg [4½ lb] to 2.7 kg [6 lb]	20–30 minutes
Larger fish, according to thickness, per 450 g [1 lb]	5–10 minutes

Place the fillets and small fish in the pan. Heat the liquid in a separate pan to near simmering. Pour this round and over the fish until it is just covered. The liquid is then brought to just below simmering point. At the appearance of the first bubble in the liquid, reduce the heat immediately to maintain a very gentle simmer. There should not be any bubbles on the surface of the liquid, just a gentle quivering.

Small flat fish may have a tendency to curl when placed in hot water and cooked fairly quickly. A good tip is to slit the fish down the backbone on the dark skinned side, and carefully snip the backbone in two places. To snip the backbone simply raise it in two places with the point of a pair of scissors, slip one blade underneath and snip through. Two cuts should be sufficient to hold the fish flat while it is cooking. Smooth the flesh back once the backbone has been cut.

POACHING TIMES

Poaching times may vary according to whether the fish has fine or coarse flesh, whether it is in a solid piece, and whether, if it is filleted, it is cooked flat or rolled. Fish is cooked when the flesh is opaque all through or when a little creamy curd appears between the scales and the flesh parts easily from the bone when the point of a skewer is inserted.

NO-COOK POACHING METHODS

There are two no-cook ways of poaching fish—one is ideal for smoked fish, and the other for a large whole fish to be served cold.

The 'jug' method

Kippers, bloaters and other small whole smoked fish can be poached without being cooked at all and can be served hot or cold.

Choose a heatproof jug into which you can lower the fish without folding or bending it. It should be deep enough to hold the whole fish except the inedible tip of the tail.

Lower the fish into the jug, head first, and pour the liquid, which should be boiling, over it. Fill the jug completely. Leave it to stand for 5–10 minutes; do not leave it any longer or the fish will go soggy. Pull the fish out gently by its tail, lay it on kitchen paper and pat dry.

Step-by-step to poaching a large fish

1 Have cooled court-bouillon ready. Choose a pan and equipment for lifting and supporting the fish.

2 Cut two long, double-thickness pieces of foil. Fold to make two long slings. Place under the rack.

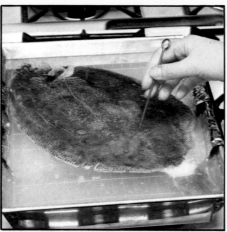

5 Time cooking period from point of simmering. Poach for the time specified in chart. Test fish.

6 Lift the fish and rack out with the foil slings allowing the liquid to drain back into the pan.

Step-by-step to 'jugging'

1 Choose a tall heatproof jug deep enough to hold the whole fish except the inedible tail tip.

2 Bring a simple white court-bouillon to the boil. Lower the fish, head first, into the jug.

3 Lower the prepared fish into the pan. Pour in the court-bouillon to barely cover. Cover with lid.

4 Place over low heat. Bring just to simmering point. Reduce heat immediately and poach gently.

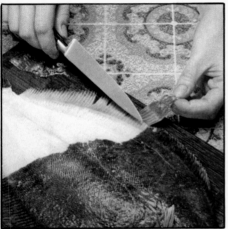

7 Lay fish on a board, dark skin up. Skin carefully with the aid of a knife and keep fish hot.

8 Make sauce from court-bouillon. Place fish on serving plate and garnish well. Serve with sauce.

3 Pour in the boiling liquid. Leave the fish to stand for 5–10 minutes, no longer.

4 Withdraw the fish gently by the tip of the tail, lay it flat on kitchen paper and pat dry.

If you wish to poach fillets of smoked fish in this manner or do not possess a tall heatproof jug, use a saucepan or other dish in which the fish can lie flat. Pour on the boiling liquid, cover with a lid or foil, and leave for 5–10 minutes. Remove the fish with a perforated fish slice, drain and pat dry. It is necessary to cover the dish or pan as the area of evaporation is far greater than that of the tall jug.

The jug method is a particularly good way of handling kippers or bloaters which you suspect may be very salty. The jugging will make them moist, less oily and less salty.

Cold start for serving cold

This method keeps the fish beautifully moist which is very important when the fish is to be served cold.

Place the whole fish in its cooking container on its supporting base. Pour in the cool liquid to barely cover the fish. Bring the liquid gently to the boil and let it bubble gently for 2–3 minutes, no longer. Remove the pan from the heat and let the fish cool in the liquid.

The beauty of this method is that the process is absolutely simple as there is no cooking time to calculate. It does not matter what size the fish is. The quantity of liquid used and the time it takes to reach the boil and then to cool down again and cool the fish will ensure that a fish of any size will be cooked right through. Wait until the fish is completely cold before removing it from the liquid.

If you are serving fillets this method cannot be used. Treat the fish as though you were serving it hot. When cooked, remove from the pan, drain thoroughly and place on the serving platter. Allow to become cool, cover and keep chilled.

Handy hints

Fish is always improved by the inclusion of wine in the cooking liquid. If you have no wine for the court-bouillons in the chart, you can use instead:
- dry cider or a mixture of cider and water
- $\frac{2}{3}$ quantity of fish stock with $\frac{1}{3}$ quantity of white wine vinegar with a pinch of sugar
- dry vermouth and water mixed half and half.

SOLE VERONIQUE

This classic dish was named after the first-born child of one of the chefs; she was born the day the dish was created. Seedless white grapes are added to the fish in its creamy sauce. You will need a quantity of béchamel sauce for this recipe and this can be prepared in advance or while the fish fumet is simmering. Have this ready in a small saucepan. Make the fish fumet as described in the chart on poaching liquids.

SERVES 4

8 fillets of sole weighing in total about 700 g [1½ lb]
salt and white pepper
550 ml [1 pt] fish fumet
100 g [¼ lb] seedless white grapes
150 ml [¼ pt] béchamel sauce
2 medium-sized eggs
60 ml [4 tablespoons] thick cream
30 ml [2 tablespoons] softened butter

1 Season the fillets with salt and pepper and lay them flat in a shallow flameproof dish. Pour over sufficient fumet to cover.

2 Bring the pan to simmering point and adjust heat immediately to maintain a bare simmer. Poach the fillets for 6–8 minutes depending on thickness.

3 Lift the fillets out of the dish with a perforated fish slice. Reserve the fumet in the dish. Drain the fillets well and lay on a serving dish. Keep warm.

4 Pick the stems off the grapes and drop them into near boiling water to heat through. Remove them from the water after a few moments using a perforated spoon. Drain well and arrange around the fish.

5 Taste the fish fumet remaining in the flameproof dish. Boil for a few minutes to reduce if a stronger flavour is needed. Measure off 250 ml [½ pt] fumet and strain into the pan holding the béchamel sauce; stir in while pouring.

6 Separate the eggs and reserve the whites for another dish. Cream together the yolks and 30 ml [2 tablespoons] cream.

7 Add 30 ml [2 tablespoons] of warm sauce mixture to the cream and yolks, blend thoroughly and then stir into the sauce.

8 Heat the sauce slowly without boiling, stirring continuously, until it thickens. Place the pan in a baking tin containing hot water to keep warm.

9 Heat the grill to hot. Whip the remaining cream until thick but not stiff. Stir the butter into the sauce and then add the whipped cream.

10 Pour the sauce over the fish and the grapes. Place under grill for about a minute to brown lightly, and serve immediately.

TWO TURBOT MEALS IN ONE

◨◨◨ *Justify the expense of this large prime fish by making two distinctive meals with it, one served hot and the other cold. The hot dish is served with a bowl of freshly grated horseradish and a sauce-boat of melted butter, and the chilled turbot is covered with a herb-flavoured vinaigrette dressing.*

Serve the hot dish for dinner one evening and the turbot vinaigrette for a light lunch with crusty brown bread and butter the next day. The second dish has a completely different flavour from the hot dish served the night before.

SERVES 4 (TWICE)
**1.8 kg [4 lb] chicken turbot
about 1.7 L [3 pt] general-
purpose court-bouillon**

Cold turbot with vinaigrette dressing is the second meal from one fish. A lemon and watercress garnish adds a touch of colour.

For the hot garnish:
**1 large egg
20 ml [1¼ tablespoons] butter
15 ml [1 tablespoon] parsley
1 lemon**

For the cold garnish:
**150 ml [¼ pt] vinaigrette
    dressing
22.5 ml [1½ tablespoons] mixed
    fresh parsley, tarragon and
    chives
1 egg
6 capers
5 walnuts**

1 Gut the fish if this has not already been done, wipe with a damp cloth and place, dark side uppermost, in a genuine or improvised fish kettle. Make a muslin or 2 foil slings and put slings under the fish to aid removal.

2 Pour in enough general-purpose court-bouillon just to cover the fish.

3 Bring the liquid to simmering point slowly, and adjust heat to maintain a bare simmer. Poach the fish for 15–18 minutes or until tender.

4 Hard boil both the eggs (one for the hot dish, one for the cold). Plunge them into cold water, shell and leave in cold water until needed.

5 Remove the fish from the heat. Lift the fish out of the liquid on to a board. Pat the fish dry.

6 Skin the upper dark-skinned surface of the fish. Trim the fins and cut down along the backbone. Remove the upper two fillets from the fish, loosening and lifting each fillet from the bone. This will leave the head and tail intact with the backbone and the two fillets underneath. The upper, thicker fillets are served hot. The rest of the fish should be allowed to become cool, covered loosely with foil and chilled.

7 Place the two fillets close together on a serving platter to look like a fish. Melt 20 ml [1½ tablespoons] butter over a low heat and brush most of it over the turbot. Use the rest to butter a piece of grease-proof paper, cover the turbot and keep warm.

8 Chop one hard-boiled egg evenly, and chop the parsley finely.

9 Slice the lemon thinly to get enough slices to cover the length of the turbot.

10 Lay the slices of lemon down the centre of the turbot fillets, to hide the join. Scatter over the chopped egg and parsley and serve immediately.

11 To serve the turbot vinaigrette lay the fish in a shallow serving dish with the backbone uppermost. Remove the backbone by snipping through at the head and tail, loosening with a knife, and lifting out. Leave the head and tail in place if you wish, or remove.

12 Finely chop the mixed fresh herbs and mix into the vinaigrette. Chop the remaining hard-boiled egg, the capers and the nuts and stir into the dressing. Check the seasoning and pour over the fish.

13 Cover the dish lightly and chill the fish for at least 4 hours with its dressing.

SKATE WITH BLACK BUTTER

Once despised, we now appreciate the lovely flavour of this easily-digested, rosy-white fish. It has a soft bone, unlike the normal spiky fish bones, from which the flesh parts willingly, making the eating easier and all the more enjoyable. The pieces of skate which we eat are nearly always from the wing, and the whole kite-shaped creature is a rare sight.

Black butter (beurre noir) is traditional with wing of skate and is quick and simple to make. In a basic recipe the proportion of vinegar is less, but the amount of vinegar in this recipe has been increased for extra zest.

SERVES 4
1 kg [2¼ lb] wing of skate
1 L [1¾ pt] simple
   court-bouillon

For the beurre noir:
75 g [3 oz] unsalted butter
15 ml [1 tablespon] capers
15 ml [1 tablespoon] white
   wine vinegar

1 Cut the skate into serving portions; the bone is easy to cut through although it looks tough.

2 Place the skate portions in one layer in a shallow flameproof pan or baking tin, or a deep skillet.

3 Pour the cool court-bouillon over the skate, just covering it. Bring slowly to simmering point, then adjust the heat to maintain a bare simmer. Cover and poach for 8–15 minutes, until the skate is tender.

5 Transfer the skate from the pan to a board. Scrape off any skin with the blunt side of a knife. Place the fish on a warmed serving dish, and keep warm while making the beurre noir.

6 Melt the butter in a heavy-based pan over low heat and cook very gently until it turns dark golden brown. This will take about 1 minute.

7 Meanwhile chop the capers. Add the vinegar and capers to the butter, stir once and remove from heat.

8 Pour the black butter over the skate and serve immediately.

FILETS DE MERLAN A LA DIEPPOISE

This is a simple yet good dish from a French port renowned as a fishing centre. It is worth taking time over although its ingredients seem quite ordinary. The liquid from the mussels is used in place of a court-bouillon. You can use canned mussels but these must be in brine, not in vinegar. You will need a 150 g [5 oz] can. Fresh mussels must be cleaned carefully. This process is described in detail on pages 412–413 in the Star Recipe for moules à la marinière.

SERVES 4
1.15 L [2 pt] fresh mussels
8 whiting fillets weighing, in
   total, about 700 g [1½ lb]
salt and pepper
175 g [6 oz] button
   mushrooms
half a lemon
75 g [3 oz] butter

250 ml [½ pt] dry white wine
30 ml [2 tablespoons] plain
   flour

1 Put cleaned fresh mussels in a large shallow pan. Cover and place over gentle heat. Shake the pan gently until the mussels open. Throw out any which remain shut.

2 Drain all the liquor from the fresh mussels into a bowl. Remove fresh mussels from shells and reserve the flesh. Discard the shells.

3 If using canned mussels, drain off the brine and dilute with water to give a lightly salted flavour.

4 Season the whiting fillets with salt and pepper, and lay them flat in a flameproof pan, side by side.

5 Wipe the mushrooms with a damp cloth and trim the stalks. Squeeze the juice from the lemon and sprinkle the mushrooms with it. Melt a third of the butter. Fry the mushrooms gently until just soft. Remove the mushrooms and reserve with the mussels.

6 Pour the butter and mushroom juice over the whiting. Add the wine and sufficient mussel liquor or diluted brine to just cover the fish.

7 Bring the liquor to simmering point and adjust the heat immediately to maintain a bare simmer. Poach the fish for 6–10 minutes. Be careful not to overcook.

8 Lift the whiting with a perforated fish slice on to a warmed serving dish. Surround with the reserved mussels and fried mushrooms and keep warm. Reserve the poaching liquid in the dish.

9 Heat the grill to hot. Boil the poaching liquid for 3–4 minutes to reduce it a little.

10 Meanwhile, cream together the remaining butter and the flour to make a smooth paste (beurre manié).

11 Over low heat, stir the buerre manié into the liquid in small spoonfuls, and stir until melted. Simmer gently until the sauce thickens, stirring continuously.

12 Pour the sauce over the fish. Place under the hot grill for a minute or two, to brown the top. Serve at once.

Three poached fish dishes with very different flavours: whiting with mussels and mushrooms, buttery skate with capers and creamy sole Véronique with grapes.

TRUITE AU BLEU

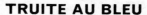

Cooking trout in this way makes the natural slime on their skins turn a dreamy slate blue. The fish should be live but if you have no fisherman in the family to produce live trout, you can use fresh trout from the fishmonger. Cooked, these will be greyish rather than blue. The important thing is not to wash the natural sheen from the skin. Do not mask the fish or hide its flavour with a thick sauce. Rather, serve the fish just with melted clarified butter and its traditional garnish of lemon quarters and chopped parsley. To make clarified butter, melt and strain through a muslin-lined sieve.

SERVES 4
4 medium-sized live or fresh trout
2.3 L [4 pt] simple court-bouillon
2 lemons
45 ml [3 tablespoons] freshly chopped parsley
175 g [6 oz] clarified butter

1 Kill the trout with a sharp blow on the back of the head. Gut the fish but handle them as little as possible. Do not cut off the fins, scrape or rinse.

2 Place the fish in a large flameproof dish or saucepan. Pour over just enough very hot court-bouillon to cover them. Bring to simmering point and adjust heat immediately to maintain a bare simmer. Poach 8–15 minutes, depending on size. Test the fish with a thin skewer after 8 minutes and continue cooking if necessary.

3 Meanwhile, quarter the lemons and chop the parsley.

4 Put the clarified butter in a small pan to melt over a low heat.

5 When the trout is cooked, remove the pan from the heat, and discard the court-bouillon. Slide the fish, or lift out gently, on to a warmed serving platter. Tilt the platter to drain off any remaining court-bouillon. Mop up with soft kitchen paper around the fish.

6 Sprinkle the parsley over the fish and garnish with lemon wedges. Pour the melted butter into a heated sauce-boat and serve immediately.

Fisherman's fare

Enjoy a real fisherman's meal with fresh fish, locally grown vegetables and herbs and some well-flavoured liquid. Every variety of fish can be used, either by itself or mixed with other fish—and nearly all the meals can be prepared in under an hour. Many fish stews, created by villagers from ingredients immediately to hand, have become part of classical French cuisine.

Stews and casseroles made with fish fresh from the sea are real fishermen's meals. All the unusual fish collected in a fisherman's nets and not sold on the quayside went into his family's cooking pot. In times gone by this was literally one big iron pot on the open fire, and the fisherman's wife put everything into it. The assorted fish with locally grown vegetables and herbs made a simmering rich broth which was ladled out and the solid food made a fragrant main-course dish.

These one-pot meals are still served everywhere. From north to south, in Europe and America, every coastal community makes its own version. The ingredients and flavour-ings vary to some extent in differing climates, but the method does not. The reason for their continuing popularity, since we do not now have to cook in one pot, is that they offer real value; the extra ingredients used are nearly always cheap. Exotic and extravagant vegetables and fruit are not necessary, nor are rich dairy products.

STEW OR CASSEROLE?

A fish stew and a fish casserole use much the same ingredients, although technically a stew should be cooked on the top of the stove and a casserole in the oven. As when made with meat, these words are used interchangeably nowadays. The main difference, when fish is used, is the quantity of liquid.

A fish stew is really a nourishing fish soup flavoured by the fish and vegetables which are cooked in it. The stew can be served as it is or can be served as two courses: the strained broth, followed by the fish and vegetables as a main course. The pot contains a substantial amount of liquid.

A casserole contains less liquid than a stew, sometimes just enough to make a sauce, and cannot be served as two courses. The fish is not cut up as it is in a stew and the resulting dish is more similar to a baked dish than to a stew.

PRINCIPLES OF STEWING FISH

When making a fish soup, the fish is boiled so that it gives up all its goodness and flavour to the liquid. The fleshy remnants are then strained out and only the liquid is served.

The dishes described in this course are different: they are a combination of a soup and a stew. The fish is cooked so that it keeps its nourishment and juices, and vegetables and herbs are added to flavour both the fish and the liquid. If the liquid is already a well-flavoured fish stock prepared from fish trimmings so much the better.

The method

The cooking method is simple in theory and practice. The vegetables that are to be included in the dish are fried briefly in hot fat or oil, in the stew pan. The cooking liquid and herbs are added and the pan is heated gently until the contents are boiling. The fish, usually cut up into chunks, is put straight into the boiling liquid so that the heat stiffens the outer flesh at once, sealing in the juices. The heat under the pan is lowered and the fish is cooked in simmering liquid for a short time: barely long enough for it to cook through. It is preferable, in fact, to slightly undercook the fish as it will continue to cook slightly in its own heat after it has been strained from the liquid.

The important fact is that the liquid must always be hot when it comes into contact with the fish. If it is added to the pan after the fish, it should be heated to boiling point first. In some recipes, where extra oil would be unpleasant, the vegetables are not fried first but are simply cooked in the hot liquid with the fish.

PRINCIPLES OF CASSEROLING FISH

The ingredients of a casserole are virtually identical to a stew except that the quantity of liquid is considerably smaller. It is usually a spicy sauce and not just plain stock. The principles are the same as stewing, in that the fish is sealed to retain its goodness and juices, and vegetables are added to increase the flavour, but the method is different.

The method

The fish is sealed, not in hot liquid but by the acid ingredient, such as lemon juice, wine or soured cream that is included in the liquid. First, as in stewing, the vegetables are put in the bottom of the casserole dish. They are sometimes fried but in other recipes are simply cooked with the fish. The fish goes in next, not cut into chunks, followed by the sauce, or the sauce followed by the fish. The sauce can be added hot or cold as it is the acid that seals the fish. The oven temperature is sufficient to bring the pot to the required temperature and to maintain this temperature throughout cooking. The liquid should be actually simmering, as in stewing. The fish is served from the casserole dish with the sauce spooned over it.

INGREDIENTS

A fisherman's wife would choose whether she would make a casserole or a stew by the types of fish that were available. This is a sensible rule to follow. If you have firm-fleshed white fish which can be cut easily into chunks, then make a stew. If you have small whole fish, thin fillets or soft fish which may disintegrate in a large quantity of liquid, it is wiser to make a casserole.

Whichever dish you are cooking, the fish must be absolutely fresh. If you cannot get a particular fish that your recipe includes, substitute another of the same type—as the fisherman's wife would. Buying mixed fish for both stewing and casseroling gives you the opportunity to try out one or two of the more unusual fish on display. They are often cheap, not because they are inferior, but because people find them strange. Don't be put off by their appearance. Some, for instance, have odd spiky heads but these can be used to make fish stock and will then be thrown away; only the flesh actually appears on the table.

You can use sea or freshwater fish, although not together. You can, and should, use a proportion of firm oily fish such as eel with your white fish, when you can get it.

You can use fresh or frozen fish and buy it whole, in steaks or fillets and treat it as necessary for your cooking method, when you get home. Cook fresh fish the day you buy it.

Fish for stewing

There is a huge choice of fish that can be used for stewing. The fish needs to be firm because the large quantity of liquid bubbling around the chunks would break them up if they were soft. Choose from the following: brill, carp, char, cod, coley, crayfish (rock lobster), grayling, grey mullet, gurnard, haddock, hake, halibut, John Dory, lobster, monkfish, mussels, oysters, pike, pollock, prawns, red mullet, river bass, rock salmon, scallops, sea bream, squid, tench, turbot, weever.

Shellfish, which are discussed in detail on pages 375–383 are absolutely ideal for use in stews as they can

be popped into the hot liquid for the few minutes they take to cook.

Fish for casseroling

Casseroling disturbs the fish very little and enables you to select the softer fish and those that are often sold in thin fillets, such as plaice. The fish lie on a bed of vegetables and can be cooked in steaks or fillets. Casseroling is suitable for coarser flavoured fish which stands up well to the aromatic, pungent flavours used in Spanish, Italian and southern French dishes. Several of the fish suitable for casseroling are firm enough for stewing and appear in both lists. Choose from: carp, cod, dab, flounder, haddock, hake, hali-

SOME FAMOUS FISH STEWS

Bouillabaisse is a famous saffron-flavoured fish stew from the Mediterranean coast of France. A true bouillabaisse cannot be made in areas where the scorpion-fish (or rascasse as the French call it) is unobtainable, since this is considered an essential ingredient to the dish.

Bouride, a stew from Provence, is very strongly flavoured with garlic. The soup and the fish are served separately.

Cotriade is a fish stew from Brittany which can be made in many areas because the varieties of fish that the Bretons use are widely available elsewhere. The other main ingredient is potatoes and the Americans have adopted this dish and called it a chowder. Newfoundland and New England are areas associated with chowder.

Matelote is the name given to a stew in which the fish is cooked in wine. Strictly speaking freshwater fish should be used but the dish varies according to the region from which it comes. In the dairy districts of Normandy, for instance, sea fish are used and the stew is thickened with eggs and cream, and cider made from the apples grown locally is included.

Meurette is a matelote from Burgundy (matelote à la bourguignonne) which uses red wine.

but, herring, John Dory, mackerel, pike, plaice, red mullet, salmon, salmon trout, sole, tunny, turbot and whiting.

The liquid for stewing

The basic liquid for a fish stew can be just water, or water and milk, but any stew is infinitely better made with stock and a fish stew with fish stock. Use the heads, trimmings, skin and bones of the fish to make a stock, before making the stew itself. If you buy the fish already prepared as steaks or fillets, always ask for some fish heads and bones at the same time. If you buy frozen fish you will either have to buy extra and use some for making the stock, which is rather extravagant, or make do without fish stock.

If you do make your own fish stock, remember it must be used, or frozen, within 24 hours. If frozen, it will keep for up to one month.

The liquid for casseroling

The liquid in a casserole is more likely to be a sauce than plain stock; it gives a richer flavour than stock. The other flavouring liquid which you will find in a number of casseroles from the European continent is wine or another liquor. Both red and white wine can be used despite the tendency to associate white wine with fish and red wine with meat.

Vegetable and flavourings

The liquid provides some of the flavouring for your stew or casserole but other ingredients are always added. Freshly chopped herbs are nearly always included, varying according to where the dish originates from: a Swedish recipe will often include dill, a Spanish one, garlic.

Two flavourings, however, occur in practically every fish stew or casserole. These are onions and parsley which are used frequently, no matter where the recipe comes from.

Other vegetables are often added to the onions and can be cooked in chunks to be served with the fish, or sieved after cooking in order to thicken the liquid or sauce. Tomatoes, potatoes and peppers are often included.

Various other ingredients are used for thickening and bulk in the stews originating from southern Europe and bread, often toasted, appears in recipes from France and Spain.

PORTUGUESE FISH SOUP

With its hard-boiled eggs, shellfish and a garnish of almonds, this is a handsome dish. It's a quick one too, for you can boil the eggs ahead of time and use frozen prawns.

SERVES 4

225 g [½ lb] fresh, skinned haddock fillet
1 medium-sized onion, finely chopped
30 ml [2 tablespoons] olive oil
1 L [1¾ pts] fish stock
100 g [¼ lb] frozen prawns
30 ml [2 tablespoons] freshly chopped parsley
salt and pepper
2.5 ml [½ teaspoon] dried oregano or tarragon
4 thick slices of bread
2 hard-boiled eggs
10 ml [2 teaspoons] butter
30 ml [2 tablespoons] flaked almonds

1 Put the onion and oil in a saucepan big enough to take all the ingredients. Cut haddock into pieces about 5 cm [2"] in size. Put the fish on the onion.

2 Pour the prepared fish stock into the pan. Add the prawns and parsley. Season well with salt and pepper. Add the herbs.

3 Bring the stock up to simmering point. Skim well. Simmer for 10 minutes, uncovered.

4 While the pan is simmering, toast the bread lightly on both sides. Chop the hard-boiled eggs. Heat the butter in a small pan over low heat and fry almonds until golden.

5 Put the toast into 4 warmed soup bowls. Put a quarter of the chopped egg on each toast slice. Ladle the soup over the toast.

6 Sprinkle the almonds over each bowl and serve at once.

MACKEREL CASSEROLE

Straight from Scandinavia, this quick, simple casserole dish is one of the few using oily fish. It is all the more welcome, since mackerel is so cheap and so good! In this recipe, the lemon juice and acid cream seal the fish as firmly as boiling liquid would.

SERVES 4
2 mackerel, each weighing about 450–700 g [1–1½ lb]
40 g [1½ oz] butter
salt
2 leeks
225 g [½ lb] canned tomatoes
15 ml [1 tablespoon] dill seeds
2.5 ml [½ teaspoon] paprika
juice of half a lemon
150 ml [¼ pt] soured cream

1 Wash and fillet the mackerel and skin if preferred. Heat the oven to 180°C [350°F] gas mark 4.

2 Use 15 g [½ oz] butter to grease the inside of a casserole which will just hold the fillets in one layer and lay the fish in it.

3 Wash the leeks and slice the white part finely. Melt the remaining butter in a frying-pan and sauté the leeks until soft. Add the tomatoes, dill seeds and paprika, mix together and transfer to the casserole.

4 Sprinkle in the lemon juice and pour the sour cream over the top.

5 Cover the dish. Put into the oven and cook for 20 minutes. Serve hot from the dish.

Warming and filling Portuguese fish soup.

SPANISH FISH SUPPER

⊠⊠⊠ *This is a splendid one-pot family meal for when you are too busy to cook your fish the day you buy it—the marinade will preserve the fish overnight. Any white fish fillet or steaks, such as coley, cod, bass, hake or haddock may be used.*

SERVES 4
1 kg [2¼ lb] white fish
4 medium-sized onions
3 garlic cloves
2 parsley sprigs
1 bay leaf
15 ml [1 tablespoon] white wine vinegar
75 ml [3 fl oz] olive oil
salt and pepper
50 g [2 oz] plain flour
8 thick slices French bread
15 ml [1 tablespoon] chopped chives

1 Skin the fish and remove any bones (keep them for making fish stock). Cut the fish into big pieces, 7.5–10 cm [3–4"] in size.

2 Peel and chop the onions and garlic and chop the parsley coarsely, including the stalks.

3 Put these ingredients into a deep non-corrodible container. Add the bay leaf, vinegar and oil. Season well with salt and pepper.

4 Put in the fish, and turn it over gently to coat thoroughly. Leave it for at least several hours or overnight.

5 In a large saucepan, bring 1.5 L [2½ pt] water to the boil. Add the fish and simmer for one minute. Add all the marinade, including the vegetables and flavourings. Season with salt and pepper.

6 Bring back to the boil. Cover the pan. Lower the heat and simmer for 15 minutes.

7 Mix the flour with 30 ml [2 tablespoons] cold water to make a smooth cream. Add a little of the hot soup and then stir it into the pan of soup. Simmer for another 5 minutes, stirring.

8 Toast the bread very lightly on both sides. Put 2 slices of toast in each of 4 heated individual soup bowls. Gently strain the fish soup, so as not break up the fish, over the bread in the bowls. Place the strained fish in a warmed, shallow dish. Sprinkle it with the chives.

9 Serve a bowl of soup to each person. Hand round the fish and onion mixture separately, so that each person can put some into his soup.

STEWED EELS, 1880

⊠ *Not all fish stew recipes are imported! This one comes from England's Mrs Beeton. Eels are rich in nourishment and well worth making into a family meal. The stock may be made with a cube.*

SERVES 4
1 kg [2¼ lb] eels or 4 conger eel steaks weighing about 225 g [½ lb] each
salt and pepper
2 large onions
4 cloves
1 strip lemon zest
575 ml [1 pt] chicken stock
75 ml [3 fl oz] port or Madeira
75 ml [3 fl oz] thick cream
30 ml [2 tablespoons] flour
cayenne pepper
a few drops of lemon juice

1 If you have bought whole eels, wash and skin them and remove their heads. Cut them into pieces 7.5 cm [3"] long.

2 Lay the pieces of eel or the conger steaks in a stewpan which will just hold them in one layer. Season them with salt and pepper.

3 Peel the onions and stick the cloves into them. Place the onions on the fish. Add the strip of lemon rind.

4 Mix together the stock and the port or Madeira. Bring to the boil in a small saucepan. Pour the liquid over the fish. Bring the pan up to the boil over medium heat.

5 Reduce the heat so that the liquid just simmers. Cover the pan. Simmer for 30 minutes or until the fish is tender.

6 Discard the onions. Take out the pieces of eel or conger with a slotted spoon; drain them over the pan. Put them in a heated shallow serving dish. Keep them warm under buttered paper.

7 In a small bowl, mix the cream and flour. Add a little of the hot liquid from the pan. Blend thoroughly, leaving no lumps.

8 Off the heat, stir this mixture into the sauce in the pan. Replace the pan over moderate heat, and stir until the mixture thickens. Reduce the heat and allow the flour to cook for a few minutes.

9 Stir a few grains of cayenne pepper and a few drops of lemon juice into the sauce. Check the seasoning.

10 Strain the sauce over the fish and serve at once.

Matelote Normande is a particularly tasty fish stew. It is a rich and nourishing dish from a lush region of France, making use of many delicious local ingredients.

MATELOTE NORMANDE

This is a creamy dish from the rich dairy districts of Normandy in France. It is a good example of a dish making use of local ingredients. Use a mixture of white fish, including some eel. Serve with a garnish of triangular shaped croûtons and with some mushrooms sautéed in butter.

SERVES 6

1.6 kg [3½ lb] firm white
   fish
225 g [½ lb] conger eel
1 L [1 quart] mussels
   in shells
1 large onion
60 g [2½ oz] softened butter
850 ml [1½ pt] dry still cider
15 ml [1 tablespoon] freshly
   chopped parsley
50 g [2 oz] flour
30 ml [2 tablespoons] thick
   cream
chopped parsley to garnish

1 Remove skin and bones from all the fish. Cut the flesh into pieces about 10 cm [4"] in size.

2 Wash and scrub the mussels thoroughly. Discard any which are open.

3 Peel and chop the onion. Melt 15 g [½ oz] butter in a large flameproof casserole and fry the onion gently until soft and transparent.

4 Put the mussels into a saucepan with 175 ml [6 fl oz] of the cider. Cover the pan and heat gently until the mussels open.

5 Remove the pan from the heat. Pour the mussel liquor into the casserole. Remove the mussels from their shells, set aside and keep warm.

6 Add the parsley to the casserole and cook very gently for 5 minutes.

7 Pour in the remaining cider and 575 ml [1 pt] water and bring to the boil.

8 Add the fish, cover the casserole and bring back to simmering point. Simmer for 10 minutes.

9 Remove from the heat. Take out the fish, draining for one minute, over the casserole. Put the fish in a warmed shallow serving dish, and keep warm under buttered paper.

10 Mix the remaining butter and the flour to make a beurre manié and add this, in small spoonfuls, to the liquid in the casserole. Stir until the butter melts.

11 Replace the casserole over medium heat and bring to the boil, stirring. Stir until the sauce thickens slightly. Stir in the cream and remove from the heat.

12 Sprinkle the mussels on top of the fish and pour sauce over. Garnish.

BOURIDE

Even if we cannot make an authentic bouillabaisse, we can make a bouride which is very similar. Creamy and garlicky, it has the real southern flavour of its French home in Provence. You will need 275 ml [½ pt] homemade or bought egg-based mayonnaise. If you cannot find one of the fish listed, choose another variety of firm white fish.

SERVES 4-6
450 g [1 lb] each of fresh haddock, cod and rock salmon or halibut
salt
freshly ground black pepper
6 small slices of bread
45 ml [3 tablespoons] olive oil
1 garlic clove

For the fish stock:
700 g [1½ lb] fish heads, bones and trimmings from white fish
1 medium-sized onion
1 leek
50 ml [2 fl oz] white wine
20 ml [4 teaspoons] white wine vinegar
zest of orange quarter

For the garlic mayonnaise:
15 ml [1 tablespoon] fresh white breadcrumbs
15 ml [1 tablespoon] white wine vinegar
4 garlic cloves
275 ml [½ pt] mayonnaise
a few drops of lemon juice
salt and pepper
2 egg yolks

1 Remove any skin and bones from the fish and reserve for the stock. Cut the fish into 5 cm [2"] pieces and season. Refrigerate.

2 Make the fish stock. Peel and slice the onion and wash the leek and slice the white part. Put all the ingredients in a large saucepan with 850 ml [1½ pt] water. Bring to the boil. Skim well. Lower the heat so that the liquid just simmers. Half cover the pan and simmer for 30 minutes. Do not leave it for any longer.

3 While the stock is simmering, prepare the garlic mayonnaise. Mix the breadcrumbs into the vinegar. Leave to soak for 5 minutes. Drain and squeeze the crumbs dry in kitchen paper.

4 Peel and crush the garlic well. Mix it with the crumbs until blended to a smooth paste. Add, little by little, 15 ml [1 tablespoon] mayonnaise. Work it in with the back of a spoon to make a smooth cream.

5 Mix this garlic cream into the remaining mayonnaise. Sharpen the mayonnaise with lemon juice, and add salt and pepper to taste. Reserve.

6 Toast the slices of bread very lightly on both sides. Heat the olive oil in a frying-pan, over low heat. Fry the toast on both sides until well soaked with oil, and golden. Peel and cut the garlic clove in half. Rub over toast while still hot. Keep warm.

7 Strain the fish stock into a bowl. Squeeze as much stock as you can out of the solid matter. Discard the solids. Rinse out the pan and put back the liquid stock.

8 Bring the stock to simmering point. Add the pieces of fish with a large spoon. Simmer until the fish is firm, about 6–10 minutes. Do not overcook.

9 Remove the fish with a slotted spoon. Put it on a warmed serving dish. Keep it warm under buttered paper. Reserve the stock in the pan.

10 Measure 150 ml [¼ pt] garlic mayonnaise into a bowl. Put the rest into a sauce-boat, cover it and set aside.

11 Beat the egg yolks into the garlic mayonnaise and transfer to a saucepan.

12 Trickle the hot fish stock into the mayonnaise, stirring quickly all the time. Set over very low heat and stir until the mixture thickens slightly. Do not let it boil.

13 Check the seasoning of the garlic soup. Add extra lemon juice, salt and pepper if needed.

14 Strain the garlic soup into a hot tureen. Serve with the dish of fish, the garlic toast and the sauce-boat of mayonnaise.

Bouride is a very rich and creamy dish, strongly flavoured with garlic.

FISH AND 'CHIPS' CASEROLE

To casserole 'chips' sounds crazy, but these 'chips' are not fried potatoes, they are chipolatas! If you do not think fish and sausages go together, try this dish and see how delicious it is. Serve with baked potatoes and hot grilled tomatoes putting the potatoes in the oven well before the casserole. Fish cutlets or steaks should be used for this dish.

SERVES 4
4 cod or haddock cutlets, each 175 g [6 oz]
350 g [¾ lb] onions
175 g [6 oz] mushrooms
150 ml [¼ pt] tomato juice
dash of Worcestershire sauce
salt and pepper
5 ml [1 teaspoon] dried marjoram
4 cooked chipolata sausages

1 Heat the oven to 160°C [325°F] gas mark 3. Peel and chop the onions finely. Wipe and chop the mushrooms and put both the onions and mushrooms in the bottom of an ovenproof casserole.

2 Wipe the fish cutlets and lay them in a single layer on top of the vegetables in the casserole.

3 Mix the tomato juice with the Worcestershire sauce. Pour it into the casserole. Sprinkle the dish with salt and pepper, and the marjoram.

4 Cover the dish, and cook for 10 minutes. Cut the chipolata sausages into 1.25 cm [½"] slices. Add them to the casserole and continue cooking for 10–15 minutes until the fish is tender.

5 When the fish is ready, serve it hot from the casserole.

SPICY STAND-BY CASSEROLE

A keen fisherman might be shocked, but frozen fish fillets in an unusual spicy sauce make a super stand-by for the busy cook. This casserole which has an Italian flavour about it is a joy, since you can make the store-cupboard sauce ahead of time and use the fillets still frozen. Use white fish such as coley, haddock or plaice. Serve with sautéed potatoes and a green salad.

SERVES 4
700 g [1½ lb] frozen white fish fillets
2 medium-sized onions
1 large garlic clove
15 ml [1 tablespoon] olive oil
30 ml [2 tablespoons] tomato purée
10 ml [2 teaspoons] ground cinnamon
4 bay leaves
salt and pepper

1 Peel and chop the onions and garlic. Heat the oil in a small flame-proof casserole. When hot, fry the onion and garlic until soft.

2 Stir in the tomato purée and the cinnamon. Add the bay leaves and 225 ml [8 fl oz] water and season well with salt and pepper. Bring to simmering point.

3 Simmer for 20 minutes, uncovered, to make a thick sauce. Remove the bay leaves.

4 Heat the oven to 180°C [350°F] gas mark 4. Lay the frozen fillets in 3 or 4 layers in the casserole. Spoon some of the hot sauce over them.

5 Cover the casserole. Put it in the oven for 20–30 minutes until the fish is white and flaky. Serve hot from the casserole.

MATELOTE ROUGE

Red wine is used here with white fish: it sounds and looks a little strange but the flavour is excellent. It is so good that the dish can be made wholly with the cheaper varieties of white fish but, if you feel extravagant, use 100–175 g [4–6 oz] firm fish such as trout or halibut in place of the cheaper fish. This version of a matelote is unusual in another way too; the fish pieces are fried to seal them instead of being put into hot liquid. Be generous with the fried croûtons.

SERVES 4
600 g [1¼ lb] mixed fillets of cod, hake and whiting
75 g [3 oz] peeled prawns, fresh, or frozen and thawed
50 g [2 oz] seasoned flour
2 medium-sized onions
1 medium-sized carrot
575 ml [1 pt] dry red wine
1 sprig thyme

The combination in this recipe, red wine and fish, is rather strange but it offers an original and attractive variation.

1 sprig rosemary
15 ml [1 tablespoon] freshly
   chopped parsley
2 strips lemon zest
1 large garlic clove
salt and pepper
30 ml [2 tablespoons] oil
50 g [2 oz] butter
175 g [6 oz] button mushrooms

For the garnish:
5–6 slices white bread
15 ml [1 tablespoon] olive
   oil
30 ml [2 tablespoons] butter
50 g [2 oz] drained peeled
   prawns
30 ml [2 tablespoons] freshly
   chopped parsley

1 Skin the fish fillets and pat dry. Cut them into 2.5 cm [1"] pieces. Drain the prawns. Toss all the fish in the flour. Set aside.

2 Peel and chop one onion and slice the carrot. Put the wine, parsley, onion and carrot, herbs, lemon zest and peeled garlic into a large saucepan. Season with salt and pepper. Cover the pan, bring to simmering point, and simmer for 30 minutes.

3 When the pan is simmering safely, chop the second onion finely. Heat 25 g [1 oz] butter and the oil in another saucepan, which will hold all the ingredients. Fry the white fish and prawns, in batches, until just cooked through and golden, about 5 minutes.

4 Take out the last batch of fish and prawns. Put in the chopped onion. Add the remaining butter if necessary. Lower the heat, cover the pan, and cook very gently until the onion is just soft and golden but not browned.

5 Meanwhile, wipe and quarter the mushrooms. Add them to the pan. Cook very gently for 5 minutes with the pan uncovered and then remove from the heat.

6 Put the fish back in the pan on top of the onions and mushrooms. Strain the cooked wine sauce into the pan. Put over very low heat and simmer until the sauce reduces enough to be slightly thickened.

7 While the stew is simmering, make the garnish. Remove the crusts from the bread and cut each slice into 4 or 5 rounds. Heat the oil and butter in a frying-pan and fry the bread until golden. Remove from the pan and fry the prawns for 1 minute.

8 Turn the stew into 4 individual earthernware dishes or 1 large one. Lay the round croûtons over the stew and scatter on the prawns and parsley.

Flavourful fish

Here are more delicious ways of cooking fish, including main dishes and rare and interesting hors d'oeuvres. No special equipment is needed, no intricate techniques are involved, no time-consuming preparation is called for; just choose your fish and produce a variety of flavours from the naturally juicy to the unusually spicy. There's a dish for every occasion and every palate.

Explained in full detail are no less than four different methods of cooking fish, suitable for both oily and white fish.

The first three methods, oven poaching, braising and sousing, all involve cooking in the oven while the fourth, pickling, involves no cooking.

Oven poaching and braising are two straightforward and effective ways of cooking fish for main meals. Oven poaching is used for those cuts of fish which are not suitable for poaching on top of the cooker. Braising introduces vegetables to the baking dish which not only add flavour to the fish while cooking and help to keep it moist, but also improve the appearance of the finished dish by adding colour.

Both sousing and pickling involve the use of a marinade which softens the fish bones (which can be spiky) and imparts a distinctive flavour. The dishes are prepared in advance as many are at their best after 2–3 days' marinating. These methods are more suitable for oily fish as the marinade successfully counteracts the richness of the fish. Soused and pickled fish are generally served cold as an hors d'oeuvre or are made into a meal with salad vegetables in season and some fresh bread.

OVEN POACHING

Many of the principles discussed in connection with poaching fish on top of the cooker (see pages 329–339) apply also to oven poaching, as do the general principles (such as taking care to season well and not to overcook) which apply to all methods of cooking fish. Poaching on top of the cooker is particularly suitable for whole fish, fillets and smoked fish. Oven poaching is better suited to steaks and portions, and is also suitable for fillets.

However, oven poaching can be compared more readily, in practical terms, with baking. Oven temperatures and cooking times are the same for both processes. There are several automatic advantages when using the oven as opposed to the hob: fishy smells are kept to a minimum and service is straight from the baking dish. This means less handling of the fish and consequently less fear of it breaking up. It also means less washing-up.

The main difference between oven poaching and baking (and this is where the term poaching is justified and the association with poaching on top of the cooker comes in) is the use of liquid. Oven-poached fish is cooked in sufficient liquid to come

half-way up the fish. A little less liquid is used than when poaching fish on top of the cooker as evaporation in the oven is very slight. After poaching, the liquid can be used to create some of the most delicious sauces.

When poaching prime quality fish such as sole or turbot the liquid used is usually fish fumet (see pages 332–333), dry white wine, dry vermouth or dry cider. Additions are by no means essential but you can use mildly flavoured additives, such as mushrooms, which will not mask the fine flavour of the fish.

When cooking less tasty fish, such as cod or mock halibut, the liquid can be more strongly flavoured with herbs and vegetables to enhance the flavour of both the fish and the sauce. The recipe for fillet of cod bretonne is a good example: the creamy vegetable sauce brings a little glamour to an otherwise ordinary fish.

BRAISING FISH

This is another method of oven cooking fish to be compared to, but

Grey mullet braised with vegetables is garnished with slices of lemon.

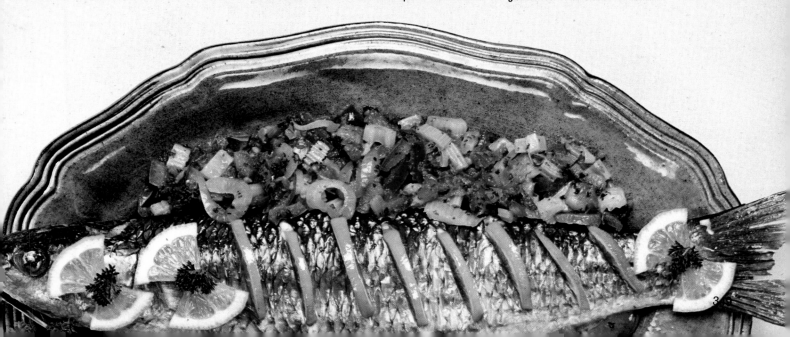

not confused with, baking. The cooking times and temperatures are the same but the results are different.

Braising is a method of cooking whole fish of a medium size, steaks or thick slices of fish on a bed of vegetables. The tougher cuts of meat are usually cooked in this way and the principles are basically the same for fish. The recipe given here which illustrates this method of cooking fish is grey mullet with lemon.

The fish is prepared in the same way as for any other method of cooking fish. Whole fish are laid raw on the bed of prepared vegetables. Fish steaks or slices need to be fried for a few minutes on each side in hot fat to seal the surfaces, before being laid on the vegetable bed.

The vegetables used are usually chosen from the following: onions, celery, leeks, carrots, peppers and tomatoes. The vegetables are cleaned and diced or finely sliced and are fried gently in butter to soften, before being spread over the base of the dish. Vegetables add both flavour and colour, and herbs such as bay leaves and garlic are often included too.

The vegetables are served with the fish as an integral part of the finished dish. For attractive presentation the cooked fish is usually transferred to a warmed serving platter and the vegetables arranged around the sides as a garnish.

The liquid which is added to the dish is normally fish stock or fish fumet (pages 332–333), white wine or cider. The amount is very small, just sufficient to cover the bed of vegetables, and is added cold. The dish is then covered tightly so that evaporation is minimal. If tomatoes are being used there is no need to use any liquid. Enough juice will run from the tomatoes as they cook to keep the

other vegetables and the fish moist.

By the end of braising time the liquid in the dish should be well flavoured. You may find you have too much, though. Serving fish swamped in liquid, however well-flavoured, looks unappetizing.

If there is too much liquid you can reduce it by rapid boiling, having first drained it off the vegetables and fish. This will not only improve the flavour and consistency but also the appearance of the finished dish. Alternatively, the liquid can be thickened by the addition of a little beurre manié. Again, the liquid is strained off and thickened on top of the cooker and then poured back over the fish and vegetables on the serving platter.

SOUSING AND PICKLING

Soused and pickled (sometimes called spiced) are the terms used to describe fish which has been marinated in an acid solution. This is one area of cooking where the terms are not clearly defined. In Britain, sousing means to cook the fish in the oven in an acid-based solution. The fish is then cooled and allowed to marinate in the cooking liquid. In Europe, the fish is usually cooked beforehand (either by frying or grilling) and is then immersed in the vinegar solution to marinate.

The British method of sousing is used for fish rich in oil such as herring and mackerel, rather than white fish as the acidity of the marinade ingredients offsets the richness of the fish giving it an appetizing, piquant flavour. The acid also softens the small bones in the fish and acts as a preservative. Fish soused by the British method should be eaten within three days.

A vinegar marinade is also used to pickle fresh herrings which have been lightly salted beforehand. With this method the fish is not cooked by heat at all. Instead of cooking the fish is simply cured by acid in the marinade. This process is an excellent way of preserving herrings and provides one of the best known pickled fish dishes—rollmops. If immersed in the marinade and kept refrigerated in an airtight jar, herrings will keep in perfect condition for several weeks.

The marinade

The ingredients of the marinade must be well balanced to produce a

pleasing dish and it is important that the mixture is not too harsh. The quantity should be sufficient to cover the fish generously.

In Britain, malt vinegar is more commonly used because of the brewing tradition which makes malt readily available. If it is too harsh, the vinegar can be used diluted, roughly one part water to three parts vinegar or up to half and half.

Vinegar is not always used and the marinade is then flavoured with dry wine or dry cider. The recipe given for soused mackerel is an example. The fish is cooked in the wine and then soused in the liquid resulting in a finer flavour.

Herbs, spices, sugar and vegetables are added to the marinade for flavouring. The herbs that are used include bay leaves, parsley, tarragon and fennel.

Step-by-step to

MAKES 8
8 fresh herrings
50 g [2 oz] coarse salt
550 ml [1 pt] white wine or cider vinegar
1 large onion

3 Drain fish. Lay skin side down on a board. Peel and slice onion. Cut gherkins in half lengthways.

Sousing fish

Prepare the fish by gutting it. Herrings, pilchards and small mackerel can be soused whole or can be deheaded and boned (see pages 292–293). Larger mackerel should be cleaned and split down the belly and the bones removed. They can be filleted if preferred. Do not skin the fish.

Mix the marinade ingredients and season well. Arrange the fish flat in a close-fitting dish and pour over enough marinade to completely cover the fish. Cover the dish with a lid or foil and bake at 150°C [300°F] gas mark 2 for about 1 hour or until the fish is tender. Remove the dish from the oven, leave to cool, and refrigerate the fish in its marinade until needed. The fish should be served very cold with a little of the marinade strained over it. The fish will keep for three days.

Pickled fresh herrings

The way in which fresh herrings are pickled is an effective preservative and provides a very well-known dish, rollmops. In this case the herrings are boned and pickled whole; fillets, which are pickled flat, are called Bismarcks. The fish should be really fresh and is at best after five days' marinating but can be preserved in perfect condition for several weeks.

It is important that the fish is stored carefully. Once prepared, the rollmops should be placed in a wide-necked container and sufficient marinade should be poured over to completely cover them. A sterilized glass jar is the best container: the seal must be airtight and the lid non-corrosive. The container should be kept under refrigeration. Stored this way, the fish will remain in perfect condition for at least 5–6 weeks.

The fish is cleaned, deheaded,

split down the belly and boned (see pages 292–293). Fillet the fish if you prefer but do not skin either the boned fish or the fillets. Two recipes are given here: one for rollmops and a sweet pickle recipe for herring fillets. Both are good preservatives, but the fish can, of course, be eaten once the marinating process is completed.

The fresh herrings are pickled raw. They are 'cooked' by the acid in the marinade, which is vinegar. As an extra preservative the fish is lightly salted before being marinated, either in pure salt (overnight) or in brine. Both methods are very simple. Always use kitchen salt which has no chemical additives to make it free-flowing. The brine is made by dissolving 50 g [2 oz] salt in 550 ml [1 pt] water and the herrings should be soaked for at least two hours. The herrings can also be filleted and salted in pure salt overnight. Place

making rollmops

4 small pickled gherkins
2 bay leaves
6 white peppercorns
15 ml [1 tablespoon] mixed pickling spice

1 Dissolve salt in 550 ml [1 pt] cold water. Bone herrings and lay open in the brine. Leave for 2 hours.

2 Bring the vinegar and spice to the boil slowly. Set aside and leave to infuse for an hour.

4 Halve onion slices. Put some onion and half a gherkin on each herring and roll up from the head.

5 Pack in a wide-necked container. Strain in the spiced vinegar and add bay leaves and peppercorns.

6 Add any remaining onion, cover and leave in a cold place to marinate, or seal and store.

the fillets in layers in a dish and cover each layer of fish generously with salt. Cover and refrigerate overnight.

Once salted, the herrings must be drained thoroughly (if soaked in brine) or rinsed under cold running water and drained thoroughly (if salted in pure salt). Finally, pat the fish dry with kitchen paper.

Mix the marinade ingredients together and place in a saucepan. Bring to the boil and leave for at least an hour for the flavour to infuse. The marinade is then ready for use.

If you wish to store the fish lay the fillets in a suitable lidded container or prepare your rollmops and place them in a wide-necked container. Pour the marinade over the fish to completely cover it. Seal securely and store in the refrigerator.

If the fish is to be served immediately after marinating, place the fillets in a suitable glass or china dish. Pour the marinade over to completely cover the fish, cover the dish lightly and leave in a cold place to marinate for at least eight hours. Rollmops should be marinated in a deeper wide-necked container for at least four days before being used.

Since time immemorial gluts of fish have been preserved for eating in leaner times. Wind drying, salting, smoking and pickling are all age-old methods of preserving fish. In spite of modern methods of preservation such as the deep-freeze, forms of these are still in use today simply because people enjoy the flavours.

Salt herring: the genuine salt herring is the gutted fish preserved between layers of pure salt in wooden casks. The fish is sold from the casks and, once common, is now available only in a few delicatessens serving Jewish communities, or in those specializing in Eastern European food. Salt herring needs thorough soaking, in milk, before being used.

Rollmops: although easily made at home, as with most foods today they can be bought ready made. They are available at most chilled food counters and are sold loose or in jars for longer keeping. (See step-by-step for rollmops.)

Bismarcks: are prepared in the same way as rollmops, but the fillets are left flat instead of being rolled. Available at chilled food counters.

Matjes: this is a Dutch word meaning virgin herrings. The skinned and brined fillets are sweet pickled and have a full, rich flavour. They are also

available from chilled food counters. Allow one fillet per serving. The flavour can vary in strength and if too strong, soak them in milk and water, then pat dry, before serving alone or in a mixed salad.

SOUSED MACKEREL

This hors d'oeuvre can also be made with herring but is particularly good with small, really fresh mackerel which you serve whole. If only large mackerel are available, fillet and roll them before cooking.

This is a dish that can be prepared ahead and refrigerated. Serve the fish within two days with the reduced cooking liquor poured over and garnish with slices of lemon and possibly fresh bay leaves and whole black peppercorns.

SERVES 4
**4 small fresh mackerel,
    weighing about 250–350 g**
[9–12 oz] each
15 ml [1 tablespoon] oil
1 medium-sized carrot
1 medium-sized onion
1 lemon
salt
6 black peppercorns
1 dried red chilli
1 bay leaf
250 ml [½ pt] dry white wine

1 Heat the oven to 150°C [300°F] gas mark 2.

2 Use the oil to grease a shallow ovenproof dish into which the fish will fit in a single layer.

3 Peel and finely slice the carrot and onion. Strew these over the base of the dish. Slice the lemon and place two slices in the dish. Reserve the remaining slices for the garnish.

4 Gut the fish, cut the fins off and leave

and skin the dark-skinned fillets for you, and ask for the heads, bones and skin for the stock. According to their thickness, the fillets can be poached flat, folded or rolled.

SERVES 4
700 g [1½ lb] fillets of brill
150 ml [¼ pt] fish stock
25 g [1 oz] softened butter
1 shallot or ½ small onion
salt and white pepper
150 ml [¼ pt] dry white wine or
dry vermouth
15 g [½ oz] flour
150 ml [¼ pt] thick cream
1 lemon
15 ml [1 tablespoon] milk
(optional)
30 ml [2 tablespoons]
Parmesan cheese
fresh parsley sprigs

1 Heat the oven to 180°C [350°F] gas mark 4.

2 Use 12 g [½ oz] butter to grease a shallow flameproof dish into which the fish will fit in one layer, and to butter a piece of grease-proof paper or foil large enough to cover the dish.

3 Peel and finely chop the shallot or onion and strew over the base of the greased dish.

4 Season the fillets with salt and pepper. According to their thickness leave flat, fold in half (skin side inside, if unskinned), or roll up from the tail, skin side inside. Arrange side by side in the dish.

5 Pour the wine and stock around the fish and cover the dish with the buttered paper or foil.

6 Poach in the centre of the oven for 15–20 minutes depending on the thickness of the fish and its arrangement in the dish. Test it after 15 minutes, and take care not to overcook.

7 Drain the poaching liquor into a saucepan and boil rapidly, un-covered, until reduced to about 150 ml [¼ pt]. This will evaporate the alcohol and concentrate the flavour. Keep the fish warm in the covered dish.

8 Cream the remaining butter and the flour to a soft paste (beurre

---

the heads on or cut them off as you prefer and depending on how the fish fit the dish.

5 Lay the fish in the dish, head to tail, and sprinkle them with salt.

6 Crush the peppercorns coarsely and add to the dish with the chilli, bay leaf and wine. Cover the dish.

7 Cook in the centre of the oven for about one hour or until the fish is tender.

8 Test the fish with a skewer and, if cooked, remove the dish from the oven.

9 Allow the fish to cool in its container. Arrange the reserved slices of lemon on the mackerel. Cover the dish and refrigerate.

10 The soused fish must be served very cold and within three days of

Mackerel soused in white wine is served cold with the liquid in which it has been marinated.

being made. To serve transfer the fish to a serving dish.

11 Strain the marinade and pour some of the liquid over the mackerel. Garnish with lemon slices.

FILLETS OF BRILL IN WINE AND CREAM SAUCE

This is a classic way of poaching fillets of prime flat fish such as sole, chicken turbot or halibut, or brill as suggested here. Because all these fish have a fine flavour and texture, very little additional flavouring is necessary. You will need some fish stock either home-made or made with a fish stock cube. Remember to adjust the quantity as you only need 150 ml [¼ pt].

Ask the fishmonger to fillet the fish

manié). Reduce the heat to low and beat the beurre manié into the reduced liquid, little by little. Simmer gently for a few minutes, stirring.

9 Heat the grill to high.

10 Add the cream to the sauce, off the heat, and then bring gently almost to boiling point, stirring continuously.

11 Check the seasoning and add a squeeze of lemon juice to sharpen the flavour very slightly. Add any extra liquid that has run from the fish. The sauce should be of coating consistency; if it is too thick add the milk.

12 Spoon the sauce over the fish to coat it completely. Grate the cheese and sprinkle evenly over the dish.

13 Slip the dish under the hot grill for 2–3 minutes until the surface is golden. Garnish with a few parsley sprigs and serve immediately.

Variation

Use a less prime fish and add extra flavouring. Try paupiettes of plaice with prawns. Add 150 ml [¼ pt] peeled prawns to the original recipe and omit the cheese and the grilling.

Lay the fillets of plaice flat on a board, skin side uppermost if un-skinned. Season well and, reserving one prawn to garnish each fillet, put a few prawns on each. Roll up from head to tail and stand upright in the dish. (If close together they will stay rolled, if not, secure the ends with a cocktail stick and remove before serving.)

Poach in liquor and when cooked prepare the cream sauce, seasoning it well with lemon juice, and pour over the fillets. Garnish the top of each fillet with a prawn and a small sprig of parsley, and serve immediately.

FILLET OF COD BRETONNE

This recipe can be used for oven poaching steaks, portion-sized pieces of thick fillet or chunks of fish. The choice of fish is wide and depending on the season and availability, any of the following could be used: haddock, cod, hake, saithe, mock halibut, rockfish or dogfish. Cod fillets are used for this version. If wished, they could just as easily be cut into 2.5 cm [1"] chunks.

Skin the fillets before cooking or ask your fishmonger to do this—don't forget to ask for some fish trimmings for the stock. Make this in advance. If you don't have time, however, water is a satisfactory substitute.

SERVES 6
1 kg [2¼ lb] cod fillet
75 g [3 oz] butter
1 small onion
1 medium-sized carrot
2 celery sticks
2 medium-sized leeks
salt and white pepper
250 ml [½ pt] dry cider or white wine
150 ml [¼ pt] fish stock
25 g [1 oz] flour
150 ml [¼ pt] thin cream
half a lemon

1 Use 25 g [1 oz] butter to grease a shallow ovenproof, dish, into which the fish will fit in a single layer, and a piece of greaseproof paper or foil to cover the dish.

2 Peel and finely chop the onion and strew it over the base of the dish. Portion the fish if in large pieces, and lay the portions on the onion.

3 Heat the oven to 190°C [375°F] gas mark 5.

4 Wash the carrot, celery and leeks, peel as necessary and cut into julienne strips about 3 mm [⅛"] wide and 2.5 cm [1"] long.

5 Melt 25 g [1 oz] butter in a small saucepan over low heat, put in the vegetables, stir, cover and sweat for 8–10 minutes until beginning to soften. Season lightly.

6 Spoon the soft vegetables evenly over the fish and pour in the cider or wine, and fish stock or water. Cover the dish with the buttered paper or foil.

7 Place in the centre of the oven and cook for 15–20 minutes according to the thickness of the fish. Take care not to overcook.

8 Drain the poaching liquid into a saucepan. Leave the fish and vegetables in the covered dish and keep warm.

9 Boil the liquid rapidly, uncovered, until reduced to 250 ml [½ pt].

10 Cream together the remaining butter and flour to make a soft paste (beurre manié). Beat the beurre manié into the liquid over low heat, piece by piece. Cook for a few minutes until thickened. Remove from the heat and stir in the cream.

11 Replace over heat and bring slowly to just below boiling point. Season to taste with salt and pepper and lemon juice and pour over the fish and vegetables. Serve immediately.

GREY MULLET WITH LEMON

This attractive recipe for braising a whole fish is particularly suitable for a firm-fleshed fish such as grey mullet. Mullet is a heavily scaled fish and needs to be carefully scaled before cooking. Ask the fishmonger to clean and scale the mullet but leave the head on, otherwise simply lay the fish flat and use the back of a knife to remove the scales, working from the tail to the head. No liquid is used in this recipe because the tomatoes provide sufficient juice to keep the fish moist. The vegetables are boiled rapidly at the end to evaporate any excess juice.

SERVES 4–5
1 grey mullet, weighing about 1–1.1 kg [2–2½ lb]
salt
1 lemon
1 green pepper
1 medium-sized onion
2 celery sticks
25 ml [1 fl oz] olive oil
2 garlic cloves
4 tomatoes
30 ml [2 tablespoons] fresh parsley
freshly ground black pepper
bay leaf
thyme sprig

1 Heat the oven to 190°C [375°F] gas mark 5.

2 With a sharp knife make deep incisions across the fish, spacing them at 2.5 cm [1"] intervals.

3 Sprinkle the fish liberally with salt. Scrub the lemon, slice thinly and cut each slice in half. Press half a slice into each cut in the fish.

Vegetables are used to add flavour when poaching cod fillets.

Cover and refrigerate until needed.

4 Wash, de-seed and finely chop the green pepper. Peel and finely slice the onion. Wash and finely slice the celery.

5 Heat the olive oil over medium heat in a flameproof casserole large enough to accommodate the fish.

6 When hot, fry the pepper, onion and celery together gently over low heat until they begin to soften.

7 Meanwhile, peel and chop the garlic. Peel, de-seed and chop the tomatoes and chop the parsley.

8 Add all these to the frying vegetables and cook gently for a minute or so. Season with salt and pepper.

9 Remove the casserole from the heat, lay the fish on top of the vegetables and baste it well. Tuck the bay leaf and thyme on either side of the fish and cover. (If you have no lid use oiled greaseproof paper.)

10 Braise in the centre of the oven for 30–40 minutes depending on size, basting several times. Test the fish after 30 minutes to see if it is cooked.

11 To serve, lay the whole fish on a hot serving plate and keep warm. Boil the vegetables rapidly, uncovered, until most of their juice has evaporated. Spoon the vegetables along either side of the fish.

SWEET PICKLED HERRINGS

Herring fillets pickled in this manner have a richer, sweeter and less acid flavour than traditional rollmops. Preparation must start the day before as, instead of being lightly salted in brine, the fish is filleted and salted overnight in pure salt. Make sure the herrings are really fresh when you buy them and clean and fillet them yourself (see pages 292–293) or ask the fishmonger to fillet them for you.

These pickled herrings, once refrigerated will keep for several months but are best eaten within a few weeks.

Serve the fillets either whole or cut into pieces and arranged in a dish with a garnish of the onion rings, a couple of fresh bay leaves and some sliced stuffed olives.

SERVES 6
3 large fresh herrings
block or coarse salt
150 ml [¼ pt] distilled malt vinegar or wine vinegar
100 g [¼ lb] granulated or soft brown sugar
25 g [1 oz] mixed pickling spice
1 large onion
2 bay leaves

1 Trim the fillets into a neat shape and remove all visible bones.

2 Layer the fillets flat into a glass or china dish, sprinkling each layer thickly with salt. Cover and refrigerate overnight.

3 Next morning, rinse the fillets thoroughly in cold running water, drain well and pat dry with kitchen paper. Wipe out the dish.

4 Put the vinegar, sugar and pickling spice into a saucepan with 150 ml [¼ pt] water and bring slowly to the boil. Remove from the heat and allow to become cold.

5 Peel the onion and slice finely into rings. Layer the fillets and onion rings into the cleaned dish, or into a plastic box if you wish to store them.

6 Strain the cold spiced vinegar over the fillets (it should just cover them) and tuck the bay leaves down the sides.

7 Cover the dish and refrigerate for 8 hours before draining and using the fillets, or seal the box securely and store in the refrigerator.

A Friday fry-up

Crisp and golden and piping hot, fish and chips can make a very delicious meal. Here is explained how to fry fish to perfection, so that when the fish itself is cooked the coating is evenly browned and crisp. The method is popular all over the world; this course includes many well-known favourites like English fish and chips, Italian fritto misto and Japanese tempura.

It is much easier to achieve first class results by frying fish in deep rather than shallow fat. The temperature of the fat is so high and the cooking so rapid that, as the coating browns to perfection, the fish inside is cooked to just the right degree.

The fish itself is protected from direct contact with the hot fat by a substantial coating, yet it cooks rapidly because it is virtually surrounded by heat. The fat is really very hot, which means that immediately the coating touches the hot fat it sets, imprisoning all the juices and flavour of the fish. The coating browns quickly and evenly, less fat is absorbed, and the result is crispy, grease-free and succulent at the centre.

To deep fry successfully, however, you must have the right equipment and oils, the fish should be prepared correctly and cooked at an exact temperature. Care and attention are key words to successful deep frying.

THE FISH

Fish for frying, whether in shallow or deep fat, should not be more than 2.5 cm [1"] thick. It is important that the heat is able to penetrate and cook the fish in the time it takes to brown and crisp the coating. A burnt coating or undercooked fish will render the result inedible. As long as this rule is observed, the fish can be fried whole, in fillets or in chunks.

The fish can also be beaten with potato to make fish cakes. This is an ideal cooking method for cheaper, less flavoursome varieties of white fish, which can be cheered up with generous seasoning and rich, creamy potato. Fish cakes can also be shallow fried and a recipe is given on page 372.

As soon as you get the fish home, remove it from its wrappings, rinse under cold running water and drain thoroughly. Keep the fish chilled, covered with polythene or foil until needed.

The most suitable fish for deep frying is given below.

Small whole fish such as sprats, sardines, smelts, whitebait, portion-sized dabs, sole and plaice, and small shellfish, such as scampi, prawns and mussels.

Fillets of haddock, cod, whiting, coley and hake.

Chunks of large fish, such as halibut, turbot, brill and monk fish.

THE COATING

All fish for frying must be carefully and thoroughly enclosed in a coating which will protect it from the hot fat and seal in all its juices and flavour. The coating must be fairly substantial, in order to be effectively protective. Dipping fish in egg and then white breadcrumbs which have been dried in the oven is one way of coating the fish. The other is to use batter. There are many variations on a basic flour, water and oil batter (see right).

One exception is whitebait. These are so small and need such brief cooking that they are at their best simply lightly coated in seasoned flour. No further coating is necessary.

Egg and breadcrumbs

It is not necessary to measure the quantities for egg and breadcrumbing as the flour can be applied from a dredger and any breadcrumbs that are left over can be put back into storage. If, though, you are coating small pieces of fish and a dredger is not very satisfactory, allow between 25–50 g [1–2 oz] for each 450 g [1 lb] fish.

Batter coatings

Batter is the most popular coating for deep frying fish. Batter cannot be shallow fried, whereas egg and breadcrumbed fish can. The batter must be sufficiently sticky to cling to the surfaces of the fish and not run off. To coat 450 g [1 lb] fish you will need up to 425 ml [¾ pt] fritter batter.

The batter that is used to coat fish for that traditional dish, fish and chips is plain fritter batter. For 425 ml [¾ pt] fritter batter, sift 100 g [¼ lb] plain flour with salt. Make a well in the centre and pour in 30 ml [2 tablespoons] oil and 150 ml [¼ pt] cold water. Draw flour in from the sides, mix until thick; leave for 30 minutes.

The batter is very easily lightened by adding beaten egg whites just before the batter is to be used. Use two egg whites for 425 ml [¾ pt] batter. The egg whites must be whisked to their maximum volume to ensure a light and crisp batter. This egg white batter makes a very satisfactory coating for all types of fish and the results are always much lighter than plain batter and particularly crisp and mouthwatering.

Batters for coating fish can be made even more light and airy by using a light alcoholic liquid, such as cider, beer or lager, in place of plain water in the batter mix. When an alcoholic liquid is used, the batter must be allowed to stand before it is used so that it can ferment and effervesce to lighten it. Beaten egg whites are always used in these batters.

Tempura batter is heavier than plain batter. Sift 100 g [¼ lb] plain flour with salt. Break one egg into another bowl and whisk in 15ml [1 tablespoon] soy sauce. Gradually add 150 ml [¼ pt] iced water. Add flour to the liquid 15 ml [1 tablespoon] at a time and whisk vigorously. This makes 275 ml [½ pt] batter. A recipe for tempura is given on page 364.

FATS FOR DEEP FRYING

To store the oil, after each frying session allow the oil to cool. Strain through a sieve lined with absorbent kitchen paper to remove sediments and bits of coating. Strain the oil again into a container with a tight fitting lid and store in a cool dark place. Never pour hot fat into a plastic container.

The best medium in which to deep fry fish is undoubtedly oil. There are various types of oil, some with a distinctive flavour, others with no flavour at all. The prices also vary enormously and, as a large quantity is needed, some of the prices are prohibitive.

Vegetable, nut or corn oil are best for deep frying as they reach frying temperature fairly quickly and, having a high smoke point, can be raised to the high temperature necessary for deep frying without burning. Lard and clarified dripping can also be used for deep frying but both burn easily at a lower temperature than oil and are, therefore, difficult to regulate.

Quantity of oil

Because of the danger element, it is unwise to fill a pan to more than one-third or a half full of oil. A fire can flare up instantly from fat bubbling over the sides of the pan if you are cooking on gas. It will also burn and smoke very unpleasantly on an electric cooker.

For safety's sake use no more than the quantities given here:
● for a pan 23 cm [9"] in diameter, 12.5 cm [5"] deep with a capacity of 4 L [7 pt] use 1.5–1.75 L [2½–3 pt] oil;
● for a pan 20 cm [8"] in diameter, 9cm [3¾"] deep with a capacity of 2.75 L [5 pt] use 1.2 L [2 pt] oil.

EQUIPMENT

The one piece of special equipment that is essential for deep frying is, of course, the pan. There are many types available nowadays, so pick one to suit your particular need. It is possible, if you do not possess a deep fat fryer, to use a heavy-based saucepan with a folding basket that is made to fit any pan. The basket is, in fact, only used for fish coated with egg and breadcrumbs as batter would stick to the mesh. The pan must be large enough to completely cover the source of heat and deep enough to take the required quantity of oil safely.

The easiest and most accurate way of testing the temperature of the fat is to use a frying thermometer. It is certainly worth investing in one if you deep fry food regularly.

Lifting the fish out of the batter and into the fat is best done with a skewer. This means that no batter is scraped off and your hand is at a safe distance from the hot fat.

A perforated spoon is invaluable for lifting the fish out of the hot fat. It ensures that excess fat can drain back into the pan rather than be spooned out with the fish. With larger slices of fish it may be easier to use a fish slice.

Absorbent kitchen paper will efficiently complete the task of draining the fish.

THE METHOD

Far too many fires start in the kitchen with blazing fat pans, so make sure the pan is clean, the fat is heated slowly, the handle does not jut out over the cooker and there is no water about. Never carry a pan of hot oil.

Because frying is such a quick method of cooking, it is more than ever essential to be thoroughly organized with everything in its proper place. It is important not only to know exactly what you will need but also in what order.

Preliminary steps

Several things must be done before you contemplate actually frying the fish. The fish should already have been rinsed and chilled as soon as it was brought home from the fishmonger.

The first step, then, is to prepare

the batter or breadcrumb coating. Make the batter, apart from adding the egg whites, and chill it until needed. For a breadcrumb coating, assemble the dredger of flour, the bowl of beaten egg and the breadcrumbs piled on a large sheet of greaseproof paper.

Preparing the fish

Small whole fish generally need to be topped and tailed and gutted. The gutting of round fish is described in detail on pages 292–293 and of flat fish on pages 314–315.

The exception here is whitebait, which is so small that it is fried and eaten, quite literally, whole. Whitebait is a very small silvery fish. It is the small fry of herring and sprats. As to when a whitebait becomes a sprat, the unofficial definition is when it is large enough to need gutting and beheading before it is cooked.

The fish can be cleaned (gutted) in advance, lightly seasoned and stored, chilled, until needed. However, the cleaning of fish is best done as near cooking time as possible, and with a tasty coating the preliminary seasoning is not so important.

Mussels are prepared as described on pages 412–413 and are then shaken in a pan over gentle heat until they open. They are then removed from their shells. Discard any mussels which remain closed. The preparation and cooking of other small shellfish are described on pages 375–379.

Fillets of fish, if small enough, can simply be wiped over with a damp cloth, seasoned if wished and kept chilled if not needed immediately. If they are too thick for frying, the fillets can be cut into portions 150–175 g [5–6 oz] in weight and not more than 2.5 cm [1"] thick.

Chunks or pieces of fish can be cut from fillets, steaks and cutlets. It is important that the chunks be boneless as it is difficult to locate and remove bones inside a piece of fish that has been coated, and coming across one inadvertently could ruin the enjoyment of the dish. The chunks or pieces should not be much larger than bite sized.

Before the fish is coated with batter, it is given a light dusting of seasoned flour. Shake well to dislodge surplus flour. This should be applied just before the fat is heated so that the flour does not have time to absorb moisture from the fish and become soggy.

An egg and breadcrumb coating can be applied now, rather than after the fat has been heated, as it is quite a long operation and hot fat cannot be kept waiting.

All accompaniments and garnishes should be ready to be served before you start frying. Heat all the serving dishes and plates so that the fish will not be cooled when it is served. Keep vegetables, serving dishes and plates hot in the oven while frying the fish.

Arrange some crumpled kitchen paper on a baking tray ready to drain the fish. This can be put into the oven to keep the first batch of fish hot while the rest is being fried.

Heating the oil

It is exceedingly important that the fat is at the right temperature for frying before the fish is lowered into the pan. It must be hot enough to seal the coating on contact. Fat that is too cool will soak into the coating and the result will be unappetizing.

The best temperature varies a little with different oils and also with the nature and size of the pieces of fish. Recommended temperatures can, therefore, only be guidelines. The usual temperature is between 180°C [350°F] and 195°C [380°F], the lower temperature being for larger portions of fish needing a slightly longer time for the heat to penetrate and the higher temperature for small pieces of fish needing brief cooking.

Pour the correct quantity of fat carefully into the pan with the basket in position if you are using a bread-crumb coating. Remove the basket and put it away if you are using a batter coating. Put the pan over low heat, stand the thermometer in it, and heat very gently to the correct frying temperature.

Finishing the batter

While the oil is heating you will have time to finish the batter. Keep a very careful watch over the pan of oil and on no account leave the kitchen.

Whisk the egg whites to their maximum volume and fold lightly into the chilled batter mixture. Put the batter into a deep bowl so that the pieces of fish can be entirely immersed and evenly coated all over. Put the bowl on a firm surface near the cooker.

The oil will probably have reached frying temperature during this time. If you do not have a thermometer, drop a small chip of raw potato into the pan from the end of a spoon. Moderate

bubbling means that the fat is hot enough, but not too hot, for frying.

Coating the fish with batter

When frying temperature is reached you can start coating the fish with batter. Dip the fish, one or two pieces at a time, into the batter. Make sure all the surfaces are evenly coated. Lift out on a skewer, one at a time, holding briefly over the bowl to allow excess batter to drip back. Immediately transfer the pieces of fish to the pan of oil, one at a time, lowering each piece gently into the hot oil. Skewers are particularly use-

ful here, as they can safely be dipped into the hot fat, whereas fingers cannot!

Breadcrumbed fish should be put into the basket with a skewer or tongs and the basket lowered slowly into the fat.

Fry as many pieces as the pan will take comfortably. Do not overcrowd the pan or the temperature of the fat will be lowered. In a pan containing 1.5–1.75 L [2½–3 pt] oil do not attempt to fry more than three portion-sized pieces of fish at one time.

Fry the fish until the coating is crisp and golden brown and the fish cooked through. This will take between 1½–5 minutes, depending on the size and thickness of the pieces. Turn once with a perforated spoon or skewer to brown both sides evenly.

Lift out the battered fish with a perforated spoon or fish slice, hold over the pan momentarily to drain, then lay on the crumpled paper on the baking tray. Breadcrumbed fish can be lifted out in the basket and transferred to the baking tray with tongs. Put the baking tray in the oven to keep hot while the remaining fish is fried.

When all the fish is fried, transfer it to a hot serving dish which can be lined with a paper doily. Serve piping hot, handing vegetables and a piquant sauce or wedges of lemon separately.

FRIED WHITEBAIT

Despite the fact that they are eaten whole, complete with heads and eyes, you have only to try this uniquely English delicacy to become addicted. Crispness is the all important quality, and frying whitebait in deep fat is the best way to achieve it. Because they are so small and fry so quickly, a higher fat temperature is used than for larger portions of fish. Choose very fresh whitebait (the fish should separate easily and not stick together), and handle the fish as little as possible to avoid bruising or crushing. Have everything for the meal ready before you start to prepare the fish because, once coated with flour, it should be fried and eaten without delay. Quick-frozen whitebait can give as good a result as fresh, but allow time for the fish to defrost thoroughly before cooking. Serve fried whitebait as a first course with plenty of lemon to squeeze over and some fresh brown bread and butter to eat with the fish. The fish will be at its best while hot.

SERVES 4
450 g [1 lb] whitebait, fresh or defrosted
45 ml [3 tablespoons] seasoned flour
1.2–1.75 L [2–3 pt] oil
salt
cayenne pepper (optional)

For the garnish:
parsley sprigs
lemon wedges

1 Start heating the pan of fat. Heat the oven to 180°C [350°F] gas mark 4.

2 Put the whitebait into a colander and submerge gently in cold water. Remove any foreign matter such as pieces of weed, if any. Drain well and pat dry with kitchen paper.

3 Spread the flour on a large piece of greaseproof paper and put the fish, a few at a time, in the centre. Lift the edges of the paper so that the fish roll over until lightly coated with flour and are quite separate from each other.

4 Transfer fish to a sieve and shake gently to dislodge surplus flour. Repeat until all fish are well coated. Put some crumpled kitchen paper on a baking tray.

5 When the oil reaches a temperature of 195°C [380°F] lower the basket, containing not more than a handful of whitebait, into the fat. Fry for 1 to 2 minutes, until the fish is very crisp and golden, shaking the basket now and then to prevent the fish clinging together.

6 Lift the basket out of the fat, drain over the pan for a few seconds, then turn the whitebait on to kitchen paper to drain, and keep hot in the oven.

7 Repeat with successive batches of whitebait, checking that the fat has returned to frying temperature before adding a fresh batch.

8 When all are fried, sprinkle with salt and a light sprinkling of cayenne pepper as well.

9 Line a hot serving dish with a plain paper doily and pile the whitebait into it. Garnish with lemon and parsley and serve at once.

SOLE COLBERT

This classic dish is not difficult to cook provided you remember to measure the diameter of your frying basket before buying the fish! You need one small sole, complete with head and tail, for each person. It is fried flat, hence the need to check that the fish will fit into your frying basket.

Although Dover sole is the traditional fish for this recipe because of its firm texture and fine flavour, lemon sole and dab are also delicious cooked this way and considerably less expensive. As you can fry only one fish at a time it is not a dish to undertake for more than a few people. If the worst happens and the fish is, after all, a little too big for the pan, try cutting off its tail. If it is then still too large, look for a wider pan which is still sufficiently deep and use a fish slice and palette knife to lift the fish in and out, instead of a frying basket.

Again, prepare the garnish in advance and have the plates heating in the oven. Making lemon butterflies is simple but effective. The Colbert butter can be made well in advance and refrigerated until needed.

SERVES 4
4 sole, each weighing about 250–350 g [9–12 oz]
2 medium-sized eggs
100 g [¼ lb] dried white breadcrumbs
a dredger of seasoned flour
1.2–1.75 L [2–3 pt] oil

For the Colbert butter:
100 g [¼ lb] unsalted butter
60 ml [4 tablespoons] finely chopped fresh parsley
10 ml [2 teaspoons] finely chopped fresh tarragon
30 ml [2 tablespoons] lemon juice
15 ml [1 tablespoon] meat jelly from underneath beef dripping
salt
freshly ground black pepper

For the garnish:
sprigs of parsley
lemon butterflies

1 To make the Colbert butter, cream the butter until soft, then beat in the herbs, the lemon juice little by little, the meat jelly and salt and pepper to taste. Form into a roll about 2 cm [¾"] in diameter, wrap in greaseproof paper and chill in the refrigerator until needed.

2 If the fishmonger has not already done so, remove the dark skin of the sole (see pages 314–315) and trim the tail, small fins and edges of the fish. Rinse the fish and pat dry.

3 With a sharp knife make an incision right along the backbone on the skinned side of each fish.

4 Slide the knife under the flesh and ease the fillets away from the bone, leaving them attached at the head, tail and outer edge only, thus forming a large 'pocket' on each side of the backbone and freeing the bones.

5 Using scissors, cut through the backbone at the head and tail and in the middle. The purpose of this is to make it easier to remove the bone after frying.

6 Break the eggs into a flat dish, add 15 ml [1 tablespoon] water and beat lightly to mix.

7 Spread the breadcrumbs on a large piece of greaseproof paper.

8 Coat each sole with seasoned flour from the dredger, then with beaten egg and finally with breadcrumbs.

9 Press the breadcrumbs on firmly with a palette knife. If time allows, cover the fish loosely with greaseproof paper and leave in a cool place for about half an hour for the coating to firm up.

10 Cover a flat baking sheet with crumpled kitchen paper ready to drain the fish. Heat the oven to 180°C [350°F] gas mark 4.

11 When ready to fry, heat the fat, with the frying basket in position, to 190°C [375°F].

12 Raise the frying basket, put in one fish, cut side uppermost, and lower gently into the fat. Fry for about 3–4 minutes until golden and cooked through.

13 Lift out the basket, drain for a moment over the pan, and then gently lift out the fish with a slice and lay on the crumpled paper to drain.

14 Using a sharp knife, ease out and discard the back bone with the bones attached on either side. Keep the fish hot in the oven while frying the other fish.

15 While the last fish is frying, cut the Colbert butter into thin rounds.

16 Immediately before serving, insert several pieces of Colbert butter into the long central slit along the top of each fish. Garnish with sprigs of parsley and lemon butterflies. Serve immediately.

FISH AND CHIPS

For many people, juicy fish encased in a crisp golden batter and served with a pile of rustling, crisp potato chips, is an unbeatable combination. Everyone needs to know how to cook a creditable version of this British speciality and how to avoid the pitfalls of soggy, pallid chips and pale, flannelly fish. Chips are fried once until soft and again at a higher temperature.

Although a heavier batter makes the portions larger, a light, crisp batter is infinitely more pleasant to eat. Use 425 ml [¾ pt] plain fritter batter (see recipe on page 358); make this in advance and chill it. The optional egg whites will be added at a later stage. Keep them in a small container at room temperature until needed.

Boneless portions of almost any kind of white fish are suitable; chunky portions of cod, haddock, coley, rock salmon, hake or whiting are more traditional than fillets of flat fish, but there are no hard fast rules.

Serve with a piquant tartare sauce or a freshly made tomato sauce and wedges of lemon.

SERVES 3
3 fish fillets, each weighing about 175 g [6 oz]
1.2–1.75 L [2–3 pt] oil
seasoned flour in a dredger
700 g [1½ lb] raw chipped potatoes
2 large egg whites
425 ml [¾ pt] plain fritter batter

1 Fill a deep pan one-third to a half full of oil with the basket in position. Put in a thermometer and put pan to heat gently. Heat the oven to 180°C [350°F] gas mark 4.

2 Meanwhile, coat the fish lightly with seasoned flour, shaking to dislodge excess flour. Set aside.

3 When frying temperature for the potatoes is reached, remove the basket from the pan, put in the chips and lower the basket slowly into the hot fat.

4 Fry the chips at 180°C [350°F] for 5 minutes. Drain on absorbent kitchen paper then fry them again at 200°C [400°F].

5 While the chips are frying, finish the batter. Whisk the egg whites to their maximum volume and fold them into the prepared plain fritter batter. Transfer to a deep bowl and place it near the cooker.

6 When the chips are ready transfer them to some crumpled kitchen paper on a baking tray and keep them hot in the oven.

7 Make sure the oil is at the correct temperature for frying fish. It should not be more than 180°C [350°F].

8 When frying temperature is reached, submerge a piece of fish in the batter, lift out with a skewer, drain momentarily over the bowl and lower gently into the hot oil.

9 Repeat the process with the other pieces of fish. Have some crumpled kitchen paper ready for draining.

10 Fry until the batter is crisp and golden and the fish cooked through, about 3–5 minutes depending on thickness.

11 Lift the fish out with a skewer, drain over the pan for a moment and transfer to crumpled kitchen paper to drain.

12 Place each portion on a hot plate and add a portion of hot chips.

Sole is fried whole for this classic dish and garnished with Colbert butter.

JAPANESE TEMPURA

▨▨▨ *Tempura is a traditional Japanese way of cooking and serving food. The food is chosen for contrast in colour, flavour and texture and each Japanese cook will vary the ingredients according to taste, using eel, snapper, prawns, plaice, crab, flounder, scallops, squid, cod, green pepper, aubergine, lotus root, bamboo shoot and cauliflower. The food is fried in a special tempura batter (see page 358) which gives a particularly golden coating, and dipped in a soy-based sauce. Unlike plain fritter batter, the tempura batter must be used as soon as it is made. Remember to put the water into the refrigerator in advance to cool. The preparation of mussels is described on pages 412–413. The sauce must be made the day before.*

The nicest way to serve tempura is from a fondue pot. The guests can then fry the food themselves and will appreciate the selection chosen. The food can just as easily be battered and fried in the kitchen by the hostess and served on a large serving dish.

The exotically named fuji foo yong is simply stuffed mushrooms which are battered and fried with the other vegetables.

Tempura would obviously, in Japan, be served with other Japanese dishes. Suitable accompaniments outside Japan would be a selection of salads, and fried rice.

SERVES 4
12 peeled fresh prawns
12 fresh mussels
4 spring onions
12 French beans
12 mange-tout
4-8 parsley sprigs
425 ml [¾ pt] tempura batter
1.2-1.75 L [2-3 pt] oil

For the tempura sauce:
1 small fresh ginger root
225 ml [8 fl oz] soy sauce
90 ml [6 tablespoons] granulated sugar
juice of half a lime or lemon
225 ml [8 fl oz] dry sherry
225 ml [8 fl oz] vegetable stock

For the fuji foo yong:
1 dried black mushroom

6 fresh peeled prawns
3 fresh or canned water chestnuts
2 spring onions
75 g [3 oz] bean sprouts
8 large flat mushrooms
1 small piece fresh ginger root
salt

For the garnish:
lemon wedges
parsley sprigs

1 To make the tempura sauce, finely slice the ginger root. Combine the ginger, soy sauce, sugar, lime or lemon juice, sherry and stock in a screw top jar. Leave to stand overnight.

2 Place the prawns on a board and score across the underside to prevent them curling up when fried.

3 Scrub mussels in several changes of water, remove beards, put in a large pan and shake over fierce heat until they open. Remove from the shells and discard the shells and any mussels that do not open.

4 Trim ends of the spring onions, green beans and mange-toute. Wash the parsley sprigs.

Japanese tempura is a colourful mixture of food including bean sprouts, mushrooms and prawns.

5 Arrange the prawns, mussels and vegetables on a plate and chill until ready to use.

6 To make the fuji foo yong, place the dried mushroom in a mixing bowl and pour over enough boiling water to barely cover. Leave until soft—about 15 minutes.

7 Dice the prawns. If using fresh water chestnuts peel them. Cut chestnuts into thin slices and cut the slices into thin strips.

8 Trim and finely chop the spring onions.

9 If canned bean sprouts are used, rinse them before chopping lightly.

10 Drain and chop the dried mushroom.

11 Wipe clean the fresh mushrooms. Remove and finely chop the stalks.

12 Grate the ginger.

13 Combine all the ingredients for the fuji foo yong, except the fresh mushroom caps, in a mixing bowl and season with salt.

14 Fill each cap with the mixture, arrange on the plate with the rest of the tempura ingredients and keep chilled.

15 Fill a deep fat fryer one-third full of oil. Heat to 180°C [350°F]. Heat the oven to 180°C [350°F] gas mark 4 and put a large serving dish and plates to warm.

16 Meanwhile, make the tempura batter following the instructions on page 358.

17 Dip individual pieces of food into the batter and transfer immediately to the hot fat.

18 Deep fry in small batches, turning once or twice until golden brown. Drain and keep hot on crumpled kitchen paper in the oven. Pour the sauce from the jar into four individual bowls.

19 Serve the fried food on a large serving dish garnished with wedges of lemon and parsley sprigs with an individual bowl of sauce for each diner.

FRITTO MISTO DI MARE

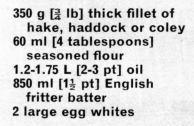

Under this name, but with local variations according to the region, restaurants all around Italy's coast serve the most delectable mixtures of fried fish. The fish used varies according to the local catch and the season and is often an ingenious way of making use of the little fish that are too small for other purposes. There should be at least three different kinds of fish and shellfish, preferably more, providing if possible a variety of shapes. A typical Italian mixture might include prawns or scampi, rings of previously boiled squid, small whole fish and bite-sized cubes of fish fillet from larger species. The important points are that the fish must be very fresh, the coating light, and the frying oil hot enough to crisp and brown the coating rapidly. Fry similar-sized fish together in a batch, so that the frying time and temperature can be adjusted to suit the size of the pieces.

The coating can be either egg and breadcrumbs or an egg white batter. Make the batter in advance and chill, but do not add the egg whites. A sharp, piquant sauce is always served with the fish, and instead of the customary mayonnaise-based tartare sauce you may prefer a less rich version made with hardboiled eggs and cream.

SERVES 4
24 cooked prawns
8 small whole fish, such as sardines, smelts or sprats
350 g [¾ lb] thin fillets of sole, plaice or dab

350 g [¾ lb] thick fillet of hake, haddock or coley
60 ml [4 tablespoons] seasoned flour
1.2-1.75 L [2-3 pt] oil
850 ml [1½ pt] English fritter batter
2 large egg whites

For the garnish:
lemon wedges
orange wedges
fresh parsley sprigs

1 Shell the prawns if necessary.

2 Cut the heads off the small whole fish.

3 Cut the thin fillets into 2.5 cm [1"] wide diagonal strips.

4 Skin the thick fillets if necessary and cut into 2.5 cm [1"] cubes.

5 Toss each variety of fish separately in seasoned flour and shake in a sieve to remove surplus flour.

6 Heat the oven to 180°C [350°F] gas mark 4 and put a large serving dish and plates to heat.

7 Pour the oil into the pan and put to heat slowly to 190°C [375°F].

8 Whisk the egg whites stiffly and fold gently but thoroughly into the chilled batter. Transfer to a deep bowl.

9 Cover a baking sheet with crumpled kitchen paper

10 Arrange the fish in separate piles, according to size.

11 Dip the pieces of fish in the batter on the end of a skewer and transfer to hot fat, briefly frying each batch separately. Check that the fat has regained frying temperature before frying each batch. The smaller pieces will need 1-2 minutes, and the larger pieces 3 minutes at the most.

12 Drain, and keep hot in the oven until all are fried.

13 Line the serving dish with a paper doily and pile fish in it in groups. Garnish with lemon and orange wedges and parsley sprigs.

MONK FISH 'SCAMPI'

Since it was discovered that the tail meat of a monk fish can be cut up into small pieces and fried to make a very good imitation scampi, the demand for it has increased. You might be lucky enough to find some in a local fish shop or market, especially if you live on the coast. Although no longer cheap, it is still good value for money because there is no wastage. It provides a mock 'scampi' which will deceive all but the experts and at roughly half the cost.

Remember to have the garnish and the accompaniments ready before starting to fry the fish. The three sauces are optional but delicious. If you are pressed for time when preparing the meal, the fish can be coated in advance, as it needs to rest for at least an hour to firm up. This quantity is enough to serve 4 as a starter, 2-3 as a main course.

SERVES 3-4
450 g [1 lb] tail piece of monk fish
15 ml [1 tablespoon] seasoned flour
2 small eggs
100 g [¼ lb] dried white breadcrumbs
1.2-1.75 L [2-3 pt] oil

For the garnish
fresh parsley sprigs
wedges of lemon

To serve:
thin slices of brown bread and butter
275 ml [½ pt] rémoulade tartare sauce or mayonnaise verte

1 Cut the fish into small pieces about 4 × 1.2 cm [1½ × ½"] and 1.2 cm [½"] thick. You should have about 30 pieces.

2 Put the seasoned flour on a piece of greaseproof paper and place next to the fish.

3 Break the eggs into a shallow dish, add 10 ml [2 teaspoons] water and beat lightly with a fork to mix well. Place next to the flour.

4 Pile the dried breadcrumbs on a large piece of greaseproof paper and place next to the bowl of beaten egg.

5 Have a clean board or flat tray

available on which to collect the coated fish until you are ready to fry it.

6 Put a few pieces of fish at a time into the flour and lift the edges of the paper to coat them.

7 Using tongs, lift out each piece of fish in turn, shake lightly so that surplus flour falls back on to the paper, and lower the fish into the beaten egg.

8 Coat each piece of fish with the beaten eggs and dried white breadcrumbs. Sift any remaining breadcrumbs and put back into storage.

9 When all the pieces of fish are coated, cover loosely with greaseproof paper and leave for an hour to firm up.

10 When ready to fry, heat the oven to 180°C [350°F] gas mark 4 and put some crumpled kitchen paper on a baking tray.

11 Heat a pan one-third to a half full of oil, with the basket in position, until a thermometer registers 190°C [375°F].

12 Lift out the basket and carefully place about a quarter of the fish pieces in it.

13 Lower the basket gently into the fat and fry for 1-2 minutes until the

coating turns golden brown and becomes crisp.

14 Immediately lift out the basket, drain over the pan for a second or two, then tip the fish on to the crumpled paper to drain. Put into the oven to keep hot.

15 Check that the fat has regained frying temperature, then fry the next batch of fish—and transfer to the oven in the same manner.

16 When all the pieces of fish are fried and drained, pile them on a hot, shallow doily-lined serving dish, garnish with the parsley and lemon and serve at once. The sauce should be served separately.

Variations

●For goujons, little strips of crispy fried fish, you can use any thin fillets, such as lemon sole, plaice, dab or megrim. They are often made from sole and, naturally, the finer the fish the better the flavour. Skin any dark-skinned fillet (pages 292–293) and rub over with half a lemon. A little of the juice can be squeezed on to the fish. Cut each quarter-cut fillet on the diagonal into 2.5 cm [1"] strips. Coat with flour, egg and breadcrumbs, fry in oil, drain and serve as above.
●For mock whitebait, instead of 2.5 cm [1"] strips, cut the fillet into very thin strips, 8 mm [⅓"] wide. The very slender goujons which result make a good substitute for whitebait.

Frying tonight

Frying is a particularly quick and attractive way of cooking all types of lean white fish and small, whole oily fish. The white fish loses its often rather bland appearance and gains a deliciously crisp and golden surface which contrasts with its fragile flesh. Prime quality fish can be served simply with wedges of lemon—the basis of some classic dishes. Cheaper but equally wholesome varieties can be fried and served with many delicious sauces.

The principles of shallow frying fish in an open pan are the same as those for shallow frying meat, in fat and relatively quickly. The main difference between frying meat and frying fish is that fish is more fragile, which means that the fat is used at a slightly lower temperature and the food must be handled with greater care. A fish slice is an essential piece of equipment for lifting and turning the fish. Almost invariably, the fish is coated before frying. Frying is carried out in an open pan to ensure a crisp coating. There are many different coatings which can be used for fish and there is a list of several on page 368 which are suitable.

THE FISH
Fish for shallow frying should not be more than 2.5 cm [1"] thick. The following are the most suitable types:
small, whole flat fish such as dabs, plaice, sole, megrim and witch

small, whole oily fish such as trout, mackerel, herrings and sardines
fillets of sole, plaice, whiting, John Dory and mackerel
steaks and cutlets of cod, hake, halibut, turbot, brill and mock halibut.

Preparing the fish
Fish should always be removed from their wrappings as soon as possible, rinsed under cold running water and drained thoroughly. Keep the fish chilled, lightly covered with polythene or foil until needed.

While a fishmonger will always clean a whole fish for you, you can, of course, do this yourself. The process is described on pages 292–293 for round fish and on pages 314–315 for flat fish. The cleaning is, in fact, best done as near cooking time as possible. Once cleaned, the fish can be seasoned although, if being coated in seasoned flour, this is not strictly necessary.

Fillets of fish, steaks and cutlets can simply be wiped with a damp cloth, seasoned if wished and kept covered and chilled until needed.

The special preparation necessary for frying fish is to give it a coating to protect the delicate flesh from the intense heat of the fat and, at the same time, to add an attractive crispy surface. The softer the fish, the greater the need for a really protective coating which will set firmly on contact with hot fat.

SUITABLE COATINGS

Food that is to be fried is often given a coating to help retain the juices and flavour within the food. This protects the food from the intense heat of the fat and also stops it from absorbing an unnecessary amount of fat. A coating makes the food easier to handle, especially soft food such as fish, and gives it an attractive contrasting texture of a crisp, golden skin.

The coatings listed below are all very successful when used with fish. If you feel adventurous, experiment with different coating ingredients.

Flour, fine oatmeal and matzo meal are suitable for fillets, steaks and cutlets and small whole fish. The fish should be thoroughly dried before being rolled completley in the well-seasoned flour or the meal. A firmer coating can be achieved if, after being floured, the fish is dipped in milk, drained and given a second coating of flour.

Egg and breadcrumbs give a firmer, crisper and more protective coating than flour. Adding grated cheese or herbs to the breadcrumbs gives extra flavour.

Coarse oatmeal and rolled oats make attractive coatings for oily fish, particularly herrings. The flavour is improved if the oatmeal is first crisped in the oven or shaken in a pan over heat for a few minutes.

Crushed potato crisps and cornflakes make rough-textured coatings, particularly good for fish cake mixtures.

Packet stuffing mixtures make readily available, easy to apply, useful coatings for less tasty fish.

FAT FOR SHALLOW FRYING

The fats used for shallow frying fish are butter, dripping and oil. The flavour of the fat is important when frying fish; butter and oil, mixed half and half, are very satisfactory. As with frying meat, it is customary in some recipes to use butter alone. To prevent the butter from burning it should first be clarified; melt and strain the butter through a muslin-lined sieve. Fish which is prepared 'à la meunière' is always fried in clarified butter. If you are using oil alone, olive oil has a distinctive flavour, but many people prefer the cleaner, less noticeable taste of vegetable oil.

The temperature of the fat

Fish needs more gentle treatment than meat and the temperature of the fat is, therefore, not quite so high. It must, though, be sufficient to seal and crisp the coating.

Oil and butter or butter alone: put in the fish while the butter is still foaming and maintain a steady heat so that the fish sizzles gently and the butter does not burn.

Oil alone or clarified dripping: heat the fat until a small cube of bread dropped in turns brown in 30 seconds. This heat is correct for thin fillets but for thicker pieces of fish such as steaks allow the temperature to drop slightly before lowering in the fish. The slightly lower temperature is needed so that the heat can penetrate to the centre of the fish without overbrowning the surface.

FRYING

Put 60 ml [4 tablespoons] butter and oil mixed into a large, heavy-based frying-pan. Heat gently until frying temperature is reached. While the butter is still foaming, lower in the fish, one at a time, skin side up. The fish should lie flat, with a small space between each one. Always allow the fat to regain frying temperature before lowering in the next piece. When frying in batches, do this between each batch.

Fry the fish until golden brown and turn once to brown the other side. To turn the fish, slide a fish slice under the fish and use a palette knife or spoon to hold it steady.

Frying times: allow two to three minutes each side for thin pieces of fish, and four to five minutes each side for whole fish and pieces 1.25-2.5 cm [½-1"] thick.

DRAINING AND SERVING

Like all fried food, fish should be well drained on crumpled kitchen paper and must always be served piping hot. Fish which is served in a sauce or dressing made from the pan juices is, obviously, not drained.

Remember to heat serving dishes in advance and have the garnishes and accompaniments prepared so that there is no delay in serving.

GARNISHES AND SAUCES

Vegetable garnishes are served with the fish primarily to add colour and

succulence. The vegetables are cooked briefly after the fish has been prepared and coated, but before it is fried. In this way, the vegetables are ready to serve immediately the fish is cooked. Once cooked, they are kept warm while the fish is being fried and are spooned over the fish just before serving. The vegetables that are most suitable are the more moist varieties, such as tomatoes, onions, mushrooms, celery and leeks.

Fried fish is enhanced by the sharp contrast of piquant flavours. Not without reason, lemon juice is the classic companion of fried fish. For a change, try lime juice or orange juice.

Sauces should be well flavoured

SERVES 4
2 sole, each weighing about 500 g [18 oz]
30 ml [2 tablespoons] seasoned flour
50 g [2 oz] clarified butter
50 g [2 oz] butter
10 ml [2 teaspoons] lemon juice
15 ml [1 tablespoon] freshly chopped parsley

4 Fry gently over medium heat until golden, 3–4 minutes. Turn carefully and fry until golden.

and spicy or piquant. Fish sauces can be either hot or cold. For hot sauces, try melted butter sauce, anchovy butter sauce, egg sauce, mushroom sauce, dill sauce, beetroot sauce, mustard sauce or cucumber sauce. Cold sauces include the favourite mayonnaise-based tartare sauce, walnut sauce, almond sauce or mayonnaise curry sauce. Experiment with different ingredients and flavourings for an individual sauce.

MARINATING
Marinating in a piquant dressing is an excellent way to impart flavour and variety to some of the less tasty varieties of fish. Lemon juice or vinegar is used for its acidity and herbs, garlic, spices, onions, anchovies and vegetables for extra flavour. This is a popular method in Europe and in the Middle East, where the fish is marinated sometimes before and sometimes after frying or grilling.

Fish marinated before cooking is more often served hot, with a little of the marinade spooned over just before serving. Fish marinated after cooking is served cold and makes an unusual first course.

Almost any firm-fleshed fish, both oily and white, is suitable for marinating: small fish can be cleaned and left whole but larger fish are better filleted, sliced, or cut into strips.

FRYING FROZEN FISH
Commercially frozen fish products usually carry full instructions and cooking times on the pack. Frozen fish is best cooked from the near frozen state, preferably within half an hour of being taken from the freezer. It is better coated, and the slight softening of the surface as the fish defrosts helps the coating to adhere more firmly.

Cook the fish in exactly the same way as fresh fish, allowing half as long again on each side.

Step-by-step to frying fish à la meunière

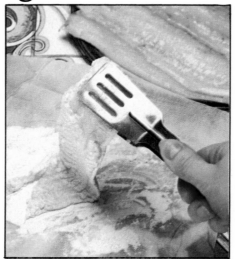

1 Fillet fish into quarter-cut fillets (see pages 314–315). Skin dark-skinned fillets. Rinse, pat dry.

2 Spread seasoned flour on greaseproof paper. Press fillets into flour. Shake off surplus.

3 Heat clarified butter in large frying-pan. While butter foams, lower in four fillets.

5 Arrange fillets, overlapping, on a hot dish. Keep hot. Fry remaining fillets and transfer to dish.

6 Wipe out frying-pan and heat fresh butter rapidly, watching it carefully, until golden brown.

7 Pour butter promptly over fish, followed by the lemon juice. Scatter on the parsley and serve.

MARINATED ROCK SALMON

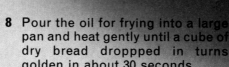Italians are very keen on marinating fish, either before or after cooking. Rock salmon is an inexpensive, firm-fleshed fish usually sold skinned and filleted. Any firm-fleshed fish cut into small pieces can be used—Italians like filleted fresh sardines cooked in this way. In Italy, the fish would be served with a green salad and fresh bread, but sautéed potatoes and a fresh green vegetable would be equally appropriate.

SERVES 4
450 g [1 lb] rock salmon
1 lemon
2.5 ml [½ teaspoon] freshly
    ground black pepper
5 ml [1 teaspoon] dry English
    mustard
2.5 ml [½ teaspoon] dried
    oregano
10 anchovy fillets
45 ml [3 tablespoons] olive
    oil
15 ml [1 tablespoon] freshly
    chopped parsley
45 ml [3 tablespoons] plain flour
1 large egg
90 ml [6 tablespoons] oil

1   Remove any bones from the fish and cut the flesh into lengths of 5 cm [2″].

2   Squeeze the lemon and put the juice, pepper, mustard and oregano into a bowl and mix.

3   Chop the anchovy fillets finely and add to the marinade with the olive oil and parsley. Mix well.

4   Put in the fish, stir gently for a few seconds to mix the marinade with the fish. Cover the dish loosely and leave in a cool place for at least 1–2 hours.

5   Lift the pieces of fish out of the marinade, one by one, pausing a moment to let surplus marinade drain back into the basin. Reserve the marinade.

6   Spread the flour on a sheet of greaseproof paper. Roll each piece of fish in flour to coat thoroughly and shake to remove surplus flour.

7   Beat the egg lightly in a shallow dish.

8   Pour the oil for frying into a large pan and heat gently until a cube of dry bread droppped in turns golden in about 30 seconds.

9   Dip the fish, piece by piece, in the beaten egg to coat lightly, and immediately lower into the hot fat. Do not crowd the pan. Fry for 2–3 minutes, turning once or twice, until golden and crisp all over.

10 Lift the fish out with a perforated spoon, drain briefly on crumpled kitchen paper and pile up on a hot serving dish. Keep hot and repeat with the remaining fish.

11 Immediately before serving sprinkle with a little of the marinade.

TROUT WITH ALMONDS

The charm of this popular dish depends on frying the fish in butter so that the skin of the trout is crisp and golden and the fish cooked through. The nutty flavour and texture of the almonds contrast well with trout but, portions of brill or halibut, which also seem to have a natural affinity with almonds, can be cooked in the same manner despite the lack of skin. Ask the fishmonger to clean the trout through the gills but to leave the head on. If frozen rainbow trout is used instead of fresh, it can be cooked from near frozen if fried very gently for about 15 minutes.

Garnish the dish with wedges or twists of lemon and watercress.

SERVES 4
4 fresh trout, each weighing
    about 200 g [7 oz]
60 ml [4 tablespoons] seasoned
    flour
75 g [3 oz] clarified butter
25 g [1 oz] butter
50 g [2 oz] flaked almonds
15 ml [1 tablespoon] lemon
    juice
salt
freshly ground black pepper

1   Spread the seasoned flour on a sheet of greaseproof paper and roll the fish in it, one at a time, to coat thoroughly all over. Shake off surplus flour.

2   Heat 50 g [2 oz] clarified butter in a large frying-pan and, while still foaming, put in two trout and fry gently over medium heat for 4–5 minutes until golden.

3   Turn the fish carefully and continue cooking for another 4–5

370

Trout with almonds is fried à la meunière as in the step-by-step instructions. Other less expensive fish, such as lemon sole, dabs, megrim and witch can also be fried this way for a simple and light meal.

minutes on the other side. Check that the fish is cooked through to the bone by making a small incision with the point of a knife in the thickest part. Lift the fish out without draining, arrange on a serving dish and keep hot.

4 Add the remaining clarified butter to the pan and cook the next two fish in the same way.

5 When all the fish are cooked, remove the pan from the heat and wipe out with kitchen paper. Put in the butter, return to the heat and, when hot, fry the almonds, stirring frequently until pale and golden brown.

6 Add the lemon juice to the pan with a light seasoning of salt and pepper. Stir, spoon over the trout and serve immediately.

BRETON-STYLE FLAT FISH

This is an attractive, quick and useful recipe for cooking flat fish such as dabs, lemon sole or megrim when they happen to be available in single portion sizes. You can ask the fishmonger to remove the heads and dark skin and trim the fins, or do this at home with a sharp knife. Use whichever fresh herbs are available, choosing from parsley, chervil and chives.

SERVES 4
**4 flat fish, each weighing
    about 350 g [12 oz]
45 ml [3 tablespoons] seasoned
    flour
2 shallots
1 lemon
100 g [¼ lb] unsalted butter
30 ml [2 tablespoons] oil
50 g [2 oz] shelled shrimps
20 ml [4 teaspoons] drained
    capers
20 ml [4 teaspoons] chopped
    fresh herbs**

1 Spread the seasoned flour on a sheet of greaseproof paper. Press each fish in turn into it, to coat thoroughly on both sides. Shake off surplus flour.

2 Chop the shallots finely and squeeze the lemon.

3 Heat 25 g [1 oz] butter and 15 ml [1 tablespoon] oil in a small pan. Fry the shallots gently for a minute or two until soft. Add the shrimps, capers and herbs to the pan with the lemon juice. Reduce the heat to minimum and cover the pan.

4 Heat 50 g [2 oz] butter and the remaining oil in a large, heavy-based frying-pan and, when hot, fry two of the fish gently over medium heat for 4–5 minutes. Turn carefully and brown the other side. Remove to a hot serving dish and keep hot.

5 Melt the remaining butter in the pan and repeat the frying process with the remaining two fish. Transfer to the serving dish.

6 Spoon the shrimp mixture over the fish and serve immediately.

FANCIFUL FISH CAKES

Fish cakes need never be the dreary wodges of vaguely fish-flavoured potato. They should be tasty, well-seasoned mixtures, containing at least as much fish as potato, enclosed in a crunchy golden coating. The fish and potato mixture must be cooled before being coated and fried, so the mixture can be made in advance. Although traditionally round, the cakes can be made in fish shapes, balls or ovals, and coated with cornflakes, crushed potato crisps or coarse oatmeal instead of the more usual egg and breadcrumbs. If being served to children, the cakes can be decorated with quartered slices of lemon for the gills and a slice of stuffed olive for the eyes. Serve plain for breakfast, or with a freshly made tomato sauce or a creamy smooth parsley sauce.

SERVES 4
275 g [10 oz] old potatoes
350 g [12 oz] white fish fillet
40 g [1½ oz] butter
salt
white pepper
15 ml [1 tablespoon]
freshly chopped parsley
5 ml [1 teaspoon] lemon juice
1 small egg
2 small packets potato crisps
90 ml [6 tablespoons] oil

1 Peel the potatoes and boil in lightly salted water until tender, then drain very thoroughly. Mash in the saucepan.

2 Meanwhile, put another saucepan of water to boil and cut the fish fillet into several pieces. Use a little of the butter to grease a plate and a piece of greaseproof paper to cover the fish. Lay the fish on the buttered plate, season with salt and pepper and cover with the buttered greaseproof paper.

3 Set the plate over the saucepan of boiling water, cover with the lid and steam for 10 minutes. Drain off the liquid, remove any skin and bones and flake the fish.

4 Beat the remaining butter into the mashed potato and add the fish and the parsley. Add the lemon juice and seasoning to taste. Beat until smoothly mixed.

5 Turn on to a plate, cover loosely and leave until cold and firm.

6 Divide the cooled mixture into 6 or 8 equal portions and, on a lightly floured surface, shape the portions into ovals. Beat the egg.

7 Tip the potato crisps into a strong plastic bag and crush finely with a rolling pin. Dip fish cakes in egg.

8 Turn the crushed crisps on to a piece of greaseproof paper and coat each fish cake thoroughly. Use a palette knife to press the crumbs on and to reshape the cakes.

9 Heat the oil in a large frying-pan over medium heat. When very hot, fry a single layer of fish cakes until golden, then turn carefully and brown the other side. Lift out with a fish slice, draining briefly over the pan, then thoroughly on crumpled kitchen paper. Keep hot while frying the remaining cakes and serve immediately.

Variations

●For herring roe fish cakes, replace the white fish with 225 g [½ lb] soft herring roes, poached for 10 minutes in a little milk.
●For salmon fish cakes, replace the white fish with a 200 g [7 oz] can of pink salmon, drained and flaked.

COLD MARINATED FRIED FISH

Although the swordfish generally used for this dish in the Middle East is not often available in other countries, the dish can be made with slices of any firm fish, such as mock halibut or rock salmon, or with small, whole fresh mackerel. The fish is not coated before frying. Ask the fishmonger to slice it or buy steaks. The dish does not take long to prepare but you must allow at least an hour before serving for it to chill sufficiently.

SERVES 6
1 kg [2¼ lb] mock halibut
60 ml [4 tablespoons] olive oil
225 g [½ lb] onions
2 green peppers
2 garlic cloves
400 g [14 oz] canned tomatoes
15 ml [1 tablespoon] tomato purée
30 ml [2 tablespoons] freshly chopped parsley
salt
freshly ground black pepper
50 g [2 oz] black olives

1 Pat the fish thoroughly dry with kitchen paper.

2 Heat the oil in a large sauté pan (with a lid) over medium heat and, when hot, fry the pieces of fish fairly quickly until golden on both sides, but not cooked through. Lift out carefully and reserve.

3 Peel and thinly slice the onions; halve, de-seed and thinly slice the peppers; peel and crush the garlic.

4 Add the onion to the oil remaining in the pan, which should be about 45 ml [3 tablespoons], and fry gently for about 5 minutes until beginning to soften.

5 Add the sliced peppers and continue frying gently for a further 5 minutes.

6 Add the crushed garlic and fry for another minute.

7 Drain the canned tomatoes in a sieve over a measuring jug. Make the tomato liquid up to 150 ml [¼ pt] with water and dissolve the tomato purée in it.

8 Roughly chop the tomatoes and add to the sauté pan, with the liquid and parsley, and salt and pepper to taste. Bring to the boil and simmer for 5 minutes.

9 Lay the reserved pieces of fish gently in the pan, spooning the sauce over them if not completely covered.

10 Cover the pan and cook very gently for 10–15 minutes until the fish is cooked through.

11 Lift out the fish and arrange the pieces side by side in a shallow dish.

12 Boil the liquid rapidly, uncovered, until reduced to the consistency of a thin sauce. Add the whole black olives for the last few minutes of cooking and check the seasoning before pouring over the fish.

13 Allow to become cold and chill in the refrigerator before serving.

COD PROVENCAL-STYLE

This recipe is a useful way of adding both colour and flavour to any kind of white round fish fillets. It is particularly suitable for coley, whiting and cod, with fresh or frozen fillets. Serve with creamy mashed potatoes.

SERVES 4
700 g [1½ lb] cod fillets
30 ml [2 tablespoons] seasoned
   flour
1 medium-sized onion
2 garlic cloves
450 g [1 lb] tomatoes
60 ml [4 tablespoons] olive oil
5 ml [1 teaspoon] freshly
   chopped parsley
salt
freshly ground black pepper
25 g [1 oz] black olives

1 Skin the fillets and cut the fish roughly into 4 cm [1½"] squares.

2 Put the seasoned flour into a plastic bag. Put in the fish and toss until well coated. Remove the fish and shake off surplus flour.

3 Peel and slice the onion; peel and crush the garlic cloves; peel, de-seed and chop the tomatoes.

4 Heat 30 ml [2 tablespoons] oil in a sauté pan over low heat. When hot, put in the onion and fry gently for about 6–8 minutes until soft. Add the garlic and cook for another minute or so, then add the tomatoes, chopped parsley and salt and pepper to taste.

5 Toss over fairly brisk heat for several minutes until the tomato begins to soften, then reduce heat to minimum and cover pan.

6 Heat the remaining oil in a large frying-pan and, when sizzling hot, put in the pieces of fish. Fry over moderate heat, turning frequently, until cooked through and lightly browned on all sides. This will take about 8 minutes.

7 Remove the fish with a perforated spoon, drain on crumpled kitchen paper and transfer to a hot shallow serving dish.

8 Spoon the vegetables over the fish, garnish with whole black olives and serve immediately.

Cod Provençal-style is a tasty and colourful dish of fried fish and juicy vegetables.

MACKEREL FILLETS ANTIBOISE

⊠ *Large mackerel tend to be coarse but can still make a pleasant luncheon dish if filleted, fried and served with a succulent and colourful vegetable garnish as in this recipe. For an added touch of colour, prepare some grilled tomatoes in advance as an extra garnish.*

SERVES 4
**4 mackerel fillets, each
   weighing about 175 g [6 oz]
30 ml [2 tablespoons] seasoned
   flour
2 medium-sized leeks
4 young celery sticks
45 ml [3 tablespoons] olive
   oil
salt
freshly ground black pepper
50 g [2 oz] butter
half a lemon**

1 Spread the seasoned flour on a sheet of greaseproof paper and press each mackerel fillet in turn into the flour to coat each side. Shake off surplus flour.

2 Remove the coarse outer leaves and trim the leeks. Wash them thoroughly in cold salted water, drain and then cut across into 6 mm [¼"] slices. Wash and trim the celery and cut across into 6 mm [¼"] slices.

3 Heat 30 ml [2 tablespoons] oil in a heavy-based saucepan over medium heat. Fry the leeks and celery, covered, shaking the pan frequently, for about 15 minutes or until tender. Season with salt and pepper.

4 Meanwhile, heat 25 g [1 oz] butter and the remaining oil in a large frying-pan and fry the mackerel fillets, skin side uppermost, for 4–5 minutes. Turn carefully and fry the other side for 3–4 minutes. Lift out and arrange on a hot serving dish with a space between each fillet.

5 Spoon a little of the leek and celery mixture along the space between each fillet.

6 Wipe out the pan in which the fish was cooked and put in the remaining butter. Heat briskly until it is nut brown, then immediately spoon a little over each fillet, followed by a squeeze of lemon juice. Serve immediately.

HERRINGS FRIED IN OATMEAL

⊠ *This favourite Scottish recipe is one of the best ways of cooking herrings. The crunchy overcoat of nutty-flavoured oatmeal is a perfect foil for rich and succulent fish. Splitting and boning the herrings give a larger surface area to be coated. Make sure the fish used is really fresh. Fresh, coarse oatmeal is best for coating, but if not available use rolled oats or porridge oats, lightly crisped under the grill before use. Bacon dripping makes a tasty alternative to oil for frying. Serve plain for breakfast, or with a fluffy mustard sauce for supper. Generously garnish the fish with wedges of orange and small cluster of watercress.*

SERVES 4
**4 fresh herrings, each
   weighing about 250-350 g
   [9-12 oz]
15 ml [1 tablespoon] coarse
   salt
freshly ground black pepper
60 ml [4 tablespoons] coarse
   oatmeal
90 ml [6 tablespoons] oil**

1 Split and bone the herrings (see on pages 292–293), removing both head and tail

2 Rinse the fish in cold water and pat dry with kitchen paper. Sprinkle generously with salt and pepper.

3 Spread the oatmeal on a piece of greaseproof paper and press each fish in turn into the oatmeal so that it is coated on both sides.

4 Heat the oil in a large frying-pan over medium heat and, when hot, lay two of the herrings in the pan, cut side down, and fry for about 4 minutes until brown and crisp.

5 Turn the fish carefully and cook the other side for another 3–4 minutes. Watch that the fat does not get too hot or the oatmeal may burn. Reduce heat if necessary.

6 Lift out the fish and drain on kitchen paper. Place on a serving plate and keep hot while frying the remaining fish. Serve very hot.

HERRING ROE TOASTS

⊠ *Soft herring roes have a rich flavour and a creamy texture. They are excellent lightly floured, fried in butter and served on toast. For this recipe you need fresh roes which will retain their shape. Roes which have been frozen in bulk are often a soft, shapeless mass when thawed and although very suitable for fish cakes or other soft mixtures, they cannot be separated into individual roes for frying. Prepare the garnish first to avoid any delay in serving.*

SERVES 2
**225 g [½ lb] fresh, soft
   herring roes
30 ml [2 tablespoons] seasoned
   flour
pinch cayenne pepper
25 g [1 oz] butter
15 ml [1 tablespoon] oil**

**For the garnish:
2 slices of bread
15 g [½ oz] butter
half a lemon
fresh parsley**

1 Toast the bread and butter it. Cut off the crusts if wished. Cut the lemon into wedges and wash the parsley and divide into small sprigs. Set aside.

2 Put the roes in a colander and wash very thoroughly with cold water. Drain well and remove any pieces of black membrane. Blot dry with kitchen paper.

3 Put the seasoned flour on a large piece of greaseproof paper, add a large pinch of cayenne pepper and mix thoroughly.

4 Put the roes, a few at a time, into the flour, lifting the corners of the paper to coat the roes completely. Lift out with tongs and shake off surplus flour.

5 Heat the butter and oil in a small frying-pan and, when hot, fry the roes, a few at a time, for about 2 minutes or until golden. Turn carefully and fry the other side until golden. Lift out and reserve while frying remaining roes.

6 Drain the roes carefully and pile on to the toast. Add a sprig of parsley and some wedges of lemon before serving.

Sea shell specials

Prawns, shrimps and scampi have always ranked among the most desirable of all seafood to eat and this course explains the difference and shows how to cook and serve these shellfish for the tastiest of meals.

Crustaceans are aquatic creatures with brittle jointed shells. These shellfish have always been sought after and, consequently, they are far from cheap. This means there is all the more reason for knowing how to choose and cook them so that, when you do buy them, they prove a real treat.

Shrimps and prawns, so delicate to look at, are in fact the scavengers of the sea shore. They feed on coastal debris and are very nutritious.

Fresh shellfish are unbeatable for flavour—whether they are the large crayfish of Australia and New Zealand, the popular Italian scampi or Dublin Bay prawn (shown on the left at the bottom of the picture below) or the tiny British common or brown shrimp.

Shrimps

This name is given to a small species, called the crevette grise in France and the gamberetto in Italy. In many countries, however, no distinction is made between prawns and shrimps.

Shrimps are found in inshore waters, and bury themselves in sand. In northern Europe there are two types: the common or brown shrimp is a grey transparent colour and goes pink when cooked. The pink shrimp is almost colourless and transparent but again turns pink when cooked. Shrimps are nearly always sold boiled.

Prawns

Prawns range in size from about 5 cm [2"] to 15 cm [6"] depending on which part of the world they come from. British prawns are greyish and partly transparent when raw, turning pink, with firm flesh, when boiled. They are usually sold ready boiled. Like shrimps they are sold in pints: one pint is equivalent to 225 g [8 oz] which after peeling will weigh 125-150 g [4-5 oz].

Prawns from Norway and Greenland are slightly larger—about

10 cm [4"] long, with a lovely melting texture. They are often imported into Britain and sold ready boiled.

The Mediterranean prawn is the largest European prawn—about 12.5 cm [5"]. It is known as crevette rose in France and gambero in Italy.

Pacific prawns are still larger, and are much darker in colour than the European prawns. They are a greenish brown colour, with a pink tinge. The flesh turns pale pink when cooked.

Frozen prawns: the larger types of prawn are often frozen for export. Pacific or king prawns are shipped frozen raw from China and Malaysia. Australian Pacific prawns are usually shipped whole if they are boiled before freezing, but have their heads removed if they are frozen raw. A dark, greenish brown freshwater prawn is exported from Bangladesh. Prawn catches from Mexico are shipped to the United States. Mediterranean prawns are also frozen and shipped all over the world.

Frozen peeled prawns can be divided into two classes. Those with the better taste and texture are caught in cold waters, in places like Canada, Greenland and Norway. Warm water prawns are caught off Malaysia, Thailand, Japan, China and Australia. They have a harder, more chewy texture, and less flavour.

Scampi

Scampi is the Italian name (scampo in the singular) for a specific type of shellfish known as the Dublin Bay prawn in Britain, but also called the Norway lobster. In France, scampi are called langoustines.

They are up to 20 cm [8"] long, although in Europe they do not usually grow to more than half this length. They have a hard, spiky, orangey pink shell with a greyish tinge, which does not change colour much when cooked. They have long pincers, but the meat is all in the tail.

They are sold ready boiled or frozen, without the head. For a main course for six people, buy 1.4 kg [3 lb] if they are in their shells, or 700 g [1½ lb] if shelled.

A selection of some of the most popular types of prawn and shrimp:
top, from the left: British prawns in their shells; shelled British prawns.
Bottom, from the left: Mediterranean prawns; the common or brown shrimp; pale pink shrimps; scampi, known as Dublin Bay prawns, Norway lobsters, or langoustines, with and without a coating of breadcrumbs; Pacific prawns, which can be identified by their dark colour, without their heads.

Crayfish

These freshwater shellfish (ecrevisses if French) are similar to scampi. They are up to 15 cm [6"] long, a greenish brown colour, with pincers like small lobsters. They are caught in the United States and in Australia, where they are very good, as well as in Europe. They are not the same as crawfish, a larger, seawater shellfish which is known as crayfish in many parts of the world.

BOILING LIVE SHELLFISH

If you do buy or catch fresh (live) scampi, prawns or shrimps, they will need to be boiled and this should be done as soon as possible. Keep them in a bucket of salted water until you are ready to cook them.

They are very quick to cook and the flavour can easily be ruined by over cooking. It is only necessary to parboil them if recooking or re-heating them later.

Bring a pan of seawater to the boil, or tap water plus enough salt to make a brine strong enough for an egg to float in (about 175 g [6 oz] salt to 2.3 L [4 pt] water). Put in the shrimps, scampi or prawns and bring back to the boil. By the time it boils, the shrimps, scampi or prawns will probably be cooked, or will need only another ½–1 minute. You can test one to see if they are cooked. If it is under-done it will be soggy; over-done and it will be hard. Larger prawns will need another 4–5 minutes.

Alternatively, put prawns in a tightly covered pan and set over a high heat to cook in their own juice. Shake the pan occasionally and cook for about ten minutes or until the prawns are cooked.

SERVING FRESHLY BOILED SHELLFISH

Fresh boiled shellfish can be used for composite dishes or sauces or they can be served immediately after boiling and this, of course, shows off their fresh salty, yet sweet, taste to best advantage.

● Serve while still warm with a hollandaise-type sauce if they are large or simply with wedges of lemon if tiny shrimps.

● If only parboiled, large prawns and scampi can be placed on an oiled rack and brushed with herb-flavoured oils or herb butter and finished off under the grill.

● Wait until they are cold and serve with mayonnaise.

● To make a meal of fresh boiled prawns, serve them on a bed of crushed ice accompanied by a bowl of fresh hard-boiled eggs, some radishes or tomatoes, a bunch of watercress or lettuce hearts. Fresh brown bread, butter, a bowl of coarse salt, and a bowl of olive oil flavoured with lemon and plenty of fresh chopped herbs complete a simple but magnificent feast.

To shell or not to shell

Whether or not you shell before serving dishes such as those de-scribed above is up to you. They look prettiest in their shells and it has certain advantages. You can serve soon after cooking, and it puts some of the work into other peoples hands!

Moreover, people like to suck the juices contained in the shells as they peel them. If your guests are peeling their own prawns, it is a good idea to provide them with finger bowls.

1 Take the head in forefinger and thumb of one hand and the tail in the other and straighten out.

2 Pull the head and tail back towards each other and then gently pull them apart.

3 The tail and body shell should come off in one piece, leaving the body attached to the head.

FROZEN AND SHOP BOILED

Shellfish that is bought ready boiled, and frozen shellfish that was boiled before freezing can be used in recipes calling for fresh prawns or shrimps but the flavour is not quite as good.

Breadcrumbed and battered frozen shellfish need to be fried while frozen or the coating will come off but all other prawns and shrimps and scampi need to be thoroughly thawed. This needs to be done slowly as quick de-frosting toughens them and spoils the flavour. The liquid needs to be drained off or the dish will taste very waterlogged.

COOKING SCAMPI, PRAWNS AND SHRIMPS

The type of dish you make with these shellfish depends on two factors.

The first is whether the scampi, prawns or shrimps are fresh or frozen. As already explained, the fresher the shellfish the simpler the dish can be but frozen shellfish may need stronger accompanying flavours to mask a possible lack of taste.

The second factor is how many people you want to stretch the shellfish to feed. Obviously, rice based dishes are more economical if you want to feed several people.

The type of shellfish to be used for a dish is largely a question of individual taste and budget. Basically any shellfish can be used for any of the recipes given here. From a practical point of view, however, the larger shellfish are best in dishes where you want chunks of decorative colour, whereas tiny brown shrimps are every bit as good as larger varieties for pounded dishes such as potted shrimps, soups and sauces.

Handy hints

● The use of firm white fish is an excellent way of supplementing expensive shellfish. Dogfish and monkfish have a similar texture and go very well with shellfish. Other white fish such as coley also blend quite well with them.

● In a prawn cocktail you can use less prawns per person and substitute nuts and celery which adds a nice crunch. Try your own selection of vegetables for a different flavour.

● Make use of every bit of flavour by using fish stock, made with some prawn or shrimp shells included, as a base for sauces and soups.

COLEY AND PRAWN PIE

This is a lovely pie, using coley for economy. A good fish stock is important and both stock and wine need to be reduced to strengthen the flavour. Traditionally, savoury pies are highly decorated so use the pastry trimmings for decoration. Either make your own flaky pastry or use a bought kind. Cod is less economical.

SERVES 4
700 g [1½ lb] coley or cod fillet
100 g [¼ lb] peeled prawns
1 medium-sized onion
100 g [¼ lb] mushrooms

This pie is a deliciously creamy combination of white fish and juicy prawns served in a thick, tasty sauce.

prawns and shrimps

4 If the fish is to be used for a garnish, leave the head on the body. If not just twist and separate.

5 Check that the black vein which runs along the back is removed, some people are allergic to it.

6 Don't discard the shells as they can be saved for making fish stock for fish pies, sauces and soups.

4 sticks celery
freshly ground black pepper
salt
175 g [6 oz] flaky pastry
575 ml [1 pt] fish stock

150 ml [¼ pt] dry white wine
60 ml [4 tablespoons] thin
cream

50 g [2 oz] butter
30 ml [2 tablespoons] flour
1 small egg for glaze

1 Skin the coley and cut into 2.5 cm [1"] pieces. Put in a large saucepan, cover with the fish stock and poach for 5 minutes. Lift out with a slotted spoon and put into a 1.15 L [2 pt] pie or soufflé dish.

2 Strain the stock then put it in a pan with the wine and boil until it has reduced to 575 ml [1 pt].

3 Melt the butter in another pan. Peel and chop the onion and cook in the butter until softened. Finely slice the celery and add to the onion and cook for 5 minutes.

4 Wipe the mushrooms, chop the stalks and slice the caps. Add to the pan and cook for 3 minutes.

5 Stir the flour into the vegetables taking care not to break them. Remove from the heat and blend in the stock and the wine. Season.

6 Return the pan to heat and bring the sauce to the boil. Simmer for 2-3 minutes, and stir in the cream.

7 Scatter the prawns over the coley, pour over the sauce and allow to cool for 15 minutes before putting the pastry over the top.

8 Meanwhile heat the oven to 200°C [400°F] gas mark 6.

9 Roll out the pastry 6 mm [¼"] thick, large enough to overlap the pie dish. Roll the remainder thinner and cut 2 strips, each 12 mm [½"] wide.

10 Cover the prepared pie, seal edges and decorate with the trimmings. Brush with beaten egg and cook for 20-30 minutes until well risen and golden brown.

PRAWNS CREOLE

◪ This is a lovely main course dish served with boiled long grain rice. Shrimps can be used instead of prawns and frozen ones can be used. They need to be well drained before adding to the sauce.

SERVES 4
225 g [8 oz] peeled prawns
1 small onion
1 small green pepper
25 g [1 oz] butter
30-45 ml [2-3 tablespoons] flour

650 g [1 lb 7 oz] canned tomatoes
5 ml [1 teaspoon] each of rosemary, thyme and oregano
salt and pepper
5-10 ml [1-2 teaspoons] sugar

1 Skin and finely chop onion, deseed and chop pepper and fry both in the butter for 5-10 minutes until soft.

2 Stir in the flour and gradually add the tomatoes, roughly chopped, and the herbs, salt, pepper and sugar.

3 Simmer gently for about 15 minutes until the sauce thickens and the flavours are blended.

4 Add the prawns and cook for a further 5 minutes to heat them through. Serve with the boiled rice.

PRAWNS EN COCOTTE

◪ This is a delicately flavoured dish which can be served in small individual ramekin dishes or scallop shells. (For fish stock see the recipes on pages 332–333). If you are not making this dish in advance it can be finished by browning the breadcrumbs under the grill instead of reheating and browning in the oven.

SERVES 4
175 g [6 oz] large peeled prawns
1 small bulb fennel
150 ml [¼ pt] milk, infused for 15 minutes with 5 ml [1 teaspoon] fennel seeds
150 ml [¼ pt] fish stock
225 ml [8 fl oz] dry white wine
1 shallot, chopped or 1 slice of onion
1 blade mace
1 small bay leaf
6 black peppercorns
45 ml [3 tablespoons] thin cream
25–30 g [1–1¼ oz] butter
25 g [1 oz] flour
salt and pepper
fresh white breadcrumbs
a little extra butter

1 In a small saucepan boil the wine with the chopped shallot or onion and the blade of mace, bay leaf and peppercorns, until it is reduced to

150 ml [¼ pt]. Strain the wine.

2 Wash fennel and slice into 12 mm [½"] thick strips. Poach for 5 minutes in the strained, infused milk. Strain and set aside milk and fennel.

3 Add 15 ml [1 tablespoon] of the fennel to each ramekin dish. Divide the prawns between the dishes.

4 To make a velouté sauce, melt the butter in a saucepan. Remove from heat and stir in the flour.

5 Return to the heat and cook gently without stirring until it is pale straw colour. Remove from the heat and blend in the fish stock and strained wine.

6 Slowly bring to the boil, add the milk and simmer for 2–3 minutes. Add the cream and season with salt and pepper.

7 Pour the sauce over the prawns and fennel. This can all be done in advance.

8 Heat the oven to 200°C [400°F] gas mark 6.

9 To finish, cover the top of the ramekin dishes with the breadcrumbs, dot with the extra butter and bake for 15 minutes or until the top is golden.

PRAWN NEWBURG

◪ This delicious dish can also be made with lobster or shrimps. It can be served with either boiled rice or hot buttered toast.

SERVES 4
225 g [8 oz] peeled prawns
25 g [1 oz] butter
60 ml [4 tablespoons] Madeira or sherry
2 large egg yolks
425 ml [¾ pt] thin cream
salt
cayenne pepper
chopped chives or parsley to garnish

1 Sauté the prawns (reserving a few for garnishing) very gently in the butter for about 5 minutes. Stir in the Madeira or sherry and cook for another 2–3 minutes.

2 Mix the cream and egg yolks and pour into the prawn mixture. Add seasonings to taste.

3 Heat very gently until a thickened creamy consistency is obtained. Serve poured over boiled rice or with toast.

4 Sprinkle with chives or parsley and garnish with the reserved prawns.

POTTED SHRIMPS

This recipe makes a lovely first course served on its own with brown bread or on Melba toast.

SERVES 4
450 g [1 lb] shelled shrimps
100 g [4 oz] butter
2.5 ml [½ teaspoon] ground mace
a pinch of cayenne pepper
2.5 ml [½ teaspoon] ground nutmeg
clarified butter

1 Melt the butter in a pan and add the shrimps. Heat them up slowly but do not let them boil.

2 Add the seasonings and then pour the shrimps into small pots or glasses.

Potted shrimps are sealed in clarified butter, so can be kept for a few days. They look attractive in individual ramekins, in small jars or in chunky tumblers.

3 Leave them to become quite cold and then cover each pot with a little clarified butter. Use within a few days.

4 Leave in the pots if they are really attractive, otherwise turn them out and serve on individual plates lined with a few lettuce leaves, trying to retain the shape of the pot.

PRAWN PASTE

The combination or prawn and basil makes a delightful, delicately flavoured paste. It can be made in a hurry, if necessary, by putting all the ingredients in a liquidizer and blending at top speed.

SERVES 3–4
225 g [½ lb] cooked, peeled prawns
20–30 ml [4–6 teaspoons] olive oil
2.5 ml [½ teaspoon] finely chopped basil
pinch of cayenne pepper
juice of 1 lime or half a lemon
1.5 ml [¼ teaspoon] crushed coriander or cumin seed (optional)

1 Pound or mash the prawns to a paste and very gradually add the olive oil.

2 Season with the cayenne pepper and finely chopped basil. Add the strained lemon or lime juice.

3 When the mixture is smooth, add the coriander or cumin and check the seasoning—salt may or may not be necessary depending how much has been cooked with the prawns.

4 Pack the paste in a little jar or terrine. Cover and store in the refrigerator (but not for more than 2 days). Serve chilled with toast.

SCAMPI ON SKEWERS

This is a delicious dish of Italian origin. The scampi are coated with egg and breadcrumbs and put on skewers, fried in butter and then served with lemon wedges. It can be used as a starter or as a main course on a bed of plain boiled rice with a side salad.

SERVES 4
8 pieces of scampi
8 rashers of bacon
225 g [½ lb] button mushrooms
60 ml [4 tablespoons] white breadcrumbs
15 ml [3 teaspoons] chopped sage
zest of 1 large lemon
1 large egg, beaten with a pinch of salt
30 ml [2 tablespoons] seasoned flour
50 g [2 oz] butter

1 Dry the scampi (if thawed). Wipe the mushrooms. Put the seasoned flour and beaten egg on two separate plates.

2 Mix the breadcrumbs with two thirds of the sage and the lemon zest and put on another plate.

3 Coat the scampi with flour, egg and breadcrumbs, pressing the flavoured crumbs on firmly.

4 Melt the butter in a medium-sized frying-pan—there should be enough to cover the bottom of the pan, and add the rest of the sage.

5 Thread the scampi lengthways on the skewers. Roll the rashers of bacon and thread these and the mushrooms alternately.

6 When the butter is foaming put the skewers into the pan and fry over a moderate heat for 6-8 minutes, turning 4-5 times until golden brown all over. Serve immediately.

Variation
● Scampi kebabs with cream is a nice dish. Use 1 kg [2¼ lb] of mixed monkfish, scampi, blanched baby onions and wedges of red pepper on skewers. Season and brush with melted butter. Pour 30 ml [2 tablespoons] sherry and about 150 ml [¼ pt] water into the bottom of a gratin dish. Place the kebabs in this and grill, basting while they cook. Keep the fish hot and strain the liquid into a pan and allow to bubble up and reduce until syrupy. Add 125 ml [4 fl oz] fresh thin or sour cream mixed with 15 ml [1 tablespoon] French mustard and cook until hot and reduced a little. Serve with the kebabs.

SCAMPI FILLETS

This makes a delicious luxury dish which actually isn't very expensive.

SERVES 4
8 fillets of John Dory or other flat fish
8 peeled scampi
30 ml [2 tablespoons] seasoned flour
50 g [2 oz] melted butter
125 ml [4 fl oz] white wine or cider
chopped parsley

1 large egg, hardboiled
5 ml [1 teaspoon] sage

1 Plunge the fillets of John Dory into hot water. Drain and dry well and sprinkle with seasoned flour.

2 Roll each fillet round a peeled scampi and secure with a toothpick. Put into a buttered gratin dish and brush with the melted butter and sage.

3 Cook uncovered at 180°C [350°F] gas mark 4 for 20 minutes. Gradually add the wine or cider during this time by adding and basting every 5 minutes.

4 Cover with buttered paper and cook for a further 10 minutes. Garnish with chopped parsley and sieved hard-boiled egg yolk and chopped white of egg.

ICED SHRIMP SOUP

This delicately flavoured iced soup is a delicious first course for a summertime dinner party.

SERVES 4
225 g [½ lb] boiled shrimps
350 g [¾ lb] white fish fillet
1 small lemon, and juice of half a lemon
2 large tomatoes
1 small onion
5 ml [1 teaspoon] dried dill
45 ml [3 tablespoons] white breadcrumbs
pinch of nutmeg
15 ml [1 tablespoon] thick cream
cucumber for garnish

1 Peel the shrimps and place the shells in a pan with the white fish, complete with skin.

2 Slice the lemon, tomatoes, and onion and add to the pan with the dill and 850 ml [1½ pt] water. Simmer for 20 minutes and then strain.

3 Put the shrimps (except for a few for garnishing) in a blender with the breadcrumbs, the juice of half a lemon and the nutmeg. Add the strained stock and liquidize.

4 Chill and then blend in a swirl of cream and garnish with paper thin slices of cucumber and a few whole shrimps.

The king of the river

To cooks, gourmets and fishermen alike, the salmon is the king of the river. Handsome to serve and delicious to eat, this elegant, pink fish will turn any meal into a very special occasion. The salmon is both elusive and expensive in its finest form but cheaper alternatives are available, such as frozen Pacific salmon, grilse and salmon trout.

The salmon is a migratory fish, dividing its time between river and sea. It spawns in the gravel beds in the upper reaches of the salmon rivers and there the tiny salmon or 'fingerling' stay and develop for two or three years. Then, as 'smolts', they swim in a shoal down the river and far out to sea. At sea they feed and develop for one, two or even three years until they are ready to return to the river to spawn. Miraculously, the salmon invariably return to the river in which they were born and swim upstream against endless hazards until the survivors reach the spawning grounds and the life cycle begins again.

The salmon 'run', or swim up the river, either in the early months of the year, when they are known as spring or first run fish, or later in summer when they are called summer or second run fish. Fresh, first run fish are the finest, with a particularly delicate flavour and command a correspondingly high price. As the season when fishing is allowed progresses and supplies increase the price usually falls.

TYPES OF FISH
Fresh salmon is very delicious but also very expensive. It can be bought frozen but the flavour cannot be

compared to that of fresh salmon. Grilse and salmon are cheaper but equally delicious alternatives.

Atlantic salmon

This is the species fished in countries bordering the north Atlantic ocean. Those caught in the rivers of Scotland, Ireland, Wales, England and Norway are especially esteemed for their quality and fine flavour. If you buy fresh salmon in Britain it will certainly be Atlantic salmon.

The body of the salmon is plump and the head small in comparison with Pacific salmon. The fish has a forked tail and its shining skin varies from steely grey on the back, through silver to a white belly. Black spots appear above the lateral line. The weight of a whole fresh salmon can vary from 3-9.1 kg [7-20 lb].

In Britain, the season lasts roughly from February to the end of the summer, exact dates varying a little between Scotland, England and Ireland. The peak season for fresh salmon, when supplies are at their greatest, is June to July. Early season fresh Atlantic salmon is best prepared by very simple methods so that the delicate flavour is not lost.

Pacific salmon

The salmon which proliferate in the Pacific ocean are fished in American, Canadian and Russian rivers and are eaten fresh in these countries. There are five different species of Pacific salmon and several of them are exported canned or frozen.

Frozen Pacific salmon is available exported all the year round and is usually considerably cheaper than fresh salmon. It is gutted and beheaded before freezing and, although similar to the Atlantic salmon, its body is flatter and the skin duller once it has thawed. The average weight of the fish is 2.2-3.6 kg [5-8 lb].

Frozen salmon, although by no means as fine as fresh salmon, is excellent served with well-flavoured sauces or made into dishes such as mousse or kedgeree.

Grilse

This is the name given to a young salmon returning to its native river to spawn for the first time. It is sold fresh or frozen and is available during the early summer. It looks the same as fresh salmon, except that it is, of course, smaller. The average weight of a grilse is between 1.4-3.6 kg [3-8 lb]. Grilse is ideal for a small dinner party and can be served in any of the ways suitable for salmon.

Salmon trout

This fish is also known as sea trout, sewin and peal as well as by many other local names. Many people consider this to be the best of all river fish, combining as it does the finest qualities of salmon and trout.

Its silvery skin, streamlined shape and pink flesh resemble a grilse or young salmon, but it is, in fact, a migratory member of the brown trout family. Its head is blunter and the tail not so forked as that of a salmon. The fish usually has dark spots below as well as above the lateral line and weighs between 1-1.8 kg [2¼-4 lb], although they can reach 4.5 kg [10 lb].

Fresh Atlantic salmon (top) is identified by its size and by its being whole. Grilse (middle right) is smaller but similar in appearance, while salmon trout (middle left) is smaller still. Frozen salmon (bottom right) is always headless. Salmon cuts reveal the pink flesh.

The fish can be cooked and served in the same way as salmon but being small is particularly good cooked whole.

BUYING THE FISH

Always buy salmon and salmon trout from a high quality fishmonger. When you are buying expensive fish you want to be certain that you are also buying quality.

Fresh whole fish: a fresh salmon or salmon trout is stiff and firm with a sparkling silvery glint to its skin. The eyes should be full and bright and the gills bright red. Be wary of dull, flabby fish with sunken eyes. A fish that is headless will probably have been imported and, therefore, have been frozen.

Salmon is a substantial and firm-fleshed fish and portions do not need to be large. Apart from the central bone, there are few bones to worry about, but if buying a whole, fresh fish, remember to allow for the head and tail wastage. Consider also the size of your pan and preferably buy a fish that will fit in whole. If need be, it can be cut in half. If the fish weighs less than 1.5 kg [3½ lb] including the head and tail, allow 200-225 g [7-8 oz] per portion. If it weighs more than 1.6 kg [3½ lb], allow 150 g [5 oz] per portion.

Ask the fishmonger to leave the head and tail on but to remove the gills and eyes and gut the fish. If the fish is to be served whole, it need not be scaled or the fins trimmed unless it is to be served in its skin. If you prefer to prepare the fish yourself, instructions for all these processes are given on **pages 292–293**.

Cuts and steaks: ask to see the whole fish and then have taken from it the cut that you want. If this is not possible, look carefully at the skin on the individual portions to make sure it is bright and silvery and that the flesh is firm, pale pink and freshly cut. Cutlets are taken from the head end, where the fish has been gutted, and steaks from below the belly, down to the tail. Steaks cut from the tail piece will be cheaper but this part of the fish does contain more bone and you will need to allow a greater weight per portion. For middle cut steaks and cutlets allow 150-175 g [5-6 oz] per portion and for tail piece steaks, 200 g [7 oz]. The slices will be about 2-2.5 cm [¾-1"] thick from a medium-sized fish. If the fish is particularly large

and one slice too much for one portion, it can be divided in half after cooking.

When buying steaks and cutlets it is sensible, whenever possible, to have as large a surface area of skin as possible. This acts as a natural waterproof barrier, helps to keep the fish moist and protects it while it cooks. The fish can be sliced into portions after cooking.

STORING THE FISH

Ideally, salmon should be cooked as soon as possible after it has been caught, when it is at its most succulent and the cooked flesh has traces of a creamy curd-like substance between the flakes. This is unlikely to be possible unless you live in the immediate vicinity of the salmon rivers. All fish should preferably be cooked on the day it is bought and should never be kept uncooked for longer than 24 hours.

Clean the fish, if not already done by the fishmonger, and wipe it with a clean, damp cloth. Scrape the belly cavity and remove any congealed blood. Season the cavity generously with salt and pepper and keep covered and refrigerated until needed.

Salmon can be packaged and quick frozen for longer storage, whole or in portions. A whole fish should be very thoroughly scaled and cleaned and can be left complete, head and tail intact. Small or medium-sized salmon are better suited to freezing than large fish and can be kept safely for two months.

Cooked fish can be stored loosely wrapped in foil or cling film in the refrigerator for a few days; some people prefer it when the creamy curds have disappeared and the flesh is firmer.

COOKING SALMON
Fresh salmon

Although our 19th century forbears suffered from a surfeit of salmon, at today's prices our problem is not finding new ways of serving it, but cooking the occasional fish that comes our way with infinite care to conserve every scrap of its fine flavour and succulence.

The one cardinal rule is never to overcook salmon. Although it is an oily fish, overcooking makes the flesh dry and dense and it can become quite chewy in texture. Cooking

should always be gentle and cuts or slices must be wrapped loosely in foil so that all the juices are retained.

Spring salmon caught in the first weeks of the season is so delicate and delicious that it should be cooked in the simplest possible manner. The traditional Scottish method is to poach whole salmon lightly in salted water. A whole fish can also be poached in a simple court-bouillon. Two methods are described here: One where the fish can be served hot or cold, and one specially designed for serving the fish cold.

Baking is the alternative to poaching a whole fish: the fish is wrapped in foil and baked in the oven (see pages 322–323). A section on poaching fish can be found on pages 329–338 and baking fish on pages 320–328. The methods are the same for poaching or baking salmon but because the fish is very large, the timing varies slightly. Times for poaching and baking salmon are given in the chart and, for poaching, are taken from the moment the liquid reaches simmering point.

Cuts and slices of salmon, having been wrapped loosely in foil with the ends secured (so that cut surfaces do not come into contact with water) can be poached or baked. Unwrapped slices can also be grilled, steamed or shallow fried, and these processes are described in great detail on pages 292–308, 309–319 and 367–373 respectively.

Sauces for early season salmon are best confined to melted butter for hot salmon and mayonnaise for cold salmon. Later in the season, as the fish become more plentiful, the flesh firmer and the flavour less delicate, both cooking methods and added flavours can be more robust.

Frozen salmon

To avoid the risk of overcooking, it is best to completely thaw whole salmon or large cuts so there is no danger of the outside becoming overcooked before the centre is cooked through. Ideally, leave the salmon in its packaging in a refrigerator, allowing about 18 hours for a 1-1.8 kg [2½-4 lb] piece to thaw and from 24-36 hours for a whole medium-sized fish. For speedier thawing at room temperature, allow roughly 3-4 hours per 450 g [1 lb].

Steaks or cutlets are thin enough for the heat to penetrate fairly quickly, so these can be cooked from frozen, allowing about half as long again as when cooking fresh or fully thawed fish.

Equipment for poaching
The average salmon is a fairly large fish and may cause some problems in the kitchen finding a pan large enough to take the fish whole. If you cook whole salmon or other large fish fairly frequently, a fish kettle is a useful piece of equipment. This is a long, deep pan fitted with a perforated plate with long handles. The fish lies on the plate, just above the base of the pan, so that the liquid just covers it. The perforated plate makes lifting the fish in and out easy and there is no danger of burning or scalding yourself.

There are various ways in which a fish kettle can be improvised and these are detailed on pages 330–331. You will, however, still need a pan that is long enough to take the length of the fish. The alternative to this, if you have no such pan, is to cut the fish in half and wrap the cut surfaces securely in foil. This will prevent any of the natural juices seeping into the water. The two pieces can then be cooked side by side.

Fish poached in this way can be served hot or cold. There is an alternative method for poaching salmon that is to be served cold which is designed to keep the fish moist while it cools.

No-cook poaching method for salmon to be served cold
This method avoids any possibility of overcooking the fish, by giving it a very brief simmering time. It is then allowed to cool slowly in the liquid so that the flesh remains beautifully moist and succulent.

A whole fish or any size cut of fish can be cooked by this method, provided you have a fish kettle or pan large enough and deep enough to contain the fish plus enough water to cover it completely with 2.5 cm [1″] to spare. The larger the fish the more water will be required and the longer it will take to cool, thus the method adapts itself to any size of salmon or salmon cut.

COOKING TIMES FOR FRESH SALMON		
Weight	**Poaching**	**Baking**
1.4 kg [3 lb]	25–30 minutes	45 minutes
2.2 kg [5 lb]	40–50 minutes	65-68 minutes
3.2 kg [7 lb]	50–60 minutes	80 minutes
3.6 kg [8 lb]	55–65 minutes	88-90 minutes
4.5 kg [10 lb]	60–75 minutes	95 minutes
5.4 kg [12 lb]	65–80 minutes	100 minutes
6.8 kg [15 lb]	75–90 minutes	110 minutes
8.2 kg [18 lb]	85–100 minutes	118 minutes
9.1 kg [20 lb]	95–105 minutes	125 minutes

You must allow time for complete cooling which, in the case of a whole salmon, will be overnight. Cuts of fish should be wrapped in foil to prevent any juices escaping into the water. The juices are retained in the foil and can be used for flavouring sauces.

If cooking a piece of fish, cut a piece of foil large enough to enclose the fish generously and brush it with oil. You must use oil, not melted butter, as this would solidify as it cooled. Place the prepared fish in the foil, wrap it loosely and twist the edges together tightly to make a loose but completely waterproof parcel.

Place the parcel, or the unwrapped whole fish, in your chosen cooking vessel and add enough cold water to cover the fish by 2.5 cm [1″]. Bring the water to the boil, reduce the heat to maintain a simmer and simmer the fish for 5 minutes. Do not cook fish for longer.

Remove the pan from the heat, cover it tightly and transfer it to a cool place where it can stand undisturbed. Leave the pan until the water is cool but not absolutely cold as it is much easier to remove the skin from the fish while it is still faintly warm. The skinned fish can be stored, loosely covered, in the refrigerator until it is needed.

SKINNING AND BONING COOKED SALMON

The distinctive colour of the flesh of a salmon is part of its attraction. It can vary from a very delicate pale pink to a much deeper shade, verging on red. It is a shame not to present the fish to its best advantage and the time needed to skin the fish is well worth it.

Salmon to be served hot can be left in its skin, provided the fish has been scaled and the fins trimmed, or can be served with the upper surface revealed. If the fish has been cooked unscaled or is to be served cold, it should be completely skinned.

Whole fish

If these are large they will require careful handling, but the method is the same for any size fish. Lay the fish on a piece of damp greaseproof paper on a flat surface. Use a sharp knife and cut through the skin across the tail, around the head and down the length of the backbone. Peel off the skin with the knife, taking any fins with it, until the upper surface is revealed. Gently scrape away the shallow layer of brown-coloured flesh that usually runs along the centre of the fish and reserve this for a made-up dish. With the help of the greaseproof paper, roll the fish over and repeat the operation on the other side.

Boning is not essential, but it does make the portioning and serving of the fish easier. First, loosen the upper fillet by inserting a knife between it and the bone. Lift off the fillet and reserve. In the case of a large fish, it may be easier to divide the fillet along the middle and lift it off in two pieces. Snip through the bone at the head and tail and peel it off from one end. Carefully replace the upper fillet. Move the fish very carefully to a serving dish, either with fish slice or by sliding it off the greaseproof paper. If the fish breaks during this process the 'joins' can easily be concealed by a garnish.

Steaks and cutlets

These are very simple to skin. Ease a knife around the fish and peel away the skin gently. Loosen the central bone and lift out.

SERVING SALMON

The choice of accompaniments depends entirely on the quality of the salmon being served. If you are

Step-by-step to skinning and boning

1 Take the fish and lay it on a large sheet of damp greaseproof paper on a flat surface.

2 Take a sharp knife and cut the skin across the tail, round the head and along the top of the fish.

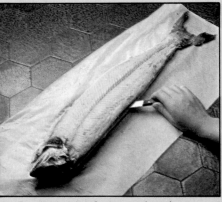

6 Pass the knife in under the upper fillet, flat against the bone, and work it along the fish.

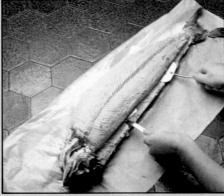

7 Lift off the upper fillet very carefully, using two fish slices, and lay it on greaseproof paper.

fortunate to have some fresh spring salmon, or later in the season some grilse or salmon trout, you will not want to overpower their delicate flavour with heavy sauces and robust vegetable dishes; reserve these for late season or imported frozen fish.

Sauces and butters

The ideal accompaniment for prime quality salmon served hot is plain melted butter and served cold, a light, lemon-flavoured, home-made mayonnaise. Later in the season the melted butter can be replaced by any of the following sauces: hollandaise, béarnaise or mousseline. Home-made mayonnaise can be flavoured with several variations such as chantilly, rémoulade, mayonnaise verte, gribiche and tartare. If using bought mayonnaise, use an egg-based one.

When serving cold salmon there are two alternatives to providing a separate sauce. The fish can be coated with aspic or a chaudfroid sauce. These make the presentation particularly handsome and are recommended for a special occasion. Making aspic and chaudfroid is a very involved process so allow yourself plenty of time.

Vegetables

Vegetables should be kept very simple so as not to detract from the fish and only a limited number should be served. The obvious accompaniment to cold salmon is a crisp, green salad with a light dressing and some potatoes, either new, boiled and tossed in butter or a potato salad. New potatoes, boiled in their skins and tossed in butter are ideal with hot salmon and can be lightly flavoured with chopped parsley, dill, chives or tarragon. Sautéed vegetables, such as cucumber, courgettes and mushrooms, young spinach, asparagus and French beans are all suitable.

a whole salmon

3 Peel the skin away from one end, using the knife to prize it away from the flesh.

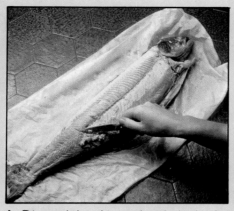

4 Discard the skin and with the knife, scrape away the brown flesh from the middle of the fish.

5 Using the greaseproof paper, roll the fish over and repeat the skinning process on the underside.

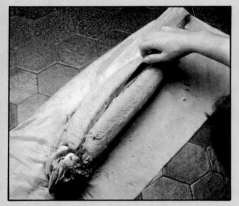

OR run a knife along the length of the fish to divide the upper fillet in two. Lift off each half.

8 Snip through the backbone at the tail and the head and peel it away from the lower fillet.

9 Lift the upper fillet back into position. Transfer the whole fish to a serving dish and garnish.

POACHED SALMON

If you are poaching a large fish, a fish kettle will be very useful. If you have not got one, try one of the improvisations given on pages 330/1. A recipe for the court-bouillon appears on page 332; it must be cool when it is used. Choose your accompaniments according to the season but be careful not to detract from the delicate flavour of the fish. The suggestion given here is for a sauce called a mousseline which is a creamier version of a hollandaise sauce, excellent served with fine-flavoured salmon. The fish can, of course, be served cold with a mayonnaise.

SERVES 15–18
1 fresh salmon, weighing 2.7 kg [6 lb]
salt and pepper
1.7 L [3 pts] general-purpose court-bouillon
575 ml [1 pt] sauce mousseline

1 Wipe the salmon with a clean damp cloth, remove any congealed blood from around the belly cavity and season with salt and pepper.

2 Place the fish on the perforated plate and, using the long handles, lower the plate into the kettle. Pour in sufficient cool court-bouillon to barely cover the fish.

3 Put the lid on the pan and bring the liquid to simmering point on a low heat. Adjust the heat to keep the bouillon at just below simmering point: it should quiver but not bubble.

4 Poach the fish for the calculated time, taken from the moment the water reaches simmering point. Test with a thin skewer to see if it is cooked.

5 Raise the perforated plate out of the pan and lay it across the kettle to drain for 5 minutes.

6 Carefully remove the fish to a warm serving dish. Skin the upper surface if desired and garnish as wished.

Variation
●To serve the fish cold, after draining transfer the fish to a shallow dish or pan and leave undisturbed in a cool place. When cool, skin the fish and if you have not got a large enough serving dish put the fish on a foil-covered board with the head and tail on some sprigs of watercress. Use slices of cucumber to garnish the fish and arrange slices of lemon against the sides of the fish.

When salmon is cold it can be garnished in a variety of ways. Bearing in mind that the flesh is pink, try to include some greenery and colourful tomatoes.

SALMON TROUT BAKED IN FOIL

This is one of the best methods of cooking fresh salmon trout. The method can also be used for grilse, salmon cuts and whole small and medium-sized salmon and is very useful when you do not have a pan large enough to use for poaching. A large fish can be cut in half and wrapped in two separate parcels, the timing being calculated on the weight of each parcel rather than the total weight. A medium-sized fish may need to be 'persuaded' to fit into the oven by curving it on its stomach. The head and tail may touch the sides of the oven but will be protected by the foil. Fish cooked in this way can be eaten hot or cold.

The hollandaise sauce is the perfect accompaniment to baked trout. Serve with new potatoes, tossed in butter and chopped parsley.

If you wish to serve the fish cold, grease the foil with oil rather than butter and when baked, remove the parcel to a cool place and leave the fish until cool but not cold, before skinning and refrigerating until needed.

SERVES 6
1 salmon trout weighing 1.4 kg [3 lb]

salt and pepper
15 ml [1 tablespoon] melted butter
425 ml [¾ pt] hollandaise sauce
fresh dill for garnish

1 Heat the oven to 180°C [350°F] gas mark 4. Put a baking tray on the centre shelf.

2 Make sure the belly cavity of the fish is quite clean and season it well with salt and pepper if you have not already done so.

3 Weigh the fish and calculate the cooking time.

4 Cut a large piece of foil in which to wrap the fish and grease this generously with melted butter.

5 Lay the fish in the middle of the foil. Fold the foil over and twist the edges together firmly. The parcel must be loose but secure.

6 Place the parcel on the hot baking tray or, if the fish is large and has to be curled slightly, directly on the oven shelf.

7 Bake for 45 minutes and remove from the oven.

8 Leave the fish to rest in the unopened foil for 10 minutes. Transfer the whole parcel to a warm serving dish and carefully fold back the foil. With a sharp knife, skin the upper surface of the fish and garnish with the fresh dill.

KOULIBIAC

This is a traditional Russian recipe, originally made with a yeast pastry but nowadays usually with puff or flaky pastry. Although some recipes suggest using leftover cooked salmon it is much better made with freshly cooked salmon. The recipe is a very rich one, so the traditional custom of pouring melted butter into the vent holes just before serving has been omitted. If you want to do this, use 25 g [1 oz] extra butter. Season the filling really well, adding the lemon juice to offset the richness. The chicken stock may be made with a cube. The cold cucumber sauce is a good lubricant and contrast.

Baking in foil is particularly recommended for fresh salmon trout to preserve its delicate flavour. It makes a lovely party dish, hot or cold. Koulibiac is a delicious pie made with puff pastry.

SERVES 8–10

450 g [1 lb] middle cut salmon
100 g [¼ lb] long grain rice
275 ml [½ pt] cold chicken
   stock
salt
freshly ground black pepper
75 g [3 oz] butter
100 g [¼ lb] mild onion or
   shallots
100 g [¼ lb] small button
   mushrooms
30 ml [2 tablespoons] freshly
   chopped parsley
juice of a lemon
pinch of grated nutmeg
400 g [14 oz] puff pastry
2 hard-boiled eggs
1 egg beaten

To serve:
sour cream and cucumber
   sauce

1 Put the rice, stock and 1.25 ml [¼ teaspoon] salt into a saucepan and bring to the boil. Stir, cover tightly and simmer for 15-20 minutes until all the stock has been absorbed and the rice is dry and fluffy.

2 Cut the salmon into 6 mm [¼"] slices and season them with salt and pepper.

3 Melt 50 g [2 oz] butter in a large frying pan and lightly fry the slices of fish for 2-3 minutes each side. Lift out and leave to cool.

4 Meanwhile peel and finely chop the onion or shallots.

5 Add the remaining butter to the frying pan, put in the onion and fry gently for about 10 minutes until soft and golden.

6 Meanwhile wipe and finely slice the mushrooms.

7 Add the mushrooms to the onions, stir well and continue frying gently for another 4-5 minutes.

8 Meanwhile remove the skin and flake the fish coarsely, carefully removing all bones as you do so.

9 Add the cooked rice, flaked fish and chopped parsley to the onion and mushroom mixture and season with lemon juice, nutmeg and salt and pepper to taste. Mix well and set aside to cool.

10 Heat the oven to 200°C [400°F] gas mark 6.

11 Divide the pastry in half and roll out each piece into an oblong measuring 30 × 23 cm [12 × 9"]. Cut a 2.5 cm [1"] strip off the shorter side of each piece and reserve.

12 Lay one oblong of pastry on a flat baking sheet. Cover it with the cold rice and fish mixture, leaving a 1.25 cm [½"] margin around the edges.

13 Slice the hard boiled eggs thinly and lay over the mixture.

14 Dampen the edges of the pastry with water, lay the second oblong

of pastry on top and press the edges together to seal them. Seal the edges with the back of a knife.

15 Make two vent holes in the centre of the top layer of pastry for the steam to escape. Cut the reserved strips of pastry into leaves and use to decorate around the holes

16 Brush pastry with beaten egg.

17 Bake towards the top of the oven for about 30-40 minutes, until the pastry is cooked and golden.

18 Serve hot, with cold cucumber

sauce handed separately.

SALMON TROUT EN GELEE

This is a lovely dish for summer supper parties and very simple to prepare. Cook the fish in the morning so that it is cold and ready to decorate in the afternoon. If you haven't a dish long enough on which to serve it, use a clean plank of wood covered with foil instead, and adjust the garnish accordingly. For mayonnaise chantilly season 425 ml [¾ pt] with the juice of half a lemon and then fold in 40 ml [3 tablespoons] whipped cream.

SERVES 6
1 salmon trout weighing 1.4 kg [3 lb]
salt
freshly ground black pepper
oil
575 ml [1 pt] aspic jelly

For the garnish:
1 cucumber, thinly sliced
1 sprig fresh tarragon or fennel
2 hard-boiled eggs, quartered lengthways

To serve:
425 ml [¾ pt] mayonnaise Chantilly

Two very different dishes which both make tasty meals. Serve salmon kedgeree as a change from the usual smoked fish version and salmon trout when you want to impress. Left-over salmon may be used for the salmon kedgeree, but the salmon trout dish requires fresh fish.

1 Heat the oven to 180°C [350°F] gas mark 4 and put a baking tray on the centre shelf.

2 Wipe·the fish with a clean damp cloth, scrape the body cavity and season it with salt and freshly ground black pepper.

3 Cut a piece of foil 15 cm [6"] longer than the fish and brush it liberally with oil.

4 Lay the fish on the foil and twist the foil edges together to make a loose but watertight parcel.

5 Place on the baking tray and bake in the centre of the oven for 45 minutes.

6 When the fish is cooked remove the parcel from the oven and leave in a cold place, unopened, until cool.

7 Open the parcel and skin the fish before it becomes cold, following the directions for skinning given in the step-by-step instructions.

8 Carefully lift the fish, supporting the head and tail as you do so, and lay flat on a serving dish.

9 Check that the aspic jelly is cold and almost setting (if not, stand it over crushed ice and stir until it coats the back of the spoon), then spoon a thin film of jelly over the fish. Leave to set.

10 Arrange a very simple garnish on the fish such as a spray of tarragon leaves or a frond of fennel. Set the garnish by glazing with another layer of jelly.

12 Leave in a cold place to set, and chill the remaining aspic.

13 To serve, chop the aspic jelly on a piece of wet greaseproof paper and arrange along either side of the fish. Border the dish with overlapping slices of crimped cucumber and arrange the pieces of egg on either side. Just before serving, tuck a few small fronds of fennel into any gaps. Hand round the mayonnaise Chantilly separately.

SALMON KEDGEREE

A kedgeree of salmon is one of the prettiest of dishes, as well as an excellent way of making a small amount of cooked salmon into a rather special supper or buffet party dish. Use left-over or freshly cooked salmon. This recipe uses a fairly high proportion of fish to rice, so if an extra guest turns up unexpectedly you need have no fear about adding an extra 50 g [2 oz] rice. The quantity of butter ensures a creamy tasting kegeree, but if you like a soft creamy texture add the optional cream.

SERVES 4-6
225 g [½ lb] long grain rice
5 ml [1 teaspoon] salt
1 medium-sized onion
100 g [¼ lb] butter,
preferably unsalted
450 g [1 lb] cooked salmon
1 hard-boiled egg
30 ml [2 tablespoons] chopped
chives (optional)
salt
freshly ground black pepper
4 shakes cayenne pepper
45 ml [3 tablespoons] thick
cream (optional)

For the garnish:
3 hard-boiled eggs, quartered
lengthways
parsley sprigs

1 Put the rice and salt into 575 ml [1 pt] cold water in a saucepan, bring to the boil, stir, cover tightly and cook gently for 15-20 minutes, until all the water has been absorbed and the rice is dry and fluffy.

2 Meanwhile peel and finely chop the onion.

3 Melt 50 g [2 oz] butter in a large saucepan and fry the onion very gently until soft but uncoloured.

4 Free the fish of all skin and bone and flake it with a fork.

5 Remove the white from one of the hard-boiled eggs and chop it roughly. Reserve the yolk.

6 Add the cooked rice, salmon, chopped egg white, chives and remaining butter to the onion, with seasonings of salt, pepper and cayenne pepper.

7 Toss together lightly with a fork and heat gently until hot through.

8 Check the seasoning and stir in the cream if used.

9 Pile on to a hot serving dish, press the reserved hard-boiled egg yolk through a sieve to garnish the top, and surround the base with alternate quarters of hard-boiled egg and sprigs ot parsley.

Canny ways with fish

When you want a tasty meal in a hurry, when you feel too tired to go shopping, or when unexpected guests arrive and you need to extend what was planned to be a family meal . . . that's the time to turn to your store cupboard. Take a tip from the ideas given here and use your cunning to turn a can of fish into a splendid and appetizing dish!

Most prudent cooks keep well-stocked store cupboards, so they never run out of everyday basic foods such as flour, sugar, tea, coffee, jam, herbs and spices. But cooks who are both well organized and shrewd see to it that their store cupboard shelves also include a good selection of canned fish. Convenience foods are clearly a boon when it comes to coping with an emergency, and few canned goods keep as well or prove quite so useful as canned fish.

Canned fish is nutritious food and it is marvellously easy to use—no lengthy preparation or cooking is needed—all of which means it is the perfect standby for making interesting hors d'oeuvres, savouries or main course salads at very short notice.

It is worth spending time and imagination on canned fish and you will find that it is very versatile: its flavour and texture go well with so many other foods, so it is a pity to serve it always plain and simple, just as it comes out of a can. You can use it to create delicious sauces, to form the basis of many tasty composite dishes and to add sparkle to lots more: some substantial enough to please a hungry family and some delicate and decorative party dishes to delight your guests.

TYPES, STORAGE AND USES

Canning is a good method of preserving fish and, apart from being neatly packaged, it also has a long shelf-life. Providing your store cupboard is cool and dry, fish canned in tomato sauce will keep well for at least a year, canned in natural juices it will remain in good condition for two years, and fish canned in oil will retain excellent eating qualities for up to five years. Although not essential, it helps the maturing process of fish canned in oil if the cans are turned over at six-monthly intervals.

Anchovy fillets. The best anchovies come from the Bay of Biscay. They are salted for six months before being skinned, filleted and packaged in olive oil in long narrow cans. For certain dishes, and for people who don't like salty foods, it is a good idea to soak anchovies in milk or (cheaper and quicker) to rinse them under cold running water before use.

Almost more than any other fish, anchovy lends zest and dramatic interest to a host of different dishes. Cut them in half lengthways and arrange in lattice patterns, roll them neatly, snip them into little pieces or pound them in a mortar with a pestle for pasties and sauces.

Brisling. These are often described as sardines, but in fact they are sprats which are members of the herring family (brisling is the Norwegian word for sprats). They are much smaller than sardines—averaging 16-24 fish to a 100 g [$\frac{1}{4}$ lb] can. They are lightly smoked before canning and make a good alternative to sardines in hors d'oeuvres and savoury dishes.

Crab. This is a very tasty shellfish and quite a bit cheaper than lobster. The white meat is canned in its natural juices and various graded qualities are sold. Dressed crab contains other ingredients and is suitable for salads. Use pure crab-meat for mousses and pâtés and hot savouries and hors d'oeuvres.

Herrings. These are canned in various forms including small whole fish, fillets and also soft herring roes. Fillets in oil or natural juices are useful for salads, open sandwiches and cooked dishes. Fillets in various savoury sauces can be simply heated

through and served on hot toast, or added to rice and vegetable dishes for pilafs.

Soft roes are taken from mature male fish found mostly off the Norwegian coast during the early months of the year. Dipped in seasoned flour, carefully fried then served on buttery toast, they make a traditional British savoury.

Kippers. Like herrings, these are available in cans whole or, more often, filleted. They are useful for salads, hors d'oeuvres and snacks.

Lobster. Usually considered the king of shellfish, canned lobster is not quite as tasty as freshly boiled lobster. The flavour and texture of fresh lobster is probably shown off to best advantage when served plain and unadorned as lobster salad. It makes sense, however, to use the

canned variety to bind in sauces (where flavour will be affected by the addition of other ingredients) for filling vol-au-vents to make soufflés, mousses and seafood risotto.

Mackerel. Cuts of mackerel canned in natural juices have proved a popular and inexpensive product. They are excellent for pâtés and salads. Fillets in white wine can be served as an hors d'oeuvre.

Pilchards. Larger and meatier than sardines, these are usually canned in tomato sauce. Good value for money, they are very useful for main meal salads, substantial snacks and cooked dishes.

Prawns and shrimps. Usually canned in natural juices, these small

shellfish are great favourites. They look decorative too, which makes them a good choice for garnishing soups and canapés. Use them to make your own prawn paste and to add a touch of class and colour to sauces for poached or baked fish.

Pressed cod's roe. Hard roes are taken from large North Sea cod and cooked in the can. Serve cold in slices, or slice and fry.

Salmon. Various species are caught for canning with the result that there is a variety of grades and prices to choose from. So-called red salmon has the most flavour and is the most

expensive and a pink salmon is the cheapest. Use the best salmon for salads, mousses and other cold dishes, and the cheaper grades for cooked dishes.

Sardines. These are small pilchards mostly caught off the north-west coast of Africa and Portugal. After preparation, they are lightly cooked in olive oil, and then canned in the same oil. Cans of Brittany sardines sometimes include a few slices of onion and carrot used in the cooking process to add extra flavour. Sardines are sometimes canned in tomato sauce and these make tasty hot snacks on toast.

The fish vary in size, averaging 4-8 fish to a 100 g [$\frac{1}{4}$ lb] can. The best and most expensive sardines are matured in the can for at least a year before they are to be sold.

Sild. These are similar to brisling but are even smaller. Like brisling, they

can be used instead of sardines in many dishes.

Smoked oysters and mussels. Canned in oil, these rich-tasting and exotic seafoods are delicious in bacon rolls, to serve on sticks for snacks or to add to a fish pie to give it a lift.

Tuna. This is the generic name for several related species of fast swimming fish caught in many parts of the world. The best varieties have a soft, tender texture when canned. The very finest and most expensive comes from the underpart of the fish known as 'ventresca'. Tuna has many uses in the kitchen, for sauces, salads and pâtés as well as hot dishes.

QUICK IDEAS

●For sardine bites, drain the oil from sardines, spread the fish with a little French mustard, dip in an egg and breadcrumb mixture and deep fry. Serve with wedges of lemon for an appetizer or to accompany cocktails.

●Chop anchovy fillets finely and add them to lemon and parsley stuffing for extra piquancy. This is excellent with fish, veal and rabbit.

●For eggs with shrimps, a simple but luxurious first course, put a few canned and drained shrimps in cocotte dishes before adding eggs, seasoning and cream. Bake in a bain-marie.

●Summer seafood salad makes an attractive main course for a summer lunch party. Stir some vinaigrette dressing into 225 g [½ lb] cold, boiled rice. Mix in a good handful of finely chopped herbs such as parsley, chives and dillweed, 50 g [2 oz] each of cooked peas and diced cucumber. Arrange in a ring around the edge of the dish. Mix together 50 g [2 oz] sliced raw button mushrooms, 100 g [¼ lb] peeled, seeded and quartered tomatoes and 200 g [7 oz] of flaked crabmeat. Coat lightly with mayonnaise and pile into the centre of the dish. Arrange 75 g [3 oz] canned prawns decoratively on top. Serve with watercress salad.

●For a warming and inexpensive supper make pilchard potatoes. Bake very large potatoes until tender. Cut off the tops and carefully scoop out most of the flesh. Mash this together with pilchards in tomato sauce and season well with salt and pepper. Pile the mixture back into the potato skins and top with a little grated cheese. Return to the oven to heat through and allow the cheese to melt.

●Drained tuna in mayonnaise with a pinch of black pepper and the juice of half a lemon makes an unusual filling for avocado pears.

●For seafarer's rarebit—a tasty snack for anyone who is really hungry—wrap brisling in thin rashers of streaky bacon, grill, then serve on top of cheese on toast.

●Serve grilled bacon and brisling on cocktail sticks for an unusual nibble to accompany aperitifs.

●Tuna and anchovies combine well with French beans, lettuce, cold cooked potatoes, tomatoes, olives and capers for a delicious salade nicoise.

●Almost any canned fish can be used for stuffed eggs. Mash the fish, mix with sieved hard-boiled egg yolks and either a little cream, sour cream, butter or mayonnaise, until of piping consistency. Add complementary seasonings and use to fill halved hard-boiled egg whites.

●Omit egg yolks from the above mixture and use it as a party dip for crisps, potato sticks or crudités.

●For sardine fish cakes, mash drained canned sardines with a squeeze of lemon juice and mix with well-seasoned mashed potato. Form into small rounds, dust with flour and fry. These are very popular with children. Use sild or brisling instead of sardines, if you wish.

●Salmon kedgeree makes a substantial brunch. Stir boiled rice into a pan of melted butter over low heat. Add some thick cream, plenty of freshly chopped chives, parsley, and salt and black pepper. Stir to mix well and allow to become very hot. Gently incorporate canned, drained and flaked pink salmon and chopped hard-boiled eggs just before serving.

●Pound anchovy fillets to a paste, mix with softened butter and spread on rounds of hot toast. On top place grilled or fried tournedos or noisettes of lamb. A cheaper alternative is to spread the mixture on fingers of toast to serve with boiled eggs.

●For tuna bake, mix together a can of flaked tuna fish, a can of sweetcorn kernels and a can of pimentos, all well drained. Stir the mixture into a cheese sauce flavoured with a little nutmeg. Top with breadcrumbs and grated cheese and bake until very hot and golden and bubbling on top.

ANCHOVY AND POTATO PIE

Here is a delicious and unusual dish in which commonplace ingredients are given a lift by the piquancy of anchovies and the richness of cream. Serve it as a supper dish for three or as a vegetable accompaniment to a main course dish of grilled fish, in which case it is sufficient for six.

SERVES 3-6
50 g [2 oz] canned anchovy fillets
3 leeks
40 g [1½ oz] butter
4 tomatoes
550 g [1¼ lb] potatoes
freshly ground black pepper
250 ml [½ pt] chicken stock
150 ml [¼ pt] thin cream

1 Heat the oven to 200°C [400°F] gas mark 6.

2 Drain the anchovies and rinse well under cold running water to get rid of excess salt. Pat dry and set aside.

3 Wash, trim and finely slice the leeks, using tender green parts as well as the white stems.

4 Melt 25 g [1 oz] butter in a small pan, add the leeks, cover and sweat over low heat for about 10 minutes, shaking the pan or stirring from time to time to prevent sticking.

5 Meanwhile, skin and slice the tomatoes, and peel and slice the potatoes very thinly.

6 Use the remaining butter to grease the base and sides of a large shallow dish.

7 Cover the bottom of the dish with a layer of potato slices, using about one-third of the potatoes. Spread half the leeks on top, season with pepper (but not salt because the anchovies contain plenty). Add half the sliced tomatoes and arrange half the anchovies on top.

8 Repeat with another layer of potatoes, the remaining leeks, tomatoes and anchovies, and top with a layer of potatoes.

9 Bring the stock to boiling point and pour it over the dish. Press the mixture down well (a potato masher is the best implement to use for this).

10 Bake in the centre of the oven for 1 hour, occasionally pressing the mixture down into the liquid. By the end of cooking time, the potatoes should be quite tender and have absorbed most of the liquid.

11 Turn off heat and remove dish from oven. Pour the cream over the dish and shake the dish gently so that the cream can seep down to the lower layers.

12 Return the dish to the oven for about 10 minutes to allow the cream to become hot and to be absorbed by the vegetables.

TONNO E FAGIOLI

◩ This classic Italian salad can be served as a hearty appetizer for six to eight (it is filling so the main course which follows should be light). It will make a main course salad for four in which case baked potatoes filled with anchovy butter make a tasty accompaniment. If you want to stretch the dish further to feed an extra person, add any of the following: black olives, sliced hard-boiled eggs, left-over cooked rice or peas but the contrast between fish, nutty beans and cool cucumber is best left alone.

SERVES 4
200 g [7 oz] canned tuna
425 g [15 oz] canned red kidney beans
1 small onion
1 small cucumber
2.5 ml [½ teaspoon] dried dillweed
60 ml [4 tablespoons] freshly chopped parsley
75 ml [3 fl oz] vinaigrette dressing

In Portuguese pâté the richness of sardines is balanced with mustard and lemon juice.

1 Rinse the kidney beans under cold running water. Drain thoroughly and turn the kidney beans into a salad bowl.

2 Peel and chop the onion finely. Cut the cucumber into large dice but do not peel it.

3 Add the vegetables and herbs to the salad bowl. Pour on vinaigrette dressing well flavoured with salt and pepper. Toss the mixture until well coated.

4 Drain the tuna fish, flake it and add it to the salad bowl.

5 Mix lightly and serve.

PORTUGUESE PATE

◩ This sardine pâté is marvellously quick and easy to make. The sharp flavours of mustard, lemon and onion act as an excellent foil for the richness of sardines and combine to produce a tasty hors d'oeuvre at reasonable cost. Serve the pâté garnished with slices of lemon and accompany it with fingers of hot buttered toast sprinkled with chopped parsley.

SERVES 6-8
225 g [½ lb] canned sardines in oil
20 ml [4 teaspoons] French mustard
20 ml [4 teaspoons] lemon juice
45 ml [3 tablespoons] curd cheese
salt and pepper
1 shallot or pickling onion

1 Drain the oil from the sardines, turn the fish into a mixing bowl and mash to a pulp with a fork.

2 Stir the mustard and lemon juice into the curd cheese, then add this mixture to the bowl.

3 Season with salt and pepper and mash again until a smooth paste is achieved and flavours are well blonded.

4 Peel and grate or very finely chop the shallot or pickling onion. Stir it into the pâté.

5 Scrape the bowl clean with a rubber or plastic spatula and pack the pâté into a small dish.

397

Two distinguished hors d'oeuvres: kipper cocktail is garnished with crisp celery leaves; scalloped crab is served hot.

6 Garnish and serve immediately or cover (ungarnished) and refrigerate until required. The pâté will keep for 24 hours.

Variation

●Substitute 4-6 finely chopped spring onions for the shallot or pickling onion and use mayonnaise instead of curd cheese.

KIPPER COCKTAIL

Cheaper and more original than shrimp or prawn cocktail, this makes an elegant appetizer. Serve it in small wine or sherry glasses. Stand each glass on a small plate with a teaspoon for eating the cocktail. Serve with brown bread and butter rolls. Make these using thin slices of buttered, fresh bread with crusts removed and roll up tightly like miniature swiss rolls.

SERVES 6
200 g [7 oz] canned kipper fillets
150 ml [¼ pt] sour cream
half a lemon
15 ml [1 tablespoon] tomato ketchup
10 ml [2 teaspoons] French mustard
45 ml [3 tablespoons] mayonnaise
salt and pepper
2 large dessert apples
3 celery sticks
50 g [2 oz] cashew nuts
parsley sprigs or celery tops

1 Drain the kippers and cut the flesh into fairly small pieces.

2 Turn the sour cream into a mixing bowl and beat with a fork until smooth and creamy.

3 Grate the lemon zest and add it to the sour cream together with the ketchup, mustard and mayonnaise.

4 Stir to mix well. Season to taste with salt and pepper and mix again.

5 Peel and core the apples and cut into small chunks. Put into a bowl

with the kippers and sprinkle with a little lemon juice to prevent discolouration.

6 Clean and slice the celery and add it to the kipper and apple mixture together with half the nuts.

7 Pour the sauce over and toss lightly to coat all the ingredients.

8 Divide the mixture between six glasses. Cover and chill for 1 hour—but no longer than 3 hours or the nuts will be softened by the sauce.

9 Garnish with remaining nuts and parsley or celery just before serving.

SCALLOPED CRAB

Here is a first course dish which is really in the luxury class. Use canned lobster or prawns instead of crab if you wish. Serve in scallop shells, ramekins or individual soufflé dishes.

SERVES 6
400 g [14 oz] canned crabmeat
45 ml [3 tablespoons] sherry or brandy
60 ml [4 tablespoons] butter
30 ml [2 tablespoons] plain flour
250 ml [½ pt] thick cream
30 ml [2 tablespoons] grated Parmesan cheese
salt and pepper
freshly grated nutmeg
50 ml [2 oz] toasted breadcrumbs

1 Drain the crabmeat, (reserve juices) put it into a bowl, sprinkle with sherry or brandy.

2 Melt half the butter in a small heavy-based saucepan and make a thick white sauce with the flour and cream adding the cream very gradually.

3 Gently stir in the crabmeat and its can juices. Cover and simmer very gently for 5-10 minutes so that the crabmeat heats through.

4 Meanwhile heat the grill to very hot and grease the scallop shells or dishes with a little butter.

5 Remove the saucepan from the heat. Stir in the grated Parmesan

cheese and season to taste with salt, pepper and nutmeg.

6 Divide the contents of the saucepan between the shells or dishes. Scatter the breadcrumbs over the shellfish mixture and top with the remaining butter cut into flecks.

7 Cook under the grill for 1-2 minutes until browned and very hot, then serve immediately.

SURPRISE MACARONI

Macaroni cheese is cheap, easy to make and very filling—a favourite mid-week dish in many households. This variation on the traditional recipe gives you extra colour, flavour and nutritive value. Make the cheese sauce by making a basic white sauce and stirring in grated Cheddar cheese.

SERVES 4
200 g [7 oz] canned pilchards in tomato sauce
175 g [6 oz] macaroni
1.5 ml [¼ teaspoon] salt
15 ml [1 tablespoon] oil
550 ml [1 pt] cheese sauce
225 g [½ lb] tomatoes
50 g [2 oz] Cheddar cheese

1 Turn the pilchards and their tomato sauce into a flameproof dish, cover the dish with foil and place in a low oven to heat through while you cook the macaroni and make the cheese sauce.

2 Bring a large pan of water to boiling point. Stir in the macaroni plus the salt for flavour and add the oil to prevent the pasta from sticking together. Cook at a fast boil until tender.

3 Slice the tomatoes, grate the cheese and heat the grill.

4 Turn the cooked macaroni into a colander to strain off all liquid, then stir the drained macaroni into the cheese sauce.

5 Remove the pilchard dish from the oven, uncover and spoon the macaroni cheese on top.

6 Arrange the sliced tomatoes in a layer over the macaroni and top the dish by sprinkling on the cheese.

7 Brown the dish under a hot grill.

Fishing for compliments

Nothing beats an appetizer of smoked fish or roes when you want to give your meal a distinctive air of opulence. Smoked salmon and osetr caviare are clearly in the luxury price bracket and, therefore, reserved for the occasional splash. But humbler goodies such as smoked mackerel, kippers, mock caviare and cod's roe are affordable more often and can easily be made into elegant dishes. Learn how to choose and serve all sorts of smoked fish and roes for the maximum delight of diners and with minimum fuss for the cook.

LUXURIOUS ROES

Hard roe is the egg sack of the female fish and is made up of numerous tiny eggs. Soft roe comes from the male fish and is never smoked. Roe is always impressive as an appetizer, whether it is the expensive caviare or the more modest smoked cod's roe which can be used in a number of ways.

Caviare

This is the salted hard roe of a sturgeon. Large sturgeons are now found only in the Caspian Sea so caviare is almost exclusively a Russian and Iranian product and, consequently, it is extremely expensive.

To be enjoyed at its best you need to eat caviare as fresh as possible. Needless to say, most people have to be content with the slightly muted flavour of pasteurized caviare from pots and cans from specialist food stores.

The three kinds of true caviare are named after the species of sturgeon that supplies the roe—beluga, osetr and sevruga.

Beluga comes from the largest fish (between 16 and 20 years old) and is the most expensive. Colour varies from pale grey to pitch black and the grains are large.

Osetr comes from slightly smaller fish and is the rarest. It has a stronger flavour than beluga. The colour can vary from golden brown through to grey, green and black.

Sevruga comes from smaller (7-10 year old) fish and the grains are therefore smaller too. It has a superb flavour, is the most readily available and is also the cheapest.

Pressed caviare. This is made from left-over roes of various species of sturgeon and pressed into tins. The flavour is very good although more

heavily salted than fresh caviare. It is much less expensive than fresh caviare and is widely used by caterers for fillings and garnishes.

Mock caviare
Mock caviare comes from the roe of fish, such as cod and salmon, as opposed to sturgeon.

Red caviare comes from salmon and it is greatly appreciated for its beautiful golden-red colour. Its taste is unlike true caviare but it has a good individual flavour of its own – somewhere between smoked cod's roe and a fine kipper. It makes stylish cocktail snacks or a tasty filling with sour cream for blini (pancakes).

Lumpfish caviare is a black-or red-dyed mock caviare produced from the roe of the lumpfish. Although it is nothing like caviare in flavour, it makes a dramatic garnish to smoked salmon canapés and open sandwiches and can be used to decorate cold savoury mousses. It is widely available in small pots at relatively modest cost.

Other roes
Botargo is the salted and dried roe of the grey mullet which is native to Mediterranean countries. It is recognizable by its black skin and orange-brown centre. The roe can be served cut into thin slices with bread, olive oil or butter, and a slice of lemon or a fresh fig.

Smoked cod's roe is the firm roe of a large cod which is lightly brined and smoked. It is sold by weight and available from fishmongers. The skin colour of cod's roe can vary a great deal according to the smoker, but the roe should feel soft when pressed otherwise it may be hard and wasteful. If too salty, cod's roe can be soaked in water. Smoked cod's roe is also sold skinned and ready to use in jars. This saves on preparation time and makes a useful store cupboard item for emergencies, but it is an extravagant way to buy smoked cod's roe, which is really very easy to prepare yourself.

Serving caviare
Once bought, the important thing is always to keep fresh, pasteurized or mock caviare chilled but not frozen. Keep it just below the frozen food compartment in a refrigerator and eat it within a day or two.

To appreciate fully the fine flavour of real caviare it should be served

Smoked cod's roe   *Sevruga*   *Red lumpfish caviare*   *Beluga*   *Black lumpfish caviare*   *Red caviare*   *Pressed caviare*

absolutely alone and unadorned, with nothing except a dry biscuit or thin toast. Send it to the table in its container surrounded with ice-cubes. For an average portion allow 25-40 g [1-1½ oz]. Pressed caviare can be served on small dry biscuits as cocktail snacks.

SMOKED FISH
Fish loses its freshness very quickly and can be dangerous if eaten when stale. The eating period can be extended if fish is treated immediately after it is caught. Preservation methods include salting, pickling, smoking, drying, freezing and canning.

The oldest method is brining (immersing fish in heavily salted water) and this process is still used today to tenderize, flavour and preserve fish. Oily fish need more than brine to preserve them if they are to be kept for any length of time so they are smoked afterwards, which also flavours the fish. In fact it gives fish such a delicious piquant taste that even non-oily fish which do not need the additional preservatives are often smoked simply for the flavour.

Smoked fish provide one of the best possible first courses to any meal, and even modest varieties such as mackerel and buckling have an air of opulence.

Although the principles of different types of curing and smoking are basically similar, the same species of fish tastes different when bought from different smokers. So shop around to find the cure most to your liking.

There are two main methods of smoking fish—at a high or relatively low temperature.

Hot-smoked fish. After brining, the fish is smoked in a kiln with the temperature raised to a degree high enough to cook the fish right through. Fish smoked in this way can be served without further cooking. They include buckling, trout and eel, all of which are usually available from delicatessens and fishmongers.

Cold-smoked fish. After brining, the fish is smoked at a relatively low temperature. Most fish prepared in this way need to be lightly cooked before eating. They include haddock, bloater, kipper, whiting and fillets of cod.

Inevitably there are exceptions to these rules. Smoked salmon, which is cold smoked, is nearly always served without further cooking. And some hot-smoked fish, such as Arbroath smokies, although technically completely cooked, are at their most palatable if just heated through before serving.

Choosing and storing smoked fish
The flavour of smoked fish is best when freshly cured, so when buying always look for signs of freshness. These are (as shown in the picture) firm flesh, glossy skin and a wholesome fresh smoked smell. Avoid tired-looking fish that has shrivelled and lost its bloom.

Before the days of refrigeration, heavy salting and prolonged smoking were necessary to preserve fish. Nowadays brining and smoking are light as they are intended mainly as a means of giving fish a delicious flavour. The preservative effect is slight. Therefore smoked fish should be refrigerated and kept for not much longer than the fresh equivalent.

SMOKED FISH

Type and description	Serving ideas
Smoked eel: a rich and satisfying fish with a firm buttery texture. Look for a meaty eel and avoid skinny or dried up specimens. Eel can sometimes be bought filleted in long strips.	Allow about 40 g [1½ oz] per portion. To serve, peel off the skin, ease the two fillets off the bone and arrange side by side on a plate with a wedge of lemon and a sprig of parsley. Serve brown bread and butter separately.
(1) Smoked salmon: there are various qualities which account for the varying prices. Top quality smoked Scotch and Irish salmon is relatively pale in colour with dense glossy flesh. Canadian is much brighter in colour and less oily. It is the cheapest and the least good quality. Salmon can be bought as a whole side, in vacuum packs, canned or by weight.	All smoked salmon is best sliced freshly and very thinly, straight from a whole side. Allow 100 g [¼ lb] for 3-4 portions as hors d'oeuvres. Serve with a piece of lemon and have a pepper mill on the table. Paper-thin slices of buttered brown bread, decrusted and rolled, are the best accompaniment. End pieces of smoked salmon can sometimes be bought more cheaply and these do excellently for making canapés, pâtés, stuffed eggs and quiches.
Smoked sturgeon: a seasonal fish, not always available, provides a rare treat. The roe from some of this family is salted and known as caviare.	Slice and serve as for smoked salmon.
(2) Smoked trout: a delicately flavoured fish prepared by hot smoking. It must be fresh and succulent to be enjoyed at its best.	Allow 175-200 g [6-7 oz] trout per person. Remove the skin just before serving (not before or the flesh may dry up) but leave the head and tail on. Serve with lemon quarters and buttered brown bread. A light horseradish cream enhances the flavour. Makes an excellent pâté.
(3) Smoked mackerel: a new product and one of the great success stories of the modern fishing industry. Hot-smoked mackerel is ready to serve and has a delicious flavour. A cold-smoked mackerel is also available but needs light cooking.	One smallish fillet weighing 75-100 g [3-4 oz] makes an ample portion. Head, tail, skin and bone the fish and serve with lemon and brown bread and butter. It makes excellent salads and pâtés.
(4) Smoked haddock: a cure originally developed in the village of Findon in Scotland, where whole haddock were first split open and smoked.	Grilled or lightly boiled, it can be served with cucumber or mayonnaise.
Arbroath smokies: small haddock, beheaded and gutted but left whole and hot smoked.	Can be eaten as it is or brushed with butter and heated through under the grill before serving.
Buckling: the aristocrat of the smoked herring tribe. The fish is beheaded and gutted, and then hot smoked until the skin has a beautiful golden sheen.	Skin the buckling and serve it whole or, if large, filleted. The skin will peel off easily if you cover the fish with boiling water for a minute and then drain it. Buckling makes an excellent pâté and is good in salads.
Bloater: a Yarmouth herring speciality which is rather difficult to find.	It must be lightly grilled or baked within 24 hours of buying.
(5) Kipper: a fine fat herring which is split, lightly brined and then cold smoked over wood chips. Available whole, boned, filleted and as 'boil-in-the-bag' and canned products. It is customary for producers to dye kippers, but undyed kippers can still be found in speciality shops.	Marinated in lemon or vinegar, kipper fillets are superb served raw, but to do this safely the kippers must be very fresh. Kippers are also excellent grilled or lightly boiled. Keep kippers refrigerated and use within 5 days.
(6) Smoked sprats: a good, relatively cheap and very tasty mouthful from the herring family. Fiddly to eat so you will win laurels if you manage to fillet and skin them first.	Serve with plenty of lemon and brown bread and butter. They can be heated under the grill for a few minutes if preferred hot.

Step-by-step to filleting smoked mackerel

1 Cut off the tail and, if the head is present, remove that too.

2 Cut through the skin along the length of the back.

3 Cut through the skin from the end of belly cavity to the tail.

4 Lift skin with the tip of a knife and peel it back.

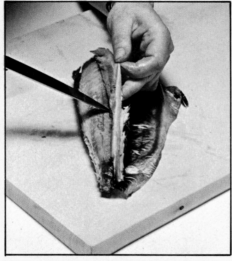

5 Carefully turn the fish over. Peel skin off the other side.

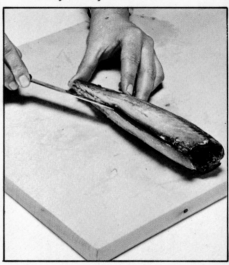

6 Cut through the flesh from the belly cavity to the tail end.

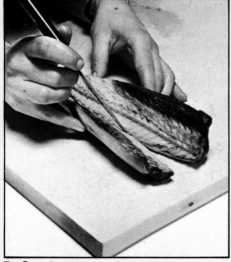

7 Gently ease the fish open to lie flat, exposing the backbone.

8 Lift out the backbone starting at the head end.

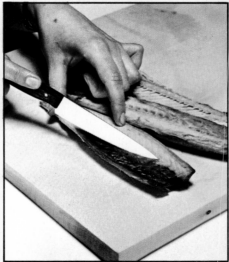

9 Scrape away the dark skin of the belly cavity and remaining bones.

SERVING SMOKED FISH

The classic way to serve smoked fish is very simple: with wedges of juicy lemon to season it and brown bread and butter as an accompaniment. This is not only a treat for diners but a sheer delight for the cook since so little work is involved. Diners can either skin and fillet the fish themselves or this can be done in advance, which is very easy as shown in the step-by-step pictures.

For the richer, oilier smoked fish, such as mackerel and buckling, it is a good idea to serve an accompanying sharply flavoured sauce—either as a substitute for or in addition to wedges of lemon. Two delicious cold sauces are given in the recipe section.

Some smoked fish can be marinated to make delicious salads and various types make excellent bases for pâtés, creams and mousses. These are all popular first courses and are equally useful for buffet parties and to accompany drinks, topping cocktail canapés, filling miniature pastry cases, stuffing celery 'boats' and so on.

The richest pâtés are simply made from skinned and filleted fish pounded with unsalted butter and seasoning. Lighter textured, less rich mixtures can be made by replacing some of the butter with cream, cream cheese, cottage cheese, hard-boiled egg, or even a small proportion of fresh breadcrumbs (which also makes the pâté go a little further).

HORSERADISH CREAM

This piquant cream requires no cooking and makes a delicious accompaniment to smoked fish. If you are unable to get fresh horseradish, use 30 ml [2 tablespoons] bottled horseradish sauce instead.

SERVES 6-8
fresh horseradish
150 ml [5 fl oz] thick cream
30 ml [2 tablespoons] milk
5 ml [1 teaspoon] lemon juice
salt
2.5 ml [½ teaspoon] sugar

1 Peel and finely grate the horse-radish to yield 15 ml [1 tablespoon].

2 Pour the milk and the cream into a small basin and whisk until thick but not stiff.

3 Stir in the lemon juice, horse-radish, salt and sugar.

4 Serve lightly chilled.

Variation
● For mustard cream, substitute 15 ml [1 tablespoon] English mustard for the horseradish.

SMOKED MACKEREL MONACO

The richness of smoked mackerel is beautifully contrasted with a sharp crunchy salad of raw celery, apple and sour cream. This is a rich dish so there is no need for large portions.

SERVES 4
450 g [1 lb] smoked mackerel
2 crisp dessert apples
22.5 ml [1½ tablespoons] lemon juice
3 celery sticks
150 ml [¼ pt] sour cream
freshly ground black pepper

For the garnish:
half a small sweet red pepper or canned pimento
30 ml [2 tablespoons] freshly chopped parsley

1 Cut off the head and tail of the mackerel. Carefully cut through the skin along the length of the belly and the back and remove the skin.

2 Open the mackerel and lift out the backbone and as many of the small bones as possible.

3 Using two forks, break up the mackerel flesh into small rough chunks about the size of sugar lumps.

4 Wash the apples, quarter them and remove the cores but do not peel.

5 Chop the apples into fairly small dice. Put into a basin with the lemon juice and stir thoroughly. The lemon prevents the apples from discolouring.

6 Clean the celery sticks and chop into pieces the same size as the apples.

7 Add the celery to the apples, pour over sour cream and add a good

grinding of pepper. Mix together.

8 Divide the sour cream mixture into 4 portions and spoon on to four small plates.

9 Divide the mackerel into 4 portions and arrange the chunks around the sour cream mixture.

10 Cut the red pepper into thin strips, discarding pith and seeds, or drain and thinly slice the canned pimento.

11 Criss-cross the strips of red pepper or pimento on the mackerel and sprinkle the chopped parsley over the sour cream mixture.

SMOKED FISH APPETIZER

This hors d'oeuvre is a selection of smoked fish divided into portions and arranged on an individual plate for each person. Prepare the fish as neatly as possible, arrange it on the plates in a uniform pattern and the result will be an enticing start to a meal.

SERVES 6
50 g [2 oz] smoked salmon, thinly sliced
1 small smoked trout or buckling
1 small smoked mackerel
3-4 marinated kipper fillets (see recipe on following page)

For the garnish:
1 lemon
1 seedless orange
12 small gherkins
watercress sprigs

1 Divide the salmon into 6 and form the slices into rolls.

2 Skin and fillet the trout (or buckling) and cut each fillet into 3 portions.

3 Skin and fillet the mackerel and cut into very small, rough-shaped pieces.

4 Drain the kipper fillets from the marinade and cut each across into strips about 1 cm [⅓"] wide. Use scissors to do this as it is easier than using a knife.

5 Arrange a portion of each type of fish on each plate.

Tasty first courses: smoked trout pâté with lemon twists, buckling-stuffed lemons and marinated kipper fillets.

6 Wipe the fruit clean and cut each into 6 segments.

7 Cut the gherkins into fans and wash and drain the watercress.

8 Garnish each plate with gherkins, watercress, lemon and orange.

BUCKLING-STUFFED LEMONS

The inclusion of butter makes this pâté very rich. It is best accompanied by slender fingers of hot, freshly made toast. The mixture is too thick and dry to blend in a liquidizer so you will need a mortar and pestle to make it.

SERVES 4

1 large buckling, about 200 g [7 oz]
4 lemons
100 g [¼ lb] unsalted butter at room temperature
half a garlic clove [optional]
freshly ground black pepper
4 bay leaves

1 Slice the tops off the lemons and set aside. Cut a sliver off the other end of each lemon so they will stand upright.

2 Scoop out the pulp with a tea-

spoon and place in a nylon sieve resting over a small bowl. Press the juice through.

3 Put the buckling in a basin, cover with boiling water and leave to stand for 1 minute.

4 Drain and cut off the tail. Carefully cut through the skin along the length of the belly and the back and peel away skin.

5 Open the fish. Lift out the backbone and as many small bones as possible.

6 Put the fillets into a mortar. Add the butter. Peel and slice the garlic and add.

7 Pound with a pestle until fish and butter have blended and are reduced to a thick smooth paste.

8 Stir in 15 ml [1 tablespoon] of the reserved lemon juice and add a good grinding of black pepper.

9 Check seasoning and add more lemon juice if wished.

10 Spoon the mixture into lemon shells, replace caps and decorate each with a bay leaf. Refrigerate for 30 minutes or until required.

SMOKED TROUT PÂTÉ

This is a delicately flavoured pâté and less rich than most because sour cream and cream cheese are used. The ingredients are blended most easily in a liquidizer. You could use a large pestle and mortar instead but it will take you slightly longer. Serve the pâté in one large dish or six small individual dishes or cocottes. Garnish with lemon twists and serve with crisp dry biscuits.

SERVES 6

2 fresh smoked trout, 175-200 g [6-7 oz] each
150 ml [¼ pt] sour cream
5 ml [1 teaspoon] horseradish sauce
5 ml [1 teaspoon] lemon juice
15 ml [1 tablespoon] freshly chopped parsley
100 g [¼ lb] cream cheese
25 g [1 oz] butter at room temperature
black pepper

1 Cut off the heads and tails from the trout.

2 Carefully cut through the skin along the length of the belly and the back and peel away the skin.

3 Open out the fish and lift the flesh off the backbones, taking care to

remove all the small bones.

4 Put the trout into a liquidizer. Add the sour cream, horseradish sauce, lemon juice and parsley and blend until smooth.

OR pound the smoked trout, a little at a time, in a mortar with a pestle. Stir in the sour cream, horseradish sauce, lemon juice and parsley to make a smooth, creamy paste.

5 Add the cream cheese, butter and pepper and blend again until smooth. Do this either in the liquidizer or by creaming and beating the mixture in a mortar.

6 Check seasoning. Turn the mixture into a large dish or six individual dishes, packing the mixture firmly and smoothing the top with a palette knife. Cover and refrigerate until required.

MARINATED KIPPER FILLETS

◨◨◨ *You will need four kippers for this dish. It is essential that they are fresh and of top quality. Ask the fishmonger to fillet them as this is a tricky job or buy frozen kipper fillets. The marinade will break down any little bones.*

SERVES 4
8 kipper fillets
1 small onion
45 ml [3 tablespoons] lemon juice
60 ml [4 tablespoons] olive oil
6 black peppercorns
2 bay leaves

1 Skin the kipper fillets and remove any obvious bones.

2 Lay the kippers flat in a small dish just large enough to hold them.

3 Peel the onion, slice thinly and lay on top of the kippers.

4 Mix the lemon juice and oil together and pour over the kippers.

5 Tuck the peppercorns and the bay leaves between the fish.

6 Cover and refrigerate overnight.

7 To serve, drain the fillets and serve 2 per portion.

WATERCRESS AND WALNUT SAUCE

◨ *Here is another excellent cold sauce to serve with smoked fish. Purists would say that the walnut skins should be rubbed off before making the sauce. This does give a finer flavour but takes hours to do unless the walnuts are very fresh and moist, in which case the skins rub away easily if the shelled nuts are plunged in boiling water for 1 minute.*

SERVES 6-8
25 g [1 oz] walnuts, shelled weight
1 bunch watercress
150 ml [¼ pt] sour cream
salt and pepper

1 Put the walnuts, a few at a time, in a mezzaluna or mortar and chop or pound until quite finely ground.

2 Wash the watercress and pull the leaves off the stems. Reserve stalks for soup or stock and plunge the leaves in boiling water for 1 minute.

3 Turn into a sieve to drain and squeeze the watercress dry, then chop finely.

4 Stir the sour cream until smooth and turn into a small mixing bowl.

5 Add the walnuts and watercress and mix well. Season to taste with salt and freshly ground black pepper.

Star recipe

HALIBUT MAYONNAISE

Halibut or turbot are both delicious eaten cold with salad. The secret of serving fish cold is to eat it as soon as possible after cooking and cooling, then it will be moist and succulent. Don't therefore, cook it the day before. Halibut steaks from the tail end look attractive and are virtually boneless once the centre bone is removed.

SERVES 4

**4 halibut steaks, weighing
   about 175 g [6 oz] each
salt and white pepper
half a lemon
30 ml [2 tablespoons]
   of thin cream
200 ml [7 fl oz] home-made
   mayonnaise
100 g [¼ lb] black grapes
2 seedless oranges
crisp lettuce leaves
watercress sprigs**

1 Lightly oil a large piece of kitchen foil or greaseproof paper and lay the fish on it.

2 Season the fish with salt and white pepper. Squeeze the lemon and pour juice over the fish.

3 Wrap the foil round the fish to form a secure parcel and refrigerate until ready to be cooked.

4 Prepare a steamer and steam fish for 15–20 minutes. Remove parcel and open it to cool the fish.

5 Halve and de-seed the grapes. Peel the oranges and remove pith. Cut the orange in thin slices.

6 Using a fish slice transfer the fish to a wire rack over a dish. Remove the centre bones and skin.

7 Stir the thin cream into the mayonnaise and coat each halibut steak thickly with the mayonnaise.

8 Decorate the coated steaks with the prepared grapes and a sprig of watercress.

9 Line a dish with lettuce leaves. Transfer the fish on to it and garnish with orange slices.

Star recipe
Paella

This traditional one-pot Spanish dish gets its name from the heavy iron frying-pan with two handles in which it is customarily cooked and served. In the absence of a proper paella, use a frying-pan, sauté pan or a wide-bottomed flameproof casserole. However, note that whatever you use it must be large enough to contain 1.4 litres [2½ pt] of stock plus the large quantity of rice in addition to the chicken, shellfish and vegetables. If necessary, divide your ingredients into two pans and cook side by side.

The result is a pretty and colourful party dish, which looks and tastes just as good cold. Saffron is one of the main ingredients of a true paella because of its unique flavour and rich yellow colour. But in this recipe it has been listed as an alternative as it is expensive. Instead turmeric can be used for colouring, although, it must be admitted, the flavour is not quite the same.

SERVES 8
4 chicken joints
15 ml [1 tablespoon] turmeric
or 4 ml [¾ teaspoon]
powdered saffron
2 large bay leaves
500 g [1 quart] prawns in
their shells
225 g [1 pt] shrimps in
their shells
1 kg [1 quart] mussels in their
shells
salt
freshly ground black pepper
cooking oil
1 large green pepper
1 large red pepper
2 Spanish onions
4 garlic cloves
350 g [¾ lb] long-grain rice
700 g [1½ lb] tomatoes
125 g [¼ lb] frozen peas

1 Put the chicken joints in a pan. Add the turmeric. If using saffron, dissolve the powder in 15 ml [1 tablespoon] of boiling water but do not add to the pan at this stage.

2 Cover the chicken joints with water and add the bay leaves. Bring the water to the boil, cover and simmer for 25 minutes.

3 When the time is up, take out the chicken joints and discard the bay leaves. Reserve the stock.

4 Shell half the prawns and all the shrimps, reserving the shells.

5 Prepare the mussels (see step-by-step instructions on pages 412–413). If any of the mussel shells are open, given them a sharp tap with the back of a knife. If they do not close, discard them—as this will mean they are dead. Pull away beards, scape off encrustations and scrub shells thoroughly under cold running water. Put the prepared mussels in a saucepan. Cover with water and boil rapidly until they open.

6 Reserving the mussel stock, remove the mussels from the pan and remove top shell. Discard any that have remained closed.

7 Strain the mussel stock through a fine sieve to catch any sand or grit.

8 Skin the chicken and shred the flesh from the bones. Reserve these bones.

9 Measure both the mussel stock and the reserved chicken stock into a large pan and make up to 1.7 L [3 pt] with water. Add the re-

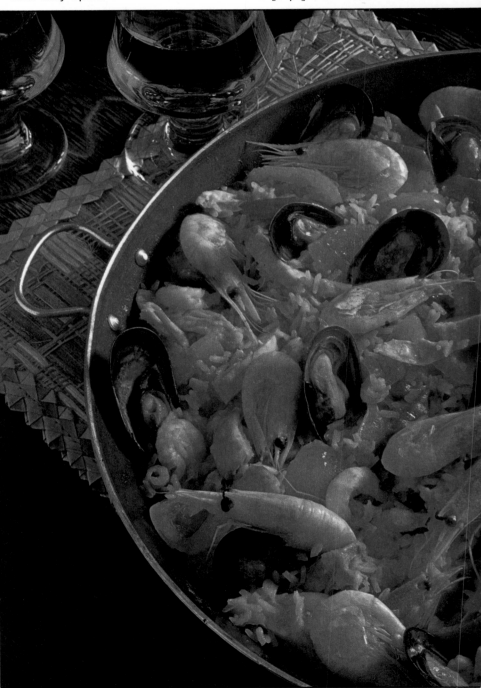

served chicken bones and prawn and shrimp shells to the pan.

10 Boil rapidly until the liquid in the pan has reduced to 1.4 L [2½ pt]. Taste and season with salt and black pepper if necessary.

11 Take the dish in which the paella is to be cooked and cover the bottom with oil. Place over a moderate heat.

12 Rinse, quarter and de-seed the peppers. Cut across into 6 mm [¼"] wide strips. Fry gently in the oil for 2-3 minutes. Take out and reserve.

13 Peel and chop the onion and garlic finely. Fry in the same oil until soft.

14 Pour in the rice and turn over and over in the oil to heat through.

15 Strain the hot reduced stock into the paella pan and add the shredded chicken meat. Stir until the mixture is bubbling.

16 Lower the heat and continue stirring until the rice begins to absorb the stock.

17 Meanwhile scald the tomatoes in a pan of boiling water for 1 minute in order to skin them. Then chop roughly, de-seeding where possible.

18 Stir the chopped tomato into the paella. Add the shelled prawns, shrimps and mussels. If using saffron, add the infused powder at this stage too. Cover the paella pan tightly with foil. Turn to the lowest possible heat and cook gently, without disturbing, for 20 minutes.

19 When the time is up, stir the paella. Add the reserved peppers and the peas and stir again.

20 Strew the remaining prawns (unshelled) over the top. Re-cover tightly with foil and cook for a further 5-10 minutes. By this time the rice should have absorbed all the liquid but still be firm.

21 Serve hot from a paella pan or, if cooking in a substitute pan, transfer to one or two large, warmed serving dishes before taking to the table.

Star recipe

Moules à la marinière

▲*Shellfish add a touch of luxury to any meal; mussels are a great treat and fortunately they do not cost a luxury price.*

This dish comes from France's Atlantic coast and is excellent, providing that the mussels are fresh and thoroughly cleaned. Gritty mussels are unpleasant to eat, while sand left in the soup will collect in the liquor, turning it grey. Dead mussels can give you nasty food poisoning, so be sure that they are alive, by the means described here.

Serve moules à la marinière as a meal-in-a-bowl for two people or a first course for four. For a meal-in-a-bowl buy 1 kg [2¼ lb] of mussels per person if sold by weight, or 1 L [1 qt] if sold by volume.

If a large number of mussels in the fishmonger's tray are open or the shells are broken, do not buy them because these will be dead. (Live mussels usually keep their shells closed when they are out of water.)

When you get home, clean the mussels thoroughly. This is not difficult but it does take time. Keep the cleaned mussels immersed in a bowl of water until required for cooking, changing the water several times.

Eat mussels on the day of purchase whenever possible. If you have to leave them overnight, add some salt to the water. If wished you can add a little flour or oatmeal, too, to feed the mussels so they become plump and white. Cover the bowl with a clean cloth and put in a cool place.

After cooking, check again that your mussels are fresh. Heat should force the shells open so discard any that remain closed.

It is usual to remove half the shell from each mussel before serving. This is to reduce the amount of shell in the soup bowls. Put an empty plate in the centre of the table for the remaining halves of the shells as each person discards them.

Serve in soup bowls with the mussels piled up, and provide spoons for the soup liquid. To eat the mussels, you pick the shell up in your fingers and tip the mussel into your mouth, discarding the empty shell. It is therefore a good idea to provide big napkins to wipe sticky fingers, and finger-bowls would also be useful.

SERVES 2
2 kg [2 quarts] mussels
1 onion
1 shallot (or a second onion)
1 garlic clove
4 parsley stalks
thyme sprig or dried thyme
salt and pepper
40 g [1½ oz] butter
**200 ml [7 fl oz] dry white wine
  or dry cider**
75 ml [3 fl oz] water
**15 ml [1 tablespoon] chopped
  parsley**

1 Mussels should be absolutely fresh. Tap any open mussel. Discard it if it does not shut.

5 When ready to cook, drain the mussels. Chop the garlic, onion and shallot very finely.

6 Melt butter in a large saucepan over low heat. Add vegetables, cover and sweat for 10 minutes.

10 Reduce the heat and cook for a further 3 minutes to make sure the mussels are cooked.

11 Strain the liquor through a colander into a second saucepan. Discard the herbs.

2 Using your hands, pull away beards (any hanging seaweed gripped between the two shells).

3 Scrub the mussels under cold running water. Scrape away encrustations with a sharp knife.

4 Keep the mussels in a bowl of cold water until ready to cook. Change the water several times.

7 Tie parsley stalks and thyme with a piece of fine string. Or tie up dried thyme in buttermuslin.

8 Add the herbs, wine or cider and water to the pan. Heat through slowly until almost boiling.

9 Add the mussels, cover and shake gently over fierce heat for 2 minutes to open the shells.

12 Discard any mussels that are still tightly shut. Remove half a shell from each that is open.

13 Add the mussels on their half shells to the liquor in the pan. Reheat gently and season to taste.

14 Ladle soup into a tureen or bowls, heaping up the mussels in the centre. Garnish with parsley.

413

Star recipe

TARAMASALATA

⧖ *The name literally means salad of 'tarmara'. This is the salted grey mullet roe but, as this fish is seldom found beyond the Mediterranean, smoked cod's roe makes an excellent substitute.*

There are many ways of making taramasalata but the easiest way is to use a liquidizer. If you do not have one, pound the roe with a pestle in a mortar, although it will take longer.

The easiest way to remove the outer skin of the roe is to immerse the roe in boiling water. You lose less roe this way than the alternative method of scraping the soft eggs from the skin with a blunt knife.

Traditionally, taramasalata is served with pita bread but, if this is not available, thin slices of toast or brown bread are perfectly acceptable.

You can turn taramasalata into a dip to serve with crudités by stirring in sour cream to make the basic smoked cod's roe pâté slightly thinner.

SERVES 6
150 g [5 oz] smoked cod's roe
1 thick slice white bread
60 ml [4 tablespoons] water
1 garlic clove
freshly ground black pepper
250 ml [½ pt] olive oil
30 ml [2 tablespoons] lemon juice

For the garnish:
black olives
2 lemons

1 Put the cod's roe in a bowl. Pour on boiling water to cover completely and leave for 1 minute.

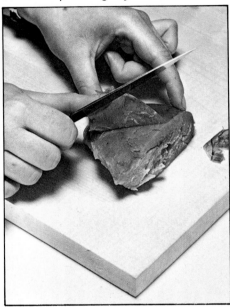

2 Drain the roe. Make a nick in the skin with the point of a sharp knife and peel away skin.

3 Cut crusts from the bread and pour on water. Press with a spoon until bread is soft and pappy.

4 Gently squeeze the bread with your fingers to remove excess liquid and leave a soft white pulp.

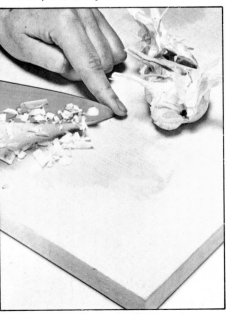

5 Using a sharp knife, peel away garlic skin and chop the flesh into small pieces.

6 Add the garlic, 30 ml [2 tablespoons] oil and some pepper to the bread and blend.

414

Add a walnut-sized piece of roe and some more oil. Blend the mixture until smooth.

8 Continue blending, adding a little roe and oil at a time, until a thick smooth paste is formed.

9 Blend in the lemon juice. Correct seasoning if necessary. Cover and refrigerate until required.

Transfer to a serving dish and garnish with whole black olives and lemon cut into wedges.

Star recipe

Smoked trout with mustard cream sauce

◻ *This is an hors d'oeuvre from the luxury class which deserves to be eaten just as it is—merely garnished with lettuce and lemon wedges and accompanied with brown bread and butter. The mustard cream sauce makes a superb alternative to the more usual but tasty horseradish. If you wish, the fish can be filleted and the heads and tails removed beforehand (which is a very easy process and one that you can do yourself). This will be essential on an occasion when the fish is larger and a portion is only half a fillet. It is, however, more usual—if less convenient for the diners—to serve the fish unfilleted. Serve the sauce in a separate bowl.*

SERVES 3
**3 small smoked trout
1 lettuce heart
half a lemon
3 slices brown buttered bread
parsley for garnish (optional)**

**For the sauce:
30 ml [2 tablespoons] Dijon
mustard**

**90 ml [6 tablespoons] soured
cream**

1   Make the sauce. Put the mustard and the soured cream into a jug and stir until thoroughly blended. Chill lightly in the refrigerator.

2   Wash and dry the lettuce leaves. Put these on a serving plate and arrange the trout on top decoratively.

3   Cut the lemon into wedges and arrange on the trout as a garnish. Use parsley, too, if wished.

4   Serve bread and butter separately.

INDEX

Picture Credits

Rex Bamber: 10, 13, 16, 17, 18/9, 34/5, 36/7, 38/9, 40, 73, 82/3, 85, 87, 90, 91, 92/3, 111, 114/5, 120/1

John Cooke: 178, 179

Alan Duns: 51, 52/3, 55, 57, 58/9, 60, 88/9, 146/7, 148/9, 150/1, 153, 193, 196/7, 200/1, 203, 286, 287, 288, 295, 296, 298, 320/1, 322, 324/5, 326/7, 359, 360/1, 362/3, 364/5, 366, 406/7

Melvin Grey: 25, 26/7, 31, 32/3, 182/3, 184B, 185B, 229, 231, 236/7, 238/9, 240/1, 242/3, 244/5, 246/7, 249, 278/9, 338/9, 357, 367, 370/1, 373

Anthony Kay: 250/1, 253, 255, 256/7, 375, 376/7, 378/9B, 381, 383, 384/5, 387

Paul Kemp: 20/1, 23, 24, 95, 96/7, 100, 135, 136, 137, 138, 142/3, 144/5, 165, 166/7, 172/3, 290/1, 299, 300/1, 302/3, 304, 305, 306, 308, 309, 310/1, 312/3, 319, 384/5, 388

John Lee: 269, 276/7

David Levin: 4/5, 9, 12, 14, 15, 28/9, 45, 46, 56, 64/5, 75, 76/7, 99, 101, 102, 104/5, 112/3, 113, 116, 118/9, 126/7, 128, 128/9, 139, 140/1, 155, 158/9, 160/1, 168, 170/1, 175, 176/7, 180/1, 184T, 185T, 186/7, 188, 189, 190/1, 192, 195, 198/9, 207, 208/9, 211, 212/3, 222/3, 224/5, 226/7, 234, 235, 271, 272, 273, 282, 283, 284, 285, 289, 292/3, 314/5, 317, 334/5, 349, 350/1, 368/9, 378/9T, 400, 401, 403, 404, 408, 409, 414/5

Meat Promotion
Executive: 10

Moulinex Ltd: 205

Roger Phillips: 61, 68/9, 84, 103, 105TR, 106, 108/9, 260/1, 263, 264, 266, 268, 275, 356

Paul Radkai: 352/3, 355

Iain Reid: 122, 123, 125, 130/1, 131, 132/3, 134, 206, 214/5, 216/7

Swiss Turkey: 222/3, 224/5

Paul Williams: 162/3, 259, 262, 340/1, 342/3, 344/7, 346/7, 348, 388/9, 410/1

George Wright: 1, 3, 6, 8, 41, 48/9, 50, 62/3, 66, 57, 70, 72, 78/9, 80/1, 157, 164, 204, 280/1, 329, 330/1, 332/3, 336/7, 412/3, 416